Philosophical Foundations of Evidence Law

Philosophical Foundations of Evidence Law

Edited by

CHRISTIAN DAHLMAN, ALEX STEIN, AND
GIOVANNI TUZET

OXFORD
UNIVERSITY PRESS

OXFORD
UNIVERSITY PRESS

Great Clarendon Street, Oxford, OX2 6DP,
United Kingdom

Oxford University Press is a department of the University of Oxford.
It furthers the University's objective of excellence in research, scholarship,
and education by publishing worldwide. Oxford is a registered trade mark of
Oxford University Press in the UK and in certain other countries

First Edition published in 2021

Impression: 1

Published in the United States of America by Oxford University Press
198 Madison Avenue, New York, NY 10016, United States of America

British Library Cataloguing in Publication Data

Data available

Library of Congress Control Number: 2021935103

ISBN 978–0–19–885930–7

DOI: 10.1093/oso/9780198859307.001.0001

Printed and bound in the UK by
TJ Books Limited

Table of Contents

List of Contributors   vii

Introduction   1

I. EVIDENCE, TRUTH, AND KNOWLEDGE

1. Evidence and Truth   11
   Hock Lai Ho

2. The Naturalized Epistemology Approach to Evidence   25
   Gabriel Broughton and Brian Leiter

3. Proven Facts, Beliefs, and Reasoned Verdicts   40
   Jordi Ferrer Beltrán

4. The Role of the Expert Witness   53
   Lena Wahlberg and Christian Dahlman

II. LAW AND FACTFINDING

5. The Role of Rules in the Law of Evidence   69
   Frederick Schauer

6. Excluding Evidence for Integrity's Sake   83
   Jules Holroyd and Federico Picinali

7. Second-Personal Evidence   96
   Alex Stein

8. Burdens of Proof   108
   Mark Spottswood

9. Weight of Evidence   123
   Dale A. Nance

10. Cost-Benefit Analysis of Evidence Law and Factfinding   137
    Talia Fisher

III. EVIDENCE, LANGUAGE, AND ARGUMENTATION

11. Linguistic Evidentials and the Law of Hearsay   157
    Lawrence M. Solan

12. The Pragmatics of Evidence Discourse   169
    Giovanni Tuzet

13. Argumentation and Evidence   183
    Floris Bex

IV. EVIDENCE AND EXPLANATION

14. Inference to the Best Explanation, Relative Plausibility, and Probability   201
    Ronald J. Allen and Michael S. Pardo

15. The Scenario Theory about Evidence in Criminal Law   215
    Anne Ruth Mackor and Peter J. van Koppen

16. Coherence in Legal Evidence   231
    Amalia Amaya

V. EVIDENCE AND PROBABILITY

17. The Logic of Inference and Decision for Scientific Evidence   251
    Franco Taroni, Silvia Bozza, and Alex Biedermann

18. Bayesianism: Objections and Rebuttals   267
    Norman Fenton and David Lagnado

19. The Problem of the Prior in Criminal Trials   287
    Christian Dahlman and Eivind Kolflaath

20. Generalizations and Reference Classes   301
    Michael S. Pardo and Ronald J. Allen

VI. PROOF PARADOXES

21. Paradoxes of Proof   317
    Mark Spottswood

22. The Problem with Naked Statistical Evidence   332
    Christian Dahlman and Amit Pundik

VII. BIASES AND EPISTEMIC INJUSTICE

23. Evidence Law and Empirical Psychology   349
    Justin Sevier

24. Relevance through a Feminist Lens   364
    Julia Simon-Kerr

25. Race, Evidence, and Epistemic Injustice   380
    Jasmine B. Gonzales Rose

26. De-Biasing Legal Factfinders   395
    Frank Zenker

Index   411

List of Contributors

Ronald J. Allen is the John Henry Wigmore Professor of Law at Northwestern University in Chicago, Illinois, USA.

Amalia Amaya is British Academy Global Professor in the School of Law at the University of Edinburgh, United Kingdom, and Research Professor of Philosophy at the National Autonomous University of Mexico.

Jordi Ferrer Beltrán is Associate Professor of Philosophy of Law at the University of Girona, Spain.

Floris Bex is Professor of Data Science and the Judiciary at the Department of Law, Technology, Markets and Society, Tilburg University and Associate Professor at the Department of Information and Computing Sciences, Utrecht University, The Netherlands.

Alex Biedermann is Associate Professor at the School of Criminal Justice of the Faculty of Law, Criminal Justice and Public Administration at the University of Lausanne (UNIL), Switzerland.

Silvia Bozza is Associate Professor in the Department of Economics at Ca' Foscari University in Venice, Italy.

Gabriel Broughton is a PhD candidate in philosophy at Princeton University, USA.

Christian Dahlman is Professor in Jurisprudence (Samuel Pufendorf Chair) in the Faculty of Law at Lund University, Sweden.

Norman Fenton is Professor of Risk Information Management at Queen Mary College, University of London, United Kingdom.

Talia Fisher is Professor of Law at the Tel-Aviv University Faculty of Law, Israel.

Jasmine B. Gonzales Rose is Professor of Law at Boston University Law School, USA.

Hock Lai Ho is the Coomaraswamy Professor of the Law of Evidence in the Faculty of Law at the National University of Singapore.

Jules Holroyd is a Vice-Chancellor's Fellow in the Department of Philosophy at the University of Sheffield, United Kingdom.

Eivind Kolflaath is Professor in the Department of Philosophy and the Faculty of Law at the University of Bergen, Norway.

David Lagnado is Professor of Cognitive and Decision Sciences in the Department of Experimental Psychology, University College London, United Kingdom.

Brian Leiter is Karl N. Llewellyn Professor of Jurisprudence and Director of the Center for Law, Philosophy & Human Values at the University of Chicago Law School, USA.

Anne Ruth Mackor is Professor in the Department of Transboundary Legal Studies at the Faculty of Law, University of Groningen, The Netherlands.

viii   LIST OF CONTRIBUTORS

Dale A. Nance is Albert J. Weatherhead III & Richard W. Weatherhead Professor of Law at the Case Western Reserve University School of Law in Cleveland, Ohio, USA.

Michael S. Pardo is Professor of Law in the Law Center at Georgetown University in Washington D.C., USA.

Federico Picinali is Associate Professor in the Department of Law at the London School of Economics and Political Science, United Kingdom.

Amit Pundik is Senior Lecturer at the Tel-Aviv University Faculty of Law, Israel.

Frederick Schauer is David and Mary Harrison Distinguished Professor of Law at the University of Virginia Law School, USA.

Justin Sevier is Charles W. Ehrhardt Professor of Litigation at the Florida State University College of Law, USA.

Julia Simon-Kerr is Professor of Law at the University of Connecticut School of Law, USA.

Lawrence M. Solan is Don Forchelli Professor of Law at Brooklyn Law School in New York, USA.

Mark Spottswood is the David and Deborah Fonvielle Professor of Law at the Florida State University College of Law, USA.

Alex Stein is Justice of the Israel Supreme Court.

Franco Taroni is Full Professor in the School of Criminal Justice at the Faculty of Law, Criminal Justice and Public Administration at the University of Lausanne (UNIL), Switzerland.

Giovanni Tuzet is Full Professor of Philosophy of Law at Bocconi University in Milan, Italy.

Peter J. van Koppen is Professor Emeritus of Legal Psychology in the Faculty of Law at the VU University Amsterdam and Maastricht University, The Netherlands.

Lena Wahlberg is Associate Professor of Jurisprudence in the Faculty of Law at Lund University, Sweden.

Frank Zenker is Assistant Professor in the Department of Philosophy at Boğaziçi University in Istanbul, Turkey.

Introduction

This volume presents contributions from scholars spread across three continents and domiciled in twelve different countries, whose common interest is evidence theory as related to law.

Evidence theory as related to law stayed mostly dormant until the advent of the "New Evidence Scholarship" in the mid-eighties of the twentieth century.[1] Before that time, a small number of scattered, yet remarkable, works by John Kaplan, Per Olof Ekelöf, Laurence Tribe, Jonathan Cohen, Judith Jarvis Thomson, and others have identified and rationalized the alleged alignments and misalignments between mathematical probability and adjudicative factfinding.[2] The publication of William Twining's book, *Theories of Evidence: Bentham & Wigmore* in 1985[3] and the 1986 *Boston University Law Review Evidence Symposium* volume[4] have changed things around. These publications have irreversibly changed the direction of the study of evidence by shifting evidence scholars' focus from rules to reasons.[5]

The shift from rules to reasons was transformative along two dimensions: interdisciplinarity and internationalization. The realization that reasons moving the factfinding process forward are antecedent to, and consequently more important than, evidentiary rules has opened up new paths of inquiry that connected adjudicative factfinding to epistemology, mathematics, economics, psychology, sociology, political morality, and linguistics and led to further and richer explorations of how theories of probability and induction affect the understanding and reform of the law of evidence.[6] The primacy of reasons has also created a sizable common ground for theorizing for evidence scholars from different countries. With a focus on reasons rather than rules, the differences between factfinding in the more regulated Anglo-American systems vis-à-vis the freer European systems—once understood as dramatic—became less important.

These important developments motivated us to initiate the publication of this volume. The principal idea of this project was to assemble and present the major philosophical and interdisciplinary insights that define evidence theory, as related to law, in a single book. We divided these insights into seven parts, best read in the order presented.

Part I, "Evidence, Truth, and Knowledge," presents the core ideas as to what evidence law is about. These ideas define and explain the principal goal of all systems of evidence situated in what Twining described as the rationalist tradition:[7] discovery of the truth and the resulting accuracy of verdicts.

---

[1] See Tillers and Green 1988; Park 1991; Twining 1985. See also Park and Saks 2006.
[2] See Ekelöf 1964; Kaplan 1968; Tribe 1971; Cohen 1977; Thomson 1986. See also Park 1991.
[3] Twining 1985.
[4] Reedited as Tillers and Green 1988.
[5] See Twining 1990; Stein 2005; Laudan 2006; Ho 2008.
[6] See Twining and Stein 1992.
[7] See Twining 1990, 32–91.

Christian Dahlman, Alex Stein, and Giovanni Tuzet, *Introduction* In: *Philosophical Foundations of Evidence Law*. Edited by: Christian Dahlman, Alex Stein, and Giovanni Tuzet, Oxford University Press. © Christian Dahlman, Alex Stein, and Giovanni Tuzet 2021. DOI: 10.1093/oso/9780198859307.003.0001

Chapter 1, "Evidence and Truth" by Hock Lai Ho, defends the classical—yet not universally accepted—proposition that *trials aim primarily at determining the truth* of disputed propositions of fact, and that evidentiary rules ought to promote the realization of that goal. Ho defends this proposition by exploring its conceptual implications and by taking truth to be a prerequisite for "rectitude of decision"—an objective only realized when courts correctly combine substantive law with true facts.

Chapter 2, "The Naturalized Epistemology Approach to Evidence" by Gabriel Broughton and Brian Leiter, considers the law of evidence and its pursuit of accuracy in factfinding from the perspective of naturalized social epistemology. With everything else being equal, there are good reasons to prefer accurate verdicts to inaccurate ones. As a corollary, the task of naturalized epistemology and empirical science, as applied to adjudication, is to assess evidence law *veritistically*. Broughton and Leiter discuss in particular the contribution of jury simulation studies to this assessment and the applications of naturalized epistemology on eyewitness testimony and character evidence.

Chapter 3, "Proven Facts, Beliefs, and Reasoned Verdicts" by Jordi Ferrer Beltrán, challenges a subjectivist conception of factfinding by tying the very concept of "proof" and the applicable proof standards and burdens to the duty of *giving reasons* for trial verdicts. According to Ferrer Beltrán, if "proof" were conceptually identical to the factfinders' beliefs and convictions, satisfying the need for a reasoned justification for decisions about facts would be impossible.

Chapter 4, "The Role of the Expert Witness" by Lena Wahlberg and Christian Dahlman, maps out the scope of the *epistemic authority* of expert witnesses as interpreters and explainers of evidence and uncertainties that fall within their expertise. They argue that experts should only testify about questions of fact and ought not to express their opinions on questions of law and other ultimate adjudicative issues such as the probability of a hypothesis given the evidence. Rather, experts should facilitate the factfinder's assessment of how strongly the evidence supports the underlying hypothesis, given all the uncertainties involved.

Part II, "Law and Factfinding," explores the regulatory role of the law in adjudicative factfinding.

Chapter 5, "The Role of Rules in the Law of Evidence" by Frederick Schauer, starts out with Bentham's antinomian thesis that rejected the very idea of setting up rules for selecting and evaluating evidence. Bentham believed that factfinding should be governed by epistemically good reasons as a process unconstrained by artificial legal rules. Schauer observes that most legal systems took up this approach by softening the hard edges of rules (as in common law jurisdictions) and by following the basically free-proof model of factfinding (as in countries that adopted the continental European approach). Yet, he claims that the law of evidence still remains substantially an *affair of rules*; and for good reasons so.

Chapter 6, "Excluding Evidence for Integrity's Sake" by Jules Holroyd and Federico Picinali, highlights the role of exclusionary rules in factfinding and the recent attempt, by both courts and scholars, to employ the concept of integrity as a rationale for suppressing *unlawfully obtained evidence*. Holroyd and Picinali contend that, as it stands, the theory of integrity can hardly play a defensible role in the factfinding process, and they set forth challenges that scholars who take integrity seriously ought to meet.

Chapter 7, "Second-Personal Evidence" by Alex Stein, draws on Hohfeld's scheme of jural opposites and correlatives to identify the *irreducibly second-personal nature of legal entitlements* and the interplay between the rightholder's authority and the duty-bearer's accountability. Based on that insight, he argues that facts that courts need to ascertain and—critically—the procedures that courts must carry out in ascertaining those facts ought to be second-personal as well. As a corollary, courts must only rely upon second-personal evidence, that is: upon information concerning the alleged jural relationship between the holder of the underlying entitlement and the bearer of the correlative duty or obligation. According to Stein, this fundamental requirement defines the modus operandi of the Anglo-American system of evidence and its core rules.

Chapter 8, "Burdens of Proof" by Mark Spottswood, carries out an inquiry—conceptual and normative—into the meaning and functioning of the probability thresholds that evidence needs to surpass to justify an award of sanctions. This discussion explores the *inputs* that burdens of proof should draw from and then moves on to consider the suitability of varying burden structures adjusted to the *levels of sanctions* in civil and criminal cases.

Chapter 9, "Weight of Evidence" by Dale Nance, analyzes and operationalizes the concept of "weight" as denoting the *relative degree to which evidence has been developed on the basis of which to determine disputed claims.* This concept was coined by John Maynard Keynes and further developed in the context of judicial proof by L. Jonathan Cohen, Dale Nance, and Alex Stein. Nance distinguishes weight from the degree to which evidence favors one side over the other, and then assays the different ways this concept of weight can be operationalized. He identifies the strengths and weaknesses of various theories, and advocates a conception of weight that emphasizes its connection to fundamental policy choices about the importance of accuracy in litigation and, perhaps, the allocation of the risk of error. He argues that a common failure to appreciate the differences between ordinary decision-making under uncertainty and formal adjudication is responsible for many confusions about the concept of weight.

Chapter 10, "Cost-Benefit Analysis of Factfinding" by Talia Fisher, describes and analyzes two economically driven models of evidence and proof: the *cost-minimization model,* geared toward minimization of the cost of errors and the cost of accuracy as a total sum, and the *primary behavior model* aiming to incentivize socially optimal behavior and interactions. This analysis identifies the models' difficulties, engendered, for the most part, by the misalignment between the private and the social costs and benefits of adjudication, and addresses the models' relationship to the existing evidentiary rules and institutions.

Part III, "Evidence, Language, and Argumentation," explores the role of language and argumentation in the factfinding process by viewing this process a "linguistic affair:" that is, as an interplay of language and speech acts.

Chapter 11, "Linguistic Evidentials and the Law of Hearsay" by Lawrence Solan, focuses on the testimonial—and hence linguistic—nature of evidentiary rules as related to the trial process. Specifically, Solan uses insights from linguistics and the philosophy of language to juxtapose—against each other—the ways in which natural language expresses degrees of certainty in the truth of an assertion of fact and the ways in which the law does the same. This discussion focuses, in particular, on the hearsay doctrine and on the linguistic elements identified as "evidentials:" expressions that include information about *how speakers came to know the assertions they make.*

Chapter 12, "The Pragmatics of Evidence Discourse" by Giovanni Tuzet, explores a number of pragmatic aspects of the evidentiary discourse. This discussion restates the basic distinction between semantics and pragmatics and then addresses the nature of the *speech acts* in evidence discourse, the role of *implicatures* and *presuppositions*, and the place of *deixis*, i.e. the use of indexicals and demonstratives. Tuzet claims that evidence discourse is predominantly assertive; that problems associated with implicatures are abated as questioners are skilled and questions are specific; that exploitation of presuppositions is avoided by attorneys' vigilance and judicial control; and, finally, that deixis reveals the discourse's *ostensive dimension*.

Chapter 13, "Argumentation and Evidence" by Floris Bex, underscores the centrality of argumentation to legal and evidential reasoning: the prosecution *argues* that the suspect committed the crime; attorneys present their *arguments*; the plaintiff *argues* his case by citing a relevant precedent; the court presents concurring and dissenting *arguments*; and so on. Bex reviews the different accounts of argumentation developed in the academic literature and then relates those accounts to the context of evidence and proof. Specifically, he focuses on the construction of arguments and counterarguments as involving consecutive reasoning steps, starting with identifying an item of evidence and then reasoning towards some conclusion with the help of general rules of inference and generalizations.

Part IV, "Evidence and Explanation," focuses on the *explanationist* approach to judicial evidence and proof. This approach accommodates different methods for explaining evidence—claimed to be superior to mathematical probability—that correlate degrees of persuasion with explanatory power. These methods include *inference to the best explanation, relative plausibility, scenario theory*, and *coherence*.

Chapter 14, "Inference to the Best Explanation, Relative Plausibility, and Probability" by Ronald Allen and Michael Pardo, juxtaposes an *explanation-based account of juridical proof* against different probability accounts, develops an argument about the descriptive superiority of the explanation-based account over its competitors, and sets forth the theoretical and practical implications of this argument.

Chapter 15, "The Scenario Theory about Evidence in Criminal Law" by Anne Ruth Mackor and Peter van Koppen, presents the Dutch Scenario Theory, developed in the 1990s by van Koppen in collaboration with Willem Wagenaar and Hans Crombag. The Scenario Theory builds on the descriptive psychological account featuring factfinders who think in terms of a story when they reason about evidence to develop a normative theory of adjudicative factfinding. This theory claims that factfinders ought to assess the strength of the scenario underlying the indictment by reference to *alternative scenarios*, the evidence, and their general knowledge of the world. The theory ascribes a piece of evidence the status of a *discriminating fact* when one scenario explains it better than another competing scenario.

Chapter 16, "Coherence in Legal Evidence" by Amalia Amaya, discusses the *coherence approach* to judicial proof that builds on Paul Thagard's theory of coherence as *constraint satisfaction*. Amaya maps out a five-step procedure for coherence-based inference in adjudicative factfinding: (1) specification of a base for coherence; (2) construction of a contrast set; (3) identification of alternative factual accounts or theories of the case; (4) evaluation of the coherence of these alternative accounts; and, finally, (5) selection of the account that best satisfies the coherence criteria.

Part V, "Evidence and Probability," focuses on the Bayesian and other statistical approaches to adjudicative factfinding.

Chapter 17, "The Logic of Inference and Decision for Scientific Evidence" by Franco Taroni, Alex Biedermann, and Silvia Bozza, lays out the fundamentals of inference and decision-making under uncertainty with regard to forensic evidence. Taroni, Biedermann, and Bozza explicate the *subjectivist version of Bayesianism* and analyze the usefulness of the likelihood ratio in measuring the degree to which the evidence discriminates between competing propositions in a trial. They also underscore the importance of *decision analysis* as a framework that forces decision-makers to formalize preference structures.

Chapter 18, "Bayesianism: Objections and Rebuttals" by Norman Fenton and David Lagnado, explains the advantages of using *Bayesian networks* in adjudicative factfinding. The chapter addresses a number of common objections to the Bayesian approach, such as "There is no such thing as a probability of a single specified event;" "The Bayesian approach only works with statistical evidence;" "The Bayesian approach is too difficult for legal factfinders to comprehend;" and "A Bayesian network can never capture the full complexity of a legal case." Fenton and Lagnado offer rebuttals to each of these objections.

Chapter 19, "The Problem of the Prior in Criminal Trials" by Christian Dahlman and Eivind Kolflaath, addresses a classical challenge to the Bayesian approach. The chapter examines different ways of setting the prior probability of the prosecutor's hypothesis in a criminal trial, in particular, the classical Bayesian solution of setting the prior at $1/N$, where N is the number of possible perpetrators in the geographical area where the crime was committed. Dahlman and Kolflaath argue that this solution is at odds with the presumption of innocence, and that other proposals are also problematic, either theoretically or in practice. According to Dahlman and Kolflaath a *presumed prior determined ex lege* is less problematic than other solutions, and the problem of the prior can be avoided by a reconceptualization of the standard of proof.

Chapter 20, "Generalizations and Reference Classes" by Michael Pardo and Ronald Allen, examines the implications of the *reference-class problem* for attempts to model the probative value of evidence in mathematical terms. This examination makes three distinct contributions to evidence scholarship. First, and most importantly, it articulates and explains the problematic relationship between algorithmic tools and legal decision-making. Second, it points out serious pitfalls to be avoided for analytical or empirical studies of juridical proof. Third, it indicates when algorithmic tools may be more or less useful in the evidentiary process. As such, the chapter offers yet another demonstration of the very complex set of relationships involving human knowledge and rationality, on the one hand, and attempts to reduce either to a set of formal concepts, on the other.

Part VI, "Proof Paradoxes," revisits the debate that started in the 1970s when L. Jonathan Cohen and other scholars argued that the conceptualization of judicial factfinding in terms of Pascalian probability gives rise to paradoxes and anomalies.

Chapter 21, "Paradoxes of Proof" by Mark Spottswood, takes a fresh look on the classic debate on the proof paradoxes and the problem of naked statistical evidence, illustrated, alongside some real-world cases, by the *Gatecrasher* case, the *Prison Riot* case, the *Blue Bus* case, the problem of conjunction (and disjunction), and the group-decision problem.

Chapter 22, "The Problem with Naked Statistical Evidence" by Christian Dahlman and Amit Pundik, joins the most recent debates on naked statistical evidence, in particular the objections to naked statistics based upon sensitivity, normalcy, incentives for lawful conduct, and free will. Dahlman and Pundik argue that the problem of naked statistical evidence is not an epistemic problem, as some assume, but is actually a *moral problem*.

Part VII, "Biases and Epistemic Injustice," addresses structural problems present in the rationalist account of factfinding in social settings characterized by race- and gender-based inequities and disparities in power, wealth, and social status.

Chapter 23, "Evidence Law and Empirical Psychology" by Justin Sevier, unfolds a brief historical account of the relationship between empirical psychology and the law of evidence, specifies the major contributions that psychologists have made to our understanding of evidence law, highlights recent, cutting-edge research, and makes several suggestions for how future research can assist in maintaining the *relevance of psychology to sound evidentiary policy*.

Chapter 24, "Relevance through a Feminist Lens" by Julia Simon-Kerr, evaluates and criticizes the established evidentiary rules and institutions through the lens of feminist theory. Contrary to accepted wisdom, Simon-Kerr argues that these *rules and institutions are neither epistemically neutral nor value-free*. She develops this argument through the doctrine of relevance that determines whose stories are told and how they are told. These stories' relevancy and veracity critically depend upon generalizations from experience or expertise that are irreducibly socialized. As such, they predominantly reflect the experiences of the white men acting as judges and comprising the vast majority of jurors, while silencing the experiences and voices of women and people of color. Simon-Kerr claims that understanding this contingency holds the potential for validating alternative ways of knowing and for expanding the process of arriving at truth.

Chapter 25, "Race, Evidence, and Epistemic Injustice" by Jasmine Gonzales Rose, starts off with the definition of "racist evidence" as any evidence suggesting "that one racial group is inferior to or superior to another racial group in any way." Based on this definition, the chapter identifies and analyzes the *epistemic problems posed by racialized factfinding* and relates them to the broader notion of cultural cognition. This discussion focuses on the epistemic failings of "racial character evidence" and the unequal evidentiary treatment of white—as opposed to Black and Brown—"racialized reality evidence," especially on matters of structural racism and race relations with law enforcement. While white racialized reality evidence receives "implicit judicial notice" and is fast-tracked to the jury box, the racialized reality evidence of Black and Brown people is subject to the full rigors of evidentiary scrutiny and oftentimes suppressed. This system results in a pervasive epistemic injustice.

Chapter 26, "De-Biasing Legal Factfinders" by Frank Zenker, examines the psychological studies of biases and de-biasing measures in human decision-making with special reference to adjudicative factfinding. Research shows that factfinders are prone to *cognitive biases* (such as anchoring, framing, base-rate neglect, and confirmation bias) as well as *social biases*. Driven by this research, multiple studies have been carried out to examine the extent to which those biases can be mitigated by de-biasing measures like "consider the opposite" and "give reasons." Zenker reviews these studies and concludes that empirical research on de-biasing measures has so far delivered less than one would hope for.

We hope that this volume will enhance the understanding of the factfinding process taking place in the courts of law, stimulate future research, and promote interdisciplinary debates in the field of evidence and proof. That philosophy and other disciplines can ameliorate the study of evidence in law has become common knowledge a long time ago. Works assembled in this volume demonstrate that the amelioration is bidirectional: for their part, studies of evidence in law can also contribute a lot to philosophy and other disciplines.

Christian Dahlman, Alex Stein, and Giovanni Tuzet

References

Cohen, L. J. (1977). *The Probable and the Provable*. Oxford: Oxford University Press.

Ekelöf, P. O. (1964). "Free Evaluation of Evidence," *Scandinavian Studies in Law*, 8: 45–66.

Ho, H. L. (2008). *A Philosophy of Evidence Law: Justice in the Search for Truth*. Oxford: Oxford University Press.

Kaplan, J. (1968). "Decision Theory and the Factfinding Process," *Stanford Law Review*, 20: 1065–92.

Laudan, L. (2006). *Truth, Error, and Criminal Law: An Essay in Legal Epistemology*. Cambridge: Cambridge University Press.

Park, R. C. (1991). "Evidence Scholarship, Old and New," *Minnesota Law Review*, 75: 849–73.

Park, R. C. and Saks, M. J. (2006), "Evidence Scholarship Reconsidered: Results of the Interdisciplinary Turn," *Boston College Law Review*, 47: 949–1031.

Stein, A. (2005). *Foundations of Evidence Law*. Oxford: Oxford University Press.

Thomson, J. J. (1986). "Liability and Individualized Evidence," *Law and Contemporary Problems*, 49: 199–219.

Tillers, P. and Green, E. D. (eds.) (1988). *Probability and Inference in the Law of Evidence: The Uses and Limits of Bayesianism*. Dordrecht: Kluwer. (Reedited symposium originally published in *Boston University Law Review*, 66(3-4), 1986: 377–952).

Tribe, L. H. (1971). "Trial by Mathematics: Precision and Ritual in the Legal Process," *Harvard Law Review*, 84: 1329–93.

Twining, W. L. (1985). *Theories of Evidence: Bentham & Wigmore*. London: Weidenfeld & Nicholson.

Twining, W. L. (1990). *Rethinking Evidence: Exploratory Essays*. Oxford: Blackwell.

Twining, W. L. and Stein, A. (1992). "Introduction," in W. L. Twining and A. Stein (eds.), *Evidence and Proof*, xv–xxx. New York: New York University Press.

PART I

EVIDENCE, TRUTH, AND KNOWLEDGE

1

Evidence and Truth

Hock Lai Ho

1. Introduction

The view is taken by many judges[1] and legal scholars,[2] and reflected in some codes of evidence,[3] that a trial aims primarily at determining the truth of disputed propositions of facts, and that evidentiary rules regulating the trial ought, therefore, to promote the realization of that end. But not everyone agrees with this.[4] I interrogate this view by addressing the following: what do we mean by "truth" in the present context? Is truth the aim of a trial? What other roles or functions might the concept of truth have? How is truth related to justice? If the trial is a system for ascertaining the truth, how should evidentiary rules be designed?

2. Concept of Truth

Many things have truth-value. Beliefs, propositions, sentences, assertions, and more can be true or false. Most of us are competent in applying the truth predicate and have an entirely serviceable understanding of what truth means. For Ramsey, the meaning is "perfectly obvious." "Suppose a man believes that the earth is round; then his belief is true because the earth *is* round."[5] Putting this in general form: "a belief is true if it is a 'belief that *p*' and *p*, but false if it is a 'belief that *p*' and *–p*."[6] Ramsey notes that this view is "substantially that of Aristotle, who ... declared that 'To say of what is, that it is not, or of what is not, that it is, is false, while to say of what is that it is, and of what is not that it is not, is true.'"[7] Ramsey's theory has been taken as a version of deflationism. Deflationary theories of truth deny that truth is a substantive property and endorse the equivalence thesis. This thesis may be stated in various forms, for example, as a thesis about meaning ("that p is true" has the same meaning as "that p") or one about speech acts (to assert that p is true is just to assert that p). To quote Ramsey, "that 'it is true that Caesar was murdered' means no more than that

---

[1] Here are two representative references. In *Tehan v United States ex rel Shott* (1966) 382 US 406, 416, the United States Supreme Court declared that the "basic purpose of a trial is the determination of truth." Similarly, in the Supreme Court of Canada case of *R v Nikolovski* [1996] 3 SCR 1197, 1206, Cory J stated: "The ultimate aim of any trial, criminal or civil, must be to seek and to ascertain the truth."

[2] See, e.g., Wigmore 1983, §37.1, 1019: not "many ... will take seriously the claim that the law of evidence ... should have its predominant purpose something other than the search for truth."

[3] See, e.g., Rule 102 of the Federal Rules of Evidence in the United States.

[4] For a discussion of dissenting views, see Ho 2008, 51–70.

[5] Ramsey 1991, 9.

[6] Ibid., 11.

[7] Ibid., 11.

Hock Lai Ho, *Evidence and Truth* In: *Philosophical Foundations of Evidence Law*. Edited by: Christian Dahlman, Alex Stein, and Giovanni Tuzet, Oxford University Press. © Christian Dahlman, Alex Stein, and Giovanni Tuzet 2021.
DOI: 10.1093/oso/9780198859307.003.0002

Caesar was murdered, and 'it is false that Caesar was murdered' means that Caesar was not murdered."[8] This account of truth, as he acknowledges, is "merely a truism"[9] and a "trivial formalism."[10]

Inflationary theories of truth, on the other hand, insist that truth is a substantive property though there is much dispute on what the property is. Their focus is metaphysical rather than linguistic; the search is for what truth consists in, the underlying structure, essence or nature of truth. It is claimed that what makes the belief that the earth is round true is not (contrary to what Ramsey thought) simply that the earth is round. What makes the belief that the earth is round true is, on one account, that the proposition believed in "corresponds" to reality (the "facts"), or, on another view, that it "coheres" with other beliefs within a set.

A distinction is sometimes drawn between the property and the concept of truth.[11] By way of analogy, consider the concept of "water." A person who is competent in the use of the predicate "water" has a grasp of the *concept* of water (it is the colorless liquid that flows out of taps, falls when it rains, fills lakes, etc.). That person possesses the concept even if he does not know the *property* of water (for instance, that it has the chemical composition of H_2O). Similarly, even if truth is a property with features that are not captured in the ordinary concept of truth, we do not need to know what those features are to be able to deploy the concept competently.

As Haack has argued, the nominal (as opposed analytical) definition of truth of the sort offered by Aristotle and Ramsey is all that we need for present purposes.[12] Metaphysical speculation on the property of truth is ultimately unhelpful.

3. Legal Truth versus Plain Truth?

The literature on legal factfinding frequently speaks of "procedural truth" or "formal legal truth" and contrasts it with "substantive truth" or "plain truth." Summers for instance distinguishes between "formal legal truth" and "substantive truth" and "define[s] as 'formal legal truth' whatever is found as fact by the legal fact-finder ..., whether it accords with substantive truth or not."[13] He notes that Kelsen "drew a similar distinction." In Kelsen's own words:[14]

> In case a fact is disputed, the judicial decision which determines that the fact occurred in truth "creates" legally the fact and consequently constitutes the applicability of the general rule of law referring to the fact .... If a court of last instance declares ... that an individual has committed murder, the ... commission of murder are legal facts, even if, in reality, ... the accused [has not] committed murder. As a "legal" fact, that is as a fact to

---

[8] Ramsey 1927, 157.
[9] Ramsey 1991, 12.
[10] Ibid., 14.
[11] See Alston 1996, 37–8; Alston 2002.
[12] See, e.g., Haack 2004, 45.
[13] Summers 1999, 498.
[14] Kelsen 1944, 218. See also Kelsen 1949, 136.

which the law attaches certain consequences (duties or rights), the fact and, accordingly, its consequences are "created" by the judicial decision; and it is only as a legal fact that it has significance.

Golding believes that Kelsen's theory lends support to the argument that "the law has its own standards or criteria of truth, and its own definition of 'truth.'"[15] To my mind, none of these should lead us to think that factual adjudication in law employ a special or extraordinary concept of truth.

Suppose Brutus is charged with the murder of Caesar. The court cannot lawfully convict Brutus unless it finds in favor of all of the material propositions of facts that are necessary to constitute the offense. Let us assume that murder is defined by substantive criminal law as the intentional causing of the death of another person. The court's findings of facts have to be made in accordance with the law. The law requires, for instance, that the court bases its findings on evidence that is admissible and has been adduced in the proper manner at the trial and that the evidence meets the legal standard of proof. It is only when certain legal conditions are satisfied that the court may find that Brutus intentionally caused the death of Caesar. If all that is meant by the statement that "the law has its own standards or criteria of truth" is that there are legal criteria that must be met before the court may lawfully find that Brutus intentionally caused the death of Caesar, the statement is unobjectionable. Now, should the criteria be met and the court find that Brutus intentionally caused the death of Caesar, the meaning of the finding is plain enough.[16] To find that Brutus intentionally caused the death of Caesar is to find that *it is true* that Brutus intentionally caused the death of Caesar. And this finding is true if Brutus intentionally caused the death of Caesar and false if Brutus did not intentionally cause the death of Caesar. There is nothing special or mysterious about the concept of truth here (which is not to say that there are no other complications; I deal with these later).

The distinction between "legal fact" and "natural fact" is Kelsen's way of emphasizing that it is the court's finding and not the truth that has legal effect. The court has to find Brutus guilty of murder if and only if the court finds that Brutus intentionally caused the death of Caesar. It may be true that Brutus intentionally caused the death of Caesar but there is insufficient evidence of this at the trial. Since the court cannot lawfully find that Brutus caused the death of Caesar, it cannot convict him of murder. Conversely, if the evidence available at the trial is such that it calls for the finding that Brutus intentionally caused the death of Caesar, the court must find the same and consequently convict Brutus of murder. Suppose it turns out that it is false that he intentionally caused the death of Caesar. While we may concede that the court was lawfully required to make the finding which it did and to attach to the finding the relevant legal consequences, the conviction was unjust. We are able to criticize the outcome as a miscarriage of justice precisely because what the finding presents as true is false (more on this later).

---

[15] Golding 1978, 108.
[16] The meaning of a finding of "not guilty" is more complicated: Ho 2008, 24–7.

4. Truth as the Aim

When it is claimed that the predominant purpose of the trial is to "search for" or "determine" or "ascertain" the truth, truth means truth in the ordinary sense, and it is obfuscatory to speak of "legal truth," "formal truth," or "procedural truth."

But is truth the aim of the trial? Let me consider briefly four possible responses that either reject or qualify this claim: that truth is not *a* goal, not the *ultimate* goal, not the *only* goal, and not the *direct* goal.

If truth is not a goal, and the trial is not about ascertaining the truth, what can the trial be about? One controversial suggestion is that the system should ensure, not so much that the verdict speaks the truth, but that the public believes that it does. According to Nesson, the value of many rules of evidence lies in procuring and preserving public acceptance of a positive verdict; they protect the appearance of truth in the material propositions of fact on the basis of which the defendant is found guilty or liable.[17] This suggestion has drawn criticism, not least because it is normatively objectionable to treat the stability of verdicts as the end in itself, regardless of the truth, and a trial system that adopts this as the principal goal lacks legitimacy.[18] Truth surely matters. Golding rightly observes that, quite apart from truth being a condition for legal justice (giving parties their legal due), "it is hard to see why a society should expend funds to support a system of public courts unless it expects its laws to be enforced. Laws are enforced only when correct answers are given to the questions of fact in a case."[19]

Others have emphasized that the pursuit of truth is not the *ultimate* goal of the trial. Truth is pursued not for its own sake but for a purpose for which the trial exists. Among the possible ways of describing the purpose are the enforcement of the law, the vindication of legal rights, and the determination of legal liability. It must be remembered that the trial is only one facet of the legal process. Law can be enforced, legal rights can be vindicated, and legal liability can be determined in the legal process without the need for a trial: for one, the relevant facts might not be disputed and only issues of law fall for adjudication. The trial is the mechanism that is invoked only when facts are disputed, and it is the process by which findings of fact are made. That factfinding is conducted for a higher purpose—to enforce the law or determine legal rights and liabilities—is consistent with the claim that the adjudication of factual disputes, which is the definitive business of the trial, is aimed at ascertaining the truth.

Others accept that truth is a goal, or even the primary goal, of the trial, but emphasize that it is not the *only* goal. Among them is Weinstein:[20]

> Trials in our judicial system are intended to do more than merely determine what happened .... Among the goals—in addition to truth finding—which the rules of procedure and evidence ... have sought to satisfy are economizing of resources, inspiring confidence, supporting independent social policies, permitting ease in prediction and application, adding to the efficiency of the entire legal system, and tranquilizing disputants.

[17] Nesson 1985.
[18] See further, Ho 2008, 57–61, and the literature cited therein.
[19] Golding 1978, 107.
[20] Weinstein 1966, 241.

We should not confuse the goal of an enterprise with the desirable features of the enterprise. The features may be desired for reasons other than advancing the achievement of the goal. It is certainly desirable for the trial system to be efficient and not to waste resources, but we do not conduct a trial *in order* to achieve efficiency or conserve resources. The positive qualities of legal rules and the purposes that they serve are also distinguishable. It is desirable that rules of procedure and evidence are easy to apply and predictable in application, but "ease of prediction and application" is not what the rules *are for*. "Independent social policies" do shape the rules of evidence but, as will be discussed later when I address countervailing interests, they act largely as side constraints rather than as goals of the trial enterprise.

It is a good thing that disputants are, as Weinstein puts it, "tranquilized" by the manner in which their trial is conducted. The related suggestion is often made that the purpose of the trial is to settle or resolve disputes. If we take "disputes" to refer to the disputes that are presented, and in the form as presented, for resolution at the trial, it is obviously true that trials aim to resolve disputes. Just as obviously, this is not what is meant by the suggestion. The reference to disputes must be to the root quarrels that cannot be settled out of court or by a guilty plea and have to be brought to court for a binding verdict. Psychological studies claim that the willingness of the parties to accept and abide by the trial outcome are enhanced by certain process attributes, such as fairness, respectful treatment, willingness to hear the parties out, and so forth. Some rules of evidence may be appraised from this angle. Weinstein recognizes this. He notes that the hearsay rule is of "psychic value to litigants, who feel that those giving evidence against them should do it publicly and face to face."[21]

But the effects that we hope a trial might have must not be identified with the task facing the trial court. The trial process is fundamentally different from various forms of "alternative dispute resolution" (ADR) such as mediation, conciliation, and arbitration. It may well be that "a dispute-resolver's untrammeled search for truth can backfire—unearthing matter capable of intensifying rather than absorbing the underlying controversy."[22] But parties turn to the court typically when there is no hope of resolving the underlying conflict. The trial is not about achieving compromises and smoothing ruffled feathers. As Viola puts it: "The distinction between a judge and a mediator consists specifically in the fact that the former is appointed to apply preexisting normative criteria."[23] The court's task is to decide the legal dispute before it and if the legal process is to hold true to form, the court has to decide according to the law, and to do that, it has to get the facts that are legally material right.

Lastly, it is claimed, for want of a better expression, that truth is not the *direct* goal of an adversarial system. In this connection, a comparison is often made with the inquisitorial approach which is allegedly more truth-oriented. Haack contends that "the purpose of [an adversarial] trial is to arrive at a determination of guilt . . . in a legally-correct way" and this is not the same as seeking or discovering the truth.[24] But, as she is quick to add, this does not mean that the truth is irrelevant:[25]

[T]he hope is that arriving at conclusions in a legally-correct way will mean that, by and large and on the whole and in the long run, justice is served; and part of what this means is

---

[21] Ibid., 245.
[22] Damaška 1998, 304.
[23] Viola 1995, 214.
[24] Haack 2019, 203.
[25] Ibid., 203. She likens this to Adam Smith's "Invisible Hand" theory of markets in Haack 2016, 326.

that, if all those involved do their jobs adequately, often enough *the truth about what actually happened will come out.*

5. Truth-Related Norms

The point is well taken that the trial is vastly different from a scientific or historical inquiry. But getting the truth is more than a hope in legal factfinding. The role or function of the concept of truth can be elucidated by exploring how it engages with the various activities of which the trial is comprised and sets expectations of the participants. The principal actors are the witnesses, the lawyers, and the factfinders (by whom I include both the jury and the judge conducting a bench trial). Truth-related norms underpin many of the legal rules by which these actors are bound in carrying out their duties.

Let me deal first with witnesses and the rules that apply to them. They are sworn to tell "the truth, the whole truth and nothing but the truth," and perjury is made a crime. The purpose is not only to place them under a duty of sincerity and deter lies; it is also to raise consciousness of the solemnity of the occasion and consequently of the importance of accuracy in their testimony. There are also rules that disqualify persons from acting as witnesses if they are unable to engage in the competent communication of truth; on one formulation of the competency rule, the disqualification applies to all persons who "are prevented from understanding the questions put to them or from giving rational answers to those questions by tender years, extreme old age, disease, whether of body or mind ...."[26] Witnesses are supposed to testify only on matters of which they know to be true (that is, matters of which they have direct knowledge). No leading question is allowed during examination-in-chief on the theory that we want the witnesses to speak the truth instead of being prompted to say simply what counsel would like to hear. Witnesses are subjected to cross-examination so that their credibility as informational sources can be tested. The overall picture that emerges is not merely that we hope that witnesses will tell the truth; more than that, we expect them to do so, and the trial is structured with a view to having that expectation met.

There may appear to be less emphasis on truthfulness when we turn to the role of counsel in an adversarial setting. Their job is advocacy. The goal is to win the argument, to persuade the judge to accept the factual hypotheses that favor their clients, and to reject those advanced by the opposite side. Management of the case and the presentation and challenging of evidence at the trial are strategized towards this end; they are not aimed at fostering the revelation of truth in some objective, disinterested sense. For instance, parties are under no general obligation to produce or elicit evidence at the trial that is or may be adverse to their interest in securing victory in the adjudicative contest.

Even so, in discharging their professional responsibilities, lawyers are bound by legal rules that demand fidelity to truth. According to one set of rules, lawyers are expected to "always be truthful and accurate in [their] communications with any person involved in or associated with any proceedings before a court."[27] They must not "knowingly mislead or attempt to mislead" the court, opposing counsel, or any witness;[28] "fabricate any fact or

---

[26] Evidence Act, §120 (Singapore).
[27] Legal Professional (Professional Conduct) Rules 2015, §9(1), Principle (c) (Singapore).
[28] Ibid., §9(2)(a).

evidence;"[29] include any statement in any document used for legal proceedings that they know to be false;[30] or "concoct any evidence or contrive any fact."[31]

Importantly, when the parties engage in the activity of proving facts, they are making and supporting truth claims. In seeking to persuade the judge to accept their theory of the case, the party carrying the burden of proof is seeking to persuade the judge to find that its factual theory *is true*; and in seeking to undermine their opponent's competing factual hypothesis, they are seeking to persuade the judge to find that it *is false* or at least to cast doubt on its truth (that is, dissuade the judge from finding that it is true). Proof of facts is about establishing that those facts are indeed facts, that they are true.[32] This carries implications for the sort of evidence, arguments, and reasoning that counsel may deploy in advocacy. Only relevant evidence—evidence that has logical connections with the truth or falsity of relevant facts—may be adduced. Persuasion is by means of advancing a hypothesis the truth of which explains, fits, and may be rationally inferred from the evidence, and also by means of responding to and explaining away evidence that causes logical friction with the hypothesis. The hypothesis is presented to the court, not as a coherent fiction but as the truth.

Lastly, let me deal with the judge of fact. The factfinder in an adversarial trial plays a passive role. It is not his job—and it is improper for him—to actively investigate and gather evidence. The jury has no opportunity to question witnesses and there are substantial limits on the extent to which the judge at a bench trial may do the same. The factfinder has to make do with such evidence as the parties are able to adduce, and choose to adduce, at the trial, and critical evidence may be unavailable or withheld. Further, the judge of fact is not on a "general voyage of discovery,"[33] conducting a wide-ranging inquiry into all matters that may be legally relevant or material to the merit of the verdict. The trial is normally confined to those questions of fact that the parties have decided to put in issue. If both sides choose, for different strategic reasons, not to raise an issue, the adversarial judge may not pursue the truth of the matter even though it is otherwise of substantive relevance to what the verdict ought to be.[34] There is, further, the constraint of time: the verdict must be reached one way or the other after the lawyers are done with their submissions, and there is no option of suspending judgment and prolonging investigation.

Many of these features are born out of practical interests and necessities and respect for party autonomy. For example, trials cannot be allowed to drag on without compromising our interest in bringing prompt closure to legal disputes. Despite the apparent implications or consequences of these features, theoretical arguments have been mounted in epistemological defense of the adversarial system. The division of labor and the incentive structures that are put in place may make it as effective a system of ferreting out the truth as we may hope to achieve, given the practicalities we find ourselves in; and, even if it is not as effective as we would want it to be, it is (so the supporters claim) superior to the inquisitorial system. Self-interest provides compelling motivation for parties to be thorough in seeking out and

---

[29] Ibid., §9(2)(b).
[30] Ibid., §9(2)(c).
[31] Ibid., §9(2)(g).
[32] Tuzet 2013, 207, argues that there is a conceptual relation between proof and truth.
[33] Derham 1963, 345.
[34] See, e.g., Damaška 1986, 113, reporting that in some American jurisdictions, "even where the factual grounds supporting the finding of insanity are overwhelming, so that a verdict of not guilty by reason of insanity seems appropriate, the defendant who fails to raise the defense can be convicted." The position appears to be different in inquisitorial systems: Weigend 2003, 171.

eliciting evidence that supports their case or rebuts those of their opponents. On the "truth-finding theory" offered to justify the adversarial system, "each side will, with partisan zeal, bring to the court's attention all the material favorable to that side, and, therefore no relevant consideration will escape its notice."[35] If the system works as it should, "the part of the truth that one side omits will be brought to light by the other side."[36] Leaving the task largely in the hands of an inquisitorial judge faces the risk of bureaucratic disinterest. Further, the judge may not be as attuned to the intricacies and complexities of the facts as the parties are and therefore may not be as effective in examining witnesses.[37] The inquisitorial judge may also suffer from a version of confirmation bias: having reached a conclusion early on in the investigation, he may stick to it in the face of inconsistent or contrary evidence that emerges later.[38] For Summers, there is less risk of prejudgment in the adversarial system because it institutionalizes suspension of judgment on the part of the factfinder until both sides have been fully heard.[39] Lord Eldon is often quoted in this connection on the effectiveness of partisan argumentation; "truth," he said, "is best discovered by powerful statements on both sides of the question."[40]

These are theoretical arguments. How well they translate into practice depends on many contingencies. The system is unlikely to realize the epistemological hopes that theory pins on it if, for instance, there is serious inequality of resources and unequal access to lawyers of equal skills.

Whether the system is adversarial or inquisitorial, there is, I suggest, an internal connection between findings of fact and truth. I now address the complications that I had foreshadowed. Earlier, I suggested that to find that Brutus intentionally caused the death of Caesar is to find that *it is true* that Brutus intentionally caused the death of Caesar. Certain conditions must be met before the court may make this finding. Among other things, the evidence must satisfy the legal standard of proof; it must, in the present instance, establish beyond reasonable doubt that Brutus intentionally caused the death of Caesar. The proper interpretation of proof beyond reasonable doubt is heavily contested.

One approach to interpreting the standard is psychological. For proof to be established beyond reasonable doubt, the judge of fact (whether the actual factfinder or a hypothetical ideal factfinder) must be in a certain psychological state (of which possible candidates are feeling sure, belief and knowledge) with respect to the relevant propositions.[41] The relevant proposition, in our example, is that "Brutus intentionally caused the death of Caesar," and not that "more good than harm will result if we act as if Brutus intentionally caused the death of Caesar."

I think the relevant psychological state is linked to what a finding of fact amounts to. If to find positively that p is to assert that p, and if it is a norm of assertion that one asserts that p only if one believes or knows that p, then one ought to find that Brutus intentionally caused the death of Caesar only if one believes or knows the same. But this is simplistic. Although there are some judicial statements that endorse belief as the appropriate state,[42] for a variety

[35] Golding 1978, 106.
[36] Haack 2008, 33.
[37] Taruffo 2006, 515.
[38] Fuller 1972, 44–5.
[39] Summers 1978, 125.
[40] *Ex parte Lloyd* (1822) Mont. 70, 72n, per Lord Eldon LC, quoted by Denning LJ in *Jones v National Coal Board* [1957] 2 QB 55, 63.
[41] Yaffe 2019, 98.
[42] Ho 2008, 106–7.

of reasons, a personal and subjective belief on the part of the factfinder that Brutus intentionally caused the death of Caesar is neither sufficient nor necessary.[43] One reason is that it ought to matter how the state of belief was arrived at.[44] Another reason is that the factfinder is bound by various legal rules when deliberating on the verdict. I have argued elsewhere that we should draw on the concept of "selfless assertion" and accommodate the various restrictions that evidentiary rules impose on verdict deliberation. The main consideration, putting it in broad terms, is whether an epistemically responsible and rule-abiding factfinder would be justified in believing that Brutus intentionally caused the death of Caesar.[45]

6. Truth and "Rectitude of Decision"

The usual way of articulating the importance of getting the truth is that it is necessary to achieve justice understood as "rectitude of decision." This goal is attained only when the substantive law is correctly applied to findings of fact that are true.[46] On this view, we seek the truth in order to do justice.[47]

What are we to make of the claim that the trial aims at the truth? For ease of discussion, let me concentrate on a guilty verdict. Is the court to find Brutus guilty of the offense of murdering Caesar—more briefly, to find that Brutus murdered Caesar—if and only if (it is true that) Brutus murdered Caesar? As already noted, this is not the case. It may be true that Brutus murdered Caesar but the prosecution is unable to produce the evidence needed to prove his guilt; in that event, the court must find Brutus not guilty. Truth is different from justification.[48]

Should we say instead that justification, not truth, is what we are really looking for? The court is to find that Brutus murdered Caesar if and only if the evidence adduced at the trial is strong enough to legally justify the decision of the court to accept (the truth of) the proposition that Brutus murdered Caesar. But the evidence may only *seem* strong enough but actually is not. Suppose Brutus is innocent. But witnesses called by the prosecution lie flawlessly in their testimony and evidence that would show the accused to be innocent or throw doubt on his guilt is missing. The court is, in a sense, justified in convicting—indeed, it is legally obligated to convict—Brutus.

Even though the court has acted lawfully in convicting Brutus, and the conviction has legal effect, surely something has gone wrong. He has suffered a miscarriage of justice. To explain this, one may draw on a distinction between substantive criminal law and adjectival law (comprising of rules of evidence and procedure). Substantive criminal law sets out conduct rules addressed to the general public and adjectival law sets out rules that regulate

---

[43] Ferrer Beltrán 2004, 43–6. The position is less clear on the French standard of *intime conviction*: Damaška 2019, 118–21.

[44] Ho 2011, 241–63.

[45] In Ho 2008, 93, I proposed the following: "The fact-finder must find that p only if (i) one would be justified in believing sufficiently strongly that p if one were to take into account only the admitted evidence, ignore any inadmissible evidence to which one might have been exposed and avoid reliance on any line of evidential reasoning that the law might forbid in the case at hand; and (ii) if one found that *p*, one would find that *p* at least in part because one would be justified in believing that *p* under (i)."

[46] Twining 2006.

[47] This is not the only connection between truth and justice. It is not only that truth must be found to do justice, justice must be done in the search for truth: Ho 2008.

[48] See generally Mazzarese 1995, 165–9.

the trial process, including decision rules directed at the judge.[49] In this instance, as we are supposing, the judge has followed the decision rules in deciding to convict the accused. The conviction was, in this sense, lawful and, for that reason, legally effective as it stands.

The rules of substantive criminal law, on the other hand, are addressed to members of the general public for the purpose of guiding their behavior. The substantive criminal law defines murder, makes it an offense, forbids the public from committing murder, and warns them of certain sanctions if they do. The message is "do not commit murder," and *not*: "do not commit murder unless you can get away with it," and the accompanying warning is "you are liable to these sanctions if you commit murder" and *not*: "you are liable to sanctions for murder if and so long as you are unlucky enough to have the evidence at your trial turn strongly against you." The substantive law authorizes the imposition of sanctions for murder only on those who have committed that offense. Brutus did not deserve, under the norm that is addressed to him, to be sanctioned for a murder that he has not committed. He has thereby suffered a miscarriage of justice. His conviction lacks "rectitude."[50]

7. Designing the Trial System: Accuracy and Countervailing Values

If we think of a trial, especially a criminal trial, "as a tool for ferreting out the truth,"[51] the ideal system is one where the court will convict those and only those who committed the offenses with which they have been charged, and acquit those and only those who did not commit the relevant offenses. This ideal is unattainable in practice (it is practically impossible to eliminate all errors), and, in theory, needs to be qualified (it is fanatical to wish for a system that would brook no interference in pursuit of these and only these twin goals).

Since a perfectly accurate system is beyond reach, the law has to manage the risks of errors. Minimization and apportionment of such risks are seen as principal objectives of evidence law, especially in fixing the legal standards of proof.[52] In adjudicating factual disputes, the judge is supposed to decide what to do based on what he thinks the truth is, and since there is a practical interest in finality, the judge has to decide here and now (at the end of the trial) how the verdict should go. To acquit when in reasonable doubt is a practical decision, founded on some principle of political morality that defend the Blackstonian idea that "it is better that ten guilty persons escape, than that one innocent suffer."[53] The trial is therefore not wholly an epistemic exercise and truth is not the only relevant consideration. Of course, that the trial system cannot always succeed in getting the truth does not mean that it should not aim at getting the facts right. Since we have a fundamental interest in the truth, we would want the system to achieve a high frequency in getting the facts right. The critical question, then, is whether trial systems which "purport to be seeking the truth are well engineered to lead to true beliefs about the world."[54]

---

[49] See Dan-Cohen 1984.
[50] See Bulygin 1985, 160–163; 1995, 21–4.
[51] Laudan 2006, 2.
[52] See, e.g., Stein 2005.
[53] Blackstone 1769, 352.
[54] Laudan 2006, 2.

If true beliefs about the facts of the case is the goal, we might think that a well-engineered system is one that would generally allow any evidence that can potentially assist in revealing the truth to be admitted. Thus, Thayer states as a leading principle of evidence law that everything that is relevant (that is "logically probative of some matter requiring proof," or, effectively, anything that facilitates the ascertainment of truth) "should come in, unless a clear ground of policy or law excludes it."[55] The qualification recognizes that while truth is a fundamental goal, there are legitimate side constraints in the pursuit of truth. As the famous judicial dictum goes: "Truth, like all other good things, may be loved unwisely—may be pursued too keenly—may cost too much."[56]

Rules that exclude, or have the effect of excluding, relevant evidence have been grounded in various countervailing considerations that are thought to outweigh the interest in finding the truth in the respective domains of operation. They include the value of protecting certain relationships (evidential privileges), efficiency (discretion to exclude needlessly cumulative evidence), upholding the rule of law (inadmissibility of illegally obtained evidence), respecting human rights or dignity (right of silence, the privilege against self-incrimination), preserving the stability of transactions (treating certain records as conclusive), and preventing harm by prompt removal of dangerous conditions (rule excluding evidence of subsequent remedial measures). It is arguable whether some of these considerations are really of a countervailing nature. For example, legal professional privilege may serve to protect the lawyer-client relationship *and* advance our interest in getting the truth by encouraging the client to disclose critical information that he might otherwise conceal, and the exclusion of confessions obtained by torture can be explained by the demand of basic humanity *and* by epistemic concerns about their reliability.

The last point puts in question the assumption that more relevant evidence is always better than less in determining the truth. As Haack has maintained, while "comprehensiveness of evidence is an epistemological desideratum, it doesn't follow that exclusionary rules of evidence are simply epistemologically indefensible."[57] Some rules purport to render evidence inadmissible in order to promote accuracy and not because of stronger countervailing non-epistemic considerations. Thus, hearsay is generally inadmissible, on one rationale, because it is unreliable given the lack of opportunity to cross-examine the maker of the original statement, and one reason given for excluding evidence of "similar facts" and bad character is that it is overly prejudicial, having the tendency to be given too much weight by the factfinder.

It does not follow that just because a type of evidence is generally unreliable, it is epistemologically sound to exclude all tokens of that type. Where there is reason to think that a token is reliable, its exclusion under a rule that applies generally to the type of evidence would seem objectionable from the epistemic standpoint. But this is less clear at the systemic level. It could be that, in the long run and on aggregate, having a rule that excludes a type of evidence will result, overall, in fewer instances of the factfinder being misled than if the admissibility of tokens of such evidence were determined on a case-by-case basis.[58] Complicating the choice to be made is the availability of the further option of admitting the

[55] Thayer 1896, 530.
[56] *Pearse v Pearse* (1846) 1 De G & Sm 12 at 28–29; 63 ER 950 at 957.
[57] Haack 2014, 22; see especially Haack 2014, ch. 2, which is a reprint of Haack 2004.
[58] See generally Schauer 2008.

type of evidence and meeting the danger of unreliability in non-exclusionary ways. The law allows certain classes of risky evidence to be admitted but requires the factfinder to exercise special caution in determining its weight. This is done by having or requiring the judge to deliver the appropriate direction or warning to the jury and, for bench trials, by having rules that require the same caution to be exercised by the judicial factfinder.

Another challenge in assessing the truth-fostering capacity of various features of a trial system is that they often have opposing effects. For example, zealous cross-examination, though not quite "the greatest legal engine ever invented for the discovery of truth,"[59] can be an effective method of exposing lies, testing credibility, and eliciting vital evidence kept from the light during examination-in-chief. Equally, cross-examination can be used to confuse and rattle a truthful witness and distort the facts, and, further, the vigor with which cross-examination is conducted may deter persons with useful information from coming forward for fear of suffering abuse in the witness box. It would seem then that we have to consider the net overall effect of this feature of the trial in deciding whether, on the whole, it facilitates more than it hinders the revelation of truth, and this complication adds to the challenge of empirical verification.

Acknowledgment

I thank Giovanni Tuzet for his helpful comments on a draft of this chapter.

References

Alston, W. P. (1996). *A Realist Conception of Truth*. Ithaca and London: Cornell University Press.

Alston, W. P. (2002). "Truth: Concept and Property," in Richard Schantz (ed.), *What is Truth?*, 11–26. Berlin and New York: De Gruyter.

Blackstone, W. (1769). *Commentaries on the Laws of England* (vol. 4). Oxford: Clarendon Press.

Bulygin, E. (1985). "Norms and Logic: Kelsen and Weinberger on the Ontology of Norms," *Law and Philosophy*, 4: 145–163.

Bulygin, E. (1995). "Cognition and Interpretation of Law," in L. Gianformaggio and S. Paulson (eds.), *Cognition and Interpretation of Law*, 11–35. Turin: Giappichelli.

Damaška, M. (1986). *Faces of Justice and State Authority—a Comparative Approach to the Legal Process*. New Haven: Yale University Press.

Damaška, M. (1998). "Truth in Adjudication," *Hastings Law Journal*, 49: 289–308.

Damaška, M. (2019). *Evaluation of Evidence: Premodern and Modern Approaches*. Cambridge: Cambridge University Press.

Dan-Cohen, M. (1984). "Decision Rules and Conduct Rules: On Acoustic Separation in Criminal Law," *Harvard Law Review*, 97: 625–77.

Derham, D. P. (1963). "Truth and the Common Law Judicial Process," *Malaya Law Review*, 5: 338–49.

Ferrer Beltrán, J. (2004). "'It is Proven that p': The Notion of Proven Fact in the Law," *Associations*, 8: 29–54.

Fuller, L. (1972). "The Adversary System," in H. J. Berman (ed.), *Talks on American law*, 35–48. Washington DC: Voice of America.

---

[59] Wigmore 1940, 29. Similarly, Ravenshear 1899, 76 ("the most powerful weapon conceivable for exposing falsification").

Golding, M. P. (1978). "On the Adversary System and Justice," in R. Bronaugh (ed.), *Philosophical Law—Authority, Equality, Adjudication, Privacy*, 98–121. Westport, CT: Greenwood Press.

Haack, S. (2004). "Epistemology Legalized: Or, Truth, Justice, and the American Way," *American Journal of Jurisprudence*, 49: 43–61.

Haack, S. (2008). "The Whole Truth and Nothing but the Truth," *Midwest Studies in Philosophy*, 32: 20–35.

Haack, S. (2014). *Evidence Matters—Science, Proof, and Truth in the Law*. Cambridge: Cambridge University Press.

Haack, S. (2016). "La Justicia, la Verdad y la Prueba: No tan Simple, Después de Todo [Justice, Truth, and Proof: Not so Simple, After All]," in Jordi Ferrer Beltrán and Carmen Vázquez (eds.), *Debatiendo con Taruffo*, 311–40. Madrid: Marcial Pons.

Haack, S. (2019). "'Scientific Inference' vs. 'Legal Reasoning'?—Not So Fast!" *Problema*, 13: 193–213.

Ho, H. L. (2008). *A Philosophy of Evidence Law—Justice in the Search for Truth*. Oxford: Oxford University Press.

Ho, H. L. (2011). "Virtuous Deliberation on the Criminal Verdict," in A. Amaya and H. L. Ho (eds.), *Law, Virtue and Justice*, 241–63. Oxford: Hart Publishing.

Kelsen, H. (1944). "The Principle of Sovereign Equality of States as a Basis for International Organization," *Yale Law Journal*, 53: 207–20.

Kelsen, H. (1949). *General Theory of Law and State*. Cambridge, MA: Harvard University Press.

Laudan, L. (2006). *Truth, Error, and Criminal Law*. Cambridge: Cambridge University Press.

Mazzarese, T. (1995). "Cognition and Legal Decisions Remarks on Bulygin's View," in L. Gianformaggio and S. Paulson (eds.), *Cognition and Interpretation of Law*, 155–75. Turin: Giappichelli.

Nesson, C. (1985). "The Evidence or the Event? On Judicial Proof and the Acceptability of Verdicts," *Harvard Law Review*, 98: 1357–92.

Ramsey, F. P. (1927). "Facts and Propositions," *Proceedings of the Aristotelian Society*, 7(Supplementary volume: Mind, Objectivity and Fact): 153–70.

Ramsey, F. P. (1991). *On Truth: Original Manuscript Materials (1927–1929) from the Ramsey Collection at the University of Pittsburgh*, in N. Rescher and U. Majer (eds.), Dordrecht: Kluwer.

Ravenshear, A. (1899). "Testimony and Authority," *Mind*, 8: 63–83.

Schauer, F. (2008). "In Defense of Rule-Based Evidence Law—and Epistemology Too," *Episteme*, 5: 295–305.

Stein, A. (2005). *Foundations of Evidence Law*. Oxford: Oxford University Press.

Summers, R. S. (1978). "Comment: 'On the Adversary System and Justice'," in R. Bronaugh (ed.), *Philosophical Law—Authority, Equality, Adjudication, Privacy*, 122–6. Westport, CT: Greenwood Press.

Summers, R. S. (1999). "Formal Legal Truth and Substantive Truth in Judicial Fact-Finding—their Justified Divergence in Some Particular Cases," *Law and Philosophy*, 18: 497–511.

Taruffo, M. (2006). "Principles and Rules of Transnational Civil Procedure: An Evidentiary Epistemology," *Pennsylvania State International Law Review*, 25: 509–18.

Thayer, J. B. (1896). *A Preliminary Treatise on Evidence at the Common Law—Part I: Development of Trial by Jury*. Cambridge, MA: Harvard University Press.

Tuzet, G. (2013). "Arguing on Facts: Truth, Trials and Adversary Procedures," in C. Dahlman and E. Feteris (eds.), *Legal Argumentation Theory: Cross-Disciplinary Perspectives*, 207–23. Dordrecht: Springer.

Twining, W. (2006). "The Rationalist Tradition of Evidence Scholarship," in W. Twining *Rethinking Evidence—Exploratory Essays*, 35–98. Second edition. Cambridge: Cambridge University Press.

Viola, F. (1995). "The Judicial Truth: The Conception of Truth in Judicial Decision," in L. Gianformaggio and S. Paulson (eds.), *Cognition and Interpretation of Law*, 203–16. Turin: Giappichelli.

Weigend, T. (2003). "Is the Criminal Process about the Truth?: A German Perspective," *Harvard Journal of Law and Public Policy*, 26: 157–74.

Weinstein, J. B. (1966). "Some Difficulties in Devising Rules for Determining Truth in Judicial Trials," *Columbia Law Review*, 66: 223–46.

Wigmore, J. H. (1940). *A Treatise on the Anglo-American System of Evidence in Trials at Common Law* (vol. 5). 3rd edn. Boston: Little, Brown & Co.

Wigmore, J. H. (1983). *Wigmore on Evidence—a Treatise on the Anglo-American System of Evidence in Trials at Common Law* (vol. 1A) (revision by P. Tillers). Boston: Little, Brown & Co.

Yaffe, G. (2019). "When does Evidence Support Guilt 'Beyond a Reasonable Doubt'?," in L. Alexander and K. Ferzan (eds.), *The Palgrave Handbook of Applied Ethics and the Criminal Law*, 97–116. Cham: Palgrave Macmillan.

2
The Naturalized Epistemology Approach to Evidence

Gabriel Broughton and Brian Leiter

1. Introduction

At the core of epistemology, as the philosophical study of knowledge, is the critical examination of our methods of inquiry. The epistemologist wants to know how we should manage our beliefs about the world. What counts as good evidence for a conclusion? What can we reasonably infer from a given body of information? On a traditional view, these questions must be answered a priori—by the light of pure reason, as it were—without appeal to any supposed empirical knowledge. Naturalism rejects this view. A good method of inquiry must be *reliable*, in the sense that it consistently leads to the truth. But whether any given method is reliable depends on facts about the world that we can't discover from the armchair. Accordingly, naturalists insist that epistemology must be an a posteriori discipline, continuous with and dependent upon empirical science.

Naturalized epistemology has an individual and a social part. Individual epistemology concerns the intellectual practices of particular agents considered in isolation. Social epistemology takes up the social practices that inculcate belief. More specifically, it evaluates those practices instrumentally, in terms of how likely they are to yield true beliefs on important questions. Call this *veritistic* evaluation.[1] Since the effects of any given practice on the beliefs of relevant agents is an empirical question, amenable in principle to scientific investigation, naturalized social epistemology draws on the sciences. Still, its ultimate conclusions are *evaluative*. When the social epistemologist finds that a practice is more likely to lead to true beliefs than the alternatives, she identifies a reason to implement it. But practices that rate well on the veritistic dimension may perform so poorly on others that, all things considered, they should not be implemented. The social epistemologist focuses on the veritistic reasons without necessarily taking a stand on how they stack up against the rest.

In this chapter, we consider the law of evidence from the perspective of naturalized social epistemology, provisionally setting aside the other values implicated by rules of evidence and focusing on the promotion of accurate fact finding.[2] Of course, there are good reasons, all else being equal, to prefer accurate verdicts to inaccurate ones. For instance, a criminal prohibition's deterrence value depends on how reliably violators are convicted.[3] Indeed, many of the key aims of primary legal rules—from corrective justice

---

[1] Goldman 1999.
[2] cf. Allen and Leiter 2001.
[3] Kaplow 1994.

Gabriel Broughton and Brian Leiter, *The Naturalized Epistemology Approach to Evidence* In: *Philosophical Foundations of Evidence Law.*
Edited by: Christian Dahlman, Alex Stein, and Giovanni Tuzet, Oxford University Press. © Christian Dahlman, Alex Stein, and Giovanni
Tuzet 2021. DOI: 10.1093/oso/9780198859307.003.0003

to economic efficiency—can only be performed if the disputes arising under them are generally decided accurately. And there are other reasons too, having to do with justice in the individual case, with rule-of-law values, and with the perceived legitimacy of the law and its institutions.

The law of evidence matters to naturalized epistemology because it affects the accuracy of adjudication. But accurate adjudication depends on more than evidence law. It depends, for example, on civil and criminal procedure. It depends on the funding allocated to prosecutors and public defenders, on the contents of law school curricula, and on much else besides. The study of evidence law thus falls into place as one component of the broader project of studying *adjudication* as part of naturalized epistemology. This turns out to be important. For in the epistemological study of evidence law one sometimes identifies a persistent fact finding error that evidence law seems helpless to address. In such cases, one must remember that there may be other ways, outside of evidence law, to fix the problem.

2. Prospects

Studying evidence law as part of naturalized epistemology means (i) evaluating evidence law veritistically (ii) using the tools and results of the sciences. Start with (i). Rules of evidence can be evaluated along many dimensions. Do they produce outcomes that are generally accepted as fair or legitimate? Do they express respect for the parties? Do they keep administrative costs down? Studying evidence law as part of naturalized social epistemology means evaluating it in terms of the accuracy of the verdicts that it can be expected to produce. And this brings us to (ii). Rather than appeal to armchair intuition or the authority of tradition, naturalized epistemology examines evidence law with the help of empirical science.

How much can the sciences tell us about the veritistic value of different rules of evidence? Not all that much, according to some commentators.[4] These skeptics point out that we generally lack the sort of independent access to the facts of legal disputes that would allow us to reliably determine whether a given verdict is correct. And there are obvious practical, legal, and moral impediments to running actual legal trials under "experimental" rules of evidence. But how, then, are we supposed to empirically assess the reliability of alternative rules of evidence?

Many psychologists and social scientists interested in legal decision-making have focused on conducting controlled experiments known as *jury simulations*. These are studies in which participants acting as mock jurors observe a "trial" and then render a "verdict" or answer questions about the case. Typically, jury simulations involve randomly assigning participants to view different versions of the trial—one version might include an eyewitness or an expert, say, that another omits—in order to measure the effects of these differences. Critics claim that jury simulations tell us nothing about real juries.[5] They argue that

---

[4] See, e.g., Redmayne 2003, 866; Friedman 2001, 2034.
[5] See, e.g., Nunez et al. 2011. See also *Lockhart v. McCree*, 476 U.S. 162, 172 (1986).

simulation studies are unrealistic—they lack *ecological validity*—because (i) they use college students as mock jurors rather than drawing on a more representative sample; (ii) they
use brief written case summaries instead of live testimony and real evidence presented over
days or weeks; (iii) they omit jury deliberations and focus on the "verdicts" of individual
jurors; and (iv) they use mock jurors who know that their decisions will have no real consequences. As a result, simulation studies don't generalize. And, the critics reason, since jury
simulations are the best that social science—and, so, naturalized epistemology—can do,
this means that naturalized epistemology has little to offer evidence law.

We think this overstates the case, for four reasons.

(i) *Simulation studies don't exhaust the naturalized epistemology of evidence law.*
When a rule of evidence excludes relevant information, the rationale is often that,
while the evidence has *some* probative value, the jury may significantly miscon-
strue that value (or misuse the evidence in some other way). So the rule is based on
two distinct claims, one about the actual value of the evidence and another about
the value the jury will attribute to it. Jury studies address the second claim, but
other empirical findings bear on the first. Consider, for instance, the reliability of
various (so-called) forensic sciences. We don't need jury studies to find the error
rates associated with spectographic voice identification, microscopic hair comparison, or bite mark analysis. This suggests that even if the sciences had nothing to
tell us about juries, they would still have something to contribute to the veritistic
evaluation of evidence law.

But even when it comes to jury psychology, we are not limited to simulations. We
also have (a) surveys, (b) archival analyses, and (c) field experiments.[6] While none
of these methodologies has been as popular among social scientists as simulations,
each has contributed to our understanding of juries. Start with surveys. Many surveys in this area involve contacting jurors after a trial and asking why they decided as
they did. But other sorts of surveys can also be useful. For example, courts have frequently insisted that jurors understand the factors affecting the reliability of eyewitness identifications. A properly conducted survey can put this empirical claim to the
test.[7] Archival analyses use large datasets to discern relationships between case characteristics and outcomes. Such analyses can be used to study, for instance, whether
juries are more likely to convict a defendant if she has a criminal record, or whether
experienced jurors are more likely than inexperienced ones to find civil defendants
liable. Field experiments involve randomly assigning actual juries to different procedural conditions and then measuring differences between experimental groups
on various dependent variables. While understandably rare, field experiments have
been used to study the effects of permitting juror discussion during civil trials,[8]
among other procedural innovations.

(ii) *Low ecological validity is probably not as worrisome as the objection suggests, since
what really counts is external validity.* An experiment's ecological validity is the

---

[6] See Bornstein 2017.
[7] More on this in the following section.
[8] Diamond et al. 2003.

extent to which it mimics salient surface features of a real-world target setting. Its external validity is the extent to which its results generalize. There is, of course, a relationship between the two. Increasing ecological validity sometimes increases external validity by eliminating differences between the experimental and the target context that affect important dependent variables. But sometimes there is no payoff in external validity, because the eliminated differences are causally irrelevant. The question is whether the differences between simulations and trials really matter.

Suppose that we are interested in the effects of admitting a certain kind of "bad character" evidence against criminal defendants. We might run a jury simulation experiment that sacrifices some level of ecological validity by using college students as mock jurors. And suppose that we find that the admission of the character evidence causes a rise in convictions. Now, what kind of differences between student jurors and *realistic jurors*, as we'll call them, should we be worried about? One possibility is that realistic jurors are simply more (or less) likely to convict than student jurors. In fact, this would *not* limit our ability to generalize the effect observed in our simulation, because it would involve student jurors and realistic jurors reacting to the character evidence similarly, qualitatively and quantitatively, even if they differ in other ways. The simulation's external validity would only be limited if there were some interaction between juror type and character evidence, for instance if admission had no effect on realistic jurors. Of course, whether student jurors and realistic jurors differ in these ways is an *empirical* question.

The verdicts of student jurors and realistic jurors have now been compared in dozens of experiments, involving a variety of civil and criminal cases and the manipulation of numerous independent variables beyond juror type, thus facilitating consideration of both main effects and interaction effects. Both types of effects are rare, and interaction effects are especially so. In one review of twenty-six studies, for instance, main effects of juror type were observed in just five, while interaction effects were only found in two. Thus, "interactions are the exception rather than the norm."[9] Subsequent research confirms this result.[10] Similar studies suggest that concerns about the medium in which trials are presented to mock jurors as well as the presence or absence of deliberation may be somewhat overblown.[11]

(iii)   *Jury simulation studies are becoming increasingly realistic.* Even skeptics about the preceding can take solace in the fact that ecological validity in jury studies is improving. Critics conjure an image of college sophomores scanning a brief case summary and declaring a personal verdict, but this is no longer how most jury simulations are done. A review of every jury simulation reported over two recent years in *Law and Human Behavior* showed that the majority did *not* use student jurors or written case summaries.[12] Instead they used a more representative sample of community members and, in the usual case, a video presentation of a mock trial performed by professional actors. And while most of the studies still bypassed jury deliberation, a substantial minority (about 20%) did not.

[9]   Bornstein 1999, 80.
[10]   Penrod et al. 2011, 205
[11]   See, e.g., Kerr and Bray 2005.
[12]   Bornstein 2017.

(iv) *Triangulation and conceptual replication can help address reasonable concerns about external validity.* Even more realistic simulation studies differ from trials, of course. While a two-hour video is certainly better than a two-paragraph summary, it is still a far cry from two weeks or even two days in a courtroom. More important, none of these improvements in ecological validity addresses the problem of *consequentiality*.[13] No matter how representative the sample or how realistic the trial presentation, mock jurors still know that they are not real jurors. They still know that their decisions do not have real consequences. A handful of experimental studies have attempted to determine whether this difference limits the external validity of jury simulations. One study arranged for two separate juries, an actual jury and an experimental one, to hear a number of criminal cases.[14] The mock jury consisted of a random sample of potential jurors from the pool who were not selected or questioned by the attorneys. For each trial, the mock jury, like the actual one, was present in the courtroom during the proceedings and eventually deliberated in private before rendering a verdict. A few additional studies have attempted to test the effects of consequentiality in other ways.[15] Unfortunately, these isolated studies point in different directions, so that no firm conclusion can be drawn. This is clearly an area where further research would be useful.

Ultimately, though, no single methodology can give us everything that we want in a study. Simulations offer the benefit of internal validity. In a laboratory setting, because we can randomly assign mock jurors to trial conditions distinguished only by some particular variable of interest, we can be confident that any differences in juror behavior between conditions is the result of the experimental manipulation. The disadvantage of simulations is that we have no a priori guarantee of external validity. Laboratories and courtrooms are different, and it's always possible that an effect observed in one will not be observed in the other. Archival analyses and other field studies, by examining the behavior of actual juries deciding actual cases, offer stronger assurances of external validity. Unfortunately, they do so at the expense of internal validity. Outside the laboratory, cases that differ in one way are liable to differ in many others as well. As a result, we can seldom draw causal conclusions with any confidence based on field studies alone. Every study is imperfect in some way.

The proper response is not to wash our hands of the investigation. It is to (i) *replicate* our simulation results in a variety of contexts, and (ii) *triangulate* those results with evidence from the field.[16] Suppose, for instance, that the admission of a certain kind of statistical testimony in a simulated products liability trial causes a massive increase in jurors' liability judgments. To establish the external validity of this result, we would next want to replicate it in another simulation using deliberating juries rather than individual jurors, or using a different products liability trial. We might also conduct an archival analysis to test for a correlation between such testimony and plaintiff judgments. If we continue to observe the same effects in many different simulation studies, and we find converging evidence from outside the laboratory, then we can be reasonably confident in generalizing our findings to actual trials.

---

[13] Bornstein and McCabe 2005.
[14] Diamond and Zeisel 1974.
[15] See, e.g., Kaplan and Krupa 1986; Suggs and Berman 1979.
[16] Saks 1997, 5.

3. Applications

For naturalized epistemology, the proof is in the pudding. Accordingly, we turn, in the remainder of this chapter, to two applications of the approach: eyewitness testimony and, more briefly, character evidence.

3.1 Eyewitness Testimony

An eyewitness identification likely represents the *principal* evidence in upwards of 100,000 criminal prosecutions in the United States each year.[17] And the law generally takes eyewitness identifications to be very *good* evidence, as appellate courts have consistently sustained guilty verdicts based on the testimony of a single eyewitness, even where that testimony is undermined by other evidence. Yet eyewitnesses are often wrong. Mistaken eyewitness identifications contributed to at least 258 of the 375 wrongful convictions (69%) in the US that have so far been overturned based on DNA evidence.[18] These exonerations suggest that mistaken eyewitness identification is the single leading cause of wrongful convictions in our criminal justice system today.

This raises, but does not settle, the question of the reliability of identification evidence. The science of eyewitness memory, developed over the last forty years, helps to provide an answer. Research psychologists most often study eyewitness memory by conducting laboratory experiments in which participants view a simulated crime and later attempt to pick the culprit out of a lineup. In one study, for example, participants signed up for an experiment on "complex information processing." In fact, the experimenters had arranged for someone to interrupt each session by bursting into the lab and stealing an expensive piece of electronic equipment.[19] Having become eyewitnesses to a crime, the participants were later shown either a target-present or a target-absent lineup and asked to identify the thief. Eyewitnesses perform surprisingly poorly in such studies. A review of ninety-four experiments found that among subjects shown target-present lineups, just 46 % correctly identified the culprit, while 21% incorrectly identified a filler.[20] (The remainder declined to make an identification.) Among subjects shown target-absent lineups, 48% incorrectly identified an innocent person. Experiments conducted outside the laboratory suggest that these results generalize.[21]

These results converge with the findings of field studies of lineups conducted in actual police investigations. Unlike in the experimental context, researchers observing eyewitness identifications at a police station don't know who actually committed the crime. The lineup consists of a suspect and several fillers known to be innocent. If an eyewitness identifies the suspect, then she may or may not have identified the actual culprit. We simply don't know whether her identification is accurate. If she identifies a filler, however, then we know that she has made a mistake. The published field studies include data from 6,734 lineups

---

[17] See Goldstein et al. 1989.
[18] Innocence Project 2020.
[19] Lindsay 1986.
[20] Clark et al. 2008.
[21] See, e.g., Pigott et al. 1990, in which forty-seven unwitting bank tellers were confronted by, and later asked to identify, a man trying to cash a crudely forged money order.

conducted in a variety of jurisdictions.[22] All told, eyewitnesses identified the suspect 2,746 times (40.8%), identified a known-innocent filler 1,599 times (23.7%), and declined to make an identification 2,389 times (35.5%). Thus, nearly one in every four eyewitnesses (23.7%) identified someone known to be innocent. Setting aside the cases in which no identification was made, 36.8% of the choosers pointed to someone known to be innocent. Since some suspect identifications were surely mistaken as to the actual culprit, the true rate of mistaken identification is even higher.

Of course, eyewitnesses perform better in some circumstances than others. In the research literature, factors related to eyewitness accuracy are divided into *system variables* and *estimator variables*.[23] A system variable is a variable that is potentially under the control of the criminal justice system, such as the size of the lineup shown to an eyewitness. An estimator variable is one that is outside the system's control, such as the age of the eyewitness. Some research on estimator variables has produced predictable results, for instance that eyewitness accuracy falls when the culprit is seen only briefly, or only in the dark, or only from a great distance. But the literature includes some startling findings as well. For instance, eyewitness accuracy falls when the culprit's race differs from the eyewitness's,[24] when the eyewitness only sees the culprit under highly stressful conditions,[25] and when the culprit openly displays a weapon,[26] among other conditions.

Concerning system variables, we note three significant findings. First, research shows that accuracy is significantly affected by whether the eyewitness has been warned that the culprit might or might not be in the lineup. Pre-lineup instructions that lack this warning—what are called *biased instructions*—produce a negligible increase in correct identifications and a massive increase in false positives as compared to unbiased instructions.[27] Second, research shows that *filler selection* is extremely important. In particular, using fillers that make the suspect stand out—for instance, by failing to match eyewitness descriptions of the culprit—severely undermines the reliability of an identification.[28] Third, if the lineup administrator knows who the suspect is, then she can influence the identification, and undermine its reliability, in a variety of ways.[29]

In fact, an unblinded lineup administrator can cause problems even after an identification has been made. For instance, she can raise the confidence a mistaken eyewitness has in her identification by providing positive feedback. Research has repeatedly shown that even modest encouragement ("Good, you picked out the suspect") significantly inflates both the eyewitness's confidence that her identification was correct and the confidence that she *recalls* having when she originally made the identification.[30]

The courts have often touted eyewitness confidence as an important index of accuracy.[31] Are they right about this? Are confident eyewitnesses reliable? We need to distinguish between (i) an eyewitness's confidence in her identification at the time she makes it, (ii) her

---

[22] Wells et al. 2020.
[23] Wells 1978.
[24] Meissner and Brigham 2001.
[25] Deffenbacher et al. 2004.
[26] Steblay 1992.
[27] Steblay 1997.
[28] Fitzgerald et al. 2013.
[29] See, e.g., Greathouse and Kovera 2009.
[30] Semmler et al. 2004; Wells and Bradfield 1998.
[31] See, e.g., *Neil v. Biggers*, 409 U.S. 188, 199–200 (1972).

confidence at the time of trial, and (iii) her belief at the time of trial about her confidence at the time of identification. It is quite clear that because of the malleability of eyewitness confidence and retrospective assessments of confidence, neither (ii) nor (iii) is a remotely reliable index of accuracy.[32] The real question is whether initial eyewitness confidence, if accurately recorded by a blinded administrator, reliably tracks accuracy.

A consensus has emerged that, under certain conditions, it does.[33] But the boundary conditions of this phenomenon are not yet clear. Some argue that initial confidence reliably predicts accuracy so long as the testing conditions are *pristine*—so long, that is, as (i) the lineup includes only one suspect; (ii) the lineup is fair, in the sense that the suspect does not stand out; (iii) the pre-lineup instructions are unbiased; and (iv) the lineup administrator does not know who the suspect is (i.e., double-blind administration).[34] Others argue, with some empirical support, that pristine testing conditions are not good enough.[35] In addition, they claim, the *witnessing conditions* must be favorable: the eyewitness must have a relatively long look at the culprit's face, from a relatively close distance, in relatively good light, and so on. This remains an open question. Even if pristine testing conditions turned out to be sufficient to ensure a strong confidence-accuracy relationship, however, the problem would remain that, although the situation is improving, most eyewitness identifications in the United States are not conducted under pristine conditions.[36]

Even if eyewitness identifications are not especially reliable, an identification will typically still be relevant. It will typically still make the defendant's guilt more probable than it otherwise would have been. The research goes to the probative value of eyewitness identifications, and we only have a problem if juries take them to be more or less probative than they actually are. Unfortunately, the evidence suggests that jurors do indeed *overbelieve* eyewitnesses. Consider an experiment in which a number of factors in a staged crime were manipulated to yield low (33%), moderate (50%), or high (74%) proportions of correct eyewitness identifications.[37] Jurors then watched as defense counsel cross-examined an eyewitness drawn from one of these conditions. Under every condition, jurors' belief rates were higher than witnesses' accuracy rates. The disparity was especially severe when witnessing conditions were poor. Under those conditions—in which only 33% of eyewitnesses were accurate—jurors believed eyewitnesses 62% of the time.[38]

A number of US courts have suggested that jurors are at least sensitive to the factors affecting eyewitness accuracy.[39] They insist that the results just canvassed are simply common sense, perfectly familiar to the average juror. Survey research shows that this is wrong. In one study, experimenters asked jury-eligible adults to judge the truth or falsity of thirty statements concerning various issues affecting eyewitness accuracy (e.g., "The presence of a weapon impairs an eyewitness's ability to accurately identify the perpetrator's face").[40] They then compared these responses to those of research psychologists in the field. The

---

[32] Bradfield et al. 2002; Wells et al. 1981.
[33] See, e.g., Wixted and Wells 2017; Palmer et al. 2013.
[34] Wixted and Wells 2017.
[35] See, e.g., Lockamyeir et al. 2020.
[36] See, e.g., McNabb et al. 2017; Greene and Evelo 2015; Police Executive Research Forum 2013.
[37] Lindsay et al. 1981.
[38] These results were replicated in Wells et al. 1980. See also Brigham and Bothwell 1983.
[39] See, e.g., *United States v. Rodriguez-Felix*, 450 F.3d 1117, 1125 (10th Cir. 2006); *State v. Coley*, 32 S.W. 3d 831, 833–834 (Tenn. 2000).
[40] Benton et al. 2006.

results showed that jurors generally agreed with the experts on just four out of the thirty statements. For instance, while 98% of experts said that police instructions can affect an eyewitness's willingness to make an identification, just 40% of jurors agreed. And while 90% of experts said that eyewitnesses are more accurate when identifying members of their own race, just 50% of jurors agreed.

These data converge with the results of experimental investigations of the factors that actually influence verdicts. For instance, one study involved mock jurors watching a video of an armed robbery trial in which an eyewitness identification was the key prosecution evidence.[41] Ten factors relevant to eyewitness accuracy were systematically manipulated, including culprit disguise, retention interval, weapon visibility, instruction bias, and lineup fairness. The *only* factor that significantly affected verdicts was eyewitness confidence *at the time of trial*, which, as we saw, is effectively worthless. The remaining factors had at most trivial effects, often in the wrong direction. This basic result—that jurors are highly sensitive to eyewitness confidence at trial but insensitive to important factors bearing on eyewitness accuracy—has been replicated repeatedly.[42]

A variety of possible reforms could improve the accuracy of the system. These reforms fall into three distinct categories. The first involves attempts to improve the reliability of the eyewitness identification evidence that law enforcement collects along the lines discussed earlier. If law enforcement agencies were forced to use best practices, the resulting identifications would be more reliable, and more in line with jurors' expectations.[43] This might be accomplished through legislation requiring their use or, indirectly, through a rule of evidence excluding identification evidence resulting from dubious procedures. (Such a rule of evidence might itself be adopted by legislation or by judicial interpretation of constitutional due process. The US Supreme Court has rejected this approach,[44] but a number of states have adopted something like it.[45])

The second category of reforms involves using the existing rules of evidence to exclude the least reliable eyewitness identification evidence. This could overlap with the previous reforms in jurisdictions that use evidence law to deter shoddy identification procedures, but courts should also exclude some identification evidence whose unreliability is not due to procedural defects. For instance, an eyewitness should not be allowed to testify at trial (or in pretrial hearings) about her confidence that the defendant (i.e., the person she has identified) is in fact the culprit. We have seen that eyewitness confidence can be inflated by dubious procedures. But a variety of additional variables have also been shown to inflate eyewitness confidence even in the absence of procedural defects.[46] As a result, an eyewitness's confidence at trial is liable to reflect factors unrelated to memory strength. In many cases, eyewitness confidence at trial may actually be strictly irrelevant, but even if not, given its likely influence on the jury, courts should exclude it as "prejudicial" or "confusing" under Rule 403 of the Federal

---

[41] Cutler et al. 1988.

[42] See, e.g., Jones et al. 2020; 2008.

[43] For an extended discussion of best practices, see Wells et al. 2020.

[44] See *Neil v. Biggers*, 409 U.S. 188 (1972); *Manson v. Brathwaite*, 432 U.S. 98 (1977). Compare *Stovall v. Denno*, 388 U.S. 293 (1967); *Manson v. Brathwaite*, 432 U.S. 98, 118–124 (1977) (Marshall J, dissenting). The empirical evidence shows the Court's current due process approach to identification evidence to be irredeemably flawed. See, e.g., Wells and Quinlivan 2009.

[45] See, e.g., *Com. v. Johnson*, 420 Mass. 458, 472 (1995); *People v. Adams*, 53 N.Y.2d 241, 251 (1981).

[46] See, e.g., Odinot et al. 2009; Shaw 1996; Wells et al. 1981.

Rules of Evidence (FRE) or the state equivalent. Other plausible candidates for exclusion include evidence from eyewitnesses whose initial confidence in an identification was low,[47] as well as courthouse identifications generally.[48]

The final category of possible reforms involves trying to improve jurors' ability to evaluate the eyewitness identification evidence that they do see. If jurors fail to appropriately evaluate identification evidence because their knowledge of the factors affecting identification accuracy is limited, perhaps their performance would improve if this information were provided to them. This might be done, for instance, through expert testimony from a qualified research psychologist.[49] Historically, eyewitness expert testimony was excluded as invading the province of the jury.[50] Under FRE 702, it's admissible if (i) it is based on reliable scientific knowledge, and (ii) it will help the jury evaluate the eyewitness testimony at issue. While courts generally allow that eyewitness expert testimony is based on reliable scientific knowledge, many still routinely exclude it as unhelpful, claiming that eyewitness psychology is just common sense for the average juror.[51] As we have seen, this is false.

The question remains, though, whether expert testimony will actually improve jurors' evaluations of identification evidence. If it has any effects at all, it might produce (i) *confusion*, leading to perverse evaluations of eyewitness identifications; (ii) *skepticism*, leading to fewer guilty verdicts regardless of the strength of the evidence; or (iii) *sensitivity*, leading to verdicts that track the strength of the evidence.[52] Given that jurors tend to over-believe eyewitnesses, some form of skepticism effect would arguably be salutary. But accuracy would hardly recommend that jurors be led to dismiss identifications made quickly and confidently in pristine testing conditions based on memories formed in ideal witnessing conditions. Such identifications remain, by all accounts, very strong evidence. Thus, sensitivity is ultimately the more desirable result.

Research shows that expert testimony can sometimes improve juror sensitivity to the factors that affect eyewitness accuracy.[53] The more common result, however, has been increased skepticism of eyewitness testimony in general.[54] This, at least, is the more common result when discrimination is measured at the level of *verdicts*. Interestingly, though, in many cases where expert testimony does not produce verdicts that are sensitive to the quality of the identification, it nevertheless improves jurors' general understanding of eyewitness factors. The problem, in other words, seems to be that of applying this knowledge to the particular case. Recent experiments with expert testimony modeled on the interview-identification-eyewitness (I-I-Eye) teaching aid[55] suggest that this problem can be solved.[56]

---

[47] See Wixted and Wells 2017.
[48] See Garrett 2012.
[49] Alternatively, it might be done through jury instructions. We ignore jury instructions for reasons of space.
[50] See, e.g., *Criglow v. State*, 183 Ark. 407 (1931).
[51] See, e.g., *State v. Young*, 35 So.3d 1042, 1050 (La. 2010).
[52] Cutler et al. 1989.
[53] See, e.g., Wise and Kehn 2020; Cutler et al. 1989.
[54] See, e.g., Jones et al. 2017; Lindsay 1994.
[55] Pawlenko et al. 2013.
[56] See, e.g., Wise and Kehn 2020.

3.2   Character

FRE 404(a) prohibits the use of evidence of someone's "character"—evidence that she is careless, or that she is aggressive—to prove that she acted accordingly on a particular occasion (subject to some exceptions). This basic prohibition extends to evidence of previous *actions* when offered to show character in order to prove action in accordance. Yet FRE 404(b) permits evidence of past actions to be used for other purposes, for instance, to show motive, or opportunity, or absence of mistake. When specific acts evidence is admitted under FRE 404(b), the court may instruct the jury to consider it only for a specified permitted purpose and not as the basis for the prohibited character inference. FRE 404(a) does contemplate an exception for impeachment in accordance with FRE 608, which permits evidence of a dishonest character to impeach a witness.

There is a large social psychology literature examining the explanatory power of the notion of character. Do people act in keeping with stable personality traits across a diverse range of situations? Or is behavior so situation-specific that personality traits lack predictive value? *Situationism* holds that, in fact, people's actions are primarily the result of situational factors—often factors operating outside conscious awareness—rather than reflecting stable dispositions constitutive of character. Thus, situationism repudiates the core premise underlying the most obvious use of character evidence—namely, that character can be used to predict behavior on a particular occasion. As Ross and Nisbett note, "standard correlation coefficients determined in well-controlled research settings" show that "personality traits" lack substantial "explanatory and predictive power."[57] If situationism is correct, then the FRE 404(a) bar on character evidence is sound.

But consider the FRE 608 exception for impeachment by evidence of dishonest character. If "manipulations of the immediate social situation can overwhelm in importance the type of individual differences in personal traits or dispositions that people normally think of as being determinative of social behavior,"[58] then why think a witness's dishonest behavior at work or in her personal life bears on her truth-telling *in court, under oath, before a judge, under threat of perjury*? The situation giving rise to the impeachment evidence and the situation in which the witness testifies are usually nothing alike.

Many also worry that permitting evidence of past actions under FRE 404(b) will lead juries to draw officially forbidden inferences about the "bad character" of criminal defendants. In fact, there is substantial experimental evidence to suggest that any limiting instruction associated with the admission of such evidence is likely to be ineffective.[59] Given situationism, the danger of "unfair prejudice" under FRE 403 appears substantial: if the jury draws (forbidden) inferences from putative traits of character, the jury will be misled and prejudiced, since situationism teaches that character traits have relatively little predictive power. Should such evidence generally be excluded?

Caution is required here. Consider the famous situationist study of Good Samaritan behavior,[60] which found that "[i]f the subjects were in a hurry . . . , only about 10 percent helped [the person needing assistance]. By contrast, if they were not in a hurry . . . about 63 percent

---

[57] Ross and Nisbett 1991, 91.
[58] Ross and Nisbett 1991, xiv.
[59] See, e.g., Lieberman and Arndt 2000.
[60] Darley and Baton 1973.

of them helped."[61] But what about that 10%? Would it not be reasonable to invoke their good character in explaining their behavior, unlike the majority? Indeed, other researchers have argued that character traits can have quite large impacts on behavior. Suppose we want to know whether a trait of "honesty" can be used to predict the degree to which children will engage in a broad array of related behaviors. If we try to predict just *one* such behavior on the basis of one other behavior, we obtain a correlation that explains only 5% of the behavioral variance. However, if we look at the overall honesty that a child shows across a whole battery of tests and then try to predict the honesty that the same child will show in another battery of tests, we obtain a much higher correlation—this time, explaining a full 81% of the variance.[62] This suggests that it is the *quality* of the evidence that matters: we need *better proof* of character.

Existing rules, however, permit rather weak evidence of character: the opinion of those who know the person or her reputation, or evidence that she committed a serious crime, or committed any crime involving dishonesty. Moreover, at trial, we are concerned with a single instance of conduct—Did the defendant act in accordance with character *on the occasion that resulted in charges*? Did the witness tell the truth *today*?—which is precisely where situationism counsels skepticism about the predictive value of character evidence. In this context, the case for excluding evidence that supports inferences about character deserves more serious consideration from courts, although sometimes the probative value of prior bad acts for permissible purposes will outweigh the danger of unfair prejudice.

References

Allen, R. J., and Leiter, B. (2001). "Naturalized Epistemology and the Law of Evidence," *Virginia Law Review*, 87: 1491–550.

Benton, T. R., Ross, D. E., Bradshaw, E., Thomas, W. N., and Bradshaw, G. S. (2006). Eyewitness Memory is Still Not Common Sense: Comparing Jurors, Judges and Law Enforcement to Eyewitness Experts. *Applied Cognitive Psychology*, 20: 115–29.

Bornstein, B. H. (1999). "The Ecological Validity of Jury Simulations: Is the Jury Still Out?" *Law and Human Behavior*, 23(1): 75–91.

Bornstein, B. H. (2017). "Jury Simulation Research: Pros, Cons, Trends, and Alternatives," in M. B. Kovera (ed.), *The Psychology of Juries*, 207–26. Washington, DC: American Psychological Association.

Bornstein, B. H., and McCabe, S. G. (2005). "Jurors of the Absurd: The Role of Consequentiality in Jury Simulation Research," *Florida State University Law Review*, 32(2): 443–68.

Bradfield, A. L., Wells, G. L., and Olson, E. A. (2002). "The Damaging Effects of Confirming Feedback on the Relation between Eyewitness Certainty and Identification Accuracy," *Journal of Applied Psychology*, 87(1): 112–20.

Brigham, J. C. and Bothwell, R. K. (1983). "The Ability of Prospective Jurors to Estimate the Accuracy of Eyewitness Identifications," *Law and Human Behavior*, 7(1): 19–30.

Clark, S. E., Howell, R. T., and Davey, S. L. (2008). "Regularities in Eyewitness Identification: The Role of System and Estimator Variables," *Law and Human Behavior*, 32(3): 233–58.

Cutler, B. L., Dexter, H. R., and Penrod, S. D. (1989). "Expert Testimony and Jury Decision Making: An Empirical Analysis," *Behavioral Sciences and the Law*, 7: 215–25.

Cutler, B. L., Penrod, S. D., and Stuve, T. E. (1988). "Juror Decision Making in Eyewitness Identification Cases," *Law and Human Behavior*, 12(1): 41–55.

---

[61] Ross and Nisbett 1991, 4.
[62] Hartshorne and May 1928.

Darley, J. M. and Baton, C. D. (1973). "From Jerusalem to Jericho: A Study of Situational and Dispositional Variables in Helping Behavior," *Journal of Personality & Social Psychology*, 27: 100–8.

Deffenbacher, K. A., Bornstein, B. H., Penrod, S. D., and McGorty, E. K. (2004). "A Meta-Analytic Review of the Effects of High Stress on Eyewitness Memory," *Law and Human Behavior*, 28(6): 687–706.

Diamond, S. S., Vidmar, N., Rose, M., Ellis, L., and Murphy, B. (2003). "Inside the Jury Room: Evaluating Juror Discussions during Trial," *Judicature*, 87(2): 54–9.

Diamond, S. S., and Zeisel, H. (1974). "A Courtroom Experiment on Juror Selection and Decision-Making," *Personality and Social Psychology Bulletin*, 1(1): 276–7.

Fitzgerald, R. J., Price, H. L., Oriet, C., and Charman, S. D. (2013). "The Effects of Suspect-Filler Similarity on Eyewitness Identification Decisions: A Meta-Analysis," *Psychology, Public Policy, and Law*, 19(2): 151–64.

Friedman, R. D. (2001). "E is for Eclectic: Multiple Perspectives on Evidence," *Virginia Law Review*, 87: 2029–54.

Garrett, B. L. (2012). "Eyewitnesses and Exclusion," *Vanderbilt Law Review*, 65(2): 449–506.

Goldman, A. (1999). *Knowledge in a Social World*. Oxford: Oxford University Press.

Goldstein, A. G., Chance, J. E., and Schneller, G. R. (1989). "Frequency of Eyewitness Identification in Criminal Cases: A Survey of Prosecutors," *Bulletin of the Psychonomic Society*, 27(1): 71–4.

Greathouse, S. M., and Kovera, M. B. (2009). "Instruction Bias and Lineup Presentation Moderate the Effects of Administrator Knowledge on Eyewitness Identification," *Law and Human Behavior*, 33(1): 70–82.

Greene, E., and Evelo, A. J. (2015). "Cops and Robbers (and Eyewitnesses): A Comparison of Lineup Administration by Robbery Detectives in the USA and Canada," *Psychology, Crime & Law*, 21(3): 297–313.

Hartshorne, H., and May, M. A. (1928). *Studies in Deceit*. New York: Macmillan.

Innocence Project (2020). *DNA Exonerations in the United States*. Available at https://www.innocenceproject.org/dna-exonerations-in-the-united-states/ (Accessed: March 29, 2021).

Jones, A. M., Bergold, A. N., Dillon, M. K., and Penrod, S. D. (2017). "Comparing the Effectiveness of *Henderson* Instructions and Expert Testimony: Which Safeguard Improves Jurors' Evaluations of Eyewitness Evidence?," *Journal of Experimental Criminology*, 13: 29–52.

Jones, A. M., Bergold, A. N., and Penrod, S. (2020). "Improving juror sensitivity to Specific Eyewitness Factors: Judicial Instructions Fail the Test," *Psychiatry, Psychology and Law*, 27(3): 366–85.

Jones, E. E., Williams, K. D., and Brewer, N. (2008). "'I had a Confidence Epiphany!': Obstacles to Combating Post-Identification Confidence Inflation," *Law and Human Behavior*, 32: 164–76.

Kaplan, M. F., and Krupa, S. (1986). "Severe Penalties under the Control of Others can Reduce Guilty Verdicts," *Law & Psychology Review*, 10: 1–18.

Kaplow, L. (1994). "The Value of Accuracy in Adjudication: An Economic Analysis," *Journal of Legal Studies*, 23(1): 307–401.

Kerr, N. L., and Bray, R. M. (2005). "Simulation, Realism, and the Study of the Jury," in N. Brewer and K. D. Williams (eds.), *Psychology and Law: An Empirical Perspective*, 322–64. New York: Guilford Press.

Lieberman, J. D., and Arndt, J. (2000). "Understanding the Limits of Limiting Instructions: Social Psychological Explanations for the Failures of Instructions to Disregard Pretrial Publicity and other Inadmissible Evidence," *Psychology, Public Policy, and Law*, 6(3): 677–711.

Lindsay, R. C. L. (1986). "Confidence and Accuracy of Eyewitness Identification from Lineups," *Law and Human Behavior*, 10(3): 229–39.

Lindsay, R. C. L. (1994). "Expectations of Eyewitness Performance: Jurors' Verdicts do not Follow from their Beliefs," in D. F. Ross, J. D. Read, and M. P. Toglia (eds.), *Adult Eyewitness Testimony: Current Trends and Developments*, 362–84. New York: Cambridge University Press.

Lindsay, R. C. L., Wells, G. L., and Rumpel, C. M. (1981). "Can People Detect Eyewitness-Identification Accuracy within and Across Situations?," *Journal of Applied Psychology*, 66(1): 75–89.

Lockamyeir, R. F., Carlson, C. A., Jones, A. R., Carlson, M. A., and Weatherford, D. R. (2020). "The Effect of Viewing Distance on Empirical Discriminability and the Confidence-Accuracy

Relationship for Eyewitness Identification," *Applied Cognitive Psychology*, 34(5):1047–60. doi: 10.1002/acp.3683.

McNabb, N. S., Farrell, B. R., and Brown, C. R. (2017). "Voluntary Adoption of Evidence-Based Practices by Local Law Enforcement: Eyewitness Identification Procedures in Arkansas, Iowa, Kansas, Missouri, and Nebraska," *Journal of Gender, Race, and Justice*, 20(3): 509–42.

Meissner, C. A., and Brigham, J. C. (2001). "Thirty Years of Investigating the Own-Race Bias in Memory for Faces: A Meta-Analytic Review," *Psychology, Public Policy, and Law*, 7(1): 3–35.

Nunez, N., McCrea, S. M., and Culhane, S. E. (2011). "Jury Decision Making Research: Are Researchers Focusing on the Mouse and not the Elephant in the Room?," *Behavioral Sciences and the Law*, 29: 439–51.

Odinot, G., Wolters, G., and Lavender, T. (2009). "Repeated Partial Eyewitness Questioning causes Confidence Inflation but not Retrieval-Induced Forgetting," *Applied Cognitive Psychology*, 23: 90–7.

Palmer, M. A., Brewer, N., Weber, N., and Nagesh, A. (2013). "The Confidence-Accuracy Relationship for Eyewitness Identification Decisions: Effects of Exposure Duration, Retention Interval, and Divided Attention," *Journal of Experimental Psychology: Applied*, 19(1): 55–71.

Pawlenko, N. B., Safer, M. A., Wise, R. A., and Holfeld, B. (2013). "A Teaching Aid for Improving Jurors' Assessments of Eyewitness Accuracy," *Applied Cognitive Psychology*, 27(2): 190–7.

Penrod, S. D., Kovera, M. B., and Groscup, J. (2011). "Jury Research Methods," in B. Rosenfeld and S. D. Penrod (eds.), *Research Methods in Forensic Psychology*, 191–214. Hoboken, NJ: Wiley.

Pigott, M. A., Brigham, J. C., and Bothwell, R. K. (1990). "A Field Study on the Relationship Between Eyewitnesses' Descriptions and Identification Accuracy," *Journal of Police Science and Administration*, 17(2): 84–8.

Police Executive Research Forum (2013). "A National Survey of Eyewitness Identification Processes in Law Enforcement Agencies" (March 8).

Redmayne, M. (2003). "Rationality, Naturalism, and Evidence Law," *Michigan State Law Review*, 4: 849–83.

Ross, L., and Nisbett, R.E. (1991). *The Person and the Situation: Perspectives of Social Psychology*. Philadelphia, PA: Temple University Press.

Saks, M. J. (1997). "What do Jury Experiments tell us About how Juries (should) make Decisions?," *Southern California Interdisciplinary Law Journal*, 6(1): 1–53.

Semmler, C., Brewer, N., and Wells, G. L. (2004). "Effects of Postidentification Feedback on Eyewitness Identification and Nonidentification Confidence," *Journal of Applied Psychology*, 89(2): 334–46.

Shaw, III, J. S. (1996). "Increases in Eyewitness Confidence Resulting from Postevent Questioning," *Journal of Experimental Psychology: Applied*, 2(2): 126–46.

Steblay, N. M. (1992). "A Meta-Analytic Review of the Weapon Focus Effect," *Law and Human Behavior*, 16(4): 413–24.

Steblay, N. M. (1997). "Social Influence in Eyewitness Recall: A Meta-Analytic Review of Lineup Instruction Effects," *Law and Human Behavior*, 21(3): 283–97.

Suggs, D., and Berman, J. J. (1979). "Factors affecting testimony About Mitigating Circumstances and the Fixing of Punishment," *Law and Human Behavior*, 3(4): 251–60.

Wells, G. L. (1978). "Applied Eyewitness Testimony Research: System Variables and Estimator Variables," *Journal of Personality and Social Psychology*, 36: 1546–57.

Wells, G. L., and Bradfield, A. L. (1998). "'Good, you Identified the Suspect': Feedback to Eyewitnesses Distorts their Reports of the Witnessing Experience," *Journal of Applied Psychology*, 83(3): 360–76.

Wells, G. L., Ferguson, T. J., and Lindsay, R. C. L. (1981). "The Tractability of Eyewitness Confidence and its Implications for Triers of Fact," *Journal of Applied Psychology*, 66(6): 688–96.

Wells, G. L., Kovera, M. B., Douglas, A. B., Brewer, N., Meissner, C. A., and Wixted, J. T. (2020). "Policy and Procedure Recommendations for the Collection and Preservation of Eyewitness Identification Evidence," *Law and Human Behavior*, 44(1): 3–36.

Wells, G. L., Lindsay, R. C. L., and Tousignant, J. P. (1980). "Effects of Expert Psychological Advice on Human Performance in Judging the Validity of Eyewitness Testimony," *Law and Human Behavior*, 4(4): 275–85.

Wells, G. L., and Quinlivan, D. S. (2009). "Suggestive Eyewitness Identification Procedures and the Supreme Court's Reliability Test in Light of Eyewitness Science: 30 Years Later," *Law and Human Behavior*, 33(1): 1–24.

Wise, R. A., and Kehn, A. (2020). "Can the Effectiveness of Eyewitness Expert Testimony be Improved?," *Psychiatry, Psychology and Law*, 27(2): 315–30.

Wixted, J. T., and Wells, G. L. (2017). "The Relationship between Eyewitness Confidence and Identification Accuracy: A New Synthesis," *Psychological Science in the Public Interest*, 18(1): 10–65.

3

Proven Facts, Beliefs, and Reasoned Verdicts

Jordi Ferrer Beltrán

1. Introduction

A careful reading of the literature on evidence and proof and national and international case law allows the conclusion that the assumptions of the subjectivist conception of proof continue to be accepted by most authors and courts in both common law and civil law countries—assumptions founded on the constant conceptual link between proof and the conviction of the trier of fact.[1] This link is common in legal systems from the Roman-Germanic tradition as the presentation of the evidence is intended to convince the trier of fact and that, considering the result, a fact is proven if, and only if, the trier is convinced that it took place.

A quick look at the attention the doctrine and case law of English-speaking countries has paid to determining standards of proof might lead to the conclusion that things are very different in this legal tradition. It is not unusual for English-speaking authors to reach such a conclusion. Many of them, such as Clermont and Sherwin, are surprised that the majority of the Continental legal systems do not contain rules establishing thresholds of sufficiency of proof and rely on the conviction of the trier of fact to decide on the facts of the case.[2] However, this is an over-simplification. In fact, three crucial factors push the English-speaking evidential systems toward convergence with the Romano-Germanic ones in terms of subjectivity: firstly, the extreme vagueness of the formulas commonly used to indicate standards of proof and the lack of definition of their key concepts. Secondly, the thesis, maintained in part of the doctrine and the American case law, of the flexible nature of both "beyond all reasonable doubt" and the "preponderance of evidence" or "balance of probabilities," depending on the circumstances of the particular case, where the trier of fact has to specify the levels of proof required.[3] Thirdly, the majority of the doctrine and almost all the case law from the higher courts conceive of standards of proof in terms of the degree of firmness or confidence that must be reached by the triers of fact in their own beliefs before they can consider a factual hypothesis to be proven. It is therefore clear that, despite the extensive use in the English-speaking tradition of the

---

[1] The subjectivist conception is opposed to the rationalist conception of proof. With respect to the latter, see Twining 1994, 243 ff.

[2] Clermont and Sherwin 2002, 243 ff. A commentary on the weaknesses of Clermont and Sherwin's work from the point of view of comparative law can be seen in Taruffo 2003, and the response to this in Clermont 2009. There is also a comparative presentation of the evidence evaluation systems and standards of proof applicable in common law and civil law countries in Tuzet 2020, 98 ff. For a more careful look at the legislation on standards of proof in different European countries, see the articles included in Tichý 2019.

[3] See, e.g., Bartels 1981, 907–908; Stoffelmayr and Diamond 2000, 783; Lillquist 2002, 162 ff.; Ho 2008, 179 ff., 186, 198; Hamer 2011, 425. It should be stressed that it is also possible to find the thesis that judicial conviction can be graduated in the literature on evidence from civil law countries. Along these lines, for example, see Schweizer 2019, 20, 40–41.

Jordi Ferrer Beltrán, *Proven Facts, Beliefs, and Reasoned Verdicts* In: *Philosophical Foundations of Evidence Law*. Edited by: Christian Dahlman, Alex Stein, and Giovanni Tuzet, Oxford University Press. © Christian Dahlman, Alex Stein, and Giovanni Tuzet 2021. DOI: 10.1093/oso/9780198859307.003.0004

concept of standard of proof, the way in which it has largely been understood brings it closer to, rather than distinguishing it from, the evidential subjectivism which still predominates in civil law countries in the name of the free evaluation of evidence.[4]

At the same time, the idea that reasons should be given for judicial decisions and trial verdicts as a requirement of due process is clearly established in countries following the Romano-Germanic tradition[5] and this has been reinforced by international human rights case law. Meanwhile, although in English-speaking countries the existence of a duty to give reasons on which decisions on law and on the facts have been based has triggered a more recent debate, in many of them the current discussion is not so much about whether or not reasons should be given for decisions as about how far this duty extends.[6]

I therefore hope to show in this contribution that there is a close relationship between the concept of proof, standards of proof, and the way in which the duty of giving reasons for trial verdicts, and even the possibility of complying with this duty, are understood. Specifically, I will maintain that if proof is conceptually linked to the beliefs or convictions of the trier of fact, it is impossible to sustain the idea of giving reasons as a justification of the decisions about facts. And, as a corollary to this, if we do not have methodologically well-formulated standards of proof it is not possible to comply with the duty of giving reasons for these decisions, understood as justification.

2. The Conceptual Link between Proof and the Beliefs of the Trier of Fact

There are various ways of approaching the relationship between evidence and the beliefs of the trier of fact. For the purposes of this contribution, I am particularly interested in the establishment of a conceptual relationship between the proof of F (as an evidential result or proven fact) and the acquisition of belief in F by the trier of fact. I will focus on the analysis of this link and on the implications this has for the possibility of justifying factual decisions.

The conceptual relationship between belief in a particular proposition on facts and the proof of this proposition has been established, maintaining that it is a necessary condition for the proposition to be proven that the trier of fact should have the belief (or the conviction, which amounts to the same thing) that this proposition is true.[7]

In many cases, this link is found not only in the academic literature and in case law, but is also expressly set out in the legislation. Procedural codes or statutes use criteria such as "*intime conviction*" or any of the formulations which in one way or another refer to the trier of fact's belief in order to define the conditions for being able to say that a fact is proven.[8]

In the English-speaking literature, by contrast, this link is commonly established via standards of proof, demanding a certain degree of firmness of belief, or that belief should depend on the degree of probability of the proposition of fact. This approach maintains,

---

[4] The title of a work by Stein 1997, *Against Free Proof*, is significant in terms of following the line maintained here.
[5] One, now classic, analysis of this can be seen in Taruffo 1975, 321 ff. together with a historical analysis in Aliste Santos 2018, 31 ff.
[6] Instead, the discussion is focused on whether, and in what way, juries should give reasons for decisions on the facts. On this point, in relation to England and Wales, see Jackson 2002; Roberts 2011; Coen and Doak 2017, 788 ff. With respect to the United States, see Nepveu 2003, 266 ff.; Burd and Hans 2018.
[7] See, e.g., Cabañas García 1992, 21.
[8] See, e.g., Spanish Criminal Proceedings Act, Art. 741.1; German Code of Civil Proceedings (ZPO), Art. 286.1.

for example, that the trier of fact must believe that the proposition is more likely to be true than false for it to be proven in civil proceedings. In fact, the criteria used in the standards of proof to identify the evidential threshold are linked to the conception held of evidence assessment. For this reason, the appeal to beliefs (and their graduation) in standards of proof is a reflection of a more general subjectivist concept of proof. Along these lines, it is worth repeating, because of its historical importance for US law and its clarity, Harlan J's statement in the case *In re Winship*:

> [A] standard of proof represents an attempt to instruct the factfinder concerning the degree of confidence our society thinks he should have in the correctness of factual conclusions for a particular type of adjudication. Although the phrases "preponderance of the evidence" and "proof beyond a reasonable doubt" are quantitatively imprecise, they do communicate to the finder of fact different notions concerning the degree of confidence he is expected to have in the correctness of his factual conclusions.[9]

At doctrinal level, *McCormick on Evidence*, one of the most important American handbooks on evidence, says:

> [T]he "reasonable doubt" formula points to what we are really concerned with, the state of the jury's mind, whereas the other two [preponderance of the evidence and clear and convincing evidence] divert attention to the evidence, which is a step removed, being the instrument by which the jury's mind is influenced.[10]

In one way or another, either through the definition of the notion of "proof" or through the selection of the criteria establishing a threshold of sufficiency so that a hypothesis can be considered proven, the result is the establishment of a conceptual relationship between proof and beliefs of the trier of fact: it is a necessary condition for a factual hypothesis to be proven that the trier of fact comes to believe that the facts occurred in that particular way. But is this a good idea? I think the answer is clearly no, for at least three reasons, each of which would, on its own, be sufficient.

The first problem is found when we observe that, in reality, it is not unusual for triers of fact to make decisions that go against their own beliefs. Both in criminal and civil proceedings, for example, the trier of fact may believe that the defendant was responsible for certain facts but also understands that there is not sufficient evidence to convict them. The trier of fact may also have pieces of evidence (on which to base their belief) that have not been incorporated into the trial or that have subsequently been excluded and which they can therefore not use as a basis for their decision.[11] The causes of the dissonance between beliefs and facts declared to have been proven are very diverse, and the conception that considers that the trier of fact's beliefs are a necessary condition of proof can only conclude that in these cases the facts are not proven, which does not seem satisfactory.

---

[9]   *In re Winship*, 397 U.S. 358 (1970).
[10]   Broun et al. 2006, 568. In English doctrine, the same idea can be found in Redmayne 1999, 187, n. 104, with respect to the formula for the standard of "clear and convincing proof."
[11]   Thomas 2013, 490–1 offers empirical information, according to which, for example, 7% of English juries admit having sought information on the internet about the parties' legal teams and 1% "visited" the scene of the crime via Google Earth. With respect to these situations, see also Jackson 2016, 288.

In addition, as has been seen, in some of the circumstances mentioned, the trier of fact not only can, but also must, set aside their beliefs to select the proven facts they incorporate into their reasoning. Because of this, if the trier of fact has to set aside their beliefs about the facts of the case to determine the proven facts but does not set them aside, it might be said that the judge considered hypothesis F to be proven even though it was not actually proven.

Secondly, it must be emphasized that the link is established between the fact that the trier of fact acquires the belief that F took place and the proof of F, not between F's credibility and its proof. However, the fact that the trier, you, the reader or my mother might have a certain belief does not in itself have any capacity to justify F, nor is it an indicator of its truth value.[12] It is not surprising, then, that some epistemologists who have devoted their attention to legal proof should be surprised and horrified that the beliefs of specific subjects could be considered a necessary (or even sufficient) condition of the proof of a factual hypothesis. Would anyone consider that the proof of a medical hypothesis depends on my traumatologist believing it?[13] Of course, if that were the case, there would be no way of attributing that doctor any responsibility for a poor diagnosis.

Thirdly, a careful analysis of the notion of belief as a propositional attitude shows that there is a characteristic of it that makes it particularly inadequate to take account of the mental state involved in the declaration of proven facts. In fact, it can be said that beliefs are something that happen to us. In other words, the act of having a belief is involuntary.[14] Williams's argument in this respect appears to be especially convincing: if we can decide to have a belief, we can then decide to have a false belief. But we cannot actually decide to have a false belief and, therefore, we cannot decide to have a belief, fundamentally because of the pretension of truth intrinsic, by definition, in beliefs. This does not exclude the possibility that beliefs about the occurrence of a fact could be based on pieces of evidence, but this is simply causal, in the sense that if an individual is provided with pieces of evidence supporting the truth of a proposition, these elements can *cause* that individual's belief in the occurrence of the fact. However, under no circumstances can the individual in question *decide* to have a particular belief in that respect.[15]

Now, if this is the case, it follows that having a particular belief about an event cannot, in itself, be justified, because only deliberate acts can be justified. If we accept that the result caused by the pieces of evidence presented at the trial is the production of a particular propositional attitude about the proposition it is intended to prove, it follows that, under the reconstruction being analyzed, the result could be formulated as "I believe *p*." If the fact of having a belief cannot, in itself, be justified, then there is no possibility of justifying this result, or the evaluation of the evidence made by the trier of fact, which amounts to the same thing. In other words: for those who propose that a factual hypothesis is proven if the trier of fact achieves a certain mental state (*intime conviction*, certainty, belief, etc.) about it, coherence of reasoning necessarily forces them to maintain a subjectivist conception of evidence where the sole ground necessary for the decision adopted is that it should

---

[12] For this reason, it is not coherent to accept a subjectivist conception of proof (which links the concept of proof with the beliefs of the trier of fact) at the same time as the objective of finding out the truth (understood as correspondence). This incoherence is clearly found, for example, in Schweizer 2019.

[13] In the same sense, see Haack 2003, 76; Laudan 2006, 124–5.

[14] See Engel 1998, 143; 2000, 3, 9, whom I follow on this point. Along similar lines, see, for example, Williams 1973; Cohen 1989, 369; 1991, 467; Bratman 1992, 3; Redondo 1996, 183 ff.

[15] Williams 1973, 141 ff. Also Van Fraassen 1984; Losonsky 2000.

correspond to the trier of fact's *intime conviction*—their belief. It is enough to say, then, that the trier of fact has reached this belief and that, as this is not a voluntary act, no justification in the strict sense of the word can be required. The justification of the propositional content of the belief—the factual hypothesis—is something else. Of course, it is possible to justify this propositional content, but whether or not a factual hypothesis based on pieces of evidence is justified does not depend on whether or not it is believed by any particular subject. Debating the possibility of justifying the act of having a belief is, in fact very different from discussing the justification of the propositional content of that belief. What the conception of proof I am criticizing adopts as a necessary condition for a proposition to be proven is not the justification of this proposition based on evidence, but rather the fact that the trier of fact has a belief that the proposition is true.

In this context, the trier of fact could only include in a reasoned verdict, in systems where this is required, an explanation (not justification) of the causes that have led to their belief in "p." This result is in line with the thesis of those who have maintained that the free evaluation of evidence by the trier of fact cannot be more than the expression of the trier's *deep* conviction about the facts that have occurred, and this goes beyond any possibility of control and justification. By contrast, this is an undesirable consequence for those who would conceive the evidential reasoning in a way compatible with due process, which allows its justification to be overseen by a higher court or by third parties (either the parties, the legal community, or society itself). To get round this obstacle, it will be necessary to abandon the link between proof and the beliefs of the trier of fact, and reconstruct the propositional attitude of the trier toward the facts themselves so that the element of deliberate decision in selecting the proven facts is included.[16]

Belief, as a propositional attitude, also has a second specific feature, which is problematic if the trier of fact's belief is used as a necessary condition of proof or as a criterion to identify the threshold of evidential sufficiency through standards of proof. I am talking about independence of context.[17] In other words, our beliefs are caused by a multitude of factors and pieces of information, and they can change over time. At any time "t" we can believe "p" or not believe it, but we cannot believe "p" in relation to context "c_1," and believe "not-p" in relation to context "c_2." We cannot, for example, believe or not believe that London is a noisy city depending on whether it is Monday or Tuesday or on whether we are being asked by the mayor of the city or by an ecologist.[18] And a member of the jury or a judge cannot, for example, believe that John killed Peter when doing their official job and not believe it when they are not on duty (as a *simple* citizen).[19]

[16] For all these reasons, in previous studies, following Cohen 1989; 1991, I have suggested reconstructing the propositional attitude of the trier of fact with respect to the proposition declared to have been proven through the notion of acceptance. Unlike belief, acceptance is deliberate and contextual, which fits in better with evidential decisions. However, if the criterion for considering a proposition to be proven was the trier of fact's acceptance, we would once again look at a subjective criterion. Because of this, acceptance is the propositional attitude that allows us to reconstruct the declaration of proven facts which is, in fact, made by the trier of fact. However, it is the acceptability of the facts in the light of the evidence and the standards of proof that determines what can be considered proven. For a discussion at greater length, see Ferrer Beltrán 2002, 90 ff.; Ferrer Beltrán 2006, 294 ff.

[17] In this respect, see Bratman 1992; Engel 1998, 143–4; Engel 2000; Clarke 2000, 36 ff.

[18] Although it is perfectly possible to answer differently to one or other for strategic reasons, in one of the two cases we will be lying with respect to the belief we have.

[19] We must be aware that when the propositional content of the belief includes deictic terms (like "this," "you," "now," "here," etc.), it is obvious that the truth value of this proposition is dependent on the context. So, for example, the truth value of "today it's raining in Barcelona" always depends on the day referred to by the proposition. In these circumstances, the (truth value of) the propositional content of the belief will depend on the context, but the belief itself—and the propositional attitude—will not. In this respect, see Bratman 1992, 3, n. 4.

The contextual independence of the beliefs raises serious problems in reconstructing the propositional attitude involved in stating proven facts in circumstances where the trier of fact is asked to make a decision about the proof of "p" without taking into account a piece of information they have. This happens, for example, when the judge (or the jury, as appropriate) has become aware of a piece of evidence which has later been declared inadmissible for reasons of form or because it has been obtained in breach of fundamental rights, etc. In these cases, it is inevitable that the information provided by the rejected item of evidence operates in the formation of the judge's or jury's belief about the facts. By contrast, this piece of evidence cannot be taken into account for the purposes of determining the proven facts of the case. There can also be a dissociation of this kind if the trier of fact has knowledge of the case from outside the proceedings that has not been included by either of the parties. It is obvious that this outside knowledge will affect the formation of the trier's beliefs but at the same time such knowledge cannot be used to determine the proven facts of the case.

In these circumstances, the trier of fact's belief about "p" (believing "p," believing "not-p," or not believing "p") cannot be dissociated in such a way that they have one belief as a citizen and another as trier.

A similar problem can occur in a situation where a decision must be made on whether the same fact is proven applying different standards of proof. For example, this would apply when determining possible criminal and civil liabilities. If this has to be decided by the same judge or jury based on an identical set of evidence, it is impossible for the trier of fact to believe, for civil purposes, that the fact occurred and not to believe it for criminal purposes. However, the applicability of different standards of proof makes it possible for the same fact to be proven in one sphere and not in the other.

There are two possible ways of solving this problem, depending on how we interpret what the graduation of the evidential requirements established in the standards of proof refers to. The first way involves understanding that the trier of fact's belief should not concern "p" but rather "the probability of p based on the evidence presented."[20] In line with this, if the trier of fact believes that the probability of "p" is "x," there is the possibility that this belief will lead to the defendant losing the case in accordance with the civil standard of proof, but being acquitted in accordance with the criminal standard of proof, for example.

The problem is that this assumes the criterion for determining the evidential sufficiency threshold used for the standard of proof is not now the (Baconian) probability that a fact happened in the light of the evidence, but the trier of fact's belief in this probability. We should remember, however, that the fact that any subject believes that the probability an event has occurred is "x" is absolutely independent of whether this is actually the probability, because the relationship between beliefs and reality is a contingent one.

However, if standards of proof resort to the trier of fact's belief about the probability of the hypothesis in order to identify the evidential threshold, it is impossible for it to fulfil its function of distributing the risk of error on the basis of a greater or lesser evidential requirement. It is quite reasonable to maintain that the higher the level of requirement imposed by the standard of proof, the greater the risk of error imposed on the party that has the burden of proof. However, it is not said that the evidential requirement imposed by a standard, E_1, requiring the trier of fact's belief in a probability x to consider a hypothesis H proven is

---

[20] It seems that Tichý 2019, 296 and Schweizer 2019, 20, for example, see things that way.

lower than that imposed by a standard E_2 requiring the trier of fact's belief in a probability of x' for the same purposes (where x' > x). The two standards are simply different, but they do not require one more than the other. Whether it is more or less demanding to meet a standard of this kind depends on whether it is necessary to produce in each trier of fact the respective beliefs and it may easily be that if E_2 is applied, belief in H is achieved with a lower level of evidence than E_1 would have had to apply. And if the criterion established by the standards is that the respective beliefs are achieved there is nothing more to say.

The second way of simultaneously taking into account the fact that standards of proof require different levels of evidence, and that they do so referring to the beliefs of triers of fact, involves maintaining that what changes from one standard of proof to another is the degree of firmness or confidence the trier must have in their beliefs about the factual hypotheses.[21] Done in this way, the proposition that the trier of fact should believe is the one that confirms the occurrence of a fact, and the probability would be a magnitude that would classify the degree of confidence that the trier has in their belief. It is easy to see that this is precisely the basis of what the classical supporters of subjective probability called the subject's disposition to bet on to the truth of the hypothesis. It is no coincidence, then, that this second path leads to the problems of trying to take account of the evidential reasoning through subjective probability.[22]

Ultimately, including as a necessary condition for a factual hypothesis to be proven that the trier of fact must believe that the hypothesis is true necessarily involves a subjectivist conception of evidence. And this is an obstacle to checking the correctness of the evidential reasoning precisely because the decision-making parameter is the decision-maker's conviction.

3. Giving Reasons for Verdicts as a Requirement of Due Process

The requirement to give reasons for judicial decisions has been a constant both in Spain and internationally. The European Court of Human Rights (ECtHR) has considered that grounds or reasons being given for judicial decisions forms part of the right to a fair trial (Convention for the Protection of Human Rights and Fundamental Freedoms, Art. 6.1).[23] In the same way, the Inter-American Court of Human Rights (I/A Court HR) has maintained that:

> the duty to state reasons is one of the "due guarantees" included in Article 8(1) [of the American Convention on Human Rights] to safeguard the right to due process.[24]

---

[21] To this interpretation can be ascribed Harlan J's words in *In re Winship*, which is followed by a good part of American jurisprudence and doctrine. Along the same lines, see, among many others: Dennis 2017, 491; Lowey 2009, 68, 71.

[22] I cannot develop the reasons why subjective probability is not, as I see it, an adequate instrument for taking account of the structure of evidential reasoning here. On this subject, I refer the reader to Ferrer Beltrán 2007, 108 ff. and the classic Cohen 1977, 49–120.

[23] See, among many others, the judgment of the ECtHR in the cases *Van de Hurk v. the Netherlands*, of April 19, 1994, para. 61; *Ruiz Torrija v. Spain*, of December 9, 1994, para. 29.

[24] *Decision of the I/A Court HR of August 5, 2008*, case: *Apitz Barbera and others ("Corte Primera de lo Contencioso Administrativo") v. Venezuela*, Series C, no. 182, para. 78.

However, when that duty refers to decision on facts, it is not at all clear what is understood by reasons and what their scope is. We can distinguish two broad conceptions of reasoned verdict, which we will call "psychologist" and "rationalist." The first of these identifies reasons with the linguistic expression of motives that have led to the adoption of a decision. The second, by contrast, sees reasons as justification: a reasoned decision would therefore be a decision that has reasons that justify it. The two conceptions have the linguistic support of the ambiguity of the expressions "reasoned decision" or "reasoned verdict," which denotes both the expression of motives and the reasons for a decision. But the two must not be confused.[25]

A statement that confirms that c is one of the causes of a human belief, decision, or behavior is, of course, a descriptive statement and, as then, it can be true or false. Concerning decisions on facts, the link between proof and the trier of fact's beliefs (either via the concept of proof or the requirements of the standards of proof) would mean the trier should describe the motives that have led them to acquire the belief that the facts would have occurred in that particular way. Put another way, while giving reasons means linguistically expressing the motives (the factors that have caused the belief in what the decision on the facts is based on), the reasoned verdict must explain the mental *iter* that has led the trier of fact to become convinced. The problem is that the causal factors of our beliefs are partially inaccessible to us.[26] Only we are capable of describing some of the most immediate circumstances leading us to acquire a belief but, of course, this description, even if made conscientiously, would be no more than limited and partial with respect to the causes of the decision. It is not surprising, then, that reasons, understood as an expression of the causes of the decision, is limited to very partial descriptions of the mental *iter* and is often replaced by long and pointless descriptions of the evidential course of the trial.

In contrast with this way of understanding the obligation to give reasons, the rationalistic conception sees it as the justification of the verdict. So, saying that reasons are given for a decision will mean that it is duly justified. It means, then, that the evidential decision has good epistemic and normative reasons to give it sufficient basis.[27] The former will result from an individual and joint evaluation of the evidence for the purposes of determining the degree of corroboration that the pieces of evidence given at the trial provide for the different, conflicting, factual hypotheses. The normative reasons, by contrast, point to the sufficiency or insufficiency of this corroboration which will have to be justified on the basis of the standards of proof applicable to the case.

Here again two possibilities open up: a decision can be considered justified if there are sufficient reasons to base it on or if these reasons not only exist but have also been analytically formulated (i.e., linguistically expressed in the decision). In other words, it is a matter of distinguishing between *having* reasons for x and *giving* reasons for x.[28]

Based on this, it can be maintained that the requirement to give reasons for verdicts has two main functions. The first is aimed, on the one hand, to make possible for the parties to

[25] The distinction between motives and reasons was considered by Nino 1993, 37 and is a fundamental distinction of analytical philosophy. In this respect, see also, among others, Raz 1978, 3–4; Bayón Mohíno 1991, 43 ff; Redondo 1996, 79 ff.

[26] In the case of collegiate bodies, it is also particularly difficult.

[27] On the requirements for giving reasons for the justification of judicial decisions, see Igartua Salaverría 2003, 96 ff. and, specifically, on the reasons for evidential decisions, Igartua Salaverría 2003, 135 ff.

[28] Schauer 2009, 175 ff.

check the justification of the verdict and any possible challenge via appeal and, on the other, to make it possible for the superior judge or court to review the decision, so that they can check whether decision being challenged is correct using the reasons given in it.[29] So, if a reasoned verdict is conceived as a justified verdict, the duty to give reasons is a guarantee of the proper administration of justice and, therefore, of due process.[30] Secondly, giving reasons allows the whole of society to monitor judicial decisions through the publicity given to the decisions and the basis for them.

4. Standards of Proof as a Precondition for the Possibility of Justified Verdicts

Having reached this point, it is appropriate to ask whether it is possible to justify decisions on facts if we assume a concept of proof or standards of proof that establish, as a criterion for a fact being proved, that the trier of fact should believe that the fact has occurred. And the answer to that question can only be negative.

It should be remembered that those who maintain a subjectivist conception of proof, linking proof to the beliefs of triers of fact, consider it conclusive that they should actually acquire the belief that facts occurred in a certain way, not that the corresponding hypothesis should have credibility in the light of the evidence presented. Considering that, as we have seen, having a belief is not a deliberate act, it is impossible to provide a justification for it. We cannot ask the trier of fact to justify the act of acquiring a belief, just as we cannot ask them to justify the reflex movement of their leg on receiving a blow at a certain point on their knee. The propositional content of beliefs can be justified (and reference is made to this when talking about justified beliefs) but not the mental fact of having the belief. Therefore, if the criterion for making a decision is the fact that the trier of fact have the belief (or the conviction, or a firm belief, or a belief in the fact that an event happened with a certain degree of probability) it makes no sense to ask them to offer a justification of it, just because it is conceptually impossible to give. It is no surprise, then, that the subjectivist conception of proof has never required reasons to be given for evidential decisions. Nor have subjectivist formulations of standards of proof traditionally been designed in the English-speaking sphere for jury decisions, which do not require reasons to be given.

The problem, once more, lies in the incompatibility of this conception with the right to due process. If the duty to give reasons for decisions is a requirement of due process, as we have seen in the previous section, a conception of proof that makes giving reasons

---

[29] In this respect, the decision of the English Court of Appeal in the case of *Flannery v Halifax Estate Agencies Ltd* is very clear, maintaining that "[w]here because no reasons are given it is impossible to tell whether the judge has gone wrong on the law or the facts, the losing party would be altogether deprived of the chance of an appeal unless the court entertains an appeal based on the lack of reasons itself," *Flannery v. Halifax Estate Agencies Ltd* (1999) 149 NLJ 284. The ECtHR has also placed the emphasis on reasons being given within a trial to make possible to exercise the right to appeal. In this respect, see, for example, the judgment of the ECtHR in the case *Hadjianastassiou v. Greece*, of December 12, 1992, para. 33. And the I/A Court HR, along the same lines, has considered that "the reasons for judicial decisions are a condition making it possible to guarantee the right to defence" (Judgment of February 15, 2017, case: *Zegarra Marín v. Peru*, Series C, no. 331, para. 155).

[30] Along the same lines, Roberts 2011, 215, to which I refer also for the English case law mentioned there. It is worth mentioning again the English Court of Appeal in the case *Flannery v. Halifax Estate Agencies Ltd*, in which the duty to give reasons for decisions is considered as a function of due process and, therefore, of justice, *Flannery v. Halifax Estate Agencies Ltd* (1999) 149 NLJ 284.

conceptually impossible is also incompatible with due process. And formulating standards of proof appealing to the beliefs of the trier of fact as a criterion is not compatible with the fair trial either. Respect for this fundamental right therefore requires that the standards of proof are formulated relying on criteria that can be monitored intersubjectively, referring to the capacity the evidence has to justify the factual hypotheses to be proven, and that there should be a threshold of evidential sufficiency which avoids vagueness as far as possible.[31]

Considering this conclusion, both the ECtHR and the I/A Court HR are forced to make pronouncements on compatibility with the right to due process of jury trials that do not require them to justify their decisions. The ECtHR did so in the Judgment of the Grand Chamber, *Taxquet v. Belgium*, of November 16, 2010[32] and the I/A Court HR in the Decision *V.R.P., V.P.C. and others v. Nicaragua*, of March 8, 2018, which almost entirely follows the argument strategy of the former.

It is important to highlight, because of the importance of this issue in this contribution, that both Belgian and Nicaraguan legislation on criminal proceedings which applied in the cases that finally reached these international courts, established that jury decisions that had to be made on facts would be based on their *intime conviction*, and reasons would not be given. However, for the ECtHR or the I/A Court HR, these regulations would not appear to be contrary to due process if "the accused, and indeed the public, must be able to understand the verdict that has been given."[33] Finally, although the ECtHR has not expressly made any pronouncement concerning *intime conviction* as a criterion for evidential decisions, the I/A Court HR has, considering that "intime conviction is not an arbitrary conviction."[34]

Beyond the clear doctrinal inconsistencies on the duty to give reasons for decisions between these judgments of the ECtHR and the I/A Court HR and the line of previous case law, it is appropriate to ask whether, with respect to a verdict in which reasons have not been given to justify it, it is possible to "understand the verdict" or to "reconstruct the logical course of the jury's decision."[35] Unfortunately, one example is not enough to show this: as in any country where the rule of law applies criminal proceedings must be governed by the presumption of innocence, we need to know the conditions in which this presumption can be removed or, in other words, when the accusatory hypothesis will be sufficiently corroborated to be considered proven. This is precisely the function of a standard of proof: to determine the threshold of evidential requirement so that a hypothesis is considered proven. But there is not necessarily only one threshold: the same hypothesis, with the same evidence and same degree of corroboration, can be considered proven if the standard of proof is x and not proven if it is x' (where $x' > x$). For a decision on the proof of hypothesis H to be justified, we must show that the available evidence gives H a certain degree of corroboration and that this degree of corroboration is sufficient in accordance with the applicable standard of proof. However, if we do not know the applicable standard of proof or if

---

[31] On the methodological requirements for a correct formulation of standards of proof, see Ferrer Beltrán 2018.

[32] On the decision in the case of *Taxquet v. Belgium* and the obligation to give grounds for verdicts, see, among other studies: Coen and Doak 2017, 795 ff.; Cohen 2016, 422 ff.; Jackson 2016, 296 ff.; Roberts 2011; Thaman 2011, 613 ff.

[33] Judgment of the Grand Chamber, *Taxquet v. Belgium*, of November 16, 2010, para. 90.

[34] Judgment *V.R.P., V.P.C. and others v. Nicaragua*, of March 8, 2018, para. 262.

[35] Even if it were possible to speculate in this way, one thing is knowing that the evidence presented could lead us to imagine the reasons on which the decision could hypothetically be based and another very different matter is that these might actually be reasons that the jury has taken into account. Without a reasoned verdict, function of reasons within a trial (i.e., providing the parties with the basis for an appeal and allowing the higher court to monitor whether this basis is correct) is undermined. See Jackson 2016, 301.

it has not been determined, there is no way of justifying that the corroboration is sufficient. Without a standard of proof, it is impossible to give reasons (understood as justification).[36]

Tuzet has shown that, in general, in countries with an English-speaking legal culture, the stress has been placed on standards of proof for the purposes of offering the triers of fact decision-making criteria, while in countries with a Romano-Germanic legal culture more attention has been paid to the requirements evaluating the evidence and giving reasons for decisions as a means to check them.[37] The attempt to respect the characteristics of the two traditions has put international courts of human rights in difficulties, as we have just seen. However, in my opinion, both cultural traditions have necessary but insufficient elements for fully developing due process: if we do not have methodologically well-formulated standards of proof that determine the thresholds of evidential sufficiency in an acceptably precise way and intersubjectively monitorable form, it is impossible to give reasons for (i.e., justify) the fact that a factual hypothesis has achieved a sufficient degree of corroboration in the light of the evidence presented in the trial. Without standards of proof, it is impossible to justify the verdict. And if reasons are not expressly required for decisions, we have no way of ensuring that the evidential reasoning is correct or checking the application of the standards of proof, which is also an obstacle to the parties exercising their right to appeal. Having duly formulated standards of proof as pre-established general rules for evidential decisions and requiring justification of these based on the evidence presented and the applicable standards are two inescapable conditions for avoiding decisions being made arbitrarily and they therefore make due process possible.

References

Aliste Santos, T.-J. (2018). *La Motivación de las Resoluciones Judiciales*. Madrid: Marcial Pons.

Bartels, R. D. (1981). "Punishment and the Burden of Proof in Criminal Cases—a Modest Proposal," *Iowa Law Review,* 66(4): 899–930.

Bayón Mohíno, J. C. (1991). *La Normatividad del Derecho: Deber Jurídico y Razones para la Acción*. Madrid: Centro de estudios Constitucionales.

Bratman, M. E. (1992). "Practical Reasoning and Acceptance in a Context," *Mind,* 101(401): 1–16.

Broun, K. S., Dix, G. E., Imwinkelried, E., Kaye, D., et al. (2006). *McCormick on Evidence*. St Paul, MN: Thomson/West.

Burd, K. A., and Hans, V. P. (2018). "Reasoned Verdicts: Oversold?" *Cornell International Law Journal* 51(2): 319–60.

Cabañas García, J. C. (1992). *La Valoración de las Pruebas y su Control en el Proceso Civil: Estudio Dogmático y Jurisprudencial*. España: Trivium.

Clarke, D. S. (2000). "The Possibility of Acceptance without Belief," in P. Engel (ed.), *Believing and Accepting,* 31–53. Dordrecht: Springer.

Clermont, K. (2009). "Standards of Proof Revisited," *Vermont Law Review,* 33, 469–487.

Clermont, K., and Sherwin, E. (2002). "A Comparative View of Standards of Proof," *The American Journal of Comparative Law,* 50(2): 243–75.

Coen, M., and Doak, J. (2017). "Embedding Explained Jury Verdicts in the English Criminal Trial," *Legal Studies,* 37(4): 786–806.

Cohen, L. J. (1977). *The Probable and the Provable*. Oxford: Clarendon Press.

---

[36] Along the same lines, among others, Gascón Abellán 2005, 138; Laudan 2006, 64; Tuzet 2020, 94. Nor is there the possibility of determining whether the presumption of innocence has been respected or violated because we do not know the threshold of evidential sufficiency for removing it.

[37] Tuzet 2020.

Cohen, L. J. (1989). "Belief and Acceptance," *Mind,* XCVIII(391): 367–89.

Cohen, L. J. (1991). "Should a Jury say What it Believes or What it Accepts," *Cardozo Law Review,* 13: 465–83.

Cohen, M. (2016). "The French Case for Requiring Juries to give Reasons: Safeguarding Defendants or Guarding the Judges," in J. E. Ross and S. Thaman (eds.), *Comparative Criminal Procedure,* 422–50. Cheltenham and Northampton, MA: Edward Elgar.

Dennis, I. H. (2017). *The Law of Evidence.* London: Sweet & Maxwell, Thomson Reuters.

Engel, P. (1998). "Believing, Accepting, and Holding True," *Philosophical Explorations,* 1(2): 140–51.

Engel, P. (ed.) (2000). *Believing and Accepting* (vol. 83). Dordrecht: Springer.

Ferrer Beltrán, J. (2002). *Prueba y Verdad en el Derecho.* Madrid: Marcial Pons.

Ferrer Beltrán, J. (2006). "Legal Proof and Fact Finder's Beliefs," *Legal Theory,* 12(4): 293–314.

Ferrer Beltrán, J. (2007). *La Valoración Racional de la Prueba.* Madrid, Barcelona, and Buenos Aires: Marcial Pons.

Ferrer Beltrán, J. (2018). "Prolegómenos para una Teoría de los Estándares de Prueba. El Test Case de la Responsabilidad del Estado por Prisión Preventiva Errónea," in D. M. Papayannis and E. P. Fredes (eds.), *Filosofía del Derecho Privado,* 401–30. Madrid, Barcelona, Buenos Aires, and Sao Paulo: Marcial Pons.

Gascón Abellán, M. (2005). "Sobre la Posibilidad de Formular Estándares de Prueba Objetivos," *Doxa. Cuadernos de Filosofía del Derecho,* 28: 13.

Haack, S. (2003). "Clues to the Puzzle of Scientific Evidence," in S. Haack (ed.), *Defending Science—within Reason: Between Scientism and Cynicism,* 139–206. Amherst, NY: Prometheus Books.

Hamer, D. (2011). "A Dynamic Reconstruction of the Presumption of Innocence," *Oxford Journal of Legal Studies,* 31(2): 417–35.

Ho, H. L. (2008). *A Philosophy of Evidence Law: Justice in the Search for Truth.* Oxford: Oxford University Press.

Igartua Salaverría, J. (2003). *La Motivación de las Sentencias, Imperativo Constitucional.* Madrid: Centro de Estudios Políticos y Constitucionales.

Jackson, J. D. (2002). "Making Juries Accountable," *The American Journal of Comparative Law,* 50(3): 477–530.

Jackson, J. D. (2016). "Unbecoming Jurors and Unreasoned Verdicts: Realising Integrity in the Jury Room," in J. B. Hunter, P. Roberts, S. N. M. Young, and D. Dixon (eds.), *The Integrity of Criminal Process. From Theory to Practice.* Oxford: Hart Publishing.

Laudan, L. (2006). *Truth, Error, and Criminal Law: An Essay in Legal Epistemology.* Cambridge: Cambridge University Press.

Lillquist, E. (2002). "Recasting Reasonable Doubt: Decision Theory and the Virtues of Variability," *UC Davis Law Review,* 36(1): 85–197.

Losonsky, M. (2000). "On Wanting to Believe," in P. Engel (ed.), *Believing and Accepting.* Dordrecht: Springer.

Lowey, A. H. (2009). "Taking Reasonable Doubt Seriously," *Chicago-Kent Law Review,* 85(1): 63–75.

Nepveu, K. H. (2003). "Beyond 'Guilty' or 'Not Guilty': Giving Special Verdicts in Criminal Jury Trials," *Yale Law & Policy Review,* 21(1): 263–300.

Nino, C. S. (1993). "Derecho, Moral, Política," 14: 35–46.

Raz, J. (1978). "Introduction," in J. Raz (ed.), *Practical Reasoning,* 1–18. Oxford: Oxford University Press.

Redmayne, M. (1999). "Standards of Proof in Civil Litigation," *The Modern Law Review,* 62(2): 167–95.

Redondo, M. C. (1996). *La Noción de Razón para la Acción en el Análisis Jurídico.* Madrid: Centro de Estudios Constitucionales.

Roberts, P. (2011). "Does Article 6 of the European Convention on Human Rights Require Reasoned Verdicts in Criminal Trials?" *Human Rights Law Review,* 11(2): 213–35.

Schauer, F. (2009). *Thinking like a Lawyer: A New Introduction to Legal Reasoning.* Cambridge, MA and London: Harvard University Press.

Schweizer, M. (2019). "Standard of Proof as Decision Threshold," in L. Tichý (ed.), *Standard of proof in Europe,* 19–50. Tübingen: Mohr Siebeck.

Stein, A. (1997). "Against 'Free Proof'," *Israel Law Review,* 31(1–3): 573–89.

Stoffelmayr, E., and Diamond, S. (2000). "The Conflict between Precision and Flexibility in Explaining 'Beyond A Reasonable Doubt'," *Psychology, Public Policy, and Law,* 6(3): 769–87.

Taruffo, M. (1975). *La Motivazione della Sentenza Civile.* Padova: CEDAM.

Taruffo, M. (2003). "Rethinking the Standards of Proof," *The American Journal of Comparative Law,* 51(3): 659–77.

Thaman, S. (2011). "Should Juries give Reasons for their Verdicts?: The Spanish Experience and the Implications of the European Court of Human Rights Decision in Taxquet v. Belgium," *Chicago-Kent Law Review,* 86(2): 613–68.

Thomas, C. (2013). "Avoiding the Perfect Storm of Juror Contempt," *Criminal Law Review,* 6: 483–503.

Tichý, L. (2019). "Standard of Proof: Fundamental Problems through the Perspective of Comparative Analysis," in L. Tichý (ed.), *Standard of Proof in Europe,* 287–316. Tübingen: Mohr Siebeck.

Tichý, L. (ed.) (2019). *Standard of Proof in Europe* (vol. 158). Tübingen: Mohr Siebeck.

Tuzet, G. (2020). "Assessment Criteria or Standards of Proof? An Effort in Clarification," *Artificial Intelligence and Law,* 28(1): 91–109.

Twining, W. (1994). *Rethinking Evidence: Exploratory Essays.* Evanston, IL.: Northwestern University Press.

Van Fraassen, B. C. (1984). "Belief and the Will," *The Journal of Philosophy,* 81(5): 235–56.

Williams, B. (1973). "Deciding to Believe," in B. Williams (ed.), *Problems of the Self: Philosophical Papers 1956–1972,* 136–51. Cambridge: Cambridge University Press.

4

The Role of the Expert Witness[*]

Lena Wahlberg and Christian Dahlman

1. Introduction

Expert witnesses play an important role in legal factfinding. In the modern criminal trial, an increasing part of the evidence presented by the prosecution is reported and explained to the factfinder[1] by forensic scientists. In civil litigation, for example, in tort cases, medical and other experts regularly testify on the relations of causes and damages. In this chapter, we will discuss the role of the expert witness in legal factfinding.

The first question that needs to be addressed with regard to the role of the expert witness is whether we are dealing with a witness or an expert. Is the expert witness just another witness reporting observations, like a non-expert who testifies as an eyewitness? Or, is the expert witness testifying on a meta-level with regard to witness observations, assessing reported observations from the point of view of expert knowledge? The answer to this question is that both of these functions belong to the role of the expert witness, and they are often intertwined with each other. Consider, for example, a coroner who has performed an autopsy on a murder victim, and testifies in court that the victim had *petechiae* (tiny red spots) on the eyeballs, suggesting strangulation as a cause of death. In the first part of this statement, the coroner reports a first-hand witness observation (*petechiae*), in the second part the coroner helps the factfinder to assess to what extent this observation supports the hypothesis that the victim was strangled.[2] A notable difference between these two functions is that the expert witness is replaceable with regard to the second part, but not with regard to the first. With regard to his or her expert knowledge, the expert can be replaced by another expert with the same expertise, but with regard to first-hand observations, the expert is unreplaceable, just like an eyewitness.

In this chapter, our focus will be on the part where the expert is replaceable (not on first-hand observations). We will discuss the role of the expert witness in the assessment of evidence. As we have seen, the expert witness helps the factfinder assess how strongly a certain piece of evidence supports a certain hypothesis. In the following sections, we will discuss how this role should be understood and constrained.

It should be pointed out that each legal system has its own set of rules for expert testimony. These rules of procedural law have many features in common, but they also display

[*] This chapter is based on research funded by Riksbankens Jubileumsfond, The Swedish Foundation for Humanities and Social Sciences (grant M14:0139:11), and Torsten Söderbergs stiftelse (grant R6/18).

[1] In this chapter, the term "factfinder" is used to refer to the legal factfinder. Depending on the legal system and the case at hand, the factfinder can be a jury or a judge.

[2] As stated in the *Federal Rules of Evidence*, Rule 702, the role of the expert witness is to "help the trier of fact to understand the evidence or to determine a fact in issue."

Lena Wahlberg and Christian Dahlman, *The Role of the Expert Witness* In: *Philosophical Foundations of Evidence Law*. Edited by: Christian Dahlman, Alex Stein, and Giovanni Tuzet, Oxford University Press. © Christian Dahlman, Alex Stein, and Giovanni Tuzet 2021. DOI: 10.1093/oso/9780198859307.003.0005

notable differences. The purpose of this chapter is not to account for the rules of evidence of any particular legal system. We will discuss the role of the expert witness in principle, on a theoretical level that we believe has general relevance. Even so, procedural rules in a particular jurisdiction might in some respects hinder the fulfilment of the expert's role as it is described here. When this is the case, our outline of the expert's role can instead be used to discuss the appropriateness of these rules.

Our discussion will take as its starting point that the expert witness is an epistemic authority, and we fully agree with the view that non-experts, like factfinders, should regard experts as more trustworthy than themselves in some domains.[3] At the same time we recognize that both expert testimony and legal factfinding are highly composite. Neither is the result of objective observations alone, but depend in part on subjective evaluations, and on the assessor's values. Moreover, the factfinder must ultimately answer questions of fact that often go beyond and include other evidence than the expert's testimony. For these reasons, we do not think that the mere fact that a certain conclusion has been drawn by an expert gives the factfinder a preemptive reason to draw the same conclusion. Rather, we believe that the ideal function of expert testimony is to help factfinders to arrive at the assessment that they would have made on their own, had they possessed the required expert knowledge.

Later, we will develop the expert's role in ways that will promote this ideal function of expert testimony. The job description that we outline for the expert is rather demanding and cannot be met in every detail. For example, subjectivity is undesirable in a legal setting but cannot be completely eliminated. We believe, however, that the expert should nevertheless *try* to avoid it, and play the role described in this chapter to the very extent possible.

2. Educator or Advocate?

A factfinder evaluates evidence on the basis of his or her background knowledge about the world. As an example, a factfinder will assess the credibility of an eyewitness who saw the perpetrator run down a dark alley and later identifies the defendant as the perpetrator on the basis of background knowledge about the difficulties of making correct observations under such conditions. For some pieces of evidence, however, the factfinder's world knowledge is insufficient. Some evidence requires expert knowledge in the assessment of how strongly a certain piece of evidence (E) supports a certain hypothesis (H), for example, how strongly the observed matching features between a shoe print at the crime scene and the defendant's shoe (E) supports the hypothesis (H) that the shoe print was made with the defendant's shoe.

Some expert witnesses are appointed by the court to serve exactly this function, but what about expert witnesses that are hired by the parties (which is often the case in common law systems)? Do they also serve this function as an objective educator? Or should they be viewed as advocates on the team that hired them? It has been argued by Lubet and others that the principal loyalty of an expert witness ought to be with the court and the factfinder: "the single most important obligation of an expert witness is to approach every question with independence and objectivity."[4] We agree with this view. The

---

[3] Walton 1997; Zagzebski 2012.
[4] Lubet 1999, 467.

role of expert witnesses in the assessment of evidence is to assist the factfinder with expert knowledge, not to act as additional advocates for the party that hired them. Expert witnesses should apply their expertise to the evidence at hand regardless of whether it favors or disfavors the party that called them to the witness stand. As Lubet puts it "an objective expert views the facts and data dispassionately, without regard to the consequences for the client."[5]

This call for objectivity follows from the function of the expert witness in the assessment of evidence. As we have seen, the factfinder turns to the expert witness for expert knowledge that the factfinder lacks. All factfinders want to arrive at the assessment that they would have made on their own if they had possessed the required expert knowledge, and they trust the expert to help them with this. The trust they bestow on the expert witness therefore presupposes that the expert is objective. A partisan expert, who always testifies that the evidence at hand strongly supports the case of the party that hired him or her serves no purpose for the factfinder in the assessment of the evidence.

Unfortunately, expert witnesses do not always live up to this ideal.[6] It is a well-known problem that parties seek expert witnesses that will testify in their favor and find experts who are ready to do this for a fee (so-called *expert shopping*). This phenomenon can give rise to a situation where each party has hired an expert and the expert witnesses make contradictory assessments of the same evidence.

There are expert witnesses who try to be objective, but that does not guarantee that they live up to this ideal. Studies have shown that people tend to underestimate the extent to which secondary interests, as a payer-provider relationship, influence their judgment.[7] Expert witnesses who see themselves as objective could therefore be unconsciously biased. As an example, forensic experts who work in the police force occasionally display a bias in favor of the prosecution that they are unaware of themselves.

An example of biased expert testimony can be found in the Quick case, a much discussed[8] Swedish murder case, where a mental patient, Thomas Quick, told his therapist that he was a serial killer, responsible for a number of unsolved murders in Sweden and Norway. Quick was prosecuted for eight murders on the basis of his confessions. At the trials a professor of psychology at Stockholm University testified as an expert witness, certifying that Quick's confessions were genuine. The psychology professor referred to scientific research on the phenomenon of false confessions and said that there was nothing in the present case to indicate that Quick's confessions were false. The factfinders trusted the professor's assessment, and Quick was convicted for all eight murders. Some years later Quick retracted his confessions and said that he had made the whole thing up. The case was reopened, and after a thorough investigation, Quick was exonerated on all charges. One of the things that the new investigation exposed was that the psychology professor had been working closely with the police from the beginning, actively participating in the search for evidence to build a case against Quick.[9] The psychology professor was strongly committed to the hypothesis that Quick was guilty, and was not the impartial unbiased expert that he appeared to be when he testified that Quick's confessions were genuine. Contrary to what the psychology professor

---

[5] Ibid.
[6] Posner 1999, 93.
[7] See, e.g., Moore and Loewenstein 2004; Moore et al. 2010; Gold and Appelbaum 2011.
[8] See, e.g., Råstam 2013.
[9] Josefsson 2015, 298–9, 303–5, 310.

had said in his testimony, several factors that are regarded as indicators of false confessions in the psychological literature were clearly present in Quick's confessions (Quick was attention seeking, his confessions were vague and tentative, and he used the confessions to obtain extra prescriptions of the tranquilizer drugs that he was addicted to).

3. Sticking to the Assigned Question

Legal decision-making involves a multitude of questions and sub-questions of various kinds. With regard to expert witnesses, these questions can be divided into questions that lie within the role of the expert witness and questions that fall outside that role. It is important that expert witnesses restrict themselves to the questions assigned to them by their role in the assessment of evidence. As we will explain in the following three sections, the expert witness should (1) only speak on questions of fact, never on questions of law, (2) only assess how strongly a piece of evidence supports a certain hypothesis, never how probable the hypothesis is given the evidence, and (3) stay within his or her area of expertise.

3.1 Questions of Law versus Questions of Fact

Typically, an adjudication process raises questions of two kinds: questions of law and questions of fact. The details of this distinction are much debated[10] but for the purpose of this chapter some rough definitions will suffice. Questions of law will here be defined as questions about the meaning of legal norms, including questions about what states of affairs must obtain for the legal consequences prescribed by these norms to ensue. Questions of fact, on the other hand, will be defined as questions about whether a state of affairs that some legal norm designates as relevant obtains. With these definitions, it is readily seen that the issue of what is a legally relevant question of fact is in itself a question of law.

The distinction between questions of law and questions of fact can be used to delineate the division of labor between factfinders and experts by delimiting the expert's role to the answering of questions of fact. Of course, this does not mean that an expert's role is to answer all questions of fact that arise in adjudication. As mentioned in the previous section, the expert must not answer questions outside the domain of his or her expertise. However, the distinction can help to define the expert's role negatively, by disqualifying the expert from answering questions of law.

There are at least two reasons why experts should not answer questions of law. The first reason is a special case of the principle, developed below in Section 3.3, that the expert should not answer questions outside the domain of his or her expertise. Questions of law, like questions of medicine or questions of forensic science, require a certain kind of expertise. Answering a question of law includes identifying and interpreting legal norms, taking into account all relevant sources of law. This task requires legal expertise of a kind that can be expected from a judge in a court of law, but that falls way outside the domain of knowledge and experience that make someone qualified as a scientific expert. Secondly, and perhaps

---

[10] See, e.g., Allen and Pardo 2003; Sevelin 2019.

more importantly, the role of being a judge confers on the legal decision-maker a legitimacy in settling questions of law, including the discretion to fill in the gaps or come to a decision when the law fails to provide a single right answer. With the role of being a scientific expert, in contrast, comes neither the expertise nor the legitimacy to settle questions of law.

In adjudication, questions of law include (among other things) the demarcation of the relevant *factum probandum* (the fact to be proven), and the definition of the applicable standard of proof. The *factum probandum* is demarcated by the meaning of concepts that make up the applicable legal norm (e.g., the legal meaning of "negligent behavior" or "personal injury") and formed by considerations pertaining to the limits of legal liability. The legal standard of proof tells us how strong the evidence must be for a fact to be accepted as proven by a court. The severity of this standard depends on the different interests and values at stake in adjudication, including, for example, the standpoint that it is more important to avoid wrongful convictions than to avoid wrongful acquittals—a standpoint which is inherent in the presumption of innocence. Just like the question of what is a relevant *factum probandum*, the question of what standard of proof applies is a question of law. As a result, what facts are legally relevant and how certain these facts must be to trigger legal consequences are legal questions that must not be answered by the expert.

This division of labor between courts and experts may appear rather straightforward but is more complicated than the distinction between questions of law and questions of fact might suggest. For one, the tenet that the expert must not answer questions of law does not come with the mirrored rule that the court must not answer questions of fact. Rather, the task of the court is to answer all questions of law and some questions of fact. In the next section, we will discuss the complicated issue of the distribution of labor between courts and experts with respect to the settlement of questions of fact.

In the remainder of this section, we will address a predicament that might hamper a straightforward application of the principle that experts must not answer questions of law. More precisely, we will discuss how failure to observe subtle legal dimensions of seemingly factual questions creates a risk not only that experts trespass the boundary to questions of law, but also that they provide incorrect, non-legal answers to legal questions. Consider, as an example, the tightly framed question "Did the head trauma cause the plaintiff's mental disorder?" Answering this question does not presuppose any understanding of clearly legal concepts like "negligence" or "personal injury." Even so, the question includes legal elements and is not a pure question of fact. To begin with, the meaning of the question depends on the interpretation of the term "cause." When this term is used in a legal provision, it is a question of law whether it means that the effect must not have occurred but for the cause (the but-for test), or that the alleged cause must have been a necessary element of a set that was sufficient for the effect to occur (the NESS-test), or something else.[11] Taking this into account, the question spells out "Did the head trauma cause [in a legal sense] the plaintiff's mental disorder?"

Moreover, questions like this can rarely be answered with certainty. This is not necessarily a problem in itself, since in law it suffices to establish the causal relation according to the applicable standard of proof. Depending on the type of case and legal system at hand, the standard might require the *factum probandum* to be proven by a "preponderance of the

---

[11] For discussions on causation in the law, see, e.g., Hart and Honoré 1985; Wright 1985; Moore 2009.

evidence," "beyond reasonable doubt," or some other standard of proof. Which standard of proof to apply is a question of law, which means that our question now reads: "Is it proven [according to the applicable legal standard of proof] that the head trauma caused [in a legal sense] the plaintiff's damage?"

It is readily seen that the legal dimensions in this question risk getting lost in interdisciplinary translation. Conceptions of causation are used in most disciplines and discourses, but not necessarily defined in the same way there as they are in law. When asked whether there is a causal relation between a and b, it is natural for experts to answer using their own conception of causation. Indeed, medical experts called upon to assist courts in answering such questions have sometimes focused more on whether the trauma was the most significant cause of the injury, or on the possibility to identify a causal mechanism between the trauma and the injury, than on whether there was a legally relevant causal relation between them, such as a relation which would pass the but-for test or the NESS-test.[12]

Similarly, standards of proof are not unique to law but are used in science too.[13] In a scientific study, it is common practice to require rather strong evidence for establishing a correlation between two parameters. It is often said that from a scientific point of view, false positives/Type I errors (the error of incorrectly rejecting the null hypothesis that the parameters are uncorrelated) are considered much worse than false negatives/Type II errors (the error of failing to reject a false null hypothesis). In law, where non-epistemic considerations are important and suspension of judgment is not an option, the risk of Type I errors and Type II errors is often balanced differently. In legal factfinding, the choice and application of standards of proof is a question of law,[14] and the expert should convey information that will allow the factfinder to apply the legal standards.

What has now been said implies that if experts answer the question, "Did the head trauma cause the plaintiff's mental disorder?" by applying their own standards of proof and their own conception of causation, they will have answered the wrong question (a question not assigned to the expert). This error—the error of providing the right answer for the wrong question—has sometimes been referred to as a Type III error.[15] To find the way out of this predicament, and make sure that the expert plays the role of expert and not of judge in adjudication, both factfinders and experts must pay close attention to what information the questions posed to the expert ask for, and what information the answers provided by the expert convey.

3.2 Assessing Support versus Assessing the Hypothesis

As we have seen, the role of an expert witness in the evaluation of evidence is to help the factfinder assess how strongly a certain piece of evidence supports a certain hypothesis, for example, how strongly the observed matching features between a shoe print at the crime scene and the defendant's shoe supports the hypothesis that the shoe print was made with the defendant's shoe. Factfinders need such help whenever the assessment in question

---

[12] Wahlberg 2017.
[13] Allen 1994, 1166.
[14] Ibid.
[15] Mitroff and Featheringham 1974; Kriebel at al. 2001; Wahlberg 2010.

requires some kind of expert knowledge. In the case of a shoe print, the expert knowledge could, for example, consist in knowledge of the prevalence of a certain sole pattern or a certain wear mark.

The role of the expert witness in the evaluation of evidence is limited to how strongly the evidence supports the hypothesis.[16] As discussed in the previous section, it is not the role of the expert witness to assess if the hypothesis is sufficiently supported with regard to the standard of proof. Whether the hypothesis is proven or not is an issue of law that should be decided by the factfinder. It is not even within the role of the expert witness to assess the probability of the hypothesis given the evidence that the expert is helping the factfinder to assess. There are two reasons for this restriction. To begin with, evidence assessment in a criminal case starts with the presumption of innocence, and the probability of a hypothesis put forward by the prosecution may therefore depend on how the presumption of innocence is interpreted and applied in the case at hand, which again is an issue of law, and therefore not for the expert witness to decide. Furthermore, the probability of the hypothesis may depend on other pieces of evidence that have been presented at the trial, but are unknown to the expert witness, and the expert witness is therefore not in a position to assess the probability of the hypothesis all things considered.

This becomes apparent in the Bayesian approach to legal evidence. As Bayes' rule dictates, the probability of the hypothesis given the evidence at hand $P(H|E)$, commonly referred to as the *posterior probability*, is calculated on the basis of the probability that the hypothesis is true before the evidence at hand has been considered $P(H)$, commonly referred to as the *prior probability*, updated with the *likelihood ratio* $P(E|H)/P(E|-H)$. The prior probability depends on how the presumption of innocence is interpreted and applied in the case at hand, for example, the interpretation that the probability that the defendant is guilty before any evidence has been presented by the prosecution should, according to the presumption of innocence, be viewed as $1/N$, where N is the number of possible perpetrators in the area where the crime in question was committed.[17] The prior probability also reflects all the evidence that has already been assessed and integrated in it. Bayes' rule makes it obvious that an assessment of the posterior probability presupposes assessments regarding the prior probability that are not for the expert witness to decide. Expert witnesses who are faithful to their role provide the factfinder with information about likelihood ratios that the legal and ultimate factfinder can integrate with other factors in an overall assessment of the posterior probability, and leaves the latter task to the factfinder.

To speak on the likelihood ratio and be silent on the posterior probability was established as a maxim for expert testimony in the infamous French case known as the Dreyfus Affair. In 1894, the French artillery officer Alfred Dreyfus was accused of communicating military secrets to the Germans. The main evidence against Dreyfus was an unsigned letter to a German military attaché in Paris. According to the testimony of Alphonse Bertillon, a self-proclaimed expert on handwriting, the letter was written by Dreyfus. The court relied on Bertillon and convicted Dreyfus for treason. It later turned out that Dreyfus was innocent. In an appeal trial in 1906, Dreyfus' lawyer submitted a report by the brilliant mathematician Henri Poincaré and two of his colleagues at the French Academy of Sciences (Jean Gaston Darboux and Paul Appell). The report criticized Bertillon's methodology, and emphasized

---

[16] Wagenaar 1988, 502; Robertson et al. 2016, 19.
[17] See Chapter 19, Dahlman and Kolflaath, "The Problem of the Prior in Criminal Trials," in this volume.

that an expert witness should be silent on the probability of the hypothesis given the evidence and speak only on how strongly the evidence supports the hypothesis.

> Since it is impossible for us to know the probability a priori, we cannot say that the observed coincidence proves that the ratio of the probability that it is a forgery to the inverse probability has a particular value. From the observed coincidence we can only say that the ratio becomes so many times greater than before the observation.[18]

3.3 Staying within the Area of Expertise

It goes without saying that an expert witness ought not to speak outside the area of expertise. Since the role of the expert witness in the assessment of evidence is justified by his or her area of expertise, an expert witness has no legitimate role to play outside it. This is, however, easier said than done. When expert witnesses testify in court they often get questions that stretch their area of expertise, and some questions fall outside it. It is not easy for an expert witness who wants to be helpful to know when to answer and when to respond that the question falls outside his or her expertise.

The Canadian case *R. v. Marquard* is an illuminating example.[19] A three-year-old girl had been injured when she was staying with her grandmother. The girl had a burn on the side of her face. The grandmother claimed that her granddaughter had burnt herself on a cigarette lighter. According to the prosecution, the grandmother had put the girl's face to a hot stove in order to discipline her. The grandmother was prosecuted for aggravated assault and the prosecution called two expert witnesses to testify. Unfortunately, the experts did not stay within their area of expertise. The first witness was an expert in child abuse and pediatrics, but not an expert in burns. Nevertheless, she testified that the child had suffered a contact burn and not a flame burn. The second witness was an expert on the nature and origin of burns but asserted in his testimony that the girl's passivity during the medical examination was characteristic of abused children.

4. Standing on Solid Ground

Legal factfinding should not be based on bad science. Even so, there is no shortage of examples of when expert testimony based on poor scientific reasoning has found its way into the courtroom. To give a recent example, a study published in 2019 concluded that a large number of the psychological assessment tools used by psychologists in forensic settings were not generally accepted in their field.[20] The need for the legal system to find strategies to minimize the risk that expert testimony based on "junk science" distorts the legal factfinding process has been noted by many and for a long time.[21]

---

[18] "Dans l'impossibilité de connaître la probabilité à priori, nous ne pourrons pas dire telle coïncidence prouve que le rapport de la probabilité de la forgerie à la probabilité inverse a telle valeur. Nous pourrons dire seulement, par la constatation de cette coïncidence, ce rapport devient tant de fois plus grand qu'avant la constatation," (Darboux et al. 1904, 7).

[19] *R. v. Marquard* (1993) 4 S.C.R. 223.

[20] Neal et al. 2019.

[21] See Hand 1901; Huber 1993; Angell 1996; Walton 1997; Goldman 2001; Meester et al. 2006; Råstam 2013.

In our view, an expert witness has a personal responsibility to present testimony that rests on good science. This is so because an element of trust is inevitable in appeal to expert opinion, as it is in science more generally.[22] There will always be parts of the expert's observations, assumptions, etc. that are impossible for an external assessor to control without redoing the expert's job. Actions taken by a legal system or a court can therefore at most promote but not guarantee that an expert's testimony rests on solid ground. It is symptomatic that the 2019 study of psychological assessment tools found that the most scientifically suspect tools were almost never legally challenged.[23] Consequently, for the system to work, expert witnesses must take action to ensure that the testimonies they give rest on good science, and do not risk misleading the factfinder.

What, then, distinguishes good science from poor science or non-science? Many philosophers of science have attempted to answer this question, but their efforts have so far not resulted in any uncontroversial demarcation criterion. The matter is further complicated by the fact that the scientific world is highly complex and heterogeneous. The prevalent scientific ideals, standards and methodological approaches differ both across and within disciplines. For example, the questions asked and methods used in quantitative studies differ considerably from those of use in qualitative studies, and researchers versed in one of these traditions do not always look kindly upon the other. The lack of agreement as to fundamental questions such as the role and value of truth and objectivity in scientific research makes the question of how to identify good science even more difficult to answer.

Difficult to answer as it may be, the question of what demarcates good science from junk science becomes pivotal when courts must decide whether or not to admit or rely on an expert's testimony. In the well-known US case *Daubert v. Merrell Dow Pharmaceuticals,*[24] the Supreme Court, inspired by Carl Hempel and Karl Popper, listed several questions that a judge can consider when deciding on the admissibility of expert testimony. These questions, the "Daubert factors" pertain to whether the theory or technique can be and has been tested, whether it has been subjected to peer review and publication, the known or potential error rate, the existence and maintenance of standards controlling the technique's operation, and whether it is generally accepted in the scientific community.

The Daubert factors have not stood undisputed and have, among other things, been criticized for misconstruing the original ideas of the cited philosophers of science.[25] However, the factors are continuously used in federal courts as well as in some state courts in the United States, and they can provide a valuable contribution to discussions on what should be the appropriate standards for an expert's testimony in other legal systems too. Perhaps most importantly, the Daubert factors take a clear stand for objectivity and testability as virtues of expert testimony.

Irrespective of the observation that objectivity and testability cannot be fully obtained in practice, it seems to us that these are necessary ideals that an expert witness must strive for. It may be the case that subjectivity is unavoidable in scientific research, but it is also the case that expert subjectivity impedes the testimony's function to assist factfinders in arriving at the assessment that they would have made on their own, had they possessed the required

[22] Hardwig 1991; Zagzebski 2012.
[23] Neal et al. 2019.
[24] *Daubert v. Merrell Dow Pharmaceuticals* (1993) 509 U.S. 579.
[25] See, e.g., Allen 1994; Haack 2010.

expert knowledge. We have already noted that the expert should not act as a hired gun acting only on behalf of one of the parties, and nor should the expert's personal perspective or subjective speculations influence the legal factfinding. Rather, the expert's job is to assist the court, the ultimate factfinder, to attain knowledge of the world. In this respect, the expert can be thought of as a replaceable instrument. This means that the expert, in assessing whether his or her testimony stands on sufficiently solid ground, should ask whether other experts would be likely to come to the same conclusion. If not, this does not necessarily mean that the expert's conclusion is erroneous, but it does mean that the expert should reflect on why the conclusions would differ. Theoretical disagreement is not uncommon in science but needs to be communicated to the factfinder. The expert should therefore inform the court about the testimony's sensitivity to theoretical standpoints and other elements in the reasoning that are likely to be disputed by others.

So far, we have talked about the expert's responsibility to ensure that his or her testimony is based on good science. But how about the strategies available for a legal system to control that the expert's testimony is indeed well founded? Which strategies are available depends in part on the legal system. Many common law jurisdictions, such as the United States, have rather comprehensive requirements for the admissibility of expert testimony. Testimony that does not meet the criteria will be rejected as inadmissible by the legal judge, and testimony that passes can be scrutinized by the other party's expert and in cross-examination. In civil law jurisdictions, courts will rarely reject an expert's testimony as inadmissible due to poor scientific reasoning. Instead, the reliability of an expert's testimony is normally assessed as part of the court's evaluation of evidence. In these systems, experts hired by the parties and cross-examination are usually less common. Irrespective of the legal system, it is no easy task for a judge who lacks relevant scientific expertise to assess the scientific quality of an expert's testimony or to judge who is right of two experts with opposite views. In an article published in the *Harvard Law Review* in 1901, Judge Learned Hand asked the rhetorical question:

> [H]ow can the jury judge between two statements each founded upon an experience confessedly foreign in kind to their own? It is just because they are incompetent for such a task that the expert is necessary at all.[26]

As said earlier, the predicament described by Learned Hand cannot be completely evaded. However, it is not the unsolvable paradox that it might seem. Checklists and other devices have been developed to allow non-experts to challenge at least parts of an expert's testimony and the reasoning leading up to it.[27] This possibility complements, but does not replace, the expert's own responsibility to provide testimony that rests on solid grounds.

5. Communicating Uncertainty

As we have seen, expert testimony communicates knowledge from the expert to the factfinder. This transfer of information presents a challenging communication task, since the

---

[26] Hand 1901, 54–6.
[27] Walton 1997, 223; Posner 1999, 93–5; Goldman 2001; Gooden and Walton 2006, 278–9.

factfinder is unfamiliar with the area of expertise and its terminology. What words should the expert use to express how strongly a certain piece of evidence supports a certain hypothesis? How should the expert explain the uncertainties of this support? An evidence assessment always entails a number of uncertainties. How can the expert witness make sure that the factfinder gets a full and accurate picture of these uncertainties?

A first obstacle is the vagueness of ordinary language. Degrees of support can be expressed by words like "strong" or "weak," but such words are notoriously vague. How strong is "strong support"? People understand the word "strong" differently, and empirical studies show that verbal quantifiers in expert testimony are interpreted differently among factfinders.[28] Expert witnesses can avoid this problem by expressing degrees of support numerically. As we have seen in Section 3.2, a *likelihood ratio* quantifies how strongly a piece of evidence supports a hypothesis. Using numbers instead of words makes the assessment more precise.

Some expert witnesses display a behavior that can be described as *uncertainty reticence*. They voice an assessment when the evidence supports the hypothesis so strongly that it is practically certain that the hypothesis is true (or the evidence supports the negation of the hypothesis so strongly that it is practically certain that the hypothesis is false), but they abstain from an assessment in all other cases, saying that the evidence is "inconclusive." Such behavior is psychologically understandable but undermines the function of the expert witness in two ways. First of all, to say that the evidence is "inconclusive" across a scale where the degree of support varies considerably denies the factfinder valuable information. An expert witness should try to quantify how strongly the evidence supports the hypothesis. Secondly, experts who classify a result as inconclusive are in effect applying their own standard of proof. As elaborated in Section 3.1, this means that the expert is using a non-legal norm to answer a question of law. Instead, the expert should provide information that allows the factfinder to answer the question of law, by applying the legal standards of proof to the information that he or she conveys, in combination with the other evidence that is available in the case.

Sometimes, especially when the hypothesis is probabilistic, it might be possible for the expert to quantify and communicate how strong support the evidence provides by adjusting the hypothesis. As an example, consider the situation where the scientific evidence is very weak in support of the preponderant view that a widely used medical test has the high diagnostic value x. In a situation like this, it might be the case that the available evidence nevertheless provides strong evidence for another hypothesis, namely that the diagnostic value of the test amounts to at least the lower value y. Instead of saying that the support for the test having diagnostic value x is low or inconclusive, the expert could say that given the available scientific evidence, the diagnostic value must be at least y. The value y might be way too low to make the test useful in a medical setting, but it can be sufficiently high for the test to provide evidence that in combination with other evidence amounts to the applicable legal standard of proof.

When an expert witness explains the uncertainty in the support that a certain piece of evidence lends to a certain hypothesis it is important that the expert addresses all the uncertainties involved. Let us, as an example, consider a case where a shoe print at the crime scene

---

[28] Nordgaard et al. 2010.

matches the defendant's shoe with regard to sole pattern and wear marks, and a forensic expert testifies that the observed matching features strongly support the hypothesis that the defendant's shoe is the source of the shoeprint. This assessment includes several uncertainties that the expert should explain to the factfinder. First of all, there is an element of subjectivity in the forensic analysis of wear marks that creates uncertainty. There is a risk that another footwear expert would have interpreted the wear marks differently. Secondly, there is the risk of a random match. How strongly an observed match supports the hypothesis depends on the probability of a match if the hypothesis is false, in this case, the probability that a random shoe that is not the source of the shoe print happens to match the shoe print. This probability can be assessed on the basis of expert knowledge on the prevalence of the sole pattern and the wear marks in question, and can be expressed in numbers, for example, "the probability of a random match is 1 in 100 000." Thirdly, there is a risk that the expert's assessment of the random match probability is based on poor reference data. In our example, it could be the case that if the expert would obtain more data on the frequency of certain sole patterns and certain wear marks, the expert would need to adjust the random match probability from 1/ 100,000 to 1/ 10,000. This uncertainty is sometimes described as the weight or robustness of the evidence.[29] All of these uncertainties should be addressed by the expert witness.

One way of helping the court to assess these uncertainties is, as mentioned in Section 4, to inform the court about elements in the expert's reasoning that are likely to be disputed by other experts, and the probability that another expert would come to another conclusion.

This kind of reflection is probably irrelevant from the point of view of experts who are convinced that their own assessment is the right one, but it is nevertheless highly relevant to the factfinder who has to make the ultimate assessment. Because the expert, by definition, cannot deliberately communicate uncertainties that she is not aware of, the expert's assessment of uncertainty can only help but not replace the factfinder's own assessment.

6. Concluding Remarks

In this chapter, we have discussed the expert witness's role in the legal factfinding process. We have taken as our starting point that the role of the expert is to assist the factfinders to arrive at the assessment that they would have made on their own, had they possessed the required expert knowledge. This means that experts should not act as additional advocates for the party that hired them. We have stressed the importance that the expert witness sticks to the assigned question. This means that the expert should give opinions only on questions of fact, never on questions of law, and assess only how strongly a piece of evidence supports a certain hypothesis, never how probable the hypothesis is given the evidence. Moreover, experts must stay within their area of expertise.

We have argued that the role of being an expert witness comes with a personal responsibility to ensure that the testimony rests on solid scientific ground. Expert witnesses should therefore ask themselves whether other experts would come to the same conclusion. Finally,

---

[29] See Chapter 9, Nance, "Weight of Evidence," in this volume. See also Sahlin 1983 on "epistemic risk."

we have stressed that experts should address all uncertainties involved, including the possibility that they would have assessed the evidence differently if they had gathered more reference data, and the possibility that other experts would have come to a different conclusion. The expert should explain all uncertainties to the factfinder in a clear and transparent way and avoid *uncertainty reticence*—the tendency to self-censor to what degree the evidence supports the hypothesis, by categorizing the support as "inconclusive."

References

Allen, R. (1994). "Expertise and the Daubert Decision," *Journal of Criminal Law and Criminology*, 84: 1157–75.

Allen, R. and Pardo, M. (2003). "The Myth of the Law-Fact Distinction," *Northwestern University Law Review*, 97: 1769–808.

Angell, M. (1996). *Science on Trial: The Clash of Medical Evidence and the Law in the Breast Implant Case*. New York: W.W. Norton.

Darboux, J., Appell, P., and Poincaré, H. (1904). *Rapport de M. les Experts Darboux, Appell, Poincaré, Affaire Dreyfus*. Available at https://www.maths.ed.ac.uk/~v1ranick/dreyfus/dreyfustyped.pdf (Accessed: March 25, 2021).

Gold, A., and Appelbaum, P. S. (2011). "Unconscious Conflict of Interest: A Jewish Perspective," *Journal of Medical Ethics*, 37: 402–5.

Goldman, A. (2001). "Experts: Which Ones should you Trust?" *Philosophy and Phenomenological Research*, 63: 199–220.

Gooden, D., and Walton, D. (2006). "Argument from Expert Opinion as Legal Evidence: Critical Questions and Admissibility Criteria of Expert Testimony in the American Legal System," *Ratio Juris*, 19: 261–86.

Haack, S. (2010). "Federal Philosophy of Science: A Deconstruction—and a Reconstruction," *New York Universal Journal of Law and Liberty*, 5: 394–435.

Hand, L. (1901). "Historical and Practical Considerations regarding Expert Testimony," *Harvard Law Review*, 15: 40–58.

Hardwig, J. (1991). "The Role of Trust in Knowledge," *Journal of Philosophy*, 88: 693–708.

Hart, H., and Honoré, A. (1985). Causation in the Law. Oxford: Clarendon Press.

Huber, P. (1993). *Galileo's Revenge: Junk Science in the Courtroom*. New York: Basic Books.

Josefsson, D. (2015). *The Strange Case of Thomas Quick: The Swedish Serial Killer and the Psychoanalyst who Created Him*. Translated by A. Paterson. London: Portobello Books.

Kriebel, D., Tickner, J., Epstein, P., Lemons, J. et al. (2001). "The Precautionary Principle in Environmental Science," *Environmental Health Perspectives*, 109: 871–6.

Lubet, S. (1999). "Expert Witnesses—Ethics and Professionalism," *Georgetown Journal of Legal Ethics*, 12: 465–88.

Meester, R., Collings, M., Gill, R., and van Lambalgen, M. (2006). "On the (Ab)Use of Statistics in the Legal Case against Nurse Lucia de B," *Law, Probability and Risk*, 5: 233–50.

Mitroff, I., and Featheringham, T. R. (1974). "On Systemic Problem Solving and the Error of the Third Kind," *Behavioral Science*, 19: 383–93.

Moore, D., and Loewenstein, G. (2004). "Self-interest, Automaticity and the Psychology of Conflict of Interest," *Social Justice Research*, 17: 189–202.

Moore, D. A., Tanlu, L., and Bazerman M. H. (2010). "Conflict of Interest and the Intrusion of Bias," *Judgement and Decisionmaking*, 5: 37–53.

Moore, M. (2009). *Causation and Responsibility: An Essay in Law, Morals and Metaphysics*. Oxford: Oxford University Press.

Neal, T., Slobogin, C., Saks, M., Faigman, D., and Geisinger, K. (2019). "Psychological Assessment in Legal Contexts: Are Courts Keeping 'Junk Science' Out of the Courtroom?" *Psychological Science in the Public Interest*, 20: 135–64.

Nordgaard A., Wistedt I., Drotz W., Elmqvist J. et al. (2010). *Uppfattning av Värdeord i Sakkunnig-Utlåtanden.* SKL Rapport.

Posner, R. (1999). "The Law and Economics of the Economic Expert Witness," *Journal of Economic Perspectives,* 13: 91–9.

Robertson, B., Vignaux, G., and Berger, C. (2016). *Interpreting Evidence.* Second edition. Chichester: Wiley.

Råstam, H. (2013). *Thomas Quick—the Making of a Serial Killer.* Edinburgh: Canongate Books.

Sahlin, N.-E. (1983). "On Second Order Probabilities and the Notion of Epistemic Risk," in B. P. Stigum and F. Wenstøp (eds.), *Foundations of Utility and Risk Theory with Applications,* 95–104. Dordrecht: Springer.

Sevelin, E. (2019). "What about the Non-Legal Facts: Revising Allen and Pardo's Analytical Distinction between Law and Fact," *The International Journal of Evidence & Proof,* 23: 349–65.

Wagenaar, W. (1988). "The Proper Seat—a Bayesian Discussion of the Position of Expert Witnesses," *Law and Human Behavior,* 4: 499–510.

Wahlberg, L. (2010). *Legal Questions And Scientific Answers: Ontological Differences and Epistemic Gaps in the Assessment of Causal Relations.* Lund: Mediatryck.

Wahlberg, L. (2017). "Legal Ontology, Scientific Expertise and the Factual World," *Journal of Social Ontology,* 3: 49–65.

Walton, D. (1997). *Appeal to Expert Opinion.* University Park, PA: Pennsylvania State University Press.

Wright, R. (1985). "Causation in Tort Law," *California Law Review,* 73: 1735–828.

Zagzebski, L. (2012). *Epistemic Authority: A Theory of Trust, Authority and Autonomy in Belief.* Oxford: Oxford University Press.

PART II
LAW AND FACTFINDING

5

The Role of Rules in the Law of Evidence

Frederick Schauer

1. Introduction

Jeremy Bentham, one of history's great haters, hated many things, and among them was the law of evidence.[1] Indeed, his hatred of evidence law was not restricted to particular rules and doctrines, although he truly did hate many of them, especially the rules relating to privileges[2] and witness competency.[3] Rather, Bentham hated the very idea of *rules* of evidence, especially exclusionary rules,[4] believing that factual determinations could and should ordinarily be made by judges and jurors in particular cases, and with little interference from what he considered artificially constraining abstract rules.

Bentham's ideas seem less heretical now than they did when he first offered them. Most common law jurisdictions have softened the hard edges of a rule-based approach to evidence,[5] for example, by eliminating many of the exclusions based on witness competence,[6] by relaxing, in many jurisdictions almost to the point of elimination, the rules excluding hearsay evidence, especially in civil cases,[7] and by substantially weakening the rules excluding secondary evidence of writings—the so-called best evidence rule.[8] And most civil law countries persist in something resembling what has come to be known as the *free proof* tradition, the substantially rule-free approach to considering the facts that bear on the existence of criminal or civil liability.[9]

Despite these comparatively recent developments, the law of evidence, especially but not only in the common law world, remains substantially an affair of rules. Why that is the case, and whether it should be the case, is the subject of this entry.

2. The "Free Proof" Idea

What has come to be known as the idea of free proof is the notion that all relevant evidence should be considered (privileged information aside), and that each item of evidence offered

---

[1] That Bentham hated all of evidence law is an overstatement (see Nance 1988, 275), but not by much. He did, after all, claim that "[a]lmost every rule that has ever been laid down on the subject if evidence [is] repugnant to the ends of justice." (Bentham 1827, 4). The current definitive edition remains (Bentham 1843). And see also Postema 1986, 347–9, 411–12.

[2] Laudan 2006, 147–70.

[3] Allen 1995; Fisher 1997, 660.

[4] Haack 2014, 5; Haack 2005, 56; Twining 1985, 28.

[5] Stein 2005, 107–16, 212–23; Twining 2014, 208.

[6] e.g., (United States) Federal Rule of Evidence 601.

[7] Sklansky 2009. A useful table summarizing developments in the common law world can be found in Caton 2011, 129.

[8] Federal Rule of Evidence 1003; Strine, et al., 2013, 72, n. 252.

[9] Stein 2005, 117; Kunert 1966.

Frederick Schauer, *The Role of Rules in the Law of Evidence* In: *Philosophical Foundations of Evidence Law.* Edited by: Christian Dahlman, Alex Stein, and Giovanni Tuzet, Oxford University Press. © Christian Dahlman, Alex Stein, and Giovanni Tuzet 2021.
DOI: 10.1093/oso/9780198859307.003.0006

at a trial should be individually evaluated—on a "case-by-case" basis, as it is commonly put—to assess how much probative value, if any, that particular item of evidence should be given in the determination of the fact that that item is offered to prove. Where a system of free proof prevails, whether system-wide or, in particular trials, the judge or judges making the factual determination decide for themselves what weight to give each item of evidence that is offered for their consideration. And when and if applied to jury trials, the free proof idea would largely eliminate the screening function of the judge, such that any item of evidence that is presented would be heard by the jury, which then, without the interference of a judge, would similarly decide how much (if any) weight to give to that item of evidence in reaching its factual conclusions.

This brief sketch is somewhat of a caricature of the free proof idea, but it is a caricature that hews closely to the way in which people evaluate evidence in their everyday non-litigated lives.[10] When someone claiming to be knowledgeable tells us something, we typically listen to what they say and then decide how much credence to give to what they have told us, in light of what we know about their knowledge, what we know about their past reliability, what we know about their biases, what we know about their sources of information, what we know about how well what they have told us fits with what we already know or with other pieces of evidence, and so on. All of these considerations, and more, factor into how likely we think that what we have been told is true. Similarly, when considering the accuracy of a photograph or drawing, we use what we know about the circumstances under which the image was created, as well as what we know about drawing or photography, to make our own judgment in the particular instance about the likely accuracy of the representation.

The important feature of such everyday occurrences is that ordinary people reaching everyday factual conclusions are not constrained by second-order proof rules telling them how to make their first-order evidentiary evaluations.[11] Even assuming that people possessed the ability to impose rules on themselves,[12] hardly an obvious or sound assumption,[13] it is not something we think of doing in our day-to-day evidentiary evaluations. The probative value of each piece of information we receive is ordinarily evaluated on a particular or case-by-case basis, and thus we determine the probative value of an item of evidence at the same time that we become aware of the content of the item of evidence whose probative value we are assessing. And because the approach to evidence just described is what ordinary people—not judges, and not lawyers—do in their everyday affairs, and what families do in their own internal organization and governance,[14] Bentham described such an approach as the "Natural System of Procedure," including therefore the natural system of evaluating evidence. "Be the dispute what it may,—see everything that is to be seen; hear everybody who is likely to know anything about the matter; hear everybody, but most attentively of all, and first of all, those who are likely to

---

[10] "A large class of 'exclusionary' rules bars certain types of evidence from reaching the trier of fact, though these same types of evidence would cheerfully and blithely be regarded as probative in everyday life." Goldman 1990, 291.

[11] On the distinction between first-order reasons and second-order reasons about those reasons, and also about first-order decisions and second-order decisions about those decisions, see, most influentially, Raz 1990; 1979. Useful explications include Perry 1989; Sunstein and Ullman-Margalit 1999.

[12] Schelling 1985.

[13] Schauer 1991, 160–1.

[14] Postema 1986, 348.

know most about it—the parties."[15] For Bentham, this approach was to be contrasted with what he called the Technical System, the approach he abhorred and which he believed characterized English law at the time. The Technical System relied heavily on rules of exclusion—whether of witnesses or of particular pieces of evidence—and thus stood in marked contrast with the Natural System's willingness to hear everybody with relevant information, and to hear everything relevant that they had to offer.

Bentham's crusade to use the Natural System of Procedure, including but not limited to its approach to evidence, as the model for adjudication in the legal system is in a sense curious. Implicit in the Natural System, as suggested earlier, is a trust in the reasoning processes of the decision-maker, a trust, when applied to judges, that exists in at the very least some tension with Bentham's well-known scorn of "Judge and Co."[16] and the preference for codification that emerged out of it.[17] Believing that lawyers and judges were engaged in a conspiracy to make law unnecessarily complex in order to enrich the wallets of lawyers and the power of judges, Bentham insisted that a code of precise legal rules, leaving little discretion to judges and little argumentative space to those who argued before them, would forestall most of the evils that corrupt lawyers and judges were prone to bring about.

Bentham's distrust of judges and his consequent endorsement of discretion-limiting legal rules in general is thus in puzzling contrast with his view about evidence. One might suppose, after all, that someone who distrusted the power of judges to make law and distrusted the power of judges to apply law flexibly and with discretion would also distrust judges to make decisions about evidence. But although the use of something like the Natural System might grant judges more discretion than we imagine that Bentham would have endorsed,[18] it is important to remember that Bentham was writing in the context of a system in which the jury was far more prevalent in both civil and criminal cases than it is now. Perhaps, therefore, the seeming tension can be resolved by noting that the Natural System leaves evidentiary determinations largely in the hands not of judges and lawyers, but of lay jurors. And seen from this perspective, Bentham's trust in jurors more than in the judges who would keep information from them is consistent with Bentham's greater trust in non-lawyer legislators and the non-lawyer citizenry than in the legal profession and the judges who emerged from it.

Benthamite exegesis aside, however, Bentham's basic idea is important because it aligns so closely with the practices in most civil law jurisdictions. In the civil law world, which to a very rough approximation includes almost all of those nations that were never part of the British Commonwealth, lay juries are rare, something closer to the free proof tradition prevails, and few rules of exclusion limit what judges as factfinders may hear and consider.[19]

---

[15] Bentham 1843 (vol. 7), 599. The concluding phrase refers to a particular object of Bentham's vitriol—the exclusion for reasons of bias of testimony by interested parties to a civil action or of the defendant in a criminal case. Wigmore 1979, §576, 817. See also Langbein, Lerner, and Smith 2009, 247–8.

[16] Bentham 1843 (vol. 5), 481, 512; (vol. 7), 226–31. A valuable discussion is in Resnik 2011. And a nuanced (and controversial) view of Bentham's views about judges, one that sees Bentham as less uniformly contemptuous, is in Postema 1986, which discusses this exact point with reference to evidentiary determinations (Postema 1986, 411–12), and argues that Bentham viewed requirements of public reason giving as a check on judicial arbitrariness.

[17] Alfange 1969.

[18] But see the interpretation in Postema 1986, 411–12.

[19] See Damaska 1997; 1995; Blumenthal 2001; Dufraimont 2008; Langbein 1979; Tilley 2011. Free proof, more or less, is also the norm in Scandinavian countries, whose procedural aspects combine elements of both the common law and civil law traditions (Ekelöf 1964). There is, to be sure, a distinction between admission rules and

And although the preceding two sentences egregiously oversimplify a far more complex picture,[20] it remains the case that most civil law jurisdictions come closer to the pure free proof idea than do most common law ones. The importance of this conclusion, at least for this chapter, lies in the fact that free proof—evidence without rules—was not simply another of Bentham's provocative ideas, but rather represents an extraordinarily pervasive perspective on the processes of proof.

3. Enter the Jury

Given the pervasiveness and seeming sensibility of the free proof idea, a natural question to ask is why common law systems have for so long resisted free proof, and have instead relied heavily on a rule-based evidence system, especially a system containing exclusionary rules that keep from the decision-maker countless facts and inferences that a free proof system would plainly admit.

For Thayer in the late nineteenth century[21] and for Wigmore not long after, the answer to this question lay in the existence and power of juries.[22] Thayer, whose focus was principally historical rather than theoretical or doctrinal, sympathized with the Benthamite critique of the unnecessary complexity of the rules of evidence, believing that many of them were matters of substantive law rather than of procedure, and believing as well that many of them could be explained by their historical provenance more than by contemporary rationality.[23] Had it not been for the institution of the jury, Thayer argued, the law of evidence would have developed in a much simpler way, with a dominant focus on logical relevance, and a presumption, albeit rebuttable, against excluding any relevant evidence.

Thayer's primarily historical writing was scant on deep policy or doctrinal analysis, but that task was to be taken up by Thayer's student Wigmore, whose influence on the field remains strong even after the almost eighty years since his death. Although Wigmore, like Bentham and Thayer, thought the rules of evidence unnecessarily complex, and although he sometimes argued that such rules were merely transitional to a better state of affairs closer to free proof or closer to an exclusive Thayerian focus on relevance,[24] his more sustained view, especially as expressed in his monumental treatise,[25] was that the rules of evidence developed and needed to be sustained because of the deficiencies of juries, or, more precisely,

---

evaluation rules, and many of the civil law jurisdictions that have eliminated the Roman or classical rules regarding how to evaluate evidence have at least some exclusionary rules. But the exclusionary rules they have tend to be largely about privileges, and, to the extent that civil law jurisdictions have exclusionary rules that are not about privileges or constitutional limitations, those exclusionary rules are far fewer in number and far less in weight than is typical of the common law world.

[20] On why the stark contrast in the text may gloss over important complications, see Jackson and Summers 2012; Jackson 2019, 691.

[21] Thayer 1896. The definitive edition is now taken to be the 1898 edition, published by Little, Brown & Co.

[22] Twining 1985, 5–8.

[23] Thayer's historical claim was famously challenged in Morgan 1937, finding Thayer's conclusion that the exclusionary rules are "a child of the jury" and "not more than a half-truth." And an important discussion of Thayer's basic approach can be found in Twining 1994, 188–203.

[24] Twining 1985, 236, n. 44.

[25] Wigmore 1904.

of jurors.[26] "Hence the trial rules may well guard against the jurors being misled by specially plausible but weak evidence or against being perplexed and misguided by a confusion of petty data which have only trivial probative value."[27] For Wigmore, therefore, the inability of members of a jury to distinguish between valuable and trivial evidence and to give evidence no more and no less weight that it properly deserved, coupled with the tendency of those jurors to be swayed by passion and prejudice, led him to the conclusion that it was better that some evidence, even evidence that might have some probative value, be kept from the jury. And the vehicle for doing so was the exclusionary rules of evidence that Bentham scorned and that Thayer occasionally grudgingly tolerated.

Exclusionary rules thus represent an approach diametrically opposed to the free proof idea. Pure free proof, or at least the version adapted from Thayer that would employ only the single rule of relevance, is an approach that gives the decision-maker access to all relevant evidence, and allows the decision-maker to give that evidence the weight it deserves. Exclusionary rules, by contrast, keep some relevant evidence from being known or considered by the decision-maker, on the theory that the decision-maker might give such evidence too much weight, or might misunderstand or misapply the evidence in some other way.

Two brief digressions are in order here. First, there are some exclusionary rules that serve functions extrinsic to the factfinding process, and that are therefore extrinsic to the epistemic goals of maximum accuracy.[28] Such rules typically exclude evidence with at least some probative value, and thus involve an epistemic sacrifice. Nevertheless, it is thought that the epistemic sacrifice is worth making in order to achieve certain social goals extrinsic to the accuracy-maximizing goals of the trial process. One prominent example is the rule excluding even probative evidence if it has been obtained unlawfully, a rule—often and perhaps confusingly called the "exclusionary rule"—that is court-created but of constitutional status (for criminal cases) in the United States,[29] and is commonly a matter of policy in many other jurisdictions.[30] Equally pervasive, and also serving goals extrinsic to truth-finding, is the set of rules regarding privileges. Accuracy in truth-determination would likely increase were defendants in criminal trials required to testify under oath, were lawyers required to testify about discussions with their clients, and were priests, ministers, rabbis, imams, and other religious leaders required to testify about the conversations they have had with the penitents and others who talk to them in a religious setting. But the social value of uninhibited conversations in such settings and relationships is thought more important than any gains in accuracy that might come from requiring evidence in settings such as those just described.[31]

Other categories of evidence are also excluded for reasons that are extrinsic to accuracy-maximization. The inadmissibility of evidence of subsequent remedial measures in actions based on negligence or other culpable conduct,[32] for example, is based on the seeming

---

[26] The text's explicit distinction between jurors and juries is intended to reflect the fact that the collective and deliberative practices of juries may at times produce different (and typically better) conclusions than those that are reached by individual jurors. See Saks and Spellman 2016, 46–9.

[27] Wigmore 1904, 930. And see Wigmore, 1904, 250, discussing the importance of "guarding the jury from the overweening effect of certain kinds of evidence."

[28] Mueller, Kirkpatrick, and Richter 2018, 297–302.

[29] *Mapp v. Ohio*, 367 U.S. 643 (1961). On the exclusionary rule as "extraveritistic," see Goldman 1999, 293.

[30] Ma 1999.

[31] Louisell 1956.

[32] In the United States, see Federal Rule of Evidence 407.

social value of encouraging the repair of damaged premises, even though a repair by the owner of premises after an accident might be probative of the owner's recognition of the problem, and therefore probative of the owner's negligence.[33] And the typical inadmissibility of evidence relating to settlement of a civil action[34] or, where plea bargaining exists, to the compromise of a criminal prosecution,[35] is again thought to encourage the discussions leading to a settlement or to a plea bargain, and thus to facilitate processes with arguable social value.

Second, there are some exclusionary rules that are based on particular goals and values of the legal system that may not exist in extra-legal contexts, even though the exclusion may, again, come at some sacrifice to the goals of truth. For example, when generally probative evidence of a defendant's past crimes is excluded against the prosecution's attempts to use such evidence to prove that the defendant committed a similar crime on this occasion (and so too with past acts of negligence in civil action),[36] one argument for exclusion is that a defendant, having already been punished for the previous crimes, is in effect being punished again if those crimes can be used as evidence on subsequent occasions. In addition, goals of rehabilitation may argue for such a defendant being entitled to a "fresh start." But as with privileges and various other extrinsic exclusionary rules, the goals here are ones that are seen as opposed to truth-finding, and are thus imposed not to further accuracy, but instead despite the loss of accuracy.

Such extrinsic exclusionary rules apart, however, and the digression thus completed, most of the rules of evidence, and the ones that represent the stark contrast with the free proof tradition, are intrinsic in the sense of being aimed at the goal of increasing the accuracy of the factfinding process. And these rules, or so Thayer and Wigmore and their successors believed, increased the accuracy of the factfinding process by withholding from the jury some admittedly probative evidence that was so likely to be misunderstood, misevaluated, misweighed, or misapplied by the jury that the epistemic losses from excluding probative evidence were outweighed by the epistemic gains coming from the misuse of evidence that, in theory and if properly used, would have positive probative value.[37]

The classic example of such an exclusionary rule would be the typical rule in common law jurisdictions excluding evidence of past conduct to prove present behavior.[38] That a person has robbed banks in the past is typically probative that they have committed the bank robbery with which they are now charged, and someone with a record of negligent

---

[33] Most of the exclusionary rules aimed at such extrinsic goals are based on rarely tested empirical assumptions about the existence of a causal relationship between the existence of the rule of exclusion and conduct by primary actors. For skepticism about such a relationship in some contexts, see Mueller, Kirkpatrick, and Richter 2018, 240 (subsequent remedial measures); *Jaffee v. Redmond*, 518 U.S. 1 (1996) (Scalia dissenting) (patient-psychotherapist privilege).

[34] Federal Rule of Evidence 408. Relatedly, see Federal Rule of Evidence 409 (payment if medical expenses) and Federal Rule of Evidence 411 (evidence of liability insurance).

[35] Federal Rule of Evidence 410.

[36] Federal Rule of Evidence 404(b).

[37] Goldman argues, importantly, that even if we accept the basic premise of accuracy-based exclusion, it is still an open question whether and when the epistemic (Goldman calls it "veritistic") loss from excluding probative evidence is greater than the epistemic gain that would come from the admission of misused, misunderstood, and misweighted evidence. Goldman1999, 292–5. To the same effect, see Laudan 2016, 179, n. 6. And in this regard, it is worthwhile taking note of the 1972 observation by Rupert Cross, at the time Great Britain's pre-eminent scholar of evidence (and much else) that he was "working for the day when [his] subject was abolished" (as quoted in Twining 1994, 1).

[38] As in Federal Rule of Evidence 404(b).

driving is more likely than someone with no such record, everything else held constant, to have been negligent on some particular occasion. But such evidence, as well as other evidence of the propensities or character traits that such acts may reveal, is once again typically excluded not only because of the "double punishment" and "rehabilitation" justifications just described, but also, and primarily, because of a fear that jurors will overweight it. Such evidence may be probative, but if jurors will consider it conclusive, then it is better, so it has long been thought, to exclude the evidence entirely rather than to have it overused in such a way. If jurors are likely to believe that a defendant who has robbed banks in the past is *of course* the one who robbed this bank at this time, then mandatory underweighting, which is what an exclusionary rule does, is preferable to likely overweighting.[39]

So too, traditionally, with the exclusion of hearsay evidence. Most people routinely rely on hearsay in many of their personal and professional dealings and decisions. And they do so because most hearsay evidence has some probative value. But traditionally, and certainly when Thayer and Wigmore were writing, hearsay was excluded despite the fact that it has at least some probative value in many or most instances. But as with evidence of past acts, and as with the related exclusion of evidence of character, at least one argument for the hearsay rule[40] has been a fear that jurors would not understand the weaknesses (if weaknesses they are) of evidence by an out-of-court declarant offered to prove the truth of some matter but which was not originally offered under oath and could not be subject to cross-examination. And thus the traditional exclusion of hearsay (the large and increasing number of exceptions aside) is again typically understood to be based in part on the view that jurors would overvalue hearsay evidence, and accordingly on the view that mandated undervaluation—exclusion by a different name—was preferable to likely overvaluation.

4. Is It Only About Juries?

In believing that it was the institution of the jury that explained the Anglo-American preference for exclusionary rules of evidence, Thayer, Wigmore, and their successors implicitly or explicitly took the position that such rules would be unnecessary were evidence to be considered only by legally trained judges.[41] But there is a reason to doubt that in this they were correct.[42]

One might think that judges might be able to avoid many of the epistemic failures that led Thayer and Wigmore to attribute exclusionary rules largely to the epistemic risks coming from factual decision-making by lay jurors. Judges, after all, are lawyers, and we might suppose that lawyers are, on average, more intelligent than the (more or less) random cross-section of the population that serves on juries. And we might suppose as well that legal training and legal practice would make judges more attuned to the nuances of evidence, and therefore less susceptible to the various prejudices and cognitive failures that bedevil the lay

---

[39] See Lilly, Capra, and Salzburg 2012, 1–2.
[40] And not the only one by any means. See Nance 1988; 1996.
[41] Not surprisingly, this is the view of many judges, who often discard or lessen the stringency of the rules of evidence when they are presiding (and thus deciding) without a jury. Levin and Cohen 1971; Sheldon and Murray 2003.
[42] Schauer 2006.

people who serve on juries.[43] Consequently, we might think that Thayer and Wigmore were correct in supposing that jurors were prone to a range of prejudices, misunderstandings, and misevaluations that judges were generally able to avoid.[44]

But in supposing all of this, we would likely be mistaken. Judges are indeed lawyers, and perhaps lawyers (and therefore judges) are smarter, on average, than the population at large, but judges are also humans.[45] And thus the question is whether judges as lawyers and humans are less prone to the epistemic failures that we see in non-lawyer humans, or in humans generally. And a considerable amount of research indicates that they are not. Even when people, and thus judges, are aware of their own tendencies towards cognitive error, they are scarcely less susceptible to many of the familiar biases—anchoring, ignoring base rates, availability, and many others—that have been well-documented in human decision-makers generally.[46] And thus even if we were to assume, counterfactually as a historical and descriptive matter, that judges were explicitly trained in various strategies of debiasing, there is reason to doubt that such strategies would be substantially effective.

At least some of what is in the foregoing paragraph has been documented by serious research. In one particularly significant and well-designed study, for example, actual judges were shown to be largely unable to ignore inadmissible evidence of which they were aware, even though they knew of its legal inadmissibility.[47] What this and other research suggests, therefore, is that much that Thayer and Wigmore attributed to jurors could be attributed to judges as factfinders as well.[48] And to the extent that this is so, then the hypothesized difference between jurors and judges is diminished, and, accordingly, so does the argument for attributing the existence of the exclusionary rules of evidence solely or largely to the institution of the jury.

Even after the distinction between judges and jurors is understood to be largely exaggerated, the question still remains as to whether there should be exclusionary rules of evidence. In other words, do the cognitive and epistemic similarities between judges and jurors as factfinders argue for the elimination of exclusionary rules for both judges and jurors, or does it instead argue for the use of such exclusionary rules for both judges and for jurors? With respect to the former possibility, it is important to note, after all, and as Bentham recognized in describing what we now call free proof as the "natural" system of factfinding, that ordinary people in making ordinary everyday determinations of fact are not saddled with exclusionary rules. Why should not the same apply to those ordinary people, and a fortiori to judges, when they are making factual determinations in courts of law?

There are many ways to answer this question, but one starts with the idea that it is hardly clear, Bentham notwithstanding, that the so-called natural method should be taken as an

---

[43] A careful and balanced analysis of the claim that judges are in some ways better at (or different from) making factual determinations than jurors is in Spellman 2010.

[44] On the basic claim that distrust of lay jurors represents the principal justification for the exclusionary rules of evidence, see, in addition to Thayer and Wigmore, Mueller, Kirkpatrick, and Richter 2018, §1.1; Hart and McNaughton 1959.

[45] See, famously, Frank 1931. And see, more recently and informed by contemporary experimental research, Saks and Spellman 2016, 33–56; Spellman 2007.

[46] The literature is vast. Among the more prominent and/or more useful contributions are Kahneman 2011; Broomell 2020; Mellers, Schwartz, and Cooke 1998; Slovic, Fischhoff, and Lichtenstein 1977; Tversky and Kahneman 1974.

[47] Wistrich, Guthrie, and Rachlinski 2005. Relatedly, and to much the same effect, see Guthrie, Rachlinski, and Wistrich 2001; Robinson and Spellman 2005.

[48] Schauer 2006.

ideal. Enlightened by the findings of modern psychology, with Kahneman and Tversky being the most well-known and influential figures, we know that people make countless mistakes in their everyday factual determinations.[49] It is at least conceptually plausible, therefore, even if unrealistic as a practical matter, to suppose that even ordinary people making ordinary decisions outside of the legal system might make better decisions were they to be subject to some number of exclusionary rules.[50] Of course in the real world it is hard to imagine how that would work, but the practical impossibility of such an approach should not lead us to glorify so-called natural decision-making any more than we glorify smallpox, slavery, patriarchal social organizations, and countless other phenomena whose seeming naturalness, or at least longstandingness, is not seen as an impediment to human-created improvements. And perhaps so too with making factual determinations. Bentham's profound contempt for the legal system and its inhabitants[51] may have led him to exaggerate the extent to which things are better without lawyer- and judge-led institutions, but 200 years of psychological research later it is difficult to credit the idea that the way in which ordinary people make ordinary decisions is a model that the legal system should seek to emulate.

As a result, if faced with a choice between subjecting *neither* judges nor juries to exclusionary rules, on the one hand, and subjecting *both* to exclusionary rules, on the other, recognition that many of the epistemic deficiencies of jurors plague judges as well would appear to provide a stronger argument for the latter than for the former.[52] In a world of imperfect decision-makers, whether those imperfect decision-makers be professional judges or lay jurors, rule-based and rule-constrained factfinding may across the full range of decisions produce more accurate decisions than a rule-free approach that can produce better decisions in the hands of optimal decision-makers but worse decisions in the hands of the decision-makers we actually have.

5. On Law and Rules Generally

In a way it is surprising that the free proof ideal is so often taken as the appropriate goal, such that the burden of justification appears now to lie with those who would support a rule-based approach to the evaluation of evidence. And this seeming presumption against a rule-based approach to evidence is surprising because law itself is a rule-based enterprise. Legal decision-makers, after all, are not simply instructed to make the best all-things-considered possible decision for every dispute or every transaction with legal implications. Weber was mistaken in attributing to Islamic law and the figure of the *qadi* a rule-free approach to decision-making,[53] in which the decision-maker is empowered to make the decision which

---

[49] Valuable overviews also include Gilovich, Griffin, and Kahneman 2002; Plous 1993.

[50] Schauer 2008.

[51] See Lieberman 1989, 219; Keeton and Schwarzenberger 1948, 11–14.

[52] This conclusion is interestingly and importantly supported by the retention of exclusionary rules even in jurisdictions with substantial common law roots but, now, with no juries, of which South Africa is a prominent example. See Maartens and Schwikkard 2011. Much the same might be said about Israel, which also, even without juries, retains an approach to trial evidence closer to its common law origins than to the free proof ideal. See Evidence Ordinance (new version) 1971.

[53] See Rosen 1980. Weber's discussion of *qadi* justice (*kadijustiz* in Weber's original German text) is in Weber 1954.

is best, or most fair, or most just (and these are not the same) without the intervention of more specific rules. But Weber was right in describing the move from rule-free adjudication or rule-free social organization to more rule-based decision-making institutions and practices as an advance. "Do the right thing" may work well as the title of a movie,[54] but no society has yet come to the conclusion that it works well as the best approach to social organization and institutional design.[55] Much the same can be said, within the utilitarian tradition, about the difference between act- and rule-utilitarianism. Full-blown act-utilitarianism may have some theoretical appeal, but even the most committed act-utilitarians recognize that something more concrete than "maximize utility" is necessary for the actual operation of non-ideal societies.[56]

The point of the foregoing is to shift the burden of justification. We should not ask why, given the existence of a free proof tradition and its everyday counterparts, common law legal systems have developed and continue to use a different approach to factfinding. Rather, we should ask why, given the pervasively rule-based structure of all developed legal systems,[57] whether in common law or civil law jurisdictions, the determination of facts at trials should be subject to a different approach. If legal systems, in the large, recognize the undesirability of telling officials that they ought only to make the correct all-things-considered decisions about citizen behavior, and recognize the undesirability of telling citizens that their only legal obligation is to do the all-things-considered correct thing, then what is surprising is why anyone would ever have thought that what is so plainly undesirable in law's normative or prescriptive mode should become desirable in law's factfinding mode.

This is not to suggest that the arguments for and against rule-based approaches in law are identical in law's prescriptive and factfinding modes. To the extent that rules are important devices in the coordination of human behavior, for example, and thus to the extent that law exists primarily for such a coordination function,[58] or to the extent that law exists primarily for the related idea of planning,[59] such considerations are less applicable, even if not wholly inapplicable, to the determination of facts. Similarly, to the extent that rules in law serve important separation of powers (in the non-technical and non-constitutional sense) functions, again those considerations are less important when we are thinking about the determination of factual truth.

Despite these differences, however, there are important similarities. And the most important is that the rule-based approach to prescription we take for granted remains substantially based on the way in which people have widely divergent goals, widely divergent preferences, and, most importantly, widely different abilities. By simplifying decisions, the ordinary behavior-regulating legal rules we take for granted suppress many of these differences, and do so desirably and with little controversy except at the edges. When the American state of Montana quickly abandoned its experiment of replacing numerical speed limits with only the mandate to drive "reasonably and prudently,"[60] it recognized

---

[54] Lee 1989.

[55] On the divergence between law and an all-things-considered approach to moral decision-making, see Alexander and Schauer 2007.

[56] On the use of rules of thumb within the utilitarian tradition even by those who would treat those rules as defeasible if shown to produce the wrong result for a particular act, see Smart 1956, 344. On modern rule-utilitarianism generally, see Hooker 2002; Urmson 1953.

[57] And given the existence of law itself, as opposed to a law free "do-the-right-thing" society.

[58] Postema 1982.

[59] See Shapiro 2011.

[60] See Sunstein and King 1999.

that numerical speed limits desirably served to suppress differences in opinion about what speeds were reasonable and prudent at some time in some place, and desirably helped (or forced) those with lesser driving skills (or lesser appreciation of their own driving skills) to drive more safely.

Such considerations apply to factfinding as well. Evidentiary rules, and not only exclusionary rules, compensate for epistemic deficiencies just as ordinary rules compensate for deficiencies in morality or rationality on the part of those whom they regulate. And as with ordinary behavior-regulating primary rules, such an approach does not come without costs. Following ordinary legal rules may produce suboptimal decisions when those decisions are viewed in isolation, but the degree of aggregate suboptimality is commonly thought less than the degree of aggregate suboptimality that would likely exist were decidedly suboptimal decision-makers empowered to make their own determinations of the best all-things-considered decision. Similarly, a rule-based approach to evidence may produce frequent epistemic suboptimalities when it excludes genuinely probative evidence, as Bentham so memorably insisted. But, analogously, the suboptimality of such decisions, even when aggregated, may be less than the suboptimality, in the aggregate, of factfinding by decidedly suboptimal decision-makers, whether they be judges or members of a jury.

This is not to say that this or that rule of evidence in common law jurisdictions is necessarily the best one. The decline in the exclusion of hearsay, for example, appears to be based on the view that the traditional exclusion achieves too little benefit at too great a cost. But the deficiencies of particular rules of evidence should not be taken to suggest that the very idea of rules of evidence is itself deficient, and perhaps it is the free proof tradition rather than the rule-based tradition that is in need of serious reconsideration.

References

Alexander, L., and F. Schauer. (2007). "Law's Limited Domain Confronts Morality's Universal Empire," *William & Mary Law Review*, 48: 1579–603.

Alfange, D., Jr. (1969). "Jeremy Bentham and the Codification of Law," *Cornell Law Review*, 55: 58–77.

Allen, C. J. W. (1995). "Bentham and the Abolition of Incompetency from Defect of Religious Principle," *Journal of Legal History*, 16: 172–88.

Bentham, J. (1827). *Rationale of Judicial Evidence, Specially Applied to English Practice*, J. S. Mill (ed.). London: Hunt & Clarke.

Bentham, J. (1843). *The Works of Jeremy Bentham*. Edited by J. Bowring. Edinburgh: W. Tait; London: Simpkin and Marshall.

Blumenthal, J. (2001). "Shedding Some Light on Calls for Hearsay Reform: Civil Law Hearsay Rules in Historical and Modern Perspective," *Pace International Law Journal*, 13: 93–116.

Caton, M. (2011). "Abolish the Hearsay Rule: The Truth of the Matter Asserted at Last," *Maine Bar Journal*, 26;, 126–30.

Damaska, M. (1995). "Free Proof and its Detractors," *American Journal of Comparative Law*, 43: 343–57.

Damaska, M. (1997). *Evidence Law Adrift*. New Haven, CT: Yale University Press.

Dufraimont, L. (2008). "Evidence Law and the Jury: A Reassessment," *McGill Law Journal*, 53: 199–242.

Ekelöf, P. O. (1964). "Free Evaluation of Evidence," *Scandinavian Studies in Law*, 8: 45–66.

Fischhoff, B., and Broomell, S. B. (2020). "Judgment and Decision Making," *Annual Review of Psychology*, 71: 331–55.

Fisher, G. (1997). "The Jury's Rise as Lie Detector," *Yale Law Journal*, 107: 575–711.

Frank, J. (1931). "Are Judges Human? Part 1: The Effect of Legal Thinking that Judges behave like Human Beings," *University of Pennsylvania Law Review*, 80: 17–53.

Frank, J. (1931). "Are Judges Human? Part Two: As Through a Glass Darkly," *University of Pennsylvania Law Review*, 80: 233–67.

Gilovich, T., Griffin, D., and Kahneman, D. (eds.). (2002). *Heuristics and Biases: The Psychology of Intuitive Judgment*. Cambridge: Cambridge University Press.

Goldman, A. (1990). *Knowledge in a Social World*. Oxford: Oxford University Press.

Guthrie, C., Rachlinski, J. J., and Wistrich, A. J. (2001). "Inside the Judicial Mind," *Cornell Law Review*, 86: 777–830.

Haack, S. (2005). "Epistemology Legalized: Or, Truth, Justice, and the American Way," *American Journal of Jurisprudence*, 49: 43–61.

Haack, S. (2014). *Evidence Matters: Science, Proof, and Truth in the Law*. Cambridge: Cambridge University Press.

Hart, H. M., Jr., and McNaughton, J. T. (1959). "Evidence and Inference in Law," in D. Lerner (ed.), *Evidence and Inference*, 48–72. Glencoe, IL: Free Press.

Hooker, B. (2002). *Ideal Code, Real World: A Rule-Consequentialist Theory of Morality*. Oxford: Oxford University Press.

Jackson, J. D. (2019). "Common Law Evidence and the Common Law of Human Rights: Toward a Harmonic Convergence," *William & Mary Bill of Rights Journal*, 27: 689–715.

Jackson, J. D., and Summers, S. J. (2012). *The Internationalisation of Criminal Evidence: Beyond the Common Law and Civil Law Traditions*. Cambridge: Cambridge University Press.

Kahneman, D. (2011). *Thinking, Fast and Slow*. New York: Farrar, Straus & Giroux.

Keeton, G.W., and Schwarzenberger, G. (eds.) (1948). *Jeremy Bentham and the Law*. London: Stevens.

Kunert, K. H. (1966). "Some Observations on the Origin and Structure of Evidence Rules under the Common Law System and the Civil Law System of 'Free Proof' in the German Code of Criminal Procedure," *Buffalo Law Review*, 16, 122–164.

Langbein, J. (1979). "Law without Plea Bargaining: How the Germans do it," *Michigan Law Review*, 78, 199–225.

Langbein, J., Lerner, R. L., and Smith, B. P. (2009). *History of the Common Law: The Development of Anglo-American Legal Institutions*. New York: Aspen.

Laudan, L. (2006). *Truth, Error and the criminal Law: An Essay in Legal Epistemology*. Cambridge: Cambridge University Press.

Laudan, L. (2016). *The Law's Flaws: Rethinking Trial and Errors?* London: College Publications.

Lee, S. (Director) (1989). *Do the Right Thing* (Movie). 40 Acres and a Mule Filmworks.

Levin, A. L., and Cohen, H. K. (1971). "The Exclusionary Rules in Nonjury Criminal Cases," *University of Pennsylvania Law Review*, 119: 905–32.

Lieberman, D. (1989). *The Province of Legislation Determined: Legal Theory in Eighteenth-Century Britain*. Cambridge: Cambridge University Press.

Lilly, G. C., Capra, D. J., and Salzburg, S.A. (2012). *Principles of Evidence*. Sixth edition. St. Paul, MN: West Publishing Company.

Louisell, D. W. (1956). "Confidentiality, Conformity and Confusion: Privileges in Federal Court Today," *Tulane Law Review*, 31: 101–24.

Ma, Y. (1999). "Comparative Analysis of Exclusionary Rules in the United States, England, France, Germany, and Italy," *Policing*, 22: 280–303.

Maartens, P. J., and Schwikkard, P. J. (2011). "A Juryless Jurisdiction and the Epistemic Rules of Evidence," *South African Law Journal*, 128: 513–32.

Mellers, B. A., Schwartz, A., and Cooke, A. D. J. (1998). "Judgment and Decision Making," *Annual Review of Psychology*, 49: 447–77.

Morgan, E. (1937). "The Jury and the Exclusionary Rules of Evidence," *University of Chicago Law Review*, 4: 247–58.

Mueller, C., Kirkpatrick, L., and Richter, L. (2018). *Evidence*. Sixth edition. New York: Aspen/Wolters Kluwer.

Nance, D. (1988). "The Best Evidence Principle," *Iowa Law Review*, 73: 227–97.

Nance, D. (1996). "Verbal Completeness and Exclusionary Rules under the Federal Rules of Evidence," *Texas Law Review*, 75: 51–129.

Perry, S. (1989). "Second-Order Reasons, Uncertainty, and Legal Theory," *Southern California Law Review*, 62: 913–94.

Plous, S. (1993). *The Psychology of Judgment and Decision Making*. New York: McGraw-Hill.

Postema, G. J. (1982). "Coordination and Convention at the Foundations of Law," *Journal of Legal Studies*, 11: 165–203.

Postema, G. J. (1986). *Bentham and the Common Law Tradition*. Oxford: Clarendon Press.

Raz, J. (1979). *The Authority of Law: Essays on Law and Morality*. Oxford: Clarendon Press.

Raz, J. (1990). *Practical Reason and Norms*. Princeton, NJ: Princeton University Press.

Resnik, J. (2011). "Bring back Bentham: 'Open Courts,' 'Terror Trials,' and the Public Sphere," *Law & Ethics of Human Rights*, 5: 1–69.

Robinson, P., and Spellman, B. A. (2005). "Sentencing Decisions: Matching the Decisionmaker to the Decision Nature," *Columbia Law Review*, 105: 1124–61.

Rosen, L. (1980). "Equity and Discretion in a Modern Islamic Legal System," *Law and Society Review*, 15: 217–46.

Saks, M. J., and Spellman, B. A. (2016). *The Psychological Foundations of Evidence Law*. New York: New York University Press.

Schauer, F. (1991). *Playing by the Rules: A Philosophical Examination of Rule-Based Decision-Making In law and in Life*. Oxford: Clarendon Press.

Schauer, F. (2006). "On the Supposed Jury-Dependence of Evidence Law," *University of Pennsylvania Law Review*, 155(1): 165–202.

Schauer, F. (2008). "In Defense of Rule-Based Evidence Law—and Epistemology Too," *Episteme*, 5: 295–305.

Schauer, F. (2015). *The Force of Law*. Cambridge, MA: Harvard University Press.

Schelling, T. (1985). "Enforcing Rules on Oneself," *Journal of Law, Economics, and Organization*, 1: 357–74.

Shapiroi, S. (2011). *Legality*. Cambridge, MA: Harvard University Press.

Sheldon, J., and Murray, P. (2003). "Rethinking the Rules of Evidentiary Admissibility in Non-Jury Trials," *Judicature*, 86: 227–31.

Sklansky, D. (2009). "Hearsay's Last Hurrah," *Supreme Court* Review, 2009: 1–82.

Slovic, P., Fischhoff, B., and Lichtenstein, S. (1977). "Behavioral Decision Theory," *Annual Review of Psychology*, 28: 1–39.

Smart, J.J.C. (1956). "Extreme and Restricted Utilitarianism," *Philosophical Quarterly*, 6: 344–54.

Spellman, B. A. (2007). "On the Supposed Expertise of Judges in Evaluating Evidence, *University of Pennsylvania Law Review PENNumbra*, 156: 1–9.

Spellman, B. A. (2010). "Judges, Expertise, and Analogy," in D. Klein and G. Mitchell (eds.), *The Psychology of Judicial Decision Making*, 149–64. Oxford: Oxford University Press.

Stein, A. (2005). *Foundations of Evidence Law*. Oxford: Oxford University Press.

Strine, L., Jr., Hamermesh, A., and Jennejohn, M. (2013). "Putting Stockholders First: Not the First-Filed Complaint," *Business Lawyer*, 69: 1–78.

Sunstein, C., and King, R. E. (1999). "Doing without Speed Limits," *Boston University Law Review*, 79: 155–91.

Sunstein, C., and Ullmann-Margalit, E. (1999). "Second-Order Decisions," *Ethics*, 110: 5–31.

Thayer, J. B. (1896). *A Preliminary Treatise on the Law of Evidence*. Cambridge, MA: Harvard University Press.

Tilley, D. (2011). "The Non-Rules of Evidence in the Ad Hoc Tribunals," *International Lawyer*, 45: 695–724.

Tversky, A., and Kahneman, D. (1974). "Judgment under Uncertainty: Heuristic and Biases," *Science*, 185: 1124–31.

Twining, W. (1985). *Theories of Evidence: Bentham and Wigmore*. London: Weidenfeld & Nicolson.

Twining, W. (1994). *Rethinking Evidence: Exploratory Essays*. Evanston, IL: Northwestern University Press.

Urmson, J. (1953). "The Interpretation of the Moral Philosophy of J. S. Mill," *Philosophical Quarterly*, 3(10): 33–9.

Weber, M. (1954). *Max Weber on Law in Economy and Society*. Edited by M. Rheinstein. Translated by E. A. Shils. Cambridge, MA: Harvard University Press.

Wigmore, J. H. (1904). *A Treatise on the Anglo-American System of Evidence in Trials at Common Law*. Boston, MA: Little, Brown.

Wigmore, J. H. (1979). *Evidence in Trials at Common Law*. Revised by J. H. Chadbourn. Boston: Little, Brown.

Wistrich, A. J., Guthrie, C., and Rachlinski, J. J. (2005). "Can Judges Ignore Inadmissible Information? The Difficulty of Deliberately Disregarding," *University of Pennsylvania Law Review*, 153: 1251–345.

6

Excluding Evidence for Integrity's Sake

Jules Holroyd and Federico Picinali[*]

1. Introduction

In recent years, the notion of "integrity" has been frequently discussed by scholars, and deployed by courts, in the domains of criminal law and of criminal procedure.[1] It has been argued that integrity "offers a powerful conceptual lens through which the criminal process in its entirety, or selected phases or aspects of it, can be viewed and critically re-examined".[2]

Courts and scholars employ the concept of integrity especially in relation to two procedural problems, that of improperly obtained evidence and that of abuse of process. Our discussion is focused exclusively on how integrity is used in conceptualizing and addressing the former. We argue that it is difficult to identify in the available literature a defensible role for integrity to play; and we set forth challenges that should be met by scholars who seek to employ the notion of integrity. Before we raise these challenges, we introduce the problem of improperly obtained evidence and the roles that integrity is thought to perform in relation to it.

2. Context and a Look Ahead

The problem of improperly obtained evidence is that of deciding whether evidence that has been obtained through improper means could be admitted at trial without compromising the trial's fairness. In case of a negative answer, the mainstream view is that the evidence should be excluded. To illustrate the problem, consider the facts of the European Court of Human Rights (ECtHR) case *Jalloh v. Germany*.[3] In *Jalloh*, a suspect was forcibly administered an emetic by German police and, as a result, regurgitated a bag of cocaine that he had previously swallowed. The German court had admitted the bag of cocaine in evidence and the ECtHR was asked to rule on whether this decision compromised the fairness of the

---

[*] We presented an earlier draft at the "JC Smith Trust Fund Visiting Scholar Workshop on Epistemology and Criminal Evidence," University of Nottingham, March 21–2, 2019. We are grateful to all participants for their feedback. Special thanks to Paul Roberts, Antony Duff and Sandra Marshall for comments on an earlier draft.

[1] In addition to works cited below, see Mirfield 1997, 23–8; Choo 2008, 12–17, 106–13, 186–91; Giannoulopoulos 2019, 204–23. In addition to case law cited below, see: *A and others v. Secretary of State for the Home Department* (2005) UKHL 71; *R v. Maxwell* (2010) UKSC 48; *Warren and Others v. Attorney General for Jersey* (2011) UKPC 10. Integrity is also employed by the ECtHR in the case of *Gäfgen v. Germany*, No. 22978/05, ECHR [GC] June 1, 2010, among others. Finally, Art. 69(7) of the Rome Statute of the International Criminal Court mentions integrity as a ground for excluding evidence.

[2] Roberts et al. 2016, 1.

[3] *Jalloh v. Germany*, No. 54810/00, ECtHR [GC] July 11, 2006. Notably, the ECtHR in *Jalloh* does not explicitly resort to the standard of integrity. However, it heavily relies on balancing, which—as we will see later—is an important component of the theory of integrity.

Jules Holroyd and Federico Picinali, *Excluding Evidence for Integrity's Sake* In: *Philosophical Foundations of Evidence Law*. Edited by: Christian Dahlman, Alex Stein, and Giovanni Tuzet, Oxford University Press. © Christian Dahlman, Alex Stein, and Giovanni Tuzet 2021. DOI: 10.1093/oso/9780198859307.003.0007

trial. The ECtHR found that the conduct of the police amounted to inhuman and degrading treatment and was, therefore, in violation of Art. 3 of the European Convention on Human Rights (ECHR). It also found that admitting the improperly obtained evidence undermined the fairness of the trial, thus breaching Art. 6 ECHR. In other words, trial fairness required that the bag of cocaine be excluded.

When courts and scholars employ integrity in order to conceptualize and address the problem of improperly obtained evidence, they do so in four different, but closely related, ways. First, integrity is employed as a standard of conduct for the state actors involved in the criminal justice enterprise (the police, the prosecution, the courts). In particular, it is argued that the police must display integrity in the way in which they gather evidence.[4] Improprieties in this activity are conceptualized as departures from the standard of integrity. The integrity of criminal process crucially depends on—if it is not the same thing as—the integrity in the behavior of the criminal justice authorities involved in it. As a standard of conduct, integrity is relied upon also in a specific role, which is worth keeping separate for the purposes of our analysis. In this second role, integrity is seen as providing guidance for choosing the appropriate course of action that the state should take in response to an impropriety that has already taken place in the gathering of the evidence. In using integrity in this second role, the advocates of integrity claim—or imply—that integrity is capable of being restored once the impropriety occurred; but they also accept that in some cases integrity should be sacrificed for the sake of protecting other competing values.[5] Third, integrity is used as a device for identifying the parts of the criminal process in which the behavior of the criminal justice authorities is relevant to the assessment of the state authority to condemn and punish. In this third role, integrity has been called "integrity as integration."[6] The idea is that integrity demands that the process be considered as a whole in order to assess the authority of the state's condemning and punishing the defendant. Most significantly, what happens during the acquisition of evidence in the pre-trial phase is relevant to this assessment. Finally, integrity is itself posited as a necessary condition for the state authority to condemn and punish.[7] It is argued that for the state to have this authority, its agency throughout the process must comply with integrity as a standard of conduct.

In the following sections, we consider how integrity is thought to perform the four roles we have identified, and we raise issues with the use of integrity in each of these roles, respectively. Our aim is not to claim that integrity is a useless tool in theorizing about, and in implementing, criminal procedure; rather, it is to show the challenges faced, and as yet unmet, by proponents of integrity.

3. Integrity as a standard of conduct is superfluous

It was suggested that integrity serves as a standard of conduct for the criminal justice authorities: it provides guidance as to how these authorities should act within the criminal process.[8] According to most advocates of integrity, the standard includes more than just a

---

[4] See Roberts et al. 2016, in particular, 7, 13, 17; Dixon 2016, 75.
[5] See Ashworth 2003; Duff et al. 2007; Chau 2016.
[6] See Duff et al. 2007, 226, 236–41.
[7] See Ashworth, 2003, 108; Duff et al. 2007, 226. See also *R v. Looseley; A-G's Reference (No3 of 2000)* [2001] UKHL 53; *R v. Latif* [1996] 1 WLR 104; *R v. Horseferry Road Magistrates' Court*, ex p Bennett [1994] 1 AC 42.
[8] See Roberts et al. 2016, 30–2.

formal requirement that the authorities' agency be consistent in respecting some external substantive constraints. It also encapsulates substantive constraints on their action.[9] For example, Duff and co-authors draw on Ashworth in characterizing integrity as "underpinned by ... 'a network of supporting rules and principles',"[10] respect for which is crucial to the state's authority to condemn and punish. In particular, Ashworth focuses on fundamental rights with constitutional or supranational status, and especially on the rights enshrined in the ECHR.[11] These rights must be consistently respected for the behavior of criminal justice authorities to display integrity. Under this substantive conception, integrity is sometimes said to demand that the authorities act with "moral" coherence,[12] where the attribute is used precisely to refer to embedded substantive constraints such as those just mentioned. It is with this substantive notion that we are concerned here.

Our focus is on whether integrity plays a meaningful role as a standard of conduct for the criminal justice authorities, with specific regard to the gathering and the use of evidence. The challenge that we present concerns the division of labor between integrity and the values that are deemed fundamental to the criminal process, such as the aforementioned rights. More precisely, once we demand that action be constrained by, or be respectful of, these values, what is added by demanding integrity in respecting them?

Compare a criminal justice authority that is consistently compliant (in respecting values embedded in the standard) and one that is occasionally compliant. The latter, for instance, sometimes extracts confessions using oppressive measures (say, violating Art. 3 ECHR); or uses rogue agents to gather evidence by breaking and entering in the suspects' homes (say, violating Art. 8 ECHR). In articulating what is problematic about the authority that is occasionally compliant, one need only appeal to the fact that certain fundamental rights have been violated through its conduct. Pointing out that, therefore, this authority lacks integrity, does not add anything to the normative critique.

One may resist our intuition pump by contending that integrity does play an indispensable role as a standard of conduct *for the courts* when it comes to diagnosing, and especially repairing, breaches of the suspect's or defendant's rights committed during the gathering of the evidence. Without relying on integrity—it might be argued—courts would not be able properly to appreciate what renders problematic the scenario that they face, or to appreciate why the default remedy to the problem is the exclusion of the evidence. The argument concerns two particular cases, drawn from Duff and co-authors,[13] that may arise in the context of evidence gathering.

The first case is that in which the defendant's rights have been violated by someone other than the criminal justice authorities. If the relevant standard of conduct were merely that according to which criminal justice authorities must respect rights, and if the impropriety had been committed by such authorities, it would be reasonable to argue that the court would have to exclude the evidence. Indeed, exclusion of the evidence would be a means for the state to remedy the rights violation that it has previously perpetrated. But if the impropriety has been committed by a third party, under a standard of conduct that demands respect for rights the court has no obligation to exclude the evidence, since there is no disrespectful

---

[9] See Ashworth 2003, 108–10; Duff et al. 2007, 226.
[10] Duff et al. 2007, 226.
[11] See Ashworth 2003, 108–10. Note that Ashworth ultimately does not endorse the integrity approach.
[12] See Duff et al. 2007, 226; Roberts and Zuckerman 2010, 188.
[13] See Duff et al. 2007, 232–3.

conduct on the part of the state that needs remedying. This conclusion, however, leaves many of us uneasy.

The second case is that in which evidence has been obtained by violating rights of someone other than the defendant. In this case, one may argue that if we appeal merely to a standard of conduct according to which criminal justice authorities must respect rights, it follows that the court is under no obligation to exclude the evidence. This is because, whilst someone's rights have been violated, excluding the evidence would not remedy that impropriety. Indeed, excluding the evidence benefits the defendant, whose rights have not been violated, but it does not benefit the victim of the rights violation, i.e., the third party. Again, this conclusion leaves many of us uneasy. The argument considered here claims that appeal to the notion of integrity as a standard of conduct for criminal justice authorities can explain why it would be wrong for the court not to exclude the evidence under the two scenarios at issue. The idea is that courts would be acting inconsistently if they proclaimed rights—as they routinely do—and then relied on the fruits of rights violations, irrespective of the identity of the perpetrator and of the victim of such violations.

We concede that integrity appears to give the right answer in these cases: the evidence should be excluded. However, we doubt that appeal to integrity is at all needed to reach and implement this answer. We think that this task can be accomplished by appealing exclusively to a familiar conception of respect for the relevant rights involved. Even in these two specific cases, then, our claim is that a standard of conduct demanding respect for the relevant rights is sufficient to guide the courts to act appropriately.

Note that here we are not referring to the "remedial" or "rights thesis;" a thesis developed by Ashworth and claiming, roughly, that when evidence would not have been obtained but for the state's breach of the defendant's rights, the evidence should be excluded in order to restore the defendant to their material condition prior to the breach.[14] Following Duff and co-authors, we recognize the limitations of the rights thesis. These include, precisely, the fact that it does not give the right answer in the above problematic scenarios: it is apparently indifferent to violations of rights not committed by the state and of rights other than the defendant's. As a result, we argue that the rights thesis does not offer a comprehensive account of what respect for rights requires.[15]

In our view—and this is certainly not an idiosyncratic or ad hoc account—proper respect for rights does not simply involve refraining from violating them. It also involves taking up the proper attitude and comportment towards rights violations, whether we are responsible for these violations or not. This must include refraining from endorsing violations and refraining from benefiting from them.[16] In the two cases mentioned earlier then, we need merely note that if evidence has been obtained by breaching rights—whether or not the breach is committed by the state and whether or not the rights violated are the defendant's—respect for rights requires that the court excludes the evidence. It is by excluding the evidence that the state, through the court, can refrain from both endorsing, and benefiting from,[17] the previous rights violation. In other words, excluding evidence can be seen as a distancing mechanism through which the state signals its critical attitude towards, and

---

[14]   On the rights thesis, see, in particular, Ashworth 1977; Ashworth and Redmayne 2010, 345, 357–61; Roberts and Zuckerman 2010, 181–5.

[15]   See Duff et al. 2007, 232–3.

[16]   cf. Butt 2007; Duff 2018a, 208–9.

[17]   cf. Chau 2016, 275–7.

refuses to partake in, the violation. Of course, respect for rights would also demand that improprieties in the gathering of the evidence be addressed with measures or proceedings external to the trial at issue. This is because refraining from endorsing, or benefiting from, rights violations is not yet a sanction for these violations. The issue of external proceedings, however, lies beyond the scope of this article. We also leave aside the question whether the state may be justified in admitting evidence obtained improperly, if the impropriety is minor and the evidence is highly probative of a serious crime. We are open to the possibility that in such a case the failure of the state to remedy, or distance itself from, the rights violation is a reasonable cost to pay. Whilst, for reasons of space, we cannot discuss this possibility from within a theory of respect for rights, later in the chapter (Section 5) we consider it briefly in the context of our critical assessment of integrity.

A standard of conduct demanding respect for rights has richer explanatory and normative resources than proponents of integrity have supposed. Respect for rights can both provide the appropriate diagnosis of the problem faced by the court in the two scenarios sketched earlier, and indicate the appropriate remedial measure. We want to emphasize that our understanding of what respect for rights requires is not at all a new insight. Rather, it is one that is fundamental to the justification and operation of criminal justice itself. After all, under all reasonable construals criminal justice is premised on the idea that the state must take the appropriate attitude and action following certain violations of citizens' rights on the part of fellow citizens. The state cannot ignore, or endorse, or benefit from, these violations. It must, instead, respond to them in a way that is consistent with showing respect for the rights that have been breached. This is true when the violations are committed by its own agents in the course of the criminal process or by any agent in everyday life.

We believe that integrity as a standard of conduct is superfluous. A standard demanding respect for the values that we deem crucial to our criminal process would be substantively equivalent, as well as simpler. The problem of superfluity aside, there are other serious challenges that integrity faces. We consider these challenges in the following sections.

4. Reliance on Integrity When Responding to an Impropriety is Contradictory and Obfuscatory

Let's now assume that someone was able to show that our arguments in the previous section are wrong: in particular, that integrity is a useful standard of conduct for the court when it comes to responding to an impropriety. Granting this assumption for the sake of argument, in this section we consider additional problematic aspects of the use of integrity to diagnose and address the problem of improperly obtained evidence. In particular, there are two aspects of the theory of integrity that we find problematic. The first is the claim that in some cases the standard of integrity should be departed from. The second is the claim that this standard is capable of being ultimately satisfied by the state, notwithstanding the departure from it represented by the initial impropriety.

Once evidence has been obtained improperly, the relevant courses of action that are open to the court are the exclusion or the admission of the evidence. The advocates of integrity claim that the decision of the court should depend on a careful weighing of the factors at play. Through this balancing exercise—they say—courts should identify the course of action that best conforms with the substantive constraints to which courts are expected to adhere.[18] The relevant factors to be balanced include the seriousness of the impropriety and the importance of securing the defendant to justice—a factor that generally tracks the seriousness of the crime itself and the strength of the case against the defendant. Another relevant factor is the significance of the evidence at issue for the prosecution case. Finally, and importantly, integrity is itself treated as a factor in the balancing exercise.

The fact that integrity is treated as a factor in the balancing exercise implies that for the advocates of integrity, integrity itself is susceptible of being outweighed by other factors.[19] If this happens, integrity *should be departed from*. This is the case where the balancing exercise demands that the evidence be admitted. Admitting the evidence would be a departure from the standard of integrity, since the court would not be distancing itself from the previous impropriety; it would not be remedying the impropriety; we may go as far as to say that, by allowing the use of the fruits of the impropriety, the court would be condoning it.[20] If warranted by the balancing exercise, though, the departure from the standard of integrity would be a cost to pay for the sake of achieving goals that, in the circumstances of the case, are weightier than integrity itself.

Our worry with this approach is that we don't see how it is possible to justify such departures from the standard of integrity, whilst arguing—as the advocates of integrity generally do—that integrity is not just a standard of conduct for the criminal justice authorities, but also a condition for the state's authority to condemn and punish. Is it the case that integrity is such a condition only in some cases, but not in others? Or is it the case that, rather than integrity, one of the conditions for the state authority to punish is doing what the balancing exercise indicates that the state should do? These are questions that should be addressed by whoever subscribes to the view that integrity can be outweighed, whilst maintaining that it has a role to play in the foundation of the authority of the state in the criminal justice domain.

Now consider the scenario in which the balancing exercise demands that the state exclude the evidence. The exclusion of the evidence may be taken to signal the distancing of the state from the impropriety, or it may even be taken to be a remedy to the impropriety. It is on these grounds that the advocates of integrity argue that, by excluding the evidence, integrity—which was departed from with the initial impropriety—is effectively restored. But can this be right? Can the standard of integrity be ultimately satisfied by excluding evidence obtained improperly? Irrespective of whether the defendant is innocent or guilty and of whether she is eventually convicted or not, excluding evidence is itself a cost—if not a wrong—at least if the evidence is reliable and has sufficient probative value. Excluding evidence is the loss of information that is relevant to decision-making. Also, in some cases excluding the evidence may allow a guilty person to evade justice—either because she is acquitted or because the prosecution has to drop the charges against her. Excluding the evidence, then, involves a departure from substantive constraints, the respect for which is likely to be relevant to whether the state has authority to administer criminal justice. These

---

[18] See Ashworth and Redmayne 2010, 346–7; Ashworth 2003, 118–21; Duff et al. 2007, 241–52; Whitfort 2016, 247. The use of balancing is evident in the ECtHR case law on improperly obtained evidence, e.g., *Allan v. UK*, no. 48539/99, ECtHR [GC], November 5, 2002 and *Jalloh v. Germany* (n. 3). cf. *Gäfgen v. Germany*, (n. 1), para. 173, where the court identifies cases in which evidence obtained through a breach of the defendant's right under Art. 3 ECHR should be automatically excluded, lest trial fairness is compromised.

[19] This is how we read Duff et al. 2007, 241–2, 247, 252. See also Hungerford-Welch 2017, 16; O'Connor 2012, 673; *R v. Crawley (Scott)* [2014] EWCA Crim 1028, para. 23; *R v. Syed* [2019] Crim L Rev 443.

[20] But see Chau 2016, 274–5.

include accuracy in factfinding, but also the interests of victims and the rights of those who may be later victimized by the guilty defendant who were to avoid conviction. It is difficult to see how, given the departure from such constraints, the court could be said to have acted with integrity, and the state to have restored the integrity that was previously undermined by other criminal justice authorities. Rather, more costs have been incurred.

One may object that when the balancing exercise demands that the evidence be excluded, even if excluding the evidence consists in a departure from relevant substantive constraints, this departure would be the lesser of the two evils if compared to the alternative decision to admit the evidence and thus to condone the impropriety. But if we take integrity to be the stringent standard of conduct that we described earlier and to which advocates of integrity seem to refer (i.e., a standard demanding consistency in the respect of relevant substantive constraints), choosing the lesser of the two evils cannot possibly display or restore integrity. An evil would still be a departure from a relevant substantive constraint.

Our claim is that the use that is generally made of integrity in order to identify the action to take after evidence was obtained improperly is both contradictory and obfuscatory. If integrity is a factor in the balancing exercise, then it can be departed from. If so, though, it is unclear how integrity could be treated as a necessary condition for the state's authority to condemn and punish, without incurring in a contradiction. Also, even when the balancing exercise suggests that remedial action be taken, it is unclear how integrity could be restored by so acting, given that the relevant remedial action is itself a departure from some of the substantive constraints that we expect to be encapsulated in the standard of integrity. Talk of integrity being restored obfuscates these costs. The only way for the state to respect integrity is to not commit an impropriety in the first place. Integrity is lost once the impropriety is committed, and with it—under a coherent application of the theory of integrity—also the state's authority to condemn and punish.

5. Integrity as Balancing: A Solution?

One might avoid the problems that we have raised in the previous section by adopting an alternative notion of integrity, according to which integrity merely demands that the court act as the balancing exercise suggests. Under this construal integrity is primarily a decision-making procedure that consists in having due regard for all the reasons that are relevant to a particular decision, and in engaging in a comparative assessment of the reasons that favor different courses of action. But integrity would still be a standard of conduct, since it would enjoin the agent to act as it is indicated by the weightier reasons. We call this conception *integrity as balancing*.

Integrity as balancing accounts for the promising idea that the integrity of an individual is a practical attitude—or virtue—that is engaged in situations where there is no rule of conduct that unequivocally determines how they should act.[21] In such situations, integrity is displayed by acknowledging the facts and values that are relevant to the decision, by recognizing that these reasons may support alternative choices, by assessing the relative weight of the conflicting reasons and, ultimately, by acting in a way that reflects the result of this

---

[21] We thank Paul Roberts for inviting us to consider more carefully this understanding of integrity.

assessment. Under integrity as balancing one can act with integrity even if she departs from a substantive constraint; in other words, even if she infringes a value, right, or duty that she cherishes. Indeed, under this conception integrity is displayed precisely in situations in which a departure from a substantive constraint is inevitable, that is, in which a conflict between normative considerations cannot be dissolved. The person with integrity is aware of the costs that any decision will involve, but nonetheless takes it upon herself to act in the best possible way, given the values that she holds dear. It is precisely because departures from significant substantive constraints are tolerated by—if not constitutive of—integrity that integrity as balancing does not face the two problems highlighted in the previous section. Admitting or excluding evidence obtained improperly are both costly choices, but choices that a court can make with integrity. The questions remain whether the court's display of integrity as balancing is sufficient to remedy the prior departure from integrity (under whatever conception thereof) occurred during evidence gathering; and whether this display is sufficient to restore the integrity of state agency, considered as a whole, and to warrant the state's authority to condemn and punish. These questions would require careful scrutiny on the part of those who were to endorse integrity as balancing.

Here, we want to direct attention to a different question raised by reliance on integrity as balancing, namely: whether this notion of integrity could apply only in the context of regulating the conduct of the court when choosing the appropriate response to an impropriety, or also in the context of regulating the conduct of other criminal justice authorities—in particular, investigative authorities involved in evidence gathering. Notice that, unlike the notion of integrity discussed previously, integrity as balancing is not a superfluous standard of conduct. Rather than requiring consistent compliance with pre-existing norms, integrity as balancing enjoins the decision-maker to produce an ad hoc norm relying on the normative material available to them, and gives (at least some) guidance on how to do so. Hence, besides meeting the challenge that we raised in Section 4, integrity as balancing seems to meet also the challenge that we raised in Section 3. This explains the appeal for extending the application of this standard also to investigative authorities.

Investigative authorities often find themselves in situations characterized by the alternative between respecting the rights of the suspect and furthering the interests of the victims, of the prosecution, and of their own agencies—which regrettably may include producing results in terms of rates of arrests, convictions, etc., irrespective of the responsibility of the individuals involved. These are precisely the situations where the problem of improperly obtained evidence arises. It seems to us that it would be extremely dangerous to invite investigative authorities to exercise in these cases the discretion that integrity as balancing would afford. Even assuming that in some very limited circumstances the suspect's rights should give way, we fear that these authorities would often infringe these rights without justification if they were authorized, encouraged, or even required to act as suggested by the balancing of the conflicting normative considerations at stake. In taxing decision-making contexts such as those characteristically giving rise to the problem of improperly obtained evidence, we should not want an investigative authority to engage in any ad hoc norm-making. Instead, we should want to reduce the discretion of the authority to a minimum through clear and stringent directives—for example, do not breach the suspect's rights! This seems necessary to give these rights proper protection.

There is another important caveat regarding reliance on integrity as balancing in the context of improperly obtained evidence. As we pointed out in the previous section, we think that the decision consisting in whether to exclude or admit evidence obtained improperly is rarely such as the type of decision problem where integrity as balancing would be useful. Normally, when evidence is obtained by breaching the suspect's or defendant's rights, there is already sufficient normative material to determine how the court should act, without having to resort to any balancing whatsoever. This material is provided by the rights in question, the proper respect of which requires that the evidence be excluded, lest the state condones, and benefits from, a rights violation. It is only in the rare occasions in which the impropriety is minor and the evidence obtained is highly probative of a serious crime that a conflict between normative considerations can be said to arise and to call for resolution. In these cases only, we see the potential value of appealing to integrity as balancing as a virtuous decision-making procedure and standard of conduct.

6. The Problem of Scope

Integrity is used—by scholars especially—as a device for identifying the parts of the criminal process in which the behavior of the criminal justice authorities is relevant for the state authority to condemn and punish (Section 2). More specifically, integrity is used to rebut the so called "separation thesis." According to this thesis, pre-trial and trial should be treated as separate, discrete phases, such that an impropriety by the criminal justice authorities during the pre-trial phase does not taint the trial: the state can start the trial with a clean slate.[22] This means that the authority of the state to condemn and punish is not jeopardized by the illegal behavior of the police in the pre-trial phase. The separation thesis has obvious implications for the problem of improperly obtained evidence: if evidence has been obtained improperly during the pre-trial phase, it is still admissible at trial. This is precisely because, being pre-trial and trial separate, the conduct of the authorities in the former cannot taint the latter. It cannot render the trial unfair.

Advocates of integrity criticize the separation thesis. They argue that in assessing the authority of the state as criminal adjudicator, we cannot treat pre-trial and trial as if they were isolated from each other. Integrity demands that we consider the criminal process as an integrated whole. Hence the phrase "integrity as integration" coined by Duff and co-authors.[23] The upshot is that evidence that has been obtained improperly during the pre-trial phase cannot be uncritically admitted at trial. As discussed in the previous sections, the advocates of integrity argue that this evidence might have to be excluded in order to restore the integrity of state agency, hence the authority of the state to condemn and punish.

Our interpretation of the literature is that two main arguments are employed to defend the idea of integrity as integration. The first may be called the "argument from instrumental relation." According to this argument, the pre-trial phase is instrumental to the trial. In particular, evidence gathering is instrumental to the prosecution's choice whether to charge the defendant; and it is instrumental to securing her conviction at trial.[24] Because of this instrumental relation, what happens in the pre-trial phase must be taken into account in

---

[22] On the separation thesis, see, in particular, Ashworth 2003, 112–115; Ashworth and Redmayne 2010, 361–2.
[23] See Duff et al. 2007, 226.
[24] See Ashworth 2003, 113–15; Duff et al. 2007, 226, 236–41.

determining whether the state has the authority to condemn at trial; more specifically, whether it acted with integrity.

The second argument for treating the criminal process as an integrated whole may be called the "argument from agential link." The premise is that both the court managing the trial and the police and prosecution conducting the pre-trial phase represent or constitute the state in the criminal process enterprise.[25] If the state's authority to condemn and punish depends on the integrity of its agency—the argument goes—then the behavior of all its representatives in the delivery of criminal justice in a particular case must be taken into account. This includes the behavior of the police and of the prosecution during the pre-trial phase.

Now, if the argument from instrumental relation and the argument from agential link indeed succeed in rebutting the separation thesis—something on which we remain non-committal—they do so at the cost of raising a complex issue, which we call the "problem of scope." This is the issue of identifying the boundaries for the assessment of the state authority to condemn and punish. In other words, how wide should we cast a net when identifying the portion of state agency that is relevant for this assessment in any particular case? This issue is present irrespective of the notion of integrity that one adopts as a standard of conduct for the criminal justice authorities. Also, this issue does not concern exclusively the theory of integrity. It concerns any theory of the authority of the state as criminal adjudicator that rejects the separation thesis.

The separation thesis offers a clear answer to the problem of scope: the trial is insulated from what happens before, or outside of, it; and given that conviction is an epilogue of the trial and that punishment is crucially premised on such epilogue, we need not look beyond the trial in order to assess whether the state has the authority to condemn and punish. The advocates of integrity reject this answer to the problem of scope, but do not give a clear alternative answer. If integrity is indeed a necessary condition for the state authority to condemn and punish, the question that needs answering is which state behavior should comply with integrity for this condition to be satisfied.

To be sure, an answer to the problem of scope is generally assumed by the advocates of integrity: the assessment of integrity should concern only the conduct of the state agents in the particular proceedings at issue, from the start of the investigation until the verdict. This assumption is evidenced by the fact that improprieties on the part of state agents committed in other cases are never considered by courts or academics as facts that threaten integrity in the case at issue. Rather, courts may be interested in how such improprieties were dealt with by other courts, so as to derive guidance on how to deal with the impropriety in the case they are dealing with. Also, courts and academics do not look at the behavior of the state outside criminal proceedings, when making, or discussing, the assessment of integrity.

It should be noted, though, that the above assumption is not warranted if the advocates of integrity attack the separation thesis by relying on either of the two arguments mentioned above. To see this, consider first the argument from agential link. The argument rejects the separation thesis on the grounds that there is a link between the actions of state agents involved in different phases of the proceedings, i.e., pre-trial and trial. These actions are all constitutive of state agency in the delivery of criminal justice in the particular case and are,

---

[25] See Ashworth 2003, 115; Ho 2019, 827.

therefore, relevant to the assessment of integrity in state action. If, however, what matters for the definition of the scope of this assessment is just that an action be constitutive of state agency in the delivery of criminal justice in a given case, it is not clear why the agential link should be acknowledged only with respect to state agents involved in the trial and the pre-trial phases. Consider that the agency of the state is also implicated in a great many functions, external to these phases, which impinge to a greater or lesser degree on the delivery of criminal justice in any single case. Most obviously, the operation of the Treasury in its allocation of resources to the police and to the prosecution services; but also, the allocation of resources by police commissioners and directors of public prosecutions in terms of what crimes are to be targeted, investigated, and prosecuted. Moreover, as is frequently pointed out in the literature, state agency is involved in distributive functions affecting the material conditions of citizens and often producing poverty and deprivation, with their likely crimi-nogenic effect.[26] It follows, that even if we were to restrict our attention to state agency that is relevant to the occurrence, development, and outcome of a particular case, it would be unclear why we should not look beyond the proceedings themselves.

Indeed, it is not even clear why the argument from agential link should warrant restricting our attention to state agency that is relevant to the occurrence, development, and outcome of a particular case. Why should we not consider the conduct of state agents in criminal pro-ceedings overall? Isn't the integrity of state action in other, unrelated, proceedings relevant to whether the state has authority to condemn and punish in any given proceeding? Indeed, isn't the authority of the state to condemn and punish in any given case threatened by other failures in state agency that are not directly related to the administration of criminal justice? Isn't this authority undermined by corruption in political process or the failure of the state to meet citizen's basic rights or prevent their destitution?[27] After all, such behaviors indicate significant incoherence on the part of a state which purports to respect and enforce rights—and, more generally, to protect people—through criminal justice. If one is inclined towards such lines of argument, then, it is not at all obvious that appealing to the agential link con-necting state agents involved in the pre-trial and the trial suffices to show that the scope of an assessment of integrity should be limited to these phases only—rather than including other domains of state agency that may or may not have a bearing on the operation and the outcome of the particular proceedings at issue.

Consider next the argument from instrumental relation. The argument rejects the sep-aration thesis on the grounds that pre-trial activities are instrumental to the trial; they should, therefore, be included within the object of the assessment of integrity for the pur-poses of determining whether the state has authority to condemn and to punish. We do accept the instrumental relation that the argument is built upon. However, we doubt that this relation warrants the assumption that the assessment of integrity should concern only the conduct of the state agents in the particular proceedings at issue. For there are various activities that are instrumental to the functioning of trials in general, and of any token trial, but are not part of the proceedings at issue. We have already mentioned activities of this sort in the previous paragraphs. To give further examples, consider the appointment of police officers, prosecutors, and judges, or the legislative process through which laws are produced that define the procedure to be followed during the trial. Improprieties in these domains are

---

[26] See Tadros 2009; Green 2011.
[27] See Matravers 2006; Tadros 2009; Holroyd 2010; Duff 2010; 2018b; 2019.

not normally thought to undermine the integrity of the state for the purposes of an assessment of its authority to condemn and punish. But the argument from instrumental relation suggests that we should consider them.

We have assessed the two lines of argument advanced by advocates of integrity to show that there is a relationship between pre-trial and trial, such that improprieties in either are relevant to whether the state has integrity, thus authority to condemn and to punish. These lines of argument may well succeed in rejecting the idea—ingrained in the separation thesis—that the scope of concerns is limited to what happens at trial. But they do not suffice to show that the delimitation of those concerns is any token instance of criminal proceeding, rather than the agency of the state in wider contexts. This work remains to be done.

We conclude this section by pointing out that, so far, we dealt with only one dimension of the problem of scope, the dimension that is generally considered in the debate concerning the separation thesis. This consists in delimiting the *range of functions* of the state to which the standard of integrity should apply. However, the problem of scope has other dimensions that seem to be ignored by those who posit integrity as a necessary condition for the state authority to punish and condemn. These dimensions include: delimiting *time*—how old should an impropriety be for it to become irrelevant to the assessment of the state's integrity, and thus of its authority to condemn and punish in a particular case?; and delimiting *value*—for the purposes of such assessment, does it matter whether the impropriety of the state agents infringes values that are different from those that are infringed by the crime for which the defendant is tried?[28] Is it ever the case that, precisely because of such a difference, integrity in state agency may not be undermined by an impropriety of the state agents? In its current state, the literature on integrity provides no answer to these questions.

7. Concluding Remarks

We have argued that in any of the four roles envisaged for integrity, difficulties are faced. As a standard of conduct, integrity looks superfluous; proper respect for rights can do the work required. Using integrity in deciding how to respond to an impropriety, its advocates inconsistently claim that it can be departed from, but also that it is a necessary condition for the state's authority to condemn and punish. Moreover, they claim that integrity can be restored by excluding evidence, despite the substantive costs this involves. The alternative conception of integrity as balancing appears inapt in some crucial phases of the process. Finally, proponents of integrity need to address the problem of scope: a difficult and multifaceted problem to which satisfactory answers are presently outstanding.

Our goal was not to show that integrity can play no useful role in normative theories of the criminal process. Instead, we want to curb the growing enthusiasm for integrity, showing that a concept of integrity that can be theoretically and practically useful cannot be found in the literature to date, and pointing out the work that must be done if such a concept is to be articulated and defended.

---

[28] cf. Matravers 2006, 325–56.

References

Ashworth, A. (1977). "Excluding Evidence as Protecting Rights," *Criminal Law Review*, 3, 723–35.

Ashworth, A. (2003). "Exploring the Integrity Principle in Evidence and Procedure," in P. Mirfield and S. Smith (eds.), *Essays for Colin Tapper*, 107–25. London: LexisNexis.

Ashworth, A. and Redmayne, M. (2010). *The Criminal Process*. Fourth edition. Oxford: Oxford University Press.

Butt, D. (2007). "On Benefiting from Injustice," *Canadian Journal of Philosophy*, 37: 129–52.

Chau, P. (2016). "Excluding Integrity? Revisiting Non-Consequentialist Justifications for Excluding Improperly Obtained Evidence in Criminal Trials," in J. Hunter et al. (eds.), *The Integrity of Criminal Process: From Theory into Practice*, 267–79. Oxford: Hart Publishing.

Choo, A. (2008). *Abuse of Process and Judicial Stays of Criminal Proceedings*. Second edition. Oxford: Oxford University Press.

Dixon, D. (2016). "Integrity, Interrogation and Criminal Justice," in J. Hunter et al. (eds.), *The Integrity of Criminal Process: From Theory into Practice*, 75–97. Oxford: Hart Publishing.

Duff, R. A., Farmer, L., Marshall, S. and Tadros, V. (2007). *The Trial on Trial* (vol III: *Towards a Normative Theory of the Criminal Trial*). Oxford: Hart Publishing.

Duff, R. A. (2010). "Blame, Moral Standing and the Legitimacy of the Criminal Trial," *Ratio*, 23: 123–40.

Duff, R. A. (2018a). *The Realm of Criminal Law*. Oxford: Oxford University Press.

Duff, R. A. (2018b). "Responsibility and Reciprocity," *Ethical Theory and Moral Practice*, 21: 775–87.

Duff, R. A. (2019). "Moral and Criminal Responsibility," in D. J. Coates and N. A. Tognazzini (eds.), *Oxford Studies in Agency and Responsibility* (vol. 5: *Themes from the Philosophy of Gary Watson*), 165–90. Oxford: Oxford University Press.

Giannoulopoulos, D. (2019). *Improperly Obtained Evidence in Anglo-American and Continental Law*. Oxford: Hart Publishing.

Green, S. P. (2011). "Just Deserts in Unjust Societies: A Case-Specific Approach," in R. A. Duff and S. P. Green (eds.), *Philosophical Foundations of Criminal Law*, 352–76. Oxford: Oxford University Press.

Ho, H. L. (2019). "Exclusion of Wrongfully Obtained Evidence: A Comparative Analysis," in D. K. Brown et al. (eds.), *The Oxford Handbook of Criminal Process*, 821–39. Oxford: Oxford University Press.

Holroyd, J. (2010). "Punishment and Justice," *Social Theory and Practice*, 36: 78–111.

Hungerford-Welch, P. (2017). "Abuse of Process: Does it Really Protect the Suspect's Rights?" *Criminal Law Review*, 3–17.

Matravers, M. (2006). "'Who's Still Standing?' A Comment on Antony Duff's Preconditions of Criminal Responsibility," *Journal of Moral Philosophy*, 3: 320–30.

Mirfield, P. (1997). *Silence, Confessions and Improperly Obtained Evidence*. Oxford: Clarendon Press.

O'Connor, P. (2012). "'Abuse of Process' after Warren and Mitchell," *Criminal Law Review*, 672–86.

Roberts, P., Hunter, J., Young, S. N. M., and Dixon, D. (2016). "Introduction: Re-Examining Criminal Process through the Lens of Integrity," in J. Hunter, P. Roberts, S. N. M., Young, and D. Dixon (eds.), *The Integrity of Criminal Process: From Theory into Practice*, 1–34. Oxford: Hart Publishing.

Roberts, P. and Zuckerman, A. (2010). *Criminal Evidence*. Oxford: Oxford University Press.

Tadros, T. (2009). "Poverty and Criminal Responsibility," *Journal of Value Inquiry*, 43: 391–413.

Whitfort, A. (2016). "Stays of Prosecution and Remedial Integrity," in J. Hunter, P. Roberts, S. N. M., Young, and D. Dixon (eds.), *The Integrity of Criminal Process: From Theory into Practice*, 247–65. Oxford: Hart Publishing.

7

Second-Personal Evidence

Alex Stein

1. Introduction

Before Hohfeld, legal insiders intuited that law is second-personal in all of its operations. After Hohfeld, they knew it.

Hohfeld's scheme of jural opposites and correlatives unfolded analytical proof that every legal entitlement ultimately transforms into a person's right, or lack thereof, to use state power in order to force another person into an action or an inaction.[1] Even a so-called right in rem—such as a person's right to exclude others from her property—is, in the end, second-personal as well because it can only be enforced against individual encroachers rather than against unspecified individuals.[2] The reason for that is twofold. First, as a simple analytical matter, law enforcers cannot *physically* direct the power of the state against unspecified individuals. Second, and as importantly, one ought to separate legal entitlements from the rules that create those entitlements. Legal rules are general commands put in place by the law-makers for society as a whole. Entitlements, on the other hand, are the individualized consequences of those commands that transform the commands into specific orders coming from law-enforcers who tell identified individuals "do this" or "abstain from doing that" to the right-holder's benefit.

This insight has important implications for the law of evidence. Evidence law is a system of rules that regulate the process of factfinding in the courts of law. Rules belonging to this system help courts ascertain the facts underlying the disputed entitlements. As the structure of those entitlements and the underlying interplay between the right-holder's authority and the duty-bearer's accountability are unchangeably second-personal, facts that courts need to ascertain and—critically—the procedures they must carry out in ascertaining those facts, ought to be second-personal as well. As a corollary, courts must only rely upon second-personal evidence, that is: upon information concerning the alleged jural relationship between the holder of the underlying entitlement and the bearer of the correlative duty or obligation.

This requirement originates from the right to autonomy enjoyed by every individual in a free society.[3] Under the autonomy framework, an individual becomes accountable for her actions only when she abuses her autonomy by violating the autonomy of another person or a group of people—that is, when she commits a crime or a tort, or fails to perform a contract, and by doing so causes harm to another person or to society at large. Consequently, evidence capable of proving one of those wrongs must show what the individual actually

---

[1] See Hohfeld 1913.
[2] See Hohfeld 1917, 719–20.
[3] See Parchomovsky and Stein 2021.

Alex Stein, *Second-Personal Evidence* In: *Philosophical Foundations of Evidence Law.* Edited by: Christian Dahlman, Alex Stein, and Giovanni Tuzet, Oxford University Press. © Christian Dahlman, Alex Stein, and Giovanni Tuzet 2021. DOI: 10.1093/oso/9780198859307.003.0008

did and did not do and what happened to the victim of the alleged misdeed. To satisfy this fundamental requirement, evidence furnished against the alleged wrongdoer must be open to maximal individualized scrutiny: it cannot be purely statistical; and it also ought to allow the individual to examine whether it is applicable to the case at bar.[4] This prerequisite should also benefit the victim of the alleged misdeed—the right-holder who claims to have a legal authority to impose punishment upon or exact compensation or another remedy from the alleged wrongdoer. Evidence purporting to negate the claims made by the alleged right-holder must focus strictly on her interactions with the defendant; and it must also be fully open to scrutiny aiming to ascertain its case-specific implications.

In the pages ahead, I demonstrate that this twin requirement defines the modus operandi of the Anglo-American system of evidence. In Section 2, I explain the second-personal structure of all jural relations. In Section 3, I specify the conditions for evidence to be "second-personal" and to satisfy the twin individualization requirement, and then move on to explain the rule against naked statistical evidence, as well as the workings of the burden of proof doctrine and the rules disqualifying hearsay and character evidence. A brief conclusion follows in Section 4.

2. The Second-Personal Structure of Jural Relationships

In the Anglo-American legal systems, all jural relationships are ultimately second-personal. More precisely, jural relationships are second-personal in adjudication and subsequent enforcement.[5]

Every legal system that follows the Anglo-American tradition defines a right-holder's entitlement by the specifics of the correlative duty or obligation. By doing so, it conditions the provision of legal remedies to the right-holder and the corresponding imposition of obligations or penalties on the duty-bearer on the presence of *authority*, on one side, and *accountability*, on the other side.[6] To qualify as a right-holder, a person must show that she has the legal authority to apply the enforcement power of the state against another individual, who thereby becomes accountable to her. This is how courts work and entitlements get enforced.

Under this framework, for a plaintiff to be entitled to recover compensation from the defendant, the plaintiff must identify the legal rule that entitles her to a remedy, conditional on the occurrence of certain specified events, and then prove that these events have actually taken place. The legal rule that bestows this entitlement on the plaintiff gives her the authority to use the power of the state in order to force the defendant to pay her the requisite compensation. By doing so, the rule makes the defendant accountable to the plaintiff.

By the same token, for a prosecutor to be entitled to impose a prison sentence or another punishment on the defendant, she must identify a criminal statute that prescribes the requisite punishment for those who act in a certain way and then prove that the defendant has actually acted in that prohibited way. The statutory rule that gives this entitlement to the prosecutor, who represents all citizens, authorizes the prosecutor to use the power of the

[4] This idea was initially developed in Stein 2005, 91–106.
[5] See Hohfeld 1913; 1917.
[6] This basic idea originates from Darwall 2006.

state to force incarceration or another punishment upon the defendant, thereby making the defendant accountable to the citizens represented by her.

This second-personal structure is also present when the litigated entitlement is a right in rem that holds against the entire world. Consider the case of Jane, who owns Longacre situated in Fairfield, Connecticut, United States. Jane's ownership of Longacre is a bundle of entitlements that includes the right to exclude others, that is, the right to prevent uninvited individuals to step into Longacre. Assume that I am one of those uninvited individuals and then ask yourself what precisely is the right that Jane has vis-a-vis me—a person living overseas far away from Longacre. The answer to this question is that Jane will have no right as against me unless and until I fly to the United States, drive to the town of Fairfield in Connecticut, get myself close to Longacre, and then try to enter it without Jane's permission. Before that event, Jane only benefited from the limitation on my and other unspecified individuals' freedom of movement—on a theoretical "privilege," under Hohfeld's taxonomy—marked by Longacre's boundaries. This limitation can be described as a duty not to enter Longacre. Yet, this type of duty— a duty to abstain—gives Jane no claim-right as against me and other unspecified individuals unless and until one of us steps out of the crowd and *becomes specified* by entering Longacre without her permission or posits an imminent threat to make such an entry. It is then and only then that Jane will establish her authority over the actual or potential trespasser. Beforehand, the legal relationship between the two remains merely hypothetical or potential—a type of relationship that courts and other enforcers of the law are not interested in and do nothing about.

Critically, in a civil lawsuit, the plaintiff's authority and the defendant's parallel accountability derive from the factual correctness of the plaintiff's infringement allegation against the defendant.[7] For example, in order to succeed in a tort action, a plaintiff must establish that the defendant carelessly caused her injury. Consequently, the plaintiff must adduce evidence identifying her injury, the defendant's careless action, and the causal connection between the two. If convincing, this evidence would establish the plaintiff's authority over the defendant and make the defendant accountable to the plaintiff in the amount of compensation allowed by the law. The defendant, for his part, may present evidence disassociating his actions from the plaintiff's injury or showing that those actions were careful enough. If convincing, this evidence would make the defendant unaccountable to the plaintiff, and the plaintiff would then be denied the authority to exact compensation from the defendant.[8]

In a criminal case, too, the prosecutor's authority over the defendant and the defendant's parallel accountability to the citizens represented by the prosecutor depend on the factual correctness of the offense allegations raised in the indictment. Correspondingly, in order to get the defendant convicted and punished, the prosecutor must adduce evidence showing that the defendant perpetrated the alleged offense. If convincing, this evidence would make the defendant accountable and eligible for the requisite punishment; and if not, the court would have to acquit the defendant. The defendant, for his part, may present evidence that exonerates him, such as evidence showing that he acted in self-defense or under a mistake of fact. If the prosecutor representing the state fails to refute such evidence, the court would hold the defendant unaccountable and deny the state the authority to punish the defendant.

---

[7] See Darwall 2006, *passim*; see also Karr 2008.
[8] See Stein 2015a, 2090–2.

The upshot of this analysis is straightforward. Evidence that courts should use in deciding civil and criminal cases ought to be capable of proving the actual facts of the case: facts identifying the existence and the individual characteristics, or, alternatively, the nonexistence, of the authority-accountability relationship between the plaintiff or the prosecutor, on one side, and the civil or criminal defendant, on the other side. Evidence not capable of proving such plaintiff-specific and defendant-specific facts does not qualify as relevant. Hence, such evidence should not be admitted and courts should avoid using it. Put differently, courts should determine the disputed facts based upon strictly second-personal evidence: evidence upon which the plaintiff or the prosecutor can establish the second-personal grounds for imposing civil or criminal liability on the defendant.

3. Second-Personal Evidence

In the previous section, I have established the foundational proposition: because both civil and criminal liability are second-personal, evidence that courts should use in ascribing liability to individual defendants ought to be second-personal as well. The authority-accountability relationship—the basis of all legal rights, duties, and obligations—can only be established by second-personal evidence: evidence that unfolds the case-specific story of how the defendant wronged, or did not wrong, another person or society as a whole.

This evidentiary standard is closely tied to personal autonomy as the most basic entitlement that individuals in a free society enjoy.[9] Accountability is a both moral and jural opposite of autonomy.[10] For that reason, in order to hold an individual accountable to another person, thereby authorizing that person to punish the accountable individual, to take away her money or property, or to force her into doing something she is unwilling to do, the legal system must have good reasons for denying the individual her autonomy the way it does. For the requisite reasons to be good, they must establish that the individual misused her autonomy in some way by acting against a protected interest of another person.[11] That is, those reasons must demonstrate, as a matter of fact, that the individual accountable to another person—the victim—committed a crime, did not deliver on a binding promise she made to the victim, or harmed the victim by failing to exercise adequate care. As a corollary, evidence substantiating any such justifying reason must be capable of proving what the individual actually did or did not do and what actually happened to the victim of the alleged misdeed. To satisfy this fundamental requirement, the evidence must be open to scrutiny that might be called "maximal individualization."[12] That is, second-personal evidence cannot be purely statistical; and it also ought to allow the individual to disassociate herself from the inferences that the individual's adversary purports to draw from it.[13]

Evidence failing to satisfy the individualization requirement does not authorize the state to hold an individual accountable, for it does not identify the actual misuse of her autonomy—a moral and political prerequisite for imposing a penalty on the individual, for taking away her money or property, or for forcing her to do something against her will.[14]

---

[9] See Parchomovsky and Stein 2021, 66–8.
[10] Ibid.
[11] This prerequisite echoes Mill's harm principle: see, e.g., Smith 2006.
[12] Stein 2005, 91–103.
[13] Ibid., 69–72, 91–103.
[14] Ibid., 100.

As a corollary, such evidence falls short of establishing the plaintiff's or the prosecutor's authority over the individual. Evidence not open to individualized scrutiny ought not to be used against the individual because using it would violate her autonomy by disempowering her in court: such evidence would expose the individual to factual inferences about the alleged misuse of her autonomy without allowing her to disprove those inferences and to show that they do not apply to her case.[15] For these reasons, evidence not open to maximal individualization is not second-personal and ought not to be used as a basis for ascribing civil or criminal liability to an individual.[16]

3.1 The Rule Against Naked Statistical Evidence

Second-personal factfinding is case-specific by design: it requires evidence that reveals the specifics of the parties' authority-accountability relationship. Without knowing these specifics, courts would not be able to determine whether the plaintiff has a valid authoritative demand that makes the defendant accountable to her.[17] Courts consequently cannot rely upon naked statistical evidence as their primary source of information.[18] Because statistical distributions tell nothing about the plaintiff's authority over the defendant and about the defendant's parallel accountability to the plaintiff, they are second-personally irrelevant. Factfinders, for example, cannot base a murder conviction upon evidence showing that the defendant was one of 1,000 prisoners, of whom 999 participated in a riot that killed prison guards.[19]

Statistical distributions, however, can still play a role as second-order information: generalizations that help courts evaluate the credibility of the first-order evidence that ought to be case-specific.[20] For example, in evaluating case-specific testimony of an eyewitness, courts may take into account psychological studies identifying the general rate of eyewitness error, potential motives to lie, and similar credibility-related second-order evidence. Using such evidence does not violate the individualization requirement for the following reason. Such evidence updates the factfinders' general experience by which they evaluate case-specific evidence coming from both sides and see whether and how it combines into a concrete story about how the defendant did, or did not, wrong the plaintiff or society as a whole. Hence, although the effect of second-order generalizations on the credibility of case-specific evidence is statistical, the ultimate factual finding—the factfinders' choice among the competing stories, the plaintiff's (or the prosecutor's) and the defendant's—is not. This choice is guided by statistical distributions only at Stage I: when the court determines whether the first-order case-specific evidence has enough credibility to be relied upon. At Stage II, when the court combines the case-specific evidence identified as credible into two competing stories—the plaintiff's (or the prosecutor's) and the defendant's—and

---

[15] See Solum 2004, 286–9; and see generally Summers 1974; Bayles 1986.

[16] Stein 2005, 91–103.

[17] Not everyone agrees with this view: see Dahlman and Pundik, "The Problem with Naked Statistical Evidence," ch. 22, in this volume.

[18] See Stein 2015a, 2094.

[19] See Nesson 1979, 1192–3. For my recent decision acquitting the "statistically guilty" defendant in the Prisoners' situation, see *Crim. App. 2921, 2961/18 State v. Bezalel* (Isr. S. Ct., 27.10.2019) (English translation available on request).

[20] See Stein 2015a, 2091–5.

then juxtaposes one story against the other, its reasoning focuses on each story's quality. This quality is determined by the story's internal coherence and the richness, or density, of the credible evidence that goes into it.[21]

Consider the proverbial *Blue Cab* case.[22] The Blue Cab Company operates 85% of the cabs in town, and it has a competitor, the Green Cab Company, that operates the remaining 15%. A person is injured by an unidentified cab in a hit-and-run accident that had no witnesses. Under such circumstances, the victim cannot successfully claim that her probability of having been hit by a blue cab was 85%. Although statistically correct, this claim is not valid from a second-personal standpoint. All it can show is a distribution of multiple victims randomly hit by blue and green cabs. The victim has no concrete, factually articulated, account of the event in which *she*, as opposed to another victim, was hit by a blue cab. The victim consequently fails to establish her authority over the Blue Cab Company. Nor can she prove that Blue Cab Company is accountable to her, as opposed to a different victim. The victim's evidence is fatally deficient from the second-personal point of view, and so her case is doomed.

The plaintiff's failure to prove her case against Blue Cab is predicated on her evidence being *insensitive* to the truth. This evidence—as, indeed, any nakedly statistical evidence—fails to satisfy the epistemological criterion of sensitivity because it would also be present, without any alterations or adjustments, in a case in which the court positively knows that the plaintiff was hit by a green, as opposed to blue, cab. Note, however, that sensitivity is not epistemically necessary for rational factfinding unless it proceeds on a prior demand that the decisionmaker's findings be individualized. Satisfying the demand for individualization does not make the decision-maker's decisions more accurate.[23] In fact, satisfying this demand may well make those decisions less accurate in a long run of cases.[24] Yet, individualized proof meeting the sensitivity criterion makes courts' decisions second-personally correct.

To see why, consider now a similar case, identified as Green Cab, in which the injured plaintiff sues the Green Cab Company. In this case, the cabs distribution in town is the same as in the previous case: the Blue Cab Company owns 85% of the cabs, with the remaining 15% of the cabs belonging to the Green Cab Company. This time around, however, the plaintiff calls a witness who testifies under oath that she saw the cab that hit the plaintiff and that the cab's color was green. Assume further that the court receives statistical information indicating that similarly situated witnesses misidentify the vehicle's color in about 20% of the cases while providing accurate identification in 80% of the cases. From a purely statistical viewpoint, the probability of the plaintiff's allegation against Green Cab is 0.41—far below the preponderance of the evidence standard (>0.5) that applies in civil litigation. This probability is calculated as follows. The prior odds that the errant cab was green as opposed to blue, $P(G)/P(B)$, equal $0.15/0.85$. To calculate the posterior odds, $P(G|W)/P(B|W)$, with W denoting the witness's testimony, these odds must be multiplied by the likelihood ratio. This ratio equals the odds attaching to the scenario in which the witness identified the cab's

---

[21] See Allen and Stein 2013. These criteria for factfinding under uncertainty originate from what has become known as Baconian probability: see Cohen 1989, 4–27.

[22] This hypothetical case is modeled on the Massachusetts Supreme Judicial Court's decision, *Smith v. Rapid Transit, Inc.*, 58 N.E.2d 754 (Mass. 1945).

[23] Enoch and Fisher 2012, 202–10.

[24] Ibid.

color correctly, rather than incorrectly: P(W|G)/P(W|B). The posterior odds consequently equal (0.15 · 0.8)/(0.85 · 0.2)—that is, 12/17. The probability that the victim's allegation against Green Cab was true thus amounts to 12/(17 + 12) or 0.41.[25]

Does that mean that the court should deny the plaintiff recovery? I think not, and here is why. Green Cab offered no competing factual account of the events and produced no evidence supporting that account. The witness's testimony is case-specific: it provides a fully coherent account about what happened between the plaintiff and the defendant. Green Cab can challenge that account by cross-examining the witness. Such witnesses are generally credible. Specifically, they are credible in about 80% of the cases—and this is the statistical, second-order, component of the court's evaluation of the evidence.

The witness's testimony is also sensitive to the truth: in the vast majority of the cases, where the cab's color is blue rather than green, such testimony is not present.[26] Critically, there is no evidence suggesting that the distribution of blue and green cabs in the city influences the witness's capacity to tell blue from green.[27] Hence, the plaintiff's case is proven *qualitatively* by a preponderance of the second-personal evidence; and so the court should rule that Green Cab caused the plaintiff's injury and must compensate her for that.[28]

3.2 The Burden of Proof Doctrine

Burdens of proof refer to probabilities.[29] In civil cases, the requirement that a party proves her allegations by a "preponderance of the evidence" or as "more probable than not" can be—and often is—understood as referring to a probability of greater than 0.5. In criminal cases, the requirement that the prosecution proves its case "beyond a reasonable doubt" can be—and often is—interpreted as setting up a probability threshold for convictions somewhere between 0.95–0.99. Finally, the "clear and convincing" evidence standard that applies in some special cases can be—and often is—taken to stand for an in-between probability of 0.75.[30]

These conceptualizations are possible and perhaps even tempting to make. Yet, to the extent they purport to say what the law is, they are descriptively inaccurate. Nor are they normatively attractive from the second-personal standpoint.

Begin with a simple, but oft-neglected, observation: the coin of the legal realm is truth.[31] Courts operating in that realm reconstruct an event that involves the parties to the trial. Consequently, factfinding that courts engage in is about the actual facts, not statistical distributions. Courts focus on the specific occurrences in which the parties (or a single party, when that party is a criminal defendant) took part. Within this framework, courts receive case-specific evidence from the parties and evaluate the significance of that evidence by reference to how the world works (identified here as second-order generalizations). Courts then juxtapose the parties' conflicting accounts of the event and ask themselves which of

---

[25] See Stein 2013, 863–5.
[26] Reliance on this testimony also aligns with the normalcy, weight, and the knowledge-generation criteria: see, respectively, Smith 2018; Stein 2005, 80–91; Levanon 2019.
[27] See Stein 2013, 864.
[28] Ibid., 863–6.
[29] cf. Spottswood, "Burdens of Proof," ch. 8, in this volume.
[30] See Stein 2005, 143–53.
[31] Allen and Stein 2013, 567.

those accounts makes the most sense. By applying this method, courts try to get to the truth itself, rather than to a statistical surrogate of the truth. They do not base their decisions on the frequencies of events that merely resemble the event they are trying to reconstruct. Instead, they rely upon case-specific evidence that uncovers the actual details of the event in question.[32]

To win the plausibility contest, evidence that a party relies upon must unfold a narrative that makes the most sense. There is no mathematical algorithm for "plausibility:" what informs courts' evaluations of plausibility are all the experience-based factors that convince people that some story may be true. These factors include coherence, consistency, completeness, articulation, simplicity, and consilience. Based on these factors, courts consider the parties' competing stories and decide which is superior and wins the day. In some cases, courts construct their own account of the events in light of the parties' evidence and arguments.[33]

That is, courts determine the probability of the facts of the case—preponderance, clear, and convincing, or beyond a reasonable doubt—by the extent to which *these specific facts* are covered by the evidence, with the density of the evidential support being the key factor. This method of ascribing probability, identified as Baconian,[34] sharply differs from the mathematical system that associates probability with the general frequency of events based on the assumption that the available evidence contains everything the factfinders need to know about the case and that the unknown possibilities are not slanted in any particular direction and are consequently equiprobable.[35] The mathematical system of probability proceeds on the principle of indifference that equalizes the unknowns.[36] The probability system that informs the burdens of proof relies on what I tagged the "difference principle." Under this principle, the difference between an account's evidentiary confirmation relative to that of conflicting factual accounts determines the probability, or relative plausibility, of that account.[37] This feature makes the burden of proof doctrine, as applied in the Anglo-American systems of evidence, second-personal.

Consider again the suit filed by the injured plaintiff against Green Cab. In that suit, the plaintiff's story, "I was hit and injured by a green cab," is supported by an eyewitness whose testimony is generally credible. The defendant's story, "The plaintiff was hit by a blue cab," is supported by the fact that 85% of the cabs in town are blue rather than green. The two stories are equally coherent and consistent. Yet, the defendant's account of the events is not as simple and as articulated as the plaintiff's. The fact that 85% of the cabs in town are blue does not logically support the story "The plaintiff was hit by a blue cab" because it tells nothing about the blue, as opposed to green, cabs' propensity to cause accidents (frequency and propensity are not the same) and about what happened in the case at bar. This story is also anything but simple as it does not tell how the cab accidents are tied to the distribution of cabs' colors. That is, the story has no causal rationale or unifying causal idea. On the other hand, the plaintiff's account supported by the eyewitness is both simple and well-articulated. Critically, evidence supporting that account also wins the day on consilience

---

[32] Ibid., 567–79.
[33] Ibid.
[34] Cohen 1989, 21.
[35] See Stein 2011, 218–20.
[36] Ibid.
[37] Ibid., 236–42.

grounds: the witness's testimony and his general reputation for trustworthiness (calculated at 80%) hang together. On the other hand, the cab distribution evidence—80% blue and 20% green—is consistent with all available "hit-and-run" scenarios. Hence, the plaintiff wins the case; and let me repeat what I have already said: the plaintiff wins this case upon second-personal evidence. Had the case been decided by statistical evidence, she would have lost it because the statistical probability of her case is merely 0.41.

3.3 Disqualifying Character Evidence

Evidence about a person's dispositions and character is nakedly statistical.[38] Such evidence is also not second-personal: it says what it says about the individual to whom the character belongs, yet it says nothing about what that individual did and did not do within the second-personal relationship with her adversary and, indeed, whether she and her adversary have formed such a relationship in the first place. For example, evidence about a criminal defendant's character may well inform the factfinders as to what kind of person he is, but not whether he acted in conformity with his character on a particular occasion and harmed the alleged victim.[39]

Admitting character evidence, such as prior convictions, to prove action in conformity brings into play generalizations about a causal connection between personality and action. Such a connection may be present in some cases, but not in others, for the following simple reason: Sometimes people act in conformity with their characters and personalities, and sometimes do not. Crucially, arguments purporting to establish such a connection hang in the air: directing such an argument against a specific person and to a specified set of circumstances is virtually impossible, for there is no way to prove or disprove the proposition that a particular person—say, a criminal defendant—acted in conformity with his or her character in the event on trial. A generalization suggesting that he or she acted in this way is surely available as a matter of statistics. However, this generalization is one of many: it cannot be individuated and hence cannot say virtually anything about what the defendant did or did not do.[40]

Similarly to naked statistics, character evidence therefore does not qualify as second-personal. Such evidence, however, can still be used for discrediting a witness, but then, as I have already explained, the court will be using it as a second-order evidence. The first-order evidence upon which courts establish civil and criminal liability, or lack thereof, ought to be, and normally is, second-personal.

3.4 The Rule Against Hearsay

Under the hearsay rule, as applied in the United States and, until fairly recently, in England, an out-of-court statement (or other intentionally assertive conduct) cannot be admitted as evidence for its truth. Such statements are generally excluded for lack of cross-examination.

---

[38] See Stein 2005, 183–6.
[39] Ibid.
[40] Ibid.

Because the person who made such a statement (the declarant) cannot be cross-examined, the statement's credibility and effect on the individual case cannot be properly tested. Admitting such a statement into evidence thus disempowers the statement's opponent while giving an unfair advantage to the proponent of the statement.[41]

Hearsay statements, however, are admitted into evidence in various mitigated versions that align with the exceptions to the hearsay rule. Broadly speaking, the hearsay exceptions follow the distinction between "event statements" and "proceeding statements." The event-statements category includes any statement that the declarant makes, explicitly or implicitly, during any event outside of legal proceedings, identified as primary behavior, as contrasted with the litigation, or secondary, behavior. The proceeding-statements category includes statements made in formal legal proceedings, such as trial, grand jury hearing, police interrogation, deposition, or affidavit. A statement made by a person as part of an event (primary behavior) can generally be used as evidence for its truth when a witness testifies from his or her first-hand knowledge about the statement's contents and the circumstances in which the declarant made it. The statement becomes admissible when these circumstances contain basic information about the declarant's perception, memory, narration, and sincerity. By using this information, the statement's opponent can properly examine its credibility and effect on the case at bar. This examination would typically focus on how the statement interacted with the event. Because witnesses bringing this information to the court can be cross-examined about this interaction, the court's admission of the statement does not disempower its opponent even when the declarant is not available for cross-examination. The opponent's ability to cross-examine a first-hand witness about the interaction between the declarant's statement and the event on trial provides an adequate substitute for the declarant's cross-examination.[42]

A proceeding-statement, on the other hand, is a product of the declarant's interaction with the proceeding, rather than with the event itself. When the opponent of the statement is given a fair opportunity to question the declarant during the proceeding, the court can admit the statement as evidence for its truth.[43] Well-recognized exceptions to the hearsay rule make that happen.[44] However, when the statement's opponent is not afforded that opportunity, admitting the statement as evidence against her interest would amount to a disempowerment. For that reason, proceeding statements are generally not admissible.[45]

The disempowerment rationale has to do with the protection of the individual's autonomy.[46] Under this rationale, an individual cannot be held accountable to another person and forced to surrender his interests to that person's authority on the basis of one-sided untestable statements. By protecting every litigant against one-sided evidence, the legal system secures two-sided individualization of factfinding—a feature that helps the system carry out its second-personal operation.

[41] Ibid., 189–92.
[42] Ibid., 191–2.
[43] Ibid.
[44] Ibid.
[45] Ibid., 190–1.
[46] See Solum 2004, 288. cf. Tribe 1988, 666–7 ("Both the right to be heard from, and the right to be told why, are analytically distinct from the right to secure a different outcome; these rights to interchange express the elementary idea that to be a person, rather than a thing, is at least to be consulted about what is done with one.... For when the government acts in a way that singles out identifiable individuals—in a way that is likely to be premised on suppositions about specific persons—it activates the special concern about being personally talked to about the decision rather than simply being dealt with").

4. Conclusion

Courts following the Anglo-American legal tradition have been using the second-personal evidence paradigm for many years. As I have demonstrated in this chapter, they have been doing so for a very good reason. The second-personal evidence paradigm is the most principled approach to factfinding: it enables courts to help individuals vindicate their autonomy within the second-personal framework of substantive rights, duties, and obligations as established by the law. This method of evidence selection and factfinding outperforms its competitor: the statistical method of factfinding that relies upon mathematical probability generated on the basis of all available evidence.[47] When properly applied, the statistical method can minimize the cost of errors and error-avoidance across multiple cases[48]—a feature that makes it attractive from a purely economic standpoint.[49] This method, however, pays no regard to the ultimate object of adjudicative factfinding: the second-personal design of people's substantive rights, duties, and obligations.[50] Unsurprisingly, therefore, it exists only in the academic literature[51] where it serves most successfully as a tool for evaluating the overall performance of the legal system in terms of social welfare.[52]

References

Allen, R. J. and Stein, A. (2013). "Evidence, Probability, and the Burden of Proof," *Arizona Law Review*, 55: 557–602.

Bayles, M. D. (1986). "Principles for Legal Procedure," *Law & Philosophy*, 5: 33–57.

Cohen, L. J. (1989). *An Introduction to the Philosophy of Induction and Probability*. Oxford: Oxford University Press.

Darwall, S. (2006). *The Second-Person Standpoint: Morality, Respect, and Accountability*. Cambridge: Harvard University Press.

Enoch, D., Spectre, L., and Fisher, T. (2012). "Statistical Evidence, Sensitivity, and the Legal Value of Knowledge," *Philosophy & Public Affairs*, 40: 197–224.

Hohfeld, W. N. (1913). "Some Fundamental Legal Conceptions as Applied in Judicial Reasoning," *Yale Law Journal*, 23: 16–59.

Hohfeld, W. N. (1917). "Fundamental Legal Conceptions as Applied in Judicial Reasoning," *Yale Law Journal*, 26: 710–70.

Kaplow, L. (2012). "Burden of Proof," *Yale Law Journal*, 121: 738–859.

Karr, R. B. (2008). "The Second Person Standpoint and the Law: Symposium Introduction," *Loyola Los Angeles Law Review*, 40: 881–90.

Kaye, D. (1982). "The Limits of the Preponderance of the Evidence Standard: Justifiably Naked Statistical Evidence and Multiple Causation," *American Bar Foundation Research Journal*, 7: 487–516.

Levanon, L. (2019). "Statistical Evidence, Assertions and Responsibility," *Modern Law Review*, 82: 269–92.

---

[47] For a powerful account of that method, see Kaye 1982. For a statistical factfinding model aiming to incentivize welfare-enhancing primary behavior, see Kaplow 2012.

[48] See Stein 2005, 141–53.

[49] Ibid.

[50] Stein 2015a, 2090.

[51] See, e.g., Posner 1999; Stein 2015b.

[52] See Posner 1999; Stein 2015b. Note that individuals' incentive to generate favorable second-personal evidence may lead to distortions in their primary behavior: see Parchomovsky and Stein 2010.

Nesson, C. R. (1979). "Reasonable Doubt and Permissive Inferences: The Value of Complexity," *Harvard Law Review*, 92: 1187–225.

Parchomovsky, G. and Stein, A. (2010). "The Distortionary Effect of Evidence on Primary Behavior," *Harvard Law Review*, 124: 518–48.

Parchomovsky, G. and Stein, A. (2021). "Autonomy," *University of Toronto Law Journal*, 71: 61–90.

Posner, R. A. (1999). "An Economic Approach to the Law of Evidence," *Stanford Law Review*, 51: 1477–546.

Smith, M. (2018). "When does Evidence Suffice for Conviction?" *Mind*, 127: 1193–218.

Smith, S. D. (2006). "Is the Harm Principle Illiberal?" *American Journal of Jurisprudence*, 51: 1–42.

Solum, L. B. (2004). "Procedural Justice," *Southern California Law Review*, 78: 181–321.

Stein, A. (2005). *Foundations of Evidence Law*. Oxford: Oxford University Press.

Stein, A. (2011). "The Flawed Probabilistic Foundation of Law & Economics," *Northwestern University Law Review*, 105: 199–260.

Stein, A. (2013). "Are People Probabilistically Challenged?" *Michigan Law Review*, 111: 855–85.

Stein, A. (2015a). "The New Doctrinalism: Implications for Evidence Theory," *University of Pennsylvania Law Review*, 163: 2085–107.

Stein, A. (2015b). "Inefficient Evidence," *Alabama Law Review*, 66: 423–70.

Summers, R. (1974). "Evaluating and Improving Legal Process—a Plea for 'Process Values'," *Cornell Law Review*, 60: 1–52.

Tribe, L. (1988). *American Constitutional Law*. Second edition. New York: Foundation Press.

8

Burdens of Proof

Mark Spottswood

1. Introduction

Burdens of proof remain a lively subject of debate within the academic literature on evidence and juridical inference. Burdens consist of rules that guide judges and juries in determining what level of factual proof suffices to support an award of sanctions. In essence, they are functions that map some set of inputs, such as varying levels of confidence with respect to a defendant's guilt, onto some set of consequences, such as guilty or not-guilty verdicts.

One can describe many legal judgments that hinge on some underlying facts as involving a burden, whether or not it is commonly so labelled. For instance, *burdens of production* require a party to produce sufficient evidence to permit a reasonable jury to rule in their favor. Passing this threshold permits the party to present its case to a jury, while failing to pass it leads to the court finding against the party as a matter of law.[1] But this chapter, like the vast bulk of evidence scholarship on burdens, will focus exclusively on the *burden of persuasion* at trial. This burden determines when a factfinder should sustain or deny a plaintiff's or prosecutor's claims against a defendant. In American litigation, these burdens of persuasion take a few familiar forms: the *preponderance of the evidence* burden that is used for most civil cases, the intermediate *clear and convincing evidence* burden that is used for a smaller group of civil cases, and the high standard of *proof beyond a reasonable doubt* that governs in criminal cases.

Scholars have debated many kinds of questions with respect to burdens. Some have explored the underlying psychological mechanisms that jurors use when they analyze evidence and arrive at verdict decisions. Others have focused on describing the assumptions that are expressed or implicit in the existing law regulating burdens. Many have analyzed which sorts of burden rules are best from a normative standpoint, in terms of their abilities to generate fair decisions or to maximize social welfare. And some have tried to construct theories that bridge the different levels, providing accounts that balance descriptive accuracy with normative desirability.[2]

The remainder of this chapter will set forth some of the claims about burdens that have been made on each of these levels. For ease of analysis, we will divide the key questions into two parts.[3] First, we will explore the *inputs* that a burden of proof rule should draw upon, including a survey of potential candidates that scholars have identified and a consideration of factors that might help us assess their suitability for differing purposes. Then, we will turn our attention to the ways that proof burdens might transform those inputs into

---

[1] Nance 2016, 2–3.
[2] cf. Spottswood 2019, 75–6.
[3] See Tuzet 2020.

Mark Spottswood, *Burdens of Proof* In: *Philosophical Foundations of Evidence Law*. Edited by: Christian Dahlman, Alex Stein, and Giovanni Tuzet, Oxford University Press. © Christian Dahlman, Alex Stein, and Giovanni Tuzet 2021.
DOI: 10.1093/oso/9780198859307.003.0009

recommended levels of sanctions in civil and criminal cases, giving special attention to the normative suitability of differing burden structures.

2. Burden Inputs

The first step of applying a burden is to identify which particular case-related facts most directly determine its outcomes. This section will briefly outline several previously identified burden input possibilities, and then survey some of the particular features that might make these competing candidates more or less attractive. As we shall see, the particular features incorporated into a model will influence its suitability as a psychological, doctrinal, or normative account, and it is doubtful that a model that is optimized for one purpose can serve the others equally well.

2.1 Probability of Charged Conduct Versus Other Grounds

One common view is that burdens of proof might operate based on assessed *probabilities* of liability or guilt.[4] Using this approach, if a jury finds that the probability that the defendant committed the charged wrong against the plaintiff is greater than 50%, then the preponderance standard has been satisfied. Similarly, we might say, for the sake of exposition, that a probability greater than 66% meets the "clear and convincing evidence" threshold, while a probability above 90% meets the "beyond a reasonable doubt" standard, while acknowledging that some might prefer slightly different numerical thresholds. This approach is often linked to Bayesian decision theory, a mathematical framework that offers decision-makers normative guidance as to which choices they should make if they seek to maximize their future utility under conditions of uncertainty.[5] It has also been used within economic analyses that aim to identify which litigation outcomes maximize social welfare,[6] and some have incorporated it within psychological models of factfinding as well.[7]

Against this baseline, scholars have proposed many alternative approaches. Some rivals agree that the thresholds should be quantitative in nature but disagree with using *probability* estimates. Cheng and Sullivan have separately argued in favor of a *likelihood ratio* account.[8] This differs from the probability approach in two key ways. First, rather than relying on the isolated probability of the defendant's culpability, the likelihood ratio approach focuses on the comparative strength of each side's case. Second, this approach measures case strength by assessing the likelihood of observing the given body of evidence *assuming* that either side's proposed factual account was true. The preponderance standard would be met whenever the plaintiff's account makes the evidence more likely than the defendant's account, while heightened burdens would require higher ratios.

---

[4] See generally, Friedman 2018.
[5] See, e.g., Kaye 1982; Kaplan 1968.
[6] See, e.g., Posner 1999.
[7] See Devine 2012, 22–6.
[8] Sullivan 2019, 26–9; Cheng 2013, 1268; see also Dahlman and Kolflaath, "The Problem of the Prior in Criminal Trials," ch. 19, in this volume.

A related approach seeks to ground verdict decisions on *degrees of committed belief in wrongdoing*. Drawing on the theory of belief functions, Clermont has urged that we should model factfinders as having some degree of committed belief in wrongdoing, some degree of committed belief in innocence, and some degree of uncommitted belief (which might later be committed to either side should new evidence arise that is relevant to the case).[9] Like the likelihood theory, this account is essentially comparative. But degrees of belief do not depend strictly on the parties' proposed case theories, and the mathematics of combining them does not align with ordinary probabilistic reasoning.[10]

Another kind of theory focuses on the *weight* of accumulated evidence, either on its own or in addition to the probability of wrongdoing. Evidential weight refers to the quantity of evidence that has been collected on a question, relative to the *ideal* amount of evidence that might be considered in resolving the same question.[11] L. Jonathan Cohen, for instance, argued that some burden thresholds should depend on the comparative quantity of evidential weight offered by each party.[12] Neil Cohen offered a blended theory, in which not just the probability of wrongdoing, but also its confidence interval, would need to exceed the proof threshold to support a verdict decision.[13] Neither of these authors, however, explained how one might apply these ideas in deciding a run-of-the-mill court case based upon conflicting witness testimonies.[14]

A fifth group have argued against quantification entirely. One recent approach, championed prominently by Allen and Pardo, has drawn on the concept of inference to the best explanation. Advocates of this approach maintain that rather than determine the probability of any facts, jurors engage in a comparative evaluation of the *strength of each party's explanation of the evidence*.[15] Such explanations can consist of simple stories about how the litigated events might have actually transpired, but they can also take more complex forms. The strength of an explanation is evaluated in a holistic manner based on factors such as consistency with the evidence, internal consistency, simplicity, and coherence with background beliefs about the world.[16]

A final group of theories has arisen in the context of psychological accounts of jury decision-making, which attempt to elucidate the underlying mental mechanisms at play in juridical inference. Some of these accounts have modeled jurors' assessments of case strength in mathematical terms, although not all assume that the numbers in question are derived in a mathematically ideal fashion.[17] By contrast, Pennington and Hastie's *story model* analyzed the process in terms of a choice between salient *stories* about the litigated events. Factfinders, in their view, use the evidence to construct coherent narratives about the disputed events in a case, and then award victory to the party who has the "best" story based on factors such as evidential coverage, consistency, plausibility, and completeness.[18] More recently, I argued that juridical decisions arise out of an interaction between implicit

[9] Clermont 2018, 1068–9.
[10] See ibid., 1068–9, 1071–5. See also Spottswood, "Paradoxes of Proof," ch. 21, in this volume.
[11] Nance 2016, 130; Nance, "Weight of Evidence," ch. 9, in this volume.
[12] Cohen 1977, 252–6 (focusing on the preponderance standard).
[13] Cohen 1985, 404–9.
[14] Nance 2016, 138.
[15] Pardo and Allen 2008, 233–42; Allen and Pardo, "Inference to the Best Explanation, Relative Plausibility, and Probability," ch. 14, in this volume.
[16] Ibid. 230.
[17] See Devine 2012, 22–6.
[18] Pennington and Hastie 1991, 527–8.

cognition, which operates in a non-comparative, associative manner, and explicit reasoning, which often involves the articulation and comparison of semantic stories.[19]

2.2 Subjective versus Objective

One source of disagreement among rival theorists has been whether the input to the burden function should be understood as a *subjective* quality within the factfinder's mind versus an *objective* feature of the underlying case. Most obviously, the psychological models are clearly designed to explain how subjective aspects of reasoning lead to particular outcomes in cases. Moreover, many adherents to the probabilistic conception of burdens take a Bayesian perspective, interpreting the underlying probabilities as subjective.[20] (In practice, we must make a distinction between truly subjective accounts, which recommend outcomes based upon a factfinder's *actual* credence concerning guilt or liability, versus epistemic approaches, which also advise her what credence she *ought* to hold, given the evidence presented to her and her prior beliefs.[21]) The belief function theory likewise draws on an essentially subjective quality, by relying on a factfinder's degree of committed belief. And the likelihood ratio approach can also be framed in subjective terms.[22]

But some theorists maintain that it is undesirable to incorporate subjective facts into a model of proof burdens. Allen and Pardo, for instance, have maintained that credences have "no necessary relationship to advancing accurate outcomes." Moreover, they worry that premising trial outcomes on subjective beliefs conflicts with rules that allow judges to override jury verdicts when there is only one "reasonable" outcome in a case.[23] Thus, the relative plausibility theory explicates burdens as functions that depend on what the *true* balance is between competing explanations, rather than a particular factfinder's *beliefs* regarding that balance. Some other theorists take a similar approach.[24]

Ultimately, the desirability of basing burdens on credences versus objective features of a case will depend on our goals. At one extreme, it is simply odd to complain when *psychological* accounts draw upon subjective facts, as the goal of such theories is to link decisions to underlying mental processes. At the other extreme, reliance on a factfinder's actual degrees of belief will limit the reach of normative theorizing. After all, such a theory ought to be able to tell us how each case should be properly decided.[25] This would, ideally, include the ability to tell us when a factfinder's beliefs or preferences regarding case outcomes are poorly justified or biased. But if those beliefs are also the ground of a normative theory, that theory could then lose the power to help us identify some sources of error.

Harder questions arise when we focus on the goal of describing burden of proof doctrines. On the one hand, judges are permitted to set aside some jury results on the basis that they are unreasonable or against the clear weight of the evidence,[26] which might suggest

---

[19] See Spottswood 2013, 171–93.
[20] e.g., Friedman 1996, 276–8.
[21] See Nance 2016, 42–9.
[22] Cheng 2013, 1266–8.
[23] Allen and Pardo 2019, 12.
[24] e.g., Sullivan 2019, 35.
[25] cf. Laudan 2006, 79–81.
[26] See *Byrd v. Blue Ridge Rural Elec. Co-op., Inc.*, 356 U.S. 525, 540 (1958); *Brady v. S. Ry. Co.*, 320 U.S. 476, 479–80 (1943).

that there is something other than the jurors' subjective mental states that can serve as a yardstick. On the other hand, some jury instructions do seem to invite a decision based upon the juror's own views and beliefs concerning the evidence.[27] And on reflection, it is far from clear what *non-subjective* referents real-world decision-makers have access to that could ground burdens. Consider relative judgments of explanatory plausibility, for instance. One can tell a juror to decide based on which explanation is *truly* best, but in applying this instruction they will inevitably draw on their own beliefs regarding the strength of each explanation. A reviewing court, if they are to reverse a verdict, will likewise draw on their own judgments. It is almost unimaginable that any of them would say, "*Personally* I feel that the plaintiff has the stronger explanation, but in *truth* the defendant's explanation is better, so I will vote against liability (or find that the jury's verdict to the contrary was unreasonable)." Thus, defining burdens in putatively objective terms may obscure how they must operate in practice.

2.3 Single Quantity versus Comparative

Another key question is whether the input to a burden decision is an entity that can be meaningfully described in isolation, versus one that can only be described in comparison with something else. The classical probabilistic approach, for instance, would say that the preponderance standard is met when the jury has a confidence level in liability that is greater than 50%. Competing offers of proof and arguments from the parties might adjust this level upwards or downwards, but in the end the outcome depends upon a single numerical quantity. Some psychological models also incorporate features that require a factual account to be sufficiently strong *in isolation* to become intuitively appealing, whether or not a stronger competitor has been offered.[28]

By contrast, other approaches take an explicitly comparative approach. The likelihood ratio approach, for example, awards victory to whichever party's case makes the evidence more probable, without demanding that either party's case be more likely than not to be true.[29] In other words, the approach *ranks* the strength of each case in an ordinal fashion, without demanding that case strength be assessed relative to a fixed, cardinal scale. Similarly, the story model suggests that factfinders choose among competing stories, rather than assess the individual likelihood of any one story's truth.[30] In addition to these, the belief function[31] and relative plausibility accounts[32] also take a comparative approach.

Once again, the strength or weakness of each approach can only be considered in relation to the various uses we might have for describing burdens. At the psychological level, I have argued that both singular and comparative processes are at work in real-life juridical reasoning. First, while factfinders listen passively to the evidence, their minds are actively organizing it into an associative model that connects people, places, events, and moral

---

[27] See, e.g., Committee on Pattern Jury Instructions for the Seventh Circuit 2017, §1.27; *In re Winship*, 397 U.S. 358, 371 (1970) (Harlan, J., concurring).
[28] e.g., Spottswood 2013, 197–9.
[29] e.g., Cheng 2013, 1265, n. 17.
[30] Pennington and Hastie 1991, 527–9.
[31] Clermont 2018, 1079.
[32] Allen and Pardo 2019, 15.

categories into a single, unitary framework. Later, when the case has finished and the fact-finders are deliberating about how to decide, they will often approach their task by explicitly comparing each party's account of the case to the body of evidence and the relevant legal rules.

At the level of doctrine, the singular approach is more defensible than the comparative one. To be sure, some language in conventional jury instructions can be read in a comparative fashion. References to the "preponderance" or the "greater weight" of the evidence, for instance, do seem to ask the jury to prefer whichever party's case is stronger. Other language, however, fits more neatly within a singular account. Whether a case is "clear and convincing," or whether a doubt is strong enough to be "reasonable," do not seem to be inherently comparative questions. And some cases have made it explicit that even the preponderance standard is not meant to be purely comparative. On multiple occasions, the Supreme Court has stated that the preponderance standard is not met simply because the jury finds the plaintiff's account more convincing than the defendant's account. As the court has put it, "it is not enough to *dis*believe the [defendant]; the factfinder must *believe* the plaintiff's explanation."[33]

Courts, moreover, enforce a number of related doctrines that are at odds with a comparative approach. Plaintiffs and prosecutors can have their cases dismissed by a court if they are too weak to permit a reasonable jury to find in their favor, and such rulings can occur *before* the defendant has offered any counter-evidence.[34] Likewise, criminal defendants sometimes adopt a strategy of identifying internal weaknesses within the prosecutor's theories and evidence, without offering any counter-narrative. The comparative account might suggest that such a strategy requires a verdict for the prosecutor, given the absence of a competing story or explanation, but no such doctrine exists. Thus, although comparative *reasoning* is certainly an accepted way for juries to analyze whether a party who bears a burden of proof has satisfied it,[35] a fully comparative interpretation of the burden *itself* is harder to defend.

Lastly, there is the question of whether burdens *should* be comparative as a normative matter. There are two possibilities. One is that a comparative approach considers *all* the relevant possibilities on each side of the case, such that a plaintiff receives credit for each account that implies liability and the defense receives credit for each account that negates liability. Some theories, such as the explanatory account, permit a factfinder to proceed in this way. Taking this approach, the outcome of a comparative analysis should closely approximate the probability that the plaintiff's case is true, possibly implying that the gap between normative explanationism and normative Bayesianism may be smaller in practice than it might appear at first glance.[36]

By contrast, other comparative models do not permit the aggregation of inconsistent stories as a means of supporting a case. Cheng's likelihood ratio model, for instance, takes as an input the likelihood of each party's strongest *internally consistent* account. He explicates his approach using an automobile tort hypothetical. The plaintiff, in this example,

[33] *Reeves v. Sanderson Plumbing Prods.*, 530 U.S. 133, 146 (2000) (quoting from *St. Mary's Honor Ctr. v. Hicks*, 509 U.S. 502, 519 (1993)).
[34] Lempert 1986, 471–2.
[35] cf. *Anderson v. Griffin*, 397 F.3d 515, 521–22 (7th Cir. 2005) (noting that one way of raising the estimated probability of an event's occurrence is to rule out competing possibilities).
[36] See Lipton 2004, 107–17; Nance 2016, 80–1.

114 BURDENS OF PROOF

claims that the crash occurred because the defendant was speeding and that she suffered a neck injury as a result. The defendant argues that he was not speeding and that in any event the neck injury was a pre-existing condition. Cheng's approach compares the likelihood of the plaintiff's account (speeding and caused neck injury) with the likelihood of whichever *single story* offered by the defendant is most probable.[37] Imagine, for instance, that the overall likelihoods are as follows in Table 8.1.

Table 8.1   Probabilities of Separate Versus Aggregated Stories

	Separate Probability	Aggregated Probabilities
Speeding and new injury	33%	33% Chance across all plaintiff stories
Not speeding and new injury	22%	66% Chance across all defense stories
Speeding and pre-existing injury	22%	
Not speeding and pre-existing injury	22%	

With a pattern like this, Cheng's theory would conclude that the plaintiff should prevail, because no single defense story is more likely than 33%. This might be useful in a psychological model, if we think jurors are irrationally reluctant to give due credit to arguments in the alternative.[38] It *may* also have merit as a doctrinal account, given that courts sometimes instruct jurors in ways that diverge from what is mathematically ideal.[39] But as a normative guide to inference, it has grave deficiencies. Put simply, when parties argue in the alternative, the overall likelihood that they are right on one of their points is always *greater* than the likelihood that their strongest argument is correct. Thus, precluding aggregation will, in general, cause us to give too little credit to accounts that are disjunctive in form, and thereby create an excessive risk that we will erroneously find parties liable. We would do better either by relying on the strength of the plaintiff's claim alone or by comparing it to the *aggregated* probability that one or more of the defendant's accounts is true.

2.4 Quantified versus Unquantified

The last question is whether the criteria upon which burdens operate should be quantified or not. Many approaches, including the probabilistic frameworks, the likelihood ratio theories, the belief function account, and some psychological models, agree that burdens depend on something that can be described in numerical terms. Other approaches, including the relative plausibility account and the story model, avoid such quantification. As we shall

---

[37] Cheng 2013, 1263–5.
[38] See Spottswood 2016, 281–2.
[39] See ibid., 267, 282. On the other hand, some legal rules allow parties to make inconsistent arguments in the alternative. See, e.g., Federal Rule of Civil Procedure 8(d)(3) (providing that "[a] party may state as many separate claims or defenses as it has, regardless of consistency").

see, the desirability of using numerical quantities as inputs will depend on whether we are offering a psychological, doctrinal, or normative account of burdens.

At the psychological level, it is doubtful that many judges or jurors pause in their deliberations to attach explicit numbers that represent their belief in the strength of a case.[40] Thus, a quantified model will fail to capture important aspects of the internal experience of fact-finding. Of course, there may still be uses for quantified *descriptions* of the process, purely for analytic purposes. For instance, if we wish to assess whether jurors' votes line up with a quantified *normative* model of inference, it may help to elicit a quantified statement regarding their confidence in guilt, even if that would not normally be a part of the decisional process, and use that to construct a mathematicised account of their actual decisions.[41] But if we are trying to get closer to the root causes of how cases are typically decided, modeling burdens in a way that depends on quantified levels of confidence in wrongdoing may obscure as much as it clarifies.

Doctrinally, some courts describe the preponderance standard as requiring the jury to think it more than 50% likely that the plaintiff's claim is correct.[42] However, when we shift our focus to the burden of proof beyond a reasonable doubt, we find that judges display an open hostility to the notion of quantification.[43] So as before, although there may be utility to modelling these doctrines mathematically for some analytic purposes, such simplifications will fail to capture important features of existing law.

Finally, scholars have fiercely debated whether a normative model of burdens should incorporate quantification. Views on this topic will necessarily depend, at least in part, on broader notions concerning the inferential process by which jurors should decide cases. If one thinks that sequential probabilistic adjustments in response to evidence will help fact-finders reach more accurate verdicts,[44] then it might make sense to retain the quantified output of such a process as the basis for decision. Similarly, some normative proposals suggest that it would be desirable to vary sanctions fluidly in response to varying likelihoods of wrongful conduct, and thus require the input side of the equation to be a sliding scale.[45] If we think such proposals are attractive, representing the input side of the equation as a continuously variable numeric quantity will ease its implementation. More pragmatically, quantification might yield special benefits when judges or jurors must determine how to incorporate explicitly statistical evidence into their decisions.[46]

Others have worried that the seeming precision of a quantified burden presents a false hope. Most evidence does *not* present itself in a quantified form, and if one considers the vast multitude of sequential inferences needed to decide even a simple case, one must quickly conclude that any attempt to give numerical assignments of strength to each item of evidence must involve a great deal of rough guesswork.[47] Moreover, if we wish to constrain our estimates of evidence strength through reliance on real-world frequency data, we will find that there is no data to be had on some questions, while others force us to make potentially arbitrary choices among competing reference classes.[48] Ergo, if we employ burden

---

[40] See Devine 2012, 23.
[41] e.g., Koehler, Chia, and Linsdey 1995.
[42] See, e.g., *Brown v. Bowen*, 847 F.2d 342, 345 (7th Cir. 1988).
[43] See, e.g., *McCullough v. State*, 657 P.2d 1157, 1159 (Nev. 1983).
[44] cf. Spottswood 2019, 80.
[45] See Part 3 of this chapter, *infra*.
[46] cf. National Research Council 1996, 200–2.
[47] See Allen 1997, 269–70.
[48] See Pardo and Allen 2008, 259–60.

rules that specify their input functions quantitatively, in practice most factfinders will derive the required numbers from vague intuitive impressions rather than strict mathematical analysis.

But this observation, while important, does not foreclose further normative discussion. Even if jurors produce numerical estimates intuitively, perhaps asking for a number will induce them to consider potential sources of error more carefully before deciding. Alternatively, perhaps combining each juror's probabilistic judgments using averaging would return a more trustworthy result than all-or-nothing voting with respect to the overall outcome.[49] Or maybe unquantified burdens are interpreted in inconsistent or unpredictable ways by decision-makers, and quantifying them might help us better implement our goals regarding distribution of errors and equality of treatment.[50] Although these ideas are speculative, they do suggest that there could be benefits to quantifying burden inputs even if the numbers are generated by holistic intuition rather than mechanistic analysis.

We have seen that the differing approaches to modeling burdens can be classified along several interesting dimensions. Some operate on subjective states of mind, while others focus on objective case features. Some depend upon a single factor, while others draw on a comparison between alternatives. And some rely upon a factor that can be expressed numerically, while others eschew quantification. As the foregoing analysis has shown, the treatment of these details will affect the degree of fit a model has at the psychological, doctrinal, and normative levels of analysis. Moreover, the approach that works best at one level can be suboptimal for the others.

3. Transforming Inputs into Outputs

Next, let us consider how potential burdens transform representations of case strength into varying levels of sanctions. Doctrinally, the most common approach is a discontinuous, "all or nothing" rule, which awards zero sanctions up to a specified level of confidence and full sanctions above it. But interesting variations exist, including some that have been tried by courts in isolated areas, and others that have been studied theoretically but never implemented. The variations include rules that vary the threshold from case to case, rules that permit intermediate steps between zero sanctions and full sanctions, and rules that vary the sanction size continuously in response to variations in a factfinder's confidence in liability or guilt.

3.1 Potential Approaches

Most commonly, burdens of proof take a simple form, generating zero sanctions below some input threshold and full sanctions above it. In ordinary civil cases, for instance, the plaintiff gets nothing if she proves her case by less than a preponderance of the evidence,

---

[49] Imagine two cases that must be decided by six-member juries. In the first, three jurors agree that liability is 95% likely, while the others think it is 45% likely. In the second, all six jurors agree that liability is 55% likely. The former case has a higher average confidence level (70% in the first versus 55% in the second), but if we lump each judgment into a dichotomous decision on liability, we will obscure that fact.

[50] See Kagehiro 1990, 196–8.

and she gets full damages once that point has been exceeded. In criminal cases, the defendant is subject to no punishment unless the prosecutor can prove her case beyond a reasonable doubt; past that point, he is subject to full punishment (often within a range defined by statute). Affirmative defenses, meanwhile, must be proven to some fixed threshold by a defendant in order to negate these consequences. And in all of these scenarios, the party who "bears" the burden of proof must convince the factfinder that the applicable threshold has been exceeded, with ties going to their opponent.[51]

If one chooses this *single-stepped* rule, one must also decide whether its threshold will be fixed or variable. The clearest example of a fixed threshold rule is the civil preponderance standard, which places the tipping point fairly clearly at the 50% mark, for all cases to which it applies. But we can also employ a threshold that *moves*, so that some cases require more proof than others to justify sanctioning the defendant. And indeed, our system already employs a variable threshold in one sense: we apply a heightened burden in criminal cases, a more balanced burden in ordinary civil cases, and an intermediate burden in a subset of civil cases in which wrongful ascriptions of liability are thought to be especially costly.

There may also be subtler ways that our proof thresholds vary in practice. At the psychological level, factfinders who are given vague burden definitions might demand stronger proof when the costs of error seem high, while permitting weaker cases to suffice when the cost of making a mistake seems less grave. For instance, consider the notion of proof "beyond a reasonable doubt." Multiple mock-trial experiments have shown that both judges and jury-eligible laypeople would ask for higher levels of proof before convicting defendants when the cases involve more serious crimes or longer sentences.[52] It has also been suggested that juries who are tasked with deciding whether to sentence convicted defendants to death are often reluctant to do so unless they think the guilt has been proven to a *higher* level than the beyond-a-reasonable-doubt standard would require on its own.[53] Some courts have agreed that this is appropriate, permitting advocates to openly advocate for a life sentence on the basis of such residual doubts, while other courts disagree.[54]

Multi-stepped approaches add one or more intermediate steps between zero and full sanctions. Historically, continental courts employed a system where "full proof" enabled stricter consequences than "half proof," for instance.[55] Likewise, modern Scotland employs a three-tiered verdict system in criminal cases, permitting verdicts of not guilty, not proven, and guilty.[56] The former system imposed reduced punishment at the intermediate proof level, while the only impact of Scotland's intermediate verdict is potential stigma due to the lack of an innocence finding.

Some courts have gone further, replacing single- or multi-stepped thresholds with a smooth transition across the full range of case strength. In toxic tort cases, plaintiffs sometimes have difficulty proving which among multiple manufacturers competing in the relevant market actually sold them the product that caused an injury, as many years can elapsed between exposure and the onset of illness. Starting with the *Sindell* decision, some courts have permitted plaintiffs to recover a *pro rata* share of their full damages based on

---

[51] See Nance 2016, 3–4.
[52] See Stoffelmayr and Diamond 2000, 780–1.
[53] See Antkowiak 2005, 582–3.
[54] Fisher 2012, 840–1 (surveying cases).
[55] Picinali 2018, 556.
[56] Ibid.

the proportion of products sold by each company in the relevant market, in order to avoid letting companies with minority market positions escape all liability.[57] Thus, with respect to the question of factual causation of harm, the fixed threshold is replaced by a smoothly continuous scale. Some scholars have suggested that this model be generalized to a fully *continuous* burden.[58] Such burdens abandon thresholds entirely, and instead provide for a steady escalation in sanctions levels across the full range of case strength. Thus, a jury that was 25% confident in liability might award 25% of the damages, while a jury that was 75% confident might award 75%. The most commonly discussed continuous burden takes a linear form, but in recent work I have offered arguments in favor of a logistic transformation between confidence and penalties.[59]

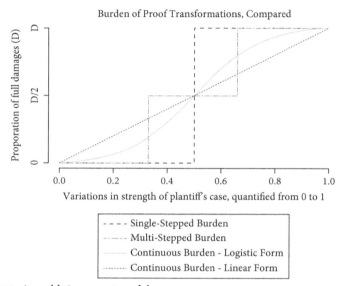

Figure 8.1 Posterior odds in correct model

Thus, the doctrinal landscape with respect to these issues is fairly clear. As set forth above, the single-stepped approach strongly dominates, and the few areas in which an alternative approach has been used have been clearly delineated. Moreover, although we have some reasons to think burden thresholds might behave fluidly as a psychological matter, courts have rarely encouraged this, except occasionally in the context of capital sentencing.

3.2 Normative Issues

Despite the doctrinal stability in this area, many scholars have contested which of these approaches function best at a normative level. In the space remaining, I will briefly review

---

[57] See, e.g., *Sindell v. Abott Labs*, 26 Cal 3d 588 (1980); *In re "Agent Orange" Prod. Liab. Litig.*, 597 F. Supp. 740 (E.D.N.Y. 1984).
[58] See generally, Spottswood 2021a (reviewing literature and advocating for continuous burdens).
[59] Ibid., Part III; Spottswood 2021b, Part IV.

some key arguments that have been made in defense of conventional, fluid-threshold, and continuous approaches.

One way of proceeding is to compare the *expected error costs* of differing burdens. Expected errors represent the average amount of error that we should expect to arise in a case based on the decision rule, the damages, and the factfinder's confidence level when deciding. For instance, assume that a judge finds that Alice's damages are $1,000 and believes there is a 75% chance that Bob caused her damages through tortious conduct. Following the preponderance rule, the judge would order Bob to pay the full $1,000. And because the judge believes there is a 25% chance that this decision would be wrong, his expected amount of error would be $250 (25% of $1,000).

Kaye compared expected error rates across several different types of cases, using both the conventional fixed-threshold civil burden and the alternative of a continuous burden that is linear in form. The latter rule instructs the jury to determine the size of an award by multiplying the found damages by the probability of liability, so that in the above hypothetical the defendant would pay $750 (75% of $1,000) instead of the full $1,000. Kaye showed that the linear rule generally produces an elevated expected error rate, as compared with the traditional rule, in cases that involve a single defendant. He also showed that, if we assume that the cost of an error in favor of either the plaintiff or the defendant is equally problematic, it will generally minimize expected errors to set the threshold between no damages and full damages at 50%, rather than at any other level.[60]

Others have accepted this argument, while arguing that the preponderance rule has other, offsetting defects. Orloff and Stedlinger argued that we should also aim to reduce the chances that individual parties would be subjected to particularly *large* errors.[61] In the example above, the traditional rule imposes an expected error of $250, and because Alice is receiving full compensation, Bob bears the entire risk. By contrast, the linear rule would impose an expected error of only $187.50 on Bob (representing a 25% chance that he has paid $750 to a person who should receive nothing) with Alice expecting to suffer an error of equal size (representing a 75% chance that she has been underpaid by $250). In general, the linear rule spreads the risk of error more evenly across parties, reducing the risk that any one party will suffer from a particularly large error.[62]

Another benefit of multi-stepped or continuous burdens is that, by reducing the chance that small variations in perceived case strength cause large variances in outcomes, they may also reduce the impact of various biases and other unfair influences on a litigation system.[63] Both common sense and economic theory[64] suggest that defendants will often wish to settle cases that should be easy wins for a plaintiff, and that plaintiffs will fail to bring, or voluntarily dismiss, cases if they think their chances of success at trial are low. This means that our systems will be biased towards trying fairly hard cases while settling easier ones.

This tendency can have problematic implications. The strength of the evidence is generally a strong predictor of how juries will decide cases[65], but other factors, such as differences

---

[60] Kaye 1982, 499, n. 42. Kaye proved a different result for cases in which multiple defendants might have harmed a plaintiff. Ibid., 503–8.

[61] Orloff and Stedinger 1983, 1165–8.

[62] See Spottswood 2021a, Part III (showing that the use of a logistic function, instead of a linear one, can further reduce the risk of large errors).

[63] Ibid., Part II.

[64] See Spottswood 2021b, Part II; Priest and Klein 1984, 3.

[65] Devine 2012, 122–3 (reviewing experimental and field evidence).

in advocacy quality,[66] in-group/out-group bias,[67] or the impacts of emotionally inflammatory evidence of little true relevance[68] might tip the scales when the evidence is closely balanced. Under the conventional rule, such influences can easily tip cases across the line from no damages to full damages, becoming the source of sizable errors and unfairness. Rules that involve steps of smaller size, or smooth transitions across the full range of confidence, will not eliminate these sorts of influences, but they will cabin the size of errors that they tend to cause. Thus, under a linear rule, the same movement from 45% to 55% confidence leads to a change of only 10% of the full damages, instead of an all-or-nothing change.

Finally, some have suggested that variable thresholds or continuous approaches can produce a more optimal pattern of deterrence of wrongdoing, as compared with what we see under the traditional rule. Consider cases in which proof will hinge on scientific evidence that makes the likelihood that a particular person was harmed a matter of purely probabilistic knowledge. A drug manufacturer might know that its drug will raise the rate of a certain form of cancer by just 50% above existing levels. If there is no known way to distinguish the other cases from the cancers that are caused by the drug, then any plaintiff could prove, at best, a 33% chance that the drug had caused their particular cancer. This, in turn, can lead to the troubling result that the law gives no deterrence against wrongs of this kind.[69] A continuous burden, by contrast, could give 33% damages to all the persons who ingested the drug and later contracted cancer, which would force the manufacturer to internalize the harm its product is causing to the public.[70]

Nor is this kind of underdeterrence unique to toxic torts. Many potential wrongdoers might be able to predict, at the time that they act, that they are unlikely to receive any punishment due to an anticipated deficit of evidence, and thus fail to be deterred by the threat of sanctions.[71] Some have argued that this type of underdeterrence may be particularly acute in the context of the criminal law, which tends to give quite severe sanctions with relatively low probability. This may arise if people value the first year of a prison sentence far more negatively than additional years far down the road, either due to habituation effects or a tendency to steeply discount future utility versus costs and benefits in the "here and now."[72] If that is right, then the system might deter far more crime by issuing modest sanctions at lower-than-traditional levels of proof[73]—an approach which can easily be realized using multi-stepped or continuous burden structures.[74] Thus, although much work remains to be done in this area, existing research tends to suggest that single-stepped burdens reduce expected errors. By contrast, other burdens may be advantaged in their ability to spread errors, reduce the impact of some problematic influences on verdicts, and produce more optimal levels of deterrence.

---

[66] See, e.g., Wheeler, Cartwright, Kagan, and Friedman 1987, 408–9, 440–1 (finding that better counsel provided a small but measurable advantage in State Supreme Court litigation).

[67] Spottswood 2011, 847–8.

[68] Grady, Reiser, Garcia, Koeu, and Scurich 2018, 513–14.

[69] See Shavell 1987, 115–17.

[70] Ibid.

[71] See Spottswood 2021a, Part I-A.

[72] Fisher 2012, 857–8.

[73] See Nagin 2013, 227–8.

[74] Due to space constraints, some interesting arguments concerning the ideal structure of proof burdens could not be discussed. See, e.g., Kaplow 2012; Picinali 2019.

4. Conclusion

Burdens of proof can be understood as functions that map a measure of case strength onto variations in the level of applicable sanctions. On the input side, scholars have hotly debated how case strength should be measured, and there may be differing "best" answers at the psychological, doctrinal, and normative levels of analysis. With respect to the best way of transforming case strength judgments into sanctioning levels, the picture is clearer at the levels of psychology and doctrine, but scholars have hotly debated which approach is most desirable at the normative level. This literature remains quite active, and I expect that the coming years will bring many new and interesting insights, both about how burdens currently operate and how they could be improved.

References

Allen, R. J. (1997). "Rationality, Algorithms and Juridical Proof: a Preliminary Inquiry," *International Journal of Evidence & Proof*, 1: 254–75.

Allen, R. J. and Pardo, M. S. (2019). "Relative Plausibility and its Critics," *International Journal of Evidence & Proof*, 23: 5–59.

Antkowiak, B. A. (2005). "Judicial Nullification," *Creighton Law Review*, 38: 545–610.

Cheng, E. K. (2013). "Reconceptualizing the Burden of Proof," *Yale Law Journal*, 122: 1254–79.

Clermont, K. M. (2018). "Common Sense on Standards of Proof," *Seton Hall Law Review*, 48: 1057–80.

Cohen, L. J. (1977). *The Probable and the Provable*. Oxford: Oxford University Press.

Cohen, N. B. (1985). "Confidence in Probability: Burdens of Persuasion in a World of Imperfect Knowledge," *New York University Law Review*, 60: 385–422.

Committee on Pattern Jury Instructions for the Seventh Circuit (2017). *Federal Civil Jury Instructions for the Seventh Circuit*. Available at http://www.ca7.uscourts.gov/pattern-jury-instructions/7th_cir_civil_instructions.pdf. (Accessed: March 23, 2021).

Devine, D. J. (2012). *Jury Decision Making: The State of the Science*. New York: New York University Press.

Fisher, T. (2012). "Conviction without Conviction," *Minnesota Law Review*, 96, 833–85.

Friedman, R. D. (1996). "Answering the Bayesioskeptical Challenge," *International Journal of Evidence & Proof*, 1: 276–91.

Friedman, R. D. (2018). "The Persistence of the Probabilistic Perspective," *Seton Hall Law Review*, 48: 1589–600.

Grady, R. H., Reiser, L., Garcia, R. J., Koeu, C., and Scurich, N. (2018). "Impact of Gruesome Photographic Evidence on Legal Decisions: A Meta-Analysis," *Psychiatry, Psychology and Law*, 25: 503–21.

Kagehiro, D. K. (1990). "Defining the Standard of Proof in Jury Instructions," *Psychological Science*, 1: 194–200.

Kaplan, J. (1968). "Decision Theory and the Fact-Finding Process," *Stanford Law Review*, 20: 1065–92.

Kaplow, L. (2012). "Burden of Proof," *Yale Law Journal*, 121, 738–859.

Kaye, D. H. (1982). "The Limits of the Preponderance of the Evidence Standard: Justifiably Naked Statistical Evidence and Multiple Causation," *American Bar Foundation Research Journal*, 7(2): 487–516.

Koehler, J. J., Chia, A., and Lindsey, S. (1995). "The Random Match Probability in DNA Evidence: Irrelevant and Prejudicial?" *Jurimetrics*, 35: 201–19.

Laudan, L. (2006). *Truth, Error, and Criminal Law: An Essay in Legal Epistemology*. New York: Cambridge University Press.

Lempert, R. O. (1986). "The New Evidence Scholarship: Analyzing the Process of Proof," *Boston University Law Review*, 66: 439–77.

Lipton, P. (2004). *Inference to the Best Explanation*. Second edition. New York: Routledge.

Nagin, D. S. (2013). "Deterrence in the Twenty-First Century," *Crime and Justice*, 42: 199–263.

Nance, D. A. (2016). *The Burdens of Proof: Discriminatory Power, Weight of Evidence, and Tenacity of Belief*. Cambridge: Cambridge University Press.

National Research Council (1996). *The Evaluation of Forensic DNA Evidence: An Update*. Washington, D.C.: National Academy Press.

Orloff, N. and Stedinger, J. (1983). "A Framework for Evaluating the Preponderance-of-the-Evidence Standard," *University of Pennsylvania Law Review*, 131(5): 1159–74.

Pardo, M. S. and Allen, R. J. (2008). "Juridical Proof and the Best Explanation," *Law and Philosophy*, 27: 223–68.

Pennington, N. and Hastie, R. (1991). "A Cognitive Theory of Juror Decision Making: The Story Model," *Cardozo Law Review*, 13: 519–57.

Picinali, F. (2018). "Do Theories of Punishment Necessarily Deliver a Binary System of Verdicts? An Exploratory Essay," *Criminal Law and Philosophy*, 12: 555–74.

Picinali, F. (2019). "Justice In-Between: The Decision-Theoretic Case for many Valued Criminal Verdicts." Available at http://dx.doi.org/10.2139/ssrn.3363666 (Accessed: March 12, 2021).

Posner, R. A. (1999). "An Economic Approach to the Law of Evidence," *Stanford Law Review*, 51: 1477–546.

Priest, G. L. and Klein, B. (1984). "The Selection of Disputes for Litigation," *Journal of Legal Studies*, 13: 1–55.

Shavell, S. (1987). *Economic Analysis of Accident Law*. Cambridge, MA: Harvard University Press.

Spottswood, M. (2011). "Live Hearings and Paper Trials," *Florida State University Law Review*, 38: 827–82.

Spottswood, M. (2013). "The Hidden Structure of Fact-Finding," *Case Western Reserve Law Review*, 64: 131–200.

Spottswood, M. (2016). "Unraveling the Conjunction Paradox," *Law, Probability and Risk*, 15: 259–96.

Spottswood, M. (2019). "On the Limitations of a Unitary Model of the Proof Process," *International Journal of Evidence & Proof*, 23: 75–81.

Spottswood, M. (forthcoming 2021a). "Continuous Burdens of Proof," *Nevada Law Journal*, 21: xx–xx.

Spottswood, M. (2021b). "Proof Discontinuities and Civil Settlements," *Theoretical Inquiries in Law*, 22(1): 201–62.

Stoffelmayr, E. and Diamond, S.S. (2000). "The Conflict between Precision and Flexibility in Explaining 'Beyond A Reasonable Doubt'," *Psychology, Public Policy, and Law*, 6: 769–87.

Sullivan, S. P. (2019). "A Likelihood Story: The Theory of Legal Fact-Finding," *Colorado Law Review*, 90: 1–66.

Tuzet, G. (2020). "Assessment Criteria or Standards of Proof? An Effort in Clarification," *Artificial Intelligence and Law*, 28, 91–109.

Wheeler, S., Cartwright, B., Kagan, R. A., and Friedman, L. M. (1987). "Do the 'Haves' come out Ahead? Winning and Losing in State Supreme Courts, 1870–1970," *Law & Society Review*, 21: 403–45.

9

Weight of Evidence

Dale A. Nance

1. Two Senses of Weight

1.1 The Keynesian Distinction

There are two distinct meanings of the phrase, "weight of evidence," in regard to adjudication or any other form of decision-making under conditions of uncertainty. One sense, the one more familiar to lawyers, is comparative as between the contentions of the opposing parties. One then speaks of the weight of evidence favoring one party, of the weight of evidence strongly favoring one party, of the weight of the evidence not favoring either party, and so forth. This sense of weight differentiates between competing hypotheses, and so may be called "Δ-weight." The obvious application is to think of the various burdens of persuasion, including various standards of proof, used in litigation as different requirements regarding which party must be favored by the Δ-weight of the evidence, and the extent to which the weight must favor that party in order for that party to prevail.

Another sense of the phrase is not comparative in this sense. Rather, it is comparative in the sense that one body of evidence with respect to contending hypotheses may (or may not) be weightier than another body of evidence with respect to the same contending hypotheses. This sense of weight was first systematically developed by John Maynard Keynes as an adjunct to a general theory of probability.[1] He observed:

> As the relevant evidence at our disposal increases, the magnitude of the probability of the argument may decrease or increase, according as the new knowledge strengthens the unfavourable or the favourable evidence; but something seems to have increased in either case—we have a more substantial basis upon which to rest our conclusion. I express this by saying that an accession of new evidence increases the weight of an argument. New evidence will sometimes decrease the probability of an argument, but it will always increase its "weight." . . . . The weight, to speak metaphorically, measures the sum of the favourable and unfavorable evidence, the probability measures the difference.[2]

This general summative sense of weight may be called "Σ-weight," which is the subject of this chapter.

---

[1] Keynes 1921, ch. 6.
[2] Keynes 1921, 71, 77.

Dale A. Nance, *Weight of Evidence* In: *Philosophical Foundations of Evidence Law*. Edited by: Christian Dahlman, Alex Stein, and Giovanni Tuzet, Oxford University Press. © Christian Dahlman, Alex Stein, and Giovanni Tuzet 2021.
DOI: 10.1093/oso/9780198859307.003.0010

1.2 The Nature and Importance of Σ-Weight

The general concept of Σ-weight has been the subject of commentary among philosophers and economists, not all of which can be fully reconciled.[3] Yet some things can be said with confidence.

First, the better view is that Σ-weight does *not* serve as a basis for comparing competing hypotheses. Specifically, if H_1 and H_2 are the only competing hypotheses (where H_2 might be just not-H_1), then the Δ-weight of given evidence is a measure of the degree to which that evidence favors H_1 as compared to H_2. But the Σ-weight of the evidence for H_1 is necessarily the same as the Σ-weight for H_2, because it is a measure of the total amount of evidence being considered with respect to the decision whether to endorse H_1 or H_2. In terms of Σ-weight, it makes no sense to suggest, for example, that one reason to select H_1 over H_2 is that the evidence for H_1 is "weightier" than the evidence for H_2.[4]

Second, the work of later theorists confirmed Keynes's intuitions about the value of the concept of Σ-weight. Specifically, an increase in Σ-weight reduces the *expected error*—or, alternatively, increases the *expected certainty*—associated with assessed probabilities.[5] Beyond that, insofar as one conceives of the standards of proof as probability thresholds—that the burden of persuasion requires that the probability of the truth of a party's claim exceed a certain threshold value (hereafter, P*)—and insofar as the threshold for the various standards of proof are determined in accord with conventional decision-theory,[6] then an increase in Σ-weight increases the expected utility of decision.[7] There is as yet no proof that these relations necessarily hold if epistemic warrant is not measurable in terms of probabilities.[8] But even then, they do make intuitive sense: the main point of seeking additional evidence before making a decision is that it will give one greater confidence in the decision one reaches, even if it does not change the decision made.

Third, increases in Σ-weight entail investigation and evaluation costs, and the inevitable trade-off between increased expected accuracy and increased decision-making costs generates a practical optimization problem, one that must be resolved—explicitly or implicitly—by every decision-maker or decision-making system. This does not mean that there is a quantitative measure of Σ-weight with an identifiable optimum value that must be attained, even for a given decision problem. As a practical matter, optimizing Σ-weight typically must be pursued more pragmatically and contextually, by posing the question whether the extant state of evidence is discernibly inferior to some identifiable and obtainable state of evidence. In principle, the practical optimization of Σ-weight has an *excusable preference* structure. That is, no matter how low Σ-weight is, it satisfies the requirement of practical optimization if there does not exist a cost-effective way of increasing it; conversely, no matter how high Σ-weight is, it fails that requirement if there is a cost-effective way to increase it.[9]

---

[3] Cohen, L.J. 1985; Davidson and Pargetter 1986; Runde 1990.

[4] Nance 2016, §3.2.

[5] Horwich 1982, 127–9; Hamer 2012, 144–5.

[6] Nance 2016, §2.2.

[7] Good 1966; Skyrms 1990, 87–106.

[8] The applicability of mathematical probabilities to the decision criteria of adjudication is much disputed. Suffice it here to say that there are numerous interpretations of probability ascriptions, and insofar as assessments of Δ-weight are to be compared with standards of proof, both understood in terms of probabilities, the relevant sense of probability is neither frequentist nor subjective, but rather epistemic, as indeed was Keynes's notion of probability. Nance 2016, §2.2.

[9] Nance 2016, §3.3.

These ideas entail that a given state of the evidence can be *deficient* in terms of Σ-weight, and the various theories of the role of Σ-weight in adjudication reflect varying answers to the questions of how to characterize and what to do about such a deficiency. Of course, a large portion of the effort of any legal system to optimize Σ-weight is provided by procedural norms and incentives regarding the investigation of litigated cases.[10] What follows focuses on the remaining role of evidence doctrines in addressing Σ-weight deficiencies. Much of the theorizing in this regard has focused on burdens of proof, but the doctrines potentially implicated by such deficiencies go well beyond that topic.

Before addressing this, however, it is important to note that a deficiency in Σ-weight can be articulated in terms of the idea that certain evidence is *missing*, and understanding the role of Σ-weight requires setting aside another consequence of the idea of missing evidence. Sometimes, the *explanation* of the fact that specific evidence is missing—as contrasted with the simple fact that the evidence is missing—can reflect on the strength of a party's case, i.e., on Δ-weight, by way of an inference to a motive for concealment, destruction, or withholding of evidence. This kind of situation can affect the probability that a party's case is true, a fact that has resulted in the use of "adverse inferences," sometimes supported by jury instructions.[11] However, this does not address fully or directly the problem of deficiencies in Σ-weight. Sometimes evidence is missing under circumstances as to which no such adverse inference is appropriate, as when the missing evidence is equally available to all parties. And even when the circumstances do permit such an adverse inference, its use may not be the optimal way to address the deficiency. Obtaining the missing evidence for the factfinder's use is almost invariably superior, from an epistemic perspective, to the factfinder's trying to infer its content from the often ambiguous circumstances surrounding the deficiency.[12] Accordingly, most of the theories discussed later, explicitly or implicitly, set to one side the "adverse inference" issue. A related point concerns "gaps" in the evidence. Such gaps can undermine the plausibility of a party's theory of the case, thus affecting Δ-weight, even if the Σ-weight of the evidence has been practically optimized. On the other hand, optimizing Σ-weight can facilitate assessment of the significance of such gaps.[13]

1.3 Jonathan Cohen's Pioneering Work

An impressive, early effort to incorporate Σ-weight into legal analysis was that of Cohen.[14] He analogized the development of evidence in adjudication to the conducting of scientific experiments in the testing of a hypothesis. He imagined that a complete set of tests could be identified and prioritized, so that the most important tests of a legal (or scientific) hypothesis could be explored first, followed by tests of lower importance, until in principle the field of n plausible tests is exhausted. Although Cohen was never entirely clear about how to constitute a single test or about how this prioritization of tests is to be done, especially in the adjudicative context, one can at least illustrate it by imagining a series of n witnesses to an event, each standing at a different distance from it, so that errors in observation are more

---

[10] Nance 2016, 186–94.
[11] Kaye 1986; Friedman 1997a.
[12] Nance 2010.
[13] Nance 2016, 234–6.
[14] Cohen, L.J. 1977.

likely as the distance increases, and each asserting facts compatible with only one party's theory of the case. Then the most important test to be conducted would be to obtain the closest witness's testimony, and determine which side if supports, if either, after taking into account any appropriate credibility challenges. Then one could move on to the next witness, and so on, until the witnesses are exhausted.

Cohen then integrates this treatment of Σ-weight with that of the standards of proof, offering his reconstruction of those standards as a way to avoid certain seeming paradoxes of interpreting standards of proof as threshold probability criteria, an interpretation that Cohen rejects. For Cohen, proof beyond reasonable doubt in a criminal case requires that Σ-weight be maximized by conducting all n tests and that the prosecution's theory of the case survive every test. With regard to civil cases, the preponderance of the evidence favors one party if that party's theory of the case survives the first m tests (not in temporal order, but rather in order of importance, with $m \leq n$), but the mth test falsifies the opponent's theory of the case. The civil parties determine how many and which of the tests to conduct, and there is no requirement in civil cases analogous to optimization of weight required in criminal cases. Thus, Cohen uses Σ-weight to construct a measure of Δ-weight based on the *number* of ordered tests each competing hypothesis survives.

Cohen's theory certainly renewed legal interest in informal reasoning and inductive logic.[15] But his theory has not gained wide acceptance for at least three reasons: (1) as guidance for factfinders, there are enormous difficulties in operationalizing his theory, both in terms of identifying the tests and in specifying what exactly it means to survive such a test; (2) as a description of prevailing practice, his theory produces implications seriously at odds with that practice; and (3) as prescription, his theory generates unacceptable consequences. The first reason should be apparent from the description given earlier.[16] The other two reasons are illustrated by Cohen's argument that his theory entails that a criminal case must be dismissed because of the loss of an "important" witness without the fault of either party, regardless of how likely guilt may be.[17] Nevertheless, his work stimulated further attempts to account for the role of Σ-weight in adjudication.

2. Modern Theories of Σ-Weight

2.1 A Useful Categorization

Modern theories addressing Σ-weight can be grouped in the following ways. First, under some "holistic" theories, like Cohen's, Σ-weight is taken as something that must be addressed as a (more or less distinguishable) part of a single judgment about whether the evidence satisfies the applicable standard of proof—such as, proof by a preponderance of the evidence, proof by clear and convincing evidence, or proof beyond a reasonable doubt. These theories necessarily contemplate that the determination whether a deficiency in Σ-weight is acceptable must be made by the factfinder in the course of applying such standards. Other theories ("dualist, factfinder-focused" theories) take Σ-weight as something

---

[15] Nance 2016, §3.4.

[16] For detail, see Nance 2016, 137–40.

[17] Cohen, L.J. 1986, 642. For descriptive and prescriptive criticism of this conclusion, see Nance 2016, 129–32.

that must be assessed by the factfinder but as a judgment that is meaningfully separate from the question whether the conventional standard of proof has been met by the burdened party. These theories take the factfinder to be making two distinct decisions: whether the standard of proof has been satisfied (a matter of Δ-weight) and whether the Σ-weight supporting that judgment is adequate. Finally, some theories ("dualist, policy-maker focused" theories) take the practical optimization of Σ-weight to be a policy issue beyond the scope of a factfinder's task. That is, the factfinder's role is exhausted by determining whether the standard of proof has been satisfied in favor of the burdened party, leaving to judges and legislatures the question of whether Σ-weight has been practically optimized.

This categorization makes the role of the factfinder central. That role is most conspicuously isolated in the adversarial jury trial, in the context of which many of the modern theories of Σ-weight have been developed. But the analysis remains enlightening for adjudicative systems that combine in a single juridical actor the factfinding function with other functions, such as the Anglo-American bench trial or European quasi-inquisitorial adjudications that allow a greater role to the judge in developing evidence for the case. In all such systems, one can distinguish between the factfinding role—the analysis of the evidence presented and application of the pertinent burden of persuasion—and the other roles exercised by judicial actors, including the monitoring of pre-trial and trial processes, the collection and introduction of evidence, and the articulation of legal rules, including the pertinent burden of persuasion.

2.2 Holistic Theories

An important holistic theory is presented by Susan Haack. For Haack, a judgment of epistemic warrant for accepting a proposition, including an adjudicative factual claim, involves three interrelated factors: "supportiveness," that is, how strong the connection is between the evidence and the hypothesis; "independent security," that is, how solid the evidence itself is; and "comprehensiveness," that is, how much of the relevant evidence the evidence actually considered includes.[18] The first two of these are easily understood as relating to Δ-weight: they determine the extent to which the evidence favors one hypothesis over a competing hypothesis. But the last of these factors embraces Σ-weight, as illustrated by the fact, which Haack emphasizes, that an increase in comprehensiveness of the evidence does not necessarily increase the epistemic warrant for a given hypothesis. It may undermine that warrant, because the content of the augmented evidence may favor a competing hypothesis. Haack thus describes the third factor as "separate" in an important way, acknowledging that "the role of the comprehensiveness clause is most apparent negatively, when one judges someone unjustified or little justified in a belief because of their failure to take account of some relevant evidence."[19] Nevertheless, she takes all three factors as integral components of the factfinder's holistic judgment of epistemic warrant that is involved in determining whether or not the standard of proof is met.[20]

A similar phenomenon can be seen in the theory of Hock Lai Ho.[21] Unlike Haack, Ho is committed to the idea that the factfinder's verdict is an expression of evidence-warranted

---

[18] Haack 1993, 81–9.
[19] Haack 1993, 87.
[20] Haack 2014, 16–19, 47–64.
[21] Ho 2008.

categorical (albeit contextualized) belief, rather than an expression of evidence-warranted *degree of* belief. For a proposition, *p*, the only available categorical beliefs are to believe *p*, to believe not-*p*, and to suspend belief regarding *p*. But like Haack, Ho in one sense appreciates the distinct role of Σ-weight, for he distinguishes between the optimal "distribution of caution" and the necessary "degree of caution" exercised in arriving at a categorical belief.[22] The former implicates Δ-weight, while the latter implicates Σ-weight. These two kinds of caution affect the factfinder's determination of categorical belief in a specific way. For Ho, to believe an asserted *p*, which is required for a positive verdict, is:

>   (i) to choose *p* over some other propositions; it is to reject or dismiss the proposition(s) that compete with *p* for truth-regulated acceptance, and
>   (ii) to be sufficiently confident that *p*.[23]

Notice that (ii) does *not* say, "to be sufficiently confident in choosing between *p* and its competitor(s)." Suppose, in particular, the evidence is such that condition (i) is satisfied—because the appropriate criterion generated by a proper distribution of caution is met, but condition (ii) is not met—because the appropriate criterion of the degree of caution (i.e., evidential completeness) is not met. Because (i) is satisfied, the factfinder cannot believe not-*p*, but because (ii) is not satisfied, the factfinder cannot believe *p*. Among the three possibilities for categorical belief, this situation the only one left is to "suspend belief." Because condition (ii) is not satisfied, a verdict against the party with the burden of establishing *p* is required.

In sharp contrast, a brief suggestion by RichardFriedman suggests how a quantified Σ-weight deficiency might be taken into account in the standard of proof itself, thus accommodating the use of probability as a measure of epistemic warrant.[24] Suppose the standard decision-theoretic, probability-threshold criterion is expressed as: decide for the plaintiff if and only if the probability of the claim, given the evidence, exceeds P*. Then Friedman's suggested criterion is: decide for the plaintiff if and only if the probability of the claim, given the evidence, exceeds P*/Q, where Q ranges from 0 to 1 and measures the degree of completeness of the evidence. This suggestion presupposes that one can measure the degree of evidential completeness, which is just another way of articulating the idea of Σ-weight. This is quite controversial in the general case.[25] And even when practical measures are possible, the discounting involved in Friedman's proposal means that the deficiency in Σ-weight inevitably counts against the party bearing the burden of persuasion. This result, which is also inherent in the theories of Haack and Ho, cannot arise from purely epistemic considerations, as the want of evidence (by assumption) does not tell in favor of either party.

The central problem with such holistic theories, when applied to adjudication, is their decisional monism: they fail to recognize that deficiencies in Δ-weight and deficiencies in Σ-weight present different problems, as to which distinct decisions are required. One decision is whether the Δ-weight of the extant evidence (taking account of any applicable adverse inferences or evidentiary gaps) is sufficient to warrant a positive finding, in light of

---

[22] Ho 2008, 185–233.
[23] Ho 2008, 143.
[24] Friedman 1997b, 279.
[25] Nance 2016, §3.5.

the applicable standard of proof. The other is whether the Σ-weight is sufficient to warrant *making a decision* on the present state of the evidence. Analytically, the second of these decisions takes priority; satisfying it is a pre-condition for making the first decision.[26] Collapsing these two decisions into one distorts the relevant considerations.[27] In particular, it obscures the possibility of deciding that the party *not* bearing the burden of persuasion is best situated to eliminate the existing Σ-weight deficiency. The confusion is an understandable consequence of modeling adjudicative factfinding too closely on ordinary practical decision-making. In the latter context, the two tasks may not be consciously differentiated, though they remain analytically distinct. They often operate through repeated iterations of evidence search and tentative decision-making until a final decision is made. In such contexts, it is plausible to characterize the decision-maker's epistemic warrant for a decision as embracing both tasks, and there is often no issue about which party is in the better position to cure the deficiency in Σ-weight, because there is only one "party" involved. In adjudicative contexts, roles are more complex and differentiated. For example, a jury cannot suspend judgment and insist that additional evidence be presented before the jury decides.

A related theoretical confusion that arises from not distinguishing between the two decisions is what it seems to suggest about the ability to interpret standards of proof in terms of probability thresholds. One recurring argument is that a low such probability for hypothesis H entails a high probability for not-H, because of the complementation rule for probabilities: $P(H) + P(\text{not-}H) = 1$. Yet, the epistemic warrant for H and that for not-H can *both* be low. Therefore, epistemic warrant—the subject of the standards of proof—does not follow the rules of mathematical probabilities.[28] The explanation that one encounters for the second premise in this argument is that situations arise in which there is too little evidence to warrant accepting either H or not-H, that is, a situation of inadequate Σ-weight. This argument, however, equivocates about what it means to accept H. The meaning depends on the alternative being considered. It may be that there is too little evidence in such situations to warrant accepting H, when the alternative is postponing choice until additional investigation can occur. In that case, it would be more illuminating to say that there is too little evidence *to make the choice* between H and not-H. But that is distinct from the question of one's epistemic warrant for accepting H in a context, such as rendering a verdict in adjudication, where the option of seeking additional evidence has been taken off the table. At that point, the only options are H and not-H; the want of Σ-weight is no longer pertinent, so the indicated argument against a probabilistic interpretation does not work.[29]

To be sure, an appropriate holistic theory can address a special kind of Σ-weight deficiency, one that arises not from the failure to present evidence for the factfinder's consideration, but rather from the failure of the factfinder to consider all the evidence that is presented to it. A failure by the factfinder even to consider the testimony of a witness who has testified would, in most contexts, generate a verdict that was unjustified. The holism of Haack or Ho serves to remind us of the usefulness of instructions to the factfinder to avoid such errors. In contrast, a formulation like that of Friedman's, if it were intended to address this special

[26] Nance 2016, §3.2.
[27] Nance 2016, §§3.6, 5.3.
[28] Stein 2011, 241–2; Haack 2014, 61–2.
[29] Nance 2016, 166–7. The same point applies if one measures epistemic warrant in terms of *belief functions*, measures that may not satisfy the complementation rule, because it is possible that $\text{Bel}(H) + \text{Bel}(\text{not-}H) < 1$. Nance 2019.

kind of Σ-weight deficiency (which is quite unlikely), would produce an arbitrary result. It would tell the factfinder that the appropriate way to respond to the factfinder's own negligence in ignoring important evidence presented to it is to inflate the threshold probability that the burdened party must exceed. In any event, the focus in the following discussion is on the arguably more important source of Σ-weight deficiencies, with which Friedman clearly was concerned: the failure, by those with the responsibility to do so, to develop and present to the factfinder evidence that could rationally affect the decision about Δ-weight.

2.3 Dualist, Factfinder-Focused Theories

A number of theories have perceived the distinct decision problems involved but have nonetheless allocated both decisions to the factfinder. These theories have invoked the concept of *resilience* or *tenacity* of belief. The core idea of these theories is that, even if greater Σ-weight does not change a factfinder's tentative decision on liability, it does solidify the probability on which it is made, making the probability and thus the decision more resistant to change by the potential addition of evidence.[30] According to these theories, the factfinder must take this effect into account.

Illustrative is Neil Cohen's confidence interval theory for burdens of persuasion.[31] He argues that it is not enough for the factfinder to estimate the probability that a claim is true and to compare that estimate with a quantitatively understood standard of proof, as in standard probability threshold models. Such models can take account of the risk of *factual* error, for example, a verdict for the plaintiff when the defendant in truth is not liable. Cohen argues, however, that there is another problem: the risk of *probability* error, for example, that the factfinder will estimate the probability to be higher than the threshold when, in truth, that probability is lower than the threshold. And this distinct risk must be taken into account. Accordingly, one must build into the factfinder's determination an additional, separate criterion designed to address this risk of probability error. For Cohen, the second requirement is that the factfinder must have "a certain level of confidence that the true probability exceeds" the indicated threshold.[32] Whether this second criterion is satisfied can be affected by augmenting Σ-weight, which narrows the confidence interval for the probability estimate. How narrow the confidence interval needs to be depends on what risk of probability error can be accepted. Cohen considers various candidates for optimizing this distinct risk of probability error, tentatively favoring, for civil cases, one that equates the risk of probability error favoring plaintiff with the risk of probability error favoring defendant. Thus, a factfinder that estimates the probability of a claim at a figure that exceeds the stated threshold must still withhold a positive verdict if the risk of probability error in favor of the burdened party exceeds the risk of probability error in favor of the opponent.

While Cohen focused primarily on civil cases, a similar idea is suggested for criminal cases by Davidson and Pargetter.[33] They pose a familiar problem of so-called naked

---

[30] Logue 1995, §§2.4, 4.4.
[31] Cohen, N. 1985.
[32] Cohen, N. 1985, 399. To give meaning to the idea that the assessed probability may diverge from the "true" probability, Cohen invokes the difference between the probability actually assessed by the factfinder under the evidence presented and the probability that the factfinder *would* assess if it were presented the totality of available (and admissible) evidence (or, in other words, if the Σ-weight were practically optimized). Cohen, N. 1987, 85.
[33] Davidson and Pargetter 1987.

statistical evidence and endorse the intuition that even a very small statistical probability that a randomly selected person is innocent will not suffice for criminal conviction of that person under the "beyond a reasonable doubt" standard. What is required to satisfy the burden is additional individuating evidence, but what kind of individuating evidence will suffice, and how much? To answer this kind of question, they suggest that an explicit Σ-weight requirement be coupled with the requirement of a sufficiently high probability of guilt. Specifically, they suggest a requirement of resilience in the probability determination. This resilience depends on the likelihood that some fact may be true that would, if true, change the assessed probability of guilt. It also depends on how much it will change that probability if that fact is true. It does not matter, however, how likely it is that such a possible fact can be shown by obtainable evidence. The requirement thus seems to be indifferent to the practical optimization of Σ-weight. Instead, they would require an acceptable degree of resilience. Yet, they are noncommittal when it comes to the question of how high resilience must be in order to be acceptable.

There are two related problems with these theories. First, they fail to grasp the excusable preference structure of the requirement that Σ-weight be practically optimized. By analogy to the assessment of Δ-weight, they assume that the factfinder is required to assesses Σ-weight against a standard of adequacy, some minimum that does not depend on the availability of additional evidence. The notions of confidence intervals and resilience seem to permit that kind of test, provided that a suitable criterion of adequate confidence or resilience can be determined and meaningfully communicated to (or intuited by) the factfinder. In the end, however, no such criterion can be identified that differs from that degree of confidence or resilience that results from the practical optimization of Σ-weight. A probability resulting from practically optimized Σ-weight but with a relatively wide confidence interval (or low resilience) is a suitable basis for decision, whereas a probability of relatively narrow confidence interval (or high resilience) that results from Σ-weight that can yet be practically increased is not.[34] In the end, whatever value there is in the notion of adequate confidence or resilience is better captured by the notion of practical optimization.[35]

The second problem is that, unlike the assessment of Δ-weight, the practical optimization of Σ-weight in ordinary decision-making involves active choice by the decision-maker. The decision-maker must *select* the level of the Σ-weight of the evidence as a condition on making a decision about Δ-weight, and this often means doing something, conducting further investigation if the Σ-weight is deficient.[36] Yet, factfinders acting as such do not make such active choices. This is most conspicuous in an adversarial jury trial, where the factfinding function is isolated and assigned to the jury, which has no control over the investigation of the case. They must decide for one side or the other based on the evidence that has been presented, making them poor institutional managers of Σ-weight.[37]

---

[34] Moreover, while an increase in Σ-weight necessarily increases expected certainty, it does not necessarily increase the resilience of the resulting probability estimate; the resulting probability may actually be *less* stable. Hamer, 2012.

[35] Nance 2016, §§5.1, 5.2.

[36] Richard Swinburne distinguishes between *synchronic* justification of beliefs—justification at a given time and with given evidence—and *diachronic* justification of beliefs—synchronic justification that results from, and is conditioned on, adequate investigation. He argues that one's beliefs at a given time and on given evidence cannot be *chosen*, whereas the extent of the investigation that informs one's beliefs can be. Swinburne 2001, 3, 23–4.

[37] Nance 2016, §4.2.

2.4   Dualist, Policy-Maker Focused Theories

Recognizing that selecting an appropriate level of Σ-weight is entirely distinct from the assessment of Δ-weight and involves important judgments of public policy, two scholars see the regulation of Σ-weight as a task for policy-makers—legislatures and judges.[38] This perspective allows a broadening of focus beyond burden of proof rules to include practices and doctrines concerning procedure, discovery, and admissibility—rules that regulate Σ-weight but are obviously not applied by the factfinder. The theories presented by Alex Stein and Dale Nance both emphasize this feature, but they also accept that, after all reasonable efforts to enhance accuracy have been taken, real-world adjudication inevitably suffers from the presence of a residual uncertainty, at which point risk-allocation is unavoidable.[39] Their theories differ, however, in the role of Σ-weight in the latter of these two stages.

Stein argues that risk-allocation is not limited to the norms that constitute the burden of persuasion, but animates a variety of other rules. Stein also argues that the risk-allocation of burdens of proof sometimes involve not just criteria of Δ-weight, but also criteria of adequate Σ-weight. These criteria emerge from judgments of political morality that are necessary to limit what would otherwise be an overly demanding "principle of maximal individualization" (PMI), which he describes as requiring that factfinders have and consider all case-specific evidence pertaining to the case (a quantitative weight requirement) and that they make no finding without subjecting the evidence to maximal individual testing (a qualitative weight requirement).[40] In regard to the collective impact of both quantitative and qualitative requirements, he explains:

> The principle of maximal individualization performs two functions. Like the best evidence principle, it aims at securing that factfinders base their decisions on the best individualized evidence that the parties can reasonably be expected to produce. This function of the maximal individualization principle is epistemic. This principle, however, also allocates the risk of error—an altogether separate and markedly non-epistemic function that the best evidence principle does not perform.[41]

Thus, Stein argues that PMI in its epistemic branch has an excusable preference structure, but PMI in its supra-epistemic branch does not. The latter branch helps to allocate the risk of error between the parties. The preferential, epistemic regulation of Σ-weight does, of course, involve its own judgments of political morality, including but not limited to the questions of how much accuracy is affordable and of which party should bear the cost of curing a Σ-weight deficiency once identified.[42] But for Stein, the judgment determining whether or not to accept the Σ-weight as adequate is sometimes part of risk-allocation between the parties: additional evidence is required, even if it cannot be produced, when doing so shifts the risk of error in a way that is morally required.

On what grounds does Stein think there is or should be such a supra-epistemic, risk-allocating function in the law's norms regarding Σ-weight? His answer to the descriptive

---

[38]   Stein 2005, chs. 5–7; Nance 2016, ch. 4.
[39]   Stein 2005, 34–5; Nance 2016, §3.8.
[40]   Stein 2005, 64, 72, 100.
[41]   Stein 2005, 40.
[42]   Nance 2016, §§3.3, 4.3.

question is, essentially, that one must infer it from things like the law's rejection of civil or criminal liability based on naked statistical evidence even when that is all the evidence that the parties can reasonably produce.[43] There are, of course, other ways to explain this supposed reluctance.[44] But Stein argues that such reluctance is based on norms of rational inference that invoke a component of PMI not subject to an excusable preference structure. Stein argues from the premise that there is a notion of the "ideal" or "complete" evidence package that is, or at least can be, more demanding than the evidence package that is the best that the parties are able to adduce. And in some contexts, specifically criminal cases, this notion should play a critical role because of the moral judgment that criminal defendants must be specially protected from any "evidentially confirmed" risk of erroneous conviction.[45] Here he reproduces Jonathan Cohen's conclusion about the innocently missing witness in a criminal case:

> Thus, if a potentially important piece of evidence is unavailable and its contents are unknown, the defendant's conviction on whatever evidence is available would never satisfy the demands of PMI .... For that reason alone, the defendant is entitled to an acquittal.[46]

Like that of Cohen, this claim is subject to a serious *reductio*. What acceptable principle of political morality would distinguish between two strong cases, otherwise identical, on the basis of the fact that a potentially important witness has died (or piece of material evidence has disappeared) accidentally in one case, whereas he or she (or it) never existed in the other? Both cases involve a counterfactual situation that could, if somehow realized, yield important information. What makes one counterfactual problematic but not the other? And if both are unacceptable, then no case will ever satisfy the requirement, because one can always imagine additional evidence that would, if taken into account, reduce uncertainty about the case and possibly affect the verdict. Stein's application illustrates the considerable difficulties in identifying an implementable stopping point between practically optimized Σ-weight, on the one hand, and certainty about the facts, on the other.[47]

In contrast, the theory offered by Nance does not rely on risk-allocation in determining the level of Σ-weight upon which a verdict may be based.[48] He understands risk-allocation as properly implicated primarily, if not entirely, in the setting of an appropriate burden of persuasion, the standard of proof against which Δ-weight is compared. The practical optimization of Σ-weight remains within what Stein calls the epistemic domain, where the best evidence principle controls and where the legal system is called upon to make a judgment whether the gains in expected accuracy from steps to augment Σ-weight are worth the anticipated costs. This, once again, is a kind of judgment of political morality, and is appropriately committed to policy-making institutional players, like judges and legislatures. But it is not one that must or should involve the intentional allocation of the risk of error. Rather, it can and should involve a judgment about reducing the aggregate risk of error, regardless

---

[43] Stein 2005, ch. 3.
[44] Nance 2016, §3.1.
[45] Stein 2005, 173.
[46] Stein 2005, 199.
[47] Nance 2007, 1138–54.
[48] Nance 2016.

of which party may be helped by doing so. Nance describes the relationship between these risk management tasks in the following way.

> The costs involved in these two steps of a decision process are different in kind. Evidence-search costs are part of litigation costs, whereas the costs that can be minimized by the proper selection of a standard of proof are the costs that follow from mistaken decisions, so-called error costs .... The former "input" costs are sunk costs by the time a verdict is required, whereas the latter "output" costs are affected by the verdict selection. When we think about the question of how much accuracy we can afford from our legal system, we are primarily thinking about the input costs. In this context, it makes sense to say that we "purchase" accuracy, or at least its expectation, with expenditure on the collection and analysis of evidence. In contrast, we do not "expend" output costs so much as we unavoidably incur them.[49]

Thus, Σ-weight management serves what are procedural policy goals, balancing accuracy enhancement against litigation cost containment. Only the residual risks of error need to be allocated between the parties, and this is the role of tests of Δ-weight, in the form of burdens of persuasion.

As compared to Nance's theory, Stein's approach to Σ-weight regulation understands it as pursuing more substantive policy goals, akin to the allocation of the risk of error by burdens of persuasion. Which theory is more successful can only be determined by careful examination of their application to particular doctrines. The question is whether a given doctrine that enforces an augmentation of Σ-weight is adequately explained or justified by the invocation of an epistemic best evidence principle or, alternatively, whether explanation or justification requires recourse to the notion of context-specific skewing of the risk of error away from that which is provided by the applicable standard of proof.[50]

To illustrate the difference, consider their competing explanations of a common-law rule to the effect that an uncorroborated, extra-judicial confession by the defendant is not enough to support a criminal conviction; it must be accompanied by corroborating evidence, usually evidence distinct from the confession and its circumstances.[51] There are reasons to be suspicious of such a confession, but then there are reasons to be suspicious of many, if not most items of evidence presented in an adversarial context. What, then, explains the need for such a distinct rule in addition to the usual rules regulating the burden of proof?

Unlike the bulk of admissibility rules, which generally apply to evidence offered by either party, such corroboration rules appear to be the best kind of support for Stein's theory in that they consistently skew decisions in favor of the defense. For Stein, PMI requires the prosecution to present a "credible piece of case-specific evidence" that "removes the

---

[49] Nance 2016, 179–80.

[50] Stein's arguments are "predominantly normative," (Stein 2005, 138), while Nance's are "interpretive" (Nance 2016, 11–12). Nance would argue that the role of the decision-maker in managing Σ-weight is not to focus on allocating risk of error, but rather on the question whether the collective "stakes" involved warrant augmentation of Σ-weight, reducing (rather than allocating) risk (Nance 2016, 135–7). It is possible that some decision-makers *in fact* make such choices with an eye to distributing risk in a preferred manner, in which case regulating such allocations may seem unavoidable. Yet, one such regulation could be simply to discourage risk-allocation in this context.

[51] Wigmore 1978, §§2070–4.

suspicion-throwing generalization from the case."[52] The reference is to generalizations such as: "sometimes people confess falsely under the pressure of interrogation," or "sometimes people falsely confess for notoriety." As to the question of which such suspicions must be taken seriously enough to be removed, presumably Stein would say only those that are plausible. Even so, he does not explain just what it takes to "remove" each such suspicion, or why one should accept the increased risk of false acquittals inherent in such a requirement, as compared to the application of the usual standard of proof for that kind of case.

In contrast, for Nance the potential explanations of a confession consistent with innocence are never truly "removed"; their plausibility can only be reduced. Why then have such a corroboration condition on a positive verdict? Because such an augmentation of Σ-weight, and associated expected certainty, is very likely to be practically feasible. One cannot say in advance what that additional evidence is likely to be, but one can be extremely confident that the prosecution can find some, at reasonable cost, if the effort is made. There are very few crimes for which the only evidence available to present is the confession itself. The rule thus deters prosecutorial laziness without causing a non-trivial number of erroneous acquittals, while at the same time preventing a non-trivial number of erroneous convictions. It may also prevent erroneous acquittals that could arise in the absence of the corroborating evidence because of factfinder skepticism toward naked confessions. With this reduction in aggregate error of both kinds, it is unnecessary to find justification for the rule by reference to skewing the standard of proof in favor of defendants.[53]

3. Conclusion

The exploration of the role of Σ-weight in adjudication is an important development in the philosophy of adjudication. Understanding that role has been slowed by a failure to appreciate differences between formal adjudication and other decision-making contexts. In particular, formal adjudication often separates roles in a way that other decision-making does not. Thus, ordinary decision-making tasks often involve complex consideration, by one person or group, of both the strength of existing evidence (an assessment) and the possible need to investigate further before making a decision (a choice). In many litigation systems, however, the task of developing evidence for consideration is assigned to one set of institutional actors, whereas the task of assessing the assembled evidence is committed to another. In that case, assuring an optimal development of the evidence must be largely committed to those who regulate the conduct of the litigation—legislatures and judges. These policy-makers must, and by their decisions do, determine the value the legal system places on accuracy of decision, which may vary according to the kind of litigation involved or even from case to case. Whether, in the regulation of Σ-weight, they should or do go beyond such concerns of procedural policy—accuracy enhancement, litigation cost-containment—to express preferences among litigants or classes thereof, in modification of what is specified by the usual standards of proof, are challenging questions.

---

[52] Stein 2005, 208.
[53] Nance 2016, 214–15.

References

Cohen, L. J. (1977). *The Probable and the Provable*. Oxford: Oxford University Press.

Cohen, L. J. (1985). "Twelve Questions about Keynes' Concept of Weight," *British Journal for the Philosophy of Science*, 37: 263–78.

Cohen, L. J. (1986). "The Role of Evidential Weight in Criminal Proof," *Boston University Law Review*, 66: 635–49.

Cohen, N. (1985). "Confidence in Probability: Burdens of Persuasion in a World of Imperfect Knowledge," *New York University Law Review*, 60: 385–422.

Cohen, N. (1987). "Conceptualizing Proof and Calculating Probabilities: A Response to Professor Kaye," *Cornell Law Review*, 73: 78–95.

Davidson, B. and Pargetter, R. (1986). "Weight," *Philosophical Studies*, 49: 219–30.

Davidson, B. and Pargetter, R. (1987). "Guilt Beyond Reasonable Doubt," *Australasian Journal of Philosophy*, 65: 182–7.

Friedman, R. (1997a). "Dealing with Evidentiary Deficiency," *Cardozo Law Review*, 18: 1961–86.

Friedman, R. (1997b). "Answering the Bayesioskeptical Challenge," *International Journal of Evidence & Proof*, 1: 276–91.

Good, I. J. (1966.) "On the Principle of Total Evidence," *British Journal for the Philosophy of Science*, 17: 319–21.

Haack, S. (1993). *Evidence and Inquiry*. Oxford: Blackwell.

Haack, S. (2014). *Evidence Matters: Science, Proof, and Truth in the Law*. New York: Cambridge University Press.

Hamer, D. (2012). "Probability, Anti-Resilience, and the Weight of Expectation," *Law, Probability & Risk*, 11: 135–58.

Ho, H. L. (2008). *A Philosophy of Evidence Law*. Oxford: Oxford University Press.

Horwich, P. (1982). *Probability and Evidence*. Cambridge: Cambridge University Press.

Kaye, D. (1986). "Do we need a Calculus of Weight to Understand Proof Beyond Reasonable Doubt?" *Boston University Law Review*, 66: 657–72.

Keynes, J. M. (1921). *A Treatise on Probability*. London: MacMillan.

Logue, J. (1995). *Projective Probability*. Oxford: Oxford University Press.

Nance, D. (2007). "Allocating the Risk of Error: Its Role in the Theory of Evidence Law," *Legal Theory*, 13: 129–64.

Nance, D. (2010). "Adverse Inferences about Adverse Inferences: Restructuring Juridical Roles for Responding to Evidence Tampering by Parties to Litigation," *Boston University Law Review* 90: 1089–46.

Nance, D. (2016). *The Burdens of Proof: Discriminatory Power, Weight of Evidence, and Tenacity of Belief*. Cambridge: Cambridge University Press.

Nance, D. (2019). "Belief Functions and Burdens of Proof," *Law, Probability & Risk*, 18: 53–76.

Runde, J. (1990). "Keynesian Uncertainty and the Weight of Arguments," *Economics and Philosophy*, 6: 275–92.

Skyrms, B. (1990). *The Dynamics of Rational Deliberation*. Cambridge, MA: Harvard University Press.

Stein, A. (2005). *Foundations of Evidence Law*. Oxford: Oxford University Press.

Stein, A. (2011). "The Flawed Probabilistic Foundations of Law and Economics," *Northwestern University Law Review*, 105: 199–260.

Swinburne, R. (2001). *Epistemic Justification*. Oxford: Oxford University Press.

Wigmore, J. H. (1978). *Evidence in Trials at Common Law* (Vol. 7; Chadbourn rev.). Boston: Little, Brown and Company.

10

Cost-Benefit Analysis of Evidence Law and Factfinding

*Talia Fisher**

1. Introduction

Utility considerations have been central to legal factfinding, at least since the days of Jeremy Bentham, the founding father of utilitarianism and a prominent evidence law theorist. A direct line can be drawn from Bentham's "principle of utility" to cost-benefit analysis (CBA)[1] so it would seem only natural that the realms of evidence law and judicial factfinding would harbor this type of reasoning.[2] However, when legal scholarship began to incorporate economic reasoning and to address issues from a CBA perspective, evidence law and the practice of judicial factfinding remained very much out of the picture.[3] While a few articles devoted to CBA of factfinding at trial were published in the early 1980s,[4] the writing remained very sporadic and quite limited in scope.[5] The lack of scholarship is particularly notable in light of the developments in CBA of related fields.

One reason why judicial factfinding has proven particularly resistant to CBA may be rooted in the subject matter of courtroom drama, which often deals with issues and stakes that strike many as non-quantifiable and antithetical to cost-benefit reasoning.[6] Notions of efficiency, rationality, minimization of cost, and maximization of benefit may seem alien to the legal realm, commonly associated with questions of moral culpability, fairness, justice, and retribution. The benefits of enhanced precision in the administration of justice or the costs entailed with privacy infringements are often deemed as irreducible to monetary metrics.[7] In the words of Raeder, "Who among us would not find it a true challenge to defend a corporation, in a case involving serious personal injury or death, by telling the jury that a cost-benefit analysis of the missing safety device demonstrated its economic infeasibility?"[8] Evidence law, continues Raeder, has more to do with fairness and less to do with efficiency.[9]

* My thanks go to Christian Dahlman, Alex Stein, Giovanni Tuzet, and the wonderful editorial board for excellent comments and suggestions.

[1] Hardin 2008, 1141.
[2] CBA can be interpreted in a host of ways. I will use the term in a loose manner, as a resort to welfare considerations for the guidance and formation of public policy and legal procedure. For further discussion, see Posner 2000, 1153.
[3] Raeder 1998, 1588. See also Shapira 1998, 1607; Friedman 1998, 1531.
[4] Easterbrook 1981, 309; Gibbons and Hutchison 1982, 119; For more recent articles, see Raeder 1998, 1585.
[5] Friedman 1998, 1531; Raeder 1998, 1585.
[6] Raeder 1998, 1588. For a comprehensive account—both descriptive and normative—of why economic analysis and CBA are ill suited for the evidentiary realm, see Lempert 2001, 1619.
[7] Friedman 2001, 2038.
[8] Raeder 1998, 1588.
[9] Raeder 1998, 1585.

Talia Fisher, *Cost-Benefit Analysis of Evidence Law and Factfinding* In: *Philosophical Foundations of Evidence Law*. Edited by: Christian Dahlman, Alex Stein, and Giovanni Tuzet, Oxford University Press. © Christian Dahlman, Alex Stein, and Giovanni Tuzet 2021. DOI: 10.1093/oso/9780198859307.003.0011

But, even if one were to reject the aptness of such narrowly constructed forms of CBA for jury persuasion and decision-making, this does not negate the potential rooted in the introduction of this tool for evidentiary policy-making.

Another reason for the initial rejection of CBA in the context of legal factfinding may be rooted in the tendency to view information and evidence as an exogenous windfall, either present or non-present after the occurrence under debate, and thereby insensitive to costs, incentives, and other economic forces. If this were the case, CBA would, indeed, seem to have very little to contribute to the analysis of evidence law and judicial factfinding. But, such a depiction of the nature of evidence and of the enterprise of unraveling the truth is, in fact, distorted. Evidence and factfinding precision are economic goods.[10] Both do not appear out of thin air. Rather, the gathering, production, and presentation of evidence, as well as its processing in court, require the investment of resources on behalf of the litigating parties and on behalf of society at large.[11] Expert testimony, DNA evidence, and forensic tests all come with a monetary price tag. Legal factfinding also entails non-monetary costs, such as privacy infringements, the pain and suffering associated with cross-examination as well as the cognitive resources of the triers of facts.[12] These monetary and non-monetary costs raise a host of issues concerning the economic desirability of the search for truth and require the making of tradeoffs. Policy-makers must place a value on factfinding accuracy—decide how much to invest in obtaining of the truth, and how to allocate the associated costs between the litigating parties (both among themselves, and between them and the taxpayer).[13] These issues are the bread and butter of CBA, which has a lot to offer in the understanding and design of evidentiary and factfinding institutions. In fact, as a historical matter, Beccaria and Bentham—whose utilitarian moral theories motivate today's CBA—addressed many issues currently underlying evidence law and criminal procedure.[14]

The object of this chapter is to highlight the prospects for integrating CBA into contemporary evidentiary policy and institutions, and to draw the general contours of the evolving scholarship in these fields of research.

2. The Geometric Space of CBA in the Theory of Evidence Law and Legal Factfinding

In the words of Allen and Stein, "*The coin of the legal realm is truth.*"[15] While it may not be entirely uncontroversial in the evidence law scholarship how important it is that courts not

---

[10] Friedman and Kontorovich 2011, 143.

[11] Levmore and Porat 2012, 690.

[12] "The costs of evaluation should not be ignored, though it may be difficult to place a monetary value upon them. Aside from the more obvious and measurable court costs, there is the important expenditure of the cognitive resources of the trier of fact. We are coming to understand how the limitations upon such normal human resources result in decision strategies that seek to optimize the allocation of the trier's mental energies." (Nance 1988, 227).

[13] Not only are the issues of how to allocate the burden of proof or of which party will bear the risks and costs of error classic economic questions, but they are often the product of evidentiary and procedural arrangements, struck between the litigating parties. This transactional dimension is, in and of itself, congruent with CBA and economic analysis. Friedman 1998, 1533.

[14] See Postema 1977, 1393.

[15] Allen and Stein 2013, 567. See also Twining 1984, 272: "The pursuit of truth in adjudication must at times give way to other values and purposes, such as the preservation of state security or of family confidences; disagreements may arise as to what priority to give to rectitude of decision as a social value and to the nature and scope of certain competing values .... But the end of the enterprise is clear: the establishment of truth;" see also Ho, "Evidence and Truth," ch. 1, in this volume.

err in factfinding, which factual mistakes are more important to avoid,[16] or what weight ought to be accorded to the veracity in the face of competing values and objectives[17]—it is considered unequivocal, that whatever the functions of law in society, fulfilling them depends on accurate judicial factfinding.[18] This view of the truth as the driving force of the law and of the legal process is virtually uncontested in evidence law scholarship, and holds true for CBA of evidentiary institutions and legal factfinding as well. Similar to other theoretical approaches to legal factfinding, CBA revolves around the veritistic core, which views the judicial process as aiming for the accurate reconstruction of the facts underlying the legal dispute.

The main difference between CBA and other, more "traditional,"[19] truth-oriented approaches to legal factfinding is that while the latter view the search for truth in monistic terms, aiming for *maximal accuracy*,[20] CBA is sensitive to the social costs associated with the unraveling of the truth, and strives for *optimal accuracy*.[21] According to CBA-oriented approaches, the object of trial and the role of evidentiary institutions are not limited simply to the unraveling of the truth, but rather refer to the cost-effective manner of doing so and to administrative expediency. This type of deliberation is captured in Posner's search model and cost minimization model, considered milestones of the CBA of legal factfinding.[22]

3. The Search Model

According to Posner, legal factfinding can be modeled as a problem in the search for truth. The search for truth is a costly, as well as a benefit-generating enterprise, both for the litigating parties and for society at large. It ought to be conducted to the point where the marginal cost of an additional piece of evidence equals its marginal benefit. The costs include monetary and non-monetary investments in evidence processing, as well as possible prejudicial effects on the triers of fact. The benefit equals the probability that the evidence will further the unraveling of the truth multiplied by the stakes of the case. The amount of evidence at the optimal point, where the marginal cost is equal to the marginal benefit,

---

[16] For instance, the "beyond a reasonable doubt" standard of proof in criminal proceedings reflects the understanding that it is more important to avoid false convictions than it is to avoid false acquittals, but debates arise as to the disutility ratio between false convictions and false acquittals. See Fletcher 1968, 888.

[17] For example, some view the unravelling of the truth as an intrinsic end of the legal process and of evidence law, while others attribute an instrumental role to the rectitude of judicial factfinding, essentially viewing it as a means for the realization of external ends (e.g. deterrence). See Damaska 1998, 301. There are those who highlight ultra-veritistic ends that are internal to the legal process, such as due process or the protection of the rights of witnesses, suspects, and defendants. Others emphasize competing social goals that are external to the realm of trial altogether, like the protection of national security or of certain relationships in society. Still others highlight the potential clash between truth seeking and the contractual underpinnings of trial in the adversarial tradition. See Weigend 2003, 157.

[18] For further discussion of accuracy versus consequences in judicial factfinding, see Kaplow 1994, 307.

[19] The term "traditional" to describe these theories was coined by Stein. See Stein 2005, 108.

[20] This position is vividly expressed in Lord Dunedin's definition of evidentiary laws as "nothing more than a set of practical rules which experience has shown to be best fitted to elicit the truth," (*Thompson v. R.* (1918), 221, 226).

[21] For further discussion of the concept of optimization in evidence law, see Fuller 1969, 15; "In a world without cost, if one can be imagined, the best evidence on an issue is all relevant evidence. In the real world, of course, litigation is a practical enterprise that must seek finality within reasonable time, money, and other resource constraints" (Nance 1988, 233). There are indications for such thinking outside the parameters of CBA as well. See, for example, the vast body of literature arguing against the use of torture as a method for eliciting the truth.

[22] Stein 2005, 141; Posner 1999, 1477. For a well-known critique of the cost-minimization model and Posner's economic analysis of evidentiary law, see Lempert 2001, 1619.

increases as the stakes of the case become higher, as the effect of the evidence on accuracy is enhanced, and as the cost of evidence processing decreases.[23] This can be expressed in the following manner:

$$B(x) = p(b)S - c(x)$$

Where x denotes the unit/amount of evidence; $B(x)$ represents the net benefit of the evidence; S represents the stakes of the case; b denotes the effect of a unit of x on the accuracy at trial; and $c(x)$ denotes the costs entailed in obtaining it.[24] Under the search model the gathering of evidence and its placement before the trier of fact ought to continue to the point where the last piece of evidence yields a benefit, in terms of its probative value and contribution given the stakes of trial, which is equal to the costs of obtaining it.[25]

4. The Cost Minimization Model

Alternatively, Posner suggests to model the presentation of evidence as a tradeoff between the costs of judicial error and the costs of error avoidance. According to Posner's cost minimization model, the optimal tradeoff is one which minimizes the overall sum of these two types of cost.[26] The costs of error avoidance include the total cost of reaching accurate determinations of matters of fact within the framework of legal procedures and at pre-court stages.[27] The costs of judicial errors include the legal entitlements and obligations that the judicial system does not successfully enforce. If false positives (legal entitlements erroneously granted to the undeserving) and false negatives (legal entitlements erroneously unenforced with respect to the deserving) are equally costly, a judicial decision-making process aimed at minimizing the overall rate of error can be expected to produce the lowest sum of error costs. This is often considered to be the case in civil proceedings where the costs of error in favor of the plaintiff are believed to be roughly equal to the costs of error in favor of the defendant.[28] Accordingly, in the civil context the standard of proof is set at the level of a preponderance of the evidence, which allocates the susceptibility to error equally between plaintiff and defendant, reflects the 1:1 disutility ratio between them, and minimizes the overall sum of error (irrespective of its type). Under this standard of proof, the court's decision is most likely to reflect factual truth.[29]

When one type of error is considered costlier than another, minimization of overall costs of error depends upon allocating risk of error in a manner, which reflects the disutility ratio between these two types of error. The paradigmatic example for asymmetrical error costs

---

[23] Posner 2004, 339.

[24] Posner 1999, 1481.

[25] See Gibbons and Hutchison 1982, 119.

[26] In the words of Stein: "Adjudicative fact-finding implicates two social costs: the cost of accuracy and the cost of errors. The cost of accuracy encompasses the legal system's expenditures on fact-finding procedures that reduce the incidence of error. The cost of errors originates from incorrect factual findings produced by the system ... the overarching goal of the law of evidence is to achieve the socially optimal tradeoff between these two costs" (Stein 2015, 430).

[27] Stein 2005, 141.

[28] Schauer and Zeckhauser 1996, 34.

[29] See Kaplow 2012, 803.

is the criminal trial, where a discrepancy exists between false positives (conviction of the factually innocent) and false negatives (acquittal of the factually guilty).[30] As the Blackstone ratio famously holds "better that ten guilty persons escape, than that one innocent suffer."[31] The beyond-a-reasonable-doubt standard of proof reflects this 10:1 disutility ratio and expresses a social preference for wrongful acquittal over wrongful conviction. It strikes a tradeoff between false convictions (false positives) and false acquittals (false negatives) that is intended to minimize the overall *cost* of error, though not necessarily the overall *rate* of error.[32]

The cost minimization model can be presented as follows: under the terms presented earlier, where p denotes the probability of a factfinding error and S denotes the stakes of such an error, pS would then stand for the cost of the error (the probability of error weighted by the stakes), and the goal of evidentiary institutions would be to minimize: $C(x) = p(x)S + c(x)$.[33] In other words, under the cost minimization model the gathering of evidence should continue to the point where the last piece of evidence yields a reduction in costs of error, which is equal to the cost of obtaining it. The legal tools designed to allow realization of this goal include burdens of proof, presumptions of fact, standards of proof, and evidentiary and procedural rules.

4.1. Motivational Failures

According to Stein, execution of the cost minimization model is contingent upon the ability to overcome motivational and informational failures.[34] The motivational failures are rooted in the fact that the private and social costs and benefits of the unraveling of the truth at trial do not correspond completely. While they often overlap, there are potential misalignments in the utility functions of the litigating parties and that of society at large: thus, as mentioned earlier, accurate factfinding in court serves social interests and is a public good, without which the wrong people will be deterred, the information made public will be skewed, the institutions of the rule of law and judicial authority will be delegitimized, etc.[35] The litigating parties, too, often have vested interests in accurate factfinding at trial, which is a pre-condition for the vindication of their substantive rights. They are entitled to courts using procedures that will render factual mistakes, ones that will jeopardize their substantive rights, sufficiently improbable. So, accuracy at trial serves both private and public interests. However, misalignments between the preferences of the parties and between the social utility function, concerning the level of accuracy at trial and the investment of social resources in achieving it, can be expected to occur: while society has an interest in preventing both types of errors that may undermine judicial factfinding accuracy—both the incorrect

---

[30] See Lee 1997, 25.

[31] Blackstone 1803, 276. Numerous variations exist, the main variation being the ratio of n guilty men who ought to be acquitted in order to spare one innocent man. See Volokh 1997, 174. See also Stein 2008, 80: "Criminal convictions require a very high, although numerically unstated, probability of guilt."

[32] Bierschbach and Stein 2007, 1207: "by decreasing the incidence of false positives (erroneous convictions of the factually innocent) a 'reasonable doubt' standard increases the incidence of false negatives (erroneous acquittals and non-prosecutions of the factually guilty."

[33] Posner 1999, 1484.

[34] Stein 2005, ch. 5.

[35] Bray 2005, 1308.

imposition of liability as well as the erroneous absolvement of legal responsibility—litigants in civil proceedings are interested in winning the case, irrespective of their factual responsibility.[36] Similarly, in criminal proceedings, the defendant is interested in acquittal, regardless of actual involvement in the alleged crime, while the public interest is to secure conviction of the factually guilty. Even in the face of a defendant's factual innocence there can be misalignments between her utility function and that of society at large, as the defendant is interested in investment of infinite public resources in securing her acquittal, while the public interest dictates the placement of a cap on the public expenditure for securing acquittal.[37]

The mismatch between the litigating parties and society refers not only to the benefits of accuracy at trial, but also to its associated costs and to the level of investment: in their quest to cut back on litigation costs, the parties may engage in deviations from the truth or in evidentiary stipulations which impair accuracy to such a degree that it compromises the supply of valuable public goods of trial.[38] Parties may also exhibit too strong a preference for the truth or customize evidence law in a way which would lead to over-investment (from a social standpoint) in accuracy at trial. Given that litigants do not fully internalize the costs of trial and of judicial factfinding, they may exhibit an over-zealousness for accuracy and for accuracy enhancing evidentiary procedures (again, as compared to the social optimum). Their evidentiary agreements may be aimed at adding extra layers of defense against judicial error, such as additional rounds of cross-examination of each witness or a jury of one hundred jurors.[39] These extra evidentiary layers may be set above and beyond the means the parties would have resorted to had they been forced to fully internalize their costs (to the taxpayer) as well as above and beyond the socially desirable level of investment in factfinding accuracy. As mentioned earlier, the social costs externalized by the parties need not necessarily be monetary in nature. They can include non-material, symbolic, or reputational harm to third parties, to the legal process, to the adjudication system, and to society at large. One such social cost, brought about by evidentiary agreements, relates to the blurring of the distinction between procedure and substance. In the spirit of the procedure and substance dichotomy, the evidentiary rules and the application of those rules should be broad enough to prevent the differential treatment of different classes of litigants. Evidentiary agreements, which open a door to the tailoring of the system of evidence to the unique interests of the parties, can create distinct classes within the pool of potential litigants. They can bias the process and its outcomes in favor of particular political groups and allow actual outcome of the judicial proceedings to be dictated by the agreed-upon evidentiary rules.

In sum, due to the fact that the private benefits in accurate factfinding may surpass or fall short of the public benefits, party control over the search for truth may result in over or under-investment, from a social standpoint, in factfinding accuracy.[40] And this brings us to the issue of the adversarial-inquisitorial dichotomy, and to the tradeoff between decentralized and centralized factfinding regimes.

Adversarial systems, prevailing in Anglo-American law and exemplified by the modern jury civil trial, are characterized by party sovereignty over trial and pre-trial proceedings.

---

[36]   Stein 2005, 142.
[37]   Stein 2005, 142.
[38]   Rose-Ackerman and Geistfeld 1987, 483.
[39]   Moffitt 2007, 508.
[40]   See Shavell 1997, 575.

The litigating parties bear most of the cost of and the responsibility for the key components of judicial factfinding. They are vested with the authority to gather the evidence, to determine the sequence and manner of its presentation, and to delineate the borders of the factual dispute.[41] Judges and jurors are designated the residual role of passive umpires "who weigh the parties' competing claims from a neutral perch."[42] In contrast, the inquisitorial model, once prevalent in the civil law systems of continental Europe, is premised upon central control over the process of judicial factfinding by state-employed, professional judges. The court is vested with the responsibility of gathering the evidence, rather than simply ruling on its basis. Evidence is collected by a judge or court-appointed commissioner, and the court determines the sequence and manner of the unfolding of the evidence and factual debate.[43] The advantage of the adversarial regime of judicial factfinding is rooted in the superior information available to the parties—typically those with the best access to the relevant information, coupled with the strongest motivation (at least one of them) to bring it before the court.[44] The adversarial system has been said to result in the court's receiving more information than under the inquisitorial system, due to the fact that under the adversarial model the court makes negative inferences with respect to the party who failed to supply supporting evidence.[45] However, these advantages can be qualified by the abovementioned inefficiencies, oftentimes associated with the private supply of the public goods of adjudicative factfinding by biased partisans, and by the potential discrepancies between the utility functions of the litigating parties and that of the public at large. Moreover, they can also be qualified in light of possible power disparities between the parties in their capacities to effectively search for, gather, and present evidence. Even the strongest proponents of the adversarial method have recognized its weaknesses in unraveling the truth in the face of structural asymmetry of power between litigating parties.[46]

4.2. Informational Failures

The qualification referring to the assumption of symmetrical access to information brings us to the second obstacle underlying the execution of the cost-minimization goal—namely, the possession of private information by criminal defendants and civil litigants concerning facts or issues that are of relevance to the factual outcome of trial. The prospect of asymmetrical information, among the parties and between them and the court, paves the way for opportunistic behavior, leading to potential deviations from the determination of truth.[47] The object of evidence law is to address and minimize the abovementioned motivational and informational failures, so as to allow for an accurate and cost efficient factfinding process, one that would align with CBA and with the cost minimization ideal. According to Stein, this goal is accommodated through four distinct sets of

---

[41] Luban 1998, 57; Damaska 1973, 513.
[42] Steinberg 2016, 899.
[43] Kessler 2005, 1188.
[44] The advantage of the inquisitorial regime is rooted in the fact that those vested with the power to collect the evidence are neutral and positioned in a manner which allows them to fully reflect the social utility function. See Froeb and Kobayashi 2001, 267.
[45] Bull 2009, 106.
[46] See Kagan 2001, 121; Langbein 1985, 843.
[47] Stein 2005, 143.

rules: (1) decision rules, which determine the burdens and standards of proof; (2) process rules, which determine evidence admissibility and define legitimate factfinding methodologies; (3) credibility rules, which elicit credibility signals from litigants with private information; and (4) the evidential damage doctrine, which allocates the risk of error to the cheapest risk avoider.[48]

Stein qualified Posner's cost minimization model in another important manner: While the cost minimization model focuses on the aggregate cost of errors and their prevention, failing to address the manner in which these costs are allocated among the litigating parties, Stein added an important distributive layer to Posner's CBA approach. As Stein claims, the goals of evidentiary institutions include appropriate allocation of the risks of error among the litigants in a manner which complies with, what he terms, "the principle of equality" and "the equal-best principle." The principle of equality applies in civil proceedings and requires the equitable distribution of the risks of error among the litigating parties, assuming a priori equality among them. The equal-best principle applies to criminal trials and assigns the majority of the risks and costs of errors to the prosecution, assuming a high disutility ratio between the social costs of wrongful convictions and wrongful acquittals.[49]

Posner's cost minimization and search models are manifestations of the "first generation" of CBA of factfinding, which is focused on systemic efficiency, on the need of the adjudicative system to unravel the truth and process cases in an efficient manner. This approach highlights the costs and benefits associated with proving the facts of the case expost. It emphasizes the backward-looking role of adjudicative factfinding in the uncovering of (mostly) *past* events.[50] In recent years we are witnessing a shift to a competing view in CBA of evidence law—one which challenges the automatic resort to factfinding accuracy, and which stresses the instrumental role played by truth at trial in the furthering of ultimate social objectives, most notably deterrence. According to this latter, "second generation" approach, the benefit of truth revelation is a function of how individuals can be expected to react to greater factfinding precision in their choice of primary behavior.[51] CBA of factfinding has thereby evolved to incorporate the role of the adjudicative process not only in the unraveling of the *past* but also, more importantly, in the shaping of the *future*.[52] It emphasizes the effects of evidentiary institutions on the CBA of potential perpetrators and on the formation of incentives, and views efficiency insofar as it relates to the optimization of primary behavior.

---

[48] Ibid., 143.

[49] Ibid., 143.

[50] The underlying premise of this first-generation CBA approach is that truth revelation is a good-enough proxy for the objects of law and trial. Kaplow described this approach as a strategy aiming at "the truth, with the expectation that this protocol will ordinary lead to good consequences. Perhaps there are some moderate deviations, occasional exceptions, and limitations, but nevertheless the applicable notion of truth might typically provide a workable guide or at least a sensible starting point" (Kaplow 2015, 1304).

[51] For instance, according to Kaplow enhanced ex post accuracy as to how much the plaintiff's future earnings are diminished by an auto accident injury may be wasteful, because it cannot be predicted ex ante and therefore cannot impact deterrence. For further discussion of accuracy versus consequences, see Kaplow 1994, 307.

[52] This new strand of CBA analysis is not focused solely on the role of the adjudicative factfinding in determining whether the defendant was, indeed, involved in the alleged offense, whether such an offense had taken place, or which of the parties failed to comply with the terms of the contract. Rather, it emphasizes the manner in which factfinding, in the event of a legal dispute erupting, would impact the decision to engage in the criminal act or to breach the terms of the contract in the first place.

5. The Primary-Behavior Approach to Legal Factfinding

According to the primary behavior approach, legal institutions, generally, and adjudicative factfinding, specifically, ought to be evaluated and understood as being also (perhaps primarily) about supplying good incentives for behavior of agents outside the courtroom: in the marketplace, in the street, and on the highway. While accurate factfinding is an appropriate goal of the judicial process, it ought to be viewed in instrumental terms, as a means for the furthering of deterrence.[53] Accordingly, the primary behavior approach uses the tools of CBA to evaluate and design judicial factfinding and evidentiary institutions in light of their capacities for shaping desirable primary behavior.

The starting point for the primary behavior approach is rooted in the application of CBA and rational choice theory to the decision-making process of potential perpetrators. The underlying assumption is that individuals act as rational maximizers of their utilities, and choose to engage in activities, including socially harmful ones, when their benefit from doing so exceeds the associated costs. The imposition of criminal sanctions or civil liability and remedies is intended to enhance the expected cost of engaging in socially harmful activities in a manner that is reflective of the social harm involved. This forces rational maximizers of their utilities to internalize the social costs of their activities into their cost-benefit calculus, and ensures resort to potentially harmful behavior only when the social benefits outweigh the social costs involved. The path to such internalization of the associated social costs into the cost-benefit calculus of agents in society passes through the courtroom, of course, as accurate judicial factfinding is a prerequisite for the creation of a causal connection between an agent's behavior and its legal outcome. Quite intuitively, in order to promote the goal of optimal deterrence legal sanctions are to be imposed upon the factually guilty, and vice versa. Accurate factfinding, in other words, can be viewed as a proxy for optimizing deterrence and for inducing socially desirable primary behavior. The consolidation of ex post error avoidance and ex ante deterrence considerations can explain the cost minimization model's emphasis on the former. However, as is the case with proxies more generally, the two objectives don't always align. Rectitude of factfinding, while typically conducive to deterrence, does not always further this goal. Inherent tensions may arise in certain circumstances between accurate factfinding and deterrence objectives. Such is the case, for instance, in the realm of bad character evidence.[54]

Criminal procedure demonstrates mixed feelings toward evidence of bad character. Such evidence is typically admitted during the sentencing phase of trial but, as a general rule, cannot serve for conviction purposes. This, despite the underlying suspicion that it has probative weight and can enhance accuracy of determinations of guilt. According to Sanchirico, there's no way of vindicating this attitude towards character evidence if one thinks of the trial simply in terms of factfinding. The bad-character rule is incompatible with the idea that trial is exclusively geared toward factfinding accuracy.[55] Rather, he suggests that the reluctance to use bad character evidence is rooted in its adverse effect in terms of ex ante incentives. This is so because at the point most relevant for incentives—when an agent is deliberating whether to break the law—her character and relevant character

---

[53] See Sanchirico 2001, 1229; Fisher and Stein 2012, 1103; Kaplow 2012, 738.
[54] Sanchirico 2001, 1229.
[55] Sanchirico 2001, 1229.

evidence are already a given. The character evidence that may be admitted against her does not depend on her current decision of how to proceed. This is the source of the incentive problem. For ideally, in order to generate the efficient incentives here, we would want the agent to know that the likelihood of her being (charged, convicted, and) punished strongly depends on whether or not she decides to break the law here and now. The weaker the dependence, the less weighty the incentive supplied by the law not to engage in this specific criminal behavior.[56] Admitting character evidence at the conviction stage of trial can thus be expected to lower the marginal cost of engaging in the criminal activity and to act counterproductively in terms of incentives. Given some plausible assumptions about the difference between the trial stage and the sentencing stage—such as which is more relevant for deterrence—perhaps this line of thought can begin to vindicate the abovementioned mixed attitude towards character evidence. Of course, a lot may be going on with character evidence. And it needn't be a part of the claim that giving the right incentives to primary behavior is the only normative consideration governing judicial factfinding, evidentiary institutions, and the rules regarding character evidence. But even if other considerations apply, still Sanchirico has succeeded in drawing attention to another kind of consideration, one that it would be foolish for CBA analysis of judicial factfinding to ignore.[57]

While the primary behavior approach views the bad character rule as an incentive model, the traditional approaches stresses its epistemic functions. According to the traditional approach, evidence of bad character may be excluded on the grounds that its probative value is outweighed by its prejudicial effect.[58] The cost minimization model, in contrast, approaches the bad character rule from the perspective of the cost-effectiveness of judicial factfinding. Under the cost minimization model, the justification for the bad-character rule is not restricted to circumstances in which the inclusion of information regarding the negative past of a defendant would decrease the overall level of factfinding accuracy. Rather, the cost minimization model would also justify the inadmissibility of previous bad conduct in circumstances in which such information is not considered a cost-effective manner of exposing the truth (for instance, because bad character evidence would dictate a broadening of the factual dispute to include prior conduct, above and beyond the allegations underlying the indictment). So, while the traditional approach to judicial factfinding focuses on the *most accurate* investigation of *past* events and the cost minimization model focuses on the *cost-effective* investigation of *past* events, the primary behavior approach maintains that judicial factfinding and the associated costs and benefits are linked more closely to the *future* than to the past.[59] From the point of view of the primary behavior approach the justification for evidentiary doctrine in general, and for the bad character rule, specifically, is not restricted to their effect on the finding of fact. This second-generation CBA conceptualizes the costs and benefits of legal factfinding in terms of incentives for disengagement in socially harmful behavior.

To conclude, like in other areas of law CBA of legal factfinding is aimed at social welfare maximization and is embedded in the normative criterion of efficiency. However, this normative setting assumes two different conceptualizations, reflective of two distinct

---

[56]   See Enoch and Fisher 2015, 557.
[57]   Enoch and Fisher 2015, 557.
[58]   Redmayne 2006, 805.
[59]   Park and Saks 2006, 1017.

theoretical approaches to legal factfinding. The first, manifested in Posner's cost minimization model, focuses on the systemic efficiency and on the cost-effectiveness of factfinding accuracy. It relates to the ex post investment of resources in exposition of the truth by the litigating parties and by society at large and defines benefits in terms of truth value The second, manifested in the model of primary behavior, focuses on the efficiency of primary behavior and stresses the instrumental role of factfinding precision. It formulates the costs and benefits, which ought to be taken into account in the utilitarian calculus, mostly in deterrence terms.

Normative considerations aside, as a practical matter CBA is increasingly becoming a staple of policy-makers' attempts to secure the efficiency of trial and judicial factfinding and their capacity to fulfill their designated social functions.[60] In the landmark case of *Mathews v. Eldridge* 424 U.S. 319 (1976), the United States Supreme Court held that the costs of providing evidentiary and procedural safeguards ought to be weighed against the benefits associated with factfinding accuracy. But, reliance on this type of reasoning has not gone unchallenged. In what follows I will address some of the central critiques, levelled against CBA, and highlight their implications for the realm of judicial factfinding.

6. Critiques of the Use of CBA in the Realm of Legal Factfinding

CBA of the type formulated by the court in *Mathews v. Eldridge* 424 U.S. 319 (1976) has been critiqued for focusing on the narrow objective of administrative expediency, and for neglecting to account for the plurality of additional ends and values underlying adjudication (some of which are not readily quantifiable or reducible to monetary terms) such as fairness, procedural justice, or human dignity.[61]

The mirror-image objection to CBA faults it precisely for attempting to place a price value on what may (otherwise) be considered invaluable. Thus, even the most enthusiastic proponents of CBA are not blind to the practical difficulties entailed in price-tagging costs and benefits, not readily quantifiable. Still others object to such price-tagging not just as a practical matter, but also in principle. For example, criticisms are levelled against placing a monetary price tag on deviations from the prescriptions of justice—whether in the form of conviction of the innocent or acquittal of the factually guilty. Price-tagging of infringements on the privacy, human dignity, or of the pain and suffering of witnesses raises similar concerns. This is also the case with respect to the psychological and moral burdens placed upon jurors and judges, facing the possibility of fateful factual oversights. All these fundamentally non-monetary values can be distinguished from other variables of the cost minimization model and of CBA of legal factfinding, which are more prone to monetary quantification, like the cost of DNA testing. CBA of legal factfinding does not allow for the drawing of an

---

[60] *Mathews v. Eldridge* 424 U.S. 319 (1976). See also Roman 2013.

[61] See Quintanilla 2015, 882. A related objection levelled against CBA, which can also be applied to the realm of legal factfinding, is rooted in alternative costs (and benefits). As mentioned earlier, Posner's models imply that we should invest 99 cents in legal factfinding to avoid a judicial error valued at $1.00. But, in a world of scarcity such a position may be difficult to defend, as the 99 cents invested in judicial error avoidance may, perhaps, be better utilized outside of the legal realm, to promote higher value social ends that have little to do with judicial factfinding. See Frank 2000, 913.

appropriate distinction between the categories, reducing all costs and benefits to unitary and monetary terms.

This leads to the related critique of incommensurability. CBA tacitly assumes that everything is commensurate with everything else; that all resources and attributes can be placed on a single metric (whether monetary or non-monetary). This, in and of itself, is highly debatable. In the words of Sunstein: *"Incommensurability occurs when the relevant goods cannot be aligned along a single metric without doing violence to our considered judgments about how these goods are best characterized."*[62] Recognizing a plurality of value scales— namely, the fact that resources differ not only in *how much* we value them but also in *how* we value them[63]—implies that the value of certain resources cannot be fully captured using a single metric, and that no common value scale can determine how all resources relate to each other. It implies that certain resources cannot be regarded as better, worse, or equal in value to other resources, thereby underscoring CBA's scaling ambitions.[64] This critique can be levelled against the implicit assumption underlying the cost minimization model, according to which the costs of error in favor of the plaintiff and the costs of error in favor of the defendant are commensurate and can outweigh each other. Similar claims may be applied with respect to the commensurability of costs of error and costs of error avoidance. The costs of error avoidance may be said to be differ qualitatively from the costs of factfinding error, and irreducible to a single scale of valuation. Error avoidance may include monetary costs like the financial investment in DNA collection, while the costs associated with legal error and with the miscarriage of justice may be non-monetizable in nature. Similar claims can be formulated with respect to the pain and suffering of witnesses upon cross examination or to the infringement of their privacy, which are qualitatively different from monetary costs of hiring expert witnesses or from the non-monetary costs of miscarriage of justice. There is room to contest the cost minimization model's flattening of these qualitatively distinct costs and benefits onto a single metric when they area weighed against each other.[65] Similar claims can be formulated with respect to the primary behavior approach and to its reduction of deterrence considerations to the qualitatively different scale of monetary costs and benefits.

Another critique, leveled against the scaling enterprise at the core of CBA, refers to the unbounded rationality assumption upon which it rests. As a scaling-based decision procedure, CBA is premised upon the fundamental notion, that when agents weigh costs and benefits, they exhibit a stable system of preferences in the face of uncertainty.[66] CBA imagines agents who act as rational maximizers of their utilities against such background, and this refers also to agents operating in the legal factfinding realm, such as judges, juries, actual and potential litigants, prosecutors, and defense attorneys. The empirical soundness of the unbounded rationality assumption has been challenged by behavioral economists and social cognition scientists. An extensive body of psychological and experimental research has cast doubt on CBA's presumption of rationality, by pointing out differences between rational choice theory and the ways human agents choose and behave in reality. The source of these

---

[62] Sunstein 1994, 796.
[63] Anderson 1993, 190.
[64] Adler 1998, 1392.
[65] Stein 2015, 2015.
[66] Becker 1976, 14.

differences lies in what Simon termed "bounded rationality."[67] According to Simon, human cognitive ability is limited in scope. In order to maximize that ability to its fullest, humans use mental shortcuts and rules of thumb (heuristics). The use of mental shortcuts can be thought of as rational behavior, that aims to minimize the aggregate cost of error and error avoidance in everyday life.[68] Bounded rationality can, thus, be considered a manifestation of the cost minimization model in the varied epistemic contexts of our lives. However, even if the use of mental shortcuts is based on rational and adaptive behavior, aimed at deriving the benefits of good judgment from the investment of cognitive resources, the actual results of this process may occasionally lead to systematic deviations from the model of perfect rationality. A significant breakthrough in the study of such deviations and cognitive biases was provided by the work of Nobel Prize Laureate, Kahneman and his colleague, Tversky. In an extensive series of experiments, Kahneman and Tversky demonstrated a variety of replicable systematic human deviations from rational choice in decision-making processes (including, "The Availability Bias," "The Anchoring Effect," "Judgmental Overconfidence," and the like).[69] In their work, *Inside the Judicial Mind*, Guthrie, Rachlinski, and Wistrich pointed to the susceptibility of judges to the various cognitive biases.[70] Irrational choice-making on behalf of judges and other key players in the justice system may distort the outcome of applying CBA to legal institutions and to judicial factfinding.

Moving beyond the welfarist framework, CBA of legal factfinding has also been criticized for the consequentialist ethics at its base, and for failing to account for justifications for factfinding rectitude, which exist above and beyond social welfare. According to deontological critiques, the level of accuracy at trial that litigating parties are entitled to is a matter of individual right rather than social welfare.[71] Rectitude of factfinding at trial bears intrinsic value, and ought not to be evaluated exclusively in terms of possible contribution to trial and social outcomes. Under this view, CBA of legal factfinding jeopardizes, or at the very least fails to comply with, the plurality of moral intuitions underlying the pursuit of truth at trial. It fails to account for the precedence of humanistic values—like fairness, equality, human dignity, liberty, or privacy—over administrative expediency and deterrence enhancement.[72]

7. Conclusion

The standard theory and real-world application of CBA to legal factfinding has been called into question due, in part, to CBA's welfarist and aggregative outlook (as manifested in the aggregation of social costs and benefits across individuals or between resources of different

---

[67] Simon 1955, 99. At the foundation of Simon's theory lie two intertwined components: one that concerns the limits of the human mind and its decision-making ability based on its limited conceptual powers and limited memory, and one that concerns effects of the environment in which the mind is functioning. There are those who argue that bounded rationality is a product of evolutionary processes.

[68] Jolls, Sunstein, and Thaler 1998, 1474.

[69] For a discussion of the development of the paradigm of heuristics and biases, see Kahneman and Tversky 1996, 582–3.

[70] Guthrie, Rachlinski, and Wistrich 2001, 778.

[71] See Dworkin 1985, 72.

[72] Under deontological thinking these and other values trump countervailing social utilities, and cannot be placed on a utilitarian calculus with—nor counterbalanced by—considerations of cost-effectiveness or overall deterrence. See Ackerman and Heinzerling 2002, 1553; Mashaw 1976, 28.

faculties on the calculus, as well as by counterbalancing human rights of intrinsic value with public welfare objectives). There is room, however, to contest this critique, and to argue that the arena of legal factfinding is predisposed to such an aggregative outlook; that it is precisely the systemic perspective, which renders CBA compatible for the evaluation and design of evidentiary and procedural institutions, more so than deontological thinking.[73]

Deontological theories of adjudication, with their emphasis on individual rights, fall short of providing a normative assessment of procedural regimes, because they do not address tradeoffs nor offer prescriptions across entire classes of cases. In the realm of criminal justice, for instance, deontological theories treat each of the deviations from the principle of just dessert, whether in the form of conviction of the factually innocent or acquittal of the factually guilty, in isolated and absolutist terms. They do not offer a prescription for balancing between errors in favor of the defendant and errors in favor of the prosecution.[74] They are, in this sense utopian theories, oblivious to the reality of life, where judicial errors are inevitable and where efforts to decrease the potential within the system for wrongful convictions increase the potential for wrongful acquittals in the system (and vice versa). Similar claims can be formulated with respect to civil trials, and to the emphasis of deontological theories on the individual rights of the litigating parties, irrespective of derivative social consequences. Prescriptions regarding factfinding and procedural regimes demand a sensitivity to the tradeoffs between various miscarriages of justice and their associated social costs.[75] The lack of account for such tradeoff undermines the deontological objection to CBA, and the argument that rights should take a precedence over systemic expedience and other public welfare considerations. The organizing logic of CBA aligns with that of the procedural arena, making it an appropriate metric for evaluating and designing institutions of legal factfinding.

References

Ackerman, F. and Heinzerling, L. (2002). "Pricing the Priceless: Cost-Benefit Analysis of Environmental Protection," *University of Pennsylvania Law Review*, 150: 1553–84.

Adler, M. (1998). "Incommensurability and Cost-Benefit Analysis," *University of Pennsylvania Law Review*, 146: 1371–418.

Allen, R. J. and Stein A. (2013). "Evidence, Probability, and the Burden of Proof," *Arizona Law Review*, 55: 557–602.

Anderson, E. (1993). *Value in Ethics and Economics*. Cambridge, MA: Harvard University Press.

Becker, G. S. (1976). *The Economic Approach to Human Behavior*. Chicago: Chicago University Press.

---

[73] See also Bierschbach and Stein 2007, 1203.

[74] For example, Reiman and Van Den Haag reasoned that retribution theories cannot justify the demand for criminal proof beyond a reasonable doubt because that demand is not congruent with the retributive obligation to punish the guilty. Should we try to convict fewer innocents and risk letting more of the guilty escape or try to convict more of the guilty and unavoidably, more of the innocent? Retributivism (although not necessarily retributivists) is mute on how high standards of proof ought to be. See Reiman and Van Den Haag 1990, 242. Moore presented a similar position in his determination that the retributivist perspective opens a door to a relatively low evidentiary standard—a balance of probabilities—in the criminal realm. According to Moore, in the absence of an a priori standard for the appropriate system-level balance between wrongful conviction and wrongful acquittal, advocates of retributivist theory could adopt a principle of symmetry between these two types of error based on the principles of retributivist justice: the retributivist might adopt a principle of symmetry here—the guilty going unpunished is exactly the same magnitude of evil as the innocent being punished—and design his institutions accordingly. See Michael 1997, 157.

[75] See also Raz 1986, 1103.

Bierschbach, R. A. and Stein, A. (2007). "Mediating Rules in Criminal Law," *Virginia Law Review*, 93: 1197–258.

Blackstone, W. (1803). *Commentaries on the Laws of England: In Four Books*. Oxford: Clarendon Press.

Bray, S. (2005). "Introducing a Third Verdict," *The University of Chicago Law Review*, 73: 1299–329.

Bull, J. (2009). "Costly Evidence and System of Fact-Finding," *Bulletin of Economic Research*, 61: 103–25.

Damaska, M. R. (1973). "Evidentiary Barriers to Conviction and Two Models of criminal Procedure: A Comparative Study," *University of Pennsylvania Law Review*, 121, 506–589.

Damaska, M. (1998). "Truth in Adjudication," *Hastings Law Journal*, 49: 289–308.

Dworkin, R. (1985). *Principle, Policy, Procedure in a Matter of Principle*. Cambridge, MA: Harvard University Press.

Easterbrook, F. H. (1981). "Insider Trading, Secret Agents, Evidentiary Privileges, and the Production of Information," *Supreme Court Review*, (1981): 309–66.

Enoch, D. and Fisher, T. (2015). "Sense and 'Sensitivity': Epistemic and Instrumental Approaches to Statistical Evidence," *Stanford Law Review*, 67: 557–612.

Fisher, T. and Stein, A. (2012). "Economic Analysis of Evidence Law," in U. Procaccia (ed.), *Economic Analysis of Law*. Jerusalem: Hebrew University Legal Publications.

Fletcher, G. P. (1968). "Two Kinds of Legal Rules: A Comparative Study of Burden-of-Persuasion Practices in Criminal Cases," *Yale Law Journal*, 77: 880–935.

Frank, R. H. (2000). "Cost-benefit Analysis: Legal, Economic, and Philosophical Perspectives: Why is Cost-Benefit Analysis so Controversial?" *Journal of Legal Studies*, 29: 913–30.

Friedman, R. D. (1998). "The Economics of Evidentiary Law: Economic Analysis of Evidentiary Law: An Underused Tool, an Underplowed Field," *Cardozo Law Review*, 19: 1531–9.

Friedman, R. D. (2001). "'E' is for Eclectic: Multiple Perspective on Evidence," *Virginia Law Review*, 87: 2029–54.

Friedman, E. and Kontrovich, E. (2011). "An Economic Analysis of Face Witness Payment," *Journal of Legal Analysis*, 3: 139–64.

Froeb, L. M. and Kobayashi B. H. (2001). "Evidence Production in Adversarial vs. Inquisitorial Regimes," *Economics Letters*, 70: 267–72.

Fuller, L. L. (1969). *The Morality of Law*. New Haven, CT: Yale University Press.

Gibbons, T. and Hutchison, A. C. (1982). "The Practice and Theory of Evidence Law—a Note," *International Review of Law and Economics*, 2: 119–26.

Guthrie, C., Rachlinski, J. J., and Wistrich, A. J. (2001). "Inside the Judicial Mind," *Cornell Law Review*, 86: 777–830.

Hardin, D. B. Jr. (2008). "Why Cost-Benefit Analysis? A Question (and some Answers) about the Legal Academy," *Alabama Law Review*, 59: 1135–82.

Jolls, C., Sunstein, C. R., and Thaler, R. (1998). "A Behavioral Approach to Law and Economics," *Stanford Law Review*, 50: 1471–550.

Kagan, R. A. (2001). *Adversarial Legalism: The American Way of Law*. Cambridge, MA: Harvard University Press.

Kahneman, D. and Tversky, A. (1996). "On the Reality of Cognitive Illusions," *Psychological Review*, 103: 582–91.

Kaplow, L. (1994). "The Value of Accuracy in Adjudication: An Economic Analysis," *Journal of Legal Studies*, 23: 307–402.

Kaplow, L. (2012). "Burden of Proof," *Yale Law Journal*, 121: 738–859.

Kaplow, L. (2015). "Information and the Aim of Adjudication: Truth or Consequences?" *Stanford Law Review*, 67: 1303–71.

Kessler, A. D. (2005). "Our Inquisitorial Tradition: Equity Procedure, Due Process, and the Search for an Alternative to the Adversarial," *Cornell Law Review*, 90: 1181–276.

Langbein, J. H. (1985). "The German Advantage in Civil Procedure," *The University of Chicago Law Review*, 52: 823–66.

Lee, T. R. (1997). "Pleading and Proof: The Economics of Legal Burdens," *The Brigham Young University Law Review*, (1997): 1–34.

Lempert, R. (2001). "The Economic Analysis of Evidence Law: Common Sense on Stilts," *Virginia Law Review*, 87: 1619–712.

Levmore, S. and Porat, A. (2012). "Asymmetries and Incentives in Plea Bargaining and Evidence Production," *Yale Law Journal*, 3: 690–723.

Luban, D. (1998). *Lawyers and Justice: An Ethical Study*. Princeton, NJ: Princeton University Press.

Mashaw, J. L. (1976). "The Supreme Court's Due Process Calculus for Administrative Adjudication in Mathews v. Eldridge: Three Factors in Search of a Theory of Value," *University of Chicago Law Review*, 44: 28–59.

Moffitt, M. L. (2007). "Customized Litigation: The Case for Making Civil Procedure Negotiable," *George Washington Law Review*, 75: 461–521.

Moore, M. S. (1997). *Placing Blame: A General Theory of the Criminal Law*. Oxford: Oxford University Press.

Nance, D. A. (1988). "The Best Evidence Principle," *Iowa Law Review*, 2: 227–98.

Park, R. C. and Saks, J. (2006). "Evidence Scholarship Reconsidered: Results of the Interdisciplinary Turn," *Boston College Law Review*, 47: 949–1032.

Posner, R. A. (1999). "An Economic Approach to the Law of Evidence," *Stanford Law Review*, 51: 1477–546.

Posner, R. A. (2000). "Cost-benefit Analysis: Definition, Justification, and Comment on Conference Papers," *Journal of Legal Studies*, 29: 1153–78.

Posner, R. A. (2004). *Frontiers of Legal Theory*. Cambridge, MA: Harvard University Press.

Postema, G. J. (1977). "The Principle of Utility and the Law of Procedure: Bentham's Theory of Adjudication," *Georgia Law Review*, 11: 1393–424.

Quintanilla, V. D. (2015). "Taboo Procedural Tradeoffs: Examining how the Public Experiences Tradeoffs between Procedural Justice and Cost," *Nevada Law Journal*, 15: 882–929.

Raeder, M. S. (1998). "Cost-benefit Analysis, Unintended Consequences, and Evidentiary Policy: A Critique and a Rethinking of the Application of a Single Set of Evidence Rules to Civil and Criminal Cases," *Cardozo Law Review*, 19: 1585–1606.

Raz, J. (1986). "Dworkin: A New Link in the Chain," *California Law Review*, 74: 1103–19.

Redmayne, M. (2006). "The Structure of Evidence Law," *Oxford Journal of Legal Studies*, 26: 805–22.

Reiman, J. and Van Den Haag, E. (1990). "On the Common Saying that it is Better that Ten Guilty Persons Escape than that one Innocent Suffer: Pro and Con," *Social Philosophy and Policy*, 7: 226–48.

Roman, J. (2013). "Cost-benefit Analysis of Criminal Justice Reforms," National Institute of Justice. Available at https://nij.ojp.gov/topics/articles/cost-benefit-analysis-criminal-justice-reforms (Accessed: March 24, 2021).

Rose-Ackerman, S. and Geistfeld, M. (1987). "The Divergence between Social and Private Incentives to Sue: A Comment on Shavell, Menell, and Kaplow," *The Journal of Legal Studies*, 16: 483–91.

Sanchirico, C. W. (2001). "Character Evidence and the Object of Trial," *Columbia Law Review*, 101: 1227–311.

Schauer, F. and Zeckhauser, R. (1996). "On the Degree of Confidence for Adverse Decisions," *The Journal of Legal Studies*, 25: 27–52.

Shapira, R. A. (1998). "The Economics of Evidentiary Law: Economic Analysis of the Law of Evidence: A Caveat," *Cardozo Law Review*, 19: 1607–34.

Shavell, S. (1997). "The Fundamental Divergence between the Private and the Social Motive to Use the Legal System," *The Journal of Legal Studies*, 26: 575–612.

Simon, H. A. (1955). "A Behavioral Model of Rational Choice," *The Quarterly Journal of Economics*, 69: 99–118.

Stein, A. (2005). *Foundations of Evidence Law*. Oxford: Oxford University Press.

Stein, A. (2008). "Constitutional Evidence Law," *Vanderbilt Law Review*, 61: 65–126.

Stein, A. (2015). "Inefficient Evidence," *Alabama Law Review*, 66: 423–70.

Steinberg, J. K. (2016). "Adversary Breakdown and Judicial Role Confusion in 'Small Case' Civil Justice," *The Brigham Young University Law Review*, 2016: 899–969.

Sunstein, C. R. (1994). "Incommensurability and Valuation in Law," *Michigan Law Review*, 92: 779–861.

Twining, W. (1984). "Evidence and Legal Theory," *The Modern Law Review*, 47: 261–83.

Volokh, A. (1997). "n Guilty Men," *University of Pennsylvania Law Review*, 146: 173–216.

Weigend, T. (2003). "Is the Criminal Trial about Truth? A German Perspective," *Harvard Journal of Law & Public Policy's*, 26: 157–73.

PART III
EVIDENCE, LANGUAGE, AND ARGUMENTATION

11

Linguistic Evidentials and the Law of Hearsay

Lawrence M. Solan[*]

1. Introduction

The rules of evidence control what it is that decision-makers may rely upon in deciding the underlying facts in a trial. Many of these rules have a linguistic aspect because so much of the evidence produced at a trial is testimonial, i.e., linguistic. In the United States, the rules of evidence[1] on which this essay focuses, require relevance, disallow irrelevant testimony, even when it is true, and generally require that the court balance the probative value of the information against its prejudicial effect in order to limit the extent to which jurors are driven more by their emotional reactions to what they see and hear than by the facts before them even when it comes to relevant information.[2]

At the same time, the rules of evidence concern themselves with the reliability of what comes before the court. For example, the Federal Rules of Evidence require that an original document be produced in order to prove its content.[3] However, the next rule holds that a copy is good enough "unless a genuine question is raised about the original's authenticity or the circumstances make it unfair to admit the duplicate."[4]

This essay, using insights derived from linguistics and the philosophy of language, explores the relationship between how natural language expresses degrees of certainty in the truth of an assertion, on the one hand, and how the law handles this issue, on the other. The hearsay rule bars certain kinds of speech acts from serving as legal evidence, in particular, assertions that report what another person earlier said, and which are offered to express the truth about the events at issue in a case. I am not the first to write about the law governing hearsay in terms of speech act theory, although discussion in the literature has been sparse. In fact, the philosopher John Langshaw Austin, to whom speech act theory is widely attributed, himself noted the connection, observing that statements offered to prove the fact of the speech act rather than the truth of the matter asserted are admissible.[5]

My goal here is to take the discussion further by discussing *linguistic evidentials* in this light as well. Consider the following scenario. A lawyer asks a witness at a trial, "Where was the defendant on June 6th when the crime took place?" The opposing lawyer should request that it first be established how the witness came to any understanding of the matter to ensure

---

[*] I wish to express my gratitude to Laurance Horn and Jennifer Glougie for advice on the literature, to Christian Dahlman and Giovanni Tuzet for comments on an earlier draft of this chapter. I am also indebted to Amanda Kadish for her excellent work as research assistant.

[1] Throughout, this essay will refer to the US Federal Rules of Evidence (FRE).
[2] FRE 403.
[3] FRE 1002.
[4] FRE 1003.
[5] Austin 1962, 13.

Lawrence M. Solan, *Linguistic Evidentials and the Law of Hearsay* In: *Philosophical Foundations of Evidence Law.* Edited by: Christian Dahlman, Alex Stein, and Giovanni Tuzet, Oxford University Press. © Christian Dahlman, Alex Stein, and Giovanni Tuzet 2021.
DOI: 10.1093/oso/9780198859307.003.0012

that he would not be giving hearsay testimony. For example: "Do you know where the defendant was?" "How do you know?" "Do you have information other than what someone told you?"

Now, imagine a language (not English) in which that information comes automatically as part of the witness's answer. The witness will use one expression if he saw the defendant at the relevant time, another expression if he knows this information from having been told, and perhaps a third if he figured it out from the circumstances. Just as English speakers include tense as part of their linguistic expressions, other languages, including Cuzco Quechua (a Peruvian language) and Turkish include information about how the speaker came to know the assertions that he makes. These linguistic elements are called *evidentials*. In essence, these languages have a built-in identifier of hearsay. They require that the speaker tip off the hearer when a statement is made based on hearsay evidence.

Moreover, there is nothing especially daunting about learning Turkish, for example, for children born into a culture that speaks that language. What this means is that a rule requiring the identification of hearsay is part of our innate linguistic endowment. Not all languages have it, but some do. When I have told Turkish law students about how their linguistic knowledge matches up with the Federal Rules of Evidence in the United States, they quickly become both amazed and entertained by the fact that there is legal consequence in a linguistic distinction that they have been making since they were young children.

2. Hearsay as a Speech Act

The most significant rule concerning the reliability of evidence is the rule against hearsay, which is the subject of much of this chapter. The US rules first define hearsay as follows:

"Hearsay" means *a statement* that:
(1) the declarant does not make while testifying at the current trial or hearing; and
(2) a party offers in evidence to prove the truth of the matter asserted in the statement.[6]

The next rule holds that hearsay is not admissible unless excepted under the rules or a law.[7] And indeed, there are many exceptions.[8]

Key to understanding this rule are the words *truth*, *statement*, and *asserted*. An assertion is one of many types of *speech act*. In his groundbreaking book, *How to Do Things with Words*, Austin created a taxonomy of speech acts, sorted by virtue of the conversational role they play.[9] Subsequently, other philosophers, most notably Searle, developed the process further.[10] Assertions are one type of speech act: statements of fact. Many, although not all assertions, are made to state a truthful proposition. When I say "Donald Trump was elected the forty-fifth president of the United States," I say it because I believe it is true, whether or not I introduce it with "I state," "I assert," "I believe," or any other expression of my relationship with the statement.

---

[6] FRE 801(c).
[7] FRE 802. There are, in fact, many exceptions, a few of which will be discussed later.
[8] See FRE 803.
[9] Austin 1962.
[10] See Searle 1969; 1979.

Of course, it is not always clear just what is being asserted. Our statements are sometimes ambiguous, and we frequently hedge to cover our bases just in case our views may not be received well. Philosophers have expressed concern with our taking assertions too seriously, seeking to parse language instead of discovering communicative intent and forgiving errors. Williams writes of "fetishizing assertion,"[11] part of lawyers' stock and trade.

Other speech acts include questions, promises, and performatives, all of which have legal relevance. In court exchanges between lawyer and witness, the lawyer is supposed to ask questions, the witness is supposed to answer them with assertions of fact. If a question asks for something other than a fact, it is generally objectionable. For example, lay witnesses are typically not permitted to offer opinions. Questions, in turn, have no truth value— they are neither true nor false. However, it is possible to embed presuppositions in a question, making them seem unfair because they may be based on an unproven assumption. The classic example is "when did you stop beating your wife?" Such questions containing embedded presuppositions are also objectionable.

Much of the literature on speech acts focuses on performatives, which are also neither true nor false. Performatives are utterances that literally perform an act when they are uttered in by an appropriate person in appropriate circumstances. Examples include: "I hereby pronounce you husband and wife," and "The court hereby sentences you to four years in prison."

Generally, the appropriate use of "hereby" is a test for whether an utterance is a performative. That word suggests that the speaker has the authority to perform the act expressed.

Perhaps surprising to some, promises are also generally considered to be without truth value, and are thus not assertions either. If I commit to buying a container of milk on my way home from work, and forgot to do it, it would be odd to say that I lied by breaking my promise. The law of contracts is all about broken promises. It holds people responsible for their failure to perform irrespective of their intent, at least for the most part.[12]

What if I never intended to keep my promise? That is considered not a lie, but rather an insincere promise. Some philosophers argue that making and then breaking an insincere promise should have greater legal consequences than a mere breach of contract,[13] although that is typically not the case in US law. Perhaps because the law regards promises as sincere, unless made when the commitment is not reasonably to be believed, making an insincere promise may be tantamount to lying, even if they are different acts of speech.[14]

The law actually recognizes the distinction between assertions and other acts of speech. It does so tacitly through the hearsay doctrine itself. But it also does so overtly by distinguishing between hearsay statements and what the law calls *verbal acts*. *Black's Law Dictionary* defines:

---

[11] Williams 2002, 100–10. I discuss this issue further with respect to legal interpretation in Solan 2014.

[12] For insightful discussion of contract law in the context of speech act theory, see Tiersma 1986.

[13] Schriffrin 2009; Ayres and Klass 2005.

[14] See, e.g., *Leonard v. Pepsico*, 88 F. Supp. 2d 116, (S.D.N.Y. 1999), aff'd 210 F.3d 88 (2d Cir. 2000). The court held that no reasonable person would believe that Pepsi, as part of an advertisement, had actually committed to selling a military jet at a large discount, as could be inferred from a television commercial in which a teenager landed a jet plane in a schoolyard. Such cases are relatively rare, but cases involving puffery—overstating the quality of a thing or service being sold—show the extent to which the law tolerates a lack of candor in commercial life. As one court described it: "Puffery cannot, by definition, mislead consumers because it is a type of statement on which no reasonable consumer would rely." *Verisign, Inc. v. XYZ.COM LLC*, 848 F.3d 292, 313 (4th Cir. 2016).

1. Verbal act. An act performed through the medium of words, either spoken or written.
2. Evidence. A statement offered to prove the words themselves because of their legal effect (e.g., the terms of a will). For this purpose, the statement is not considered hearsay.[15]

The first definition corresponds to the one used by philosophers of language for speech acts in general. The second definition is the one more relevant for our purposes in that it describes the particularly legal meaning in which verbal acts are speech acts other than assertions with truth value. Most statements in a will, to continue with *Black*'s example, are performatives, and thus verbal acts in this sense. One can leave an asset to a beneficiary by stating so in one's will. The act of bequeathing is itself a type of performative speech act as far as linguists and philosophers are concerned.

Cases using this expression come both before and after the adoption of the Federal Rules of Evidence in 1975. As for older cases, consider *Allen v. Morris*,[16] a 1912 case from Missouri. The case concerned a claim for ownership of land by virtue of adverse possession. That doctrine allows one who has occupied land owned by another to claim that land for herself after a period (traditionally twenty-one years) of continual, open possession. In other words, it is a "use it or lose it" doctrine. Relevant to such a claim is whether the occupier has adequately informed the original owner of the occupation. Such speech would constitute an admissible verbal act, because the statement is not offered for its truth, but rather to demonstrate that the original owner was properly informed. That is exactly what happened in the Allen case.

For a more modern example, consider the following scenario taken from a 2010 Maryland case, *Garner v. State*: a driver is stopped by the police for driving while his license was revoked. During the stop, the police find a collection of plastic bags, each containing cocaine, in the car's glove compartment. While all this was happening, the driver's cell phone rang, and a police officer answered. He testified: "On the other line was a male voice, sounded like a male. I said hello. He said, 'yo, can I get a 40.' I asked his name, he then hung up the telephone."[17]

Referring to both cases and evidence treatises, the court held that this testimony was not hearsay, and was thus admissible as a verbal act as evidence that the driver possessed the cocaine not for his own personal use, but rather for sale to others, which is a more serious crime.[18] Similar results occur when the police record the placement of illegal bets as proof that the defendant was engaged in an illegal gambling scheme. Speech making a contract, whether legal or illegal, is simply not the same as speech reporting an event. In contrast, if the person who called the driver stated that he had offered to buy cocaine earlier, that would be hearsay even though the original offer would remain a verbal act.

Occasionally, courts actually refer to speech as alternatively constituting a *verbal act* or a *performative*. In fact, Garner is such a case.[19] Perhaps the best articulation of this relationship can be found in Posner J's opinion in *United States v. Montana*, decided by the United

---

[15] Garner 2019.
[16] *Allen v. Morris*, 148 S.W. 905 (Mo. 1912).
[17] *Garner v. State*, 414 Md. 372, 377, 995 A.2d 694, 697 (Md. App. 2010).
[18] Ibid., 385, 702.
[19] Ibid. ("Whether the caller makes a commitment or just tries to make a bet or buy drugs, placing the call is not simply an assertion but action seeking to achieve these ends, and the performative quality of such behavior justifies nonhearsay treatment when it is proved as a means of showing that bets are taken or drugs are sold where the call is received.")

States Court of Appeals for the Seventh Circuit in 1999.[20] In that case, the defendant had driven the getaway car from a bank robbery. He asked his co-defendant (Dodd), who actually robbed the bank, to testify that he (Montana) was unaware that he was driving away from a crime scene, which was apparently not true. A federal marshal overheard some of the proposed transaction and testified as follows: "Shortly before the end of the trial, Dodd gave Montana's lawyer a note for Montana's mother, who after she read it told the lawyer that the note demanded money in exchange for Dodd's having testified favorably to Montana. The following morning, a deputy U.S. marshal heard Dodd tell Montana to tell Montana's father that 'it's going to be $ 10,000' for the favorable testimony. The district judge allowed the marshal to testify to what he had heard."[21]

Both the trial court and the court of appeals held that this testimony was not hearsay. Posner J, who is well-studied in philosophy, explained:

> The government argues that it was admissible as a "verbal act" ... thus echoing the linguist's distinction between performative and elocutionary utterances. The latter narrate, describe, or otherwise convey information, and so are judged by their truth value (information is useful only if true—indeed is *information* only if it is true); the former—illustrated by a promise, offer, or demand—commit the speaker to a course of action. Performative utterances are not within the scope of the hearsay rule, because they do not make any truth claims. Had the marshal overheard Dodd tell Montana, "your father has promised me $ 10,000," Dodd's overheard statement would have been hearsay, because its value as evidence would have depended on its being truthful, that is, on such a promise having actually been made.[22]

Courts often describe verbal acts as statements that have legal effect, separating them from statements of fact offered for their truth. This statement follows the Advisory Committee notes on Rule 801, which defines hearsay.[23] But whether a performative has a legal effect or not does not determine its status as a performative. For example, a parent who promises their child a new bicycle as a birthday present will have breached no legal duty by deciding later not to give such a lavish gift. Yet the promise is a verbal act, and not hearsay, if quoted later. Thus, having a legal effect is a sufficient, but not a necessary element of being a performative, and the same should hold for verbal acts in legal contexts.

No doubt the rule against hearsay not only leads to the exclusion of unreliable evidence, but it also leads to the exclusion of reliable evidence. The law can deal with this fact in two different ways: either by making the hearsay rule a default rule, which a judge can override when the hearsay evidence is deemed reliable, or by creating subcategories of exceptions to the rule. For the most part, US law has chosen the second path. Rule 803 lists the exceptions to the hearsay rule, which include excited utterances, records of past contemporaneous recollection, information conveyed for medical diagnosis and treatment, marriage certificates, business records kept in the regular course of business, and public and religious records.[24]

[20] *United States v. Montana*, 199 F.3d 947 (7th Cir. 1999).
[21] Ibid., 948.
[22] Ibid., 949.
[23] See FRE Advisory Committee notes to Rule 801(c): "The effect is to exclude from hearsay the entire category of 'verbal acts' and 'verbal parts of an act,' in which the statement itself affects the legal rights of the parties or is a circumstance bearing on conduct affecting their rights."
[24] FRE 803.

Moreover, an earlier statement by an opposing party falls outside the definition of hearsay, which, in practice, frees prison cellmates to testify, truthfully or not, to a defendant having boasted to having committed the crime that is the subject of the trial.

Let us explore a few more details about speech act theory. Probably the most important contribution of both Austin and Searle is the distinction between what is said and what the speaker is doing with what is said. Theorists call the former the *locution* of an utterance, and the latter the utterance's *illocutionary force*. For instance, when one utters an English sentence introduced by an interrogative word, such as "what," and with the verb preceding the subject, the utterance's illocutionary force is that of a question. Similarly, for such acts as orders, warnings, and assertions.

Utterances also have what philosophers call a *perlocutionary effect*, which is the effect that they have on the hearer. Ideally, we would wish a good match between what a speaker tries to communicate and what a hearer understands the speaker to have communicated. Some verbs, however, focus on the effect of speech on the hearer, and not on how the speaker accomplished that effect. *Convince* and *persuade* are such verbs. If I persuade someone that Trump did a great job handling the Coronavirus pandemic, it matters only that someone who did not take that position in advance now has taken that position as a result of my persuasive utterance. How I went about the persuasion is not part of the equation. I can persuade through honest argument, subterfuge, or bald-faced lies. Ethical rules governing the conduct of lawyers, and the rules of evidence themselves, combine to limit the persuasive tools that can be used in the courtroom. Centrally, lawyers may not lie, whether to a judge, to opposing lawyers, or to anyone else involved in a legal proceeding.[25]

This, however, does not mean that lawyers are straightforward in all of their communications. In interactions between lawyers and judges, there would be little tolerance for the lawyer who uses half-truths to deceive both the opposing lawyer and the court. But there is no prohibition against cajoling a witness into agreeing to the accuracy of a characterization that is true, but at the same time accurate and unfair.

Relevant to this point, linguist Schane has defined hearsay in terms of its illocutionary force.[26] The illocutionary force of a hearsay statement must be an assertion that has a truth value, and it must be offered at trial to prove the truth of the matter asserted. Examples discussed earlier confirm that there may be other reasons for which testimony is solicited, and such testimony is not hearsay.

On top of the rule against hearsay are the requirements that testimony be relevant and additional protections of its reliability.[27] These two aspects of the law of evidence—relevance and reliability—are each grounded in the philosophy of language. Let us begin with relevance. Relevance is not only significant in determining what should count as evidence in a legal case, but it also plays a large role in how we communicate with one another in everyday life. The philosopher Grice wrote that conversation is, as a general matter, a negotiated process between speaker and hearer, each participant taking a turn, and each attempting to advance the conversation by contributing to it in a way that takes into account how the contribution is likely to be understood. Grice called this the cooperative principle: "Make

---

[25] See American Bar Association 2020, Rules 3.1, 3.3.
[26] Schane 2006, ch. 3.
[27] For discussion of these and other aspects of evidence theory, see Pardo 2013; Cohen 1994.

your conversational contribution such as is required, at the stage at which it occurs, by the accepted purpose or direction of the talk exchange in which you are engaged."[28]

How does one accomplish this cooperative stance? One tries to follow four of Grice's four maxims: quantity (say all that is necessary, but not too much); quality (tell the truth); relation (be relevant); and manner (say it clearly and in an appropriate tone). Of course, we do not always conform our speech to these maxims. The further we stray, the more we risk our hearer drawing inappropriate inferences from our words. To take Grice's example, "Suppose that A and B are talking about a mutual friend, C, who is now working in a bank. A asks B how C is getting on in his job, and B replies, *Oh, quite well, I think; he likes his colleagues, and he hasn't been to prison yet.*"[29] Why would B say such a thing? The best answer is that we cannot tell without learning why he said what he said. Is C an honest person with unsavory co-workers? Does C have a criminal record and is likely to do something illegal again? Is it good or bad that C likes his colleagues? The bottom line is that we use context automatically and unselfconsciously in drawing inferences about communicative intent.

One may argue that the general rules of conversation do not apply to testimony in court and are therefore not germane to this discussion. To some extent this is fair comment because courtroom testimony is highly stylized. The lawyer asks questions, the witness answers them. That only resembles what we think of as a normal conversation. Yet it would be a mistake to overemphasize the differences. After all, the lawyer must seek relevant information (relation); the witness must answer truthfully (quality); the witness may be confined to answering the question that was asked, and not to expound in a self-serving way (quantity); and rules of courtroom decorum severely limit how the various actors may state the things they wish to say (manner). If either speaker were to say, "that's bullshit" in response to the other, for example, most judges would find the conduct intolerable.

Grice concerns himself with the pragmatics of conversation, rather than the literal meaning of what is said. The issue in Grice's philosophy is not what the words mean, but rather what the speaker intends to communicate by uttering them. Grice draws a line between the linguistic meanings of the words on the one hand, and the "conversational implicatures" on the other. It is in the service of drawing conversational implicatures and influencing the implicatures that our conversational partners are likely to draw that we use the cooperative principle. To take a classic everyday example, a dinner guest who was just served a cup of coffee may request cream by asking, "May I please have some cream," which is a direct request. That same person may also ask, "Excuse me, is there any cream?" or another such question. The host will understand such an inquiry as an indirect request for cream. It is certainly not a question about whether the world has any cream, or for that matter, even whether the host has any cream. To take a legal example, when a police officer asked a young motorist, "Does the trunk open," he was not asking about the functioning of the spring mechanism that opens the trunk of the car. Rather, he was issuing either a request or a command for the motorist to open the trunk.[30]

Grice's cooperative principle has generated a great deal of literature over the years, including some controversy. For one thing, not all of the maxims are of equal weight. In particular, some people flout the maxim of quantity by saying more than is necessary, and

---

[28] Grice 1975, 45.
[29] Ibid., 43.
[30] See *Schneckloth v. Bustamonte*, 412 U.S. 218 (1973).

others flout it by not saying enough. We all know chatterboxes and taciturn people. These issues affect conversation by virtue of their effects on relevance. A speaker who talks too much frequently provides a mixture of relevant and irrelevant information, forcing he listener to engage in the mental exercise of distinguishing one from the other, which is not always an easy task.

Recognizing these and other facts relating to the cooperative principle, some theorists have hypothesized that the entire principle can be reduced to relevance.[31] The way the conversation is advanced is by the exchange of relevant information with respect to questions under discussion. The maxim of manner can also be reduced to saying things in a way to make the relevant information sufficiently salient. This leaves us with the maxim of quality—i.e., the need to be truthful—and the maxim of relation—i.e., relevance as core principles in linguistic pragmatics.

If truthfulness and relevance are at the core of everyday conversation, it is no wonder that they are also at the core of courtroom testimony. The law of evidence concerns itself with truth-finding, and if evidence is limited, at least in part, to that which is both truthful and relevant to the questions in dispute, truth is more likely to be found. The fact that these values drive everyday conversational interaction makes the rules seem only natural, and thus easier both to enforce and to ob.[32]

As the philosopher McCreedy has demonstrated, one way of cooperating is to provide information to one's hearer on how reliable the information being conveyed is, at least in the mind of the speaker.[33] In this regard, two different sorts of judgment may be relevant. First, we can simply convey our assessment of reliability. Second, we can convey how we obtained the information, and allow the hearer to draw conclusions from that fact, generally assuming that we share such judgments. English has hints of both sorts of information. Other languages, as we shall see, incorporate them more formally as part of the grammar. These are what is known as evidentials, and shall be the subject of the remainder of this chapter.

3. Evidentials in Natural Language

Languages generally have the means for allowing us to express how it is that we came to believe in the truth of a proposition, but they differ widely in how they do so. There is some disagreement among philosophers and linguists as to whether evidentials are a matter of pragmatic inference, or whether they are actually part of the literal meaning of the assertion.[34] Moreover, researchers have found that languages differ with respect to syntactic limitations on where in a sentence an evidential may occur.[35] The arguments are complex. For our purposes, not much hinges on the resolution of these technical issues.

Consider Faller's example taken from Cuzco Quechua, which has grammatical markers for evidential information. It is not improper to make a statement that contains a hearsay evidential marker, and at the same time to say that the statement is untrue.[36]

---

[31] The groundbreaking work in this domain is Sperber and Wilson 1995. The first edition of their book was published in 1986.
[32] Tyler 1990.
[33] McCready 2015.
[34] See Murray 2017.
[35] See Korotkova 2021.
[36] Faller 2019, 18.

Pay-kuna=s (s)he-PL=REP qulqi-ta money-ACC saqiy-wa-n. leave-1o-3 Mana=**má,**
no=IMPR ni not un one sol-ta Sol-ACC saqi-sha-wa-n=chu. leave-PROG-1O-3=NEG

"They left me money (I was told)." "(But) no, they didn't leave me one sol."

In Quechua, *má,* is the hearsay marker, which is embedded in the sentence.

The same interpretive option applies to English: "I was told that I had inherited $1 million, but they didn't leave me even a single dollar" is not understood as a contradiction. We can compare this to the contradiction in "I inherited $1 million from them, but I didn't inherit any money from them." Without an indication that that one is repeating something learned through hearsay, one commits to the proposition. With the hearsay designation, one does not do so.

English is relatively impoverished in this respect. We generally use adverbs, such as *reportedly, totally, apparently,* and *actually. Actually* conveys confidence in the truth of the matter asserted. In a very interesting doctoral dissertation to which we shall return, Glougie argues that *actually* is used by witnesses in police interviews to indicate that their belief is based on evidence in which they have maximum confidence.[37] The term is most often used to correct a mistaken impression or to emphasize. Generally, this indicates that the speaker has either seen or heard evidence of the proposition conveyed, or actually experienced it herself. Reportedly, in contrast, signals hearsay and that the speaker has not committed to accepting the truth of the proposition that is repeated.

We also use the modal verb "must" as in, "I'm so tired and thirsty, I must have diabetes." "Must" in this sense, in contrast to "actually," is used when we want to convey that we have drawn an inference of the fact of the matter, but have no direct evidence. It is referred to in the literature as the *epistemic must.* The fact that we can express evidentiary reliability either by using an adverb or a modal verb is instructive. It demonstrates that languages vary considerably with respect to the grammatical forms that evidentiality take.[38]

Let us look at evidentials in Turkish as a final example.[39] Turkish distinguishes between direct and indirect knowledge. Indirect knowledge includes both hearsay and inferential knowledge, along the lines of the epistemic *must* discussed earlier. -*Miš* is the marker of indirect information. Compare these sentences, taken from an article on the acquisition of proficiency in the meaning of Turkish evidentials by young children:[40]

(1) Çocuk oyun oyna—di. Child game play PAST. Direct "The child played."
(2) Çocuk oyun oyna—mış. Child game play PAST. Indirect "The child played."

The sentences are both translated as "the child played," but the first indicates that this knowledge was acquired directly, while the second indicates that it was acquired indirectly, whether through hearsay, or by inference.

Scholars have proposed that evidential markers generally form a hierarchy with respect to the degree of commitment that the speaker has to the proposition asserted. Consider a statement in which the speaker says nothing about its evidential strength:

---

[37] Glougie 2016, 98–101.
[38] For further development of this point, see Matthewson, Davis, and Rullmann 2007.
[39] See Johanson 2003, 276–7.
[40] Ozturk and Papafragou 2008, 297.

(1) Fred flew to Los Angeles from New York last Monday.

As listeners (or readers), we assume that the speaker must have a certain level of comfort with the truth of this statement. Say, if one is 85% certain that this really happened, one will generally be comfortable saying it. Now, let us look at a range of evidential markers we use in English: *supposedly, reportedly, actually, from what I'm told,* and the epistemic *must.* An important article by Davis, Potts, and Speas[41] argues that different evidentials have the effect of adjusting the speaker's communication of probable likelihood of the statement's truth. Again referring to example (1) above, adding "actually" increases the speaker's communication of confidence above the baseline of 85%, whereas "supposedly" lowers it. The various degrees of reliability seem to form a more-or-less universal hierarchy, with certainty at the top and hearsay at the bottom, at least defeasibly. For this to work, a few preliminary assumptions must be accepted in advance. First, people must share assumptions, at least in general, about what constitutes a normal baseline of probability absent an evidential marker. Second, as Davis et al. point out, this is a pragmatic account. That is, the evidential adds context to the assertion that leads the hearer to draw an inference as to its reliability. And third, while we generally find personal experience a more reliable basis than even knowledge through sensory perception, and sensory perception more reliable than the reports of others, this is not always the case.

As Glougie and others point out, it is often possible to use an evidential marker that shows more reliability than is the norm for its use in order to signal the speaker's confidence in the information being conveyed. If I say that my sister lives in Pennsylvania (which she does), at least in some languages I can use a marker of maximum trustworthiness even if I have not visited her personally if I have a firm enough belief in the truth of that statement.

4. Conclusions

Hearsay in natural language may be the prototype of a less reliable basis for evidentiary judgment without constituting a hard and fast rule. All of this has ramifications for the relationship between our construction of a legal system and our language faculties. First, and perhaps most important, part of our innate cognitive endowment appears to include our being able to judge the reliability of the information that we absorb and communicate to others. Obviously, this ability is cognitive apart from any communicative content, since we must apprehend the information in that sense before we can convey it. And to the extent it seems best described as pragmatic, rather than purely linguistically semantic, it resides in our inferential system, rather than in our grammar, even if it is expressed through particles that are grammaticalized, as in Quechua and Turkish.[42] This creates a complicated situation, in which in some languages, but not all, evidentials play a dual role of grammatical particle and expression of attitude toward a proposition.

Second, while there is a close relationship between the rule against hearsay in law and linguistic evidential phenomena, the relationship is not a one-to-one match. For one thing,

---

[41] Davis, Potts, and Speas 2007, 76.
[42] For discussion of the architecture of the language faculty, see Chomsky 2005.

natural language generally permits ad hoc exceptions by which hearsay may be tagged as particularly reliable. The rules of evidence are just that: rules.

Third, the hearsay rule is only about hearsay, whereas languages typically create a hierarchy of evidential reliability, which move from direct experience to sensory perception, inferential evidence (circumstantial in law), followed by hearsay. It is no doubt the proliferation of categories that makes it especially necessary for evidential markers to be defeasible at the margins. Languages differ from one another in the details of what they encode, but there seems to be a core of information about reliability among languages that are not in contact with each other to suggest some kind of universality.[43]

Fourth, the exceptions to the rule against hearsay are numerous and diverse. For the most part, they attempt to exempt from the rule the kinds of statements that are most likely to be reliable. These include business records, medical records, government reports, market reports, and documents regarding property ownership among others.[44] No doubt there could be more, and those listed, while generally reliable, are not always so.

Finally, while the cognitive hierarchy of evidentiality is considered more or less universal, the existence of a rule against hearsay in law is not. For example, German law has no rule against hearsay. Rather, it is up to the judge to determine the value, if any, of hearsay evidence.[45] Even the United Kingdom has a more forgiving hearsay rule in civil cases.[46] Thus, the US rule against hearsay is built directly from an aspect of the human condition, but it is molded to meet the needs of the legal system, even if imperfectly so.

References

Aikhenvald, A. Y. and Dixon. R. M. W. (eds.). (2003). *Studies in Evidentiality*. Amsterdam: John Benjamins Publishing.

American Bar Association. (2020). *Model Rules of Professional Conduct*. Chicago: ABA.

Austin, J. L. (1962). *How to do Things with Words*. Cambridge, MA: Harvard University Press.

Ayres, I. and Klass, G. (2005). *Insincere Promises: The Law of Misrepresented Intent*. New Haven, NJ: Yale University Press.

Bastuck, B. and Göpfert, B. (1994). Admission and Presentation of Evidence in Germany, *Loyola of Los Angeles International and Comparative Law Journal*, 16(3): 609–27.

Garner, B. (ed.) (2019). *Black's Law Dictionary*. Eleventh edition. Ann Arbor, MI: Thomson Reuters.

Chomsky, N. (2005). Three Factors in Language Design, *Linguistic Inquiry*, 36: 1–22.

Cohen, L. J. (1994). Some Steps Towards a General Theory of Relevance, *Synthese*, 101: 171–85.

Davis, C., Potts, C., and Speas, M. (2007). The Pragmatic Values of Evidential Sentences, *SALT*, 17: 71–88.

Faller, M. (2019). The Discourse Commitments of Illocutionary Reportatives, *Semantics and Pragmatics*, 12(2019): 1–46. Available at https://semprag.org/index.php/sp/article/view/sp.12.8/pdf (Accessed: March 25, 2021).

Glougie, J. (2016). *The Semantics and Pragmatics of English Evidential Expressions: The Expression of Evidentiality in Police Interviews*, Unpublished Ph.D dissertation (on file with the author), University of British Columbia.

---

[43] For discussion of similarities and differences among languages in this regard, see Matthewson and Glougie 2018; Aikhenvald and Dixon 2003.

[44] FRE 803.

[45] Bastuck and Göpfert 1994, 612.

[46] Civil Evidence Act of 1995, §1(1). Section 2 requires that notice be given to opposing parties that hearsay evidence will be offered. Available at https://www.legislation.gov.uk/ukpga/1995/38/contents (Accessed: March 25, 2021).

Grice, H. P. (1975). "Logic and Conversation," in P. Cole and J. Morgan (eds.), *Syntax and Semantics 3: Speech Acts*. New York: Academic Press.

Johanson, L. (2003). Evidentials in Turkic, in A. Y. Aikhenvald and R. M. W. Dixon (eds.), *Studies in Evidentiality*, 273–90. Amsterdam: John Benjamins Publishing.

Korotkova, N. (2021). The Embedding Puzzle: Constraints on Evidentials in Complement Clauses, *Linguistic Inquiry*, 52(1): 210–26. Available at https://www.mitpressjournals.org/doi/pdf/10.1162/ling_a_00363 (Accessed: March 25, 2021).

Matthewson, L., Davis, H., and Rullmann, H. (2007). Evidentials as Epistemic Modals: Evidence from St'at'imcets, *The Linguistic Variation Yearbook*, 7: 201–54.

Matthewson, L. and Glougie, J. (2018). Justification and Truth: Evidence from Languages of the World, in M. Mizumoto, S. Stich, and E. McCready (eds.), *Epistemology for the Rest of the World*. Oxford: Oxford University Press.

McCready, E. (2015). *Reliability in Pragmatics*. Oxford: Oxford University Press.

Murray, S. E. (2017). *The Semantics of Evidentials*. Oxford: Oxford University Press.

Ozturk, O. and Papafragou, A. (2008). The Acquisition of Evidentiality in Turkish, *University of Pennsylvania Working Papers in Linguistics*, 14: 296–309.

Pardo, M. S. (2013). The Nature and Purpose of Evidence Theory, *Vanderbilt Law Review*, 66: 547–613.

Schane, S. (2006). *Language and the Law*. London: Continuum.

Schriffrin, S. (2009). Could Breach of Contract be Immoral? *Michigan Law Review*, 107: 1551–68.

Searle, J. (1969). *Speech Acts: An Essay in the Philosophy of Language*. Oxford: Oxford University Press.

Searle, J. (1979). *Expression and Meaning: Studies in the Theory of Speech Acts*. Oxford: Oxford University Press.

Solan, L. M. (2014). Multilingualism and Morality in Statutory Interpretation, *Language & Law/Linguagem e Direito*, 1(1): 1–17.

Sperber, D. and Wilson, D. (1995). *Relevance: Communication and Cognition*. Second edition. Oxford: Blackwell.

Tiersma, P. (1986). The Language of Offer and Acceptance: Speech Acts and the Question of Intent. *California Law Review*, 74: 189–232.

Tyler, T. R. (1990). *Why People Obey the Law*. Princeton, NJ: Princeton University Press.

Williams, B. (2002). *Truth and Truthfulness: An Essay in Genealogy*. Princeton, NJ: Princeton University Press.

12

The Pragmatics of Evidence Discourse

Giovanni Tuzet[*]

1. Introduction

This chapter focuses on the pragmatic aspects of evidence discourse. By calling them "pragmatic," I mean the aspects that are typically the province of "pragmatics," generically defined as the study of the use of language in context. By "evidence discourse" I roughly mean the discourse that is carried out about juridical evidence. Some clarifications are in order to supplement these starting points.

The definition of "pragmatics" is notoriously a thorny issue.[1] Some take it as the study of the relations between signs and their users; others prefer to focus on the ways in which speakers use language; others insist it has to do with the use of language in context or in concrete communicative situations; others contend it concentrates on meaning in social interactions. Be that as it may, one of the disputed points is the distinction between semantics and pragmatics. I need not take a position here on the exact boundary, if any, between the two. I will simply assume, for the purpose of this work, that the discourse on evidence has syntactic, semantic, and pragmatic aspects. I will focus on some aspects that most scholars take to be pragmatic, and will keep away from the fantastic claims that all semantic aspects can be reduced to pragmatic ones or vice versa.

Taken as above, "evidence discourse" comprises the discourse on juridical evidence carried out by various subjects in different contexts, namely, in particular, parties and factfinders in a legal case, law-makers determining some aspects of evidence law, and scholars discussing evidentiary issues. The most interesting context among these is arguably the first, that is, the context of a legal case in which parties and factfinders discuss about evidence for the purposes of its admission, presentation, and evaluation. This context includes discourse which is evidence itself, namely testimony. The interaction between parties, witnesses, and factfinders offers a great deal of linguistic material and phenomena susceptible to pragmatic analysis and philosophical reflection. This is the context the present contribution is about. The discipline called "forensic linguistics"[2] studies the linguistic features of courtroom interaction, and some specific works address the "pragmatics of evidentiality" as the study of

[*] I thank Christian Dahlman, Paolo Labinaz, Francesca Poggi, Alessio Sardo, and Iza Skoczeń for comments on earlier versions of this work.

[1] See, e.g., Levinson 1983, ch. 1; Horn and Ward 2004. As starting points of the nineteenth century literature on pragmatics, see Morris 1938; 1946 (drawing on Peirce's reflections on signs and basically claiming that semiotics divides into syntax, semantics, and pragmatics, defined as the study of the relations of signs to other signs, objects, and interpreters respectively; then refining the former definitions in behaviorally oriented terms).

[2] See Coulthard and Johnson 2010; Tiersma and Solan 2012a, Part VI; Solan, "Linguistic Evidentials and the Law of Hearsay," ch. 11, in this volume. Among others, cf. Levinson 1979; Bülow-Møller 1991; Hansen 2008; Sønderberg Mortensen and Mortensen 2017; Liao and Sun 2017.

Giovanni Tuzet, *The Pragmatics of Evidence Discourse* In: *Philosophical Foundations of Evidence Law*. Edited by: Christian Dahlman, Alex Stein, and Giovanni Tuzet, Oxford University Press. © Christian Dahlman, Alex Stein, and Giovanni Tuzet 2021.
DOI: 10.1093/oso/9780198859307.003.0013

epistemic or doxastic stances expressed in linguistic exchange (with phrases like "I know," "I think," "For sure," "Probably," etc.). Being a philosopher of law, I will rather point at the philosophical and legal issues that one can find in such context and matters.

It is of some importance that in this context "discourse" is more appropriate than "conversation," if, by the latter, we mean the "familiar predominant kind of talk in which two or more participants freely alternate in speaking, which generally occurs outside specific institutional settings like religious services, law courts, classrooms and the like."[3] Courtroom interaction has obviously numerous institutional features that make it different from everyday talk and interaction. For one thing, turn-taking is not left to the spontaneous interaction of participants, and it is in great part pre-allocated rather than determined on a turn-by-turn basis. There are legal constraints on turn-taking and allowable contributions. For another thing, courtroom interaction is a conflicting exchange to a large extent and for obvious reasons that, again, make it different from everyday interaction generally governed by some cooperation principle.

Several philosophers of law have dealt with the pragmatics of law-making (legislation in particular) and the interpretation of statutory law.[4] Many of them contend that legislation and its interpretation are conflict-harboring activities, due to the conflicting interests of political parties, different institutional bodies, courts, and so on. Scholars discuss in this perspective whether Grice's cooperative principle and maxims apply to those activities. Those scholars rarely consider the pragmatics of evidence discourse, which is instead the subject of the present work.

The aspects the chapter deals with are the following: the nature of the speech acts performed in evidence discourse (Section 2); the role of implicatures (Section 3) and presuppositions (Section 4) in such discourse; and the place that deixis, i.e., the use of indexicals and demonstratives, has in it (Section 5). I claim in particular: that evidence discourse is mainly assertive; that problems associated with implicatures are minimized as questioners are skilled and questions are specific; that exploitation of presupposition is avoided by counsel's vigilance and judicial control; and, finally, that deixis reveals the ostensive dimension of evidence discourse. These points are relevant to an appropriate shaping and administration of evidence law.

2. Speech Acts

It is well known that speech act theory began with John Austin's protest that not every use of language amounts to a statement about how things are. Austin called "constative fallacy" the claim that any meaningful utterance amounts to a true or false statement; in fact, as he pointed out, there are utterances that do not "describe," or "report," or "constate" anything at all. They perform acts of a different sort, like making a promise, giving a name, making a bet, issuing an order, and many others.[5] Austin called them "performatives," and eventually elaborated a general theory of "illocutionary acts" (whose details can be put aside here).

---

[3] Levinson 1983, 284.

[4] See especially Marmor 2008; 2011; 2014; Capone and Poggi 2016; Poggi and Capone 2017; Moreso and Chilovi 2018; Chiassoni 2019, ch. 3; Skoczeń 2019. Several contributions discuss Marmor's claims on the strategic dimension of statutory law and legal interpretation.

[5] Austin 1975, 3 ff. Other works, such as Searle 1969; 1979, systematized and regimented the theory of speech acts.

Many jurists, especially in Europe, welcomed this theoretical achievement, since it was clear to them that legal language is mostly used to do something other than stating how the world is. Issuing orders, as making wills or establishing procedures, has a different point: it says how the world *has* to be. It is the normative use of language, broadly speaking, whose significance is not captured by standard truth-conditional semantics.[6]

Evidence discourse is different, though. To make a couple of examples, "I saw the defendant run away from the building" (uttered by a witness) and "The witness didn't hesitate to answer" (uttered by a juror) are uses of language that report what happened. They have truth-values, and of course they can be treated with truth-conditional semantics. Insofar as evidence utterances belong to this category, evidence discourse is assertive. It reports, truly or falsely, how the world is, or was, or will be, in certain respects. This is not to deny that evidence discourse in courtroom and other legal contexts has specific features which make it different from discourse about scientific evidence outside the courtroom, or other than discourse about historical evidence just for the sake of historical knowledge. Some of its institutional features make evidence discourse in legal contexts different from evidence discourse in other contexts. Still, the point of reporting what a witness perceived, or a juror perceived about the witness' demeanor, is assertive. It consists in making an assertion, as empirical science and history make assertions about the world. As an additional example, consider "This biological trace belongs to the defendant" as uttered by an expert witness. It is an assertion on the source of the biological material; it is requested and made for the sake of deciding a case, for a practical purpose; but this does not change its nature, as the practical use of science does not turn it into politics or morality.

Not every utterance that has to do with juridical evidence belongs to that category, though. When participants in this discourse make points about evidentiary items, it can be for the purpose of applying a legal rule or standard. Take the sentence "This evidence is inadmissible." If uttered by counsel, it is rather a request that the judge exclude the evidence, given a certain rule of exclusion. At the same time, it must be clear from the context why the evidence is inadmissible according to counsel. That is, the discourse must be on some property of the evidence which makes it inadmissible in the relevant legal system. For instance, the evidence is inadmissible because it is hearsay. Then, when this is made clear, the speaker performs a complex speech act, or more than a single speech act: the evidence is categorized as hearsay and, because of the relevant rule, it has to be excluded. This is assertive in part (the evidence is hearsay and there is a rule that mandates its exclusion) and in part it amounts to a request addressed to the judge (the evidence has to be excluded).

Now imagine that the judge utters the same sentence ("This evidence is inadmissible"). The complex speech act performed by the judge can be reconstructed as an assertion about the evidence (it is hearsay), plus an assertion about the relevant rule (there is a rule mandating its exclusion) and a decision on the merits (the evidence is excluded). The last component is obviously absent from the counsel's speech act, where a request is prominent. Given the institutional powers of the judge, "This evidence is inadmissible" becomes a decision which excludes the evidence. To use a different terminology, such a judicial utterance

---

[6] It is interesting to note that contemporary deontic logic was born some years earlier (see von Wright 1951) and originated from the difficulty of giving, in terms of truth-values, a logical account of the inferences involving imperatives, requests, pleas, etc. (see Jørgensen 1937; Ross 1944). It was a way of avoiding the embarrassing conclusion that such uses of language amount to nonsense (as defined by the standards of logical positivism; see Ayer 1936).

has some "constitutive" effects that the counsel's utterance of the same sentence cannot have. But the assertive component is dominant if the sentence is uttered by an external observer who makes no request and has no institutional powers; that observer would only point out that, according to the relevant rule, the evidence is inadmissible (and should be excluded).

Alternatively, one can use the distinction between direct and indirect speech acts, and claim that by uttering "This evidence is inadmissible" one makes an assertion about the evidence and can perform different indirect speech acts depending on the context and the speaker's institutional role. (Constructing a complex speech act made of different components, and individuating direct and indirect speech acts, are different strategies from a theoretical viewpoint; but their difference is of no great concern here.)

A similar point can be made about the factfinders' verdict. Simply put, the question is this: is a verdict assertive or constitutive? If you subscribe to the former view, it is presumably because the verdict is either true or false (the defendant either did or did not what he or she is charged with). If you subscribe to the latter view, it is presumably because the verdict produces legal effects. For Austin, there is a class of performatives, which he called "verdictives," that are exemplified by "Guilty" declared by the jury.[7] He differentiated them from assertions because their content exceeds a description or report of the relevant facts. Some important legal theorists went farther than this and claimed that judicial determinations on facts are constitutive in that they produce legal effects (conviction when a criminal defendant is found guilty, liability in a civil case).[8]

Actually, I think there is a false dichotomy fallacy in the problem if presented as above. A verdict like "Guilty" can be reconstructed as a complex speech act, or, alternatively, as a direct speech act connected with indirect ones. In one understanding, it is the conclusion of an inference like the following: given the evidence (minor premise) and given the relevant legal norm (major premise), the defendant is found guilty (conclusion). It is a complex speech act, being an argument made of premises and conclusion.[9] When only the conclusion is stated, as it happens with juries giving no reasons for their verdicts, the premises are left implicit. When also the premises are made explicit, as it happens with courts giving written reasons for their decisions, the full argument is made explicit and available for subsequent uses (appeal, scholarly comment, etc.). And, again, the utterance context affects the nature of those premises and conclusions. "Guilty" uttered by an external observer is not the same as uttered by the prosecutor, and not the same as uttered by the jury. The observer's utterance sounds like an assertion, while the prosecutor makes a normative request and the jury's verdict establishes a conclusion with legal effects.

A verdict, not surprisingly, was for Austin a paradigmatic case of a "verdictive" speech act; but in his words it also has an "exercitive" dimension, being an exercise of power, and a "commissive" dimension, generating some specific commitments.[10]

---

[7]   Austin 1975, 42–3, 45, 88, 151, 153–5. Austin sees that verdicts need to be *justified*, and if they are not so they are "bad," though not infelicitous (ibid., 43); he adds that "for a certain performative utterance to be happy, certain statements have *to be true*" (ibid., 45), but the truths concerned in this respect are quite trivial ones—e.g., it is true that when I am apologizing I am doing something (ibid., 46).

[8]   See Ross 1944, 45–6; Kelsen 1945, 135–6.

[9]   On evidence and argumentation, see Bex, "Argumentation and Evidence," ch. 13, in this volume. By the way, it is an insight from Peirce that the (pragmatic) meaning of a proposition is fully grasped when one understands it as premise or conclusion of possible arguments (cf. Bellucci 2014).

[10]   Austin 1975, 153, 155. This accommodates some claims of the jurists on the verdict's going beyond assertion. Another example of exercitive speech act is the awarding of damages (ibid., 154).

In any case, the minor premise of the above argument retains its assertive nature. It is properly understood as an assertion about the evidence. It is true that evidence in legal contexts must be collected, presented, and evaluated according to legal criteria. But, as has been pointed out, taking evidence discourse as (nothing but) constitutive makes it impossible to make errors in factual determinations.[11] The possibility of false positives and false negatives requires evidence discourse to be assertive. It must be on the relevant facts, the probative facts and the facts to be proved. By uttering "I saw the defendant run away from the building," the eyewitness makes an assertion, as the opposing counsel does by claiming that the visual capacity of the eyewitness was impaired at the time, and so on. If we follow this line of argument the assertive nature of the claims on the evidence is transmitted, as it were, to the claims on the facts to be proved. Then "Guilty" becomes a statement on the facts to be proved, either true or false. It is precisely this what we need for the claim that verdicts are either true or false, and that true ones divide into true positives (in favor of deserving claimants) and true negatives (against undeserving claimants), while false ones divide into false positives (in favor of undeserving claimants) and false negatives (against deserving claimants).

The assertive dimension of evidence discourse is indeed prominent in the utterances of witnesses, both lay and expert, elicited by questions. A specific issue arising in this context is the definition of "perjury," since to qualify an assertive utterance as perjury we need to know not only what counts as an assertion, but also what the perjury qualification stands for. Is falsity a necessary condition of perjury? Is the intent to deceive or mislead also needed? And what if the assertion is literally true but misleading? This will be one of the points of the next section.

To sum up what we have been saying so far, evidence discourse is mostly assertive, but not exclusively so. Witnesses answer questions, and questions are not assertions, but are asked for the purpose of prompting assertions. Assertion is a prominent speech act in the discourse about evidence, *a fortiori* in the discourse that is evidence itself (testimony); still, assertion is not the only speech act performed in evidence discourse. Participants ask questions, advance pleas, make requests, suggest inferences, and produce decisions with legal effects. Courtroom interaction is a complex pragmatic affair.

3. Implicatures

The British philosopher Paul Grice is probably the most important figure in contemporary pragmatics. Many recent debates (which exceed the scope of this work) turn around positions described as Neo-Gricean or Post-Gricean. One of his main contributions, as is well know, was the claim that speakers usually follow what he labeled "Cooperative Principle"[12]

---

[11] See Ferrer 2004; "Proven Facts, Beliefs, and Reasoned Verdicts," ch. 3, in this volume. Also performative and constitutive words need to be appropriate to the situation. Errors are also possible within a performative or constitutive framework, as shown by Austin's doctrine of "infelicities," divided into "misfires" and "abuses;" but Austin's focus is on procedural errors, as it were, not on substantive ones (see Austin 1975, 14 ff.).

[12] "Make your conversational contribution such as is required, at the stage at which it occurs, by the accepted purpose or direction of the talk exchange in which you are engaged" (Grice 1989, 26).

together with four maxims falling under this principle: the maxims of Quantity, Quality, Relation, and Manner.[13]

(1) The *Quantity* Maxim is made up of two submaxims: (1.1) make your contribution to conversation as informative as required (for the current purposes of the exchange); and (1.2) do not make your contribution more informative than is required.

(2) The *Quality* Maxim states, "Try to make your contribution one that is true," and is made up of two submaxims: (2.1) do not say what you believe to be false; and (2.2) do not say that for which you lack adequate evidence.

(3) The *Relation* Maxim is "be relevant" (which is terse but conceals, as Grice said, a number of problems, such as questions about kinds of relevance, shifts in conversation, topic changes, and so on).

(4) Finally, the *Manner* Maxim (concerning *how* what is said is to be said) amounts to "be perspicuous" and comprises four submaxims at least: (4.1) avoid obscurity of expression; (4.2) avoid ambiguity; (4.3) be brief (avoid unnecessary prolixity); and (4.4) be orderly.

Those maxims are framed as if the general purpose of conversation were a maximally effective exchange of information, but Grice's prospect was to generalize them to allow for other purposes such as influencing the actions of others. Legal contexts belong in fact to the category of conflicting scenarios, where the point is not so much the exchange of information but the discussion of conflicting views and the making of decisions that impact people's life. Courtroom interaction is a case in point. Still, it is reasonable to claim that, with qualifications and possible exceptions (more on this later), also speakers in legal contexts, and in courtroom in particular, are expected to comply with the maxims. We expect participants to: (1) give the appropriate amount of information (quantity maxim, as too little evidence generates adverse inferences, and too much generates side issues like waste of time, unnecessary expenses, credibility issues, etc.); (2) be truthful or at least be able to evidentially justify what is said (quality maxim, especially for witnesses); (3) be relevant (relation maxim); and (4) be perspicuous (manner maxim). As a matter of fact, we know that courtroom interaction is strategic. This holds especially for parties and counsel. The strategic dimension depends of course on the conflicting interests. So, it is not unreasonable to suspect that at times some of the participants violate some of the maxims for the purpose of prevailing. In addition, to mark the difference with out-of-court interaction, there are definite procedures (e.g., formal turn-taking), privileges (some subjects can be exempt from testimony), and rules of exclusion (e.g., hearsay).

Continuing with Grice's account, he noted that maxims may be violated in a variety of ways, including intent to mislead, open unwillingness to cooperate, clash of requirements (quantity versus quality), and intentional *flouting* as blatant failure to fulfill a maxim. He put his attention on this phenomenon. Suppose you are asked an opinion about a politician and you answer that he sings very well. The answer blatantly violates the relation maxim. But, assuming the speaker is cooperative, hearers can realize that what is meant is a different thing,

---

[13] Grice 1989, 26 ff. The status of (some of) the maxims has been disputed; see, for instance, Sperber and Wilson 1995 (replacing the maxims with a principle of relevance); Poggi 2016 (claiming that, as it happens with customary rules, pervasive uncertainty about their application makes the maxims inapplicable).

namely that he's not a good politician. So, in a case like this, what you mean is different from what you say. When a maxim is so exploited, a *conversational implicature* is generated.[14] This makes sense of the maxims' open violations. But now suppose you are explicitly asked whether, by uttering that sentence, you meant he is not a good politician. You may answer: "Oh no, he sings very well and is a good politician." This might puzzle your hearers but does not contradict what you said earlier. Conversational implicatures have this trait: they are *cancelable*. Speakers can cancel them without contradiction.[15]

Now, if the witness says "I saw the defendant run away from the building," we can infer that what is meant is that he or she saw the defendant do that *on that day* (even more precisely, on that day at a given time). This is worked out assuming that the speaker follows the maxim of quantity. The utterance does not specify the time of the action, but construction in line with the requirement of optimal information takes the utterance as referred to the day in question. If it is found out that the defendant was in a different place on that day, the witness may add: "Well, I meant I saw that the day before." This does not contradict the earlier statement and cancels the implicature. To avoid embarrassing situations of this sort, skilled questioners are always after explicitness and disambiguate tricky statements. As a vivid example, consider the following exchange from the oft-quoted case, *Bronston v. United States*:[16]

Q. Do you have any bank account in Swiss banks, Mr. Bronston?
A. No, Sir.
Q. Have you ever?
A. The company had an account there for about six months, in Zurich.

The implicature, according to the maxim of quantity, would be that Bronston never had a personal account in Swiss banks, which in fact he had. A skilled questioner would have smelled the trick, or suspected at least what was going on, and would have further questioned Bronston. As a theoretical rendering of the issue, one can claim that in ordinary interactions we usually take our interlocutors to be benevolent and competent, whereas in special contexts we rightly adopt different strategies and proceed with more caution, processing what we are said in more sophisticated ways.[17] Courtroom interaction is not just conflicting; in adversarial systems it is adversarial, as spectacularly shown by cross-examination. In the *Bronston* case it was appropriate to suspend the benevolence-cum-competence assumption, and adopt a different strategy of questioning and interpreting what was said. After all, sometimes people brag about things they don't know, or just like to lie, and especially when interests diverge they have an incentive not to tell the whole truth.

---

[14] The implicature, to be conversational, must be "worked out" by the hearer; otherwise it is a *conventional implicature* depending on the conventional meaning of some words, like "but" in "He's poor but honest" (Grice 1989, 25–6). Grice (ibid., 37–40) also considered *generalized conversational implicatures* as different from both conventional and particularized conversational ones, given the general kind of situation in which they are generated (in the absence of special circumstances).

[15] Conventional implicatures, instead, are non-cancelable. Grice (1989, 39) also pointed out that conversational implicatures—with the exception of those due to the manner maxim—are *non-detachable*, i.e., they cannot be detached from an utterance simply by changing the words of the utterance for synonyms, whereas conventional ones can.

[16] *Bronston v. United States*, 409 U.S. 352 (1973). See, among others, Green 2001; Hansen 2008, 1398; Horn 2017, 37–8; Robbins 2019.

[17] This account, that departs from Grice and borrows from Sperber 1994, has been proposed by Bianchi 2016, 195–6.

Bronston was a case of alleged perjury. Bronston was charged with perjury for the above exchange, and was eventually acquitted by the US Supreme Court. The case raised many issues.[18] What are the conditions of perjury taken as lying under oath? Falsity and intention to deceive? As Alex Stein pointed out, under its common law definition, perjury is any false statement regarding a material matter that a witness makes knowingly and under oath in a judicial proceeding.[19] Now, as a first issue, what counts as a "statement"? Demeanor too if deliberately used as a form of communication? Second, and more importantly, what classifies as "false" in this context? Also what is genuinely considered to be false? Also what is not believed to be true? Just what is false as a matter of fact? Imagine two witnesses declaring under oath, with the intention to deceive, what they do not believe; but in one case the assertion is true and in the other false: are we going to treat them the same way? Third, how all this impacts the *mens rea* determination? Stein favors a distinction between *liars* and *evaders*, where the latter just deliver "evasive testimony that obfuscates the truth without making any affirmative attempts to mislead the court."[20] He adds that courts generally interpret perjury broadly and resolve any ambiguities in the prosecution's favor, which has the bad result of pooling liars with evaders and overenforcing the law (which is however attenuated by the common law corroboration requirement that bars conviction for perjury on the testimony of a single witness; any such testimony must be corroborated by additional testimony or other evidence).

Going back to pragmatics, the distinction between liars and evaders suggests that evaders are those who generate misleading implicatures, as Bronston did. The fact that he was acquitted could be explained and justified by the idea that in courtroom interaction speakers are supposed to follow Grice's maxims *literally*.[21] They do not commit themselves beyond the literal content of the sentences uttered. As a different diagnosis, one can say that in adversarial contexts like cross-examination some maxims (especially that of quantity) are "in abeyance."[22] As a matter of fact, strategic speakers strive to implicate more or less than they would be willing to make explicit, given misalignment of interests and uncertainty about the maxims' normativity.[23] Insinuation is an example of implicating more than the speaker would be willing to make explicit; naivety is a way of implicating less. Having the jury in mind, as the relevant audience to persuade, participants may indulge in those attitudes without belaboring overt conclusions. As it was put in a classic on cross-examination, speaking to advocates, "Remember it is the minds of the jury you are addressing, even though your question is put to the witness."[24]

Hence, to restate the point made earlier, problems associated with implicatures are minimized as questioners are skilled and good at extracting the relevant information from their

---

[18] See Stein 2005, 20–4. See also Saul 2012; Horn 2017; Tuzet 2021a.

[19] Stein 2005, 21.

[20] Ibid., 22. To be noted that both the U.K. 1911 Perjury Statute (s. 1) and the U.S. Code (Title 18, §1621) apply to the scenario in which the speaker states what he or she *does not believe to be true*. So, the statement need not be a false one as a matter of fact.

[21] This diagnosis is made by Hansen 2008 (claiming inter alia that this shows the existence of literal meanings, against radical contextualism exemplified by Recanati 2004). But if Bronston did not literally violate the quality maxim, he literally violated the quantity one, and perhaps the others too (according to Tiersma and Solan 2012b, 349–50, he violated the maxim of relation).

[22] Levinson 1983, 121; cf. Levinson 1979, 374–5.

[23] Marmor 2014, 43 ff. See also Skoczeń 2019, 74–5.

[24] Wellman 1904, 32.

interlocutors.[25] Questions and answers need to be very specific, and questioners have a sort of strategic burden to this effect. As a difference with standard questions in everyday conversation, where the point is to elicit information not known by the questioner, questions from counsel often request details that are already known by the questioner, since the point is submitting them to the factfinders' attention. Of course, that applies differently in direct and cross-examination, and depending whether the witness is hostile or not. The above questioning of Bronston was disastrous as made by the opposing counsel, but it would have been strategically fine if carried out by his own counsel, unless in this case it is taken as perjury as it is an affirmative attempt to mislead the factfinders.

4. Presuppositions

Most scholars in pragmatics share the idea that presuppositions cannot be reduced to logical implications (entailments), but dispute whether presuppositions are different from conversational implicatures. Those who maintain they are different stress that presuppositions seem closer to semantic content, even if as implicatures they need a pragmatic and contextual approach. They can be inferred from what is said, but also canceled in some contexts. Some definite expressions typically trigger them,[26] like a change-of-state verb does in the proverbial example "Have you stopped beating your husband?"—the presupposition being that the addressee used to beat him. Also, factive verbs, like "know," work as presupposition-triggers; "He knew she was there" presupposes that she was there.

It has been claimed that inference under negation is an operational test for identifying presuppositions. One can take a sentence, negate it, and see what inferences survive; that is, what inferences are shared by both the positive and the negative sentence. Consider this example:[27]

(A) The driver managed to stop in time.

From (A) we can logically infer both (B) and (C):

(B) The driver stopped in time;
(C) The driver tried to stop in time.

But if we take the negation of (A), namely

(D) The driver didn't manage to stop in time

---

[25] Scalar implicatures, suggesting that the utterer had a reason for not using a more informative or stronger term on the same scale, are commonly singled out when troublesome (Hansen 2008, 1403–4). "I have a car" has to be specified as "I have only one car;" "Some of them were gone" has to be specified as "Some, but not all, of them were gone;" and so on.

[26] Levinson 1983, 174 ff. See also Stalnaker 1973 (taking presupposition as what speakers take for granted, which, by my lights, makes harder to see the strategic uses of it) and Soames 2009, Part I (expanding the view of presupposition as what would need to be taken for granted to make sense of asserted content or its relevance to conversation).

[27] I borrow from Levinson 1983, 178.

from (D) we cannot infer (B); instead we can infer (C). (C) expresses a presupposition of (A) and (D). Note also that (A) entails (B), for whenever (A) is true (B) too is true, which is not the case with (D). Negation alters a sentence's entailments, but preserves its presuppositions.

So inferability under negation marks a basic distinction between presupposition and entailment, but a more definite account of presuppositions needs more, since they are cancelable and apparently tied to surface structure; the former aspect makes them different from entailments, the latter differentiates them from implicatures.[28]

As an example of cancelable presupposition, suppose I utter "Dolores cried before she finished the service."[29] This conveys the presupposition that Dolores finished the service. But the presupposition is canceled if I add that Dolores died before she finished the service.

Let's go back to courtroom now. Remember that (well-done) questioning resolves ambiguities and problems with implicatures. A similar moral applies to presupposition. Strategic attitudes give incentives to exploit presupposition in questioning, but vigilance by opposing counsel and judicial control minimize the risks.

In some cases, the exploitation of presupposition is blatant. "Did you see your mistress that night?" presupposes of course that the respondent had a mistress. It also presupposes trivial things such as: you were able to see someone that night; you were alive; you were not a rabbit; and so on. These are not worrisome, though. A worrisome question is "Why did you stop selling amphetamines?" where the presupposition that the respondent used to sell amphetamines is triggered by a change-of-state verb. In other cases, the exploitation of presupposition is subtler, gentler, or less easy to detect. "How long have you known the victim?" sounds less aggressive than the previous examples, probably because we are used to such expressions; still it presupposes that the respondent knew the victim, which might be a point not established yet. As a subtler case, consider the question "Did you hear what she told him?", the presupposition being that she told him something. Suppose this is false, but the witness does not know it, and answers negatively; his or her testimony may appear as a poor one. So a questioner may undermine the witness' credibility or competence by exploiting presuppositions. Consider in this respect the difference between "Did you see a stop sign?" and "Did you see the stop sign?", the second question presupposing there was a stop sign.[30] A negative answer ("No") sounds quite different if related to the second question (the witness was inattentive, or had impaired visual capacity).

As said earlier, presuppositions are cancelable. So, at least in some cases, questioners can react to a presupposition exploitation protest by saying "I didn't presuppose that." And respondents themselves can react to presupposition by canceling it. The following is not a contradiction: "I have not stopped beating my husband, because I never started." Imagine this example in a sequence of question and answer:

---

[28] See Levinson 1983, 186 ff. "To sum up: semantic theories of presupposition are not viable for the simple reason that semantics is concerned with the specification of invariant stable meanings that can be associated with expressions. Presuppositions are not invariant and they are not stable, and they do not belong in any orderly semantics" (ibid., 204). Part of the difficulty is this: "what is normally called presupposition is actually a heterogeneous collection of quite distinct and different phenomena, some perhaps semantic, others different varieties of pragmatic implication" (ibid., 217).

[29] Again, I borrow from Levinson 1983, 187.

[30] The example comes from Loftus 1975. If the presupposition is knowingly false (i.e., there was no stop sign and the questioner knows it), the question is misleading.

Q. Have you stopped beating your husband?
A. No, because I never started.

I am not sure that all factfinders would appreciate the witty answer. But it would be an appropriate reaction to a presupposition exploitation attempt. The same could happen in subtler cases: "I didn't hear what she told him, for she said nothing;" "I didn't see the stop sign, because there was none." These answers require a brave respondent, or a risk-prone one given the predictable reaction of the questioner ("Are you sure?"), and it is unsure factfinders would appreciate that.

At this point the reader may ask if so-called leading questions, as questions suggesting the desired answer, exploit presuppositions. It is not necessarily so. Let us take a leading question as one which subtly prompts the respondent to answer in a particular way, by suggesting only an affirmative answer, or just a negative one, whereas is not leading a question which may be answered either yes or no, and suggests neither answer as the correct one.[31] If so, a leading question can exploit a presupposition, but need not. Compare (a) "Have you stopped beating your husband?" with (b) "Don't you think this is a very unlikely event?" On the one hand, (a) exploits the presupposition that the husband was beaten by the respondent, and prompts the respondent to answer yes in case it was true and is no longer so; but in case it was false the respondent may rightly answer "No, because I never started," or even "No, because I just started." On the other hand, (b) suggests an answer as the correct one, which the respondent need not subscribe to, and in any event the question does not exploit a presupposition; it just relies on the assumption that the event is very unlikely.

For all of that, vigilance by opposing counsel against presupposition exploitation is important, together with judicial control over the mode and order of examining witnesses, supported by an understanding of the conceptual contours of the categories invoked.

5. Deixis

Scholars claim that the Gricean distinction of what is said (sentence meaning) and what is implicated (speaker's meaning) is not sufficient to capture the full content of utterances. Some propose a threefold distinction: what is said, what is asserted, and what is implicated.[32]

Take "I was there" told by the plaintiff. Literally, it says very little: the speaker was in a place at some distance from the utterance's place. This is what is *said* as encoded meaning of the words uttered. But the utterance asserts something richer, namely that the plaintiff was in a certain place (different from the utterance's place) that must be clear to the other participants from the discourse context, as must be the time implicitly referred to. This is what is *asserted*. Then, what is *implicated* may be that the plaintiff, being there, saw what the defendant did. Or that, being there, the plaintiff was at some distance from the accident's place. It depends of course on the situation. In a criminal case uttering "I was there" may count as a confession.[33]

---

[31] This is the account given in *Porter v. State*, 386 So.2d 1209, 1211 (Fla.3d DCA 1980). Different jurisdictions allow leading questions on cross-examination and forbid them, with some exceptions, on direct examination (see, e.g., FRE 611 in the United States, and Art. 499 of the Italian Code of Criminal Procedure).

[32] See Soames 2009, Part III; Marmor 2014, chs. 1, 2. See Recanati 2001 for a similar distinction; see also Chiassoni 2019, ch. 4; Skoczeń 2019, ch. 4.

[33] Notice, as a theoretical point, that there is some overlap between implicatures and indirect speech acts; some linguistic phenomena can be treated under the two frameworks. This is also true of presupposition and implicature, as mentioned above in the text, and possibly of implicature and perlocutionary analysis (cf. Skoczeń 2019, 24).

Pragmatics calls *indexicals* words as "I," "you," "here," "now," which refer to something without naming it, nor giving a description of it, and call *demonstratives* the words that perform a similar function pointing to something, like "this" and "that." Such words belong to the domain of "deixis," a Greek word for pointing or indicating. The traditional categories of deixis are person ("I," "you," etc.), place ("here," there," etc.), and time ("now," "then," etc.); the more recent literature adds the categories of discourse deixis (references internal to discourse or text, like "That is what I meant") and social deixis (reflecting social distinctions relative to participant-roles).[34] Deixis is one of the factors that require distinguishing what is asserted from what is said.

The use of such words is often accompanied by gestures indicating their reference. Demonstrative pronouns can be used with selecting gestures, which become crucial when the uttered sentence is something like "This is the assailant, not this." A lineup is a case in point. Without being there, you have no means to determine the relevant reference. Similar gestures accompany the presentation of material evidence and witnesses. Drawing on this I have discussed elsewhere the *ostensive dimension* of evidence discourse.[35]

Let me just give a couple of examples. The first comes from the cross-examination of a rape victim by the defendant's counsel.[36] The counsel is questioning the victim about how she was dressed:

Q. It was not really a coat at all, was it?
A. Well, it is sort of a coat-dress and I bought it with trousers, as a trouser suit.
Q. That is it down there isn't it, the red one?
A. Yes.
Q. If we call that a dress, if we call that a dress you had no coat on at all, had you?
A. No.

Apart from sexist overtones (alarming indeed), the use of demonstratives and indexicals is remarkable. In particular, a phrase like "That is it down there" says very little to people who were not present. We cannot say how the dress was—as we were not there—apart from its being red. The following turns of the cross-examination (which I don't report here for lack of space) exhibit a remarkable implicature too: the questioner, after having the victim admit she had sexual intercourse with two men on previous occasions, asks if she is seventeen and a half, and the victim confirms. To what purpose? To suggest she was not a woman of good repute, and build up an implicit argument for the jury under the reasonable doubt standard. Ostension of the dress and implicature cooperate to this effect.

The second example is an extract from O. J. Simpson's civil trial.[37] Counsel for the plaintiffs is asking whether the defendant was wearing certain shoes, a rare style, since a bloody shoe print of that sort was part of the evidence against him:

Additionally, note that also the *on that day* example (Section 3 above) is a case of deixis, but there it is in the implicature, while "I was there" has deixis as part of the sentence uttered.

[34] See Levinson 1983, ch. 2; Kaplan 1989. For a Peircean account, see Atkin 2005; Short 2007.
[35] See Tuzet 2021b. Note that ostensive acts for evidentiary purposes are different from ostensive definitions. Compare "This is the weapon," uttered in the courtroom, and "This is the French horn," uttered in the class for educational purposes.
[36] It is reported in Levinson 1979, 380.
[37] I take it from Hansen 2008, 1408.

A. . . . My only opinion is I do not recognize ever owning these shoes.

Q. The shoes in these photos?

A. Yes.

Q. So you don't believe that you were wearing shoes like this in this photo; is that what you're saying?

A. I don't believe I ever owned shoes like that.

Q. Were you wearing them?

The extract is interesting for the challenged implicature from "owning" to "wearing" shoes. The defendant tries to trade on the fact that owning a pair of shoes and wearing that same pair normally go together, and, by negating the first, he tries to convey the negation of the second. The skilled questioner does not buy the implicature and insists on the explicit question. The extract is also interesting for the use of demonstrative phrases like "these shoes," "these photos," "shoes like this," and "shoes like that." Counsel shows the photos in which the defendant was wearing those shoes. Ostension of the shoes in the photos and cancelability of the implicature cooperate here against the defendant.

In a nutshell, deixis reveals the ostensive dimension of evidence discourse and shows that this is not just a form of storytelling; it's about real things, susceptible to being exhibited to factfinders and becoming the content of evidentiary arguments.

References

Atkin, A. (2005). "Peirce on the Index and Indexical Reference," *Transaction of the Charles S. Peirce Society*, 41(1): 161–88.

Austin, J. L. (1975). *How to Do Things with Words*. Oxford: Oxford University Press. First published 1962.

Ayer, A. J. (1936). *Language, Truth and Logic*. London: Gollancz.

Bellucci, F. (2014). "'Logic Considered as Semeiotic': On Peirce's Philosophy of Logic," *Transactions of the Charles S. Peirce Society*, 50(4): 523–47.

Bianchi, C. (2016). "What Did you (Legally) Say? Cooperative and Strategic Interactions," in A. Capone and F. Poggi (eds.), *Pragmatics and law. Philosophical Perspectives*, 185–99. Cham: Springer.

Bülow-Møller, A. M. (1991). "Trial Evidence: Overt and Covert Communication in Court," *International Journal of Applied Linguistics*, 1(1): 38–60.

Capone, A. and Poggi, F. (eds.) (2016). *Pragmatics and Law. Philosophical Perspectives*. Cham: Springer.

Chiassoni, P. (2019). *Interpretation without Truth. A Realistic Enquiry*. Cham: Springer.

Coulthard, M. and Johnson, A. (eds.) (2010). *The Routledge Handbook of Forensic Linguistics*. Abingdon: Routledge.

Ferrer, J. (2004). "It is Proven that p. The Notion of Proven Fact in the Law," *Associations*, 8: 29–54.

Giltrow, J. and Stein, D. (eds.) (2017). *The Pragmatic Turn in Law: Inference and Interpretation in Legal Discourse*. Berlin: De Gruyter.

Green, S. P. (2001). "Lying, Misleading, and Falsely Denying: How Moral Concepts Inform the Law of Perjury, Fraud, and False Statements," *Hastings Law Journal*, 53(1): 157–212.

Grice, P. (1989). *Studies in the Way of Words*. Cambridge, MA: Harvard University Press.

Hansen, M.-B. M. (2008). "On the Availability of 'Literal' Meaning: Evidence from Courtroom Interaction," *Journal of Pragmatics*, 40(8): 1392–410.

Horn, L. R. (2017). "Telling it Slant: Toward a Taxonomy of Deception," in J. Giltrow and D. Stein (eds.), *The Pragmatic Turn in Law: Inference and Interpretation in Legal Discourse*, 23–55. Berlin: De Gruyter.

Horn, L. R. and Ward, G. (eds.) (2004). *The Handbook of Pragmatics*. Oxford: Blackwell.

Jørgensen, J. (1937). "Imperatives and Logic," *Erkenntnis*, 7: 288–96.

Kaplan, D. (1989). "An Essay on the Semantics, Logic, Metaphysics, and Epistemology of Demonstratives and Other Indexicals," in J. Almog, J. Perry, and H. Wettstein (eds.), *Themes from Kaplan*, 481–563. Oxford: Oxford University Press.

Kelsen, H. (1945). *General Theory of Law and State*. Cambridge, MA: Harvard University Press.

Levinson, S. C. (1979). "Activity Types and Language," *Linguistics*, 17: 365–99.

Levinson, S. C. (1983). *Pragmatics*. Cambridge: Cambridge University Press.

Liao, M. and Sun, Y. (2017). "Cooperation in Chinese Courtroom Discourse," in J. Giltrow and D. Stein (eds.), *The Pragmatic Turn in Law: Inference and Interpretation in Legal Discourse*, 57–82. Berlin: De Gruyter.

Loftus, E. (1975). "Leading Questions and the Eyewitness Report," *Cognitive Psychology*, 7: 560–72.

Marmor, A. (2008). "The Pragmatics of Legal Language," *Ratio Juris*, 21(4): 423–52.

Marmor, A. (2011). "Can the Law imply More Than it Says? On Some Pragmatic Aspects of Strategic Speech," in A. Marmor and S. Soames (eds.), *Philosophical Foundations of Language in the Law*, 83–104. Oxford: Oxford University Press.

Marmor, A. (2014). *The Language of Law*. Oxford: Oxford University Press.

Moreso, J. J. and Chilovi, S. (2018). "Interpretive Arguments and the Application of the Law," in G. Bongiovanni et al. (eds.), *Handbook of Legal Reasoning and Argumentation*, 495–517. Cham: Springer.

Morris, C. W. (1938). *Foundations of the Theory of Signs*. Chicago: University of Chicago Press.

Morris, C. W. (1946). *Signs, Language, and Behavior*. New York: Prentice-Hall.

Poggi, F. (2016). "Grice, the Law and the Linguistic Special Case Thesis," in A. Capone and F. Poggi (eds.), *Pragmatics and Law. Philosophical Perspectives*, 231–48. Cham: Springer.

Poggi, F. and Capone, A. (eds.) (2017). *Pragmatics and Law. Practical and Theoretical Perspectives*. Cham: Springer.

Recanati, F. (2001). "What is Said," *Synthese*, 128: 75–91.

Recanati, F. (2004). *Literal Meaning*. Cambridge: Cambridge University Press.

Robbins, I. P. (2019). "Perjury by Omission," *Washington University Law Review*, 97: 265–94.

Ross, A. (1944). "Imperatives and Logic," *Philosophy of Science*, 11(1): 30–46.

Saul, J. (2012). *Lying, Misleading, and What is Said*. Oxford: Oxford University Press.

Skoczeń, I. (2019). *Implicatures within Legal Language*. Cham: Springer.

Searle, J. R. (1969). *Speech Acts. An Essay in the Philosophy of Language*. Cambridge: Cambridge University Press.

Searle, J. R. (1979). *Expression and Meaning*. Cambridge: Cambridge University Press.

Short, T. L. (2007). *Peirce's Theory of Signs*. Cambridge: Cambridge University Press.

Soames, S. (2009). *Philosophical Essays* (vol. 1). Princeton, NJ: Princeton University Press.

Sønderberg Mortensen, S. and Mortensen, J. (2017). "Epistemic Stance in Courtroom Interaction," in F. Poggi and A. Capone (eds.), *Pragmatics and Law. Practical and Theoretical Perspectives*, 401–37. Cham: Springer.

Sperber, D. (1994). "Understanding Verbal Understanding," in J. Khalfa (ed.), *What is Intelligence?*, 179–98. Cambridge: Cambridge University Press.

Sperber, D. and Wilson, D. (1995). *Relevance. Communication and Cognition*. Second edition. Oxford: Blackwell.

Stalnaker, R. (1973). "Presuppositions," *Journal of Philosophical Logic*, 2(4): 447–57.

Stein, A. (2005). *Foundations of Evidence Law*. Oxford: Oxford University Press.

Tiersma, P. M. and Solan, L. M. (2012a). *The Oxford Handbook of Language and Law*. Oxford: Oxford University Press.

Tiersma, P. M. and Solan, L. M. (2012b). "The Language of Crime," in P. N. Tiersma and L. M. Solan (eds.), *The Oxford Handbook of Language and Law*, 340–53. Oxford: Oxford University Press.

Tuzet, G. (2021a). "Truthful Liars," *Transactions of the Charles S. Peirce Society*, forthcoming.

Tuzet, G. (2021b). "On Probatory Inference and Ostension," in J. Ferrer and C. Vázquez (eds.), *Evidential Legal Reasoning: Crossing Civil Law and Common Law Traditions*. Cambridge: Cambridge University Press, forthcoming.

von Wright, G. H. (1951). "Deontic Logic," *Mind*, 60: 1–15.

Wellman, F. L. (1904). *The Art of Cross-Examination*. Second edition. London: MacMillan.

13

Argumentation and Evidence

Floris Bex

1. Introduction

Argumentation is central to legal and evidential reasoning: the prosecution *argues* that the suspect committed the crime, lawyers present their closing *arguments*, the plaintiff *argues* his case by citing a relevant precedent, the court presents concurring and dissenting *arguments*, and so on. There are different interpretations of the term "argument": an argument can be a single reason for a conclusion but also the combination of the reasons for and against a certain conclusion, or a dialog between parties trying to convince each other. In the literature on reasoning with evidence, however, a narrower definition is usually adhered to: argumentation is the construction of arguments by performing consecutive reasoning steps, starting with an item of evidence and reasoning towards some conclusion using general rules of inference or generalizations, where not just arguments for a conclusion but also counterarguments against a conclusion have to be considered.

This idea of argumentation was already present in Wigmore's *Principles of Judicial Proof*,[1] in which tree-like charts representing inferences from evidence to a conclusion and possible weakening counterevidence are presented. "Neo-Wigmorians," Anderson, Schum, and Twining[2] developed these argument charts, introducing the idea of common-sense generalizations as inference warrants. Walton has extensively discussed these different types of common-sense generalizations in the form of argument schemes in different contexts, including legal evidence.[3] Furthermore Bex, Prakken, and colleagues have shown that Wigmore's charts corresponds to logical models of argumentation,[4] adding semantics for formal defeasible reasoning.[5] In this chapter, I will discuss argumentation in the context of legal evidence, presenting general ideas that draw from all of the above authors and on which there is more or less a consensus in the academic community.[6]

2. The structure of Evidential Arguments

The basic idea of an argument is a basic syllogism, where a conclusion is inferred from premises. Evidential reasoning with arguments involves taking the basic evidential data as

---

[1] Wigmore 1931.
[2] Anderson, Schum, and Twining 2005.
[3] Walton 2002.
[4] Bex, Prakken, Reed, and Walton 2003; Bex 2011; Prakken 2020.
[5] Dung 1995.
[6] Parts of this chapter have been adapted from Bex 2011, ch. 3.

Floris Bex, *Argumentation and Evidence* In: *Philosophical Foundations of Evidence Law*. Edited by: Christian Dahlman, Alex Stein, and Giovanni Tuzet, Oxford University Press. © Christian Dahlman, Alex Stein, and Giovanni Tuzet 2021.
DOI: 10.1093/oso/9780198859307.003.0014

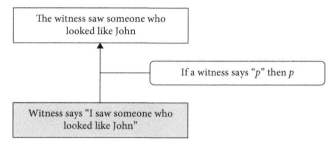

Figure 13.1 A simple evidential argument

premises[7] and inferring conclusions using *generalizations*, usually of a conditional if-then form, which justify the inference link between premises and conclusion.[8] The inferences are of an evidential nature: some evidence *e* and an evidential generalization "*e* is evidence for *p*" allows us to infer *p*. For example, a witness' testimony "I saw someone who looked like John" and the generalization "if a witness says '*p*' then (this is evidence for) *p*," where *p* is some state of affairs in the world, allows us to infer that the witness saw someone who looked like John get into the car. Figure 13.1 shows a diagrammatic representation of this argument. The evidence is represented by a grey box, the conclusion as a white box, the inference as an arrow and the generalization as a box with rounded corners.

The evidential generalization for witness testimonies can be phrased in several ways, for example, "witnesses under oath usually speak the truth," "if a witness testifies that *p* is the case then usually *p* is the case" and "If a witness is in a position to know whether *p* is true and the witness asserts *p* then *p* may plausibly be taken to be true." The exact generalization may be open to debate; do only witnesses under oath speak the truth? If a witness testifies to *p*, is then *p* *usually* the case, or perhaps sometimes or 80% of the time? However, most people would agree that, in general, conclusions can be drawn from witness testimonies, as in many legal systems a witness testimony is explicitly mentioned as a legitimate item of evidence. This does not mean that witness testimonies are always true. Rather, generalizations are often "default rules," which means that if we have no reason *not* to believe the witness, we can draw conclusions from their testimony. But such default rules have exceptions—for example, the witness may have bad eyesight, or a reason to lie about seeing John—and evidence for such exceptions can lead to a counterargument to the argument based on the witness testimony[9]. It should be noted that it is perfectly possible to have conclusive generalizations. For example, "a person can never be at two places at the same time" or, taking inspiration from classical logic, "if witness A says *p* and witness B says *p* then always (conclusively) witness A says p." Arguments based on such rules are deductive and cannot be attacked on their conclusions.

It is also possible to form more complex arguments based on multiple pieces of evidence, or in which multiple inferences are chained into arguments with intermediate conclusions. Consider Figure 13.2, where we have a witness who saw someone who looked like John get

---

[7] Evidential data are the primary sources of evidence which cannot be sensibly denied (e.g., that a witness statement was made in court, that forensic expert reports were handed to the jury).

[8] The generalization *warrants* the inference, cf. Toulmin 1958.

[9] Counterarguments and generalizations with their exceptions are discussed in Sections 3 and 4, respectively, in this chapter.

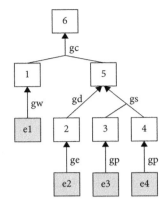

e1: Witness says "I saw someone who looked like John".

e2: Expert says that the DNA profile of the hair in the car matches John's DNA profile.

e3: Police reports that shoeprints matching Runner Pro shoes were found in the car.

e4: Police reports that John wore Runner Pro shoes when he was apprehended.

1: The witness saw someone like John getting into the car.

2: The DNA profile of the hair in the car matches John's DNA profile.

3: The shoeprints found in the car were of Runner Pro shoes.

4: John wore Runner Pro shoes when he was apprehended.

5: John was in the car at some point in time.

6: John was the man who got into the car.

gw: If a witness says "p" then p.

ge: If an expert says that "p"then p.

gp: If the police reports "p" then p.

gw: If a witness says "p" then p.

gd: If a DNA profile of person x and a hair found at location l match, then person x was at location l.

gs: If shoe prints found at location l match the shoes of person x, then person x was at location l.

gc: If a witness saw someone looking like person x get into a car and person x was in that car at some point, then it was person x that the witness saw getting into the car.

Figure 13.2 A complex evidential argument

into a car. In this car, the police later found a hair and shoe prints, which is evidence for the fact that John was in the car at some point. Thus, we can conclude that John was probably the man whom the witness saw getting into the car. In Figure 13.2, multiple smaller arguments are combined in a graph- or tree-like structure, which shows many similarities to a Wigmore chart. Thus, the argument consists of several subarguments; for example, the argument in Figure 13.1 is a subargument of the argument in Figure 13.2. Furthermore, there are different types of (sub)arguments contained in Figure 13.2. Inferences are chained, where intermediate conclusions are used to infer further conclusions (e.g., e2 → 2 → 5). In other cases, a conjunction of multiple pieces of evidence or intermediate conclusions is needed to infer a conclusion. For example, statements 3 and 4 are both needed to infer conclusion 5, denoted by the compound arrow. Note that 5 can also be separately inferred from statement 2. So there are essentially two arguments for conclusion 5: one based on

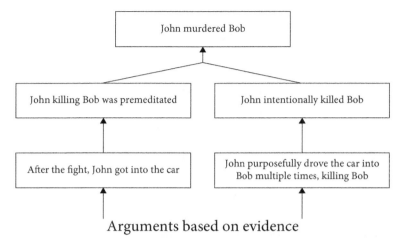

Arguments based on evidence

Figure 13.3 Legal reasoning based on arguments from evidence

e2, and another argument based on e3 and e4. These two arguments corroborate: while the conclusion can be inferred from any of them, the conclusion is stronger if we have both arguments.[10]

While legal reasoning (reasoning about the legal facts and legal consequences) seems different from evidential reasoning (reasoning about the evidence and conclusions),[11] the reasoning mechanisms employed are very much related. More specifically, we can use the facts of the case, as derived from the evidence through arguments (Figure 13.2) to further derive legal conclusions via the same kind of arguments. Figure 13.3 shows a legal argument which is itself based on arguments from evidence—in the example, the bottom left proposition that John got into the car is based on the argument in Figure 13.2. Here, the warrants for inferences in argumentation will be statutes and legal rules, and counterarguments will be based on exception to legal rules.[12] Thus, there is no real boundary between legal and evidential reasoning in argumentation, as legal arguments are based on the conclusions of evidential arguments.

3. The Dialectical Nature of Argumentation: Attack, Defeat, and Dialog

In the previous section it was shown how conclusions can be supported by evidential data through arguments of varying complexity. Note that, however, the (intermediate) conclusions cannot be drawn conclusively, as the inferences are based on generalizations with exceptions. In other words, each inference step can be doubted and actively challenged by giving counterarguments that attack the original argument. The possibility of attack

---

[10] Argument strength will be briefly discussed in Section 3.

[11] cf. the dichotomy between a "question of fact" and a "question of law," and Wigmore's separation of factual proof and legal admissibility in evidential reasoning (Wigmore 1931).

[12] See Pattaro, Rottleuthner, Shiner, Peczenik, and Sartor 2005, ch. 26.

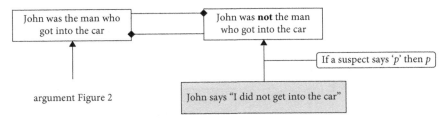

Figure 13.4 Two mutually rebutting arguments

involves the *defeasibility* of the inferences: an argument for a certain conclusion can be overturned by new information which leads to, for example, an argument for the opposite conclusion or an exception to a generalization.

In the literature, two types of attack are usually distinguished.[13] Firstly, an argument can be *rebut* by giving a counterargument with as its conclusion the negation of a proposition in the original argument. For example, if John says he did *not* get into the car, we can infer the negation of the conclusion of the argument in Figure 13.2. Figure 13.4 shows this attack between the two conclusions as arrows with diamond heads—note that rebuttal is a symmetrical attack relation: an argument with conclusion *p* attacks the argument with conclusion *not p* and vice versa. It is also possible to attack an intermediate conclusion of a subargument—in the example of Figure 13.2, by arguing that, for example, the DNA profile of the hair does not match John's profile, or by arguing that John has never been in the car.

Note that evidence cannot be attacked. In order to question, for example, a witness statement we can argue for the opposite (Figure 13.4), or we can *undercut* the argument with another argument for why a particular inference is not allowed. Unlike a rebutting argument, an undercutting argument does not deny the conclusion of an argument, neither does it deny the generalization as a whole, but rather it denies the inference step by arguing for an exception to the generalization underlying the inference. For example, say we have evidence that the expert who analyzed the DNA profiles used obsolete methods. Even though usually we would say that the opinion of experts on DNA can be trusted, in this case we might have an exception, and the argument that the DNA profile of the hair in the car matches John's profile is undercut (Figure 13.5). Note that here it is not actively denied that the two profiles match, but that the support that the evidence gives to the conclusion is effectively "broken," as the defeasible inference from the evidence is undercut. The undercut relation is not symmetrical: the undercutting argument attacks the original expert testimony argument but not vice versa.

Attacking an argument does not guarantee the argument's defeat: for this, the attacking argument has to be stronger than the other argument. With each specific (element of an) argument some measure of its *strength* or *probative force* can be associated. Often, these strengths are indicated as preferences between arguments,[14] (e.g., an argument based on a police report is always preferred to an argument based on a citizen eyewitness) and such preferences can be the object of argumentation themselves (e.g., research has shown that police officers are not more reliable witnesses than citizens). There are also various ways

---

[13] Pollock 1995.
[14] See, e.g., Modgil and Prakken 2013.

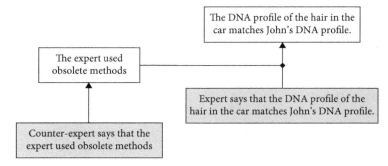

Figure 13.5 One argument (left) undercutting another argument (right).

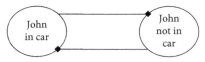

Figure 13.6 Two mutually attacking arguments

to capture the strength of arguments precisely as, for example, numerical probabilities.[15] However, the central idea is that argumentation is a dialectical process of argument and counterargument. Accordingly, we can determine the so-called *dialectical status* of arguments. Based on the formal argumentation semantics first proposed by Dung,[16] we can assign three different statuses to arguments: the *justified* arguments (those that survive the competition with their counterarguments), the *overruled* arguments (those that lose the competition with their counterarguments), and the *defensible* arguments (those that are involved in a tie).[17] Consider Figure 13.6, in which two mutually attacking (e.g., rebutting) arguments for opposite conclusions are shown[18]—for example, the argument from Figure 13.2 and the attacking argument from Figure 13.4. Now, if no preference for any argument is defined, they are both defensible. If, however, we say we prefer the left argument for "John got in the car,"[19] this argument is justified and the right argument is overruled.

The dialectical status of an argument depends on its interactions with all other available arguments. An important phenomenon here is *defense*: suppose that argument *B* attacks argument *A* but that *B* is itself defeated by a third argument *C*; in that case *C* defends *A*. In the example, say that we have a new argument that the witness who saw John get into the car lied. This argument undercuts the inference e1 → 1 in the argument from Figure 13.2, and thus attacks the complete argument for the conclusion that it was John who got into the car,

---

[15] See, e.g., Zenker 2012; Anderson et al. 2005, 230. For a more general account on Bayesianism and evidence, see Taroni, Biedermann, and Bozza, "The Logic of Inference and Decision for Scientific Evidence," ch. 17, in this volume.

[16] Dung 1995.

[17] See Prakken and Vreeswijk 2002.

[18] Following Dung 1995, Figure 13.6 only shows the overall arguments and the attack relations between them—the internal structure of the arguments is abstracted away from.

[19] After all, this was based on DNA evidence, shoeprints, and a witness, whereas the other argument was based on just John's denial.

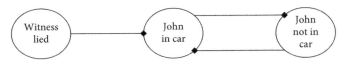

Figure 13.7 The leftmost argument defends the rightmost argument by defeating its only attacker.

see Figure 13.7.[20] Because the new argument is itself not attacked, it is justified and defeats the argument for "John in car," which is in turn overruled. The right argument for "John not in car" is now justified because its only attacker is overruled. A set of arguments that defends itself against incoming attackers can hence be seen as a coherent and defendable position.

Note that while these semantics for determining argument acceptability are dialectical in spirit,[21] they do not explicitly incorporate the dialectical *process*, where an argument can be accepted if it cannot be successfully challenged in a properly conducted *dialog*. Toulmin[22] presents his view of "logic as generalized jurisprudence": a logic for arguments should provide the essentials of a general rational process for analyzing arguments just as jurisprudence provides the essentials of the legal process. The procedural and dialogical component of argumentation has been presented more explicitly in the literature, where various protocols or sets of rules for a properly conducted rational argumentative discussion are provided.[23] For example, van Eemeren and Grootendorst's *obligation-to-defend rule* states that "discussants who advance a standpoint may not refuse to defend this standpoint when requested to do so" and the *relevance rule* states that "standpoints may not be defended by non-argumentation or argumentation that is not relevant to the standpoint." Such protocols serve not only an analytic function (is the discussion rational in that it follows the rules?) but also a heuristic function (what are our options if we want to conduct a rational discussion?). In a legal setting, dialog protocols will be partly determined by the legal procedural rules that tell us, for example, which types of evidence can be brought forward by whom and at which point in the proceedings, or whose turn it is to meet the burden of proof.[24]

The basic idea of using a dialog as a means of rationally analyzing arguments is best explained by taking an example of a *dialog game*, where a simple game is played between two players, a proponent, and an opponent. The proponent starts by moving an argument that needs to be tested and each subsequent move (by either the proponent or the opponent) contains an argument that attacks an argument of the other player. The rules of the game determine, for example, whether a player may repeat his earlier moves or whether a player may move only undercutters or rebuttals. Say, for example, that we have a game in which

---

[20] Note that there are really two arguments for "John got in the car" in Figure 13.2, one based on evidence e1, e2 and another based on evidence e1, e3, e4. Recall from the discussion of Figure 13.2 that there are two separate arguments for proposition 5, and each of these can be combined with the inference from e1 to form an argument for 6: John got in the car. Both these arguments are attacked by "Witness lied," as the witness testimony is always required to conclude "John got in the car," so for simplicity, Figures 13.6 and 13.7 show just one argument for "John got in the car."

[21] Dung implicitly assumes some sort of process in which "The one who has the last word laughs best" (Dung 1995, 2).

[22] Toulmin 1958.

[23] See, e.g., Walton 1998; van Eemeren and Grootendorst 2004; Tuzet, "The Pragmatics of Evidence Discourse," ch. 12, in this volume. For more formal approaches from artificial intelligence, McBurney and Parsons 2005.

[24] See, e.g., Prakken and Sartor 2009; Bex and Walton 2012.

the proponent starts by moving an argument and may not repeat his moves, all of the arguments in the opponent's move must defeat the proponents move and the arguments in proponent's subsequent moves must undercut the opponent's arguments in the previous move. The proponent starts by moving the argument "John not in car." The opponent must attack this argument and hence moves "John in car." The proponent must undercut this argument; this can be done by moving "witness lied." There are now no more arguments and the opponent has no more valid moves so the proponent wins. Thus, the argument game essentially provides a dialectical proof theory for arguments: the initial argument can be said to be (defeasibly) provable if the opponent can attack (and defeat) each move the opponent makes.

4. Generalizations and General Knowledge in Evidential Reasoning

Generalizations play a pivotal role in reasoning with evidential arguments. They can warrant inferences from the evidential data to conclusions and can be seen as the "glue" that keeps an argument together.[25] However, generalizations are not always true or valid, and can change over time. This is why Twining call them "necessary but dangerous"[26]: we need generalizations in order to analyze and argue about evidence, but these generalizations can also encode biases, stereotypes, and prejudices. These dangers of generalizations can be lessened by specifying exactly which generalizations we use, how we use these generalizations, and from which sources the generalizations stem. The more explicit the knowledge, the more it is open to analysis and criticism in the dialectical process of proof.

There are quite a few generalizations that, in one way or another, are consistently used by all kinds of reasoners when reasoning with evidence. Looking at evidential reasoning (or indeed at reasoning in general), it can be seen that many arguments, as well as the attacks on them, are instances of recurring patterns, such as inferences from witness or expert testimonies. In this sense, *argumentation schemes* play an important role in reasoning with evidence.[27] Argumentation schemes are forms of argument that represent stereotypical patterns of human reasoning in a conditional form, just like generalizations. The idea of defining recurring patterns of reasoning through argumentation schemes or generalizations is the subject of much study in argumentation theory, artificial intelligence, and law.

As an example of an argumentation scheme, take the well-known scheme for argument from expert opinion:[28]

Source E is an expert in domain D.
E asserts that proposition A is known to be true (false).
A is within D.
Therefore, A may plausibly be taken to be true (false).

[25]   Anderson et al. 2005.

[26]   Twining 1999. See also Dahlman 2017; Allen and Pardo, "Inference to the Best Explanation, Relative Plausibility, and Probability," ch. 14, in this volume, for an in-depth discussion on generalizations and the ways in which they may be dangerous or unacceptable.

[27]   For a discussion on argumentation schemes in the context of reasoning with evidence, see Walton 2002; Bex et al. 2003. For a general overview of argumentation schemes, the reader is referred to Walton, Reed, and Macagno 2008.

[28]   Walton et al. 2008.

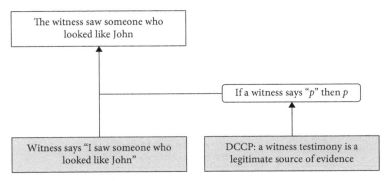

Figure 13.8 An argument for a generalization

The notion of argumentation schemes is obviously very closely related to the notion of generalizations: argumentation schemes are conditional rules based on world knowledge which can be used to draw inferences. The above argumentation scheme is a slightly more general version of the DNA expert generalization given in Figure 13.2, where the domain D would be "DNA analysis" and it is assumed that "profiles a and b match" is a statement within the domain of DNA analysis.

Looking at Figure 13.2, it can be seen that each type of evidence essentially has its own associated generalization which allows us to draw inferences from that particular type of evidence. In this way, the various types of evidence point to generalizations that are often used in reasoning with evidence. Above we already saw the generalizations for witness testimony and expert testimony. Another example is the generalization for inference from police reports. In this way, we can accept stereotypical ways of reasoning about which there is a consensus, at least in the legal and philosophical community, and thus accept that there are certain valid generalizations that can be used in rational reasoning about evidence. Because each type of evidence has its own associated generalization, the law may also point us to generalizations which are accepted by default; for example, in Dutch law witness testimonies are explicitly stated as a species of evidence on the grounds of which a judge can form his decision.[29] This means that it is highly unlikely that the legislator believed the witness testimony generalization to be false by default. In this way, we can include the *source* of the generalization in our argument—consider Figure 13.8, where the witness testimony generalization is (defeasibly) derived from source "evidence," namely the Dutch Code of Criminal Proceedings.[30]

Ideally, a generalization comes from a clearly defined source, such as an expert, scientific literature, or a legal document, so that if we are doubtful about whether the generalization should be believed we can check the original source. However, many generalizations that are not tied to specific types of evidence are often backed by experience or general knowledge. Such experience-based generalizations seem to be based on a common-sense counterpart of scientific induction and reasoning from a "general knowledge source" can

---

[29] Dutch Code of Criminal Proceedings, Art. 339, para. 3; Art. 342.
[30] Note the similarity between Figure 13.8 and Toulmin's argument scheme (Toulmin 1958). The witness testimony is what Toulmin calls the *datum*, which is the basis of the *claim* that the witness saw someone who looked like John. The generalization acts as the *warrant* and the code as the *backing*, showing why the warrant holds.

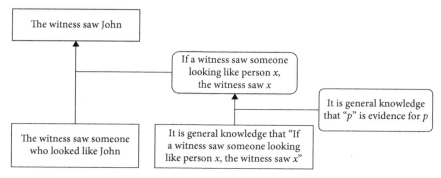

Figure 13.9 A generalization in an argument backed by general knowledge.

be formulated as a new generalization: "It is general knowledge that '*p*' is evidence for *p*."[31] Possible undercutters of this generalization are that a piece of general knowledge is infected by prejudice or value judgment. An example of a generalization backed by general knowledge is shown in Figure 13.9. Notice that the premise from which the generalization is concluded is rendered as a white box, which means that it is not considered to be evidential data but rather a general knowledge assumption which can itself be called into question (i.e., attacked by an argument).

One of the main points of looking for stereotypical patterns of reasoning is that for each generalization, some typical sources of doubt can be given. For example, the witness testimony generalization can be undercut with arguments questioning the witness' veracity, objectivity, and observational sensitivity.[32] For example, a standard undercutter for a generalization about perception is as follows: "the present circumstances are such that having a percept with content *p* is not a reliable indicator of *p*," which can be used to question a witness' observational sensitivity.[33] In the same way, the expert testimony generalization has several typical sources of doubt. Argumentation schemes capture these sources of doubt with a number of *critical questions*, which point to possible sources of doubt in an argument based on the scheme. Critical questions fit into the dialectical view on argumentation as they can be used in a question-and-answer dialog. The following six basic critical questions are associated with the expert opinion scheme:[34]

1. *Expertise question*: How credible is *e* as an expert source?
2. *Field question*: Is *e* an expert in *d*?
3. *Opinion question*: What did *e* assert that implies *a*?
4. *Trustworthiness question*: Is *e* personally reliable as a source?
5. *Consistency question*: Is *a* consistent with what other experts assert?
6. *Backup evidence question*: Is *a*'s assertion based on evidence?

---

[31] Bex et al. 2003.
[32] See Anderson et al. 2005, 67–70.
[33] Pollock 1987.
[34] Walton et al. 2008.

Answers to these critical questions can lead to various types of counterarguments. For example, a negative answer to the "field question" would undercut an argument from expert opinion and a negative answer to the "consistency question" points to a possible rebutting counterargument with an opposite conclusion.[35] In general, there are essentially four ways to attack a generalization:[36]

1. *Attacking the validity of the source of the generalization*: It is not general knowledge that "If a witness saw someone who looks like person x, then the witness saw x."
2. *Attacking the defeasible derivation from the source*: It is indeed general knowledge that if a witness saw someone who looks like person x, then the witness saw x, but this particular piece of general knowledge is based on a belief from folk psychology that people are always accurate at recognizing faces.
3. *Attacking application of the generalization in the given circumstances*: Usually it is true that "If a witness saw someone who looks like person x, then the witness saw x." However, in this case we cannot conclude that the witness saw John as John has a very common appearance.
4. *Attacking the generalization itself*: It is not the case that "If a witness saw someone who looks like person x, then the witness saw person x."

Note that the first type of attack is only possible if the source of the generalization is not evidential data but rather general knowledge. For example, it is not possible to deny the source from Figure 13.8 by arguing that "a witness testimony is not a legitimate source of evidence." In this case it is possible to attack the derivation from the source. The main difference between attacks of the third and the fourth kind is that the third kind of attack accepts the generalization as a general rule but denies its application in the case at hand, while the fourth kind of attack denies the generalization as a general rule ("it is not the case that usually ....").

5. Summary and Evaluation

This chapter has introduced arguments for reasoning with evidence in legal cases. It has been shown how arguments based on evidence to conclusions in a case can be built, how these arguments can be attacked and defended against counterarguments, and how generalizations can be used and analyzed in argumentation. The main ideas on argumentation presented in this chapter are logically and conceptually well-developed in the literature and a tradition of research on informal and formal argumentation provides the argument-based approach with the necessary academic grounding. The argument-based approach to evidential reasoning has a number of oft-cited strong and weak points[37], which will be briefly discussed below, starting with the strong points.

Arguments allow us to explicitly link the evidence to (legal) conclusions. In this way, the relevance of the evidence for a particular conclusion can be shown, and the attack relations

---

[35] The undercutting attack in the example in Figure 13.5 is an answer to another critical question of the form "Did the expert use the right method to determine the truth of *A*?"
[36] Bex et al. 2003.
[37] Verheij et al. 2016; Prakken 2020.

between arguments allow for clear identification of points of disagreement. By reasoning with arguments and counterarguments, one explicitly takes a so-called dialectical stance:[38] in argumentation, anything can be questioned, a conclusion, a generalization, the source of a generalization, and so on. These can all be tested in multiple ways and thus argumentation allows for a discussion not only of the evidential data but also of the general knowledge underlying the inferences.

More formal semantics for determining argument acceptability[39] can help in determining how the various pieces of evidence interact and why a particular combination of arguments can be believed. As the example in Figure 13.7 shows, the status of one argument may depend on attack relations between other arguments. Thus, we can determine which arguments need to be defeated if we want the arguments supporting some conclusion to be justified. For example, it might be that, for example, the testimony of one witness is important because it defends a large number of other arguments for a particular conclusion. Recent formal work also proposes algorithms for determining whether a certain conclusion is *stable*, meaning that no amount of new evidence will change the acceptability status of the argument.[40] Related to this, it can then be determined, for example, what the effect would be of finding some new piece of evidence on the main conclusions in a case.

Argumentation is often characterized as *evidential reasoning*—most of the inferences and schemes used are of the form "*e* is evidence for *c*." This type of reasoning seems to be consistent with how many decision-makers publicly justify their decisions—many motivations of decisions in Dutch criminal cases include phrases of the form "the event can be inferred from evidence e_1" and "this event is based on (or supported by) evidence e_1."[41] Evidential reasoning also seems to be the most natural way to think about inferring conclusions from evidence. For example, Van de Braak et al. showed that in the case of "testimonial knowledge," that is, information from testimonies and evidential documents, people find it significantly harder to interpret causal relations like "John bought a weapon *causes* the witness to testify that they saw John buy a weapon" than they find it to interpret evidential relations like "The witness testified that they saw John buy a weapon *is evidence for* the fact that John bought a weapon."[42] Finally, the connection between evidential and legal reasoning a case is best captured by reasoning from the evidence via the facts to legal conclusions.

The above discussion leads us to the first weakness of the argumentative approach, namely that it does not allow for reasoning with and about (explanatory) scenarios in a case. In criminal cases issues like the cause of death, but also the relations between motives and actions, are often expressed with causal generalizations of the form "*c* is a cause for *e*." While it is perfectly possible to construct a causal argument based on a scheme from cause to effect, it cannot capture the exact causal structure of a (hypothetical) scenario in a case, and the causal relations between the various the elements of this scenario (e.g., the motives and actions). Furthermore, the conclusion of an evidential argument is usually a single element of a scenario, an individual state or event (e.g., "John got into the car"). Thus, the

---

[38] Bex and Walton 2019. A stance is the level of abstraction on which certain concepts, decisions or behavior is judged. cf. Dennett's intentional stance, which views the behavior of an entity is judged in terms of the mental properties (intentions) of the entity (Dennett 1996).

[39] Dung 1995.

[40] Odekerken, Borg, and Bex 2020.

[41] Stevens 2014; Bex and Verheij 2012.

[42] Van den Braak, Oostendorp, Vreeswijk, and Prakken 2008.

overview of the case tends to be lost in a purely argument-based approach. In a case, the various hypotheses about what (might have) happened are usually not single conclusions but rather detailed scenarios or stories, coherent sets of events. These stories can explain the evidence and need to be compared to find the best explanation of the evidence. Often, when faced with evidence people will start to construct stories about what might have happened, and the police as well as decision-makers such as judges increasingly employ so-called "scenario-based" reasoning.[43] Recognizing the role of both stories and arguments, Bex has proposed a hybrid approach, in which stories about what (might have) happened in a case can be constructed and compared, and arguments based on evidence can then be used to support and attack these stories.[44] Figure 13.3 already hints at the use of scenarios or stories in a case: the two bottom claims together essentially form a short "story" about what happened—John and Bob were in a fight, which made John so mad that he drove into Bob.

Another weak point of argumentation that is often mentioned is the lack of a systematic account of degrees of uncertainty in argumentation.[45] However, one of the clear advantages of argumentation over more Bayesian approaches—in which assumptions and generalizations are encoded as (conditional) probabilities—is that discussions can take place in natural language. Bayesian analyses of a case are hard to understand for people less familiar with probabilistic reasoning (e.g., judges, jurors), and the assumptions the analysis makes might not be explicitly represented but rather included in the underlying probabilistic inference mechanisms. Recently, there has been quite some work that has compared, integrated, and discussed argument-based, story-based, and probability-based accounts to evidential reasoning.[46] This work shows that in many different approaches, ideas from argumentation, in particular dialectical processes, play an explicit role.

References

Anderson, T. J., Schum, D. A., and Twining, W. L. (2005). *Analysis of Evidence*. Second edition. Cambridge: Cambridge University Press.

Bex, F. J. (2011). *Arguments, Stories and Criminal Evidence: A Formal Hybrid Theory*. Cham: Springer.

Bex, F. J., Prakken, H., Reed, C., and Walton, D. N. (2003). "Towards a Formal Account of Reasoning About Evidence: Argumentation Schemes and Generalisations," *Artificial Intelligence and Law*, 11: 125–65.

Bex, F. J. and Verheij, B. (2012). Solving a Murder Case by asking Critical Questions: An Approach to Fact-Finding in Terms of Argumentation and Story Schemes," *Argumentation*, 26: 3, 325–53.

Bex, F. J. and Walton, D. N. (2012). "Burdens and Standards of Proof for Inference to the Best Explanation: Three Case Studies," *Law, Probability and Risk*, 11 (2–3): 113–33.

---

[43] See Pennington and Hastie 1992; Wagenaar, van Koppen, and Crombag 1993 for psychological evidence that a scenario-based approach is often used. More recent work that further develops scenario- or narrative-based accounts is Pardo and Allen 2007; Allen and Pardo, "Inference to the Best Explanation, Relative Plausibility, and Probability," ch. 14, in this volume; Mackor and van Koppen, "The Scenario Theory about Evidence in Criminal Law," ch.15, in this volume.

[44] Bex 2011.

[45] Though there has recently been work on integrating probabilistic, Bayesian approaches with argumentation, see, e.g., Zenker 2012; Hahn and Hornikx 2016.

[46] See Verheij et al. 2016; Prakken, Bex, and Mackor 2020.

Bex, F. J. and Walton, D. N. (2019). Taking the Dialectical Stance in Reasoning with Evidence and Proof, *International Journal of Evidence and Proof*, 23(1–2): 90–9. doi:10.1177/1365712718813795.

Dahlman, C. (2017). "Unacceptable Generalizations in Arguments on Legal Evidence," *Argumentation*, 31: 83–99.

Dennett, D. C. (1996). *The Intentional Stance*. Cambridge, MA: MIT Press.

Dung, P. M. (1995). "On the Acceptability of Arguments and its Fundamental Role in Nonmonotonic Reasoning, Logic Programming and n–Person Games," *Artificial Intelligence*, 77(2): 321–57.

Hahn, U. and Hornikx, J. (2016). "A Normative Framework for Argument Quality: Argumentation Schemes with a Bayesian Foundation," *Synthese*, 193(6): 1833–73.

McBurney, P. and Parsons, S. (2005). "Dialogue Games for Agent Argumentation," in I. Rahwan and G. Simari (eds.), *Argumentation in Artificial Intelligence*. Cham: Springer.

Modgil, S. J. and Prakken, H. (2013). "A General Account Of Argumentation with Preferences," *Artificial Intelligence*, 195, 361–97.

Odekerken, D., Borg, A., and Bex, F. (2020) "Estimating Stability for Efficient Argument-Based Inquiry," *Computational Models of Argument. Proceedings of COMMA 2020, Frontiers in Artificial Intelligence and Applications*, 326: 307–18.

Pardo, M. S. and Allen, R. J. (2007). "Juridical Proof and the Best Explanation," *Law and Philosophy*, 27: 223–68.

Pattaro, E., Rottleuthner, H., Shiner, R. A., Peczenik, A., and Sartor, G. (2005). *A Treatise of Legal Philosophy and General Jurisprudence*. Cham: Springer.

Pennington, N. and Hastie, R. (1992). "Explaining the Evidence: Tests of the Story Model for Juror Decision Making," *Journal of Personality and Social Psychology*, 62(2): 189–206.

Pollock, J. L. (1987). "Defeasible Reasoning," *Cognitive Science*, 11(4): 481–518.

Pollock, J. L. (1995). *Cognitive Carpentry: A Blueprint for How to Build a Person*. Cambridge, MA: MIT Press.

Prakken, H. (2020). "An Argumentation-Based Analysis of the Simonshaven Case," *Topics in Cognitive Science*, 12(4): 1068–91.

Prakken, H., Bex, F. J., and Mackor, A. R. (2020) "Models of Rational Proof in Criminal Law," *Topics in Cognitive Science*, 12(Special issue), 4.

Prakken, H. and Sartor, G. (2009). "A Logical Analysis of Burdens of Proof," in H. Kaptein, H. Prakken, and B. Verheij (eds.) *Legal Evidence and Proof: Statistics, Stories, Logic*, 223–53. Farnham: Ashgate Publishing.

Prakken, H. and G. Vreeswijk (2002). "Logics for Defeasible Argumentation," in R. Goebel and F. Guenthner (eds.), *Handbook of Philosophical Logic*, 219–318. Dordrecht: Kluwer Academic Publishers.

Stevens, L. (2014). "Bewijs Waarderen. Hoe doen Strafrechters Dat? [Evaluating Evidence: How do Judges in Criminal Cases do This?]" *Nederlands Juristenblad*, 89(40): 2842–50.

Toulmin, S. E. (1958). *The Uses of Argument*. Cambridge: Cambridge University Press.

Van den Braak, S. W., Oostendorp, H., Vreeswijk, G., and Prakken, H. (2008). "Representing Narrative and Testimonial Knowledge in Sense-Making Software for Crime Analysis," in E. Francesconi, G. Sartor, and D. Tiscornia (eds.), *Legal Knowledge and Information Systems, Proceedings of JURIX 2008: The 21st Annual Conference* (vol. 189), 160–9. Amsterdam: IOS Press..

Van Eemeren, F. H. and Grootendorst, R. (2004). *A Systematic Theory of Argumentation. The Pragma–Dialectical Approach*. Cambridge: Cambridge University Press.

Verheij, B., Bex, F. J., Timmer, S. T., Vlek, C., Meyer, J. J.-Ch., Renooij, S., and Prakken, H. (2016). "Arguments, Scenarios and Probabilities: Connections between Three Normative Frameworks for Evidential Reasoning." *Law, Probability & Risk*, 15: 35–70.

Wagenaar, W. A., van Koppen, P. J., and Crombag, H. F. M. (1993). *Anchored Narratives: The Psychology of Criminal Evidence*. New York: St. Martin's Press.

Walton, D. N. (1998). *The New Dialectic: Conversational Contexts of Argument*. Toronto: University of Toronto Press.

Walton, D. N. (2002). *Legal Argumentation and Evidence*. University Park, PA: Penn State University Press.

Walton, D. N., Reed, C., and Macagno, F. (2008). *Argumentation Schemes*. Cambridge: Cambridge University Press.

Wigmore, J. H. (1931). *The Principles of Judicial Proof or the Process of Proof as given by Logic, Psychology, and General Experience, and Illustrated in Judicial Trials*. Second edition. New York: Little, Brown and Company.

Zenker, F. (ed.) (2012). *Bayesian Argumentation: The Practical Side of Probability*. Cham: Springer.

PART IV
EVIDENCE AND EXPLANATION

14

Inference to the Best Explanation, Relative Plausibility, and Probability

Ronald J. Allen and Michael S. Pardo*[**]*

1. Introduction

In many areas of life, from hard science to managing one's everyday affairs, explanatory considerations help to guide inference. From the fact that some proposition would explain a given phenomenon we infer that the proposition is true. And when several propositions may explain a given phenomenon we infer the one that best explains it. Quantum mechanics best explains sub-atomic phenomena; evolutionary theory best explains species variations; that George Washington existed best explains the historical record concerning him; and that the Cubs won yesterday best explains why today's newspaper reports that they did. These inferences all share the same structure, typically referred to as "abduction" or "inference to the best explanation" (IBE).[1] Because legal proof falls somewhere between science and managing one's everyday affairs, it should perhaps not be surprising that the juridical proof process involves similar inferential practices.

Although juridical proof involves these inferential practices, much theorizing about the law of evidence and the proof process has focused attention elsewhere, primarily on probability theories in general and Bayesian decision theory in particular.[2] This theorizing has been helpful in understanding the process, but the neglect of explanation-based reasoning has been a mistake.[3] All of this is changing rapidly. A paradigm shift has occurred in the understanding of juridical proof, substituting explanation-based decision-making for the previous probability paradigm. In this chapter, we explain why this shift has occurred, to wit that a version of the process of inference to the best explanation best explains the macro-structure of proof at trial and the micro-level issues regarding the relevance and value of particular items of evidence. We also demonstrate that the probability-based accounts are not an alternative to but parasitic on the more fundamental explanation-based

[*] Professor Allen is indebted to the Searle Center and the Rosenthal fund for supporting his research.
[**] This chapter draws on prior work of the co-authors, but most particularly on Pardo and Allen 2008.
[1] The classic article coining the phrase and explaining the idea is Harman 1965. See also Lipton 2004; Lycan 1988; Thagard 1978; 2006; Leiter 2001; Day and Kincaid 1994; Ben-Menahem 1990.
[2] For examples, see Nance and Morris 2002; 2005; Finkelstein and Levin 2003; Davis and Follette 2002; 2003; Friedman and Park 2003; Kaplan 1968; Finkelstein and Fairley 1970; Lempert 1977; Friedman 1987; Tillers and Schum 1992.
[3] Unlike the analytical work on evidence, empirical studies of jury behavior have focused on explanatory-based reasoning, and they have concluded that jurors rely primarily on explanatory criteria in deciding cases. See Pennington and Hastie 1991. For discussions of abductive reasoning in the law, see Schum 2001; Abimbola 2001.

Ronald J. Allen and Michael S. Pardo, *Inference to the Best Explanation, Relative Plausibility, and Probability* In: *Philosophical Foundations of Evidence Law*. Edited by: Christian Dahlman, Alex Stein, and Giovanni Tuzet, Oxford University Press. © Christian Dahlman, Alex Stein, and Giovanni Tuzet 2021. DOI: 10.1093/oso/9780198859307.003.0015

considerations.[4] If this is true, one would predict that evidence scholarship would start producing efforts to modify probability accounts to embrace the essential characteristics of explanationism, and that is precisely what is occurring.[5] If probability accounts attempt to supplement explanationism, they may be helpful; to the extent they ignore such explanatory considerations, they mismodel the process under investigation.

In addition to contributing to conceptual knowledge, practical implications and real-world consequences turn on these matters. The nature of legal evidence and the process of proof have implications for virtually every legal issue that requires the evaluation of individual items of evidence, bodies of evidence, or judgments in civil and criminal cases. We demonstrate how explanatory considerations provide a better account of micro-level proof issues regarding the relevance and probative value of evidence. This conclusion, in turn, carries wide-ranging consequences for the admissibility of all types of evidence, from testimony of first-hand observations to complex scientific evidence such as DNA to other kinds of statistical evidence. This conclusion also explains and justifies the open-ended nature of the evidence rules in this area.[6] We also demonstrate how explanatory considerations provide a better account of the burden-of-proof standards employed in civil and criminal trials such as preponderance of the evidence, clear and convincing evidence, and beyond a reasonable doubt. This conclusion, also explains and justifies further aspects of the proof process such as the reliance on jurors and the existence of devices to control judgments based on the sufficiency of the evidence (such as summary judgments,[7] judgments as a matter of law,[8] and new trial motions[9] in civil cases and "sufficiency of the evidence" challenges in criminal cases[10]).

Section 2 provides a basic account of the abductive reasoning process of IBE, and it then explains how the process applies to the legal proof process at both the macro- and micro-levels. Section 3 considers possible law-specific objections from probability approaches to the version of IBE employed by the legal system (relative plausibility), which are shown to be mistaken, along with additional defects in the probability approaches that the explanation-based account avoids.

---

[4] Limitations on probability-based approaches to explain the probative value of evidence are discussed in Allen and Pardo 2007.

[5] See, e.g., Hedden and Colyvan 2019; Welsh 2020. Other examples are Franklin 2010; Franklin 2011. Franklin (2010) argues for a method to resolve the reference class problem. The method, however, only applies to cases with a quite restricted number of variables, which is atypical in litigation. See, e.g., Allen 1994, 625. In other words, Franklin restates rather than resolves the computation intractability problem. Similarly, Franklin 2011, 561, restates without resolving the reference class problem. He implicitly acknowledges that the only pertinent reference class in typical litigation is a reference class of one. That is unhelpful in litigation. In some cases, statistical proffers and a largely statistical evidence base may be workable, but generally speaking there is no knowledge of the relative frequencies and how they interact of the almost infinite number of variables applicable to the legal system generally. Ibid. See also the various articles in Symposium on Relative Plausibility and Its Critics 2019. Hedden and Colyvan largely embrace the paradigm shift but strive to preserve a place for the probability calculus. For a critique, see Allen 2019.

[6] See Federal Rules of Evidence (FRE) 401, 403.

[7] See Federal Rules of Civil Procedure (Fed. R. Civ. P.) 56.

[8] See Fed. R. Civ. P. 50.

[9] See Fed. R. Civ. P. 50(b).

[10] See Federal Rules of Criminal Procedure (Fed. R. Crim. P.) 29; see also *Jackson v. Virginia*, 443 U.S. 307, 324 (1979) (articulating standard as whether "[n]o rational trier of fact could have found proof of guilt beyond a reasonable doubt").

2. Inference to the Best Explanation

Inferences may be deductive or inductive. If the premises of deductive inferences are true, the conclusions are guaranteed to be true as well. Rarely if ever, however, will the material inferences at trial involve deductive inferences from uncontested premises. If the defendant confessed, and if her fingerprints were found at the crime scene, it may make it likely[11] that she committed the crime but it does not guarantee so. It is at least possible that she confessed and was at the scene for other reasons. The juridical proof process primarily involves inductive inferences, in the broad, non-demonstrative sense.

Inductive inferences themselves come in two varieties. First, some inductive inferences may be described as simple or "enumerative" induction. From the fact that each observed raven has been black, one infers that the next one will be black as well.[12] By contrast, some inferences may be referred to as "abductive." Abduction involves inferring a conclusion that would explain the given premises, usually but not necessarily causal.[13] From the defendant's DNA found at the scene, one infers that the defendant was there at some time. Like enumerative induction, the conclusion is not guaranteed; even if highly likely, it might be false. The pattern of inference at trial is primarily abductive rather than enumerative.[14]

2.1 Explanation as a Guide to Inference

To say that one infers the best explanation of a body of evidence to be true—whether in science, law, or everyday affairs—is not just to say that one infers the likeliest hypothesis or conclusion. Rather, explanations occur prior to and guide inference by helping to determine how likely one judges particular hypotheses or conclusions to be, and "it is for this reason that inference can be a good that explanation delivers."[15]

This process occurs in two steps: generating potential explanations of the evidence and then selecting the best explanation from the list of potential ones as an actual explanation or as the truth. Practical considerations and interests affect both steps. The domain of the inferential task will provide guidance and constraints with regard to what counts as a potential explanation.[16] This is clear in the legal context, where the substantive law determines what conduct triggers liability and hence what potential explanations to look for (e.g., did the defendant cause the plaintiff's injury). In other domains, the disciplines themselves may limit what counts as a potential explanation; what counts as potential explanations for the

---

[11] The fact that such conclusions are not guaranteed, but may be seen as more or less likely, is what invites probability-based approaches to the legal process, as it does in other areas.

[12] Lipton 2004, 9, refers to this as "more of the same." Enumerative induction may also involve inferences to general conclusions, e.g., that all or most As are B.

[13] But it need not be—one may infer, for example, mathematical, definitional, conceptual, or grammatical explanations of given premises.

[14] Inductive inferences may often be recast either as abductive or enumerative. Harman has suggested that all inductive inferences involve abduction. Harman 1965, 88–95. Fumerton, by contrast, has argued that all abduction may be described as an enumerative inference. Fumerton 1980, 589–600.

[15] Lipton 2001(a), 56; 2001(b), 93 ("we sometimes decide how likely a hypothesis is to be correct in part by considering how good an explanation it would provide, if it were correct").

[16] We do not rely on any precise definition of "explanation." It is a concept of which we assume most readers have at least a basic intuitive grasp. Explanations function by answering questions such as why, what, when, where, how, and so on. For more sophisticated accounts see Achinstein 1983; Van Fraassen 1980.

chemist may not count for the sociologist or the literary theorist. Beyond these practical considerations, however, the list of potential explanations is generally (and maybe always) limited only by the creativity of those involved.[17]

The second step, choosing among potential explanations, also varies with context and interests, and involves an open-ended set of cognitive tools. Common cognitive practices consistently entail that an explanation is better to the extent that it is consistent, simpler,[18] explains more (consilience), better accords with background beliefs (coherence), is less ad hoc, and so on.[19] There is no formula for combining such criteria. Again, practical considerations will drive this process; the scientist may be more concerned with consilience while the historian (and the jury even more so) may be more concerned with explaining a few events.[20]

A critical component—the critical component for juridical proof—is the contrastive nature of the explanations involved. Suppose one wants to explain what caused a certain event to occur—for example, why a man suffered terrible heartburn last night after eating a chili cheeseburger with extra jalapenos.[21] Events have many, many causes (from the big bang, to the man being born, to eating the chili cheeseburger with extra jalapenos). Where in the causal history of the event to look for an appropriate causal explanation will depend on one's inferential interests. For the man's wife, the decision to eat spicy food may qualify as a good explanation because the man may suffer heartburn only after eating spicy food. For the man's doctor, however, facts about the man's stomach or esophageal tract may qualify as a good explanation of the event because many of the doctor's other patients may eat spicy food without suffering any heartburn. The wife is interested in explaining why the man suffered heartburn *on this occasion* rather than on other occasions; the doctor is interested in explaining why *this man* suffered heartburn rather than other patients. The explanation in each case worked not just by picking a causal point but by picking one that contrasts it with a pertinent alternative possibility.

These points generalize. Explanations do not explain evidence in its entirety; explanations explain aspects of evidence. Explanations rarely explain why A; they explain why A rather than B. The inferential interests at stake pick out the appropriate contrasts (or "foils")—whether we want to explain why A rather than B or why A rather than C (or D, etc.). Consider whether "the maid stole the necklace" provides a good explanation of the fact that the necklace was found in the maid's pocket. It might if the other evidence is clear that someone stole it (rather than, by contrast, it being misplaced, given away, or sold).[22] But suppose the dispute is not over who stole the necklace, but whether the necklace was in fact stolen (or, by contrast, was given as a gift to the maid). Now, "the maid stole the necklace" would no longer be as good of an explanation because it does not mark a difference relevant to the inferential interests at stake ("the maid received it as a gift" also potentially explains

---

[17] For a discussion of the ways abductive reasoning aids in generating hypotheses, see Schum 2001.

[18] One reason a simpler explanation may be more likely is that more complex explanations involve more auxiliary premises and background assumptions and, therefore, more places to go wrong.

[19] Harman 1965; Thagard 1978.

[20] Wilson 1998; Thagard 1978.

[21] This example is based on one involving Adam, Eve, and an apple in White 2002, 89–90, which in turn is based on Hart and Honoré 1959, 33–4.

[22] But it might not if someone else could have easily planted it in the maid's pocket without her realizing it.

why it's in her pocket). The explanation was better, and hence an inference to it more likely, when the contrast was with someone else stealing it rather than with whether it was stolen.[23]

2.2 Explanation as a Guide to Inference at Trial

The general structure of proof at trial instantiates the two-stage explanation-based inferential process discussed earlier. At the first stage, potential explanations are generated; at the second, an inference is made to one of the potential explanations on explanatory grounds. The work at the first stage is fairly straightforward and is left primarily to the parties (including the government in criminal cases), who must offer competing versions of events that, if true, would explain the evidence presented at trial. Parties with the burdens of proof on claims or defenses offer versions of events that include the formal elements that make up the particular claims or defenses; parties on the other side offer versions of events that fail to include one or more of the formal elements. In addition, parties may, when the law allows,[24] offer alternative versions of events to explain the evidence. Finally, factfinders are not limited to the potential explanations explicitly put forward by the parties, but may construct their own, either in deliberation by suggesting them to fellow jurors or for themselves in reaching the conclusions they accept.[25]

At the second stage in civil cases where the burden of persuasion is a preponderance of the evidence, proof depends on whether the best explanation of the evidence favors the plaintiff or the defendant.[26] Factfinders decide based on the relative plausibility of the versions of events put forth by the parties, and possibly additional ones constructed by themselves or fellow jurors. Empirical evidence has confirmed that jurors[27] formulate factual conclusions by constructing narrative versions of events to account for the evidence presented at trial based on criteria such as coherence, completeness, and uniqueness.[28] This process proceeds on explanatory grounds—jurors construct narratives to explain the evidence and choose among alternatives by applying similar criteria to those invoked in the philosophy of science. These narratives function as "self-evidencing" explanations: the accepted version of events explains the evidence and the evidence provides reasons justifying acceptance of that version as the correct one.[29]

---

[23] Identifying an appropriate contrast may also help to locate the meaning of statements. See Dretske 1972, 417: "The maid stole the necklace" (rather than the butler) when asked "Who stole the necklace?" means something different than "The maid stole the necklace" (rather than received it as a gift) when asked "Why does the maid have the necklace?" Likewise, identifying appropriate contrasts also helps to locate the reasons that would support a proposition.

[24] Parties may sometimes be precluded from offering contradictory accounts. See *McCormick v. Kopman*, 161 N.E. 2d 720 (Ill. App. Ct. 1959).

[25] Empirical evidence (and common sense) suggests that juries assume in most cases the parties have put forward the explanation that best helps their case. See Nance 2001, 1579, n. 91 (citing Klonoff and Colby 1990).

[26] Allen 1991; 1994.

[27] Which is simply an instantiation of how virtually everyone reasons about the world at large. See Allen 1994 (discussion of scripts, narratives, etc.).

[28] Pennington and Hastie 1991.

[29] "Self-evidencing" does not mean circular. The worry is that the evidence (observation) is both what is explained and what is used to justify the explanation. But the evidence for the explanatory hypothesis H is not just the observation O that H explains. It is the conjunction of O together with a claim about how H would explain O (better than the disjunction of competing explanations). There are two points here that matter. First, an appraisal of the situation is not limited to O and H, but includes all the surrounding circumstances and the observer's knowledge. Second, the concern is with competing explanations. Compare whether tracks in the snow (O) evidence the

How this process proceeds at trial depends on the inferential interests of the legal system and the factfinders. Several distinct narratives (or theories) can be constructed to explain a given body of evidence, all of which are equally plausible. Indeed, as Friedman has pointed out, their number is infinite—did the accident occur at noon or 12:01 or at one of the infinite slices of time in between (which Zeno taught us to notice)?—and so on.[30] In general, how fine grained the explanation must be will depend on the context. "The accident occurred at 12:00:01" may be too detailed; "The accident occurred in the afternoon on June 16" may be good enough; and "An accident occurred sometime in the past" may be not detailed enough.

In the context of juridical proof, two factors set the inferential interests and the appropriate level of detail at which factfinders should focus in evaluating explanations. These factors are the substantive law and the points of contrast between the versions of events offered by the parties (the disputed facts). First, the substantive law will require a sufficiently detailed explanation of the evidence to show the plaintiff is entitled to relief. Sometimes, however, the substantive law allows parties to provide quite broad explanations. For example, the doctrine of *res ipsa loquitur* allows plaintiffs to recover even by offering explanations such as "My injuries were caused by *something* done by the defendant" when such a theory provides the best explanation of the evidence.[31] And second, where the parties choose to disagree focuses attention on the appropriate details for choosing among contrasting explanations. If the defendant contends that he was on vacation somewhere out of state during the car accident, then the appropriate contrast on which to focus is whether he was in state (and driving the car that caused the accident) or out of state, and not on whether he was driving or in the back seat or the trunk or any other place in the universe. Consider further Friedman's hypothetical focusing on whether an accident occurred at noon or some other time. If a defendant tries to defend on the ground that, although the accident occurred around noon, the evidence does not show precisely whether it was at 12:00 or 12:01, the defendant will obviously lose because the substantive law is indifferent to the matter. The IBE process thus accommodates the concern of too many explanations by showing how to aggregate and differentiate among them.

A complementary possible concern is having too few potential explanations. There may be cases where neither party offers a particularly plausible explanation of the evidence, either because neither side can explain key pieces of evidence or because there is such a paucity of evidence that it can be explained in multifarious ways none of which are any better (or more likely) explanations than any other. In the first scenario—where each side has problems explaining the same or different critical items of evidence—the key point is the comparative aspect of the process. A verdict will (and should) be rendered for the *better* (or best available) explanation, whether one of the parties' or another constructed by the factfinder. If the proffered explanations truly are equally bad (or good), including additionally constructed ones, judgment will (and should) go against the party with the burden of

---

hypothesis (H) that rabbits made them rather than a demon and whether the hypothesis of a rabbit explains the observation better than that of a demon.

[30] Friedman 1992.

[31] Friedman 2001, 2047, suggests that situations allowing for general explanations (like *res ipsa loquitur*) somehow pose a challenge to the theory that juries decide on the basis of the relative plausibility of competing explanations. But even quite general explanations are still explanations.

persuasion. In the second scenario—too little evidence from which to differentiate among potential explanations—should also end in judgment against the party with the burden of persuasion; they have failed to meet their burden of producing evidence from which a reasonable factfinder could differentiate among the potential, contrasting explanations.

The proof process in criminal cases is analogous but different, with a proof standard of beyond a reasonable doubt, and in cases with an intermediate proof standard of "clear and convincing" evidence. In criminal cases, rather than inferring the *best* explanation from the potential ones, factfinders infer (and should infer) the defendant's innocence whenever there is a sufficiently plausible explanation of the evidence consistent with innocence (and ought to convict when there is no plausible explanation consistent with innocence and there is a plausible explanation consistent with guilt[32]). When there is a plausible explanation of the evidence consistent with innocence, then there is a concomitant likelihood that this explanation is correct (the actual explanation) and thus that the defendant is innocent, which in turn creates a reasonable doubt (and thus should prevent the factfinder from inferring guilt).[33]

Similar alterations apply to the clear-and-convincing-evidence standard. Rather than inferring the *best* explanation from the available potential ones, factfinders should infer a conclusion for the party with the burden of persuasion if there is an explanation that is sufficiently more plausible than those that favor the other side (not just if the party with the burden has offered a better one). How sufficiently more plausible must the explanation be to meet the standard? The explanation must be plausible enough that is it clearly and convincingly more plausible than those favoring the other side. For example, the standard applies in defamation cases where the plaintiff must prove the defendant acted with "actual malice" in publishing a defamatory statement.[34] In such cases, for a plaintiff to succeed there must be a theory that explains the evidence, which incorporates actual malice by the defendant, and which is not only the best explanation but is clearly and convincingly a better explanation than those that do not include actual malice.

We acknowledge there is vagueness in how "sufficiently plausible" an explanation must be in order to satisfy either the beyond-a-reasonable-doubt or the clear-convincing-evidence standard, but this vagueness inheres in the standards themselves.[35] Lack of precision may thus be a critique of the standards, but it is not a critique of an explanation-based account. Even if the strength of a party's total evidence could be quantified (which it almost never can be), the vagueness remains for such a probability approach as well. Is 58% likelihood clear

---

[32] If both the prosecution and the defense offer implausible explanations of the evidence, the jury ought to acquit. Suggesting something quite similar to Allen 1997, 273, Professor Josephson has proposed a definition of the reasonable-doubt standard that turns on whether there is an explanation that represents a "real possibility" of innocence. See Josephson 2001, 1642 ("A real possibility does not suppose the violation of any known law of nature, nor does it suppose any behavior that is completely unique or unprecedented, nor any extremely improbable chain of coincidences.").

[33] Laudan has argued (correctly) that this is no longer a process of inference to the *best* explanation (see Laudan 2007). This is a necessary feature of the reasonable-doubt standard, however, and not a criticism of an explanatory account. IBE is, at root, based on the notion that explanatory success tracks likelihood of truth—the better the explanation, the more likely true. Because the criminal standard distributes errors unevenly (in favor of the defendant), the strength of the explanation needed for a pro-defendant verdict is therefore lower.

[34] See *New York Times v. Sullivan*, 376 U.S. 254 (1964).

[35] With "beyond a reasonable doubt," the system accommodates this vagueness by leaving it to juries to determine whether the standard has been met. See *Victor v. Nebraska*, 511 U.S. 1, 5 (1994) (citations omitted). For a critique of the court's jurisprudence in this area, see Laudan 2006.

and convincing? Is 65%? Is 72%?[36] Is 85% beyond a reasonable doubt? Is 90%? Is 95%?[37] Moreover, simply defining the standards as a certain percentage does not explain them; it changes them by fiat.[38] By contrast, we are not offering new standards; we are illuminating how explanatory factors guide the inferential processes at trial, and how the structure of the system is designed to control and foster those practices. However, the current standards are defined, they are met when explanations are plausible enough to cause and justify the desired inferences.

So much for the macro level. We next illustrate how IBE clarifies the relevance and probative value of individual items of evidence. The concepts of both "relevance" and "probative value" may be clarified by focusing on the relationship between explanations and items of evidence. Recall the "self-evidencing" nature of explanations: a hypothesis or conclusion explains evidence and the evidence in turn justifies the belief that the hypothesis or conclusion is true. An item of evidence is thus relevant if it is explained by the particular explanation offered by the party offering the evidence, which in turn justifies that explanation as correct, assuming the explanation concerns a fact that matters to the substantive law.[39] Probative value refers to the strength of the evidence in supporting an explanation;[40] the more the evidence is explained by, and hence justifies, the party's explanation, the greater the probative value and hence the stronger the inference to the truth of that explanation. The strength of that inference will depend contextually on the other evidence, and the presence of other, contrary explanations.[41] Consider again the example of the necklace found in the maid's pocket. Suppose the owner testifies that she found the necklace in the maid's pocket. This testimony is relevant because the fact that the maid stole the necklace explains the testimony. But the strength of the inference to the truth of the explanation will depend on the other available evidence. If there is other evidence that someone stole the necklace, then the testimony has greater probative value; if there is other evidence that the owner gave the maid the necklace as a gift, then the testimony has less probative value.

3. Probability

We turn now to objections to the use of IBE in explaining the nature of juridical proof, and explain where and how our account contrasts with and is superior to the probability-centered accounts in the legal literature. We have discussed at length why the objections to

[36] For an example of the vagueness, see Federal Civil Jury Instructions of the Seventh Circuit 35. Available at http://www.ca7.uscourts.gov (Accessed: March 29, 2021) (defining the "clear and convincing" standard as "highly probable that it is true").

[37] See *United States v. Fatico*, 458 F. Supp. 388, 410 (E.D. N.Y. 1978) (providing a survey of district judges on the probability they associated with various standards of persuasion—judges differed); see also Simon and Mahan 1971.

[38] Thus, Nance's lament (2001, 1593) is equally applicable to his own probabilistic account: "there is no clue how, even in principle, one can determine how probable the defendant's story must be in order to be plausible or in what other way a jury is to decide whether a story is plausible."

[39] FRE 401 defines "relevant evidence" as "having any tendency to make a fact more or less probable than it would be without the evidence" and "the fact is of consequence." Explanatory considerations establish the "any tendency" aspect of evidence (the logical relevance); the substantive law determines which facts are "of consequence." Parties must therefore construct explanations that include (or fail to include, if on the other side) the facts of consequence.

[40] Pardo 2005, 374–83.

[41] Allen 1994.

and criticisms of IBE in philosophy of science and more generally as an inferential strategy are of no significance to the best understanding of juridical proof.[42] We do not repeat those arguments here for a simple reason. Our focus is on the best explanation of juridical proof, not the deepest nor best explanation of "knowledge." Knowledge may be too high a standard for a decision-making process that always operates under uncertainty (and may be too high a standard for any decision-making process). As for criticisms of plausible reasoning in general, nothing is perfect, and it is the best that humans have. Not surprisingly, then, it is what occurs in the intensely practical setting of trials. We focus a bit more effort on the probability arguments given their once prominence in explaining juridical proof, and because they purport, like relative plausibility, to be explanatory of juridical proof. We will be brief, however, as the inadequacies of probability theory as an explanation of juridical proof have been thoroughly explored in the literature.

As a preliminary matter, it is critically important to distinguish between probability as a criterion of uncertainty and the probability calculus. Legal decision-making is obviously decision under uncertainty, and just as obviously legal systems attempt to allocate errors through various rules of evidence, which itself will involve a concept of uncertainty. How one deals with irresolvable uncertainty is different from its existence. The probability theorists have argued that the mechanism for doing so is the probability calculus. This is the mistake that they have made. For reasons that need not be rehearsed here, juridical uncertainty cannot possibly be handled as a general matter with the probability calculus, but instead is handled easily through the legal system's version of IBE—relative plausibility.[43]

The probabilists have raised various criticisms of relative plausibility, but each of them is either unavailing or applicable to their own arguments. Again, these have been thoroughly discussed in the literature[44] and we just adumbrate them here.

3.1 The Aggregation Problem

Both Friedman and Nance have raised objections to the relative plausibility of competing explanations as a macro-level theory of the proof process, each preferring Bayesian approaches. They propose articulating both the strength of a party's case and the burden of persuasion in terms of cardinal probabilities: "the claimant (plaintiff or prosecutor) should prevail if the probability that the claimant has a valid claim is greater than the standard of persuasion."[45] Nance defines the preponderance standard in a civil case with two elements, A and B, as whether $A \times B > .5$.[46]

Under their approaches, factfinders must aggregate the probabilities of all the possible stories that support each side, which they claim is handled by probability theory but not relative plausibility. But nothing in relative plausibility of competing explanations prevents aggregation. Sometimes an explanation as general as "the defendant did something that

---

[42] Pardo and Allen 2008.

[43] Allen 1994, 1997; Allen and Jehl 2004; Allen and Pardo 2019. The probability calculus may play a role in the unusual case of statistical evidence, which will also often involve forensic evidence. For a discussion, see Taroni, Bozza, and Biedermann, "The Logic of Inference and Decision for Scientific Evidence," ch. 17, in this volume.

[44] Allen and Pardo 2019.

[45] Friedman 2001, 2045.

[46] Nance 2001, 1568.

caused the accident" is good enough (in cases involving *res ipsa loquitur*) even when that something could be several things, and sometimes, *pace* Friedman, it does not matter at which of the infinite time slices between 12:00 and one second later the event occurred. Friedman's criticism of IBE is based on a misconstruction of the substantive law. But sometimes a very detailed story (explanation) will be necessary based on the appropriate contrast—for example, whether the fire occurred the day before or the day after the insurance policy expired or whether the driver's blood alcohol level was .07 or .08. Likewise, if a man gets heartburn only after he eats either chili cheeseburgers or spicy Thai food, and he now has heartburn, it is a perfectly good explanation that "he must have eaten a chili cheeseburger or spicy Thai food," even though the two may be incompatible, if, of course, the appropriate contrast is why he now has heartburn rather than not now having heartburn.

Just like a Bayesian approach, an explanation-based approach can account for aggregation of potential stories or theories and explain how and why it should proceed in the way that it does. Indeed, explanatory considerations drive key aspects of the Bayesian process. The Bayesian approach, for example, cannot offer advice on how to generate potential theories; explanatory considerations guide this process. As Nance notes explicitly: "students familiar with Bayesian thinking naturally pose the question of what circumstances or events, consistent with innocence, would *explain* the report of a match, and then inquire how likely such circumstances or events are as compared to the report of a match for an accused who is guilty [emphasis added]."[47] Obviously, explanatory considerations drive inferences as to the likelihood of various potential explanations. Indeed, there is no reason to see explanatory and Bayesian approaches as necessarily incompatible.[48] Explanatory considerations, however, are inherent and fundamental; to the extent Bayesian perspectives can clarify and improve on those considerations, they prove their worth. To the extent they do not, they do not.

3.2 The Conjunction Problem

The explanation-based account does much better than the Bayesian account in taming the conjunction paradox.[49] As just noted with respect to Nance, to solve the conjunction problem, various probability theorists argue that the standards of proof should be interpreted as involving the probability of the conjunction of the various elements.[50] The first problem with this model is that this is not how the law defines the burden of persuasion or how it instructs jurors: it does so by requiring that claimants prove *each element* to the requisite standard of persuasion.[51] A probability approach based on the proof of discrete elements to the standard of persuasion does not distribute errors evenly among parties and therefore is unlikely to increase the accuracy of outcomes.[52] Rather, it leads to paradoxical conclusions: the plaintiff in a two-element claim wins when proving each element to

[47] Nance 2001, 1609.
[48] Lipton 2001b, 103–20.
[49] On the paradox, see Allen and Pardo 2019; Pardo 2019; Allen and Jehl 2004; Stein 2001; Levmore 2001. See also, Spottswood, "Burdens of Proof," ch. 8, in this volume.
[50] Friedman 1992, 98; Nance 2001, 568.
[51] Allen and Jehl 2004.
[52] Allen and Jehl 2004, 929–36. Bell 1987.

.6 (despite a likelihood of .36) and loses when proving one element to .9 and the other to .5 (and having a likelihood of .45).

The Bayesian response is to declare that current practices are wrong and should be changed.[53] But this creates its own problem. Plaintiffs' likelihood of success will depend on how the claim is defined; more elements means that they have the burden not only of proving the additional elements, but also that their burden goes up even with regard to the other (possibly independent) elements. For example, suppose a plaintiff has to prove injury and one other independent element—on average they would have to show the probability of injury was around .707. But suppose two additional elements are added in that have nothing to do with whether the plaintiff suffered an injury. The plaintiff's burden with regard to injury now shoots up on average to around .841. By contrast, an explanatory approach based on relative plausibility ameliorates the problematic implications of the formal paradox. In civil cases, factfinders infer the best explanation of the evidence as a whole; in doing so they now have an accepted explanation that may or may not instantiate all of the formal elements of the claim. If it is does, then the claimant ought to win; if not, not.[54] This effectively neutralizes the formal paradox by spreading it over both parties' cases.

3.3   Internal Contradictions within the Probability Calculus

Conventional probability requires that the probability of events add to 1.0. At trial that would require that all the possible explanatory hypotheses will be before the court, but parties often pick the best of the explanations rather than a series, in part because the presentation of a series may itself communicate to the factfinder that none of the series is to be believed. Although perfectly allowable, one never sees at trial the defense, "I didn't do it. But if I did, it was in self-defense. And if it wasn't in self-defense, I was coerced to do it. But if I wasn't coerced, I was entrapped. And if I wasn't entrapped, I was insane." Thus, there is good reason to believe the standard problem of trials is not to accumulate all the stories for the parties and see which collectively adds up to greater than .5 (or proof beyond reasonable doubt or whatever). Rather, the standard problem may be something more like the probability of the plaintiff's case being .4, and the respective probabilities of the two defenses each being .1. In such a case, the Bayesian approach would result in a defense verdict (plaintiff has not satisfied its burden of persuasion), yet that is perverse from the point of view of reducing errors. By contrast, an explanatory account avoids this perverse result by focusing on the relative plausibility of the parties' explanations. Relative plausibility provides an easy, non-perverse answer: plaintiff wins.[55]

---

[53] See, e.g., Nance 1986 (suggesting that each element individually plus their conjunction must meet the standard).

[54] Juries are not explicitly instructed to do this, but it is plausible to suppose that they do so because explanatory criteria are used to infer holistic narratives of events before receiving jury instructions. See Pennington and Hastie 1991; Diamond, Rose, and Murphy 2006, 212 ("The deliberations of these 50 cases revealed that jurors actively engaged in debate as they discussed the evidence and arrived at their verdicts. Consistent with the widely accepted 'story model,' the jurors attempted to construct plausible accounts of the events that led to the plaintiff's suit. They evaluated competing accounts and considered alternative explanations for outcomes.").

[55] Schum 2001, 1655, has criticized IBE on a similar ground: "If we say we have the 'best' explanation ... we must also be assured we have canvassed all possibilities." The legal system, however, addresses this concern by allowing parties to present the explanations they believe to be most favorable. There are an infinite number of possible explanations; it would, of course, be nonsensical to construct a decision procedure requiring that they all be

3.4 Likelihood Ratios and Reference Classes

Probability theorists claim that probability theory in the guise of likelihood ratios gives purchase on the concept of probative value. This is the subject of another chapter in this book[56] and we will not repeat the arguments here. Suffice it to say that were the probability theorists right, they would obviously be wrong as an explanation of juridical proof. If, for example, one determines relevancy by whether a proffer of evidence might affect a decision-maker's assessment of an element, then most evidence admitted at trial is irrelevant as it is massively redundant.[57] Thus, the probability argument would amount to a criticism of trial practice rather than an explanation of it. Relative plausibility, by contrast, handles this problem seamlessly: the parties offer and support their explanation more or less how they see fit.

When it comes to assessing the probative value of items of evidence, one must focus on explanatory criteria. The probative value of evidence is the extent to which it supports an inference in a particular context.[58] The strength of this inference will depend on how well it explains the evidence, and this in turn will be determined by the inferential interests of the decision-maker and the contrasting explanations at issue in the case (recall the maid example). We suspect that those who favor the probability approaches will dislike the lack of formality and precision in this answer, but these features are part of the world, not defects in the explanation-based approach.

4. Conclusion

Explanatory considerations guide the inferential processes at trial, and the trial's structural features may be explained in terms of these considerations. Explanatory considerations illuminate micro-level issues regarding relevance and probative value, and the explanation-based account of these phenomena explains the evidence law regulating these issues. Explanatory considerations also illuminate macro-level issues regarding standards of persuasions in both civil and criminal cases, and the explanation-based account of these phenomena accords with the best understanding of the reasoning processes of jurors, avoids the formal conjunction paradox, and better aligns the standards with their purported goals regarding error distribution.

References

Abimbola, K. (2001). "Abductive Reasoning in Law: Taxonomy and Inference to the Best Explanation," *Cardozo Law Review*, 22: 1683–9.

Achinstein, P. (1983). *The Nature of Explanation*. Oxford: Oxford University Press.

Allen, R. J. (1991). "The Nature of Juridical Proof," *Cardozo Law Review*, 13: 373–422.

canvassed. The explanatory account handles this situation through a comparative approach; a probability account that must aggregate all possibilities falls prey to it.

[56] Pardo and Allen, "Generalizations and Reference Classes," ch. 20, in this volume.
[57] Allen and Jehl 2004.
[58] Pardo 2005.

Allen, R. J. (1994). "Factual Ambiguity and a Theory of Evidence," *Northwestern University Law Review*, 88: 604–40.

Allen, R. J. (1997). "Rationality, Algorithms and Juridical Proof: A Preliminary Inquiry," *The International Journal of Evidence and Proof*, 1: 254–75.

Allen, R. J. (2019). "Legal Probabilism—a Qualified Rejection: a Response to Hedden and Colyvan," *The Journal of Political Philosophy*, 27: 448–68.

Allen, R. J. and Jehl, S. A. (2004). "Burdens of Proof in Civil Cases: Algorithms vs. Explanations," *Michigan State Law Review*, 2004 893–944.

Allen, R. J. and Pardo, M. S. (2007). "The Problematic Value of Mathematical Models of Evidence," *Journal of Legal Studies*, 36: 107–40.

Allen, R. J. and Pardo, M. S. (2019). "Relative Plausibility and its Critics," *The International Journal of Evidence and Proof*, 23: 5–58.Bell, R. S. (1987). "Decision Theory and Due Process: A Critique of the Supreme Court's Law Making for Burdens of Proof," *Journal of Criminal Law and Criminology*, 78: 557–85.

Ben-Menahem, Y. (1990). "The Inference to the Best Explanation," *Erkenntnis*, 33: 209–24.

Davis, D. and Follette, W. C. (2002). "Rethinking the Probative Value of Evidence: Base Rates, Intuitive Profiling, and the 'Postdiction' of Behavior," *Law and Human Behavior*, 27: 133–58.

Davis, D. and Follette, W. C. (2003). "Toward an Empirical Approach to Evidentiary Ruling," *Law and Human Behavior*, 27: 661–84.

Day, T. and Kincaid, H. (1994). "Putting Inference to the Best Explanation in its Place," *Synthese*, 98: 271–95.

Diamond, S. S., Rose, M. R., and Murphy, B. (2006), Revisiting the Unanimity Requirement: the Behavior of the Non-Unanimous Civil Jury, *Northwestern University Law Review*, 100: 1–30.

Dretske, F. I. (1972). "Contrastive Statements," *Philosophical Review*, 81: 411–37.

Finkelstein, M. and Fairley, W. (1970). "A Bayesian Approach to Identification Evidence," *Harvard Law Review*, 83: 489–517.

Finkelstein, M. O. and Levin, B. (2003). "On the Probative Value of Evidence from a Screening Search," *Jurimetrics Journal*, 43: 265–90.

Franklin, J. (2010). "Feature Selection Methods for Solving the Reference Class Problem: Comment on Edward K. Cheng, 'A Practical Solution to the Reference Class Problem'," *Columbia Law Review*, 110: 12–23.

Franklin, J. (2011). "The Objective Bayesian Conceptualisation of Proof and Reference Class Problems," *Sydney Law Review*, 33: 545–61.

Friedman, R. D. (1987). "Route Analysis of Credibility and Hearsay," *Yale Law Journal*, 96: 667–742.

Friedman, R. D. (1992). "Infinite Strands, Infinitesimally Thin: Storytelling, Bayesianism, Hearsay and other Evidence," *Cardozo Law Review*, 14: 79–101.

Friedman, R. D. (2001). "'E' is for Eclectic: Multiple Perspectives on Evidence," *Virginia Law Review*, 87: 2029–54.

Friedman, R. D. and Park R. C. (2003). "Sometimes what Everybody Thinks they Know is True," *Law and Human Behavior*, 27: 629–44.

Fumerton, R. A. (1980). "Induction and Reasoning to the Best Explanation," *Philosophy of Science*, 47: 589–600.

Harman, G. (1965). "The Inference to the Best Explanation," *Philosophical Review*, 74: 88–95.

Hart, H. L. A. and Honoré, A. M. (1959). *Causation in the Law*. Oxford: Oxford University Press.

Hedden, B. and Colyvan, M. (2019). "Legal Probabilism: A Qualified Defence," *Journal of Political Philosophy*, 27: 448–68.

Josephson, J. R. (2001). "On the Proof Dynamics of Inference to the Best Explanation," *Cardozo Law Review*, 22: 1621–43.

Kaplan, J. (1968). "Decision Theory and the Factfinding Process," *Stanford Law Review*, 20: 1065–92.

Klonoff, R. H. and Colby, P. L. (1990). *Winning Jury Trials: Trial Tactics and Sponsorship Theory*. New York: Lexis-Nexis.

Laudan, L. (2006). *Truth, Error, and Criminal Law: An Essay in Legal Epistemology*. Cambridge: Cambridge University Press.

Laudan, L. (2007). "Strange Bedfellows: Inference to the Best Explanation and the Criminal Standard of Proof," *The International Journal of Evidence and Proof*, 11: 292–306.

Leiter, B. (2001). "Moral Facts and Best Explanations," *Social Philosophy & Policy*, 18: 79–101.

Lempert, R. (1977). "Modeling Relevance," *Michigan Law Review*, 75: 1021–57.

Levmore, S. (2001). "Conjunction and Aggregation," *Michigan Law Review*, 99: 723–56.

Lipton, P. (2001a). "What Good is an Explanation?" in G. Hon and S. S. Rakover (eds.), *Explanation: Theoretical Approaches and Explanations*, 43–59. Norwell, MA, and Dordrecht: Kluwer Academic Publishers.

Lipton, P. (2001b). "Is Explanation a Guide to Inference?" in G. Hon and S. S. Rakover (eds.), *Explanation: Theoretical Approaches and Explanations*, 93–120. Norwell, MA, and Dordrecht: Kluwer Academic Publishers.

Lipton, P. (2004). *Inference to the Best Explanation*. London: Routledge.

Lycan, W. G. (1988). *Judgment and Justification*. Cambridge: Cambridge University Press.

Nance, D. A. (1986). "A Comment of the Supposed Paradoxes of a Mathematical Interpretation of the Logic of Trials," *Boston University Law Review*, 66: 947–52.

Nance, D. A. (2001). "Naturalized Epistemology and the Critique of Evidence Theory," *Virginia Law Review*, 87: 1551–618.

Nance, D. A. and Morris, S. B. (2002). "An Empirical Assessment of Presentation Formats for Trace Evidence with a Relatively Large and Quantifiable Random Match Probability," *Jurimetrics Journal*, 42: 403–45.

Nance D. A. and Morris, S. B. (2002). "Juror Understanding of DNA Evidence: An Empirical Assessment of Presentation Formats for Trace Evidence with a Relatively Small Random-Match Probability," *Journal of Legal Studies*, 34: 395–443.

Nance, Dale A. and Morris, Scott B. (2005). "Juror Understanding of DNA Evidence: An Empirical Assessment of Presentation Formats for Trace Evidence with a Relatively Small Random-Match Probability," *Journal of Legal Studies*, 34: 395–444.

Pardo, M. S. (2005). "The Field of Evidence and the Field Of Knowledge," *Law & Philosophy*, 24: 321–92.

Pardo, M. S. and Allen, R. J. (2008). "Juridical Proof and the Best Explanation," *Law & Philosophy*, 27: 223–68.

Pardo, M. S. (2019). "The Paradoxes of Legal Proof: A Critical Guide," *Boston University Law Review*, 99: 233–90.

Pennington, N. and Hastie, R. (1991). "A Cognitive Model of Juror Decision Making: The Story Model," *Cardozo Law Review*, 13: 519–58.

Schum, D. A. (2001). "Species of Abductive Reasoning in Fact Investigation in Law," *Cardozo Law Review*, 22: 1645–81.

Simon, R. J. and Mahan, L. (1971). "Quantifying Burdens of Proof: A View from the Bench, the Jury, and the Classroom," *Law and Society Review*, 5: 319–30.

Stein, A. (2001). "Of Two Wrongs that Make a Right: Two Paradoxes of the Law of Evidence and their Combined Justification," *Texas Law Review*, 79: 1199–234.

Symposium on Relative Plausibility and its Critics (2019). *The International Journal of Evidence and Proof*, 23(1): 3–217.

Thagard, P. R. (1978). "The Best Explanation: Criteria for Theory Choice," *Journal of Philosophy*, 75: 76–92.

Thagard, P. R. (2006). "Evaluating Explanations in Law, Science, and Everyday Life," *Current Directions in Psychological Science*, 15: 141–5.

Tillers, P. and Schum, D. A. (1992). "Hearsay Logic," *Minnesota Law Review*, 76: 813–58.

Van Fraassen, B. C. (1980). *The Scientific Image*. Oxford: Oxford University Press.

Welsh, J. (2020). "Rebooting the New Evidence Scholarship," *The International Journal of Evidence and Proof*, 24: 351–73.

White, M. (2002). *A Philosophy of Culture: The Scope of Holistic Pragmatism*. Princeton, NJ: Princeton University Press.

Wilson, E. O. (1998). *Consilience: The Unity of Knowledge*. New York: Random House.

15

The Scenario Theory about Evidence in Criminal Law

Anne Ruth Mackor and Peter J. van Koppen

1. Introduction

In this chapter we discuss the Dutch scenario theory,[1] as it was further developed by van Koppen and Mackor.[2] It is a theory about reasoning about evidence and proof in criminal cases which holds that people should construct, assess, and compare competing scenarios that can explain the evidence in a case. The scenario theory has been applied to many complex criminal cases in the Netherlands.[3]

2. The Story Model of Pennington and Hastie

The starting point of the scenario approach is psychological research into the ways people actually reason when they have to deal with a lot of evidence. Wagenaar, van Koppen, and Crombag specifically refer to Pennington's and Hastie's story model.[4] Therefore, we start with an exposition of that model.[5]

The story model is a descriptive psychological theory about cognitive strategies that factfinders use to process trial information in order to take decisions about evidence and proof. Pennington and Hastie claim that factfinders typically use one central strategy, namely active story construction. In doing so, factfinders impose a narrative story organization on the trial information.[6] Their model offers an analysis both of the structure of these stories and of the dynamics of the way in which people construct and reason about stories.

Stories consist of elements, which are called episodes. Episodes consist of specific elements, namely an initiating event, a psychological response, sometimes a goal, an action, and consequences. For example, the following episode is also a simple story: a husband has an argument with his wife (initiating event), which makes him angry (psychological response). Because he intends to hurt her (goal), he beats his wife (action), which causes her death (consequence). The example illustrates that episodes have a specific structure: the

---

[1] Van Koppen 2011; Wagenaar, van Koppen, and Crombag 1993.
[2] Van Koppen and Mackor 2020.
[3] See also van Koppen 2003; van Koppen and Mackor 2020, for additional references. Also see the Project Reasonable Doubt (Project Gerede Twijfel) at VU University, Amsterdam, which is led by van Koppen. Available at https://allp.nl/projectgeredetwijfel/ (Accessed: March 29, 2021).
[4] Wagenaar, van Koppen, and Crombag 1993; van Koppen 2011; Pennington and Hastie 1992; 1993.
[5] This section is an adaptation of Dahlman and Mackor 2019, §2.1.
[6] Bennett and Feldman 2014; Pennington and Hastie 1992; 1993.

Anne Ruth Mackor and Peter J. van Koppen, *The Scenario Theory about Evidence in Criminal Law* In: *Philosophical Foundations of Evidence Law*. Edited by: Christian Dahlman, Alex Stein, and Giovanni Tuzet, Oxford University Press. © Christian Dahlman, Alex Stein, and Giovanni Tuzet 2021. DOI: 10.1093/oso/9780198859307.003.0016

elements are chronologically ordered and partly connected through physical and mental causal relationships. Stories can be thought of as a hierarchy of episodes.[7]

Pennington and Hastie built their story model on sets of three: they argue that three kinds of knowledge are relevant, that there are three kinds of reasoning procedure, and that there are three certainty principles.

Factfinders construct stories by reasoning from *three kinds of knowledge*:

(a) case-specific knowledge, i.e., evidence;
(b) knowledge about similar events to infer facts and causal relationships; and
(c) knowledge about what makes a story complete: viz —knowledge about the typical elements of stories, episodes, and their elements, and about the connections in and between episodes.[8]

Factfinders use the latter two to "fill out" a story.

Pennington and Hastie mention *three types of reasoning procedures* that factfinders use to establish intermediate and final conclusions:[9]

(a) deductive reasoning from world knowledge;
(b) reasoning from analogy to other—experienced and hypothetical—episodes; and
(c) reasoning by evaluating alternative conclusions that contradict the initial conclusion.

Pennington and Hastie propose *three certainty principles* that factfinders use to assess stories, namely coverage, coherence, and uniqueness.[10] These principles help a factfinder to determine how acceptable a story is for him and how confident he is about the truth of the story.

(a) *Coverage* deals with the question to what extent the story explains the occurrence of the evidence. The greater the coverage, the more acceptable the story and the more confident the factfinder will be.
(b) A story is *unique* if it is the only coherent story that can account for the evidence. If there is more than one coherent story, all stories are in principle acceptable, but confidence in each of them will diminish.
(c) The third certainty principle, *coherence,* has three components: consistency, plausibility, and completeness.

Consistency is about two questions, namely (1) whether the story is consistent with evidence believed to be true, and (2) whether all of its elements are consistent with other parts of the story (internal consistency).

Plausibility deals with the question whether the story fits into the factfinder's background or general world knowledge.

Completeness, finally, is about the question whether the structure of the story has all its parts, such as episodes, elements of episodes, and causal relationships in and between

---

[7] Pennington and Hastie 1993.
[8] Ibid.
[9] Ibid., 195.
[10] Ibid., 198–9.

episodes. Missing information and lack of plausible inferences makes a story incomplete and decreases confidence in the story. Pennington and Hastie argue that consistency, plausibility, and completeness can be fulfilled to a greater or lesser degree and that the values of the three components combine to yield the overall coherence of the story.

3. Scenarios, Subscenarios, and Background Knowledge

The scenario theory starts from the story model and offers a further explication of stories, called scenarios and subscenarios and background knowledge. Scenarios range from one simple proposition of how a crime may have taken place ("John shot George with a pistol") to complex stories about what happened, who was involved and how things developed over time. Scenarios, however, are not fixed entities with a singular meaning. Scenarios get their meaning from background knowledge people have. Also, scenarios are holistic and tend to change and develop.

Consider the simple scenario: *John had dinner in a restaurant last night.* First, that scenario entails much more than just these eight words, because we interpret and adjust the story almost automatically with the background knowledge we have. That background knowledge consists of generalizations that are usually true. People know that John probably is a man. They also know that he probably was going to have his third meal of that day. People also understand what a restaurant is, what the typical routine is when you go there—either pick your own table or are seated by the staff, order a drink, receive the menu, pay afterwards, etc.—and that there are different price classes for restaurants. Actually, we could go on for some pages what almost automatically comes to mind when one hears that simple eight-word scenario. At the same time, people may also differ to small or sometimes great extent in their background knowledge and thus in the manner in which they understand the scenario.

The scenario also raises questions. An obvious one is: was John going to have dinner alone? Most people have dinner in a restaurant in the company of others. Some people may ask such questions, as typically a police officer would in a crime investigation.

Scenarios paint a picture of an occasion that is as complete as people need to know. Usually, we do not want to have information about the salt and pepper set on the table or the people seated at the next table, but that may become an issue if we question John about whether he really was at the restaurant.[11] So, scenarios vary in detailedness, depending on what the scenario is for. For checking John's alibi, a very detailed scenario may be required.

Also, scenarios are dynamic and tend to change. If we learn that John is living in a very remote area without restaurants, we may want to have information about how John travelled to the restaurant. Or if we know that John always eats out with his wife but not this time, we may want to know what happened between them. Did they have a fight?

In summary, scenarios are to some extent empty vessels that are filled with background knowledge; scenarios are holistic in the sense that they cannot be equated with or reduced to the propositions that are explicitly formulated; and scenarios are dynamic, both in detailedness and in content. Much of a scenario and the interpretation of the scenario depends on common knowledge that people have, for instance, about John and about restaurants. However, people differ, slightly or extensively, in their background knowledge. Thus,

---

[11] See for an example, Strömwall, Granhag, and Jonsson 2003.

discussing scenarios and interpreting scenarios is also a social process. That also holds for topics we will discuss later, as, for instance, testing scenarios against each other and interpreting evidence and proof.

The scenario theory is typically illustrated with Figure 15.1.[12] It shows that in the end the chain of subscenarios is anchored in general background knowledge. It should be noted that background knowledge is relevant at every level: sometimes as a direct test of an unlikely scenario; always to understand scenarios; and always to understand whether and how a subscenario supports a superior scenario. Accordingly, knowledge of the world should not be perceived, as Figure 15.1 might suggest, as a "rock bottom" but rather as an ocean or a huge cloud in which scenarios and subscenarios are floating.

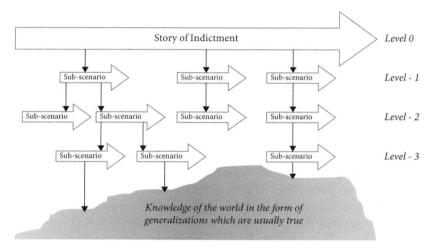

Figure 15.1 Reasoning within scenario and from scenario to evidence.

Figure 15.1 also shows that subscenarios are always the answer to the question why the indictment should be believed. For instance, if the story of the indictment is that John shot George with a pistol, and one piece of evidence may be that his fingerprint was found on the murder weapon. That answer to the question why the indictment should be believed is also a scenario, that we call a subscenario. It tells the story of the forensic detective who secured the gun at the crime scene, dusted it for fingerprints, and compared these to the one taken from John at the police station. And another subscenario is the story of the forensic detective who compared bullets from test shots with the pistol to the bullet secured from the head of the victim. And, again, these subscenarios can be probed in turn with the question why we should believe the fingerprint expert or the bullet expert. The answer will be a sub-subscenario.

The normative scenario approach instructs factfinders to keep scenarios and the evidence that is explained by a scenario separate. A scenario should not overlap with the subscenario supporting the scenario. In practice, however, people often make subscenarios

---

[12] This is a slightly adapted version of the figure in van Koppen 2011 and van Koppen and Mackor 2020.

part of their scenario. For example, when a man is prosecuted for killing his wife and there is evidence that they had marital problems, many people would include marital problems in the main scenario. However, the fact that they had marital problems is a piece of evidence for the hypothesis that the defendant had a motive to kill his wife. Therefore, the marital problems are part of a subscenario. On this point the normative scenario approach diverges from the descriptive theory.[13]

For these subscenarios the same holds as for the main scenario: we fill it or amend with our background knowledge of the world. We can readily accept the subscenarios, if we use the generalization that most experts can be relied on most of the time. But of course, that answer can be disputed. The questioning can go on indefinitely, in principle. But somewhere it ends. Sometimes it does because one of the participants to the trial is unaware of potentials problems with evidence. Good examples are fingerprints, that have more problems than most jurists are aware of,[14] and bullet comparison, that has likewise problems.[15] Sometimes the probing ends because trial participants agree on the generalizations in which the evidence is anchored. And there are also practical reasons: one cannot go on forever.

Background knowledge in the form of generalizations plays an important role in the scenario theory. First, it gives meaning to scenarios because we interpret the statements by means of background knowledge—like about John and about restaurants in the example given earlier. Such is usually an automatic process that is done without discussion. Only if people differ in their background knowledge, it may become explicit and a subject of discussion.

Background knowledge is also the stuff in which the meaning and acceptance of evidence is rooted; sometimes without much ado, sometimes after a long probe into subscenarios.

Background knowledge is also sometimes a direct test of scenarios. If a scenario holds that the same individual was in one place at noon and in a place 1,000 km away at 12:30, the scenario can be dismissed as extremely implausible or impossible, because we know there is no way to cross 1,000 km in half an hour.

4. Inference to the Best Explanation

Whereas the story model and the use of scenarios is distinctive of the scenario theory, inference to the best explanation (IBE) is at the core of all explanation-based approaches such as Allen and Pardo's relative plausibility theory, Amaya's theory of inference to the most coherent explanation, Josephson's theory of abductive inference and the scenario theory.[16] IBE was not explicitly mentioned in earlier versions of the scenario theory, but the central role of IBE has been emphasized in recent articles.[17]

Inference to the best explanation is a specific kind of abductive reasoning which is used in everyday reasoning, law, and philosophy, and also in science. It is distinguished from

[13] Also see van Koppen and Mackor 2020.
[14] Thompson, Black, Jain, and Kadane 2017.
[15] Executive Office of the President's Council of Advisors on Science and Technology 2016.
[16] See Allen and Pardo 2019; Amaya 2009; Josephson 2000. IBE is also part of the descriptive story model: Pennington and Hastie state that one reasoning strategy that factfinders use is to evaluate alternate conclusions that contradict the initial conclusion.
[17] Also see van Koppen and Mackor 2020; Mackor, Jellema, and van Koppen 2021.

deductive and inductive reasoning. We compare and contrast deduction, induction, abduction, and IBE by means of examples:

Deduction
All A's are B's
x is an A
———————————
Therefore, x is a B

Induction
Most A's are B's
x is an A
———————————
Therefore, probably x is a B

Abduction
F is a (surprising) fact
H explains F
———————————————————————————————————————
Therefore, we have reason to believe that H *might be* true
Or: Therefore, we have reason to believe that H *is* true

IBE
F is a (surprising) fact
H explains F
No other hypothesis explains F as well as H does
———————————————————————————————————————
Therefore, we have reason to believe that H *might be* true
Or: Therefore, we have reason to believe that H *is* true

The distinction between the two conclusions of abduction and IBE, "might be true" versus "is true" relates to the distinction between the context of discovery and the context of justification. Factfinders can apply IBE in the investigative phase, in the context of discovery, but also in the context of justification, in the final stage when they have to decide whether the charges have been proven. In the context of discovery, factfinders can only conclude that they have reason to believe that H might be true, but typically they should make further investigations before they can conclude that they have reason to believe that H is true. Only after they have made these further investigations, factfinders can, in the context of justification, conclude that they have reason to believe that H is true.

Two caveats about the application of IBE in criminal cases. First, in criminal law, the fact that that factfinders have reason to believe that a scenario is true is in itself not sufficient for a conviction. Conviction is possible only if the criminal act is proven beyond a reasonable doubt. Thus, there is an asymmetry between "proven" and "not proven" scenarios in that the best "proven" scenario does not always allow the judge or jury to conclude that the charges have been proven. Only if the prosecution succeeds in proving that the scenario in which the defendant committed the act is much better than all other reasonable alternative scenarios and, moreover, that it can proven beyond a reasonable doubt, fact-finders are allowed to conclude that the defendant committed the criminal act).[18] Second, often the terms "guilt scenario" and "innocence scenario" are used. This terminology is not correct since the decision about guilt is a separate step to be taken only after the decision about the proof of the facts. Here, we are only concerned with the decision about whether the defendant committed the alleged act and not yet about the further questions whether the act is punishable and whether the defendant is guilty.

The main difference between deduction on the one hand and induction, abduction, and IBE on the other is that the latter are ampliative, that is that the conclusion goes beyond what is logically contained in the premises. The difference between induction on the one hand and abduction and IBE on the other is that in the former there is only an appeal to statistics whereas in the latter there can be an appeal to statistics, but there is always an appeal to explanatory considerations.[19] The difference between abduction and IBE, finally, is that in the latter there is an explicit consideration of alternative explanations.

Abduction and IBE are both a form of indirect and explanatory reasoning. They can be contrasted with direct and evidential reasoning. In *evidential* reasoning, one reasons *directly* from the evidence to the (probable) truth of the hypothesis. In *explanatory* reasoning one first reasons from the hypothesis to the evidence and only then (and therefore the qualification *indirect* is used) from the evidence to the hypothesis. We illustrate the distinction by means of an example. We start with an example of *direct evidential reasoning*: a witness states that A and B had an argument. Therefore, we have reason to believe that the hypothesis that A and B had an argument is true. *Indirect and explanatory reasoning* would go as follows: a witness testifies that A and B had an argument. The hypothesis that A and B had an argument, explains that the witness testified what he testified and no other hypothesis (such as: the witness lied, misremembered, or misinterpreted the situation) explains that the witness testified what he testified as well as the hypothesis that A and B in fact had an argument. Therefore, we conclude that we have reason to believe that the hypothesis is true.[20]

The scenario theory holds that factfinders must use indirect explanatory reasoning, both to explain the elements of the scenario and to explain the evidence that is presented for the scenario. In that respect, the scenario theory differs from argumentative approaches, according to which factfinders should use direct evidential reasoning, and also, for example, from Bex' hybrid scenario-argumentative theory, according to which factfinders should use indirect causal explanatory reasoning in the relation between the elements, but direct evidential reasoning in the relation between the elements and the evidence.[21]

The scenario theory holds that in criminal cases explanations should be structured as scenarios consisting of episodes with the elements described by the story model, such as an initiating event, psychological response, goal, action, and consequences. In that manner IBE and the story model are combined. First, the elements take the form of hypotheses that

---

[18] See Stoffelmayr and Diamond 2000. Laudan 2007 has argued that IBE cannot be used to model the standard of proof in criminal law. See Jellema 2020 for a recent rebuttal.

[19] Douven 2017.

[20] Again, we should distinguish between context of discovery and the context of justification. For the former context, the "is" should be read as "might."

[21] Bex 2011.

together make up a scenario, analogously to how scientific hypotheses together make up a scientific theory. Since in a good scenario the elements are chronologically ordered and partially causally connected, they are not a random bunch of hypotheses, but form a more or less coherent whole, a holistic story about what may have happened.

Second, the scenario theory instructs factfinders to look for causal explanations. Within the scenario, the initiating conditions should offer a causal explanation of the psychological response which in turn should explain the goal and the action which in turn should explain the consequences. Since the elements are partially causally connected, factfinders can apply IBE to the relationship between the elements within scenarios. This line of reasoning is illustrated by means of Figure 15.2. The boxes are elements, i.e., hypotheses about what has happened, and the arrows depict chronological and causal explanatory relations.

Figure 15.2 causal explanatory reasoning with elements (hypotheses) within a scenario

Above we have seen that it seems quite natural to argue directly from the evidence to the hypothesis. For example, if the scenario hypothesizes that A and B had an argument (initiating event) which angered A (psychological response), it seems natural to reason directly from the evidence to the scenario. For example, if a witness states that he overheard that A and B had an argument and that he saw that A got angry we infer that the elements of the scenario are true. That is what both the argumentative approach and Bex' hybrid theory instruct factfinders to do.

The scenario theory, however, holds that factfinders have to apply IBE to the relation between the elements of the scenario and the evidence too. They should not ask whether the testimony is evidence for the scenario but rather whether the scenario can explain the testimony. In conclusion, the scenario theory instructs factfinders to apply IBE both to the relation between the elements within a scenario and to the relation between elements of the scenario and the subscenarios.

5. Popper's Falsificationism

We have seen that IBE instructs factfinders to construct and compare different explanations of the evidence at hand. It does not tell us, however, how to put the scenarios to the test. The normative scenario theory is empathically Popperian in nature in that it holds that factfinders should not, or at least not only, look for evidence that confirms their scenario, but instead actively search for evidence that falsifies it.[22]

In emphasizing the importance of attempts to falsify scenarios by putting scenarios to the test, the normative scenario theory diverges from the descriptive story model, since people are inclined to confirm, not to falsify. That is exemplified by a phenomenon like

---

[22] Van Koppen 2011.

confirmation bias: the general human tendency to overrate information that confirms their favorite ideas and underrate information that point to the opposite.[23] As a counterweight to these biases, the scenario theory holds that factfinders should search for evidence that falsifies the scenarios under investigation. Only if a scenario has survived serious attempts to falsification (in the context of discovery), factfinders have reason to accept the scenario as true (in the context of justification).

One way to put scenarios to the test, is to derive predictions from the scenarios under investigation and thereby to also explicitly consider what kind of evidence would falsify the scenarios. Or better put: the task of a factfinder is to decide what evidence would best discriminate one scenario from the other. Does, for instance, the prosecution's scenario better predict the evidence than the defense's scenario? If the prosecution's scenario does so, it can be concluded that the prosecution's scenario is a better story than the alternative scenario. Below we discuss in more detail the difference between evidence that strongly discriminates between the scenarios and evidence that gives a weaker test of the one scenario against the other.

Accordingly, the most important instruction that follows from Popper's falsificationist theory is: seriously attempt to falsify your scenarios, by actively searching for evidence that contradicts the scenario and by formulating predictions that follow from the scenarios under consideration and seriously investigating them.

It should be noted that if the core elements of a scenario have been falsified, there is no need for inference to the best explanation. If, for instance, there is evidence that the alleged victim of a murder is still alive, such evidence is detrimental to the prosecution's case. In such a simple case, we need not apply IBE. In that case, direct and deductive reasoning from the evidence to the falsification of the scenario suffices.

Falsification
There is ample evidence that the victim is alive.

The scenario that the victim was killed is false.

6. Creation, Accommodation, Prediction

We have already stated that the scenario theory is applicable in the context of justification when factfinders have to decide whether it is rational to conclude that the criminal act is proven, but also in investigative phases.

Normally, an investigation into a criminal case starts with some piece of evidence, for example, a broken window and a laptop missing from a house. The first hypothesis, in the context of discovery, might be that a burglary took place. Perhaps a suspect, a person carrying burglar tools, was arrested nearby. The first, still incomplete, scenario that police officers create may be that the burglar broke the window and took the laptop. In the next phase, hopefully more evidence can be gathered, perhaps a drop of blood on a piece of glass, footprints in the garden or a fingerprint on the window frame. When further evidence is discovered, the initial scenario will normally have to be accommodated to fit the new evidence and alternative scenarios will be created and accommodated too.

---

[23] Kahneman, Slovic, and Tversky 1982; Nickerson 1998.

A sufficiently detailed scenario which chronologically orders and, at least partially, caus-ally connects the elements allows factfinders to predict facts, analogous to how scientific theories allow scientists to make detailed and sometimes risky scientific predictions. That is in line with Popper's falsificationist instructions to search for falsification instead of (only) confirmation of one's theory we discussed earlier.

When a factfinder has to decide, in the context of justification, whether the criminal fact has been proven beyond a reasonable doubt, it seems relevant to know whether first the ev-idence was gathered and then a scenario was constructed, or the scenario was constructed before most of the evidence was gathered. If a scenario is constructed after the facts, it is likely to offer a neat explanation of those facts.

That is what sometimes happens when a defendant who first invokes his right to remain silent and only much later, having knowledge of all the evidence, presents a more or less plausible scenario that more or less neatly explains the evidence.[24] In contrast stands the defendant who at the very first interrogation, before he knows about the evidence that has already been gathered, offers a detailed statement about what has happened.[25] The police can use his statement as the basis for an alternative scenario and search for evidence that falsifies or confirms it. Confirmation of the statement can sometimes be interpreted as evi-dence for the validity of statements by defendants and witnesses. The analysis also holds for the scenario of the prosecution.

We end with two brief remarks about predictions. First, the status of predictions as su-perior over accommodations is still hotly debated in the philosophy of science.[26] There is, however, some agreement that confirmed predictions are not intrinsically superior to accommodations, but that testing theories by making predictions offers factfinders some protection against biases.[27] Therewith, or so it is argued, confirmed predictions can make conclusions more reliable and robust.[28]

Second, if predictions are epistemically superior to accommodations, this confronts us with the question which role they can play in criminal cases. If a scenario was tested through predictions, should evidence that was predicted receive more weight than evidence to which the scenario had to be accommodated? Even if that is epistemically defensible, how does it relate to defendant's fundamental right to remain silent?[29] The most important instruction that follows from the role that predictions can play in the scenario theory is that evidence should be given especially careful consideration if it was predicted rather than accommodated.

7. Discriminating Facts and the Likelihood Ratio

In hard cases, not all of the scenarios under consideration can be straightforwardly falsified. At most it can be said that one scenario offers a better explanation of the evidence than the

---

[24] See Mackor 2017 for a discussion of a Dutch case.
[25] See the case discussed in van Koppen and Mackor 2020.
[26] See, e.g., Harker 2008.
[27] See Peter Lipton, Testing Hypotheses: Prediction and Prejudice, Science 307 (14 January 2005), pp 219–21..
[28] More on robustness in Section 9 in this chapter.
[29] Van Koppen and Mackor 2020; Mackor 2017.

other scenarios. The scenario theory calls a piece of evidence that one scenario can explain better than the others a discriminating fact. The better the explanation, the stronger the discrimination. If, for instance, an alternative scenario entails that that defendant was at home at the time of the crime, but a witness testifies that he saw him nearby the place of the crime around that time, that piece of evidence discriminates between the prosecution and the defense scenarios. Of course, the more the testimony of the witness can be trusted, the more it supports the prosecution's scenario. Things are different, of course, if the defense can demonstrate that the witness is mistaken or lying.

Whether evidence discriminates between scenarios depends on the specific scenarios under consideration. If in the example just given, the defendant claims that he visited a friend who happens to live near the place of the crime, the same witness statement becomes less relevant and thus less discriminating between the two scenarios.

This talk of discriminating facts sounds a lot like the likelihood ratio.[30] Bayesians might want to translate the two examples as follows.

$$p(E|H_{-\text{crime}}) : p(E|H_{-\text{home}}) > 1$$

$$p(E|H_{-\text{crime}}) : p(E|H_{-\text{friend}}) = 1$$

Adherents to the scenario theory have different views on the compatibility of the scenario theory and Bayesian approaches.[31] Most adherents do not object to this translation per se, but they state it comes with a loss. First, it should be noted that the causal explanatory vocabulary of scenarios is richer than the probabilistic vocabulary.[32] Even if, in the end, the goal of factfinders is to estimate the likelihood and the likelihood ratio, it seems they first need to look for a causal explanation to be able to estimate the numbers of this ratio.

A second and more fundamental objection to such a translation is that the scenario theory is holistic in nature. As the example shows, the scenario theory does allow the factfinder to zoom in and offer "atomistic" analyses of the elements of a scenario. However, it is impossible to assess and compare all the different elements and their relations in this manner. On the scenario theory, scenarios are more than argumentative schemas or Bayesian networks and they cannot be reduced to these scenarios without loss of meaning.

Again, we see a similarity with scientific theories. Both scenarios and scientific theories are a coherent set of interlinked hypotheses. A core job of scientists is to test individual hypotheses, but they also assess the quality of a theory as a whole. The latter assessment, however, is often formulated much less precisely in terms of epistemic virtues such as simplicity, consilience, and analogy.[33] In part it has to do with the fact that scientists do not only assess scientific theories in terms of what they have achieved so far, but also in terms of their future potential. Similarly, in the investigative phase of a criminal case factfinders should take the potential of a scenario into account, but when factfinders finally have to decide about a case, they should only look at what the scenarios have achieved. However, even if we

---

[30] Mackor (in press).
[31] See Mackor, Jellema, and van Koppen (2021) for a more extensive discussion.
[32] Pearl and Mackenzie 2018.
[33] Thagard 1978.

take the distinction into account between the potential of a scenario and what it has actually delivered, it is not always clear how to assess and compare the achievements of either scientific theories or scenarios: one theory or scenario might be better in one respect, whereas an alternative does better in other respects.

8. A Critical Assessment of the "Certainty Principles" of the Story Model

Since IBE is at the heart of the scenario theory, the scenario theory too is confronted with the critical question: what makes an explanation, in the form of the overall scenario, good? When is a scenario "better" than all other reasonable scenarios? Bayesians add to that the question: what makes a scenario better than the others if it is not its probability? We have just seen that the notion of discriminating facts can be translated—with loss of meaning— in the likelihood ratio.

Accordingly, the question is whether the same holds for other notions of the scenario theory. For example, can epistemic virtues be translated in probabilistic terms?[34] According to the story model, factfinders use the "certainty principles" coverage, uniqueness, and coherence (consistency, plausibility, completeness) to assess and compare stories. Van Koppen and Mackor have argued that factfinders not only actually do, but also should, use these principles.[35] In this chapter, we offer a more critical view of the criteria of consistency and plausibility and we now stress the importance of robustness as a criterion. Let us in turn discuss the criteria.

The criterion of *coverage* states that factfinders should assess whether a scenario can explain all of the evidence in a case. A scenario that can explain all of the evidence is better than a scenario that has story gaps and thus does not explain all of the evidence. A fortiori, a scenario which explains all of the evidence is better than a scenario that is inconsistent with, that is falsified by, the evidence. Please note that in most criminal cases, elements of what happened remain obscured or simple unknown. Factfinders, thus, are used to dealing with and accepting story gaps.

The criterion of *uniqueness*, the question of how many scenarios can explain the evidence, takes us to the question of how many scenarios factfinders should compare. The scenario theory does not hold that factfinders should compare all scenarios, since that is not only practically but also theoretically impossible. Factfinders only have to compare "reasonable" scenarios, scenarios that by and large seem to fit the criteria of coverage and coherence.[36] However, since factfinders do not and cannot compare all possible scenarios, they run the risk of choosing from a "bad lot."[37] They can be accused of irrationality if their comparison is not restricted to a set of scenarios that together are both exclusive and exhaustive. However, in a criminal trial, there is seldom systematic analysis of all possible or reasonable scenarios. What is proposed by the defense and by the prosecution is also part of their trial strategy.

---

[34] Cabrera distinguishes between informational virtues (the potential of a theory or scenario) and confirmational virtues (what it has "delivered"; Cabrera 2017).
[35] Van Koppen 2011; van Koppen and Mackor 2020.
[36] Crombag and Wagenaar 2000.
[37] Van Fraassen 1989.

Moreover, the criterion of uniqueness does not offer guidance to assess how much confidence should diminish if there is more than one reasonable scenario. Should confidence diminish only in relation to the scenarios under consideration, or should factfinders also distribute some confidence over unconsidered scenarios? Again, the question is also whether their confidence can and should be translated in probabilistic terms.

Since a scenario in its ideal form is a set of chronologically ordered and partially causally connected elements, *completeness* of the scenario is an important a criterion to assess its quality. For example, if a scenario does not contain one or more of the elements it is incomplete. By putting fairly strict constraints on the structure of a good scenario, completeness is one of the criteria that distinguishes the scenario theory from other explanation-based theories.

Sometimes it is said that the emphasis on *coherence and consistency* is a serious weakness of the scenario theory, since people are inclined to believe a coherent but false story over a true but incoherent story.[38] However, this objection can easily be rebutted. Both on the story model and on the scenario theory it is not sufficient for a scenario to be internally consistent; it must also be consistent with the evidence of the case and with general background knowledge. Pennington and Hastie call the consistency of the scenario with background knowledge plausibility. Moreover, we have stated that the scenario theory emphasizes that serious attempts must be made, not (only) to confirm scenarios, but also to falsify them.

However, there is a more serious objection to coherence and consistency as criteria. First it should be noted that consistency is a formal and much less demanding criterion than IBE's criterion. IBE does not demand consistency, it demands that a hypothesis can explain an item, whether that item is a piece of evidence or another hypothesis. Again, we note that the causal explanatory vocabulary is much richer, not only than that of probability, but also than the vocabulary of logical consistency.

Another objection to the criterion of explanatory coherence is that it is merely a sloppy formulation of a probability criterion.[39] For example, it is unclear whether and how the assessment of plausibility—the consistency of a scenario with background knowledge—differs from an assessment of the prior probability of a scenario. The same holds for the criterion of consistency of a scenario with the evidence which seems to be an imprecise formulation of the likelihood ratio. Finally, this critique also holds for the criterion of internal consistency of a scenario, for what we want from a scenario is not merely internal consistency, but a proper chronological ordering and causal explanatory relations between the different elements within the scenario.

9. Robustness: The Importance of Alternative Scenarios and Falsification

The scenario theory agrees with the story model that coverage and completeness are important criteria to assess the quality of scenarios, whereas uniqueness, consistency, and plausibility seem a shorthand for a test of the quality of causal explanatory relations.

---

[38] A true story can be incoherent, among others, because it has story gaps, or because it is inconsistent with background knowledge.
[39] Dahlman and Mackor 2019.

The scenario theory adds robustness as a major "certainty principle" to the certainty prin- ciples of the story model. Robustness should function as a counterweight to biases such as the confirmation bias we discussed earlier. Robustness has been defined in different ways.[40] We focus on the definition according to which a scenario is robust when evidence for it is robust, that is, when the scenario has been confirmed in multiple and independent ways. Robustness has been defined as the extent to which different pieces of evidence: (1) are in- dependent of each other and (2) have been established by different methods, but also as the extent to which the evidence (3) discriminates between scenarios and thus allows for elimi- nation of alternative scenarios.[41]

An important problem in (criminal) law is that often there is little evidence and that part of the evidence has been used to create the scenario. Moreover, the evidence is not always independent, and often the evidence partly conflicts. Therefore, findings in criminal law are not always robust enough to allow for strong support for a scenario.

In our view, robustness does not only have to do with the robustness of the evidence and the scenarios that have been presented. Robustness is primarily an assessment of the quality of the search for evidence and possible alternative scenarios. In addition to the three cri- teria already mentioned, robustness is about the thoroughness of the search, among others via prediction, for (4) evidence and (5) counterevidence. Next to that robustness is also the criterion with which we assess the thoroughness of the search (6) for alternative sce- narios, therewith trying to diminish the risk that factfinders make a choice from a bad lot. Robustness in this sense demands that factfinders seriously think about, construct, and in- vestigate reasonable alternative scenarios, compare their "favored" scenario to these sce- narios and make serious attempts to falsify the scenarios by predicting and searching for discriminating facts. Only then, factfinders not only have reason to believe that a particular scenario *might be* true, but also that the scenario *is* true.

References

Allen, R. J. and Pardo, M. S. (2019). "Relative Plausibility and its Critics," *International Journal of Evidence and Proof*, 23(1–2): 5–59. Available at https://doi.org/10.1177%2F1365712718813781 (Accessed: March 29, 2021).

Amaya, A. (2009). "Inference to the Best Legal Explanation," in H. Kaptein, H. Prakken, and B. Verheij (eds.), *Legal Evidence and Proof: Statistics, Stories, Logic*, 135–60. Farnham: Ashgate.

Bennett, W. L. and Feldman, M. S. (2014). *Reconstructing Reality in the Courtroom: Justice and Judgement in American Culture*. Second edition. New Orleans, LA: Quid Pro. First edition pub- lished 1981.

Bex, F. J. (2011). *Arguments, Stories and Criminal Evidence: A Formal Hybrid Theory*. Dordrecht: Springer.

Cabrera, F. (2017). "Can there be a Bayesian Explanationism? On the Prospects of a Productive Partnership," *Synthese*, 194: 1245–72.

Calcott, B. (2011), "Wimsatt and the Robustness Family: Review of Wimsatt's Re-Engineering Philosophy for Limited Beings," *Biology and Philosophy*, 26(2): 281–93.

Crombag, H. F. M. and Wagenaar, W. A. (2000). "Audite et Alteram Partem," *Trema*, 23: 93–6.

---

[40] Calcott 2011; Woodward 2006.
[41] Schupbach 2018.

Dahlman, C. and Mackor, A. R. (2019). "Coherence and Probability in Legal Evidence," *Law, Probability and Risk*, 18: 275–94. Available at https://doi.org/10.1093/lpr/mgz016 (Accessed: March 29, 2021).

Douven, I. (2017). "Abduction," in E. N. Zalta (ed.), *The Stanford Encyclopedia of Philosophy*. Summer 2017 edition. Available at https://plato.stanford.edu/archives/sum2017/entries/abduction/ (Accessed: March 29, 2021).

Executive Office of the President's Council of Advisors on Science and Technology (2016). *Forensic Science in Criminal Courts: Ensuring Scientific Validity of Feature-Comparison Methods*. Report to the president. Available at pcast_forensic_science_report_final.pdf (archives.gov) (Accessed: March 21, 2021).

Harker, D. (2008). "On the Predilections for Predictions," *British Journal for the Philosophy of Science*, 59: 429–53.

Jellema, H. (2020). "The Reasonable Doubt Standard as Inference to the Best Explanation," *Synthese*. Available at 1007/s11229-020-02743-8 (Accessed: March 29, 2021).

Josephson, J. R. (2000). "On the Proof Dynamics of Inference to the Best Explanation," *Cardozo Law Review*, 22: 1621–43.

Kahneman, D., Slovic, P., and Tversky, A. (eds.) (1982). *Judgment under Uncertainty: Heuristics and Biases*. Cambridge: Cambridge University Press.

Laudan, L. (2007). "Strange Bedfellows: Inference to the Best Explanation and the Criminal Standard of Proof," *The International Journal of Evidence & Proof*, 11: 292–306.

Lipton, Peter, Testing Hypotheses: Prediction and Prejudice, Science 307 (14 January 2005), pp 219–21.

Mackor, A. R. (2017). "Novel Facts. The Relevance of Predictions in Criminal Law," *Strafblad*, 15: 145–56.

Mackor, A. R. (in press). "Different Ways of being Naked. A Scenario Approach to the Naked Statistical Evidence Problem," *IFCOLOG*.

Mackor, A. R., Jellema, H., and van Koppen, P. J. (2021). "Explanation-based Approaches to Reasoning about Evidence and Proof in Criminal Trials," in B. Brożek, J. Hage, and N. Vincent (eds.), *Law and Mind: A Survey of Law and the Cognitive Sciences*. Cambridge: Cambridge University Press: 431–69.

Nickerson, R. S. (1998). "Confirmation Bias: An Ubiquitous Phenomenon in many Guises," *Review of General Psychology*, 2: 175–220.

Pearl, J. and Mackenzie, D. (2018). *The Book of Why: The New Science of Cause and Effect*. New York: Basic Books.

Pennington, N. and Hastie, R. (1992). "Explaining the Evidence: Tests of the Story Model for Juror Decision Making," *Journal of Personality and Social Psychology*, 62: 189–206.

Pennington, N. and Hastie, R. (1993). "The Story Model for Juror Decision Making," in R. Hastie (ed.), *Inside the Jury: The Psychology of Juror Decision Making*, 192–221. Second edition. Cambridge: Cambridge University Press.

Schupbach, J. N. (2018). "Robustness Analysis as Explanatory Reasoning," *British Journal for the Philosophy of Science*, 69: 275–300.

Stoffelmayr, E. and Diamond, S. S. (2000). "The Conflict between Precision and Flexibility in Explaining Beyond A Reasonable Doubt," *Psychology, Public Policy, and Law*, 6: 769–87.

Strömwall, L. A., Granhag, P. A., and Jonsson, A.-C. (2003). "Deception among Pairs: 'Let's say we had Lunch and Hope they will Swallow it!'," *Psychology, Crime and Law*, 9: 109–24.

Thagard, P. R. (1978). "The Best Explanation: Criteria for Theory Choice," *The Journal of Philosophy*, 75: 76–92.

Thompson, W. C., Black, J., Jain, A. K., and Kadane, J. B. (2017). *Forensic Science Assessments: A Quality and Gap Analysis. Latent Fingerprint Examination*. Washington, DC: American Association for the Advancement of Science.

Van Fraassen, B. C. (1989). *Laws and Symmetry*. Oxford: Oxford University Press.

Van Koppen, P. J. (2003). *De Schiedammer Parkmoord: Een Rechtspsychologische Reconstructie* (The Schiedam Park Murder: A legal Psychological Reconstruction). Nijmegen: Ars Aequi Libri.

Van Koppen, P. J. (2011). *Overtuigend Bewijs: Indammen van Rechterlijke Dwalingen* (Convincing Evidence: Reducing the Number of Miscarriages of Justice). Amsterdam: Nieuw Amsterdam.

Van Koppen, P. J. and Mackor, A. R. (2020). "A Scenario-Approach to the Simonshaven Case," *Topics in Cognitive Science*, 12(4): 1132–51. Available at https://doi.org/10.1111/tops.12429 (Accessed: March 29, 2021).

Wagenaar, W. A., van Koppen, P. J., and Crombag, H. F. M. (1993). *Anchored Narratives: The Psychology of Criminal Evidence*. London: Harvester Wheatsheaf.

Woodward, J. (2006). "Some Varieties of Robustness," *Journal of Economic Methodology*, 13: 219–40.

16

Coherence in Legal Evidence

Amalia Amaya

1. Introduction

Coherence is a key ingredient of justification—in some views, the only ingredient.[1] What role does it play in the justification of evidentiary statements in law? How may coherence and coherence inference be characterized in evidential reasoning in law? In Sections 2, 3, and 4, I discuss three main approaches to coherence: structural coherence, narrative coherence, and coherence as constraint satisfaction. Sections 4, 5, and 6 address some problems concerning the relation between coherence and inference, coherence and virtue, and coherence and truth in the context of legal factfinding. In Section 7, I suggest some avenues for further research on coherence, evidence, and legal proof.

2. Structural Coherence

Coherence may be first understood in logical terms. On this view, a set of beliefs is coherent if it is logically consistent.[2] When the set is composed by partial, rather than full, beliefs, coherence requires that the degrees of belief should conform to the axioms of probability theory. In these structural or formal conceptions, coherence is a matter of compliance with formal rules of (deductive or inductive) logic. Logical consistency is insufficient to coherence: the coherence of a belief set seems to require that there be some sort of positive relation of support among its different elements. Intuitively, a set whose elements are deductively consistent but unrelated to each other do not exhibit the property of coherence. It is (more controversially) denied that deductive consistency is a necessary condition for coherence. At first glance, the requirement that one's beliefs be consistent seems to be a minimal requirement of coherence. However, it is an overly strong requirement—as the preface paradox and similar paradoxes of deductive consistency show.[3] That coherence does not require logical consistency is by now a fairly established point in coherentist epistemology as well as in coherentist approaches to evidence and legal proof.[4]

As far as the probabilistic approach to coherence is concerned, however, matters are far more complicated. There is an intense debate in epistemology, including the epistemology of legal proof, over whether coherence may be equated with probabilistic coherence or

---

[1] For a discussion of coherence theories of justification in different domains, see Amaya 2015.
[2] This was the position advocated by early coherentists. It also figures in current discussions on coherence and evidence; see Worsnip 2018.
[3] See Easwaran 2015, 66.
[4] See BonJour 1999; MacCormick 1984, 38; Amaya 2015.

Amalia Amaya, *Coherence in Legal Evidence* In: *Philosophical Foundations of Evidence Law.* Edited by: Christian Dahlman,
Alex Stein, and Giovanni Tuzet, Oxford University Press. © Christian Dahlman, Alex Stein, and Giovanni Tuzet 2021.
DOI: 10.1093/oso/9780198859307.003.0017

explained in probabilistic terms without residue.[5] This discussion is inscribed within a larger debate about whether theory confirmation should be explained within a quantitative, probabilistic, framework or a qualitative, explanationist, one—a discussion which has also carried over evidence scholarship. Questions about how these two paradigms of legal proof relate to each other are the subject of ongoing, exciting research—I will go back to this point later. Despite the many ways in which the project of providing a probabilistic interpretation of coherence has advanced, and is likely to further advance, the understanding of coherence, there are—to my mind—important reasons why probability theory is not well positioned to provide a useful conception of the kind of coherence that is relevant to legal factfinding (and, more broadly, a workable approach to evidential reasoning in law).

A theory of evidence and legal proof should provide legal decision-makers with valuable guidance as to how to go about reasoning and determining the facts being litigated. It is a well-established empirical finding that probabilistic approaches to reasoning are highly implausible from a psychological point of view. As a result, a probabilistic approach to coherence (and coherence-based reasoning) would fare badly as a standard that is capable to successfully guide and improve legal decision-makers' factfinding tasks. A distinction between the normative and the evaluative point of view is to the point here.[6] A model of rational proof should be normative in the sense that it not only provides an evaluative standard against which to assess beliefs but also supports attributions of blame or praise to agents and is thereby action guiding. Critically, even if a coherence theory of legal proof that rested on a probabilistic account of coherence could provide an evaluative standard, it fails to be normative in this highly relevant, action-guiding sense.

Of course, although deductive and probabilistic conceptions of coherence, for the reasons stated earlier, are wanting, this is not to say that logical and probabilistic consistency are irrelevant to coherence. There are important connections between coherence, logical consistency, and probability that a plausible conception of coherence needs to give an account of. The problems encountering structural, formal approaches to coherence arise from erecting principles of logic into principles of rationality—from failing to separate, in Ramsey's words, "formal logic," or the logic of consistency, from "human logic," or the logic of truth.[7] That is to say, we should not expect rules of inference to be derivable from rules of logic.[8] Thus, a substantive notion of coherence should be inserted within a psychologically plausible theory of evidence and legal proof that has the resources to guide legal inference and help legal decision-makers reach beliefs about the facts that are epistemically justified.

3. Narrative Coherence

A central (substantive) approach to coherence holds that the kind of coherence that is relevant to the justification of evidentiary judgments in law is of the sort that makes a story hang together, that is, narrative coherence. This is, on the face of it, plausible, given the prominent role that stories and storytelling plays in law—and prominently, but far from exclusively, in legal factfinding. Narrative coherence occupies an important place in a number

---

[5] See Dahlman and Mackor 2019.
[6] Smith 2005.
[7] Ramsey 1926.
[8] Psillos 2007.

of (otherwise wildly) different models of legal evidence and proof. Narrative conceptions of coherence figure in the context of three distinct projects, namely, the advancement of a normative theory of legal justification, empirical work in the psychology of legal fact-finding, and the development of a holistic alternative to atomistic approaches to evidence evaluation.

Narrative coherence plays an important role in some approaches to the justification of evidentiary judgments in law. One such approach is the pioneering work of MacCormick.[9] In MacCormick's view, narrative coherence is the property of a set of factual propositions that may be explained in terms of a single set of explanatory principles, more precisely, causal, and motivational principles. Narrative coherence functions, says MacCormick, as "a test of truth or probability in questions of fact or evidence upon which direct proof by immediate observation is unavailable."[10] According to MacCormick, narrative coherence plays a role in the justification of evidentiary judgments in law analogous to the role that normative coherence plays in the justification of normative judgments in law. In contrast, Jackson has advanced a conception of narrative coherence according to which narrative coherence is a standard of justification that is applicable to both normative and factual issues in law. In Jackson's narrative model, adjudication consists in matching the narrative construction of the facts under dispute with the narrative form underlying the applicable rule of law.[11] Similarly, Van Roermund has also argued for a broad model of narrative coherence in which the relation between facts and norms is also explained in terms of narrative coherence.[12]

Narrative coherence also figures prominently in some psychological models of legal fact-finding. In Hastie and Pennington's well-known "story model" of juror decision-making, jurors construct "narrative structures" to organize and interpret the evidence and then select the story that best satisfies the principles of coverage, coherence and uniqueness as the basis for their decision.[13] In a similar vein, Wagenaar, van Koppen, and Crombag have advanced a model of judicial reasoning for factfinding in criminal cases, the theory of anchored narratives or the scenario theory, according to which fact finder's decisions are based on an assessment of the credibility of the prosecutor's story, which depends on a judgment of its plausibility and of whether it is anchored on common sense beliefs which are generally taken to be true.[14] In contrast to the story model, which is exclusively empirical, the theory of anchored narratives is also normative, in that it puts forward a number of rules that provide a safeguard against common mistakes in the deployment of the anchored narratives heuristic. A thoroughly normative theory that gives to narrative coherence an important role is Bex's hybrid approach to legal proof, which combines the scenario theory with an argumentative approach to legal proof.[15]

Narrative coherence is also an important concept in holistic approaches to evidence evaluation, which hold that the mass of evidence and its probative force must be assessed as a whole.[16] Evidential reasoning, in this view, is a matter of constructing and comparing the

[9] MacCormick 1980; 1984; 2005.
[10] MacCormick 1984, 48.
[11] Jackson 1988.
[12] Van Roermund 1997.
[13] Hastie and Pennington 1991.
[14] Wagenaar, van Koppen, and Crombag 1993. See also van Koppen and Mackor 2020; Mackor and van Koppen, "The Scenario Theory about Evidence in Criminal Law," ch. 15, in this volume.
[15] Bex 2011.
[16] See Abu-Hareira 1986; Pardo 2000; Twining 2006.

explanatory goodness of alternative interpretations of the evidence. Narrative coherence is appealed to in this context as one central criterion upon which the holistic assessment of the evidence depends. An influential holistic theory is Allen and Pardo's relative plausibility theory.[17] In its first formulation, by Allen, the relative plausibility theory puts forward a rule of decision according to which factfinders should find for the guilt when there is a plausible story of guilt and no plausible story of innocence, "where such plausibility is determined by such variables like coherence, completeness, uniqueness, economy and ... probability."[18] According to Pardo's (early) pragmatic version of evidentiary holism, the parties advance competing pragmatic interpretations of various evidentiary statements, which are then organized by the factfinders in the form of narratives, from which they select the one that best explains them on the basis of "basic principles of rationality such as coverage, coherence and uniqueness."[19]

A main problem encountering narrative accounts of the kind of coherence that is relevant to legal factfinding is that they are unduly restrictive in scope, in that they are applicable only to those cases that bear a narrative structure. Because of that, a turn to an explanationist approach to legal proof, according to which factfinding involves the comparison and selection of the best explanation of the available evidence, rather than the best narrative, seems preferable. The relative plausibility theory has embraced this shift from narrativism towards explanationism; in its latest formulations, it takes explanations, rather than stories, to be central to evidential reasoning in law, thereby expanding the scope of applicability of the theory. This theory does not, however, have the resources to address what is, arguably, another main problem facing narrative models of legal proof, namely, that they rest on an underspecified notion of coherence, which gives to intuitive judgment too broad a role in evidential reasoning in law. The reliance of relative plausibility theory on judgments plausibility—of which coherence is a relevant factor—similarly fails to provide a detailed and informative test against which to evaluate and assess factfinders' reasoning.

In short, despite the many ways in which narrative theories have advanced the understanding of legal factfinding processes and the role that coherence plays wherein, there are reasons for searching for an account of coherence that is not unduly restrictive to narratives and that clearly specifies the criteria upon which judgments of coherence depends. Constraint satisfaction approaches to coherence—which give to explanatory coherence a central role—may provide us, as I will argue in the next section, with a model of legal proof that has a broad scope of application as well as the resources to avoid the charge of vagueness that may be addressed against narrative approaches.

4. Coherence as Constraint Satisfaction

A constraint satisfaction approach to coherence, developed by Thagard, may be applied to give an account of the kind of coherence that is relevant to legal factfinding. According to this approach, coherence is a matter of the satisfaction of a number of constraints, positive and negative, among a given set of elements. In order to achieve coherence, one divides the

[17] See Allen and Pardo 2019.
[18] Allen 1997, 273. See also Allen 1991.
[19] Pardo 2000, 435.

set of elements into accepted and rejected in a way that satisfices the most positive (coherence relations) and negative (incoherence relations) constraints.[20] Different applications of this abstract conception of coherence may be developed by specifying the elements, the constraints, and the kinds of coherence that are relevant in a way that takes into account the specificities of each domain.[21]

In the case of the justification of evidentiary judgments in law, there are arguably six kinds of coherence that are relevant, namely, analogical, conceptual, perceptual, deductive, explanatory, and deliberative coherence.[22] These are the same kinds of coherence that, in Thagard's view, are relevant to epistemic justification, with one major addition, deliberative coherence. This kind of coherence is necessary in factfinding contexts given the practical dimensions of legal arguments about disputed questions of fact. Each of these kinds of coherence is further specified by a set of principles. In the case of explanatory coherence—which, as in epistemic justification, remains the central one in the justification of evidentiary judgments in law—the principles are as follows:

Principle E1: Symmetry. Explanatory coherence is a symmetrical relation, unlike, say conditional probability. That is, two propositions p and q cohere with each other equally.

Principle E2: Explanation. (1) A hypothesis coheres with what it explains which can be either evidence or another hypothesis; (2) hypotheses that together explain some other proposition cohere with each other; and (3) the more hypotheses it takes to explain something, the lower the degree of coherence.

Principle E3: Analogy. Similar hypotheses that explain similar pieces of evidence cohere.

Principle E4: Priority. (a) Propositions that describe admissible evidence at trial have a degree of acceptability on their own; (b) factual hypotheses that are compatible with innocence have a degree of acceptability on their own.

Principle E5: Contradiction. Contradictory propositions are incoherent with each other.

Principle E6: Competition. If p and q both explain a proposition and if p and q are not explanatorily connected, then p and q are incoherent with each other (p and q are explanatorily connected if one explains the other or if together they explain something).

Principle E7: Acceptance. (a) The acceptability of a proposition in a system of propositions (i.e., a theory of the case) depends on its coherence with them; (b) a hypothesis of guilt may be accepted only if it is justified to a degree sufficient to satisfy the applicable standard of proof.[23]

Thus, the explanatory coherence of evidential judgments in law is a symmetrical relation between hypotheses about the facts under dispute and the evidence available (E1) that

---

[20] Thagard and Verbeurgt 1998. See also Thagard 2000.
[21] Thagard and Verbeurgt 1998.
[22] Amaya 2013.
[23] Amaya 2013.

arises from relations of explanation and analogical relations between hypotheses and evidence (E2, E3), in contrast to incoherence, which arises from relations of contradiction and competition (E5, E6). Propositions that describe admissible evidence as well as those that are compatible with innocence have a degree of acceptability on their own (E4), even if the final acceptability of any proposition depends on its coherence with the rest of propositions, provided its degree of justification satisfies the applicable standard of proof (E7). These principles are the same principles of explanatory coherence that are at work in epistemic justification, with some modifications (of principles E4 and E7), which incorporate institutional constraints that are in place in legal factfinding.

An account of coherence in terms of constraint satisfaction enjoys a high degree of psychological plausibility, as an important body of research, undertaken by Simon, Holyoak, Snow, and Read, has shown.[24] In their "coherence-based reasoning" model, legal decision-making involves a shift in the decision-maker's representation of the complex decision-task towards a state of coherence in which considerations or constraints that support one alternative are strongly endorsed and those that support the alternative are dismissed, thereby enabling the decision-maker to reach a decision with ease and confidence. This connectionist model illuminates the critical role that coherence plays in the course of legal decision-making, but, as will be argued, also shows the risks involved in coherence-based reasoning. The next two sections discuss some central features of coherence-driven reasoning and its associated perils.

5. Coherence and Inference

How may coherentist inference be characterized? Against coherence theories it has been argued that they rest on an implausible account of inference. The traditional objections raised against the conception of inference embedded in epistemic coherentism, namely, that coherence inference is circular, unfeasible, and unduly conservative, may also be directed against coherence theories. Coherence inference is circular—the objector claims—in that it licenses and inference from p to q, and then from q to p.[25] It is also unfeasible, as it requires that the agent engages in a global computation of the coherence of her whole system of beliefs, in order to determine the justificatory status of any individual belief, which outstrips human cognitive capacities.[26] Last, it is unduly conservative, as the justificatory status of any single belief depends on its coherence with a pre-existent body of beliefs.[27]

Despite their initial appeal, these objections, however, may be met. Coherentist inference, properly conceived, does not allow one to accept/reject a piece of evidence, on the grounds that it fits best with one's accepted theory of the case, which, in its turn, is accepted on the grounds that it coheres best with such a piece of evidence. The objection from circularity presupposes a linear, rather than a holistic, conception of justification that is challenged by coherentist theories.[28] It is only the idea that justification proceeds along a "pipeline," with

---

[24] For a summary of empirical findings, see Simon 2004.
[25] See BonJour 1985.
[26] See Kornblith 1989.
[27] See BonJour 1985.
[28] See BonJour 1985.

one, more foundational belief, giving support to another belief down the chain, that gives this objection its purchase.[29] Coherence relations are, to the contrary, symmetrical and judgments of coherence, holistic, so that justification emerges from mutual support among the whole body of beliefs, in a way that does not involve vicious circularity.

The holism inherent to coherentist processing does not, however, render coherence inference psychologically implausible. Even though any belief, in a coherentist approach, is up for grabs, and may be shown to be relevant to the justification of any other belief (so that, ultimately, the justificatory status of any single belief depends on its coherence with the whole body of beliefs), this is not to say that in a specific justificatory task, one could sensibly challenge the justification of any single belief or that it would be reasonable to question its justification on grounds of its incoherence with just any part of one's system of beliefs, no matter how remote.[30] Coherentist justification may be adequately sensitive to context, so that only the coherence of a subset of beliefs is relevant to the justification of the belief the epistemic credentials of which are in question in the specific case.[31] A coherence theory of evidence and proof that properly takes into account the contextual (and pragmatic) nature of justification may thus avoid the problems of feasibility associated to unrestricted versions of holism.

Last, the charge from conservatism against coherence theories of evidence and proof may be counteracted by endorsing a discriminating view of coherence-based inference, such as the view that is embedded in the principle of data priority (i.e., E4 (a), above), rather than what is called (in a somewhat emotionally loaded way) an "egalitarian," form of coherentism, in which all beliefs have an equal standing.[32] Coherence inference is discriminating in that it assigns a priority in being accepted to propositions describing the admissible evidence, thereby enabling novel information to upset the coherence of one's previous beliefs about a case. Critically, this does not amount to surreptitiously sneaking in a foundationalist element within the theory, as the assigned priority is justified on (second-order) reasons from coherence about the special role that some subsets of beliefs play in epistemic justification and, ultimately, the justification of any single belief depends on the coherence of the whole. Hence, a discriminating approach to coherence inference allows us to give to evidence its due, but also to question its epistemic credentials when there are reasons to do so.

Thus, coherence inference is bidirectional, holistic, and discriminating, in a way that is non-viciously circular, psychologically plausible, and not problematically conservative. This, however, hardly puts worries about the viability of a coherence account of inference to rest, as the problems of vagueness facing coherence theories are raised not only against the concept of coherence (discussed earlier) but also against the inference whereby such coherence is constructed in the course of legal decision-making. Coherence-based reasoning boils down to intuitionism unless we have a clear account of the inference processes the are at work in coherence judgments, and ultimately, in reaching beliefs about the events being litigated that are justified by virtue of their coherence.

My suggestion is—following the lead of proponents of coherentist interpretations of inference to the best explanation—that one may deploy the resources of explanatory

---

[29] On the "pipeline" model of justification, see Shogenji 2001.
[30] Plantinga 1993.
[31] Amaya 2015.
[32] See Haack 2000.

reasoning to provide a detailed account of coherence-driven inference in the context of legal factfinding.[33] Coherence-driven inference is, in this view, an explanatory kind of inference. Three main stages may be distinguished in an inference to the best, i.e., the most coherent explanation, namely, the discovery of a suitable set of alternatives, the pursuit and refinement of promising alternatives, and the justification of the best of them by virtue of its coherence.[34] Coherence considerations drive this inferential process at all three stages. Firstly, coherence with background knowledge helps constrain the set of alternatives that is worth pursuing. It also helps generate such a set in the first place, by prompting questions (e.g. which hypothesis could make sense of this body of evidence? Which evidence would cohere, and we should therefore expect to find, if this hypothesis were true?) which may point towards interesting, and thus far unconceived, alternatives. Secondly, an important venue for developing and refining the alternatives under discussion is the enhancement of their degree of both internal and external coherence (i.e., coherence with background knowledge) through different mechanisms such as the addition of novel information, the detraction of sources of incoherence, or the reinterpretation of available evidence with a view to increasing its coherence with working hypotheses.[35] Finally, coherence standards provide the criteria against which to compare the different alternatives and select the best one of them (e.g. the criteria layout in the previous section, if one is willing to endorse a constraint satisfaction approach to coherence).

More precisely, coherence-based inference in the determination of facts in law may be described in terms of the following procedure:

i) The *specification of a base of coherence*, that is, the set of factual hypotheses and relevant evidence over which the coherence calculation proceeds;

ii) The *construction of a contrast set* that contains a number of alternative theories of the case from which the most coherent one is to be selected;

iii) The *pursuit* of the alternative theories of the case by means of a number of coherence-making mechanisms;

iv) The *evaluation* of the coherence of the alternative theories of the case against the criteria of coherence;

v) The *selection as justified* of the most coherent of the alternative theories of the case, that is, the theory of the case that best satisfies the criteria of coherence.[36]

The conceptualization of coherence-driven inference as an explanatory kind of inference brings to light important features of coherence-based reasoning, namely, its comparative, eliminative, and defeasible nature. Coherence inference involves a comparison of

---

[33] For coherentist interpretations of inference to the best explanation, see Psillos 2002; Thagard and Shelley 1997; Harman 1986; Lycan 1988.

[34] Lipton argues for a model of inference to the best explanation which involves two filters, one that selects possible candidates and another one that selects among them. See Lipton 2004, 60. To discovery and justification, Laudan critically adds the context of pursuit. See Laudan 1977, 110.

[35] For a discussion of these mechanisms of belief revision, see Amaya, ch. 5.

[36] See Amaya 2009. Dahlman and Mackor propose that the second step be modified in that the contrast set should contain a number of alternative scenarios, rather than theories, which should further be properly, i.e., chronologically and causally connected, as well complete (Dahlman and Mackor 2019). This refinement, however, would come at the price of making the theory narrower in scope, as it would only apply to cases which bear a narrative structure.

alternatives, it works by elimination (of relevant alternatives), and it confers justification to its conclusions, which may nonetheless be defeated in light of novel, incoming, information. Failure in spotting possible defeaters to the conclusions of a coherence-driven inference (in the form of either undercutting or rebutting defeaters) detracts from their degree of justification.[37] The justification of the conclusions of a piece of coherentist reasoning turns out to depend on whether one has properly considered potential defeaters to one's claim that one explanation is best on a test of coherence and showed them not to obtain. This dependence of the justification of conclusions of an inference to the best coherent explanation on the quality of the processes whereby such conclusion is reached is at the root of a serious problem facing explanatory coherentism, namely, the coherence bias, to which I turn now.

6. Coherence and Virtue

The correctness of a piece of coherence-based reasoning, I would argue, depends upon subjective features of the subjects who perform the reasoning.[38] This sets apart coherence-based reasoning from formal reasoning patterns, for example, deductive reasoning, as personal qualities of the subjects are irrelevant for the validity of a formal argument. That coherentist reasoning is agent-based may be appreciated by considering a number of ways in which the most coherent explanation of the facts under dispute is, nonetheless, intuitively unjustified, rather than justified, as explanatory coherentism would have it. Consider the following cases:

a) A legal factfinder settles on an explanation H that is best on a test of coherence among a set of alternative explanations that, for reasons that have to do with the poor quality of the process of inquiry, fails to include relevant hypotheses and evidence, which (had they been considered) would have defeated the claim that H is the most coherent explanation, and is therefore justified.

b) A legal factfinder settles on an explanation H that is best on a test of coherence among a set of alternative explanations, and therefore justified, but the reason why it does so traces back to certain defects in the way in which the factfinder has evaluated and assessed the coherence of competing alternatives.

In these cases, the factfinder's defective inquiry and deliberation leads him to accept as justified an explanation of the facts under dispute (H) which is best on a test of coherence but, nonetheless, intuitively unjustified, for had the input to coherentist reasoning (i.e., the relevant evidence and hypotheses) be the result of epistemically blameless inquiry and had the coherence calculation been performed in an epistemically irreproachable way, the conclusion of the inference to the most coherent explanation would not have been the acceptance of H. There is, thus, an important sense in which the coherence reached through a process of reasoning that is vitiated in some of these ways fails to be epistemically valuable.

---

[37] See Psillos 2002.
[38] I have previously defended this claim in Amaya 2008.

This problem is hardly distinctive of explanatory coherentism, but it arguably affects all forms of epistemic coherentism.[39] Furthermore, the dependence of the epistemic value of a conclusion on the quality of the process whereby such conclusion is reached seems to obtain whenever we are engaged in a substantive—rather than a formal—kind of reasoning.[40] For instance, as Baehr has persuasively argued, cases of defective inquiry and reasoning also pose a problem for evidentialist theories of epistemic justification.[41] The problem for coherentism is, however, particularly acute, given that a drive for coherence seems to be ingrained in our reasoning processes and in the way in which we perform decision-making tasks. Thus, a pull towards coherence is likely to outstrip relevant evidence and hypotheses and distort their evaluation. Indeed, the existence of a "coherence bias" is well-documented in both general cognitive psychology as well as, more specifically, the psychology of legal reasoning.[42] Thus, the risks involved in coherentist reasoning are rather actual—not merely a hypothetical consequence of a (disputable) claim about the agent-based nature of coherence-driven reasoning. A coherence theory of evidence and proof should therefore be modified so as to provide some safeguards against the pitfalls of coherentist reasoning.

In previous work, I have argued for virtue coherentism, i.e., a version of coherentism according to which evidentiary statements in law are justified if they could be the outcome of virtuous coherentist reasoning.[43] Thus, the suggestion is that an inference to the best explanation of the facts under dispute (i.e., the most coherent one) yields justification only against a background of virtuous inquiry and deliberation.[44] In other words, personal virtue in conducting factfinding tasks is necessary for the coherence of the theory that is selected as explanatorily best to be justification conferring. More precisely, the virtue condition that is necessary for coherentist justification is counterfactual, so that a conclusion of an inference to the most coherent explanation is justified if it could have been virtuously reached.[45] This qualification is important to keep open the possibility that beliefs in the most coherent theory that could have been reached by virtuous factfinders be justified, even if they were actually reached by (lucky) factfinders who engage in inquiry and deliberation in an epistemically defective way or by factfinders who act in accordance with virtue, but lack virtuous motivations.

The deployment of personal virtue to correct individual cognitive biases is a well-known strategy in the literature on heuristics and biases.[46] Similarly, I would argue, virtue may also be effectively used—alongside other debiasing techniques—to counteract the coherence bias in contexts of legal factfinding.[47] By giving virtue an important constraining role (of the

---

[39] Insofar as they are committed to the view that coherence-driven inference is non-monotonic—which leaves structural approaches to coherence untouched.

[40] Which is not to say that virtuous epistemic agency is wholly irrelevant to the epistemic value of the conclusions of a formal argument. Indeed, a vicious epistemic character does not detract from the validity of a deductive argument, but it does detract from the value that its conclusions may have as guides for belief and action insofar as it may be of high consequence to the selection of its premises.

[41] See Baehr 2008, 484–5.

[42] See Kahneman 2011, 75–6; Simon 2004.

[43] Amaya 2008; 2013; 2015.

[44] See Khalifa 2010, for a defense of an account of inference to the best explanation that imposes a responsibilist constraint.

[45] In these cases, the lack of genuine virtue would deprive the factfinder of personal justification, that is to say, he would not be justified in accepting the explanation that is most coherent, even if belief in such explanation would, nonetheless, be justified.

[46] On individual virtue as a corrective for individual cognitive biases, see Kahneman 2011, 46; Roberts and West 2015.

[47] On debiasing coherence, see Simon 2004.

kind of coherence-based reasoning that yields justification), virtue coherentism can thus benefit from the drive towards coherence that is geared in our cognitive makeup in a way that avoids the risks inherent to coherentist processing, thereby providing a theory of evidence and proof that is not only psychologically plausible but also normatively appealing. This version of coherentism, as I will argue in the next section, is also better situated to address a number of problems concerning the connection between coherence and truth that threaten to undermine the case for a coherence theory of evidence and legal proof.

7. Coherence and Truth

A main problem facing coherence theory of justification is that of showing that coherence is properly connected with truth.[48] The problem of the truth-conduciveness of coherence is a forceful one in the context of legal factfinding given that truth is a momentous goal of adjudication. There is a panoply of objections against epistemic coherentism that trade on the difficult relationship between coherence and truth. One such objection is the "isolation" or "input" objection. Coherence theories—so the objection goes—do not secure that input from the external reality enters into the system of beliefs on whose coherence justification depends, thereby making justification a matter of internal relations within a system and cutting it off from the empirical world.[49] In the context of legal factfinding, this objection translates into the objection that a coherence theory of justification of evidentiary judgments in law does not secure that evidence admitted at trial play the role it ought to play in the determination of the disputed facts. This objection has been the object of a heated debate of late on the purported conflict between coherence and evidence, where such coherence is understood as structural coherence.[50] However, once we endorse a more substantive account of coherence the objection loses much of its force. BonJour's observation requirement—which ensures that the system of beliefs contain a cognitively diverse subset of observational beliefs—and Thagard's aforementioned principle of data priority, may effectively counteract the objection from isolation against epistemic coherentism, and more specifically, against coherence theories of evidence and legal proof.

Another important objection that similarly bears on the problems related to the connection between coherence and truth is the "alternative coherent systems objection." There may be many different and incompatible systems of belief that are equally coherent, among which only a purely arbitrary choice can be made, as each of them would be equally justified on a coherence theory of justification. Regardless of the merits of this objection, as addressed against epistemic coherentism, or the possibilities of coherence theories of epistemic justification of meeting it successfully, this objection does not get off the ground in the context of legal factfinding as the legal mechanisms of the burdens of proof allow factfinders to break ties among alternative, and equally coherent, explanations of the facts under dispute.[51]

---

[48] See BonJour 1985; Lehrer 2000; Thagard 2000; Davidson 2001.
[49] See BonJour 1985.
[50] See Worsnip 2018.
[51] See Nance 2001, 1586.

Last, but not least, the "truth objection," straightforwardly questions that the appropriate relation obtains between coherence and truth. Coherentist standards of justification—claims the critic—can be shown to be truth-conducive only if one identifies truth with coherence, that is, only if one endorses a (highly implausible) coherence theory of truth, according to which truth is a matter of coherence relations among beliefs. Indeed, the coherence theory of truth faces serious (and, according to many, insurmountable) problems.[52] It is, in any event, a non-starter in the context of evidential reasoning in law, given that our legal systems are deeply committed to the view that it should be possible to differentiate between justification and truth, in the traditional sense of correspondence with an independent reality, and a number of evidence rules and procedures presuppose this distinction—which is, besides, accepted by many proponents of coherence theories of evidence and legal proof.[53] Can it be plausibly shown that coherence is truth-conducive in a way that avoids a commitment to an anti-realist conception of truth?

Before discussing ways in which the truth objection may be met, it is important to clarify its import. There are two reasons why the objection, while serious, is not fatal as critics take it to be. Surely, coherentist justification is always relative to background beliefs, which may turn out to be false. It relies, as argued earlier, on a non-monotonic form of inference which may always be defeated in the light of new information. Given this defeasible character, it would be improper to require that coherence-driven reasoning be a secure route to truth—in this respect, coherentist reasoning is not worse off than other forms of non-deductive reasoning, which, by their nature, cannot secure either the truth of their conclusions. In addition, it is critical to notice that truth is a momentous, but hardly a unique, value in adjudication. The adequacy of justificatory standards for legal factfinding should be accordingly assessed against the plurality of values (epistemic and otherwise) that trials are meant to serve, rather than, exclusively, on their truth-conduciveness.

This said, it is nonetheless important to show that coherence is properly connected with truth in the understanding that this connection would be probabilistic, rather than necessary and only one criterion (among others) against which the correctness of coherentist standards of justification should be evaluated. May then, in this qualified form, the truth-objection be met? There is a number of different arguments in the coherentist literature that aim to effect a connection between coherence and truth. BonJour and Thagard have attempted to show that coherence is truth-conducive by way of appealing to inference to the best explanation (of the fact that a system of beliefs, which respects the observational requirement, is coherence and stable in the long run, in the case of BonJour, and of the fact that a coherent theory best explains the available evidence and its explanatory breadth and depth increases with time, in the case of Thagard).[54] Others, such as Davidson and Lehrer, have advanced conceptual arguments that support the view that coherence is connected with truth, through the concepts of belief and self-trust, respectively.[55] Attempts have also

---

[52] For a discussion of different coherence theories of truth and the main objections that have been directed against them, see Amaya 2015, ch. 6.

[53] See Damaška 1998, 291–5. For an acceptance of coherence as a criterion of justification but its rejection as a criterion of truth in law, see Allen 1991, 391; MacCormick, 1984, 52; Tillers 1986, 903–7. cf. Pardo 2000, 438; Jackson 1988.

[54] See BonJour 1985; Thagard 2007.

[55] Davidson 2001; Lehrer 2000; 2005.

recently made in probability theory to show that the proper connection obtains between coherence and truth.[56]

None of these strategies conclusively show that coherence is truth-conducive. Besides, these strategies are (admittedly) translatable to varying degrees to the domain of evidential reasoning in law. However, the availability of these strategies—combined with the adjustment of the import of the objection in light the proper place of truth within a theory of evidence and proof and the defeasible nature of coherentist reasoning—suggest that a coherence theory of evidence and proof cannot be straightforwardly dismissed on the grounds that it fails to show that accepting beliefs about the fact under dispute that are justified by virtue of their coherence lead us to accept beliefs that are (at least, likely) to be true.

Critically, the truth objection is not equally forceful against all versions of coherentism. In this respect, virtue coherentism is arguably in an advantaged position, as the incorporation of virtue may strengthen the truth connection of beliefs that are justified by virtue of their coherence.[57] Optimally coherent beliefs, i.e., beliefs which could be the outcome of virtuous coherentist reasoning, may, of course, turn out to be false. Fallible as we all are— the virtuous people included—there are no assurances that coherentist reasoning, even when performed against a background of epistemically responsible action, would not lead us astray. Indeed, this is as expected, for human logic is, unlike formal logic, a logic of uncertainty. The response to such uncertainty, however, is not to retreat to the comfort and safety provided by the formal, but to reason the best we can about facts the truth of which, most of the time, we cannot be sure of.

8. Conclusions

This chapter has argued that coherence has an important place in both a descriptive and a normative theory of evidential reasoning in law. In contrast to what structural approaches have it, it is not a clear-cut notion, like posterior probability or logical consistency are, but this is as it should be: reasoning about evidence is not as hard and fast an inferential process as deducing from mathematical axioms is. Nonetheless, there are less difficulties in identifying factors that are relevant to coherence judgments than critics of coherentism on grounds of vagueness seem to assume. Constraint satisfaction approaches, in contrast to narrative conceptions, provide a set of criteria of coherence that are sufficiently precise to be usable in contexts of legal factfinding. As a mode of inference, coherence-driven reasoning about evidence and legal proof may also be described in a fairly detailed way by using the tools of explanatory reasoning. Coherence, however, is not enough for the justification of evidentiary judgments in law. It is, as argued, justification conferring only against a background of virtuous epistemic action. Finally, the problems concerning the relationship between coherence and truth, while important, are not insurmountable. They are, moreover, not equally detrimental to all versions of coherentism. Virtue coherentism, as claimed, not only avoids the problem of the coherence bias that cuts off coherence from justification, but it also mitigates the problem of truth-conduciveness that cuts off coherentist justification from truth.

---

[56] See Shogenji 1999. cf. Olsson 2005; Bovens and Harman 2003.
[57] For a defense of the claim that intellectual virtue is truth-conducive, see Zagzebski 1996, 184-94.

Questions about the nature and role of coherence in evidence and legal proof (and beyond) have attracted the attention of scholars across a range of different disciplines in the last decades, and interest has not waned. Coherentism (legal and otherwise) remains a very active field of research, as new topics and problems have come on the scene. I conclude by signaling some of the most prominent areas of research in coherence studies.

Inquiry into the social dimensions of coherence is a first promising area of research. There are a number of problems in social epistemology which are highly relevant for the development of a coherence theory of evidence and legal proof. Some important issues include the relevance of coherence to testimony evaluation, the analysis of social perceptions of coherence, the connections between coherence and consensus in group deliberation, coherentist approaches to epistemic disagreement, and work in coherence building in the course of collective decision-making, which is central in the legal determination of facts by juries as well as composite courts.[58]

Another relevant line of inquiry is the study of the role that incoherence plays in evidential reasoning in law. Incoherence plays arguably an important role in triggering hypothesis formation, identifying potential sources of doubt in one's construction of the case, highlighting anomalies, and prompting inquiry and revision. The important heuristic and epistemic roles that incoherence plays in legal factfinding have not gone unnoticed in coherence-oriented work on the subject.[59] Nonetheless, a more systematic study of the relevance of incoherence, its connections to inconsistency, and its psychological profile, is likely to advance in important ways the understanding of the place that arguments from coherence should have in a theory of evidence and legal proof.

A third group of questions concerns the analysis of the potential impact that the institutional environment may have on the quality of coherentist reasoning in the context of legal factfinding. How do evidence rules and procedures impede/facilitate that legal factfinders reach coherent judgments that are epistemically valuable? Which constraints on coherence reasoning are justified (e.g. limits on its input established by exclusionary rules) in light of the plurality of values that trials are meant to serve? In which ways could factfinding institutions be redesigned to as to promote that legal factfinders' natural reasoning processes (in which coherence is prominent) work at their best? It is also important to examine and propose the revision of evidentiary rules and procedures with a view to implementing debiasing strategies which may help prevent legal factfinders from falling prey of the coherence bias.[60]

Fourth, a growth research area aims at examining the implications of the affective sciences for the theory and psychology of coherence-driven legal reasoning. There has been an interesting body of research that explores the connections between coherence and emotion in reasoning, most prominently, Thagard's model of hot coherence and Simon, Read, and Stenstrom's work on the role that hot cognitions play within the framework of coherence-based reasoning.[61] Some of the implications of this work for evidential reasoning in law have begun to be studied, but further applications and novel perspectives on the interlocking

---

[58] See Worsnip 2019; Thagard 2000; Mercier 2012.
[59] See Thagard 2000, 67; Amaya 2015; Dahlman and Mackor 2019, 279.
[60] On debiasing in legal factfinding, see Zenker, "De-Biasing Legal Factfinders," ch. 26, in this volume.
[61] See Simon, Stenstrom, and Read 2015; Thagard 2006.

roles that emotion and cognitive coherence play in evidential reasoning in law are expected to be developed in light of new research in the flourishing area of emotion studies.

Fifth, an interesting question that has recently attracted the attention of both legal scholars and philosophers concerns how probability and coherence relate to each other.[62] What role does probability play within a coherence theory of evidence and legal proof? How can probabilistic evidence be managed within such a theory? How viable is the project of developing a coherence measure for legal factfinding in probabilistic terms? The pluralistic view, already advanced by Tillers, that we should aim at determining the proper role of different theories for a diversity of inferential domains, rather than seeking to establish the validity of a one-size-fits-all method of reasoning, has found its way into the debates over probabilities.[63] Further important results on coherence and probability and their relations, in light of current work in philosophy of science and formal logic, is likely to be produced from within this pluralistic approach to evidence and proof in the future.

These are some of the key areas of (ongoing and further) research in coherentism that are particularly relevant to legal factfinding. Given the interdisciplinary nature of coherence studies (as well as evidence scholarship), collaborative endeavors among diverse research communities are a promising route to deliver novel, exciting results in these research areas as well as to open up new directions for research on coherence in legal evidence.

References

Abu-Hareira, M. (1986). "An Early Holistic Conception of Judicial Fact-Finding," *Juridical Review,* 79–106.

Allen, R. (1991). "The Nature of Juridical Proof," *Cardozo Law Review,* 13: 373–422.

Allen, R. (1997). "Rationality, Algorithms, and Juridical Proof," *International Journal of Evidence and Proof,* 1: 254–75.

Allen, R. and Pardo, M. (2019). "Relative Plausibility and its Critics," *The International Journal of Evidence and Proof,* 23: 5–59.

Amaya, A. (2008). "Justification, Coherence, and Epistemic Responsibility," *Episteme,* 5(3): 306–19.

Amaya, A. (2009). "Inference to the Best Legal Explanation," in H. Kaptein, H. Prakken, and B. Verheij (eds.), *Legal Evidence and Proof.* Aldershot: Ashgate, 135–59.

Amaya, A. (2013). "Coherence, Evidence, and Legal Proof," *Legal Theory,* 19.

Amaya, A. (2015). *The Tapestry of Reason.* Oxford: Hart Publishing.

Baehr, J. (2008). "Four Varieties of Character-Based Virtue Epistemology," *The Southern Journal of Philosophy,* 46.

Bex, F. J. (2011). *Arguments, Stories and Criminal Evidence.* Dordrecht: Springer.

BonJour, L. (1985). *The Structure of Empirical Knowledge.* Cambridge: Cambridge University Press.

BonJour, L. (1999). "The Dialectic of Foundationalism and Coherentism," in J. Greco and E. Sosa (eds.), *The Blackwell Guide to Epistemology.* Oxford: Blackwell, 117–42.

Bovens, L. and Harman, S. (2003). *Bayesian Epistemology.* Oxford: Oxford University Press.

Dahlman, C. and Mackor, R. (2019). "Coherence and Probability in Legal Evidence," *Law, Probability and Risk,* 18: 275–94.

Damaška, M. (1998). "Truth in Adjudication," *Hastings Law Journal,* 49, 289–308.

Davidson, D. (2001). *Subjective, Intersubjective, Objective.* Oxford: Oxford University Press.

---

[62] See Roche 2015; Dahlman and Mackor 2019; Olsson 2019.
[63] Tillers 1986, 922, 889–90, 934. For another pluralistic stance and its bearing on the relation between probability and coherence, see Olsson 2019.

Easwaran, K. (2015). "Accuracy, Coherence and Evidence," in T. Szabó and J. Hawthorne (eds.), *Oxford Studies in Epistemology*, 5: 61–96–. Oxford: Oxford University Press.

Haack, S. (2000). "A Founherentist Theory of Empirical Justification," in E. Sosa and J. Kim (eds.), *Epistemology*. Malden: Blackwell, 226–36.

Harman, G. (1986). *Change in View*. Cambridge, MA: MIT Press.

Hastie, R. and Pennington, N. (1991). "A Cognitive Theory of Juror Decision-Making: The Story Model," *Cardozo Law Review*, 13: 5001–39.

Jackson, B. (1988). *Law, Fact, and Narrative Coherence*. Liverpool: Deborah Charles.

Kahneman, D. (2011). *Thinking Fast and Slow*. London: Penguin Books.

Khalifa, K. (2010). "Default Privilege and Bad Lots," *International Studies in the Philosophy of Science*, 24 (1): 91–105.

Kornblith, H. (1989). "The Unattainability of Coherence," in Hackett (ed.), *The Current State of the Coherence Theory*. Dordrecht: Kluwer, 207–14.

Laudan, L. (1977). *Progress and its Problems*. Berkeley and Los Angeles, CA: University of California Press.

Lehrer, K. (2000). *Theory of Knowledge*. Boulder, CO: Westview Press.

Lehrer, K. (2005). "Coherence and the Truth Connection," *Erkenntnis*, 63(3): 413–23.

Lipton, P. (2004). *Inference to the Best Explanation*. London and New York: Routledge.

Lycan, W. G. (1988). *Judgment and Justification*. New York: Cambridge University Press.

MacCormick, N. (1980). "The Coherence of a Case and The Reasonableness of Doubt," *Liverpool Law Review*, 2: 45–50.

MacCormick, N. (1984). "Coherence in Legal Justification," in A. Peczenik, L. Lindahl, and B. van Roermund (eds.), *Theory of Legal Science*. Dordrecht: Reidel, 235–251.

MacCormick, N. (2005). *Rhetoric and the Rule of Law*. Oxford: Oxford University Press.

Mercier, H. (2012). "The Social Functions of Explicit Coherence Evaluation," *Mind and Society*, 11 (1): 81–92.

Nance, D. A. (2001). "Naturalized Epistemology and the Critique of Evidence Theory," *Virginia Law Review*, 87: 1551–618.

Olsson, E. (2005). *Against Coherence*. Oxford: Oxford University Press.

Olsson, E. (2019). "Dahlman and Mackor on Coherence and Probability in Legal Evidence," *Law, Probability and Risk*, 18 (4): 295–303.

Pardo, M. S. (2000). "Juridical Proof, Evidence, and Pragmatic Meaning," *Northwestern University Law Review*, 95 (1): 399, 442.

Plantinga, A. (1993). *Warrant*. Oxford: Oxford University Press.

Psillos, S. (2002). "Simply the Best: A Case for Abduction," in A. C. Kakas and F. Sadri (eds.), *Computational Logic*. Berlin: Springer-Verlag.

Psillos, S. (2004). "Inference to the Best Explanation and Bayesianism," in F. Stadler (ed.), *Induction and Deduction in the Sciences*. Kluwer: Dordrecht, 83–91.

Psillos, S. (2007). "The Fine Structure of Inference to the Best Explanation," *Philosophy and Phenomenological Research*, 74 (2): 441–48.

Ramsey, F. P. (1990). "Truth and Probability" (article originally published 1926), in D. H. Mellor (ed.), *Philosophical Papers*. New York: Cambridge University Press, 52–109.

Roberts, R. C. and West, R. (2015). "Natural Epistemic Defects and Corrective Virtues," *Synthese*, 192 (8): 2257–576.

Roche, W. (2015). "Probability and Coherence," in M. Araszkiewicz and J Šavelka (eds.), *Coherence: Insights from Philosophy, Jurisprudence, and Artificial Intelligence*. Dordrecht: Springer, 59–93.

Shogenji, T. (1999). "Is Coherence Truth-Conducive?" *Analysis*, 59 (4): 338–45.

Shogenji, T. (2001). "The Role of Coherence in Epistemic Justification," *Australasian Journal of Philosophy*, 79 (1): 90–106.

Simon, D. (2004). "A Third View of the Black Box," *The University of Chicago Law Review*, 71 (2): 511–86.

Simon, D., Stenstrom, D., and Read, S. J. (2015). "The Coherence Effect: Blending Hot and Cold Cognitions," *Journal of Personality and Social Psychology*, 109: 369–94.

Smith, M. (2003). "Meta-Ethics," in F. Jackson and M. Smith (eds.), *The Oxford Handbook of Contemporary Philosophy*, 3–30. Oxford: Oxford University Press.

Thagard, P. (2000). *Coherence in Thought and Action*. Cambridge, MA: MIT Press.

Thagard, P. (2006). *Hot Thought*. Cambridge, MA: MIT Press.

Thagard, P. (2007). "Coherence, Truth, and the Development of Scientific Knowledge," *Philosophy of Science*, 74 (1): 28–47.

Thagard, P. and Shelley, C. (1997). "Abductive Reasoning: Logic, Visual Thinking and Coherence," in M. L. Dalla Chiara, K. Doets, D. Mundici, and J. van Benthem, (eds.), *Logic and Scientific Methods*. Dordrecht: Kluwer, 413–27.

Thagard, P. and Verbeurgt, K. (1998). "Coherence as Constraint Satisfaction," *Cognitive Science*, 22 (1): 1–24.

Tillers, P. (1986). "Mapping Inferential Domains," *Boston University Law Review*, 66: 883–936.

Van Koppen, P. J. and Mackor, A. R. (2020). "A Scenario Approach to the Simonhaven Case," *Topics in Cognitive Science*, 12: 1132–51.

Van Roermund, B. (1997). *Law, Narrative and Reality*. Dordrecht: Kluwer.

Wagenaar, W. A. van Koppen, P. J., and Crombag, H. F. M. (1993) *Anchored Narratives*. New York: St. Martin's Press.

Worsnip, A. (2018). "The Conflict of Evidence and Coherence," *Philosophy and Phenomenological Research*, XCVI: 3–44.

Worsnip, A. (2019). "Disagreement as Interpersonal Coherence," *Res Philosophica*, 96: 245–68.

Zagzebski, L. (1996). *Virtues of the Mind*. Cambridge: Cambridge University Press.

PART V
EVIDENCE AND PROBABILITY

17

The Logic of Inference and Decision for Scientific Evidence

Franco Taroni, Silvia Bozza, and Alex Biedermann

1. Introduction

Uncertainty is an inevitable complication encountered by members of the judiciary who face inference and decision-making as core aspects of their daily activities. Inference, in this context, is mainly inductive and relates to the use of incomplete information, to reason about propositions of interest. Applied to scientific evidence, this means, for example, to reason about whether or not a person of interest is the source of recovered evidential material. More so, factfinders are required to make decisions about ultimate issues, for example, regarding a defendant's guilt. The distinct, but related roles of inference and decision require a logical assistance because unaided human reasoning is liable to fallacious conclusions. This represents a critical cause of concern because incoherent reasoning in legal proceedings places defendants at risk and can lead to miscarriages of justice. In this respect, the role of forensic scientists, whose duty is to *help* assess the probative value of scientific findings, is subjected to ongoing scrutiny. Scientists (should) provide assistance by offering to mandating authorities conclusions that are scientifically sound and logically defensible.

The choice of a normative framework—that is a coherent *standard* of reasoning—thus is widely advocated. In the current understanding, such a framework intends to implement several desirable properties for evidential assessment, such as logic, balance, robustness, and transparency. Within this general evidential context, this chapter addresses two fundamental questions. The first is "How is one to manage scientific information?" and the second is "How is one to justify a decision?" The focus will be on presenting and discussing the extent to which probability theory and decision theory, can contribute toward answering these questions. This chapter will acknowledge and distinguish between, on the one hand, perspectives on evidence evaluation in forensic science literature and, on the other hand, legal evidence and proof processes on the level of cases as a whole.

2. Forensic Science Evidence Evaluation in the Twentieth Century

Forensic science can be defined as a body of scientific principles and technical methods applied within well-defined proceedings in criminal or civil law, as well as in regulatory matters. The main purpose of forensic science is to help demonstrate the existence or past occurrence of an event of legal interest, such as a crime, and to assist members of the

Franco Taroni, Silvia Bozza, and Alex Biedermann, *The Logic of Inference and Decision for Scientific Evidence* In: *Philosophical Foundations of Evidence Law*. Edited by: Christian Dahlman, Alex Stein, and Giovanni Tuzet, Oxford University Press. © Christian Dahlman, Alex Stein, and Giovanni Tuzet 2021. DOI: 10.1093/oso/9780198859307.003.0018

judiciary, especially prosecutors and legal counsel, in determining the role of target individuals in a given contested event, as well as the *modus operandi*. On a practical account, forensic science is concerned with technical aspects such as the investigation of crime scenes and the examination of victims and persons of interests, either directly or indirectly in the form of items such as clothing, vehicles, tools, weapons, mobile phones, other electronic devices. Such aspects are not covered here. On a more conceptual side, forensic science is concerned with tasks such as classification (e.g., examining whether an unknown substance is an illegal drug). Forensic analysis also typically involves comparisons between evidential material (of unknown source) and material of known source (i.e., reference material), followed by an evaluative phase where the focus is on assessing the evidential value of findings within the particular context of the event under investigation.

The public, legal professionals and, to some extent, academic circles perceive these instances of forensic science theory and practice as both well-founded and reliable. Yet, the discovery of cases of miscarriage of justice provides a continuing stream of debate,[1] in particular with regard to scientific standards of reliability.[2] Across legal systems, courts have repeatedly stressed that forensic scientists are required to critically assess their respective domains of expertise.[3] Scientists should scrutinize both the rationale underlying the various domains of expertise as well as the ways in which scientific evidence is evaluated and presented in applied contexts. It is argued that reasoning schemes should conform to sound probabilistic principles.[4]

Instances that illustrate the unease of forensic science with fundamental shortcomings in interpretation and data evaluation can be found throughout the last century. Among the pioneering forensic scientists, few commentators faced this topic as openly and critically as did Kirk and Kingston when they wrote:

> When we claim that criminalistics is a science, we must be embarrassed, for no science is without some mathematical background, however meager. This lack must be a matter of primary concern to the educator .... Most, if not all, of the amateurish efforts of all of us to justify our own evidence interpretations have been deficient in mathematical exactness and philosophical understanding.[5]

This quote is still of relevance today, since data evaluation has been mentioned among the most neglected areas in the entire field of forensic science.[6] In the current practice of many forensic branches, evaluations of scientific evidence can hardly be regarded as anything more than an unstructured ad hoc assessment; examples are evaluations following examinations of shoe marks, tool marks, bullets and cartridges (firearms), gunshot residues, and handwriting.

At the time of Kirk and Kingston, conclusions based on robust statistical or probabilistic reasoning were rare, but they still are so today,[7] with DNA as a widely acknowledged exception. This is so even though much well-argued judicial literature has pointed out that

---

[1] Saks and Koehler 2008; National Research Council 2009; Kaye 2010; Mnookin et al. 2011; Redmayne et al. 2011; Evett et al. 2017; Garrett 2018.

[2] Law Commission 2011; President's Council of Advisors on Science and Technology 2016.

[3] Aitken et al. 2011; Murphy 2017.

[4] Saks and Koehler 2005; Garbolino 2014; Cheng 2017.

[5] Kirk and Kingston 1964, 435–6.

[6] National Research Council 2009; President's Council of Advisors on Science and Technology 2016.

[7] Koehler 2011; Thompson et al. 2013; 2018; Cole 2014; American Association for the Advancement of Science 2016.

categorical conclusions—that is, statements of certainty—cannot be justified on logical and scientific grounds.[8]

As a general starting point, it needs to be conceded that incomplete knowledge about both general aspects of scientific branches as well as particular items of scientific evidence in instant cases inevitably results in uncertainty that cannot be eliminated. It is, however, measurable by probability. In turn, this means that common patterns of forensic inference, such as inference of identity,[9] in order to be taken seriously, must be approached within a probabilistic framework.[10] While this need has already been recognized at the beginning of the twentieth century,[11] it remains an unresolved topic in contemporary debates surrounding reporting policies (see Section 5).[12] In recent years, this has led legal scholars to express their frustration at the reluctance of some parts of the forensic community to deploy more substantial efforts to critically review the foundations of identification in general, and to addressing the challenge of probabilistic evidential assessment in particular.[13] Adopting evaluative schemes that conform to logically sound principles is a priority in efforts to avoid improper forensic testimony and forensic misconduct.[14]

3. Core Needs in Forensic Science: Reasoning under Uncertainty

If forensic science should abandon the idea of certainty,[15] it becomes necessary to conceive of a way to measure uncertainty. It is natural, then, to refer to disciplines concerned with formal methods of reasoning, such as statistics, in particular methods for the assignment of probabilities to propositions of interest. That is, when the existence of uncertainty is recognized as an inherent aspect of a given inference problem, and a formal approach is possible, then this approach represents a reference in that it captures and ranks uncertainties based upon a concise and logical line of reasoning.[16]

Both judicial and psychological literature, despite relating to two fields that are different in many respects, point out the need for methods that deal with the formal analysis of rational thinking.[17] They share a common interest in challenging configurations of real-world situations that informal reasoning must confront. This is illustrated by the fact that in their reasoning tasks, investigators, scientists, and legal professionals at large (including judges, prosecutors, and lawyers) often need to consider multiple items of information with

[8] See, e.g., Finkelstein and Fairley 1970; Eggleston 1983; Twining 1994; Thompson and Cole 2007; Thompson 2012; Hahn et al. 2013; Vuille et al. 2017.

[9] Inference of identity is also commonly termed inference of source. That is, assessing whether questioned and known items come from the same source. Note, however, that propositions of common source represent only one example among several other types of propositions (e.g., propositions invoking alleged activities) that may condition the evaluation of scientific evidence (Cook et al. 1998).

[10] Lindley 1991; Robertson and Vignaux 1993; Redmayne 2002; Hahn and Oaksford 2006; Tillers 2011; Saks and Neufeld 2011.

[11] Taroni et al. 1998.

[12] Cole and Biedermann 2020.

[13] Koehler 2014; Canzio and Luparia 2018.

[14] The Innocence Project reports that, as of July 14, 2020, 367 innocent people have been exonerated in the United States, twenty-one of whom were sentenced to death. Forensic science was misapplied in 46% of DNA exoneration cases.

[15] Lindley 2014.

[16] Cole 2010; Frosini and Taroni 2015.

[17] See, e.g., Kahneman 2011; Roberts and Zuckerman 2010.

complicated interrelated structure. It is necessary, thus, to inquire about ways in which items of information occur in combination and how they stand in relation to each other. Such analyses reach further levels of complication because they need to be conducted in the light of complex frameworks of circumstances, and competing accounts regarding the alleged events.

4. Inference and Decision-Making under Uncertainty

Probability theory is among the primary candidates discussed in legal literature and philosophy of science for dealing with uncertainty in evidence evaluation as it forms a reference scheme for measuring uncertainty.[18] Throughout this chapter, the discussion will emphasize the personalist interpretation of probability, that is an interpretation that focuses on degrees of belief and how rational agents should make up their minds about events of the past, present, and future. This view is particularly helpful with respect to the needs of forensic science.[19] Even critical commentators note that "none of the conceptualizations of probability except probability as subjective degrees of belief can function at trial."[20] Notwithstanding, we acknowledge that by choosing probability as a framework for reasoning under uncertainty, it is not suggested that, descriptively, it provides a model for the working of the legal process as a whole. Instead, the argument is that probability theory helps formulate precepts for logically sound modes of reasoning, ask relevant questions and define the boundaries between the competence of expert witnesses and legal decision-makers. There is no suggestion that the responsibility for reasoning and decision-making processes is to be delegated to an abstract mathematical theory. In any case, as noted by Kaye, "additional argument is necessary to bridge the gap from a general mathematical truth to a substantive application."[21]

While providing general principles for the coherent measurement of uncertainty, probability is not a static concept. In practice, it is often necessary to reassess probabilities given newly acquired data or, more generally speaking, information. For this purpose, a standard result is available, Bayes' theorem, though its use in legal contexts has both proponents and critics. Broadly speaking, Bayes' theorem specifies how to re-organize one's state of mind based on new data, that is how to update initial beliefs (i.e., prior to data acquisition) about propositions of interest. This idea of updating beliefs in the light of new information is conceptualized in terms of the likelihood ratio, a rigorous concept for a balanced measure of the degree to which particular evidence is capable of discriminating between competing propositions put forward by parties at trial. It measures the change produced by the evidence in one's beliefs in favor of one proposition as opposed to another.[22] Likelihood ratios are mainly studied by forensic scientists as a means to quantify the probative value of scientific evidence, though further argument is necessary to convey results in a way that is understandable to recipients of expert information.

---

[18] Lindley 2014.
[19] Taroni et al. 2001; 2016.
[20] Allen 2013, 104.
[21] Kaye 1999, 27.
[22] Kass and Raftery 1995.

Probability and Bayes' theorem represent normative viewpoints, though not normative in a legal sense,[23] but in the sense of a standard that allows reasoners to think coherently in argument construction.[24] For example, when the scientist observes features of trace material and characterizes their rarity within a relevant population, such an assessment cannot be directly transposed into a conclusion regarding the proposition according to which the person of interest is the source of the trace recovered on the crime scene. The role of probability is nothing less than to ensure logical reasoning. It is in this sense that the framework is considered to provide a suitable approach to many issues that pertain to the coherent management of imperfect evidence.[25]

As much as there is debate about the suitability of probability theory and Bayes' theorem, and the extent to which practitioners are able to apply this framework, as much it is overlooked that the ultimate goal of formal methods of reasoning is not limited to quantify one's uncertainty about propositions of interest. Once all the evidence has been considered, one needs to act upon one's beliefs about what is (most probably) true. In legal contexts, acting (or deciding) means rendering a verdict in order to bring legal disputes to an end. Hence, the use of probability to deal with uncertainty is not an end by itself, but a means to an end which is decision-making.

From a formal perspective, probability theory pairs with decision theory to extend coherent reasoning to coherent decision-making. In essence, decision theory formalizes the idea that one decides on the basis of two elements. These are, on the one hand, one's beliefs about uncertain events and, on the other hand, one's expression of desirability among the various possible decision consequences. The latter aspect is captured by the concept of utility (or loss). Probability and utility operate within a general theory of decision that allows one to derive formal rules for decision-making (e.g., the maximization of expected utility).[26]

Like probability, decision theory has a difficult stand among discussants who emphasize practicality and operational feasibility. First, because decision theory involves probability which itself is challenging in fully quantified applications. Second, because it involves the quantification of the desirability of decision consequences as an additional hurdle. The conceptualist reply to this is analogous to arguments in support of probability. Kaplan has concisely noted that

> ... although we are in most legal areas far away from a usable quantification of our problems, the effort of thinking through the abstract quantitative relations among different variables turns out to provide a host of insights into the workings of our legal system.[27]

The point here is that decision theory captures the fundamental aspects of problems that decision-makers face, irrespective of their argumentative viewpoint and level of commitment to formal theories. Among these aspects is the notion of *decision* under uncertainty, in analogy to *reasoning* under uncertainty. Because, at the time a decision

---

[23] For an account on the normative perspective, as compared to descriptive and prescriptive perspectives, see, e.g., Baron 2008; 2012.
[24] Kahneman 2011; Biedermann et al. 2014.
[25] Eggleston 1991; Redmayne 2001; Aitken et al. 2021; Oaksford and Chater 2007; Canzio and Luparia 2018.
[26] See, e.g., Lindley 1985.
[27] Kaplan 1968, 1066.

needs to be made, it cannot be known with certainty which state of nature holds, one cannot directly tell which decision leads to the best consequence. What the decision analyst can do, however, is to map out the various decision paths, including the possible states of nature and associated outcomes, their probabilities, and relative (un-)desirability. Technically, this amounts to a decision tree,[28] which provides a detailed sketch of the anatomy of a decision problem.[29] By what is called "folding back" the branches of such trees, one can work out the expected value for each branch which, in turn, provides a criterion for comparing the various options. The result thus consists of a qualifier for the appropriateness of particular decisions, quantified on the basis of the (un-)desirability of the outcomes.

In this sense, decision theory is a useful framework for the exploration and scrutiny of alternative courses of action.

Decision theory forces decision-makers to formalize their preference structure and to assess the desirability of each decision outcome. It also encourages decision-makers to recognize that deciding *not* to take an action is just as much a decision as deciding which action to take, and that selecting an unnecessary action or failing to select a necessary action may represent an error. Decision theory also helps to ensure that thinking processes consider all relevant possibilities and avoid undesirable consequences. Since Kaplan's foundational paper,[30] decision theory has regularly been discussed in legal literature[31] and in forensic science.[32]

5. A Discussion of Recurrent Skeptical Viewpoints

A natural way of advocating the use of formal approaches to inference in legal contexts is by drawing an analogy to the concept of evidence and proof in science, which relies on the idea that formal procedures are easier to explain and justify than informal ones.[33] Yet, skeptical readers may wish to see further argument in support of the formalisms presented throughout this chapter. This is a critical aspect because experience shows that many scientists, when confronted with the discipline of statistics, tend to rely on definitional aspects of probability and statistical methods too uncritically. Ideally, however, researchers and practitioners would have an understanding of the rationale behind the underlying theory and refer to it because they are convinced that it is sound and addresses practical needs adequately. This raises a series of contentious issues that, in what follows, are grouped and discussed in view of two recurrent questions. The first addresses the question of why understanding probability as a degree of belief. The second addresses the question of what insight can be drawn from a decision theoretic perspective to selected aspects of evidence and proof processes.

---

[28] See, e.g., Raiffa 1968.
[29] See, e.g., Moore and Thomas 1988.
[30] Kaplan 1968.
[31] See, e.g., Kaye 1988; Cheng 2013; Cole 2014.
[32] Biedermann et al. 2014; 2018a; Taroni et al. 2005; 2020.
[33] Edwards 1988.

5.1 Why Regard Probability as a Degree of Belief?

5.1.1 Operational limitations of frequentism

Part of an argument in favor of viewing probability as a degree of belief stems from the fact that other interpretations of probability encounter applicability problems. A good example for this is the (im-)possibility to assume stable conditions between instances of long sequences of events as suggested by the frequentist definition of probability. This includes attempts to derive probabilities from base rates.

In legal contexts, it is readily seen that one cannot easily conceive of (countable) outcomes of past events to determine relative frequencies. As noteds by Lindley

> What is the chance that the defendant is guilty? Are we to imagine a sequence of trials in which the judgements, "guilty" or "not guilty," are made and the frequency of the former found? It will not work ... because it is impossible to conceive of a suitable sequence. .... The whole idea of chance is preposterous in this context.[34]

Similar observations apply to many fields including history, economics, and forensic science.[35] What events in these contexts have in common is that they are singular and unique. In anything other than idealized situations, definitions of probability other than based on the notion of degrees of belief prove unworkable.[36]

5.1.2 Justified subjectivism

The fact that subjective probability regards the probability of an event as a measure of personal belief in the occurrence of that event should not seem surprising. Even skeptics admit that it is natural to think in terms of personal probabilities, such as when betting on the outcome of a football game. A personal degree of belief is based on a person's entirety of knowledge, experience, and information with respect to the truth of a given statement or event. While it may be questioned whether uncertainties in matters of legal interest should be assimilated to uncertainties encountered in daily life, it is difficult to contest the fact that assessments of probabilities (1) *do* depend on available information, (2) may change as the information changes, and (3) may vary among individuals, not least because different individuals may have different information or assessment criteria.

Key to this understanding is that while probability can, in principle, take any value between zero and one, this does not mean that it is an arbitrary assignment from within this range of possible values. In any context of application where decision-making involves potentially adverse consequences, personal probability assignment is naturally expected to be accompanied by a justification. Stated otherwise, it is *constrained* by a warrant. This is in contrast to unconstrained, deliberate, unjustified, speculative, or fanciful assertions that lack the credentials of a justified assertion.[37]

Subjective probabilists are well aware of this subtlety, especially the fact that the rules of probability, as well as devices for eliciting probabilities, provide a liberal framework with

---

[34] Lindley 1991, 48.
[35] Kadane and Schum 1996.
[36] Press and Tanur 2001.
[37] Biedermann et al. 2018b.

rather few formal constraints. There are at least two ways to tackle this difficulty. The first is to argue that subjective probability comes with an obligation to take responsibility for one's choice, as noted by de Finetti:

> You are completely *free* in this respect and it is entirely your own *responsibility*; but you should beware of superficiality. The danger is twofold: on the one hand, You may think that the choice, being subjective, and therefore arbitrary, does not require too much of an effort in pinpointing one particular value rather than a different one; on the other hand, it might be thought that no mental effort is required, since it can be avoided by the mechanical application of some standardized procedure.[38]

The second, deeper point, is the proper distinction between subjective probability as opposed to the notions of objectivism and objectivity. Indeed, even the founding father of twentieth century subjective probabilism, de Finetti, was not opposed to objective notions.[39] Dawid and Galavotti concisely summarize this point:

> ... de Finetti's claim should *not* be taken to suggest that subjectivism is an anarchist approach according to which probability can take whatever value you like. De Finetti struggles against *objectivism*, or the idea that probability depends entirely on some aspects of reality, not against *objectivity*. He strongly opposes the "the distortion" of "identifying objectivity and objectivism," deemed a "dangerous mirage" ..., but does not deny that there is a *problem of objectivity* of evaluations of probability.[40]

5.1.3 Conceptual devices for measuring belief

Personal probabilities are sometimes viewed cautiously because it is asked how such an abstract concept could be captured in a non-trivial way. People may be reluctant to express their probabilities numerically, suggesting that this interpretation of probability remains an inaccessible concept. Such perceptions are overly restrictive because they disregard the fact that probabilities can be elicited and investigated empirically using various conceptual devices. One possibility to do this is in terms of bets that an individual is willing to accept. For instance, the probability maintained by an individual in the truth of a proposition can be compared with the probability of drawing a black ball from an urn, a setting that can be represented in terms of two gambles involving the same prize (with no stakes). This method for measuring the probability an individual entertains in the truth of a proposition consists in considering the choice between a gamble which offers a certain prize if the proposition is true and a gamble which offers the same prize if a black ball is drawn from an urn of known composition: if the person chooses the first game, this means that, for her, the probability of the proposition at issue is greater than the proportion p of black balls in the urn; if the individual chooses the second game, this means that, for her, the probability of the proposition is smaller than the proportion of black balls. Ideally, one can vary the proportion p up to the point where the person feels indifferent between the two gambles: that value p will be this person's probability for the proposition.[41] People who

---

[38] de Finetti 2017, 153.
[39] A discussion on the role of frequencies to inform a probability assignment can be found in Taroni et al. 2018.
[40] Dawid and Galavotti 2009, 98.
[41] See, e.g., Lindley 1985.

dislike the urn scheme may think of other devices, such as the spun of a betting wheel where the pointer may stop on segments of varying size that determine the probability of winning.[42]

A further method considers probability assignment as a decision.[43] It relies on proper scoring rules that are used to assign a score to the probability that the individual chooses to assert. In this conceptualization, reporting the probability that corresponds to one's actual belief is the optimal decision, because it has the minimum expected score. This should invite people to state their probability honestly.

5.1.4 The "problem" of where to start: The seemingly incommensurable prior probability

A recurrent issue is the question of how to assess probabilities measuring uncertainty about events for which only a partial reconstruction is possible, but that can be revised in the light of new information, in particular throughout Bayes' theorem. Critics refer to prior probability as something unknown, or unknowable in principle. Common reactions to this challenge are attempts to conceive devices or definitions for prior probability assignment. However, both ideas, unknowable probabilities, and the design of ad hoc definitions for their assignment are ill conceived. The reasons for this are twofold. First, unknowable probability is a contradiction in terms that de Finetti called a "pseudo-problem:"[44] probability *is* one's ascertainment as a function of the extent of one's knowledge. It is not that one does not know one's probability, the point is that one may not be willing or feel able to assert it. More forcefully he stated: "Among the answers that do not make sense, and cannot be admitted, are the following: 'I do not know,' 'I am ignorant of what the probability is,' 'In my opinion the probability does not exist.' Probability (or prevision) is not something which in itself can be known or not known: It exists in that it serves to express, in a precise fashion, for each individual, his choice in his given state of ignorance."[45]

Second, and in view of the above, attempts to define what one's prior probability ought to be, by reference to notions such as the principle of indifference, or symmetry considerations, is tantamount to breaking with the idea of (prior) probability as the expression of a person's specific degree of belief in an instant case. That is, while probability is ideally designed to capture any initial opinion, attempting to constraint this fundamental feature amounts to depriving it from one of its most powerful features.

Instead, the fact that probabilistic reasoning requires the assessment of probabilities, should be seen as an opportunity for reasoners to transparently articulate their beliefs about a phenomenon at hand. As noted by Kadane, the possibility to declare prior probabilities is a highly desirable property because it can be taken as a "step toward honesty in analysis."[46] These considerations illustrate that it is not very helpful to discuss prior probabilities without placing them into the framework to which they belong. An awareness is required of their role in Bayes' theorem in order to develop a constructive relationship between events on which we are uncertain. If this can be ensured, then one should be able to assert the

---

[42] See, e.g., Jackson et al. 2003; von Winterfeldt and Edwards 1986.
[43] See, e.g., de Finetti 2008; Lindley 1982.
[44] de Finetti 1972, 63.
[45] Ibid., 72.
[46] Kadane 1995, 314.

prior probabilities that are most suitable for the problem at hand, or ignore them if they are irrelevant.[47]

5.2 Why Should Legal Researchers and Practitioners be Aware of Decision Theory?

5.2.1 Argumentative implications of decision-theory and -analysis for forensic science

Legal practice involves two distinct, but related functions: reasoning and decision-making under uncertainty. For decades, forensic scientists have struggled, and continue to do so today, with understanding how to interact with and contribute to reasoning and decision-making processes in the law. They struggle with explaining how available information may be used to assist a judiciary action, in particular how to present the value of evidence.

The difficulty that scientists encounter has two dimensions. The first relates to the understanding of the principles and constraints of coherent reasoning and decision-making (Section 4). They experience difficulties in understanding which conclusions can and cannot legitimately be drawn from forensic evidence, and why. The second relates to confusions about the scientist's role in decision-making processes. All too often, instead of limiting their reporting to quantifying the probative value of their findings, forensic scientists tacitly make or suggest decisions. One of the most visible examples of this are so-called identification decisions, such as the attribution of a fingermark (of unknown source) to a (known) person of interest. Here, assessing the probative value of evidence would mean to assess the support the findings provide to one proposition (e.g., the fingermark comes from the person of interest) as compared to a given alternative proposition (e.g., the fingermark comes from an unknown person).[48] Yet, this is not what most examiners do. They go beyond such evaluative statements and actually make decisions: they *decide* to conclude—categorically—that a given person of interest is the source of the fingermark. Decision theory can help reveal what is involved in such decisions;[49] in particular, it can be shown that such decisions require assessments (i.e., probabilities of the state of nature and utilities or losses quantifying the desirability or undesirability of decision outcomes) which are beyond the area of competence of scientists.[50] This insight, drawn from formal decision theoretic analyses, is part of an argument to require that forensic scientists should no longer make identification *decisions*: because such decisions require value judgments for which scientists are not competent. Scientists who nevertheless make identification decisions, render their work unscientific. Stoney has concisely noted: "For over 100 years the courts and the public have expected, and fingerprint examiners have provided, expert testimony that fuses these three elements: offering testimony not as evidence, but as proof, assuming priors and including decision making preferences. This created an overwhelming and unrealistic burden, asking fingerprint examiners, in the name of science, for something

---

[47] D'Agostini 1999.
[48] Champod et al. 2016.
[49] See, e.g., Cole and Biedermann 2020.
[50] Biedermann et al. 2008; 2016.

that science cannot provide. As a necessary consequence, fingerprint examiners became unscientific."[51]

5.2.2 Decision-theoretic deconstruction of misconceived legal probabilism and Bayesianism

Legal literature is replete with attempts to model elements of legal evidence and proof processes in probabilistic terms. As much as such attempts have been accompanied with enthusiasm, as much they have attracted critiques. Consider proposals for evaluating, in colloquial terms, "the probability of a defendant's *guilt*" in the light of evidence through the use of Bayes' theorem. This is an unfruitful attempt in principle because it involves a misconception about the object to be modelled in the first place. Probability pertains to a reasoner's uncertainty about state of nature, that is a proposition regarding a real-world event. Guilt, however, is *not* a proposition; guilt is ascribed through a decision (here, a verdict). A guilty verdict is a decision to be contemplated in the light of uncertainty about the proposition of whether the defendant is the person who committed the acts of interest in the case at hand. Stated in more simple terms, probability merely addresses the question what one should believe, whereas decision is concerned with the question of what one ought to do.[52]

While the misconception about the so-called "guilt hypotheses" can be avoided by a proper reformulation of the propositions of interest, this still does not render purely probabilistic analyses suitable for modelling legal evidence and proof processes. In particular, widespread discussions about the required level of probability for deciding a case, which includes discussions concerning naked statistical evidence, do not pay sufficient attention to the fact that the anatomy of decision-making does not reduce to probability alone. Stated otherwise, one does not *only* decide based on what one believes (i.e., one's probability for a proposition of interest), but also based on one's preferences among the possible consequences. The decision-theoretic account of legal factfinding, widely attributed to Kaplan's foundational paper,[53] makes this formally precise. It defines the optimal decision in terms of the relative desirability of the various possible decision consequences, weighted by their probability of occurrence. Although this understanding can be pinned down numerically, such an advanced level of specification is not necessary to convey the underlying argumentative implications. For example, in the context of a simple decision problem with two possible options, such as liable or not liable, the decision-theoretic account maps well onto the intuitive understanding according to which the optimal decision is a function of the relative loss associated with the two ways in which the decision may go wrong. Specifically, deciding for one option based solely on a high probability for that option may not be sufficient if the loss of an adverse consequence "outweighs" the loss associated with the adverse consequence that may be incurred with the alternative option.[54]

[51] Stoney 2012, 400.
[52] Royall 1997.
[53] Kaplan 1968.
[54] See, e.g., Friedman 2018.

6. Conclusions

Normative accounts of inference and decision for scientific evidence have been studied both by scientists and legal scholars, though often in isolated streams of research. A consequence of this was a lack of exchange at the intersection between (forensic) science and the law. For example, while the law saw intensive debates around the *Collins* case, followed by movements such as the new evidence scholarship in the 1980s,[55] it was not until the early 1990s that forensic science started a systematic, in-depth study of probabilistic methods of inference.[56] At the same time, it is not always acknowledged that there are differences in the scope of the study of methods of inference and decision in science and the law. Forensic scientists often concentrate on assessing the probative value of selected items of evidence related to their respective area of interest. Lawyers are faced with the need to solve "the problem of proof" on the level of the instant case as a whole. This is one of the reasons why claims by scientists regarding the use of formal methods of reasoning cannot easily be carried over to the conceptual problems encountered by lawyers and, hence, are met with skepticism. This raises the deeper question of what formal approaches to inference and decision in science and the law can and should achieve.

The argument developed throughout this chapter is that conceptual frameworks provide standards of reasoning useable to examine whether a given argument has the necessary credentials in order to be considered sound and, thus, whether reasoners are logically entitled to their conclusions. This corresponds to a conceptually normative perspective, though it is important to understand that this standpoint does not claim to make any prescriptive statements for the functioning of the legal process. Any insight drawn from conceptually normative reflections still requires additional argument in order to be meaningfully used in legal applications. This is readily illustrated by academic discourses around largely theoretical topics such as "naked statistical evidence" which are based on peculiar sets of assumptions that hardly ever map suitably onto problems encountered by legal systems in operation, not least because the problem in the first place is not one of probability, but decision. What normative accounts of inference and decision can achieve, however, is to provide arguments in favor of the division of labor between science and the law, and ways to define the role and limitations of the use of scientific evidence in the wider perspectives of legal evidence and proof processes.

Acknowledgments

Franco Taroni and Alex Biedermann gratefully acknowledge the support of the Swiss National Science Foundation through grants No. IZSEZ0-19114 and BSSGI0_155809, respectively.

---

[55] Lempert 1988.
[56] See, e.g., Aitken and Stoney 1991.

References

Aitken, C., Roberts, P., and Jackson, G. (2011). *Fundamentals of Probability and Statistical Evidence in Criminal Proceedings Guidance for Judges, Lawyers, Forensic Scientists and Expert Witnesses*. Report prepared under the auspices of the Royal Statistical Society's Working Group on Statistics and the Law. Available at http://www.maths.ed.ac.uk/~cgga/rss/report1.pdf (Accessed: March 30, 2021).

Aitken, C. and Stoney, D. A. (1991). *The Use of Statistics in Forensic Science*. New York: Ellis Horwood.

Aitken, C., Taroni, F., and Bozza, S., (2021). *Statistics and the Evaluation of Evidence for Forensic Scientist*. Third edition. Chichester: John Wiley & Sons.

Allen, R. J. (2013). "Taming Complexity: Rationality, the Law of Evidence and the Nature of the Legal System," *Law, Probability and Risk*, 12: 99–113.

American Association for the Advancement of Science (2016). "Special Issue: Forensic Science," *Science*, 351(6278). Available at Table of Contents — March 11, 2016, 351 (6278) | Science (science-mag.org) (Accessed: March 30, 2021).

Baron, J. (2008). *Thinking and Deciding*. Fourth edition. Cambridge: Cambridge University Press.

Baron, J. (2012). "The Point of Normative Models in Judgment and Decision Making," *Frontiers in Psychology*, 3: 1–3.

Biedermann, A., Bozza, S., and Taroni, F. (2008). "Decision Theoretic Properties of Forensic Identification: Underlying Logic and Argumentative Implications," *Forensic Science International*, 177: 120–32.

Biedermann, A., Bozza, S., and Taroni, F. (2016). "The Decisionalization of Individualization," *Forensic Science International*, 266: 29–38.

Biedermann, A., Bozza, S., and Taroni, F. (2018a). "Analysing and Exemplifying Forensic Conclusion Criteria in Terms of Bayesian Decision Theory," *Science and Justice*, 58: 159–65.

Biedermann, A., Bozza, S., Taroni, F., and Aitken, C. (2018b). "The Meaning of Justified Subjectivism and its Role in the Reconciliation of Recent Disagreements over Forensic Probabilism," *Science and Justice*, 57: 477–83.

Biedermann, A., Taroni, F., and Aitken, C. (2014). "Liberties and Constraints of the Normative Approach to Evaluation and Decision in Forensic Science: A Discussion towards Overcoming some Common Misconceptions," *Law, Probability and Risk*, 13: 181–91.

Canzio, G. and Luparia, L. (eds.) (2018). *Prova Scientifica e Processo Penale*. Milano: Wolters Kluwer-Cedam.

Champod, C., Lennard, C., Margot, P., and Stoilovic, M. (2016). *Fingerprints and Other Ridge Skin Impressions*. Second edition. Boca Raton: CRC Press.

Cheng, E. K. (2013). "Reconceptualising the Burden of Proof," *The Yale Law Journal*, 122: 1254–79.

Cheng, E. K. (2017). "The Burden of Proof and the Presentation of Forensic Results," *Harvard Law Review Forum*, 130: 154–62.

Cole, S. A. (2010). "Who Speaks for Science? A Response to the National Academy of Sciences Report on Forensic Science," *Law, Probability and Risk*, 9: 25–46.

Cole, S. A. (2014). "Individualization is Dead, Long Live Individualization! Reforms of Reporting Practices for Fingerprint Analysis in the United States," *Law, Probability and Risk*, 13: 117–50.

Cole, S. A. and Biedermann, A. (2020). "How can a Forensic Result be a 'Decision'? A Critical Analysis of Ongoing Reforms of Forensic Reporting Formats for Federal Examiners," *Houston Law Review*, 57: 551–92.

Cook, R., Evett, I. W., Jackson, G., Jones, P. J., and Lambert, J. A. (1998). "A Hierarchy of Propositions: Deciding which Level to Address in Casework," *Science and Justice*, 38: 231–9.

D'Agostini. G. (1999). "Overcoming prior Anxiety," in J. M. Bernardo (ed.), *Bayesian Methods in the Sciences*, 311–20. Madrid: Revista de la Real Academia de Ciencias.

Dawid, A. P. and Galavotti, M. C. (2009). "de Finetti's Subjectivism, Objective Probability, and the Empirical Validation of Probability Assessments," in M. C. Galavotti (ed.), *Bruno de Finetti Radical Probabilist*, 97–114. London: College Publications.

de Finetti, B. (1972). *Probability, Induction and Statistics. The Art of Guessing*. New York: John Wiley & Sons.

de Finetti. B. (2008). *Philosophical Lectures on Probability, Collected, Edited, and Annotated by Alberto Mura*. New York: Springer.

de Finetti. B. (2017). *Theory of Probability: A Critical Introductory Treatment*. Chichester: John Wiley & Sons.

Edwards, W. (1998). "Hailfinder: Tools for and Experiences with Bayesian Normative Modeling," *American Psycologist*, 53: 416–28.

Eggleston, R. (1983). *Evidence, Proof and Probability*. London: Weidenfeld and Nicolson.

Eggleston, R. (1991). "Similar Facts and Bayes' Theorem," *Jurimetrics Journal*, 31: 275–87.

Evett, I. W, Berger, C. E. H., Buckleton, J. S., Champod, C., and Jackson, J. (2017). "Finding the Way Forward for Forensic Science in the US—a Commentary on the PCAST Report," *Forensic Science International*, 258: 16–23.

Finkelstein, M. O. and Fairley, W. B. (1970). "A Bayesian Approach to Identification Evidence," *Harvard Law Review*, 83: 489–517.

Friedman, R. D. (2018). "The Persistence of the Probabilistic Perspective," *Seton Hall Law Review*, 48: 1589–600.

Frosini, B. V. and Taroni, F. (2015). "Editorial," *Italian Journal of Applied Statistics*, 27: 101–3.

Garbolino, P. (2014). *Probabilità e Logica Della Prova*. Milano: Giuffrè Editore.

Garrett, B. (2018). "Forensic Fails? As Research Continues to Underscore the Fallibility of Forensic Science, the Judge's Role as Gatekeeper is More Important than Ever (Special Issue on Forensic Science)," *Judicature*, 102(1). Available at Forensic Fail? As Research Continues to Underscore the Fallibility of Forensic Science, the Judge's Role as Gatekeeper is More Important than Ever | Judicature (duke.edu) (Accessed: March 30, 2021).

Hahn, U., Harris, A. J. L. and Oaksford. M. (2013). "Rational Argument, Rational Inference," *Argument and Computation*, 4: 21–35.

Hahn, U. and Oaksford, M. (2006). "A Normative Theory of Argument Strength," *Informal Logic*, 21: 1–24.

Jackson, H. E., Kaplow, L., Shavell, S. M., Viscusi, W. K., and Cope, D. (2003). *Analytical Methods for Lawyers*. New York: Foundation Press.

Kadane, J. B. (1995). "Prime Time for Bayes," *Controlled Clinical Trials*, 16: 313–18.

Kadane, J. B. and Schum, D. A. (1996). *A Probabilistic Analysis of the Sacco and Vanzetti Evidence*. New York: John Wiley & Sons.

Kahneman, D. (2011). *Thinking Fast and Slow*. London: Allen Lane.

Kaplan, J. (1968). "Decision Theory," *Stanford Law Review*, 20, 1065–92.

Kass, R. E. and Raftery, A. E. (1995). "Bayes Factor," *Journal of the American Statistical Association*, 90: 773–95.

Kaye, D. H. (1988). "What is Bayesianism?" in P. Tillers and E. D. Green (eds.), *Probability and Inference in the Law of Evidence, the Uses and Limits of Bayesianism (Boston Studies in the Philosophy of Science)*, 1–19. Dordrecht: Springer.

Kaye, D. H. (1999). "Clarifying the Burden of Persuasion: What Bayesian Decision Rules do and Do Not Do," *The International Journal of Evidence and Proof*, 3: 1–29.

Kaye, D. H. (2010). "The Good, the Bad, the Ugly: The NAS Report on Strengthening Forensic Science in America," *Science and Justice*, 50: 8–11.

Kirk, P. L. and Kingston, C. R. (1964). "Evidence Evaluation and Problems in General Criminalistics," *Journal of Forensic Sciences*, 9: 434–44.

Koehler, J. J. (2011). "If the Shoe Fits they might Acquit: The Value of Forensic Science Testimony," *Journal of Empirical Legal Studies*, 8: 21–48.

Koehler, J. J. (2014). "Forensic Fallacies and a Famous Judge," *Jurimetrics Journal*, 54: 211–19.

Law Commission (2011). *Law Commission No 325: Expert Evidence in Criminal Proceedings in England and Wales*. London: The Stationery Office. Available at Expert Evidence in Criminal Proceedings in England and Wales HC 829 (publishing.service.gov.uk) (Accessed: March 30, 2021).

Lempert, R. (1988). "The New Evidence Scholarship," in P. Tillers and E. D. Green (eds.), *Probability and Inference in the Law of Evidence, the Uses and Limits of Bayesianism (Boston Studies in the Philosophy of Science)*, 61–102. Dordrecht: Springer.

Lindley, D. V. (1982). "Scoring Rules and the Inevitability of Probability," *Revue Internationale de Statistique* (International Statistical Review), 50: 1–11.

Lindley, D. V. (1985). *Making Decisions.* Second edition. Chichester: John Wiley & Sons.

Lindley, D. V. (1991). "Probability," in C. Aitken and D. A. Stoney (eds.), *The Use of Statistics in Forensic Science*, 27–50. New York: Ellis Horwood.

Lindley, D. V. (2014). *Understanding Uncertainty.* Second edition. Hoboken: John Wiley & Sons.

Moore, P. G. and Thomas, H. (1988). *The Anatomy of Decisions.* Second edition. London: Penguin Books.

Mnookin, J. L., Cole, S. A., Dror, I. L., Fisher, B. A. J., et al. (2011). "The Need for a Research Culture in the Forensic Sciences," *UCLA Law Review*, 58: 725–79.

Murphy, E. (2017). "No Room for Error: Clear-Eyed Justice in Forensic Science Oversight," *Harvard Law Review Forum*, 130: 145–53.

National Research Council (2009). *Strengthening Forensic Science in the US: A Path Forward.* Washington DC: National Academy Press.

Oaksford, M. and Chater, N. (2007). *Bayesian Rationality: The Probabilistic Approach to Human Reasoning.* Oxford: Oxford University Press.

President's Council of Advisors on Science and Technology (2016). *Forensic Science in Criminal Courts: Ensuring Scientific Validity of Feature-Comparison Methods.* Washington, DC: National Academy Press.

Press, S. J. and Tanur, J. M. (2001). *The Subjectivity of Scientists and the Bayesian Approach.* New York: John Wiley & Sons.

Raiffa, H. (1968). *Decision Analysis. Introductory Lectures on Choices under Uncertainty.* Reading: Addison-Wesley.

Redmayne, M. (2001). *Expert Evidence and Criminal Justice.* Oxford: Oxford University Press.

Redmayne, M. (2002). "Appeals to Reason," *The Modern Law Review*, 65: 19–35.

Redmayne, M., Roberts, P., Aitken, C., and Jackson, G. (2011). "Forensic Science Evidence in Question," *Criminal Law Review*, 5: 347–56.

Roberts, P. and Zuckerman, A. (2010). *Criminal Evidence.* Second edition. Oxford: Oxford University Press.

Robertson, B. and Vignaux, G. A. (1993). "Probability—the Logic of the Law," *Oxford Journal of Legal Studies*, 13: 457–78.

Royall, R. (1997). *Statistical Evidence: A Likelihood Paradigm.* London: Chapman & Hall.

Saks, M. J. and Koehler, J. J. (2005). "The Coming Paradigm Shift in Forensic Identification Science," *Science*, 309: 892–5.

Saks, M. J. and Koehler, J. J. (2008). "The Individualization Fallacy in Forensic Science Evidence," *Vanderbilt Law Review*, 61: 199–219.

Saks, M. J. and Neufeld, S. L. (2011). "Convergent Evolution in Law and Science: The Structure of Decision-Making under Uncertainty," *Law, Probability and Risk*, 10: 133–48.

Stoney, D. A. (2012). "Discussion on the Paper by Neumann, Evett and Skerrett," *Journal of the Royal Statistical Society. Series A (Statistics in Society)*, 175(2): 399–400.

Taroni, F., Aitken, C., and Garbolino, P. (2001). "de Finetti's Subjectivism, the Assessment of Probabilities and the Evaluation of Evidence: A Commentary for Forensic Scientists," *Science and Justice*, 41: 145–50.

Taroni, F., Bozza, S., and Aiken, C. (2005). "Decision Analysis in Forensic Science," *Journal of Forensic Sciences*, 50: 894–905.

Taroni, F., Bozza, S., and Biedermann, A. (2020). "Decision Theory," in D. Banks, K. Kafadar, D. H. Kaye, and M. Tackett (eds.), *Handbook of Forensic Statistics*, 103–30. Boca Raton: Chapman & Hall/ CRC.

Taroni, F., Bozza, S., Biedermann, A., and Aitken, C. (2016). "Dismissal of the Illusion of Uncertainty in the Assessment of a Likelihood Ratio (Discussion Paper)," *Law, Probability and Risk*, 15: 1–16.

Taroni, F., Champod, C., and Margot, P. (1998). "Forerunners of Bayesianism in Early Forensic Science," *Jurimetrics Journal*, 38: 183–200.

Taroni, F., Garbolino, P. Biedermann, A., Aitken, C., and Bozza, S. (2018). "Reconciliation of Subjective Probabilities and Frequencies in Forensic Science," *Law, Probability and Risk*, 17: 243–62.

Thompson, W. C. (2012). "Discussion Paper: Hard Cases make Bad Law—Reactions to R v T," *Law, Probability and Risk*, 11: 347–59.

Thompson, W. C. and Cole, S. A. (2007). "Psychological Aspects of Forensic Identification Evidence," in M. Costanzo, D. Krauss, and K. Pezdek (eds.), *Expert Psychological Testimony for the Courts*, 31–68. London: Lawrence Erlbaum Associates.

Thompson, W. C., Hofstein Grady, R., Lai, H., and Stern H. S. (2018). "Do Jurors give Appropriate Weight to Forensic Identification Evidence?" *Law, Probability and Risk*, 17: 133–55.

Thompson, W. C., Kaasa, S. O., and Peterson, T. (2013). "Do Jurors give Appropriate Weight to Forensic Identification Evidence?" *Journal of Empirical Legal Studies*, 10: 359–97.

Thompson, W. C. and Schumann, E. L. (1987). "Interpretation of Statistical Evidence in Criminal Trials: The Prosecutor's Fallacy and the Defense Attorney's Fallacy," *Law and Human Bahavior*, 11: 167–87.

Tillers, P. (2011). "Trial by Mathematics—Reconsidered," *Law, Probability and Risk*, 10: 167–73.

Twining, W. (1994). *Rethinking Evidence*. Evanston: Northwestern University Press.

von Winterfeldt, D. and Edwards, W. (1986). *Decision Analysis and Behavioral Research*. Cambridge: Cambridge University Press.

Vuille, J., Luparia, L., and Taroni, F. (2017). "Scientific Evidence and the Right to a Fair Trial under Article 6 ECHR," *Law, Probability and Risk*, 16: 55–68.

18

Bayesianism: Objections and Rebuttals

Norman Fenton and David Lagnado

1. Introduction

While the laws of probability are rarely disputed, the question of how we should interpret probability judgments is less straightforward. Broadly, there are two ways to conceive of probability—either as an objective feature of the world, or as a subjective measure of our uncertainty.[1] Both notions have their place in science, but it is the latter subjective notion (the Bayesian approach) that is crucial in legal reasoning. This is because we are usually concerned with events that must have either already happened or not happened, and which (from an objective viewpoint) have redundant probabilities of either one or zero. O. J. Simpson either *did* or *did not* murder his ex-wife but, with the possible exception of O. J. Simpson himself, nobody knows for certain which; thus, we aim to gather evidence to reduce our uncertainty about what actually happened. Probability theory is just as able to capture our uncertainty about whether an event did or did not happen in the past as it can capture uncertainty about an event that may or may not happen in the future. Unfortunately, a failure to understand this point about the nature of uncertainty lies at the heart of one of the most persistent objections among some members of the legal profession to the use of probability theory (especially Bayesian probability)—namely that "there is no such thing as probability." This is normally expressed informally such as in the following (these are based on actual words we have heard used on many occasions by legal professionals): "Look, the guy either committed the crime or he didn't. If he did it then the probability is one and if he didn't then the probability is 0. There is nothing in between so, there is no such thing as probability other than 0 or 1."

Indeed, it was essentially this argument used in a 2013 UK Appeal Court case ruling to reject the use of Bayes (in a civil dispute about the cause of a fire). Specifically, Point 37 of the ruling asserted (about the use of Bayes and probabilities): "I would reject that approach. It is not only over-formulaic but it is intrinsically unsound. The chances of something happening in the future may be expressed in terms of percentage. Epidemiological evidence may enable doctors to say that on average smokers increase their risk of lung cancer by X%. But you cannot properly say that there is a 25 per cent chance that something has happened .... Either it has or it has not."[2]

The "no such thing as probability" objection is also closely tied to the general objection to the notion of subjective probability on the grounds that it should not be used in legal contexts, because it depends on the vagaries of someone's personal opinion. But probabilities

---

[1] Gillies 2000, 807.

[2] *Nulty and Ors v. Milton Keynes Borough Council*, EWCA Civ 15 (January 24, 2013). It is discussed in Spiegelhalter 2013.

Norman Fenton and David Lagnado, *Bayesianism: Objections and Rebuttals* In: *Philosophical Foundations of Evidence Law*. Edited by: Christian Dahlman, Alex Stein, and Giovanni Tuzet, Oxford University Press. © Christian Dahlman, Alex Stein, and Giovanni Tuzet 2021. DOI: 10.1093/oso/9780198859307.003.0019

are always "personal" to some extent because different people will generally have different relevant information (i.e., evidence) available to them about an event (whether it already happened or may happen in the future). Your view of the probability that O. J. Simpson murdered his ex-wife will be based on incomplete information about what happened and so will certainly be different to that of O. J. Simpson himself who has the most information, or the lawyers and jurors on the case (who all have different levels of relevant information). But, crucially, subjective and personal does not mean arbitrary; the same rules of probability apply to both objective and subjective notions. For example, if you believe that the probability that someone committed a crime is p, then on pain of inconsistency you should believe that the probability that they did *not* commit the crime is $1-p$. Moreover, subjective probabilities should be updated in a rational way via Bayes' rule. So, whatever your starting point (your prior beliefs), the Bayesian framework tells you how you should update these in light of new evidence (to give your posterior beliefs). It ensures that your posterior beliefs are rationally derived from your prior beliefs, in the same way that formal logic tells you what conclusions are deductively implied by your premises.

Both the "no such thing as probability" objection and the objection to subjective probability have long been proven to be irrational because with either objection you will be open to a Dutch book:[3] this means you can be made to lose money irrespective of the outcomes of the events bet upon; also, obeying the laws of probability minimizes your overall inaccuracy.

A number of other commonly repeated objections to probability and Bayes in the law were raised in a highly influential paper by Tribe,[4] which was written as a criticism of the prosecutor's presentation in *Collins*.[5] Tribe's objections especially pertinent for Bayes[6] were:

- That an accurate and/or non-overpowering prior cannot be devised.
- That in using statistical evidence to formulate priors jurors might use it twice in reaching a posterior.
- That not all evidence can be considered or valued in probabilistic terms.
- That no probability value can ever be reconciled with "beyond a reasonable doubt."
- That due to the complexity of cases and non-sequential nature of evidence presentation, any application of Bayes would be too cumbersome for a jury to use effectively and efficiently.
- That probabilistic reasoning is not compatible with the law, for policy reasons. In particular, that jurors are asked to formulate an opinion of the defendant's guilt during the prosecutor's case, which violates the obligation to keep an open mind until all evidence is in.

However, most of these concerns have long been systematically demolished.[7] Although we revisit some of these objections in this chapter, our focus is on those objections that are most cited, even once the Bayesian framework is accepted as a rational procedure for updating our subjective probabilities. Specifically, we will deal with three common objections, all of which can at least in part be addressed by using Bayesian networks (BNs):[8] (1) that failing

---

[3] See, e.g., Fenton and Neil 2018; Pettigrew 2020.
[4] Tribe 1971.
[5] *People v. Collins*, 438 P 2d 33 (68 Cal 2d 319 1968).
[6] See Berger 2014; Fienberg and Finkelstein 1996.
[7] Edwards 1991; Koehler 1992. More recently, see Berger 2014; Tillers and Gottfried 2007.
[8] Fenton and Neil 2018.

to constrain personal priors means no reasonable consensus posterior can ever be reached; (2) that Bayes—as encapsulated by the likelihood ratio—leads to multiple problems (including legal paradoxes); and (3) that Bayes is too complex to be used in court or in legal arguments.

The chapter is structured as follows: we first review in Section 2 the historical perspective for objections to Bayes. In Section 3 we provide necessary definitions of Bayes and the likelihood ratio. In Section 4 we address the above objections to Bayes, and explain why, despite the rebuttals to the objections, the use of Bayes has been extremely limited. Section 5 points the way forward.

2. Historical Perspective

The reluctance to accept Bayes in the law is just the latest manifestation of a long-time historical reticence to accept any statistical analysis as valid evidence. Sadly, there is good reason for this reticence. When, in 1894, a statistical analysis was used in the *Dreyfus* case it turned out to be fundamentally flawed.[9] Not until 1968 was there another well-documented case,[10] in which statistical analysis played a key role. In that case another flawed statistical argument further set back the cause of statistics in court. The *Collins* case was characterized by two errors:

1) It underestimated the probability that some evidence would be observed if the defendants were innocent by failing to consider dependence between components of the evidence; and

2) It implied that the low probability from the calculation in 1) was synonymous with innocence (the so-called "prosecutor's" fallacy).

Since then the same errors (either in combination or individually) have occurred in well-reported cases such as *R v. Sally Clark*,[11] *R v. Barry George*,[12] and *Lucia de Berk*.[13] Although original "bad statistics" used in each case (presented by forensic or medical expert witnesses without statistical training) was exposed through "good statistics" on appeal, it is the "bad statistics" which leaves an indelible stain. Yet, the role of legal professionals (who allow expert witnesses to commit the same well-known statistical errors repeatedly) is rarely questioned.

Hence, although the last forty years has seen considerable growth in the use of statistics in legal proceedings, its use in the courtroom has been mostly restricted to a small class of cases where classical statistical methods of hypothesis testing using p-values and confidence intervals are used for probabilistic inference. Yet, even this type of statistical reasoning has severe limitations,[14] including specifically in the context of legal and forensic evidence.[15] In particular:

---

[9] Kaye 2007.
[10] *People v. Collins,* 438 P. 2d 33 (68 Cal. 2d 319 1968).
[11] Forrest 2003; Hill 2005.
[12] Fenton et al. 2014.
[13] Meester et al. 2007.
[14] For an extensive discussion, see Royal Statistical Society 2015; Ziliak and McCloskey 2008.
[15] Finkelstein 2009; Vosk and Emery 2014.

- The use of p-values can also lead to the prosecutor's fallacy since a p-value (which says something about the probability of observing the evidence given a hypothesis) is often wrongly interpreted as being the same as the probability of the hypothesis given the evidence.[16]
- Confidence intervals are almost invariably misinterpreted since their proper definition is both complex and counter-intuitive (indeed, it is not properly understood even by many trained statisticians).[17]

The poor experience—and difficulties in interpretation—with classical statistics means that there is also strong resistance to any alternative approaches. This resistance extends to the Bayesian approach, despite the fact that it is especially well suited for a broad range of legal reasoning.[18]

Although the natural resistance within the legal profession to a new statistical approach is one reason why Bayes has, to date, made only minimal impact, it is certainly not the only reason. Many previous papers have discussed the social, legal, and logical impediments to the use of Bayes in legal proceedings[19] and in more general policy decision making.[20]

3. Basics of Bayes for Legal Reasoning

The following terminology and assumptions will be used:

- A *hypothesis* is a statement (typically Boolean) whose truth value we seek to determine, but is generally unknown—and which may never be known with certainty. Examples include:
  - o "Defendant is innocent of the crime charged" (this is an example of an *offense level hypothesis* also called the *ultimate hypothesis*, since in many criminal cases it is ultimately the only hypothesis we are really interested in); and
  - o "Defendant was the source of DNA found at the crime scene" (this is an example of what is often referred to as *a source level hypothesis*[21]).
- The *alternative hypothesis* is a statement which is the negation of a hypothesis.
- A piece of *evidence* is a statement that, if true, lends support to one or more hypotheses.

The relationship between a hypothesis H and a piece of evidence E can be represented graphically as in the example in Figure 18.1 where we assume that:

- The evidence E is a DNA trace found at the scene of the crime (for simplicity, we assume the crime was committed on an island with 10,000 people who therefore represent the entire set of possible suspects); and
- The defendant was arrested and some of his DNA was sampled and analyzed.

---

[16] Gastwirth 2000.
[17] Fenton and Neil 2018.
[18] Fienberg and Finkelstein 1996.
[19] Faigman and Baglioni 1988; Fienberg 2011; Tillers and Green 1988; Tribe 1971.
[20] Fienberg and Finkelstein 1996.
[21] Cook et al. 1998.

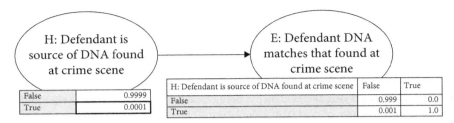

| H: Defendant is source of DNA found at crime scene | E: Defendant DNA matches that found at crime scene |

False	0.9999
True	0.0001

H: Defendant is source of DNA found at crime scene	False	True
False	0.999	0.0
True	0.001	1.0

Figure 18.1 Causal view of evidence, with prior probabilities shown in tables. This is a very simple example of a Bayesian Network (BN)

The direction of the causal structure makes sense here because *H* being true (respectively false) can *cause E* to be true (respectively false), while *E* cannot "cause" *H*. However, inference can go in *both* directions. If we observe *E* to be true (respectively false) then our belief in *H* being true (respectively false) increases. It is this latter type of inference that is central to all legal reasoning since, informally, lawyers and jurors normally use the following widely accepted procedure for reasoning about evidence:

- Start with some (unconditional) prior assumption about the ultimate hypothesis *H* (e.g., the "innocent until proven guilty" assumption equates to a belief that "the defendant is no more likely to be guilty than any other member of the relevant population").
- Update our prior belief about *H* once we observe evidence *E*. This updating takes account of the *likelihood* of the evidence.

This informal reasoning is a perfect match for Bayesian inference where the prior assumption about *H* and the likelihood of the evidence *E* are captured formally by the probability tables shown in Figure 18.1. Specifically, these are the tables for the *prior probability* of *H*, written *P(H)*, and the conditional probability of *E* given *H*, which we write as *P(E|H)*. Bayes' theorem provides the formula for updating our prior belief about *H* in the light of observing *E* to arrive at a *posterior belief about H* which we write as *P(H|E)*. In other words Bayes' theorem calculates *P(H|E)* in terms of *P(H)* and *P(E|H)*. Specifically:

$$P(H|E) = \frac{P(E|H)P(H)}{P(E)} = \frac{P(E|H)P(H)}{P(E|H)P(H) + P(E|not\,H)P(not\,H)}$$

The first table (the probability table for *H*) captures our knowledge that the defendant is one of 10,000 people who could have been the source of the DNA. The second table (the probability table for *E|H*) captures the assumptions that:

- The probability of correctly matching a DNA trace is one (so there is no chance of a false negative DNA match). This probability *P(E|H)* is called the *prosecution likelihood* for the evidence *E*.

- The probability of a match in a person who did not leave their DNA at the scene (the "random DNA match probability") is 1 in 1,000. This probability $P(E|\text{not } H)$ is called the *defence likelihood* for the evidence E.

With these assumptions, it follows from Bayes' theorem that, in our example, the posterior belief in H after observing the evidence E being true is about 9%, i.e., our belief in the defendant being the source of the DNA at the crime scene moves from a prior of 1 in 10,000 to a posterior of 9%. Alternatively, our belief in the defendant not being the source of the DNA moves from a prior of 99.99% to a posterior of 91%.

Note that the posterior probability of the defendant not being the source of the DNA is very different from the random match probability of 1 in 1,000. The incorrect assumption that the two probabilities $P(\text{not } H|E)$ and $P(E|\text{not } H)$ are the same characterizes what is known as the *prosecutor's fallacy* (or error of transposed conditional). A prosecutor might state, for example, that "the probability the defendant was not the source of this evidence is one in a thousand," when actually it is 91%. This fallacy of probabilistic reasoning has affected numerous cases,[22] but can always be avoided by a basic understanding of Bayes' theorem. A closely related error of probabilistic reasoning is the *defendant's fallacy*, whereby the defence argues that since $P(\text{not } H|E)$ is still low after taking into account the prior and the evidence, the evidence should be ignored.

Unfortunately, people without statistical training find Bayes' theorem both difficult to understand and counter-intuitive.[23] Legal professionals are also concerned that the use of Bayes requires us to assign prior probabilities. In fact, an equivalent formulation of Bayes (called the "odds" version of Bayes) enables us to interpret the value of evidence E without having to consider the prior probability of H. Specifically, this version of Bayes tells us that the posterior odds of H are the prior odds of H times the *likelihood ratio*:

$$\frac{P(H|E)}{P(\textit{not } H|E)} = \frac{P(H)}{P(\textit{not } H)} \times \frac{P(E|H)}{P(E|\textit{not } H)}$$

where the likelihood ratio (LR) is simply the prosecution likelihood of E divided by the defence likelihood of E, i.e.

$$\frac{P(E|H)}{P(E|\textit{not } H)}$$

In the example in Figure 18.1 the prosecution likelihood for the DNA match evidence is 1, while the defence likelihood is 1/1,000. So the LR is 1,000. This means that, whatever the prior odds were in favor of the prosecution hypothesis, the posterior odds must increase by a factor of 1,000 as a result of seeing the evidence. In general, if the LR is larger than one, then the evidence results in an increased posterior probability of H (with higher values leading to the posterior probability getting closer to 1), while if it is less than 1 it results in

---

[22] Balding and Donnelly 1994; Fenton and Neil 2011.
[23] Casscells and Graboys 1978; Cosmides and Tooby 1996.

a decreased posterior probability of H (and the closer it gets to zero the closer the posterior probability gets to zero). If the LR is equal to 1 then E offers no value since it leaves the posterior probability as unchanged.

The LR is, therefore, an important and meaningful measure of the probative value of evidence. In our example, the fact that the DNA match evidence had an LR of 1,000 meant the evidence was highly probative in favor of the prosecution. But as impressive as that sounds, whether or not it is sufficient to convince you of which hypothesis is true still depends entirely on the prior $P(H)$. If $P(H)$ is, say 0.5 (so the prior odds are evens 1:1), then a LR of 1,000 results in posterior odds of 1,000 to 1 in favor of H. That may be sufficient to convince a jury that H is true. But if $P(H)$ is very low—as in our example (9,999 to 1 against)—then the same LR of 1,000 results in posterior odds that still strongly favor the defense hypothesis by 10 to 1.

It is important to note that the properties of the LR (as a meaningful measure of probative value of evidence) depend both on Bayes' theorem and the assumption that the defence hypothesis is the negation of the prosecution hypothesis (i.e., the hypotheses must be mutually exclusive and exhaustive). Unfortunately, in practice there is much misunderstanding of LR by lawyers, and even by forensic experts and statisticians. An indication of the extent of the confusion can be found in one of the many responses by the latter community[24] to the RvT judgment (more on this in Section 4.3). Specifically, in the otherwise excellent position statement is the extraordinary Point 9 that asserts: "It is regrettable that the judgment confuses the Bayesian approach with the use of Bayes' Theorem. The Bayesian approach does not necessarily involve the use of Bayes' Theorem."[24]

By the "Bayesian approach" the authors are specifically referring to the use of the LR, thereby implying that the use of the LR is appropriate, while the use of Bayes' theorem may not be.

Notwithstanding these misunderstandings (and other problems with the LR that we discuss in Section 4.2) the fact that it does determine the probative value of evidence and can be calculated without reference to the prior probability of H, has meant that it has become a potentially powerful application of Bayesian reasoning in the law. Indeed, its use is a core recommendation in guidelines.[25] Forcing expert witnesses to consider both the prosecution and defense likelihood of their evidence—instead of just one or the other—also avoids most common cases of the prosecutor's fallacy.

While Bayes' theorem provides a natural match to intuitive legal reasoning in the case of a single hypothesis H and a single piece of evidence E, practical legal arguments normally involve multiple hypotheses and pieces of evidence with complex causal dependencies. For example, even the simplest case of DNA evidence, strictly speaking, involves three unknown hypotheses and two pieces of evidence with the causal links shown in Figure 18.2[26] once we take account of the possibility of different types of DNA collection and testing errors.[27]

Moreover, there are further crucial hypotheses not shown in Figure 18.2[28] such as: "Defendant was at the scene of the crime" and the ultimate hypothesis "Defendant committed the crime." These are only omitted here because, whereas the law might accept a

[24] Aitken et al. 2011.
[25] See E.N.F.S.I.; Puch-Solis et al. 2012.
[26] Dawid and Mortera 1998; Fenton, Neil, and Hsu 2014.
[27] Koehler 1993; Thompson, Taroni, and Aitken 2003.
[28] A full version of the model is provided in the supplementary material to Fenton, Neil, and Berger 2016.

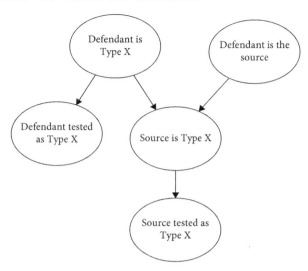

Figure 18.2 Bayesian network for DNA match evidence. Each node has states *true* or *false*

statistical or forensic expert reasoning probabilistically about the source of the forensic evidence, it is presupposed that any probabilistic reasoning about the ultimate hypothesis is the province of the trier of fact, i.e., the judge and/or the jury.

With or without the additional hypotheses, Figure 18.2 is an example of a BN. As in the simple case of Figure 18.1, to perform the correct Bayesian inference once we observe evidence we need to know the prior probabilities of the nodes without parents and the conditional prior probabilities of the nodes with parents. Assuming that it is possible to obtain suitable estimates of these prior probabilities, the bad news is that, even with a small number of nodes, the calculations necessary for performing correct probabilistic inference are far too complex to be done manually. Moreover, until the late 1980s there were no known efficient computer algorithms for doing the calculations. This is the reason why, until relatively recently, only rather trivial Bayesian arguments with over simplistic assumptions could realistically be used in legal reasoning.

However, algorithmic breakthroughs in the late 1980s made it possible to perform correct probabilistic inference efficiently for a wide class of BNs and tools.[29] These algorithms have subsequently been incorporated into widely available graphical toolsets that enable users without any statistical knowledge to build and run BN models.[30] Moreover, further algorithmic breakthroughs have enabled us to model an even broader class of BNs, namely those including numeric nodes with arbitrary statistical distributions.[31] These breakthroughs are potentially crucial for modelling legal arguments. Yet, despite widely documented examples of their use for legal arguments[32] BNs have been largely ignored. Moreover, even many experts who propose the Bayesian approach for legal reasoning continue to oversimplify their

[29] Pearl 1988; Lauritzen, S. L. and Spiegelhalter, D. J. (1988). "Local Computations with Probabilities on Graphical Structures and their Application to Expert Systems (with Discussion)," Journal of the Royal Statistical Society. Series B (Methodological) 50 (2), pp. 157–224.
[30] Agena.
[31] Neil, Tailor, and Marquez 2007.
[32] Fenton and Neil 2018; Biedermann and Taroni 2006; Dawid, Mortera, and Vicard 2007.

underlying legal arguments in order to ensure the computations can be carried out manually. This is an unnecessary and debilitating constraint on the use of Bayes.

4. Addressing Relevant Objections

4.1 Problem of Unconstrained Priors

The problem of how we attain priors that are not arbitrary and potentially biased is well covered in the chapter by Dahlman and Kolflaath in this volume.[33] Here we focus on how to avoid the problem of wildly different priors: consider, for example, the extremes whereby one juror assumes that the prior probability a defendant is guilty is 1/2 while another assumes it is 1/(7 billion) (i.e., one over the world population). Then, whereas a minimal amount of evidence supporting the prosecution hypothesis would lead to a sufficiently high posterior probability of guilt for the first juror, even enormous amounts of evidence would not be sufficient for the second juror. The novel *opportunity prior* approach[34] can—in many real-world cases—address this problem.

When the police suspect someone of a crime, one of the first questions they ask is where the suspect was at the time of the crime. This question is very diagnostic: if the suspect can show he was elsewhere, then he is ruled out. If, however, the police can show the suspect was at the crime scene, then he is ruled into a relatively small set of possible perpetrators.

Establishing opportunity is thus critical at the investigative phase. But the same logic applies at later stages of the legal process, in particular, when the suspect is charged with the crime, and we must evaluate the strength of evidence against him. Information about the suspect's whereabouts in relation to the crime scene provides a starting point for building a case, before other evidence is presented. A key point, frequently neglected in formal analyses of evidence, is that case-specific information allows us to assess the probative value of opportunity evidence.

Consider an idealized case first. Suppose we know that only five people were in a room when an item of jewelry was stolen from a small boutique. Before considering any other information, the only rational (and fair) judgment is to assign each person a probability of 1/5 of committing the theft. More generally, for n people in the room, each is assigned a probability of $1/n$. Note this does not mean that we think each person has an equal propensity to commit the crime; but just that given our current state of knowledge we should assign an equal probability to each potential perpetrator; anything else would be illogical and unfair.

The ease of estimating n depends on what is known about the location and time of the crime. For a crime committed at a solitary place and during a brief time window, we can safely assume there was only a small number of possible perpetrators. By contrast, a crime in a busy high street will include a far larger number of people. Often it will be possible to get a rough estimate or establish reasonable upper bounds for n. A crucial point here is that we are estimating the number of people who were *actually* at the crime scene at the critical time, not the number of people who *could have been* there. Thus, even if we do not know who the other people are (and might never discover this), we can still assign our suspect, who was definitely at the crime scene, a probability of $1/n$. In other words, even if many

---

33 Dahlman and Kolflaath, "The Problem of the Prior in Criminal Trials," ch. 19, in this volume.
34 Fenton et al. 2019; Lagnado 2021.

individuals *could have* been one of the other *n*-1 at the crime scene, our suspect has probability 1/*n* regardless.

This analysis does not simply see opportunity as a necessary condition for guilt. Instead, it can set a reasonable (and fair) initial probability—informed by the spatiotemporal circumstances of the case, but before considering other evidence. In cases where the suspect's presence at the crime scene is uncontested, this is a major advantage because we can set the prior at 1/*n*. For example, in a murder case where a man was accused of killing his wife, the fact that he was definitely with her when she was violently killed, and it was established that at most only three other people were in the vicinity, justifies an initial probability of about 1/4 based on this opportunity information.[35]

In many cases, however, the suspect denies being at the crime scene at the time of the crime. To apply our analysis to these contexts we introduce the notion of the *extended crime scene,* which is based on the closest proven location and time for the suspect from which he could still have got to the crime scene to commit the crime. This can include a location before or after the crime was committed. For example, it might be accepted that the suspect was at a location two miles from the crime scene, one hour after the crime took place. We use this location and time to generate the extended crime scene, which will cover all people who were in the area at most two miles from the crime and at most one hour after the crime. This gives us the number of possible perpetrators *N*, which includes the suspect. Based on this extended crime scene we assign a probability for the suspect committing the crime of *n*/*N* (as there are *n* people at the crime scene).

Estimating the number of people in the extended crime scene can be difficult, especially if the agreed locations and times are distant from the crime scene. But in many cases we can set reasonable upper limits on *N*, and thus reasonable lower bounds on the prior probability of the suspect being at the crime scene. Moreover, we can accommodate uncertainty in these estimates by using distributions rather than point values for *n* and *N*.

In sum, the opportunity prior helps us incorporate crucial information about the spatiotemporal location of the suspect in relation to the crime scene—something that detectives do intuitively. The analysis quantifies the value of this information, rather than simply concluding that the suspect "might" have been at crime scene. It also shows us how to combine opportunity with other evidence in the case. There is plenty of scope to debate the numbers, and sometimes priors will be extremely low. But some inferential edge, however small, is better than none. Moreover, this approach also helps avoid the common objection of "double-counting" statistical information about priors discussed in Section 1.

4.2 Objections to Bayes Caused by Misunderstandings and Misuse of the Likelihood Ratio Method

Alongside the prior probabilities the other main component in the Bayesian framework is the probabilistic evaluation of evidence. In simple cases (such as the two node BN in Figure 18.1) we showed in Section 3 that the strength of evidence is captured by the LR, and this is the basis for the main approach to evaluating evidence. But there are several challenges to this

---

[35] Fenton et al. 2020.

approach. For example, some commentators reject the probabilistic approach wholesale, claiming that the use of the LR to evaluate evidence leads to legal paradoxes.[36] However, it was shown[37] that these paradoxes are simply the result of a flawed approach to the use of the LR—most typically because it forces multiple different related hypotheses and pieces of evidence into a 2-node BN model rather than one which separates out the different hypotheses and evidence. In this section we identify the key problems with the LR approach which compromise the use of Bayes and describe how these problems are avoided.

4.3 The Notion that the LR can Only be Used for "Statistically Valid" Evidence

A 2010 UK Court of Appeal Ruling—known as RvT[38]—dealt the use of Bayes and the LR a devastating blow. The ruling quashed a murder conviction in which the prosecution had relied heavily on footwear matching evidence presented using Bayes and the LR. What certainly contributed to the ruling was the poorly presented evidence by the footwear expert; in particular, he did not make clear that likelihood ratios for different aspects of the evidence were multiplied together to arrive at a composite likelihood ratio. However, the ruling asserted: "We are satisfied that in the area of footwear evidence, no attempt can realistically be made in the generality of cases to use a formula to calculate the probabilities. The practice has no sound basis .... It is quite clear that outside the field of DNA (and possibly other areas where there is a firm statistical base) this court has made it clear that Bayes' theorem and likelihood ratios should not be used."

Numerous articles have criticized the ruling.[39] In fact, the judge's assertions essentially repeat the fundamental fallacy addressed in Section 1, which assumes that if probabilities are in any way subjective, then it is impossible to make rational and consistent conclusions from them. But, as explained elsewhere,[40] the idea that the statistics associated with DNA match evidence is somehow purely objective, while the statistics associated with footwear match evidence is purely subjective is a myth. All probabilities based on statistical data rely on multiple subjective assumptions about the interpretation and source of the data. Unfortunately, the ruling is having a devastating impact on the way some forensic evidence is presented with experts deliberately concealing or obfuscating their calculations.

4.4 LR Models are Inevitably Over-Simplified

The simplest and most common use of the LR—involving a single piece of forensic trace evidence for a single source level hypothesis—can actually be very complex, as already explained in Section 2 (where Figure 18.2, rather than Figure 18.1, is the correct model). Even if we completely ignore much of the context (including issues of reliability of trace sample collection/storage and potential testing errors) the LR may still be difficult or even

---

[36] Park et al. 2010.
[37] de Zoete et al. 2019.
[38] *R v. T, EWCA Crim 2439*, Case No 2007/03644/D2 (2010).
[39] Aitken et al. 2011; Berger et al. 2011; Morrison 2012; Nordgaard, Hedell, and Ansell 2012; Redmayne et al. 2011; Robertson, Vignaux, and Berger 2011; Sjerps and Berger 2012.
[40] Fenton et al. 2020.

278 BAYESIANISM: OBJECTIONS AND REBUTTALS

impossible to elicit because somehow we have to factor in to the hypothesis Hd (defendant is not the source of the DNA trace) every person other than the defendant who could have been the source (potentially every other person in the world).[41] For example, P(E|Hr) is much higher than $P(E|Hu)$ where Hr is the hypothesis "a close relative of the defendant is the source of the trace" and Hu is the hypothesis "a totally unrelated person is the source."

This means that, in reality, Hd is made up of multiple hypotheses that are difficult to articulate and quantify. The standard pragmatic solution (which has been widely criticized[42]) is to assume that Hd represents a "random person unrelated to the defendant." But not only does this raise concerns about the homogeneity of the population used for the random match probabilities, it also requires separate assumptions about the extent to which relatives can be ruled out as suspects.

It is not just the hypotheses that may need to be "decomposed." In practice, even an apparently "single" piece of evidence E actually comprises multiple separate pieces of evidence, and it is only when the likelihoods of these separate pieces of evidence are considered that correct conclusions about probative value of the evidence can be made.

Consider the evidence E: "tiny matching DNA trace found." Suppose that the DNA trace has a profile with a random match probability of 1/100 (such relatively "high" match probabilities are common in low template samples). Assuming H_p and H_d are the prosecution and defense hypotheses respectively, it would be typical to assume that

$$P(E|H_p) = 1$$

and that

$$P(E|H_d) = 1/100$$

leading to a LR of 100, thus indicating quite strong support for the prosecution hypothesis. However, the evidence E actually comprises two separate pieces of evidence:

- E1: *tiny* DNA trace found; and
- E2: DNA trace found matches defendant.

In particular, this makes clear the relevance of finding only a tiny trace of DNA when larger amounts would be expected to have been left by the person who committed the crime. So, actually $P(E|H_p)$ will be much smaller than one, because we would expect substantial amounts of DNA to be found, rather than just a tiny trace. To elicit all the necessary individual likelihood values, and to carry out the correct Bayesian calculations needed for the overall LR in situations such as this, we again need to turn to BNs as shown in Figure 18.3.

---

[41] Balding and Steele 2015; Nordgaard, Hedell, and Ansell 2012.
[42] Balding and Steele 2015.

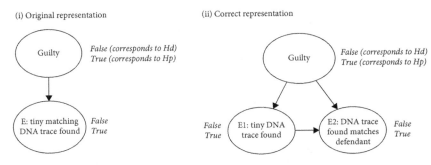

Figure 18.3 Modelling complex evidence in a BN

The oversimplistic model fails to capture the relevance of the fact that the trace was tiny. If the defendant were guilty it is expected that the investigator would have found significant traces of DNA. The significance of the tiny trace is properly captured by separating out $E1$ in the second model. A reasonable conditional probability table for $E1$ is shown in Table 18.1.

Table 18.1 Conditional Probability Table for $E1$

Guilty	False	True
Fales	0.5	0.999
True	0.5	0.0010

The conditional probability table for $E2$ shown in Table 18.2 uses the same random match probability information as was used in the oversimplified model.

Table 18.2 Conditional Probability Table for $E2$

Guilty	False		True	
E1: tiny DNA trace found	False	True	False	True
False	1.0	0.99	1.0	0.0
True	0.0	0.01	0.0	1.0

Calculating the overall LR manually in this case is much more complex, so we go directly to the result of running the model in a BN tool with $E2$ set as true (and the prior odds of guilt set at 50:50 again). This is shown in Figure 18.4. The LR is just the probability of guilty divided by the probability of not guilty, which is 0.2. So the evidence supports the defence hypothesis rather than the prosecution.

This example also indicates the importance of taking account of absence of evidence.

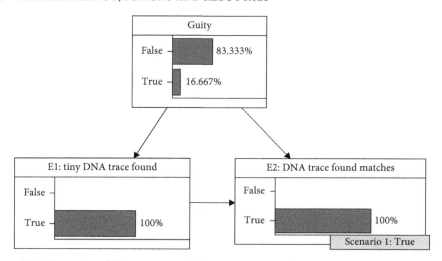

Figure 18.4 Posterior odds in correct model

We note that a frequent objection against Bayesianism is that it is practically impossible to consider *all* of the probabilistic dependencies between pieces of evidence in a case.[43] We accept that a BN does not capture the whole complexity and, like all reasoning, Bayesian reasoning makes some simplifications. But the advantage of the Bayesian approach is that it is much more nuanced and rigorous than the alternatives proposed such as relative plausibility.[44]

4.5 Bayes is Too Complex for Lawyers and Juries to Understand

This is essentially the argument that was used in *R v. Adams*.[45] This was a rape case in which the only prosecution evidence was that the defendant's DNA matched that of a swab sample taken from the victim. The defense evidence included an alibi and the fact that the defendant did not match the victim's description of her attacker. At trial the prosecution had emphasized the very low random match probability (one in 200 million) of the DNA evidence. The defense argued that if statistical evidence was to be used in connection with the DNA evidence, it should also be used in combination with the defense evidence and that Bayes' theorem was the only rational method for doing this. The defense called a Bayesian expert (Professor Peter Donnelly) who explained how, with Bayes, the posterior probability of guilt was much lower when the defense evidence was incorporated. The appeal rested on whether the judge misdirected the jury as to the evidence in relation to the use of Bayes and left the jury unguided as to how that theorem could be used in properly assessing the

---

[43] See Allen and Pardo, "Inference to the Best Explanation, Relative Plausibility, and Probability," ch. 14, in this volume.

[44] Ibid.

[45] *R v. Adams* [1996] 2 *Cr App R 467*, [1996] *Crim* LR 898, CA, and *R v. Adams* [1998] 1 Cr App R 377. It is discussed in detail in Donnelly 2005.

statistical and non-statistical evidence in the case. The appeal was successful and a retrial was ordered, although the court was scathing in its criticism of the way Bayes was presented, stating: "The introduction of Bayes' theorem into a criminal trial plunges the jury into inappropriate and unnecessary realms of theory and complexity deflecting them from their proper task. The task of the jury is . . . to evaluate evidence and reach a conclusion not by means of a formula, mathematical or otherwise, but by the joint application of their individual common sense and knowledge of the world to the evidence before them."

At the retrial it was agreed by both sides that the Bayesian argument should be presented in such a way that the jury could perform the calculations themselves (a mistake in our view). The jury were given a detailed questionnaire to complete to enable them to produce their own prior likelihoods, and calculators to perform the necessary Bayesian calculations from first principles. Adams was, however, again convicted. A second appeal was launched and was also unsuccessful, with the court not only scathing about the use of Bayes in the case but essentially ruling against its future use.

The ruling against the use of Bayes in *R v. Adams* is especially damaging because it rules against the very use where Bayes has the greatest potential to simplify and clarify complex legal arguments. The fact that the complex presentation of Bayes in the case was (rightly) considered to be its death knell is especially regrettable given that in 1996 the tools for avoiding this complexity were already widely available.

The idea that different pieces of (possibly competing) evidence about a hypothesis H are combined to update our belief in H is central to all legal proceedings. Yet, although Bayes is the perfect formalism for this type of reasoning, it is difficult to find *any* well reported examples of the successful use of Bayes in combining diverse evidence in a real case. While the spectacular failure in the above *Adams* case has not helped, a major reason for this is to do with the lack of awareness of tools for building and running BN models that enable us to do Bayesian inference for legal arguments involving diverse related evidence.

Despite the multiple publications applying BNs to legal arguments, even many Bayesian statisticians are either unaware of these breakthroughs or are reluctant to use the available technology. Yet, if one tries to use Bayes theorem "manually" to represent a legal argument one of the following results is inevitable:

1. To ensure the calculations can be easily computed manually, the argument is made so simple that it no longer becomes an adequate representation of the legal problem.
2. A non-trivial model is developed and the Bayesian calculations are written out and explained from first principles and the net result is to totally bemuse legal professionals and jurors. This was, of course, the problem in *R v. Adams*.[46]

The manual approach is also not scalable since it would otherwise mean having to explain and compute one of the BN inference algorithms, which even professional mathematicians find daunting.

---

[46] For other examples where statisticians provide unnecessarily complex arguments, see Fenton, Neil, and Berger 2016.

5. Conclusions and the Way Forward

That fallacies of probabilistic reasoning (such as the prosecutor's fallacy) continue to be made in legal proceedings is a sad indictment of the lack of impact made by statisticians in general (and Bayesians in particular) on legal practitioners. This is despite the fact that the issue has been extensively documented by multiple authors[47] and has even been dealt with in populist books.[48] There is almost unanimity among the authors of these works that a basic understanding of Bayesian probability is the key to avoiding probabilistic fallacies. Indeed, Bayesian reasoning is explicitly recommended in several works,[49] although there is less of a consensus on whether or not experts are needed in court to present the results of all but the most basic Bayesian arguments.[50]

We argue that the way forward is to use BNs to present probabilistic legal arguments since this approach avoids much of the confusion surrounding both the over-simplistic LR and more complex models represented formulaically and computed manually. Unfortunately, it is precisely because BNs are assumed by legal professionals to be "part of those same problems" that they have made little impact. Yet, ultimately, any use of probability—even if it is based on frequentist statistics—relies on a range of subjective assumptions. The objection to using subjective priors may also be calmed by the fact that it may be sufficient to consider a range of probabilities, rather than a single value for a prior. BNs are especially suited to this since it is easy to change the priors and do sensitivity analysis.[51].

A basic strategy for presenting BNs to legal professionals is based on the *calculator analogy*.[52] This affirms that since we now have efficient and easy-to-use BN tools there should be no more need to explain the Bayesian calculations in a complex argument than there should be any need to explain the thousands of circuit level calculations used by a regular calculator to compute a long division.

Only the simplest Bayesian legal argument (a single hypothesis and a single piece of evidence) can be easily computed manually; inevitably we need to model much richer arguments involving multiple pieces of possibly linked evidence. While humans must be responsible for determining the prior probabilities (and the causal links) for such arguments, it is simply wrong to assume that humans must also be responsible for understanding and calculating the revised probabilities that result from observing evidence. The Bayesian calculations quickly become impossible to do manually, but any BN tool enables us to do these calculations instantly.

The results from a BN tool can be presented using a range of assumptions including different priors. What the legal professionals (and perhaps even jurors if presented in court) should never have to think about is how to perform the Bayesian inference calculations. They do, of course, have to consider the prior assumptions needed for any BN model. But

---

[47] See, e.g., Kaye 2001; Anderson, Schum, and Twining 2005; Edwards 1991; Evett 1995; Fenton and Neil 2000; Jowett 2001; Balding and Donnelly 1994; Koehler 1993; Redmayne 1995; Thompson, and Schumann 1987; Freckelton and Selby 2005; Murphy 2003.

[48] Gigerenzer 2002; Haigh 2003.

[49] e.g., Dahlman 2020; Evett 1995; Finkelstein and Levin 2001; Good 2001; Redmayne 1995; Saks and Thompson 2003; Robertson and Vignaux 1995.

[50] Robertson and Vignaux 1995.

[51] Fenton and Neil 2018.

[52] It is described in detail in Fenton and Neil 2011.

these are precisely what have to be considered in weighing up any legal argument. The BN simply makes this all explicit rather than hidden, which is another clear benefit of the approach.

We recognize that there are significant technical challenges to overcome to make the construction of BNs for legal reasoning easier, but the lack of a systematic, repeatable method for modelling legal arguments as BNs has been addressed by using common idioms and an approach for building complex arguments from these.

Proper use of Bayesian reasoning has the potential to improve the efficiency, transparency, and fairness of criminal and civil justice systems. It can help experts formulate accurate and informative opinions; help courts determine admissibility of evidence; help identify which cases should be pursued; and help lawyers to explain, and jurors to evaluate, the weight of evidence during a trial. It can also help identify errors and unjustified assumptions entailed in expert opinions.

References

Agena. "AgenaRisk: Bayesian Network Software for Risk Analysis and Decision Making." Available at http://www.agenarisk.com (Accessed: March 31, 2021).

Aitken, Colin, Charles E. H. Berger, John S. Buckleton, Christophe Champod et al. (2011). "Expressing Evaluative Opinions: A Position Statement," *Science and Justice*, 51(1): 43–9.

Anderson, T., Schum,. D. A., and Twining, W. (2005). *Analysis of Evidence.* Cambridge: Cambridge University Press.

Balding, D. J. and Donnelly, P. (1994). "The Prosecutor's Fallacy and DNA Evidence," *Criminal Law Review*, 1: 711–21.

Balding, D. J. and Steele, C. D. (2015). *Weight-of-Evidence for Forensic DNA Profiles.* Second edition. Chichester: Chichester: John Wiley & Sons.

Berger, D. (2014). *Improving Legal Reasoning using Bayesian Probability Methods.* Queen Mary University of London.

Berger, C. E. H. et al. (2011). "Evidence Evaluation: A Response to the Court of Appeal Judgement in R v T," *Science and Justice*, 51: 43–9.

Biedermann, A. and Taroni, F. (2006). "Bayesian Networks and Probabilistic Reasoning about Scientific Evidence when there is a Lack of Data," *Forensic Science International*, 157(2–3): 163–7.

Casscells, W. and Graboys, T. B. (1978). "Interpretation by Physicians of Clinical Laboratory Results," *New England Journal of Medicine*, 299(18): 999–1001.

Cook, R. et al. (1998). "A Hierarchy of Propositions: Deciding Which Level to Address in Casework," *Science and Justice*, 38(4): 231–9.

Cosmides, L. and Tooby, J. (1996). "Are Humans Good Intuitive Statisticians After All? Rethinking some Conclusions from the Literature on Judgment under Uncertainty," *Cognition*, 58(1): 1–73.

Dahlman, C, (2020). "De-Biasing Legal Fact-Finders with Bayesian Thinking," *Topics in Cognitive Science*, 12(4): 1115–31.

Dawid, A. P. and Mortera, J. (1998). "Forensic Identification with Imperfect Evidence," *Biometrika*, 85(4): 835–49. Available at http://biomet.oxfordjournals.org/content/85/4/835.short (Accessed: March 31, 2021).

Dawid, A. P., Mortera, J., and Vicard, P. (2007) "Object-Oriented Bayesian Networks for Complex Forensic DNA Profiling Problems," *Forensic Science International*, 169(2–3): 195–205.

de Zoete, J. Norman Fenton, Takao Noguchi, David Lagnado. (2019). "Resolving the 'Probabilistic Paradoxes in Legal Reasoning' with Causal Bayesian Models," *Science & Justice*, 59(4), 367–79.

Donnelly, P. (2005). "Appealing Statistics," *Significance*, 2(1): 46–8.

Edwards, W. (1991). "Influence Diagrams, Bayesian Imperialism, and the Collins Case: An Appeal to Reason," *Cardozo Law Review*, 13: 1025–74.

E.N.F.S.I. "ENFSI Guideline for Evaluative Reporting in Forensic Science." Available at http://enfsi.eu/wp-content/uploads/2016/09/m1_guideline.pdf (Accessed: March 31, 2021).

Evett, I. W. (1995). "Avoiding the Transposed Conditional," *Science and Justice*, 35(2): 127–31.

Faigman, D. L. and Baglioni, A. J. (1988). "Bayes' Theorem in the Trial Process," *Law and Human Behavior*, 12(1): 1–17. Available at http://dx.doi.org/10.1007/BF01064271 (Accessed: March 31, 2021).

Fenton, N., , Allan Jamieson, Sara Gomes, Martin Neil et al. (2020) "On the Limitations of Probabilistic Claims about the Probative Value of Mixed DNA Profile Evidence," Cornell University. Available at http://arxiv.org/abs/2009.08850 (Accessed: March 31, 2021).

Fenton, N. E. et al. (2014). "When 'Neutral' Evidence still has Probative Value (with Implications from the Barry George Case)," *Science and Justice*, 54(4): 274–87.

Fenton, N. E., Berger D., Lagnado, D., Neil, M. (2019). "The Opportunity Prior: A Proof-Based Prior for Criminal Cases," *Law, Probability and Risk*, 18: 237–53.

Fenton, N. E. and Neil, M. (2011). "Avoiding Legal Fallacies in Practice using Bayesian Networks," *Australian Journal of Legal Philosophy*, 36: 114–51.

Fenton, N. E. and Neil, M. (2018). *Risk Assessment and Decision Analysis with Bayesian networks*. Second edition., Boca Raton, FL: CRC Press.

Fenton, N. E. and Neil, M. (2000). "The Jury Fallacy and the Use of Bayesian Nets to Simplify Probabilistic Legal Arguments," *Mathematics Today* (Bulletin of the IMA), 36: 180–87.

Fenton, N. E., Neil, M., and Berger, D. (2016). "Bayes and the Law," *Annual Review of Statistics and Its Application*, 3: 51–7. Available at http://www.annualreviews.org/doi/pdf/10.1146/annurev-statistics-041715-033428 (Accessed: March 31, 2021).

Fenton, N. E., Neil, M., and Hsu, A. (2014). "Calculating and Understanding the Value of any Type of Match Evidence when there are Potential Testing Errors," *Artificial Intelligence and Law*, 22: 1–28.

Finkelstein, M. O. (2009). *Basic Concepts of Probability and Statistics in the Law*. Berlin: Springer Science & Business Media.

Fienberg, S. E. (2011). "Bayesian Models and Methods in Public Policy and Government Settings," *Statistical Science*, 26(2): 212–26.

Fienberg, S. E. and Finkelstein, M. O. (1996). "Bayesian Statistics and the Law," in J. M. Bernardo et al. (eds.), *Bayesian Statistics*, 129–46. Oxford: Oxford University Press.

Finkelstein, M. O. and Levin, B. A. (2001). *Statistics for Lawyers*. Berlin: Springer.

Forrest, A. R. (2003). "Sally Clark—a Lesson for us All," *Science & Justice*, 43(2): 63–4.

Freckelton, I. and Selby, H. (2005). *Expert Evidence: Law, Practice, Procedure and Advocacy*. Third edition. Sydney: Lawbook Co. .

Gastwirth, J. L. (2000). "Statistical Science in the Courtroom." Springer-Verlag New York, Inc.

Gigerenzer, G. (2002). *Reckoning with Risk: Learning to Live with Uncertainty*. New York: Penguin Books.

Gillies, D. (2000). "Varieties of Propensity," *British Journal for the Philosophy of Science*, 51(4): 807–.

Good, P. I. (2001). *Applying Statistics in the Courtroom: A New Approach for Attorneys and Expert Witnesses*. Boca Raton, FL: CRC Press .

Haigh, J. (2003). *Taking Chances: Winning with Probability*. Second edition..New York: Oxford University Press.

Hill, R. (2005). "Reflections on the Cot Death Case," *Significance*, 2(1):13–16.

Jowett, C. (2001). "Lies, Damned Lies, and DNA Statistics: DNA Match Testing. Bayes' Theorem, and the Criminal Courts," *Medicine, Science and the Law*, 41(3): 194–205.

Kaye, D. H. (2001). "Two Fallacies about DNA Databanks for Law Enforcement," *Brooklyn Law Review*, 67(10): 179–206.

Kaye, D. H. (2007). "Revisiting 'Dreyfus': A More Complete Account of a Trial by Mathematics," *Minnesota Law Review*, 91(3): 825–35. Available at http://ssrn.com/abstract=944244 (Accessed: March 31, 2021).

Koehler, J. J. (1992). "Probabilities in the Courtroom: An Evaluation of the Objections and Policies," in D. K. Kagehiro and W. S. Laufer (eds.), *Handbook of Psychology and Law*. Berlin: Springer-Verlag.

Koehler, J. J. (1993). "Error and Exaggeration in the Presentation of DNA Evidence at Trial," *Jurimetrics*, 34: 21–39.

Koehler, J. J. (1993). "The Base Rate Fallacy Myth," *Psycoloquy*, 4(49): Art.1.

Lagnado, D. A. (2021). *Explaining the Evidence*. Cambridge: Cambridge University Press.

Lauritzen, S. L. and Spiegelhalter, D. J. (1988). "Local Computations with Probabilities on Graphical Structures and their Application to Expert Systems (with Discussion)," Journal of the Royal Statistical Society. Series B (Methodological) 50 (2), pp. 157–224.

Meester, R. et al. (2007). "On the (Ab)Use OS Statistics in the Legal Case against the Nurse Lucia de B.," *Law, Probability and Risk*, 5: 233–250.

Morrison, G. M. (2012). "The Likelihood Ratio Framework and Forensic Evidence in Court: A Response to RvT," *International Journal of Evidence and Proof*, 16: 1–29.

Murphy, P. (2003). *Evidence, Proof, and Facts: A Book of Sources*. New York: Oxford University Press.

Neil, M., Tailor, M., and Marquez, D. (2007). "Inference in Hybrid Bayesian Networks using Dynamic Discretization," *Statistics and Computing*, 17: 219–33. Available at http://dx.doi.org/10.1007/s11222-007-9018-y (Accessed: March 31, 2021).

Nordgaard, A., Hedell, R., and Ansell, R. (2012). "Assessment of Forensic Findings when Alternative Explanations have Different Likelihoods—"Blame-the-Brother"—Syndrome," *Science & Justice* (Journal of the Forensic Science Society), 52(4): 226–36. Available at http://www.sciencedirect.com/science/article/pii/S1355030611001468 (Accessed: March 31, 2021).

Park, R. C., Tillers, P., Moss, F. C., Risinger, D. M., and Kaye, D. H. (2010). "Bayes Wars Redivivus—an Exchange," International Commentary on Evidence, 8 (1): Art. 1. Available at https://doi.org/10.2202/1554-4567.1115 (Accessed: March 31, 2021).

Pearl, J. (1988). *Probabilistic Reasoning in Intelligent Systems*. San Francisco, CA: Morgan Kaufmann.

Pettigrew, R. (2020). *Dutch Book Arguments*. Cambridge: Cambridge University Press.

Puch-Solis, R. et al. (2012). "Practitioner Guide No 2: Assessing the Probative Value of DNA Evidence, Guidance for Judges, Lawyers, Forensic Scientists and Expert Witnesses," Royal Statistical Society. http://www.rss.org.uk/uploadedfiles/userfiles/files/Practitioner-Guide-2-WEB.pdf

Redmayne, M. (1995). "Doubts and burdens: DNA Evidence, Probability and the Courts," *Criminal Law Review*, 464, 482."

Redmayne, M. et al. (2011). "Forensic Science Evidence in Question," *Criminal Law Review*, 5: 347–56.

Robertson, B. and Vignaux, T. (1995). *Interpreting Evidence: Evaluating Forensic Science in the Courtroom*. Chichester: John Wiley & Son.

Robertson, B. and Vignaux, T. (1998). "Don't Teach Statistics to Lawyers!" 541 https://www.stat.auckland.ac.nz/~iase/publications/2/Topic4s.pdf.

Robertson, B., Vignaux, G. A., and Berger, C. E. H. (2011). "Extending the Confusion about Bayes," *The Modern Law Review*, 74: 444–55.

Saks, M. J. and Thompson, W. C. (2003). "Assessing Evidence: Proving Facts," in D. Carson and R. Bull (eds.), *Handbook of Psychology in Legal Contexts*. Second edition. Chichester: John Wiley & Sons.

Sjerps, M. and Berger, C. (2012). "How Clear is Transparent? Reporting Expert Reasoning in Legal Cases," *Law, Probability and Risk*, 11: 317–29.

Spiegelhalter, D. J. (2013). "Court of Appeal bans Bayesian Probability (and Sherlock Holmes)." Available at http://understandinguncertainty.org/court-appeal-bans-bayesian-probability-and-sherlock-holmes (Accessed: March 31, 2021).

Thompson, W. C. and Schumann, E. L. (1987). "Interpretation of Statistical Evidence in Criminal Trials," *Law and Human Behavior*, 11(3): 167–87. Available at http://dx.doi.org/10.1007/BF01044641 (Accessed: March 31, 2021).

Thompson, W. C., Taroni, F., and Aitken, C. G. G. (2003). "How the Probability of a False Positive Affects the Value of DNA Evidence," *Journal of Forensic Sciences*, 48: 47–54.

Tillers, P. and Gottfried, J. (2007). "Case Comment—United States v. Copeland, 369 F. Supp. 2d 275 (E.D.N.Y.2005): A Collateral Attack on the Legal Maxim that Proof Beyond A Reasonable Doubt is Unquantifiable?" *Law, Probability & Risk*, 5: 135–57.

Tillers, P. and Green, E. (eds.). (1988). *Probability and Inference in the Law of Evidence: The Uses and Limits of Bayesianism*. Heidelberg: Springer.

Tribe, L. H. (1971). "Trial by Mathematics," *Harvard Law Review*, 84(6): 1329–93.

Vosk, T. and Emery, A. F. (2014). *Forensic Metrology: Scientific Measurement and Inference for Lawyers, Judges, and Criminalists*. Boca Raton, FL: CRC Press.

Ziliak, S. T. and McCloskey, D. N. (2008). *The Cult of Statistical* Significance: *How the Standard Error Costs us Jobs, Justice, and Lives.* Ann Arbor, MI: The University of Michigan Press.

Legal Cases

Nulty & Ors v. Milton Keynes Borough Council, EWCA Civ 15 (January 24, 2013)
People v Collins, 438 P 2d 33 (68 Cal 2d 319 1968)
R v. Adams [1996] 2 Cr App R 467, [1996] Crim LR 898, CA, and *R v. Adams* [1998] 1 Cr App R 377
R v. T, EWCA Crim 2439, Case No 2007/03644/D2 (2010) EWCA Crim

19

The Problem of the Prior in Criminal Trials

Christian Dahlman and Eivind Kolflaath

Q: What is a Bayesian doing in a monastery?
A: Looking for a prior.

1. Introduction

If a legal factfinder uses Bayesian updating to assess the evidence in a criminal trial, what prior probability should the factfinder start out with? This is a much-debated issue in the theory of legal evidence, known as "the problem of the prior." Advocates of the Bayesian approach to legal evidence have suggested different ways to set the prior, and opponents of the Bayesian approach have pointed to the difficulties of resolving the problem of the prior as an argument against Bayesianism in legal factfinding. In this chapter, we will discuss different solutions to the problem of the prior in light of certain requirements a solution should fulfill.

The problem of the prior poses a serious challenge to the Bayesian approach in criminal trials. Different methods for determining the prior may produce prior probabilities that diverge considerably from each other. As an example, let us assume that one way of setting the prior in a given case produces a prior probability of 1%, and that given all the evidence, the posterior probability is 99%, while a different way of setting the prior produces a prior probability of 0.1% which leads to a posterior probability of 91% given the same evidence. If the threshold set by the standard of proof is 95%, the selection of method for determining the prior decides the outcome of the case. Examples like this clearly show that the problem of the prior cannot be ignored.

As we shall see, arguments for/against different ways of setting the prior are normative arguments, based on various values of criminal procedure ("fairness," "treating like cases alike," "non-arbitrariness," "the presumption of innocence," etc.). The problem of the prior is a normative problem, not a factual matter or a problem that can be solved by Bayesian epistemology.

2. The Term "Prior Probability"

A legal factfinder in a criminal case (judge or juror) is presented with a series of evidence (witness statements, forensic reports, etc.), and must assess how these pieces of information affect the prosecutor's hypothesis that the defendant committed a certain criminal act. In the Bayesian approach to legal evidence, the factfinder takes account of each piece of

Christian Dahlman and Eivind Kolflaath, *The Problem of the Prior in Criminal Trials* In: *Philosophical Foundations of Evidence Law*. Edited by: Christian Dahlman, Alex Stein, and Giovanni Tuzet, Oxford University Press. © Christian Dahlman, Alex Stein, and Giovanni Tuzet 2021. DOI: 10.1093/oso/9780198859307.003.0020

evidence separately, by updating the probability of the prosecutor's hypothesis according to Bayes' rule. Bayesian updating transforms the prior probability, i.e., the probability of the hypothesis before a certain piece of evidence has been accounted for, into the posterior probability, i.e., the probability of the hypothesis when the evidence in question has been taken into account. In a series of Bayesian updates, the prior probability applied in each update is the probability of the hypothesis given all the evidence that has already been accounted for in previous updates. After the final update, the factfinder has arrived at the probability of the hypothesis given all the evidence presented at the trial, and checks if the probability reaches the probabilistic threshold set by the standard of proof ("beyond reasonable doubt"). This chain of updates gives rise to the question known as the problem of the prior: what shall be used as the first prior probability in the sequence?

It should be noted from the start that the problem we are talking about here is not a problem of general epistemology, but a specific problem belonging to the theory of legal evidence. The question of how to determine the prior arises also when Bayesian methodology is applied in natural science, economics, and other contexts, but our discussion is concerned with the prior in criminal trials. Criminal procedure is a normative framework that creates special constraints for the assessment of evidence. A solution to the problem of the prior in criminal trials must comply with the rules of this framework, and this makes it necessary to investigate to what extent the presumption of innocence and other rules and principles of criminal procedure create constraints for the prior. It is not sufficient that the solution is satisfactory from the viewpoint of Bayesian inference. It must also satisfy the law.

The problem of the prior is situated at the intersection of law and Bayesian inference, and this creates methodological challenges. When disciplines meet it is often the case that their terminology have some term in common, and it is assumed from both sides that the term has the same meaning in the other discipline, when it actually has a somewhat different meaning. This kind of mistake can create serious misunderstandings in cross-disciplinary discussions. It should therefore be stressed from the start that several key terms in Bayesian inference have a slightly different meaning in criminal procedure, and this includes the terms "evidence" and "prior probability." In Bayesian inference, any piece of information is "evidence" if it is relevant for the probability of the hypothesis. In criminal procedure, "evidence" is information that has been presented in court in support of a certain legal claim and is accepted as legally admissible. This means that a certain piece of information can be known to a legal factfinder and relevant for the probability of the hypothesis, but since it has not been presented in court or has been rejected as inadmissible, the legal factfinder is prohibited from taking account of it as evidence when assessing the probability of the hypothesis. To distinguish between these two meanings of the term "evidence," we will refer to the latter as "trial evidence."

This distinction has consequences for the term "prior probability." What lawyers often have in mind when they talk about the prior probability in criminal trials is the probability of the prosecutor's hypothesis at the beginning of the trial, before any trial evidence has been presented. This is consistent with the meaning of "prior probability" in Bayesian inference, as it refers to the probability of the prosecutor's hypothesis before it has been updated with trial evidence, but the procedural definition adds something more. That the trial evidence has not yet been presented means that no part of the trial evidence can be considered in setting the prior. This procedural meaning of "prior probability" adds a constraint. Suppose, for example, that the trial evidence shows that a murder took place in a locked room, where the defendant is one of four possible perpetrators and the forensic evidence points at the defendant. The standard way to use Bayesian inference in this case would be to set the prior probability at 25% and update this probability with forensic evidence, but a lawyer who uses the term "prior probability" for the probability of the prosecutor's hypothesis before the trial evidence has been presented, could very well accept the inference but would not call the probability of 25% a "prior," since it is based on trial evidence.

3. The Presumption of Innocence

The idea that the prior is the probability of the prosecutor's hypothesis at the start of the trial, before any trial evidence has been presented, is connected to the presumption of innocence, a fundamental principle of criminal procedure stating that the defendant has the right to be considered innocent until proven guilty by trial evidence. The presumption of innocence implies that the factfinder should not have presumptions about any aspect of the alleged incident that the prosecutor will need to prove. Richard Friedman quotes jury instructions from the United States stating that the indictment "is only the government's claim that a crime was committed by the defendant; it is not evidence that a crime was committed or that the defendant committed it."[1] If, for example, the defendant is charged with murder, the factfinder is not entitled to assume that the deceased was murdered before he or she is presented with evidence that proves that this is the case. In case the factfinder is convinced that it was a murder, his or her certainty must be rooted in the evidence, even if the defendant does not contest that the deceased was murdered.

The presumption of innocence sets constraints on how the prior in criminal trials may be determined. Most importantly, it forbids the factfinder to base the prior on the information imbedded in the charge against the defendant presented at the start of the trial, that the case has been selected for prosecution by the prosecutor. When prosecutors decide which cases to bring to trial they pick their strongest cases, so the information that a prosecutor has decided to prosecute makes it probable that the defendant is guilty. As an example, a factfinder who believes, based on general background knowledge of the world, that 90% of all defendants are guilty of the charge that is brought against them, would epistemically assign a 90% probability to the prosecutor's hypothesis in the case at hand, at the beginning of the trial, when the only thing the factfinder knows about the case is that the prosecutor has selected it for trial. Although this is epistemically correct, it is not allowed in legal fact-finding. As Friedman points out, "[a] basic aspect of the presumption of innocence is that the jury may not treat the fact that the defendant is on trial as itself an indication of guilt."[2] A reason why this is not allowed is to avoid *double counting*.[3] The prosecutor's decision to go to trial is based on knowledge of the evidence that the prosecutor will present at the trial, and if the factfinder overlooks to factor this in when the evidence is presented, the evidence will be counted twice against the defendant, if the prior is based on the prosecutor's decision to go to trial.

[1] Friedman 2000, 880.
[2] Ibid.
[3] Stein 1996, 36.

The presumption of innocence sets constraints on what kind of information may go into the prior. It is therefore important to investigate what these constraints are. This is a matter of law. It is a question of how the presumption of innocence should be interpreted. To what extent does the presumption of innocence have scope over the prior? And what constraints does it set? In our view, the presumption of innocence obligates the factfinder to begin the Bayesian calculus with a probability that is not influenced by trial evidence, in accordance with the procedural meaning of "prior probability." This is a "strong" interpretation of the presumption of innocence, as opposed to a "weak" interpretation which does not hinder the factfinder from setting a prior based on trial evidence, e.g., evidence that that there were only four possible perpetrators in a locked room.

The strong interpretation begs a question that needs to be addressed: if the prior cannot be based on trial evidence, on what information can it be based? The answer to this question is: the factfinder's general background knowledge about the world. Criminal procedure allows the factfinder to use common knowledge that is not specific to the case at hand, and the factfinder can use this to assess the probability of the prosecutor's hypothesis, when it is presented at the start of the trial. If, for example, the defendant is charged with drunk driving, and the factfinder has not yet been presented with any trial evidence in support of this hypothesis, setting the prior according to some background knowledge about drunk driving would be consistent with the procedural meaning of "the prior."

4. Classic Bayesian Solutions

The prosecutor's hypothesis in a criminal trial can be uncertain in two different ways that require different considerations for determining the prior. Following Dahlman, we will refer to them as *uncertainty with regard to act* and *uncertainty with regard to identity*.[4] In a case where it is clear that a certain act was committed by someone but uncertain by whom, there is uncertainty with regard to identity but not with regard to act. A typical example of such a situation is a murder case where the victim is found dead with a gunshot in his back. The opposite uncertainty appears in a case where it is unclear if the defendant committed a certain act or not, but certain that if it was committed by someone it was the defendant. In such cases there is uncertainty with regard to act but not with regard to identity, which is typically the case when the defendant is charged with domestic violence. Naturally, there are also cases where there is uncertainty with regard to act as well as (potential) uncertainty with regard to identity, for example, a case where someone fell of a rooftop and it is uncertain if it was murder or suicide.

The problem of the prior in criminal trials has been discussed by Bayesians since the 1970s and there is a classic solution to uncertainty with regard to act that we will refer to as the *frequency principle* and a classic solution to uncertainty with regard to identity that we will refer to as the 1/N-principle.

According to the frequency principle, uncertainty with regard to act is handled by treating the case as randomly picked among situations of the same kind.[5] The frequency of situations where the act in question is committed among all situations of the same kind

---

[4] Dahlman 2018.
[5] Bourmistrov-Jüttner 1987, 136; Bender and Neck 1995, 237; Schweizer 2005, 161.

is assigned as the prior probability. If, for example, the defendant is charged with drunk driving, and the frequency of drunk drivers among drivers in general is one in 500, the prior is set at 0.2%. A problem with the frequency principle is how to determine "situations of the same kind." This problem will be discussed in Section 5.

According to the 1/N-principle, uncertainty with regard to identity is handled by treating the defendant as randomly picked from the pool of possible perpetrators.[6] The prior probability is calculated as 1/N, where N is the number of possible perpetrators. If, for example, a murder has been committed on an island with 1,000 possible perpetrators, the prior is set at 0.1%. A problem with the 1/N-principle is how to determine "possible perpetrators." We will discuss this problem in Section 6.

A general objection to classical Bayesian solutions like those mentioned above is that they presuppose that the prior may be based on *certainty* regarding either act or identity. As mentioned above, there is sometimes uncertainty in both dimensions. And if we take the perspective of a factfinder who acts in accordance with the presumption of innocence, there is *always* uncertainty with regard to *both* act and identity before trial evidence has been presented. But even if we accepted the premise that a prior can presuppose certainty about the other dimension, the classical solutions are problematic, as will be shown below.

5. Problems with the Frequency Principle

As we have seen in Section 4, the frequency principle instructs factfinders to set the prior by treating the case at hand as randomly picked among cases of "the same kind." The problem with this instruction is how to determine what counts as cases of the same kind. Suppose, for example, that according to the charge presented at the start of the trial, the defendant was "driving on the E18 between Oslo and Drammen on Monday, July 28, 2020 at 4 PM intoxicated with alcohol." What reference class should be used as "situations of the same kind"? All drivers in Norway? All drivers on the E18 between Oslo and Drammen? All drivers on Monday afternoons? Some other reference class differently composed? There is no easy answer to this question, and the choice between alternatives seems arbitrary. This problem is known as the "reference class problem."

Ronald Allen and Michael Pardo have claimed that the problem of the prior is unsolvable due to the reference class problem.[7] According to Allen and Pardo, the choice between different ways to determine the prior is completely arbitrary. Such arbitrariness is incompatible with fundamental principles of criminal procedure. According to other scholars, "situations of the same kind" can be determined in a non-arbitrary way.[8] James Franklin has proposed that the reference class shall be defined by all features relevant to predict the act stated in the prosecutor's hypothesis.[9] In our example, this means that if drunk driving is just as common on the E18 between Oslo and Drammen as on other roads in Norway it is not a relevant feature for predicting drunk driving, and should therefore not delimit the reference class, and the same goes for the time of the incident and other circumstances.

---

[6] Lindley 1977, 218; Dawid 1994, 11; 2002, 83–4; Bender and Nack 1995, 236; Friedman 2000, 885.
[7] Allen and Pardo 2007, 122.
[8] Cheng 2009; Franklin 2011.
[9] Franklin 2011, 559.

Franklin's solution may be tenable in principle, but his analysis shows that there is another problem with the solution. To assess which features of the situation are relevant for predicting the act, the factfinder needs large amounts of reference data on all potentially relevant features,[10] and the factfinder typically lacks this information. In our example, the background knowledge of the typical factfinder does not include statistics about the frequency of drunk driving on various roads in Norway. Determining the reference class will therefore be mostly guess work on the part of the factfinder. This means that the problem with the frequency principle has shifted, from being "arbitrary in principle" to being "arbitrary in practice."[11] So, even if the reference class problem is solvable in theory, the frequency principle is still at odds with the fundamental notion that arbitrary decision-making is unacceptable in criminal procedure.

Moreover, there is an additional worry with the frequency principle. Suppose that there is a case where frequency of criminal acts in situations of the same kind is extremely high, say 99%. In our example, we need to imagine a situation where 99% of all relevant drivers are driving under the influence (of alcohol). Should the prior then be set at 99%? If the prior is set above the threshold probability required by the standard of proof, the defendant can be convicted on the prior alone. No trial evidence is needed. This is incompatible with the presumption of innocence, and has been discussed in the literature on legal evidence as the problem of "naked statistical evidence."[12] Situations of this kind are not very realistic, but they show that something is wrong if the defendant can be convicted without any trace evidence that connects the defendant to the act.

6. Problems with the 1/N-Principle

As we have seen in Section 4, the 1/N-principle instructs factfinders to handle uncertainty with regard to identity by setting the prior at 1/N, where N is the number of possible perpetrators. The problem with this instruction is how to determine the class of "possible perpetrators." If a crime is committed in a locked room it might be easy to determine the number of possible perpetrators, but most crimes are committed in places that do not set a natural boundary on the class of possible perpetrators. Suppose that a murder is committed in Oxford. Should the class of possible perpetrators be limited to the city of Oxford? Or the county of Oxfordshire? Or should it include the whole United Kingdom? It has often been suggested by Bayesian scholars that N should equated with the population of the country where the crime was committed. Dennis Lindley suggests, that for crimes committed in the UK, the number of possible perpetrators should be equated with "the population of these islands."[13] Since the population of the UK is roughly 65 million, this country-perimeter produces a prior probability of $1/65\,000\,0000 \approx 0.000\,000\,016$.

Setting the prior in this way is problematic for several reasons. First of all, to draw the perimeter of possible perpetrators around the United Kingdom is completely arbitrary. There is no reason to set the geographical perimeter in this way, rather than setting it more

---

[10] Franklin 2010, 17.
[11] Dahlman 2018, 19.
[12] For an overview, see Dahlman 2020.
[13] Lindley 1977, 218.

narrowly around Oxfordshire, or wider to include the whole of Europe. To equate the number of possible perpetrators with the national population has the arbitrary and strange consequence that for crimes committed in small countries like Liechtenstein, the prior will be significantly higher and thus require less evidence to reach the threshold probability required for conviction, whereas crimes committed in larger countries like the United Kingdom, would have a much lower prior (a thousand times lower, as a matter of fact), and, therefore, require so much more evidence to reach a conviction. Travelers would be advised to take the opportunity to break the law when they visit large countries, and behave by the book when they pass through small countries.

Secondly, each of the mentioned perimeters (Oxfordshire, United Kingdom, Europe) is under-inclusive for a crime committed in Oxford, since it could have been committed by someone outside these populations, for example, a Japanese tourist visiting Oxford. The only way to avoid this problem of under-inclusiveness is to include the entire world population in the class of possible perpetrators. This, however, would create a huge practical problem for crime fighting. Equating possible perpetrators with the world population (roughly seven billion people) would set the prior at 0.000 000 000 14. This is an extremely low prior, that would make it almost impossible for the prosecution to produce sufficient evidence for a conviction. As an illustration, suppose that prosecutor's evidence is supported by DNA evidence where the likelihood for a false positive is one in 100 million. Normally this would be more than sufficient to satisfy the standard of proof if it is clear that the perpetrator must be the source of the DNA sample, but if the prior is 0.000 000 000 14 it would only push the probability to 1%, and not be nearly enough for conviction.[14] To reach a probability of 95% the prosecutor must produce evidence with a likelihood ratio of 133 billion to one. This makes it virtually impossible for the prosecutor to fulfill the burden of proof. With a prior that sees the whole world as possible perpetrators, almost all guilty perpetrators would escape punishment.

One way to avoid this problem is to interpret the number of possible perpetrators not as the number of people who could theoretically have come to the place where the crime was committed, but the number of people who were actually in the area where the crime was committed when it was committed. For a crime committed in Oxford, the number of possible perpetrators would then include the number of Japanese tourists who were in the area, but not every person in Japan who theoretically could have travelled to Oxford that day. This means that the factfinder needs to assess the number of tourists on a given day, but does not require that the factfinder knows which exact individuals were there. Such an interpretation of "possible perpetrators" avoids the inclusion of the entire world population, but leads back to the problem of arbitrariness. If N is equated with the number of people who actually were "in the area where the crime was committed," we need to define this area. Is it Oxford, Oxfordshire, the United Kingdom, or some other geographical area? Again, the choice of geographical perimeter seems completely arbitrary.

An attempt to come up with a non-arbitrary perimeter, is the so-called *opportunity prior*, explored by Norman Fenton, David Lagnado, Christian Dahlman, and Martin Neil.[15] The opportunity prior delimits the area where the crime was committed on the basis of the defendant's known whereabouts. If, for example, trial evidence shows that the defendant

---

[14] $0.000\,000\,000\,14/(0.000\,000\,000\,14 + 0.999\,999\,999\,86 \times 0.000\,000\,01) \approx 0.01$.
[15] Fenton et al. 2019.

was 1 km from the crime scene one hour before the crime took place, the number of possible perpetrators according to the opportunity prior is the number of people who actually were within a perimeter of 1 km from the crime scene within a timeframe of one hour before or after the crime. The opportunity prior defines the number of possible perpetrators as the number of people who had the same opportunity or better as the defendant to commit the crime, with regard to time and space. The opportunity prior avoids the problem of including the whole world population among possible perpetrators, and does not draw the geographical perimeter arbitrarily like Lindley, since the opportunity-perimeter is based on the actual whereabouts of the defendant.

Unfortunately, the opportunity prior runs into some other problems. First of all, since it is based on evidence about the defendant's whereabouts, it is incompatible with the "strong interpretation" of the presumption of innocence that the factfinder is not allowed to base the prior probability in criminal trials on trial evidence. Secondly, the opportunity prior produces results that come across as unfair in cases where the defendant was near the crime scene, and there is an explanation for this that has nothing to do with the crime, for example, that the defendant lives or works adjacent to the crime scene. In such a case, the number of people who were just as close to the crime scene as the defendant is low, which means that the opportunity prior is quite high, and only a little further evidence is needed for conviction. In other words, the opportunity prior will seriously increase the risk that innocent people are falsely prosecuted and falsely convicted, just because they happened to be nearby when a crime was committed. This does not square well with the fundamental value of "fairness" in criminal procedure.

The idea that the number of possible perpetrators can be equated with the number of people in a certain geographical area has further problems. It is obviously over-inclusive, since it includes many individuals who for natural reasons cannot be the perpetrator, for example, infants. This is the case with all geographical areas, whether it is Lindley's country-perimeter, the opportunity-perimeter, or some other geographical perimeter (the country-perimeter is over-inclusive in this respect, and, at the same time, under-inclusive with regard to foreign nationals, as we observed above). To avoid over-inclusiveness we need to exclude people who cannot have committed the crime, and this creates further problems. What does it mean to be a "possible perpetrator"? What kinds of impossibility are we talking about when we say that someone cannot have committed the crime? Suppose that someone has been murdered by a gunshot in the back. Should the class of "possible perpetrators" exclude people who do not have access to a gun? Should it exclude people on psychological grounds, and omit people who are not mentally capable of killing another human being? At a closer look, the term "possible perpetrator" is ambiguous. It could be interpreted "epistemologically" as a person the factfinder cannot yet rule out as a perpetrator, or "ontologically" as a person who could actually have committed the crime. And the latter meaning is extremely vague and needs to be specified with regard to various potential limitations. Each of these create further practical problems. Suppose, for example, that the factfinder in a murder case decides to restrict "possible perpetrators" to people in a certain population who have access to a gun. In order to determine N, the factfinder needs knowledge about the presence of legal and illegal firearms in the population, but the typical factfinder has scarce knowledge about such matters, so the assessment will be an educated guess, at best. This means that the $1/N$-principle suffers from the same problem that we observed in the frequency principle: in practice it is extremely arbitrary. It is inevitable that such arbitrariness leads to a situation where one factfinder assigns a prior probability in a case where another factfinder would assign a much higher, or much lower, prior. This violates fundamental values in criminal procedure: like cases shall be treated alike, and assessed in an objective and non-arbitrary way.

7. Presumed Prior

A different approach to the problem of the prior in criminal trials is to have a legal rule that instructs the factfinder to presume that the prosecutor's hypothesis has a certain probability (p^*) before the trial evidence has been presented. As an example, such a rule could postulate a prior probability of 1% ($p^*=0.01$) and say that, in every criminal trial, the factfinder must begin the evaluation of the evidence under the presumption that the probability of the prosecutor's hypothesis is 1% before the trial evidence has been presented. We will refer to this solution as a *presumed prior*. It is intended to reflect uncertainty with regard to both act and identity prior to trial evidence.

In cases where trial evidence makes it immediately obvious that a crime has been committed and leaves uncertainty only with regard to identity, a factfinder who applies a presumed prior of p^* will view the defendant as one of N equally possible perpetrators, where $p^* = 1/N$, before trial evidence relevant to the perpetrator's identity has been presented. If, for example, $p^* = 0.01$, the presumed prior will force the factfinder to view the defendant as one of one hundred equally possible perpetrators, before the prosecution has presented its evidence against the defendant.

If a presumed prior is used in "locked room cases," discussed above, evidence establishing that the defendant was one of n possible perpetrators in a locked room (E), will not be used by setting the prior at $1/n$. Instead, the evidence in question will be used to update the presumed prior ($p^* = 1/N$) with a likelihood ratio where $P(E|H) = 1$, since the defendant must be one of the people in the locked room given that he is guilty, and $P(E|{\sim}H) = (n-1)/(N-1)$, since this is the probability that a randomly picked person in the initial pool of possible perpetrators happens to be one of the innocent people in the locked room. This updates the prior probability of $1/N$, to a posterior probability of $1/n$, as shown below (*Bayes' Rule* in odds).

$$\frac{1/N}{(N-1)/N} \times \frac{1}{(n-1)/(N-1)} = \frac{1}{n-1} = \frac{1/n}{(n-1)/n}$$

This means that the presumed prior will not affect the posterior probability in locked room cases. The probability of the prosecutor's hypothesis given the evidence that the defendant was one of n possible perpetrators in a locked room will be the same as if $1/n$ would have been taken as the prior, with the legally important difference that the use of a presumed prior respects the strong interpretation of the presumption of innocence, that forbids factfinders from basing the prior on trial evidence.

A presumed prior obligates the factfinder (judge or juror) to act in this institutional role as if he or she believes that the prior probability of the prosecutor's hypothesis is p^*, even if his or her private belief is different. The presumed prior may, for example, require that the factfinder presumes that the probability that the defendant was drunk driving is 1% before the evidence has been presented, although the factfinder actually believes that this probability is at least 10%. This discrepancy between private belief and institutionally imposed presumptions may appear repulsing to Bayesians who are not trained in law, but is actually typical for how the law operates.[16] The law can, for example, obligate a judge to send a defendant to prison for committing an act that the judge privately believes should not be criminalized. It is a fundamental feature of the *rule of law* that legal decision-makers put their private beliefs aside, and act as if they believe in what the law instructs.

The idea of a presumed prior has been explored and discussed in the literature on legal evidence by Alex Stein, Richard Posner, and Christian Dahlman.[17] According to Posner, the presumption of innocence should be interpreted as a presumed prior of 50:50 ($p^* = 0.5$), as it instructs legal factfinders to be unbiased before the evidence has been presented.[18] This suggestion for a presumed prior has been criticized by Friedman. As Friedman points out, to presume that it is equally probable that the defendant is guilty or innocent is not to presume innocence. A presumption of innocence must presume that it is more probable that prosecutor's hypothesis is incorrect than correct.[19] Moreover, if the presumption of innocence is taken seriously with regard to a presumed prior it should not only be interpreted to require that the prior is set somewhere under 50% ($p^* < 0.5$), but rather that a presumed prior should be set way under 50% ($p^* \ll 0.5$).

In the examples above $p^*=0.01$, but a presumed prior can, of course, be postulated differently, as long as it respects the constraint of $p^* \ll 0.5$ imposed by the presumption of innocence. To boost the presumption of innocence, the prior could, for example, be adjusted to $p^* = 0.001$ or $p^* = 0.0001$. A presumed prior can be used by the criminal justice system to adjust how strongly the presumption of innocence tips the scale in the defendant's favor at the start of the trial. Just like the threshold for conviction set by the standard of proof, a presumed prior can be used as a lever to adjust how much trial evidence is required for conviction. Lowering p^* makes it harder for the prosecution, and decreases the number of wrongful convictions, at the cost of increasing the number of wrongful acquittals. Raising p^* has the opposite effect. It makes it easier for the prosecution, which decreases the number of wrongful acquittals, and increases the number of wrongful convictions.

An important merit of the presumed prior is that it does not have the arbitrariness that riddles other ways to set the prior, either in principle or in practice. As we have seen, the $1/N$-principle turns out to be completely arbitrary in principle when the number of "possible perpetrators" is equated with the population of some arbitrary geographical area, and the frequency principle, even if it is not arbitrary in principle, becomes arbitrary in practice, as factfinders have so little knowledge about potentially relevant frequencies that their assessments become pure guess work. This problem is avoided with the presumed prior. A legal rule that instructs factfinders to presume that the prosecutor's hypothesis has a certain numeric value (p^*) does not leave any room for interpretation, and its application does not involve any arbitrary assessment of facts, as it does not call for any assessment of facts at

---

[16] Cohen 1991, 475; Ho 2008, 36; de Jong and van Lent 2016, 41.
[17] Stein 1996, 37; Posner 1999, 1514; Dahlman 2018, 25–6.
[18] Posner 1999, 1514.
[19] Friedman 2000, 874.

all. As Frederick Schauer has observed, one of the advantages with rule-governed decision-making is that rules take away judgments from people with insufficient knowledge.[20]

It could be argued that a presumed prior is also arbitrary since the number p^* is arbitrary, but such an argument would be mistaken, since the presumed prior is not directed towards a factual matter such as, say, the number of possible perpetrators. When the legislator chooses a numeric value (p^*) for the presumed prior, the legislator chooses how heavy the burden of proof is that the law lays on the prosecutor. As we have seen, this choice is based on the legislator's preference between the importance of avoiding wrongful convictions and the importance of avoiding wrongful acquittals. The law's choice for a presumed prior p^* is no more arbitrary than the law's choice of a numeric value for the threshold probability required for conviction (p^{**}).

An objection that can be launched against the presumed prior is that the prior in a criminal trial should not be detached from case-specific circumstances like opportunity. On the contrary, it should be based on such circumstances, like the opportunity prior. A reply to this objection, in defense of the presumed prior, is that the presumption of innocence in the strong interpretation, forbids the factfinder to base the prior on such circumstances, since they are trial evidence (see Section 3). It is a merit of the presumed prior that it is in line with the strong interpretation of the presumption of innocence.

Another possible objection is that a presumed prior inevitably disconnects evidence assessment from the factfinder's actual degree of belief in the prosecutor's hypothesis. The presumed prior forces the factfinder to substitute his or her genuine belief about the probability of the prosecutor's hypothesis before the trial evidence has been presented with a legal imposed presumption. Consequently, the posterior probability that the factfinder ends up with after hearing all the evidence, will not necessarily correspond to the factfinder's actual degree of belief. A posterior probability derived from a presumed prior is an "institutional probability" that the factfinder applies as if it were his or her genuine belief, when acting in the institutional role as legal factfinder. This could be viewed as a problematic consequence of a presumed prior. Should the verdict not reflect the factfinder's genuine belief in the defendant's guilt or innocence? Well, if that is the case, every ruling that requires the factfinder to disregard some piece of evidence that would have affected the probability of the prosecutor's hypothesis is equally problematic, for example, a situation where a police officer testifies that a gun was found at the defendant's house and the judge instructs the jury to disregard this information, since the officer lacked a search warrant. In our view, some differences between a factfinder's private beliefs about the world and how the factfinder is constrained by the law to view the world is a reasonable price to pay, to safeguard that legal factfinding respects fundamental values of procedural justice. We share Stein's view that "[t]o postulate prior probability normatively, as, say 1/100, would certainly be more feasible than to determine it through quasi-empirical conjectures."[21]

---

[20] Schauer 1991, 150.
[21] Stein 1996, 37.

8. Moving Beyond the Problem of the Prior

If a legal system has a rule that sets a presumed prior (p^*) and a rule that sets a threshold (p^{**}) on the posterior probability required for conviction, these two rules taken together provide a normative framework for evidence assessment where the standard of proof can be expressed as the "combined likelihood ratio" of the trial evidence (E) required to update the probability of the prosecutor's hypothesis (H) from p^* to p^{**}. The required likelihood ratio (r^*) can be derived with *Bayes' Rule*.[22]

$$p^{**} = \frac{p^* \times P(E|H)}{p^* \times P(E|H) + (1-p^*) \times P(E|\sim H)}$$

$$r^* = \frac{P(E|H)}{P(E|\sim H)} = \frac{p^{**} \times (1-p^*)}{p^* \times (1-p^{**})}$$

If, for example, $p^* = 0.01$ and $p^{**} = 0.95$, the combined likelihood ratio required for conviction becomes $0.95 \times 0.99 / 0.01 \times 0.05 = 1881$. To convict the defendant, the totality of the evidence presented at the trial must be nearly 2,000 times more likely if the defendant is guilty than if he or she is innocent.

Let us, now, ask ourselves why the presumed prior is set at 1%, rather than some other degree of probability. What reason can there be to prefer $p^* = 0.01$ over $p^* = 0.1$ or $p^* = 0.001$? The only rational answer to this question, with regard to social utility, seems to be that the likelihood ratio associated with this combination of p^* and p^{**} is assumed to maximize expected utility considering the risks of wrongful convictions and wrongful acquittals. An interesting consequence of this answer is that it actually does not matter which unique combination of p^* and p^{**} is chosen among the infinitely many combinations that would result in the same required likelihood ratio (r^*). For example, the combination $\{p^* = 0.01, p^{**} = 0.95\}$ in our example is (approximately) equivalent to the combination $\{p^* = 0.005, p^{**} = 0.90\}$, as far as the required likelihood ratio is concerned, so the outcome of the trial will be the same regardless of whether the former or the latter combination is chosen. Furthermore, since there is nothing but the associated r^* that justifies that a certain degree of probability should be assigned to the presumed prior p^* when a certain degree of probability has been assigned to the threshold for conviction p^{**}, there is no need to bother with p^* and p^{**} at all. Instead of balancing p^* and p^{**} against each other to achieve the desired likelihood ratio, one could simply ignore p^* and p^{**} altogether and focus entirely on the required likelihood ratio.

This is in line with the reconceptualization of the burden of proof proposed by Edward Cheng. In Cheng's proposal, standards of proof are understood as required likelihood ratios, instead of thresholds for posterior probabilities.[23] The standard of proof in criminal trials ("beyond reasonable doubt") could, for example, be interpreted as $r^* \geq 2000$. When all the trial evidence is taken into consideration the likelihood that the prosecutor's hypothesis is true, $P(E|H)$, must be at least 2,000 greater than the likelihood that it is false, $P(E|\sim H)$.

---

[22] Dahlman 2018, 26.
[23] Cheng 2013.

As we have seen above, this is the likelihood ratio required to update the probability of the prosecutor's hypothesis from 1% to approximately 95%. Someone might say that this r^* makes it too easy for the prosecution, and will therefore produce too many wrongful convictions. This would be an argument to raise the required likelihood ratio, for example, to $r^* \geq 10,000$. Someone else might have the opposite view, and say that a required likelihood ratio of 2,000 makes it too difficult for the prosecution, and will therefore result in too many wrongful acquittals. This would be an argument to lower the required likelihood ratio, for example to $r^* \geq 500$. We do not have a numeric proposal for r^*. The point of our analysis is rather that a required likelihood ratio handles the trade-off between wrongful convictions and wrongful acquittals, and puts an end to the "problem of the prior."

9. Concluding Remarks

As we have seen, the "problem of the prior" in criminal trials can be solved in different ways, and no solution is free from objections. Every solution compromises some fundamental value of criminal procedure. The *frequency-principle* and the *1/N-principle* makes factfinding extremely arbitrary, and conflicts with a strong interpretation of the presumption of innocence. The *presumed prior* increases the gap between the factfinder's actual beliefs about the world and what they are obligated to presume in their institutional role as legal factfinders. The choice between different solutions to the problem of the prior must therefore weigh these values against each other. It cannot be settled by purely epistemological considerations. The frequency-principle and the 1/N-principle are "fact-based" in the sense that they instruct the factfinder to base the prior on some empirical fact, e.g., the number of people in a certain geographical area, while the presumed prior is "normative" in the sense that the degree of probability is given by a legal norm, but a legal decision to apply a fact-based prior instead of the presumed prior (and to apply one particular fact-based prior instead of others) still makes a *normative choice* in sacrificing the values of procedural justice compromised by the chosen the prior. The problem of the prior in criminal trials is fundamentally a normative problem.

References

Allen, R. and Pardo, M. (2007). "The Problematic Value of Mathematical Models of Evidence," *Journal of Legal Studies*, 36: 107–40.

Bender, R. and Nack, A. (1995). *Tatsachenfeststellung vor Gericht*. Second edition. München: Beck.

Bourmistrov-Jüttner, E. (1987). *Subjektive Wahrscheinlichkeitstheorie und rationale Entscheidungstheorie in Anwendung auf die Rechtspraxis*. Ph.D thesis, Ludwigs-Maximilian Universität, München.

Cheng, E. (2009). "A Practical Solution to the Reference Class Problem," *Columbia Law Review*, 109: 2081–105.

Cheng, E. (2013). "Reconceptualizing the Burden of Proof," *Yale Law Journal*, 122: 1254–79.

Cohen, L. J. (1991). "Should a Jury say What it Believes or What it Accepts?" *Cardozo Law Review*, 13: 465–83.

Dahlman, C. (2018). "Determining the Base Rate for Guilt," *Law, Probability and Risk*, 17: 17–58.

Dahlman, C. (2020). "Naked Statistical Evidence and Incentives for Lawful Conduct," *International Journal of Evidence and Proof*, 24: 162–79.

Dawid, A. P. (1994). "The Island Problem—Coherent use of Identification Evidence," Research Report No. 115, University College London, 1993. Also published in Freeman, P. and Smith, A. (eds.) (1994). *Aspects of Uncertainty—a Tribute to D. V. Lindley*, 159–70. New York: Wiley & Sons.

Dawid, A. P. (2002). "Bayes's Theorem and Weighing Evidence by Juries," in R. Swinburne (ed.), *Bayes Theorem* (Proceedings of the British Academy, 113), 71–90. Oxford: Oxford University Press.

de Jong, F. and van Lent, L. (2016). "The Presumption of Innocence as a Counterfactual Principle," *Utrecht Law Review*, 12: 32–49.

Fenton, N., Lagnado, D., Dahlman, C., and Neil, M. (2019). "The Opportunity Prior—a Proof-Based Prior for Criminal Cases," *Law, Probability and Risk*, 18: 237–53.

Friedman, R. (2002). "A Presumption of Innocence—not of Even Odds," *Stanford Law Review*, 52: 873–87.

Franklin, J. (2010). "Feature Selection Methods for Solving the Reference Class Problem," *Columbia Law Review*, 110: 12–23.

Franklin, J. (2011). "The Objective Bayesian Conceptualisation of proof and Reference Class Problems," *Sydney Law Review*, 33: 546–61.

Ho, H. L. (2008). *A Philosophy of Evidence Law—Justice in the Search for Truth*. Oxford: Oxford University Press.

Lindley, D. V. (1977). "Probability and the Law," *The Statistician*, 26: 203–20.

Posner, R. (1999). "An Economic Approach to the Law of Evidence," *Stanford Law Review*, 51: 1477–546.

Schauer, F. (1991). *Playing by the Rules*. Oxford: Oxford University Press.

Schweizer, M. (2005). *Kognitive Täuschungen vor Gericht—eine Empirische Studie*. Dissertation der Rechtswissenschaftlichen Fakultät der Universität Zürich.

Stein, A. (1996). "Judicial Fact-Finding and the Bayesian Method: The Case for Deeper Scepticism about the Combination," *International Journal of Evidence and Proof*, 1: 25–47.

20

Generalizations and Reference Classes

Michael S. Pardo[*] and Ronald J. Allen[**]

1. Introduction

Legal scholarship exploring the nature of evidence and the process of juridical proof has had a complex relationship with formal modeling. As demonstrated in so many fields of knowledge, theory formation and formal modeling have the potential to increase our comprehension of and our ability to predict and control aspects of complex, ambiguous, and unruly nature—and when applied to the legal system, perhaps also to increase the accuracy of factfinding, a tremendously important goal. The hope that knowledge could be formalized within the evidentiary realm generated a spate of articles attempting to use probability theory to explain aspects of trials.[1] This literature was both insightful and frustrating. Much light was shed on the legal system by bringing the tools of probability theory to bear upon it, but it also quickly became evident that the tools were in many ways ill-constructed for the task. Fundamental incompatibilities between the structure of legal decision-making and the extant formal tools were identified, and a number of the purported explanations of legal phenomena turned out to be internally inconsistent.[2] As a consequence, interest in this type of formal modeling declined, and attention was directed toward different kinds of explanations of the phenomena.[3]

Interestingly, a number of articles have attempted to apply mathematical models to quantify the probative value[4] of various items of evidence in ways consistent with the formal features of probability theory, and then to study decision-making from that perspective.[5] For example, the value of evidence is taken to be its likelihood ratio, that is, the probability of discovering or receiving the evidence given a hypothesis (e.g., the defendant did it) divided by the probability of discovering or receiving the evidence given the negation of the hypothesis (somebody else did it).[6] Or alternatively, the value of evidence is (more contextually) taken to be the information gain it provides, defined as the increase in probability it provides for a hypothesis above the probability of the hypothesis based on the other available

---

[*] This chapter was adapted from Allen and Pardo 2007.
[**] Professor Allen is indebted to the Searle Center and the Rosenthal fund for supporting his research.
[1] See, e.g., Kaplan 1968; Finkelstein and Fairley 1970; Lempert 1977; Friedman 1987; Tillers and Schum 1992.
[2] For example, there are attempts to defend an expected-utility approach to burdens of persuasion with an argument that is valid if, but only if, burdens of persuasion apply to cases as a whole (the defendant is liable or not, guilty or not), but this is false; they apply to individual elements. Allen 2000.
[3] Allen and Pardo 2019.
[4] "Probative value" is a relational concept that expresses the strength to which evidence supports an inference to a given conclusion. It is a crucial concept both for determining admissibility (see Federal Rules of Evidence 403, which instructs judges to exclude evidence when its probative value is substantially outweighed by its prejudicial, confusing, or duplicative effect) and for determining whether parties have satisfied their burdens of proof.
[5] Nance and Morris 2002; 2005; Finkelstein and Levin 2003; Davis and Follette 2002; 2003; Friedman and Park 2003.
[6] Nance and Morris 2002; 2005; Finkelstein and Levin 2003, 268–9; Koehler 2001; Kaye 1995.

Michael S. Pardo and Ronald J. Allen, *Generalizations and Reference Classes* In: *Philosophical Foundations of Evidence Law*. Edited by: Christian Dahlman, Alex Stein, and Giovanni Tuzet, Oxford University Press. © Christian Dahlman, Alex Stein, and Giovanni Tuzet 2021. DOI: 10.1093/oso/9780198859307.003.0021

evidence.[7] Both conceptions further assume that all of the various probability assessments conform or ought to conform to the dictates of Bayes' theorem, a formal probability theorem that maintains consistency among such assessments.[8]

As with the first wave of interest in the application of probability theory to juridical proof, this scholarship is interesting, instructive, and insightful. However, it also suffers from a deep conceptual problem that makes ambiguous the lessons that can be drawn from it—the problem of reference classes. The implications of this problem are considerable. To illustrate the problem, consider the famous blue-bus hypothetical. Suppose a witness saw a bus strike another car but cannot recall the color of the bus; assume further that the Blue company owns 75% of the buses in the town and the red company owns the remaining 25%. The most prevalent view in the legal literature of the probative value of the witness's report is that it would be determined by the ratio of blue buses to red buses, whether this is thought of or plays the role of a likelihood ratio or determines information gain (including an assessment of a prior probability).[9] But suppose the Red company owns 75% (and Blue the other 25%) of the buses in the county. Now the ratio reverses. And it would so again if Blue owned 75% in the state. Or in the opposite direction: it would reverse if Red owned 75% running in the street where the accident occurred (or on that side of the street), and so on. Or maybe the proper reference class has to do with safety standards and protocols for reporting accidents. Each of the reference classes leads to a different inference about which company is more likely liable, and nothing determines the correct class, save one: the very event under discussion, which has a likelihood of 1, and which we are trying to discover.

Now consider tests of rationality given to decision-makers that employ a problem akin to the blue-bus hypothetical. To critique the rationality of factfinders requires that one compare the answers they give to a correct answer. However, as in so much of life, even if every step one takes is perfectly rational—perfectly consistent with Bayes' theorem, for example—where one starts determines where one comes out. One has to have a correct starting point to critique an end point different from one's own, yet often no such objectively correct starting point exists. If experimenters get results different from what they believe to be appropriate, it may reflect on the rationality of the subjects, but it may just as readily be attributable to the influence of different, but equally appropriate, reference classes than those thought to be appropriate by the experimenters. Differences in outcome in such cases cannot readily be construed as reflecting on rationality, which, as we say, makes ambiguous the lessons of this renewed interest in formal modeling within the field of evidence.

In this chapter, we examine the implications of the reference-class problem for evidence scholarship that attempts to model the probative value of evidence. This chapter makes three contributions. First, and most importantly, it is a further demonstration of the problematic relationship between algorithmic tools and aspects of legal decision-making. Second, it points out serious pitfalls to be avoided for analytical or empirical studies of juridical proof. Third, it indicates when algorithmic tools may be more or less useful in the evidentiary process. At the highest level of generality, this chapter is another demonstration of the very

---

[7] Davis and Follette 2003, 668–9; Friedman 1994. We include here as well the use of data based on relative frequencies to inform prior probabilities, which is a form of information gain (it changes belief states).

[8] Finkelstein and Levin 2003; Davis and Follette 2003.

[9] See Finkelstein and Levin 2003, 268–9; Koehler 2001; Kaye 1995. As our discussion in the text indicates, the reference-class problem is ubiquitous.

complex set of relationships involving human knowledge and rationality, on the one hand, and attempts to reduce either to a set of formal concepts, on the other.

In Section 2 we elaborate on the lessons of the bus hypothetical by contextualizing it within some relevant issues in contemporary epistemology. Section 3 then applies the lessons of Section 2 to aspects of juridical proof.

2. Epistemology, Evidence, and Reference Classes: Fake Barns and Blue Buses

Evidence law has epistemic aims: to promote true conclusions arrived at via reliable evidence and rational reasoning methods and to prevent false, arbitrary, or irrational conclusions. These aims are, of course, subject to all sorts of competing considerations and goals such as time, money, protecting privacy, promoting relationships, and so on. Nevertheless, evidence law's core epistemic focus suggests that contemporary epistemological theory can illuminate epistemological issues in the law of evidence. In this section we show how one such epistemological issue regarding the concept of reliability can provide conceptual insight into the probative value of evidence—insight which, in the next section, will aid in showing the limits of attempts to model the value of evidence mathematically.

One primary epistemological project is to explain under what conditions true beliefs qualify as knowledge. One such attempt is through the concept of causation: namely, a true belief or conclusion qualifies as knowledge if some aspect of its truth causes an agent to hold the belief or accept the conclusion. For example, suppose someone drives past a barn under good observation conditions and utters to a passenger: "there's a barn." The utterance is both true and may qualify as knowledge because a real barn, in good observation conditions, caused the agent to utter the statement. The philosopher Alvin Goldman destroyed this simple causal account of knowledge.[10]

Take the above example, Goldman explains, and suppose the agent was in Fake Barn Town. Although the agent observed a real barn, it is one of the few real barns in a town filled with hundreds of barn facades, which, although they look like barns from the front, are just fake barn fronts and not real barns. Even though the agent's conclusion was true and its truth (seeing a real barn) caused the conclusion, and it was formed by a reliable process[11] (perception under good conditions), the conclusion does not qualify as knowledge because while true it is only accidentally so.[12] The agent does not know he saw a real barn. The agent would have formed the same belief even if he had observed one of the hundreds of fake barns in the town. To qualify as knowledge, the reporter would need to be able to distinguish between relevant counterfactual situations. Because the agent's capacities are not sensitive enough under these circumstances, he is an unreliable reporter of barns in this town.[13]

---

[10] Goldman 1976; see also Pardo 2005, 347–51.
[11] Reliability may be fleshed out in various ways. But it leads to a generality problem. Pardo 2005, 348–9.
[12] See also Gettier 1963; Pardo 2010.
[13] The conclusion of this artificial example has significant "real world" consequences. As persuasive psychological research suggests, testing procedures and conditions at lineups, showups, and photographic arrays may so affect a witness's choices that even accurate identifications (as confirmed after the fact) should be discarded if the witness would have made the same choices regardless of accuracy. (For an example of the psychological literature, see Wells, Olson, and Charman 2003.)

Now suppose that Fake Barn Town sits within Barn County in which real barns vastly outnumber the barn facades.[14] As if by magic, the agent, who looked unreliable in the town, now appears reliable when we attend to the fact that he in Barn County. But now suppose further that in Fake Barn State (in which the county is located) barn facades vastly outnumber real ones. The switch flips and the agent is now an unreliable reporter in the state. And so on. Or going in the reverse direction: suppose that the observation took place on Real Barn Street, in which all the barns are real. He is a reliable reporter on that street. And so forth.

Here is the critical point. The event under consideration (the observation of the barn) is a member of an infinite number of reference classes, the boundary conditions of which can be gerrymandered in countless ways, some of which lead to the inference that the agent is reliable and some that he is unreliable, given that particular class. And—outside of the reference class consisting only of the event itself—nothing in the natural world privileges or picks out one of classes as the right one; rather, our interests in the various inferences they generate pick out certain classes as more or less relevant.[15] To see the bite of this point, and in particular its bite for juridical purposes, suppose an empirical test were being run as to the ability of our agent (a witness at trial, for example) to identify barns accurately. What is the "proper" baseline (base rate) for running such a test? Is it the proportion of true barns on Real Barn Street, Fake Barn Town, Barn County, or Fake Barn State (or maybe the United Barn States of America)? There is no a priori correct answer; it depends on the interests at stake.

The probative value of juridical evidence is structurally similar to reliability in the above example.[16] Rather than being natural facts consigned to predetermined reference classes with labels attached designating the proper class,[17] the evidence, and the events on which it is based are members of an infinite number of reference classes, leading to various inferences of various strength depending on how the boundary conditions of those classes are specified.

The blue-bus hypothetical with which we began this chapter exemplifies the general implications of reference classes, and those implications would hold for practically any attempt to quantify a priori the probative value of evidence.[18] Consider another, and more realistic, example—that of an eyewitness identification made at a lineup. Any attempt to quantify the likelihood ratio of this evidence (the probability of picking the defendant given that he did it divided by the probability of picking him given that somebody else did it) quickly runs into the reference-class problem. Do we take the ratios of all identifications ever made? Those made (or not made, depending on the circumstance) across racial differences? Those made by this witness? Those made by this witness under similar lighting conditions? Those made on the same day of the week, or month, or year? And so on. In each case, the reference class will likely change and hence the quantified value will as well. But the evidence, the

---

[14] Brandom 2000, 112–16; Pardo 2005, 351–9.

[15] The problem cannot be "solved" by picking the smallest reference class, either. What matters is homogeneity within the class. How to specify the appropriate reference class for determining hypothesis confirmation has been a prominent issue in philosophy of science. Reichenbach suggested we choose the smallest class for which reliable statistics were available; Salmon, by contrast, advocated that for single cases we ought to select the broadest homogeneous class. For a discussion of these positions, see Salmon 1967, 91, 124.

[16] Pardo 2005, 374–83.

[17] See Allen 1994.

[18] The reference-class problem may be universal, but we do not need to establish that.

identification, has not changed. Thus it has no fixed, privileged, quantified value—save the event itself, which has a value of 1 or 0.

The demonstration above reveals several points. First, the value of evidence is not its likelihood ratio given a certain specified reference class. Evidence has countless likelihood ratios corresponding to its various reference classes. An explanation or justification for choosing any particular one must be provided, and there will invariably be reasonable alternatives. Second, for the same reason, the value of evidence is not, alternatively, its information gain in a given context: namely, the increase in probability of a hypothesis (e.g., the defendant did it) from the prior probability without the evidence. This view still requires a likelihood ratio calculation based upon a chosen reference class; it just combines that likelihood with the prior probability.[19] Third, rather than capturing the probative value of evidence, the various statistics or likelihood ratios flowing from various reference classes are just more evidence, and, as such, must themselves be interpreted and explained.[20] In the following section we apply these lessons to various aspects of juridical proof.

3. Modeling Probative Value

Questions at trial often focus on what happened specifically at a certain moment of time. Rarely is the ultimate issue a relative frequency about a class of events (disparate-impact issues in discrimination cases being a possible exception). The reference-class problem demonstrates that objective probabilities based on a particular class of which an item of evidence is a member cannot typically (and maybe never) capture the probative value of that evidence for establishing facts relating to a specific event. The only class that would accurately capture the "objective" value would be the event itself, which would have a probability of 1 or 0, respectively.

Any attempt to mathematically model the value of evidence, however, must somehow try to isolate an item of evidence's probability for establishing a particular conclusion. Generating these probabilities will, in turn, involve isolating characteristics about the evidence, the event, and the relationship between those characteristics. This relationship may be established by either objectively known base rates or through subjective assessments. In either case, the modeled values arise through abstracting from the specific evidence and event under discussion and placing various aspects of each within particular classes, with varying frequencies, propensities, or subjective probabilities instantiated by the various characteristics on which one has chosen to attend (for example, the frequency with which defendants who exhibit characteristic X commit crime Y). An important lesson of the fake-barn and blue-bus examples in Section 2, however, was that adjustments in the boundary conditions of the relevant classes may alter the strength of the inference from the evidence to the conclusion that the event instantiates the characteristic for which the evidence is offered (for example, whether this defendant committed crime Y).[21]

---

[19] Or, again, it simply informs the formation of a prior probability.

[20] The value of evidence, whether the original propositions or their likelihood ratios, is the strength it provides a particular inference in a particular context. This strength will be determined by the plausibility of alternative, contrary inferences. Allen and Pardo 2019.

[21] Even when the material proposition for which evidence is offered itself involves a frequency these reference-class issues still arise. For example, consider evidence establishing a racially disparate hiring practice or epidemiological studies establishing increased disease among those who took a particular drug. In the typical case, this

The reference-class problem, in other words, is an epistemological limitation on attempts to establish the probative value of particular items of legal evidence.[22] It is an epistemological limitation because different classes may point in opposite directions and nothing, other than the event itself, necessarily privileges one over another. To be sure, some will be better or worse than others because some will provide better or worse information about what we are trying to infer regarding the underlying event. But, which is which will, like any other evidence, be the subject of argument and, ultimately, judgment. These conceptual points place significant limitations on attempts to mathematically model the value of legal evidence.

We first list these limitations generally and then illustrate them with specific examples. First, and most important, the probative value of legal evidence cannot be equated with the probabilities flowing from any given reference class for which base-rate data is available. Related to this point, probative value likewise cannot be equated with the difference between prior and posterior probabilities based on such data, nor is it sensible simply to translate directly an available statistic into a prior probability. Second, the above problem regarding establishing probative value cannot be solved by merely specifying the relevant classes with more detailed, complex, or "realistic" characteristics. Third, while switching from objective to subject probability assessments better accommodates unstable probative values of evidence, it nevertheless still illustrates the pervasiveness of the reference-class problem because of its presence even when evaluating such subjective assessments. Finally, the reference-class problem is so pervasive that it arises whenever one assesses the probative value of evidence, even when one is not trying to fix a specific numeric value on particular items of evidence—for example, when assessing whether evidence satisfies a standard of proof.

We illustrate these general lessons by discussing examples of attempts to model the probative value of evidence. Our point in critiquing these models is not to criticize these models in particular. To the contrary, we think they are quite useful in helping to understand the nature of legal evidence. Our point is to show that the epistemological limitations discussed above adhere in any such attempts. Thus, our criticisms concern primarily the conclusions that may—and may not—be inferred from such models. The limitations discussed, we contend, undermine the strong conclusions drawn from such models.

3.1. Carpet Fibers

Finkelstein and Levin attempt to model the probative value of a found carpet fiber.[23] They present and analyze two variations on the following scenario: a crime has been committed and an unusual carpet fiber is found at the scene. Based on manufacturing records, an expert testifies that the frequency of such fibers in carpets is less than 1 in 500. A match is found among carpet fibers taken from a suspect, a neighbor named Jones. The authors analyze the probative value

---

evidence is being used to establish that a particular plaintiff was discriminated against or injured, and the issues discussed above will arise as to what larger class is appropriate to compare to the evidence in the case. In addition, the ratios in the evidence itself will raise issues regarding, for example, error rates and fraud, making the value of this evidence for the proposition for which it is offered not the overt statistic.

[22]   Pardo 2005, 374–83.
[23]   Finkelstein and Levin 2003, 266.

of the match assuming the police tested twenty samples from Jones's various carpets and assuming the police tested one sample from Jones and one sample from nineteen other suspects.

With regard to the first scenario, Finkelstein and Levin first argue that it would be inaccurate for a prosecutor to argue "that there is only one chance in five hundred of such a match if the crime-scene fiber had come from some place other than Jones's carpets."[24] The reason the prosecutor's argument would be inaccurate is that, because twenty samples were tested and each could have been a match, the probability of one of them matching is much higher than if only one sample fiber had been tested.[25] The authors invoke Bonferroni's inequality theorem—when there are multiple samples tested, the probability of at least one matching is less than or equal to the sum of the individual probabilities of each sample matching—and conclude: "So our prosecutor could only say that the probability of seeing a match if the crime fiber came from another source was less than 20 x 1/500, or 1 in 25, not 1 in 500," and thus "the search among the fibers of the suspect's carpets significantly reduced the probative value of what was found."[26]

With regard to the second scenario, Finkelstein and Levin conclude that the prosecutor could indeed argue "that there is only one chance in five hundred of finding such a match if the fiber did not come from Jones's carpet"[27] because this number captures the "probative value" or "probative force" or "probative effect" of the fiber evidence. (They use all three terms, apparently, interchangeably.[28]) They use this value to calculate the likelihood ratio for the evidence in order to combine it (via Bayes' theorem) with the prior odds of guilt given the other evidence:

> The likelihood ratio is thus $1/(1/500) = 500$. Given the match, the odds that the fiber came from Jones's home (versus a different home) are 500 times greater than the odds would have been ignoring the match evidence. This is undoubtedly powerful evidence.[29]

It may very well be powerful evidence, but, as with the fake barn example, there is a reference-class issue, and that issue vitiates the showing that Finkelstein and Levin are trying to make. The probative value (or force or effect) of the evidence (the fiber found at the scene and its match to Jones) is not the above-quoted likelihood ratio in the second hypothetical and it has no obvious application to the first hypothetical, either. The problem with both conclusions arises from an ambiguity in the sentence: "Based on manufacturing records, an expert testifies that the frequency of such fibers in carpets is less than 1 in 500." What does this mean? Whose records? Which records? Does the statistic refer to those who make a particular kind of carpet, or all US manufacturers, or all manufacturers in the world? Or all carpets ever made in the history of the world to date? And once we know the class to which it applies, why is this the appropriate class in which to place Jones and his carpet sample? Is the fiber more or less prevalent in his part of the world, country, state, region, age-group, gender, profession,

---

[24] Ibid.

[25] Ibid., 266–7.

[26] Ibid. This is not, however, necessarily true. If the fibers are identical, or are from the same source (a uniform rug throughout the house), multiple testing will not change the probability of a match. It is thus possible that twenty tests are equivalent to one; whether this is true or false is obviously an empirical question and cannot be resolved analytically. For that matter, why should samples of the suspect's carpeting be viewed as random samples from a population? Is there some reason to think he bought twenty different carpets randomly across the United States (or is the world the right reference class, or the local Carpet Town USA)?

[27] Ibid.

[28] See, e.g., ibid., 267, 268, 269, n. 8.

[29] Ibid., 269.

socio-economic status, etc? Each of the different classes suggested by these questions would reveal different probabilities and likelihood ratios, but the evidence under consideration has not changed. Indeed, the evidence would likely have widely varying likelihood ratios. The probative value of the evidence cannot be simply the ratio derived from any arbitrarily chosen reference class. Therefore, to argue, as Finkelstein and Levin do, that the probative value is the likelihood ratio of 500, they would first need an argument that the appropriate class has been employed, one that is not obvious given the paucity of information in the example.

A second problem with their conclusions concerns how the fiber evidence connects with other evidence. They contend:

> The presence of other evidence does not change the analysis given above because the increase in probability that Jones's house was the source of the fiber associated with finding a match is not affected by the other evidence; it is only the degree of probability based on the other evidence and the fiber matching that is so affected.[30]

Regardless of whether the *probability*—that Jones's house was the source of the fiber, given the match—is not affected by other evidence, the *probative value* of the evidence (a matching fiber) is so affected by other evidence. For example, conclusive evidence that the crime-scene fiber had been planted after the fact to frame Jones would reduce the value of the fiber evidence to zero. Even if we have no evidence about this possibility, how do we know that it was brought from the suspect's home? Even if it was, how do we know that it was from *carpeting in his home* rather than, say, from having been picked up on the shoes of the actual perpetrator when he was at a party at the home of the person wrongly accused of the crime? These possibilities further show the disjunct between the value of evidence, on one hand, and the likelihood ratio calculated based on a specified reference class, on the other. And the divergence between the two shows the mismatch that can occur when the former is modeled mathematically based on an arbitrarily chosen reference class.

The references classes employed by Finkelstein and Levin are by no means more plausible than many one can imagine. The problem, though, is that there may be no data for other plausible reference classes, meaning that the mathematics can only be done by picking these or some variant. Thus, rather than showing something true about the events under consideration, they merely show one of an enormous number of calculations that might be done if one had different data. Using the data one has does not make the proffered analysis correct or true in some sense; instead, it is reminiscent of relying on the lamp post more for support than illumination. Rather than being an objective datum that captures the value of evidence, the numbers that Finkelstein and Levin discuss are just more evidence, which itself must be interpreted to assess its value in the particular case.

---

[30] Ibid., 268. Likewise, Kaye and Koehler (2003, 651) assert that a likelihood ratio "is a constant—it does not change according to one's prior beliefs." While there is a sense it which it may be true that a likelihood ratio does not vary based on prior beliefs (although we are not sure how one could calculate such a ratio without relying on prior beliefs), it is false that likelihood ratios are "constants." Constants may exist in some scientific areas, but in most juridical contexts they can only be formed by exercises of judgment, including picking appropriate reference classes, based on ill-quantified data. Thus, rather than being "constants," they will typically be contestable propositions. Perhaps Kaye and Koehler meant to limit their remark to certain narrow aspects of scientific evidence, but even then there will be a reference-class issue. Alternatively, perhaps they meant that the process of forming prior beliefs and forming likelihood ratios are hermetically sealed off from one another, but our discussion shows this to be in error. One's investigations of the scene of the crime, coupled with increasing knowledge of the carpet industry as it bears upon the crime, plainly could affect one's construction of a likelihood ratio. Obviously forming a likelihood ratio depends on some set of "prior beliefs," and there is no reason why that set and whatever forms a prior probability must be completely distinct from each other.

3.2. Infidelity

Davis and Follette also purport to demonstrate that "the probative value of evidence can be mathematically/empirically established" if one knows the "pertinent base rates or contingent probabilities or both in the appropriate population."[31] To illustrate this they consider the value of a defendant's infidelity in the murder of his wife:

> The fact of infidelity is not probative of whether a man murdered or will murder his wife. In fact, the relative increase in likelihood that an unfaithful man will murder his wife, over the likelihood that a faithful man will murder his wife is so infinitesimal (.0923%) as to be totally insignificant.[32]

They arrive at this calculation by defining probative value as "the difference between the probability of murder given the infidelity and the probability or murder given no infidelity."[33] In order to determine this, something like a likelihood ratio (in that it compares two relative frequencies) was obtained by dividing the rate of murdered wives per million men by the rate of infidelity. This figure is used to determine what they call a "maximum probative value" of infidelity on the assumptions that faithful husbands never murder their spouses, and that at most it is only .0923% more likely an unfaithful husband will murder his wife during their marriage than a faithful husband will.[34] They then assert that those who assign greater value to the evidence are engaged in inaccurate "intuitive profiling," which simply means giving too much credence to the belief that an unfaithful husband more likely fits the profile of one who would murder his wife than a faithful one, and thus is more likely to have done so.[35] The correct probative value, under their analysis, is the value arrived at above via the chosen base rates.

As with the carpet-fiber example, the calculations work only once a particular event is placed within a particular reference class, and there is no reason to privilege the particular base rates they employ. With any given suspect, different rates exist that would vary from being highly probative to virtually irrelevant, depending on such variables as age, geographic location, types or amount of infidelities, types of murder, and so on. The evidence (infidelity) would remain the same as we vary the reference class, but the value of the evidence would change.

Davis and Follette recognize this general issue. They discuss the simplified example in order to discuss a real case.[36] According to their description of the facts, a woman and her husband were riding on a snowmobile (the woman driving and her husband on back) when the woman drowned as a result of a crash.[37] The prosecution theorized that: "the defendant had deliberately drowned his wife once they had fallen into a ditch, and that he may have somehow caused the crash, thereafter faking his own unconsciousness/inability to breathe [when paramedics arrived]. Physical evidence of each of these assertions was

---

[31] Davis and Follette 2002, 156.
[32] Ibid., 139.
[33] Ibid., 137.
[34] Ibid.
[35] Ibid., 152–4.
[36] Ibid., 135; for a discussion of the case, see Friedman and Park 2003, 640–3.
[37] Ibid., 135–6.

extraordinarily weak, particularly evidence of whether the evidence's death was the result of murder or accident."[38]

The prosecution relied heavily on motive evidence: the defendant purchased a large life insurance policy on his wife within a year and had several extramarital affairs. Recognizing the reference-class issue, the authors contend that even more favorable base rates were available to support the defendant based upon his characteristics (white, in his thirties, middle class) than the those mentioned above (about four in one million).[39] Nevertheless, they relied on the base rates for all married men in order to pick a class most favorable to the prosecution. The court refused to allow the base-rate evidence, concluding it would be misleading or prejudicial. The authors, however, contend that such testimony should be allowed "to help the jury understand that the intuitive profile or stereotype telling them the evidence is probative of guilt is misleading."[40]

As with the simplified example above, this particular defendant is part of a large number of classes, each with its own base rate, not just the general ones such as married, unfaithful, white, thirties, middle class, etc. Indeed, if one starts specifying more and more details, one will arrive at the event itself, which will have a base rate of 1 or 0, respectively. Short of that, there is no class that uniquely captures the probative value of the evidence (i.e., infidelity). This fact undermines attempts to equate probative value with probabilities based on base rates.

In response to the authors, Friedman and Park criticize the conclusions and choice of base rates.[41] They point out that the defendant's reference class will likely vary when the boundary conditions of the class are altered to account for more realistic characteristics: "not all histories of infidelity or of spousal abuse have the same probative value."[42] Second, they contend that the infidelity evidence may combine with other evidence in ways that are too complex to quantify: "[t]he insurance evidence combines with the evidence of infidelity in a way that cannot be captured by schematic quantitative analysis."[43] We agree with their criticisms, but think they do not go far enough.

The first criticism is illuminating because Friedman and Park effectively show that on the facts of the case there are very likely reference classes that suggest a much higher probability of guilt than the "most liberal base rate[s]" employed by Davis and Follette.[44] This, of course, is a partial demonstration of the central point of this chapter that there is a large class of reference classes. The reason Friedman and Park's critique does not go far enough is their suggestion that the Davis and Follette reference class is too simplistic ("Real life is far more complicated than [Davis & Follette's] scenarios"[45]), which suggests that the more complex examples they give are more realistic. This can only be true if there is a "realistic" reference class (other than the event itself), but there virtually never is. As we have tried to demonstrate, generally if not always there is a practically unbounded set of reference classes

---

[38] Ibid.

[39] Ibid., 149–50. The base rates were higher for non-white, younger married men from lower economic categories (ibid., 150).

[40] Ibid., 153. Likewise, in a subsequent response, Davis and Follette (2003, 672) argue that when jurors and judges use such evidence to construct stories, they may give it excessive weight in relation to its "true utility." The "true utility," for them, would be the result of their analysis.

[41] Friedman and Park 2003.

[42] Ibid., 639.

[43] Ibid., 642.

[44] Davis and Follette 2002, 150.

[45] Friedman and Park 2003, 639.

with probabilities within those reference classes ranging from 0 to 1 and nothing privileges any particular class. Because there is no unique base rate that would capture the value of the evidence, other than the event itself,[46] all Friedman and Park can do is articulate why they think some other reference class is more pertinent, but of course Davis and Follette could offer yet another competing class that lowers the probability, and so on. The effect of specifying more details to make the rate more realistic will depend on the relevance of those details and may or may not take one closer to the actual value, which will be 0 or 1.

With regard to combining evidence, Friedman and Park's critique seems to assume that the epistemological limitation is one of computational complexity only.[47] If we knew the likelihoods for, say, combinations of insurance and infidelity, then these values may indeed reflect the probative value of the evidence. We disagree; we think the problem is much deeper. Even if we knew those base rates, the reference-class problem, as we presented it above, would arise once again with the various combinations, or any other combination.

Replying to Friedman and Park, Davis and Follette adjust their analysis in two ways.[48] They focus more specifically on the base-rate/reference-class issue,[49] and they emphasize that their theory of probative value is not the likelihood ratio but instead the "information gain" evidence provides (the difference between prior and posterior probabilities).[50] Neither emendation removes their analysis from our critique. With regard to base rates, they assert:

> Although selection of relevant base rates that will be generally accepted will be challenging, it is our hope that this initial dialogue will serve to apprise others of the importance of the issue, and to stimulate further efforts to find objective base rates to facilitate empirically based evidentiary rulings.[51]

But, to belabor a point, there is only one empirically "objective" reference class—the event itself.[52] Among the various other reference classes, there is no other unique class that will capture the probative value of the evidence. Moreover, emphasizing "information gain" as the measure of probative value does not respond to the reference-class problem because information gain depends on base rates and thus on reference classes.

Like the carpet-fiber example, the probative value of the evidence of infidelity cannot be objectively captured mathematically.[53] Rather, the varying statistics are just themselves more evidence that must be interpreted. Like all other evidence, their value will depend on

---

[46] Of course, some could be more or less realistic, and thus tell us more about the situation, but the key point is that none of these values would uniquely capture the probative value of the evidence. That is a different question from the relative persuasiveness of arguments about reference classes. Friedman and Park present, to us, a strong argument that Davis and Follette substantially underestimated the strength of the evidence of guilt.

[47] Ibid.

[48] David and Follette 2003.

[49] Ibid., 669–70.

[50] Ibid., 668–9, 673–8.

[51] Ibid.

[52] Franklin (2010; 2011) discusses methods for addressing reference-class issues but also acknowledge the practical limitations facing such methods in litigation settings. See ibid., 561 (explaining that the ideal reference class may be "too small to be usable" or may depend on beliefs for which relevant data are unavailable). See also Allen and Pardo 2019, 12, n. 47; Allen and Pardo 2021, n. 5.

[53] Kaye and Koehler (2003) criticize Davis and Follette on the ground that the likelihood ratio is a better measure of probative value than the change in posterior probability. But as we have previously noted, this is premised upon a correct and unchanging likelihood ratio. We doubt that there is such a thing anywhere in life of any relevance to the legal system, and the DNA example they employ certain is not. DNA is very good evidence, but not because there can be no disputes about the reference class into which pieces of DNA evidence fall.

what can be inferred from them, which in turn will depend on how well they explain or are explained by the various hypotheses in issue.

4. Conclusion

Due to the epistemological limitations flowing from the reference-class issue, mathematical models do not very well capture the probative value of evidence. The statistics relied on and provided by such models are just more evidence that must be interpreted. How will this proceed? We suggest this occurs by comparing the various hypotheses that may explain the evidence. In other words, at the micro-level of determining the probative value of evidence, factfinders are engaged in a process of inference to the best explanation in which the contest is largely over the relative plausibility of the competing hypotheses advanced by the parties.[54]

References

Allen, R. J. (1994). "Factual Ambiguity and a Theory of Evidence," *Northwestern University Law Review*, 88: 604–40.

Allen, R. J. (2000). "Clarifying the Burden of Persuasion and Bayesian Decision Rules: A Response to Professor Kaye," *International Journal of Evidence and Proof*, 4: 246–59.

Allen, R. J. and Pardo, M. S. (2007). "The Problematic Value of Mathematical Models of Evidence," *Journal of Legal Studies*, 36: 107–40.

Allen, R. J. and Pardo, M. S. (2019). "Relative Plausibility and its Critics," *International Journal of Evidence and Proof*, 23: 5–58.

Allen, R. J. and Pardo, M. S. (2021). "Inference to the Best Explanation, Relative Plausibility, and Probability," in C. Dahlman, A. Stein, and G. Tuzet (eds.), *Philosophical Foundations of Evidence Law*. Oxford: Oxford University Press.

Brandom, R. B. (2000). *Articulating Reasons*. Cambridge, MA: Harvard University Press.

Davis, D. and Follette, W. C. (2002). "Rethinking the Probative Value of Evidence: Base Rates, Intuitive Profiling, and the 'Postdiction' of Behavior," *Law and Human Behavior*, 26: 133–58.

Davis, D. and Follette, W. C. (2003). "Toward an Empirical Approach to Evidentiary Ruling," *Law and Human Behavior*, 27: 661–84.

Finkelstein, M. and Fairley, W. (1970). "A Bayesian Approach to Identification Evidence," *Harvard Law Review*, 83: 489–517.

Finkelstein, M. O. and Levin, B. (2003). "On the Probative Value of Evidence from a Screening Search," *Jurimetrics Journal*, 43: 265–90.

Franklin, J. (2010). "Feature Selection Methods for Solving the Reference Class Problem: Comment on Edward K. Cheng, 'A Practical Solution to the Reference Class Problem,'" *Columbia Law Review*, 110: 12–23.

Franklin, J. (2011). "The Objective Bayesian Conceptualisation of Proof and Reference Class Problems," *Sydney Law Review*, 33: 545–61.

Friedman, R. D. (1987). "Route Analysis of Credibility and Hearsay," *Yale Law Journal*, 96: 667–742.

Friedman, R. D. (1994). "Conditional Probative Value: Neoclassicism without Myth," *Michigan Law Review*, 93: 439–77.

Friedman, R. D. and Park, R. C. (2003). "Sometimes What Everybody thinks they know is True," *Law and Human Behavior*, 27: 629–44.

---

[54] See Allen and Pardo, "Inference to the Best Explanation, Relative Plausibility, and Probability," ch. 14, in this volume; Allen and Pardo 2019.

Gettier, E. L. (1963). "Is Justified True Belief Knowledge?" *Analysis*, 23: 121–4.

Goldman, A. I. (1976). "Discrimination and Perceptual Knowledge," *Journal of Philosophy*, 73: 771–91.

Kaplan, J. (1968). "Decision Theory and the Factfinding Process," *Stanford Law Review*, 20: 1065–92.

Kaye, D. H. (1995). "The Relevance of 'Matching' DNA: Is the window half open or Half Shut?" *Journal of Criminal Law and Criminology*, 85: 676–95.

Kaye, D. H. and Koehler, J. (2003). "The Misquantification of Probative Value," *Law and Human Behavior*, 27: 645–59.

Koehler, J. J. (2001). "The Psychology of Numbers in the Courtroom: How to make DNA-Match Statistics seem Impressive or Insufficient," *Southern California Law Review*, 7: 1275–305.

Lempert, R. (1977). "Modeling Relevance," *Michigan Law Review*, 75: 1021–57.

Nance, D. A. and Morris, S. B. (2005). "Juror Understanding of DNA Evidence: An Empirical Assessment of Presentation Formats for Trace Evidence with a Relatively Small Random-Match Probability," *Journal of Legal Studies*, 34: 395–443.

Pardo, M. S. (2005). "The Field of Evidence and the Field of Knowledge," *Law and Philosophy*, 24: 321–92.

Pardo, M. S. (2010). "The Gettier Problem and Legal Proof," *Legal Theory*, 16: 37–57.

Salmon, W. C. (1967). *The Foundations of Scientific Inference*. Pittsburgh, PA: University of Pittsburgh Press.

Tillers, P. and Schum, D. A. (1992). "Hearsay Logic," *Minnesota Law Review*, 76: 813–58.

Wells, G. L., Olson, E. A., and Charman, S. D. (2003). Distorted Retrospective Eyewitness Reports as Functions of Feedback and Delay. *Journal of Experimental Psychology*, 9: 42–52.

PART VI

PROOF PARADOXES

21

Paradoxes of Proof

Mark Spottswood

1. Introduction

The literature on evidence contains many fascinating curiosities, including the so-called "proof paradoxes." Each alleged paradox consists of a stylized scenario with multiple potential outcomes, and they can be grouped into three categories. The first involves cases where a plaintiff or prosecutor attempts to sustain their burden of proof through reliance on an explicit statistical inference. The second involves cases where a judge or jury must arrive at a decision through the combination of multiple claims, elements, or defenses. And the third arises when a jury must incorporate multiple independent views of the evidence into a single verdict decision.

For each potential paradox, we can ask three distinct questions:

1. What does our intuition suggest is a fair resolution of this problem?
2. How do judges and other legal actors currently resolve this problem?
3. What resolution of this problem is normatively best, either in terms of resolving individual cases as accurately as possible or in terms of broader social policy goals?

Considering these questions separately should help to make it clear that there is no a priori reason why we must give consistent answers to each one.[1] A form of proof might, for instance, be admissible in court even if it seems intuitively problematic. Similarly, we might say that some currently admissible evidence is normatively problematic, or that some desirable evidence is currently excluded. Thus, we might legitimately wonder whether different answers to these questions are so inconsistent as to be worthy of the "paradox" label. Regardless, whether intuition, doctrine, and normative analysis align is an important question for both theorists and reformers. Accordingly, the remainder of this chapter will survey intuitions, doctrines, and normative analyses regarding each alleged paradox.

2. Statistical Evidence Paradoxes

The proof paradox literature seems to have started with Tribe's "blue bus hypothetical."[2] The scenario involves a personal injury claim by an injured pedestrian, who testifies (without contradiction) that the bus that hit him was blue. In addition, it is conceded that the

---

[1] See Spottswood 2019, 80.
[2] Tribe 1971, 1340–1.

Mark Spottswood, *Paradoxes of Proof* In: *Philosophical Foundations of Evidence Law*. Edited by: Christian Dahlman, Alex Stein, and Giovanni Tuzet, Oxford University Press. © Christian Dahlman, Alex Stein, and Giovanni Tuzet 2021. DOI: 10.1093/oso/9780198859307.003.0022

defendant operates "four-fifths" of all the blue buses in town. Tribe suggested that finding liability without more evidence would be deeply problematic in such a case despite the fact that there would seem to be an 80% probability of liability.[3]

Cohen offered a variation on this theme. His "paradox of the gatecrasher" involved a rodeo that is seeking to recover the ticket price from a person who is alleged to have snuck in without paying. Both parties agree that there were 1,000 attendees on the night of the rodeo and that only 499 tickets were sold for that performance. According to Cohen, this implies that "there is a .501 probability ... that [the defendant] did not pay."[4] Although he thought that a "mathematicist theory" requires a finding of liability, he maintained that this would be "manifestly unjust."[5]

Kaye has labelled the proof in these hypotheticals "naked statistical evidence," which we can shorthand as "NSE."[6] The term "naked" is meant to distinguish the presentation of obviously statistical evidence from the many situations in which statistical base rates might influence the weight that jurors assign to non-statistical evidence. For instance, our assumptions regarding the base rate of identification errors might affect our willingness to credit eyewitness testimony, but such evidence is not explicitly statistical in form.[7]

2.1 NSE Intuitions

Cohen felt that basing verdicts on NSE was "manifestly unjust."[8] Empirical work soon showed that his intuition was broadly shared. Wells found that both students and professional judges were far less likely to find defendants liable on the basis of naked statistics than other forms of evidence. Critically, this occurred even when they believed that the probability of fault in either scenario were essentially equivalent, negating the simple hypothesis that they did not trust the NSE in question.[9] Subsequent papers found similar patterns of intuitions among participants, while differing in their explanation of the underlying cognitive mechanism that leads people to be unwilling to impose legal consequences on the basis of NSE. Wells posited that many people may believe that evidence should only be used to support liability when "one's hypothetical belief about the ultimate fact must affect one's belief about the evidence."[10] Others proposed that people are reluctant to impose liability when the supporting evidence is *abstract* in nature (such as numerical base rates) rather than concrete (such as eye-witness accounts).[11] This may be because more vivid accounts make it easier to construct semantic stories[12], simulated scenarios,[13] or implicit associative networks[14] that are consistent with the defendant's guilt. Or perhaps finding liability based on testimony permits the factfinder to *avoid anticipated self-blame* should their finding

---

[3] Ibid., 1349.
[4] Cohen 1977, 75.
[5] Ibid. For another variation, see Nesson 1979, 1192–4 (describing the "Prison Yard" hypothetical).
[6] Kaye 1980, 603.
[7] Saks and Kidd 1980, 137–8.
[8] Cohen 1977, 75.
[9] Wells 1992, 742.
[10] Ibid., 746.
[11] Heller 2006; Niedermeier et al. 1999.
[12] cf. Pennington and Hastie 1991, 554.
[13] Kahneman et al. 1982, ch. 14.
[14] Spottswood 2013, 196–7.

turn out to be erroneous, as they can shift blame from themselves to the mistaken witness, but naked statistics provide no such cover.[15] Lastly, people may exhibit a more general bias against imposing any punishments based upon explicit inferences, even when they feel those inferences are reasonably strong.[16]

2.2 NSE Doctrine

Given the intuitions described above, one might expect that judges have roundly rejected the use of naked statistical evidence in real-life cases. Surprisingly, although a few cases limit the use of NSE, this seems to be the exception rather than the rule.

Scholarly discussions of the paradox routinely refer to a small number of cases that, on close inspection, fail to grapple directly with the admissibility or sufficiency of NSE. In *Smith v. Rapid Transit, Inc.*, for instance, the plaintiff alleged that she had been forced off the road while driving at night by a bus. Unable to describe the bus in detail, she sued the only bus company with a regular license to operate on that street. In holding this evidence insufficient to support a finding of liability, the court of appeals noted that Smith's proof "did not preclude private or chartered busses from using the street."[17] Thus, although the court offered dicta suggesting that probabilistic proof was generally problematic, the case involved only weak and *non-quantified* evidence of ownership. Many other cases that scholars routinely cite in support of the law's supposed resistance to quantified proof are similarly inapt.[18]

Likewise, unhelpful are cases in which courts reject statistical evidence that is either poorly supported or difficult to apply to the questions at hand. One court rejected expert testimony tending to show that "eighty to eighty-five percent of child sexual abuse is committed by a [close] relative ...."[19] Such statistics are not easily translated into a probability that a particular person committed an offense. For instance, knowing this frequency is little help unless one also knows the typical number of close relatives that a child has. A court might legitimately worry that without more context, the evidence is more likely to confuse than assist the jury in its task. Thus, such cases provide little warrant for concluding that the law is hostile to statistical proof in general, rather than hostile to poorly supported or misleading statistics in particular.[20]

United States v. Shonubi grappled with the issue more directly. A jury found Shonubi guilty of importing heroin from Nigeria. Although he was arrested in possession of only 427 grams of heroin, he had made seven prior smuggling trips, and the trial judge needed to determine the total amount smuggled for sentencing purposes. The judge admitted evidence of the amounts seized from 117 Nigerian heroin smugglers caught under similar circumstances, calculated likely amounts for each of Shonubi's trips, and sentenced him accordingly. The court of appeals reversed, making it plain that only "specific evidence" should be used to calculate the length of a criminal sentence.

---

[15] Heller 2006, 287.
[16] Zamir et al. 2014, 197.
[17] *Smith v. Rapid Transit, Inc.*, 58 N.E.2d 754, 755 (1945).
[18] See, generally, Brook 1985, 299–305 (surveying commonly cited cases).
[19] *Stephens v. State*, 774 P.2d 60, 64 (Wyo. 1989), overruled on other grounds by *Large v. State*, 177 P.3d 807 (Wyo. 2008). See, generally, Koehler 2001, 380 (collecting similar cases).
[20] See also *People v. Collins*, 438 P.2d 33 (Cal. 1968).

Shonubi may be an outlier, however. Compare it to *Kaminsky v. Hertz Corp.*, for example. Kaminsky was injured by a truck bearing the Hertz logo. Ninety percent of trucks bearing that logo were owned by Hertz, and 10% were owned by licensees or franchisees. The appellate court held that these facts were both admissible and sufficient to support a jury finding that Hertz owned the truck.[21]

Many other cases yield similar results. In employment discrimination cases, plaintiffs regularly use statistical disparities between actual rates of hiring, promotions, or firings of other people, and the rates that they argue would obtain in the absence of discrimination, in order to make a prima facie showing that they *themselves* were discriminated against.[22] Likewise, plaintiffs may recover in a toxic tort case on the basis that the defendant sold the majority of a product within a relevant market,[23] or show that their injury was caused by a substance on the ground that it more than doubles the base rate of the type of illness that the plaintiff suffers.[24] And in *Tyson Foods v. Bouaphakeo*, the Supreme Court recently held that class members seeking owed overtime compensation for the time it took to put on protective gear could properly rely on statistical averages of other individuals' dressing time as a means of proving the size of each class member's injury.[25]

More strikingly, courts have held that sufficiently well-supported NSE can meet the burden of proof in criminal cases. DNA match evidence, in particular, does not uniquely match a sample to one person to the exclusion of all others, but rather to a reference class of persons sharing certain discrete patterns at tested locations in their genetic code. But after some initial hurdles as courts worked to understand the new forensic technology, this evidence is routinely admitted, even when the reference class is large enough to make the probability of a random match more than a fanciful possibility.[26] And as the technology has been improved over time to shrink the size of the resulting reference class, courts have been increasingly willing to say that DNA match evidence needs no corroboration to sustain a finding of guilt, at least when the perpetrator's identity is the only disputed issue at trial and the probability of a random match is sufficiently low.[27] In short, when the statistics themselves are reasonably well-founded and pertinent, courts often hold that NSE is both admissible and sufficient to prove key facts without further corroboration.[28]

2.3 NSE and Normative Theory

Lastly, let us consider to what extent reliance on naked statistics is sound as a matter of social policy. Perhaps the simplest normative approach is to accept the recommendations of ordinary statistical theory and find these defendants liable. Probabilistic reasoning is, at bottom, simply a mathematical description of how often we should expect different kind

---

[21] *Kaminsky v. Hertz Corp.*, 288 N.W.2d 426, 427 (Mich. Ct. App. 1979). Accord *Kramer v. Weedhopper of Utah, Inc.*, 141 Ill. App. 3d 217, 220 (1986).

[22] *Int'l Brotherhood of Teamsters, Inc. v. United States*, 431 U.S. 324, 339–40 (1977).

[23] See, e.g., *Gray v. United States*, 445 F. Supp. 337 (S.D. Tex. 1978); *Namm v. Charles E. Frosst & Co.*, 427 A.2d 1121 (N.J. Super Ct. App. Div. 1981); *Sindell v. Abbott Laboratories*, 607 P.2d 924 (Cal.).

[24] See, e.g., *Manko v. United States*, 636 F. Supp. 1434 (W.D. Mo. 1986).

[25] *Tyson Foods v. Bouaphakeo*, 136 S. Ct. 1036 (2016).

[26] See, e.g., *United States v. Beverly*, 369 F.3d 516 (2004).

[27] See Roth 2010.

[28] See Koehler 2001.

of events to occur or co-vary. Thus, we might expect that we will decide more cases erroneously to the extent that we rely on intuitive rejections of probabilistic mechanics. Several writers have suggested that the intuitive resistance to resting legal decisions on naked statistics may be the result of cognitive bias, and that absent strong arguments to the contrary, we give appropriate weight to the numbers even when it feels uncomfortable to do so.[29]

Other writers agree that probabilistic reasoning should guide us but doubt that the standard of persuasion has been met in these hypotheticals. One argument, raised by both Tribe and Kaye,[30] was that the plaintiff's failure to adduce more particularized evidence was a sign that their case lacked merit. For example, if the Blue Bus company was at fault, perhaps the plaintiff could have obtained discovery showing that one of its buses was involved in a crash; the failure to produce such evidence might therefore imply either that such a search was fruitless or that the plaintiff expected it would be fruitless. But even if we think this approach works for these simple hypotheticals, it cannot justify a wholesale rejection of naked statistics. At best, it suggests that statistics that are only slightly above the proof threshold might be insufficient in cases where the plaintiff's failure to get more evidence lacks a reasonable explanation. But some cases involve statistics with far more discriminatory power, and some plaintiffs' inability to get better evidence will arise from cost constraints or other limits on discoverability. The argument also neglects the opposing inferences that might be drawn from a civil defendant's failure to present counterevidence. After all, if the person sued by the rodeo did not crash the gate, they could easily testify to that effect. If they have not done so, we might well ask why not.

Alternatively, we might exclude NSE as a means to incentivize the creation and production of higher quality evidence. A policy of exclusion might induce the rodeo to record the names of persons to whom it sold tickets, for instance. If so, we could resolve which attendees crashed the gate with a much lower error rate.[31] This may explain some hypotheticals, but it also implies that we should tolerate naked statistical proof when the parties would be unable to create better evidence *ex ante*, either because they could not reasonably anticipate lawsuits of this kind or because doing so is impossible or cost-prohibitive.

A third argument attacks the hypotheticals from the standpoint of economic efficiency. Posner framed the issue as follows: "Suppose the legal system can identify an entire class of cases in which the balance of probabilities tilts [0.51] ... in favor of the plaintiff .... If there are 1000 such cases, then allowing these to be tried can be expected to yield 510 correct decisions ... while not allowing them to be tried can be expected to yield 490 correct decisions. The social benefit of the twenty additional correct decisions ... would probably fall short of the social cost of 1000 trials."[32]

Sufficiently close cases, in other words, may not be worth trying. This argument certainly clashes with the law on a *descriptive* level, given that we regularly do allow quite close cases to receive jury trials, such as controversies hinging on close credibility contests or weak, but still admissible, scientific evidence of injury.[33] But as a normative consideration, it is harder to rebut. Perhaps, all things being equal, we might wish to raise the burden of persuasion somewhat, if we did believe that the social cost of trials outweighed the small decrement

---

[29] e.g., Redmayne 2008, 303–4; Spottswood 2013, 197–9; Shaviro 1989, 538.
[30] Tribe 1971, 1349; Kaye 1979, 106.
[31] Kaye 1979, 106.
[32] Posner 1999, 1510.
[33] See, e.g., *Wright v. Am. Home Prod. Corp.*, 557 F. Supp. 2d 1032, 1036 (W.D. Mo. 2008).

in accurate decisions that would follow.[34] Doing so, however, would only impact relatively weak NSE—and it might also justify rejecting liability in many cases involving more conventional proof.

Other theorists have argued that we must reject the conventional probabilistic framework entirely. Nesson maintained that the central goal of the factfinding process must be to deter wrongdoing, and he argued that members of the public are unlikely to internalize the law's "behavioral message" unless verdicts are presented as declarative factual pronouncements that the defendant committed a particular wrong. In his view, any verdict that plainly rests on a probabilistic foundation, such as a conviction based on naked statistics, would undermine this goal.[35] Nesson's suggestion rested merely on his own intuition, however, and we still lack empirical confirmation that such effects are real, let alone substantial enough to outweigh an expected rise in error costs from excluding NSE.

Many scholars have urged that the proof process should be understood, not as an evaluation of the probability that particular events occurred, but instead as a *comparison* of the strength of the cases presented by each party. Under such a view, a jury should find a civil defendant liable if the plaintiff's case seems stronger than the defendant's, even if the plaintiff's case by itself does not seem more likely than not to be true. These sort of theories often give slightly varying statements as to what, precisely, should be compared: candidates have included comparative degrees of inductive support,[36] ratios of the likelihoods of observing the evidence conditional on either party's theory of the case,[37] comparative degrees of committed belief in either party's case,[38] or consideration of the comparative extent to which either party's theory of the case explains the given pattern of evidence.[39]

Whether we should accept the recommendations of any of these theories with regard to NSE hinges, in part, on our trust in the underlying framework, and such analysis exceeds the bounds of this chapter. But leaving the particulars of each approach to one side, we can discuss one general feature of these arguments. Some proponents of comparative approaches have urged that NSE cannot shift the scales in such balancing because it lends no additional weight to the proponent's case. Sullivan, for example, has maintained that in the rodeo paradox, "the only 'evidence' is the contents of the ticket-box, and the contents of this box would be identical whether the defendant was one of the paying attendees or one of the gate jumpers."[40] But arguments like this seem to beg the critical question: what patterns of evidence *should* we expect to see if a randomly chosen defendant was, *in fact*, a gate-crasher? It would seem sensible to expect a higher ratio of crashers as opposed to a lower one, if the plaintiff's selection of a random attendee produced an actual gatecrasher.[41] (By analogy, if we are randomly drawing one ball from a filled urn and it is white, that should increase our confidence that the urn has many white balls, while lowering our confidence that it has very few of them.) And indeed, some proponents of comparative accounts have concluded that

---

[34] Of course, we must also acknowledge that few cases reach trial, especially when anticipated trial costs are high; to the extent that many such cases settle, the aggregate social cost of trying the remaining ones may be more tolerable.

[35] Nesson 1985, 1378–85.

[36] Cohen 1977, 245–6.

[37] Sullivan 2019, 26–29; Cheng 2013, 1267–8.

[38] Clermont 2018, 1068–9.

[39] Allen and Pardo 2019, 14–16.

[40] Sullivan 2019, 45.

[41] See Spottswood 2013, 195–6.

"there is no general distinction to be drawn . . . in terms of probative value . . . between statistical and non-statistical evidence."[42]

Lastly, there have been a number of papers in recent years that attempt to analyze these paradoxes from the standpoint of epistemology. A common method is to link various factors that have been suggested to be essential components of claims of *knowledge*, and then argue that since statistical evidence lacks these features, it cannot justify findings of guilt or liability.[43] But it is far from clear that the ordinary notion of knowledge provides either a necessary or sufficient condition for legal judgments. Consider, for instance, a simple case in which a plaintiff testifies that the defendant struck him, and the defendant testifies that he did not do so. If the jury finds the plaintiff just slightly more credible, they may find in his favor, even though it seems off to say that they *know* that the act occurred.[44] As a result, we should be cautious before accepting an argument that naked statistics are insufficient because we do not ordinarily consider them to be a sufficient basis for knowledge claims. A convincing account of these cases must also show why applying these epistemic rules would help the courts dispense better justice.[45,46]

Thus, there is substantial support in the literature for the view that we should admit some NSE, particularly when it is highly probative, when it is reliably sourced, and when exclusion would not be likely to lead to the production of better evidence. There are also many scholars who dissent from this view, offering a wide variety of theoretic defenses for our intuitive distrust of naked statistics.

3. Conjunction and Disjunction Paradoxes

The next category of paradoxes arises when factfinders must combine two or more uncertain judgments to determine a verdict. Consider what Cohen labelled "The Difficulty about Conjunction."[47] Judicial doctrine requires plaintiffs to prove each element of their case by a preponderance of the evidence—meaning, on a probabilistic interpretation, that each element must be more than 50% likely to be true. Assuming that these probabilities are statistically independent, then the chance that all are true *at once* is given by their product. In some cases, this will mean that although each element is sufficiently proven, their combination is probably false. For instance, in a case with two statistically independent elements, each proven to a probability of 70%, the probability that both are true is only 49%.

[42] Pardo 2019, 263–4.

[43] See, e.g., Ho 2008, 142 (arguing that naked statistics cannot support categorical beliefs in wrong-doing); Thomson 1986, 206 (arguing that the defect is that naked statistical evidence was not caused by the alleged acts). See, generally, Redmayne 2008, 298–307 (exploring, without ultimately endorsing, many similar arguments).

[44] Arguably, even the less demanding notion of justified belief would not be satisfied on such a thin margin of evidence.

[45] See Pardo 2019, 264; Enoch and Fisher 2015, 568–9. Pardo's work on epistemological safety does make a credible attempt to show that the concept may be normatively useful in terms of the analysis of probative value, but he makes it plain that safety does not broadly distinguish statistical from non-statistical proof. Pardo 2018, 70, n. 101.

[46] Sadly, this short treatment cannot do justice to the large literature attempting to tackle the normative sufficiency of naked statistical evidence, and many thoughtful treatments must be omitted. e.g., Dahlman 2020; Nunn 2015. These issues are further explored by Dalhman and Pundik, "The Problem with Naked Statistical Evidence," ch. 22, in this volume.

[47] Cohen 1977, 58–67.

A few variations on the conjunction problem have also been described. Imagine that a plaintiff has brought two independent claims for relief, A and B, either of which (if successful) would obligate the defendant to pay damages for a particular injury. We ordinarily assume that a plaintiff must prove any individual claim to be more than 50% likely to win. But if we once again assume statistical independence, then the likelihood that either A is true, B is true, or *both are* true, is represented by the following equation:[48]

$$P(A \ or \ B) = P(A) + P(B) - P(A)P(B).$$

For instance, imagine that a plaintiff sued a defendant for running her over with a car. The plaintiff claims the act was either an intentional act or a negligent accident. Assuming that these likelihoods are independent, if both are proven to probability of 30%, mathematically the chance that at least one of them is valid is 30% + 30% - 9%, for a total of 51%.[49] A similar scenario could arise when a defendant raises multiple affirmative defenses to a single claim, since the proof of any one affirmative defense justifies a defense verdict.

3.1 Intuitions About Conjunctive Likelihoods

There is a widespread view in the literature that it feels unfair for a plaintiff to prove all of the elements beyond the standard of proof but still lose overall.[50] This might imply that, like proof based on NSE, our intuitions reject the implications of probability theory with respect to conjunctive proof. On the other hand, Nance raised—without necessarily endorsing—the possibility that jurors might instinctively make correct judgments regarding conjunctive likelihoods, even if they could not articulate why they had done so.[51]

To date, intuitions about conjunctive likelihoods have not been explored using mock jury designs. But other evidence suggests that human beings may often fail to discount conjunctive likelihoods to the extent that probability theory would require. In a now famous experiment, Tversky and Kahneman described a fictitious person named Linda, who "was deeply concerned with issues of discrimination and social justice" in her student days. They then asked them to rate the likelihoods that "Linda is a bank teller" and "Linda is a bank teller who is active in the feminist movement." Analytically, the first statement must be more likely than the second, which incorporates the first along with an additional detail, but most participants said the second was more likely.[52] Similar results were obtained when participants were asked to predict hypothetical future events, some of which were conjunctive in form.[53]

3.2 Conjunction Doctrine

No reported court decisions appear to grapple with the conjunction paradox. Instead, the relevant doctrine is contained in the form of jury instructions. Nance drew attention to a

[48] Spottswood 2016, 263–4.
[49] At least two papers have independently raised the possibility of a disjunction paradox. See Harel and Porat 2009 (discussing criminal charges); Lombardero 1996 (discussing civil claims).
[50] See, e.g., Clermont 2013, 1100.
[51] Nance 1986, 951.
[52] Kahneman et al. 1982, 92.
[53] Ibid., 96–7. See also Saks and Kidd 1980, 142; Gettys et al. 1973, 369–70.

potential ambiguity in some instructions, such as this one: "The burden is on the plaintiff … to prove every essential element of his claim by a preponderance of the evidence. If the proof should fail to establish any essential element of plaintiff's claim by a preponderance … , the jury should find for the defendant."[54]

Nance argued that it was unclear if the words "every essential element" and "any essential element" were intended to specify that proving each element was a *sufficient* condition for liability, or merely a *necessary* one (with proof of the conjunction also being required).[55] More recently, Schwartz and Sober conducted a large-scale survey of jury instructions used across American state courts. They found that the majority of instructions made it clear that proof of each element was a necessary condition for liability, without clearly specifying that it was also a sufficient one. But a smaller fraction did include additional language instructing that finding liability was required once each element was sufficiently proven on its own.[56]

It seems doubtful, however, that the authors of jury instructions have thought about the issues raised by the conjunction paradox and made a reasoned decision to favor one outcome over the other.[57] And one piece of evidence cuts against the conclusion that courts have decided to adopt "necessary-but-not-sufficient" instructions as a means of resolving the paradox. Courts sometimes use special verdict forms, which ask juries to make separate decisions on each element. Courts commonly impose liability when the jury indicates that it has found each necessary element to be sufficiently proved, without asking whether they also believe the conjunction is probably true.[58]

3.3 Normative Approaches to Resolving Aggregation Difficulties

Some authors have taken the position that the best approach is simply to follow the dictates of probability theory. This would imply that some plaintiffs should lose despite proving each element beyond the standard of proof, and also that some defendants should win despite proving each defense to a lesser degree than the proof standard.[59] This approach, although admittedly at odds with current practices, might have a relatively modest impact on the litigation system, given that real-life cases mostly involve a fair amount of probabilistic dependence across contested elements.[60] Meanwhile, the smaller number of cases where the adjustments would be sufficient to turn a winner into a loser are precisely those in which the plaintiff was probably *not* injured by the defendant's conduct.

A second group of scholars have argued that in the context of our litigation system, the failure to adjust conjunctive likelihoods downward is valuable because it tends to offset other sources of error. Levmore focused on the possibility that the requirement of supermajority or unanimous jury agreement would inflate the effective burden of proof.[61] Stein

---

[54] Devitt and Blackmar 1977, §71.14.
[55] Nance, 1986, 948–9. Accord Friedman 2001, 2041. *But* see Allen and Jehl 2003, 900 (arguing that other portions of the same pattern instructions supported a sufficiency reading).
[56] Schwartz and Sober 2017, 674.
[57] See Nance 2016, 76–7.
[58] Spottswood 2016, 267.
[59] Ibid., 294; Friedman 1992, 97; Nance 2001, 1588.
[60] Spottswood 2016, 265; Schwartz and Sober 2017, 661–7.
[61] Levmore 2001, 734–51.

has offered a similar argument, arguing that conjunctive neglect will correct for suboptimal levels of deterrence that allegedly arise from a factfinder's reliance on information that was unavailable at the time of an allegedly wrongful act.[62] These claims are too complex to fully explore here, but they share a crucial weakness. Each invokes a (possible) biasing feature on one side of the process and relies on conjunctive neglect to counter-balance it. But in practice, we have little warrant to think that the two effects would be of similar size. Moreover, the conjunction paradox does not arise evenly in all cases; its main effects occur when there is either an unusually low degree of dependence across elements or an unusually high numbers of contested elements. Thus, if we think the problems mentioned by Levmore and Stein are pervasive, neglecting conjunctive likelihoods will be an inconsistent remedy, reserving its strongest treatment for cases where the plaintiff's case lacks merit.

Others have suggested that it is desirable for the system to compare the strength of the coherent *stories* offered by each party, rather than assessing the likelihood that the plaintiff's case is true in isolation. Nesson proposed that plaintiffs should prevail so long as the least likely element of their case is probably true.[63] Cheng preferred a probability ratio test, which compares the probability of the plaintiff's account with that of the defendant's, with the plaintiff winning only when the former is higher.[64] Nesson believes this comparative approach will make it more likely that the public will accept the verdict as a statement of what really happened, leading to greater acquiescence to the law's commands.[65] But since most juries give general verdicts without explanation, it seems doubtful that allowing juries to reject liability based upon conjunctive discounting would draw much public condemnation.[66] And as discussed above, we might also question whether the size of such an effect (if real) is worse than the harm of awarding victory to claimants whose overall claims are more likely to be false than true.

Other authors have urged that we reject entirely the application of the standard rules of probabilistic reasoning in this context. Cohen proposed *inductive* probability analysis,[67] Clermont advocated an approach based on the theories of fuzzy sets and belief functions,[68] and Allen and Pardo prefer comparatively weighing the plausibility of each party's explanation of the evidence.[69] In each case, the proposal's ability to resolve the conjunction problem depends, in part, on its strengths as a general approach to legal factfinding, which is once again beyond the scope of this chapter. But in addition, one must ask how conjunctive proof should be evaluated within each framework. We should tread cautiously before concluding that an alternative approach justifies ignoring the reality the conjunctions are normally less likely to be true than any of their constitutive elements. Since this equation describes the expected frequency of co-occurrences in reality, an approach that sets it aside will likely result in an increased rate of error in application.[70] Thus, those wishing to make these theories normatively attractive as a means of resolving cases might wish to interpret them to permit

[62] Stein 2001, 1208–13.
[63] Nesson 1985, 1389.
[64] Cheng 2013, 1262–4. His approach is formally equivalent to a likelihood ratio test, which compares the probability of observing the evidence conditional on the truth of the plaintiff's account, with the probability of observing it conditional on the defendant's account. Ibid., 1268.
[65] See Lombardero 1996, 275–6.
[66] Spottswood 2016, 291–2.
[67] Cohen 1977, 167–244.
[68] Clermont 2018, 1068–9.
[69] Allen and Pardo 2019, 14–16.
[70] Pardo 2019, 275–6.

appropriate discounting of conjunctive likelihoods, even if not done in mathematical terms. And in fact, recent work on the explanatory account of proof has increasingly converged on the notion that explanations containing more necessary conjunctive components should generally receive less credit than explanations that are simpler in form.[71]

4. Group Decision Paradoxes

The final type of paradox arises when factfinding is performed by groups such as juries or multi-judge courts. Although other problems have been raised,[72] let us focus on the *discursive dilemma*.[73] Iuliano illustrates the dilemma using the example of a six-person jury deciding a case with five elements, based upon a majority voting decision rule, with the juror's views and the possible results as summarized in Table 21.1 below:

Table 21.1   The Discursive Dilemma for Multiple Required Elements

Example 1	Element 1	Element 2	Element 3	Element 4	Element 5	Individual Conclusions
Juror 1	Proven	Proven	Proven	Proven	Proven	Liable
Juror 2	Not Proven	Proven	Proven	Proven	Proven	Not Liable
Juror 3	Proven	Not Proven	Proven	Proven	Proven	Not Liable
Juror 4	Proven	Proven	Not Proven	Proven	Proven	Not Liable
Juror 5	Proven	Proven	Proven	Not Proven	Proven	Not Liable
Juror 6	Proven	Proven	Proven	Proven	Not Proven	Not Liable
Element-by-Element Voting Results	Proven	Proven	Proven	Proven	Proven	Liable

If the jurors vote based on result only, five out of six of vote to reject liability. If instead they vote on whether to find each element sequentially, they find unanimously in favor

---

[71] Spottswood 2016, 273–80 (showing that a careful implementation of explanatory criteria should yield similar results on conjunctive and disjunctive issues as occur under a conventional probabilistic analysis); see also Pardo 2019, 280 (acknowledging that the approach "does not reject the product rule" but rather accounts for "the underlying features of reality" in a non-mathematical way).

[72] Levmore's discussion of the Condorcet Jury Theorem and related issues with respect to verdicts premised upon super-majority or unanimous agreement might provide a second example. See Levmore 2001; but cf. Allen and Jehl 2003, 16–25. Iuliano described a third candidate, but his "Lottery Paradox" is essentially the conjunction paradox recast as a problem of group agreement. Iuliano 2014, 415–23.

[73] See Iuliano 2014, 411–23; Pardo 2019, 282–8; Pardo 2015, 1832–4. Beyond the jury context, several scholars have explored the possibility of discursive dilemmas when multi-member courts decide questions of law. See, generally, Tuzet 2019 (reviewing literature).

of the plaintiff.[74] Next consider a case in which the only disputed issue is whether the defendant made a deceptive statement, and in which the plaintiff has suggested three possible statements that might fit the bill. Now, the jurors might come to the following pattern of conclusions in Table 21.2:

Table 21.2 The Discursive Dilemma for Indepently Sufficient Theories of Liability

Example 2	False Statement 1	False Statement 2	False Statement 3	Individual Conclusions
Juror 1	Proven	Not Proven	Not Proven	**Liable**
Juror 2	Proven	Not Proven	Not Proven	**Liable**
Juror 3	Not Proven	Proven	Not Proven	**Liable**
Juror 4	Not Proven	Proven	Not Proven	**Liable**
Juror 5	Not Proven	Not Proven	Proven	**Liable**
Juror 6	Not Proven	Not Proven	Proven	**Liable**
Statement-by-Statement Voting Results	Not Liable	Not Liable	Not Liable	**Not Liable**

In short, applying a decision rule step-by-step can yield different results than applying it to the overall decision, with the result sometimes favoring plaintiffs and prosecutors and at other times favoring defendants.[75]

Doctrinally, most cases are submitted to juries without any instruction regarding how the jurors are to conduct their internal deliberations.[76] Occasionally, special verdict forms or judicial polling of a jury reveals a potential instance of the discursive dilemma, but the resulting decisions reveal no clear consensus. In jurisdictions where civil cases are decided by a super-majority of jurors, some courts hold that "any [sufficient super-majority] agreeing on any interrogatory is sufficient to support the overall verdict," while others require that "the same jurors must form the majority on each interrogatory ...."[77] In criminal cases, there can be evidence of multiple potential acts, any of which might be sufficient to prove an element of the case. The United States Supreme Court has walked a delicate line, holding that jurors need not agree on the "means" by which an offense was committed,[78] but that they must agree which specific "acts" occurred when those acts constitute elements of a charged offense.[79]

On the prescriptive front, Iuliano has suggested that we re-draft special verdict forms so that jurors who have rejected one element must thereby reject each subsequent element. This

[74] Iuliano 2014, 423.
[75] cf. Tuzet 2019, 76–7.
[76] See, e.g., Eleventh Circuit Committee on Pattern Jury Instructions 2020, §§3.81–3.9 (providing pattern civil jury instructions that require unanimous agreement without instructing whether this agreement must include the rationale for a result or any internal procedures to be used in determining agreement).
[77] See *Harris v. State ex rel. Dept. of Trans. & Dev.*, 997 So.2d 849, 869–71 (La. App. 1st Cir. 2008) (collecting cases and siding with the "any majority" view).
[78] *Schad v. Arizona*, 501 U.S. 624 (1991) (plurality opinion).
[79] *Richardson v. United States*, 526 U.S. 813 (1999).

suggestion would align the results of special verdicts with how jurors would vote if they were required to vote "all-or-nothing" on a general verdict. This has the virtue of making it less likely that that the decision to use a special verdict form will be outcome-determinative.[80]

Pardo, meanwhile, has urged that fully adopting an explanatory account of proof would meliorate the discursive dilemma. He would permit jurors to vote based on result, even if they disagreed on which coherent story was most likely, provided that they each agreed that the *disjunction* of their various first choices was more likely than the opposing party's explanation of the case. But if the jurors did not think the disjunction of their first choices was a better explanation than what was offered by the opposing party, then their lack of agreement on rationale should lead the opposing party to prevail.[81] So in short, both authors ultimately elect results-based voting, but Pardo's definition of "agreeing on the result" is a bit subtler.

Nonetheless, it is not clear that we should automatically assume that the jurors' preferences over general verdicts should control from a normative perspective. In Table 21.1, above, the fact that five of six jurors would vote in favor of each element would seem to be make it far more likely than not that each element was actually true. Depending on the degree of dependence among the elements, this might lead us to conclude that overall liability is likely true as well. Ultimately, until more work is done to map the relationships between jury voting and the underlying likelihood of culpable conduct, normative analysis of this problem may be intractable.

5. Conclusion

There is still much fruitful work to be done with respect to these questions, and it is my hope that summarizing some of what has come before may help others who wish to explore new terrain. As we have seen, these problems can be analyzed on multiple levels. Whether each is a "paradox" depends in part on whether we think there is an irresolvable clash between the recommendations that human intuition, judicial doctrine, or normative analysis provide for each type of puzzle. But even when we observe such clashes, we might well ask whether we have found a mystery in need of solving, or merely an opportunity to reform our intuitions or our law.

References

Allen, R. J. and Jehl, S. A. (2003). "Burdens of Persuasion in Civil Cases: Algorithms v. Explanations," *Michigan State Law Review*, 2003: 893–944.

Allen, R. J. and Pardo, M. S. (2019). "Relative Plausibility and its Critics," *International Journal of Evidence & Proof*, 23: 5–59.

Brook, J. (1985). "The Use of Statistical Evidence of Identification in Civil Litigation: Well-Worn Hypotheticals, Real Cases, and Controversy," *St. Louis University Law Journal*, 29: 293–352.

Cheng, E. K. (2013). "Reconceptualizing the Burden of Proof," *Yale Law Journal*, 122: 1254–79.

---

[80] Iuliano 2014, 412–14.
[81] Pardo 2015, 1829.

Clermont, K. M. (2013). "Death of Paradox: The Killer Logic beneath the Standards of Proof," *Notre Dame Law Review*, 88: 1061–1138.

Clermont, K. M. (2018). "Common Sense on Standards of Proof," *Seton Hall Law Review*, 48: 1057–80.

Cohen, L. J. (1977). *The Probable and the Provable*. Oxford: Oxford University Press.

Dahlman, C. (2020). "Naked Statistical Evidence and Incentives for Lawful Conduct," *International Journal of Evidence & Proof*, 24: 162–79.

Devitt, E. J. and Blackmar, C. B. Vol 2 (1977). *Federal Jury Practice and Instructions*. Third edition. St. Paul, MN: West Publishing Co.

Eleventh Circuit Committee on Pattern Jury Instructions (2020). *Eleventh Circuit Pattern Jury Instructions (Civil)*. World Wide Web: Westlaw.

Enoch, D. and Fisher, T. (2015). "Sense and 'Sensitivity': Epistemic and Instrumental Approaches to Statistical Evidence," *Stanford Law Review*, 67: 557–611.

Friedman, R. D. (1992). "Infinite Strands, Infinitesimally Thin: Storytelling, Bayesianism, Hearsay and other Evidence," *Cardozo Law Review*, 14: 79–101.

Friedman, R. D. (2001). "'E' is for Eclectic: Multiple Perspectives on Evidence," *Virginia Law Review*, 87: 2029–54.

Gettys, C. F., Kelly, C., and Peterson, C. R. (1973). "The Best Guess Hypothesis in Multistage Inference," *Organizational Behavior and Human Performance*, 10: 364–73.

Harel, A. and Porat, A. (2009). "Aggregating Probabilities across Cases: Criminal Responsibility for Unspecified Offenses," *Minnesota Law Review*, 94: 261–310.

Heller, K. J. (2006). "The Cognitive Psychology of Circumstantial Evidence," *Michigan Law Review*, 105: 241–305.

Ho, H. L. (2008). *A Philosophy of Evidence Law: Justice in the Search for Truth*. Oxford: Oxford University Press.

Iuliano, J. (2014). "Jury Voting Paradoxes," *Michigan Law Review*, 113: 405–27.

Kahneman, D., Slovic, P., and Tversky, A. (1982). *Judgment under Uncertainty: Heuristics and Biases*. New York: Cambridge University Press.

Kaye, D. H. (1979). "The Paradox of the Gatecrasher and Other Stories," *Arizona State Law Journal*, 1979(1): 101–9.

Kaye, D. H. (1980). "Naked Statistical Evidence," *Yale Law Journal*, 89: 601–11.

Koehler, J. J. (2001). "When Do Courts Think Base Rate Statistics Are Relevant?" *Jurimetrics* 42: 373–402.

Levmore, S. (2001). "Conjunction and Aggregation," *Michigan Law Review*, 99: 723–56.

Lombardero, D. A. (1996). "Do Special Verdicts Improve the Structure of Jury Decision-Making?" *Jurimetrics*, 36: 275–315.

Nance, D. A. (1986). "A Comment on the Supposed Paradoxes of a Mathematical Interpretation of the Logic of trials," *Boston University Law Review*, 66: 947–52.

Nance, D. A. (2001). "Naturalized Epistemology and the Critique of Evidence Theory," *Virginia Law Review*, 87: 1551–618.

Nance, D. A. (2016). *The Burdens of Proof: Discriminatory Power, Weight of Evidence, and Tenacity of Belief*. Cambridge: Cambridge University Press.

Nesson, C. R. (1979). "Reasonable Doubt and Permissive Inferences: The Value of Complexity," *Harvard Law Review*, 92: 1187–225.

Nesson, C. R. (1985). "The Evidence or the Event? On Judicial Proof and the Acceptability of Verdicts," *Harvard Law Review*, 98: 1357–92.

Niedermeier, K. E., Kerr, N. E., and Messé, L. A. (1999). "Jurors' Use of Naked Statistical Evidence: Exploring Bases and Implications of the Wells Effect," *Journal of Personality & Social Psychology*, 76: 533–42.

Nunn, G. A. (2015). "The Incompatibility of Due Process and Naked Statistical Evidence," *Vanderbilt Law Review*, 69: 1407–33.

Pardo, M. S. (2015). "Group Agency and Legal Proof; Or, Why the Jury is an 'It'," *William & Mary Law Review*, 56: 1793–858.

Pardo, M. S. (2018). "Safety vs. Sensitivity: Possible Worlds and the Law of Evidence," *Legal Theory*, 2:, 50–75.

Pardo, M. S. (2019). "The Paradoxes of Legal Proof: A Critical Guide," *Boston University Law Review*, 99: 233–90.

Pennington, N. and Hastie, R. (1991). "A Cognitive Theory of Juror Decision Making: The Story Model," *Cardozo Law Review*, 13: 519–57.

Posner, R. A. (1999). "An Economic Approach to the Law of Evidence," *Stanford Law Review*, 51: 1477–546.

Redmayne, M. (2008). "Exploring the Proof Paradoxes," *Legal Theory*, 14: 281–309.

Roth, A. (2010). "Safety in Numbers? Deciding when DNA Evidence Alone is Enough to Convict," *New York University Law Review*, 85: 1130–85.

Saks, M. J. and Kidd, R. F. (1980). "Human Information Processing and Adjudication: Trial by Heuristics," *Law & Society Review*, 15: 123–60.

Schwartz, D. S. and Sober, E. R. (2017). "The Conjunction Problem and the Logic of Jury Findings," *William & Mary Law Review*, 59: 619–92.

Shaviro, D. (1989). "Statistical-Probability Evidence and the Appearance of Justice," *Harvard Law Review*, 103: 530–54.

Spottswood, M. (2013). "The Hidden Structure of Fact-Finding," *Case Western Reserve Law Review*, 64: 131–200.

Spottswood, M. (2016). "Unraveling the Conjunction Paradox," *Law, Probability and Risk*, 15: 259–96.

Spottswood, M. (2019). "On the Limitations of a Unitary Model of the Proof Process," *International Journal of Evidence & Proof*, 23: 75–81.

Stein, A. (2001). "Of Two Wrongs that Make a Right: Two Paradoxes of the Evidence Law and their Combined Economic Justification," *Texas Law Review*, 79: 1199–234.

Sullivan, S. P. (2019). "A Likelihood Story: The Theory of Legal Fact-Finding," *Colorado Law Review*, 90: 1–66.

Thomson, J. J. (1986). "Liability and Individualized Evidence," *Law and Contemporary Problems*, 49: 199–219.

Tribe, L. H. (1971). "Trial by Mathematics: Precision and Ritual in the Legal Process," *Harvard Law Review*, 84: 1329–93.

Tuzet, G. (2019). "More Votes, More Irrationality," *American Journal of Jurisprudence*, 64: 61–78.

Wells, G. L. (1992). "Naked Statistical Evidence of Liability: Is Subjective Probability Enough?" *Journal of Personality & Social Psychology*, 62: 739–52.

Zamir, E., Ritov, I., and Teithman, D. (2014). "Seeing is Believing: The Anti-Inference Bias," *Indiana Law Journal*, 89: 195–229.

22

The Problem with Naked Statistical Evidence

Christian Dahlman and Amit Pundik

1. Introduction

The three most-debated cases in the theoretical literature dealing with legal evidence are the *Blue Bus* case, the *Gatecrasher* case, and the *Prison Riot* case. They share some curious features. First of all, none of them are real cases; they are constructed by evidence scholars to make a philosophical point and are highly unrealistic. Second, they are all intended to illustrate the problem with a certain kind of statistical evidence commonly referred to as "naked statistical evidence" (NSE). The circumstances of the first two cases are described in Chapter 21 in this volume by Spottswood and we will not repeat them here. We will use the *Prison Riot* case, introduced by Charles Nesson in 1979, as our chief example of NSE. In our version:

> One hundred prison inmates participate in a riot and manage to escape. During the riot, ninety-nine of them assault and kill a guard on duty. One prisoner is caught and prosecuted for participating in the killing. It is absolutely certain that he is one of the one hundred prisoners who participated in the riot, and it is absolutely certain that ninety-nine of them participated in the killing of the guard. There is no further evidence (no witnesses or CCTV images) that makes it possible to identify the one prisoner who did *not* participate in the killing. According to the prosecutor, the prisoner who was caught should be convicted because the available evidence satisfies the standard of proof in criminal trials: it establishes that there is a 99% probability that the defendant participated in the killing of the guard.[1]

According to Nesson, the defendant should not be convicted on such evidence, since there is nothing in it that "differentiates the defendant from the other prisoners."[2] A guilty verdict is unacceptable, and this goes for all cases of NSE.[3] The peculiar nature of NSE is often illustrated by contrasting it with evidence that is not of the "naked statistical" kind, such as a witness or a fingerprint. In the *Prison Riot* case, we could imagine an alternative version with fingerprint evidence in place of the NSE that ninety-nine of the one hundred prisoners who participated in the riot also participated in the killing of the guard. In this alternative, the guard is killed by only one prisoner, who leaves a partially smudged fingerprint at the crime scene. This print is subsequently found to match the defendant. The probability that

---

[1] For those who hold the standard of proof to be higher than 99%, say 99.5%, the circumstances of the case can always be altered to satisfy this threshold, for example, by making it 1,000 prisoners where 999 participated in the killing of the guard.

[2] Nesson 1979, 1193.

[3] Nesson 1985, 1378.

Christian Dahlman and Amit Pundik, *The Problem with Naked Statistical Evidence* In: *Philosophical Foundations of Evidence Law*. Edited by: Christian Dahlman, Alex Stein, and Giovanni Tuzet, Oxford University Press. © Christian Dahlman, Alex Stein, and Giovanni Tuzet 2021. DOI: 10.1093/oso/9780198859307.003.0023

the defendant is guilty, given the fingerprint evidence, is 99%. This is the same probability of guilt—99%—as that used in the NSE version of the case. Here, though, when using fingerprint evidence for prosecution instead of the naked statistic, it is no longer unacceptable to convict the defendant of killing the guard, even though the fingerprint evidence is also "statistical" in the sense that it is based on statistics about the *prevalence* of certain fingerprint patterns. Similarly to the *Prison Riot* case, for every one hundred people whose convictions are based on fingerprints, one person, on average, would be innocent. So this raises the question: what is it about NSE that renders it unacceptable as the basis for a conviction?

The debate over NSE started in the 1970s with seminal publications by Laurence Tribe, Jonathan Cohen, and Charles Nesson,[4] and has continued with contributions from a series of eminent scholars.[5] Most agree that it is problematic to base a verdict on NSE but they disagree on *why* it is problematic, pointing to different characteristics of NSE as the root of the problem. In the last decade, the debate has been energized by publications, most notably that of Enoch, Spectre, and Fisher,[6] proposing a number of new approaches. In this book, the classical debate on NSE is covered in Mark Spottswood's chapter in this volume (Chapter 21), while the present chapter focuses on the recent debate.

2. Insufficient or Inadmissible?

Academic deliberations on NSE, mainly in philosophy but also in law, tend to conflate two distinct problems. The first is the question of *sufficiency*: is it acceptable to convict on NSE *alone*? The challenge here is to explain why conviction on NSE is unacceptable even though other kinds of evidence that establish a similarly high probability of guilt would have sufficed. The second question is that of *admissibility*: is it acceptable that NSE is presented in court as evidence and counted by the factfinder *as* evidence? Philosophical debates over NSE usually focus on the sufficiency question (see, for example, the discussion surrounding the lottery paradox).[7] In the legal context, admissibility is also a highly contentious issue. For instance, irrespective of any other evidence available, it seems highly objectionable to use the high rate of crimes involving illegal firearms in a certain neighborhood to support the conviction of an individual resident in a crime involving an illegal firearm (henceforth, *Crime Rate* case). A similar difficulty arises in other types of evidence that bear some resemblance to NSE: while no one seriously argues that a person should be convicted based on their previous convictions alone, the question of whether this evidence should be admissible is fiercely debated.[8] One might retort that the problems of sufficiency and admissibility are so different that there is no reason to expect a solution that would address both. However, both problems concern the use of the same type of evidence (NSE) in the same context (criminal proceedings) for the same purpose (finding out whether the accused is guilty). Consequently, an account that can explain and justify not only the intuitive insufficiency of NSE but also its no-less-intuitive inadmissibility seems advantageous. However, as

---

[4] Tribe 1971; Cohen 1977; Nesson 1979.
[5] e.g., Kaye 1980; Thomson 1986; Allen 1991; Wasserman 1991; Posner 1999; Stein 2005; Schauer 2006; Redmayne 2008.
[6] Enoch, Spectre, and Fisher 2012. See also Nunn 2015; Smith 2018; Pundik 2017a; Pardo 2019; Dahlman 2020.
[7] For a clear presentation of the lottery paradox, see Stein 2005, 68.
[8] e.g., Redmayne 2015.

we shall see, many of the recent solutions to the NSE problem do not pay sufficient attention to the question of admissibility.

3. An Epistemic or Moral Problem?

The debate over NSE can be broadly divided into contributions that view it as an *epistemic* problem[9] and those that regard it as a *moral* problem.[10] According to the epistemic approaches, NSE is problematic because it does not provide the right kind of *knowledge* (or the right kind of epistemic justification). The idea, broadly, is that, even though a belief that is based on NSE is very likely to be true (99% likely in the *Prison Riot* case), this belief is unwarranted because some additional condition that epistemic justification requires is missing. While the epistemic approaches differ on what is missing, they share the view that high probability is important yet insufficient. If this view is correct, NSE poses not only a legal problem but also a general problem concerning probability and knowledge. According to the moral approaches, on the other hand, the problem with NSE concerns moral justification and is specific to law and also to some other contexts where decisions based on NSE are morally unjustified. From this perspective, the problem with the NSE in the *Prison Riot* case is not that the judge who convicts the defendant lacks the knowledge or justified belief that the defendant participated in the killing of the guard, but rather that something in the underlying moral justification for criminal punishment requires some other kind of evidence. It may be rational for the judge to place a bet on whether the defendant acted the way the prosecution alleges based on the NSE, but it would not be morally right for the judge to send the defendant to prison on this evidence.

In this chapter, we will explore some epistemic approaches ("sensitivity" and "normalcy") and some moral approaches ("incentives" and "free will"). In our view, defended in more detail in the next section, the problem of NSE is not an epistemic one. We believe NSE is problematic for moral reasons. As the reader will notice, we have different views on what these moral reasons are. According to one of us (Dahlman), convictions on NSE are morally unjustified as they fail to provide incentives for lawful conduct, while the other (Pundik) believes that such verdicts are morally unacceptable because they rest on contradicting assumptions, according to which the defendant's conduct was simultaneously free *and* unfree.

4. Sensitivity and Normalcy

When considering contemporary epistemic approaches, perhaps the best place to start is with the notion of *sensitivity*, as suggested by Enoch, Spectre, and Fisher.[11] While the issue of statistical evidence has been discussed vigorously in legal scholarship for more than four decades,[12] it has been largely ignored by the philosophical community. Remarkably, Enoch, Spectre, and Fisher's work has attracted immense philosophical attention to this problem.[13]

---

[9]   e.g., Smith 2018; Moss 2018.
[10]   e.g., Dahlman 2020; Pundik 2020.
[11]   Enoch, Spectre, and Fisher 2012.
[12]   Since Cohen 1977.
[13]   e.g., Buchak 2014; Blome-Tillmann 2015; Pritchard 2017; Smith 2018; Gardiner 2019; Di Bello 2019; Bollinger 2020.

Although they come to the conclusion that "such epistemological niceties as whether a finding is sensitive are not something the law should care about,"[14] we discuss their epistemic proposal because it is elegant and appealing, and discussing it could shed some light on the advantages and challenges of the epistemic direction more generally.

Enoch, Spectre, and Fisher define sensitivity as follows: "S's belief that p is sensitive = $_{df}$ Had it not been the case that p, S would (most probably) not have believed that p."[15] Sensitivity is based on a counterfactual condition: the factfinder's belief that the defendant committed the alleged crime is sensitive if *and only if*, had the defendant not committed the alleged crime, the factfinder would most probably not have believed that the defendant had committed the crime. NSE is epistemically inferior to other kinds of evidence, the argument goes, because it is incapable of supporting a sensitive belief: even if the defendant did not commit the crime, "we would still have the exact same statistical evidence available to us."[16] In the *Prison Riot* case, the statistical evidence that ninety-nine out of one hundred prisoners participated in the killing of the guard would support the factfinder's belief that the defendant is guilty even if the defendant happened to be the only prisoner who did not participate.

There is a noticeable similarity between sensitivity and the causal approach proposed by Judith Jarvis Thomson in the 1980s.[17] Thomson argued that conviction requires "evidence which is in an appropriate way causally connected with the (putative) fact that the defendant is guilty."[18] Expressed more simply, the fact that the defendant is guilty should causally explain the fact that the evidence exists.[19] This observation has been developed independently by both Pundik and Dahlman.[20] According to Dahlman, NSE differs from other kinds of evidence with regard to the direction of causation between the act that the defendant is accused of having committed and the evidence supporting this accusation.[21] NSE has a *predictive connection* whereby causation runs from evidence to act (the fact that the prisoner participated in the riot is predictive of also having participated in the killing of the guard). By contrast, when the evidence is an eyewitness account, a fingerprint, or some other kind of trace evidence, the causal connection runs in the other direction, from act to evidence (the defendant's participation in the killing of the guard caused the eyewitness to see the incident and caused the defendant's fingerprint to be on the guard's clothes).

These observations about NSE and causation have much in common with the observations about NSE and sensitivity. Causation is commonly defined in counterfactual terms by philosophers, scientists, and lawyers. David Lewis first popularized the counterfactual analysis of causation in the 1970s,[22] which has been further developed and defended by various philosophers since.[23] This analysis is commonly deployed by scientists (following, most notably, Pearl's work)[24] and lawyers, who are accustomed to counterfactual tests of causation (either the traditional "but-for" test or the more sophisticated NESS test).[25] Under the

---

[14] Enoch, Spectre, and Fisher 2012, 200.
[15] Ibid., 204.
[16] Ibid., 207.
[17] Thomson 1986.
[18] Ibid., 214.
[19] Ibid., 203.
[20] Pundik 2017a, 209–10; Dahlman 2020.
[21] Dahlman 2020, 166–7.
[22] Lewis 1973.
[23] e.g., Collins, Hall, and Paul 2004.
[24] Pearl 2000.
[25] Wright 1985.

counterfactual analysis of causation, the sensitivity approach and the causal approach yield similar tests: "Had the defendant not been guilty, would the factfinder have believed the defendant was guilty, given the evidence?" versus "Had the defendant not committed the act, would the evidence have been created?"

Not surprisingly, sensitivity has attracted similar objections to those raised against Thomson's approach. Smith, for example, rejects sensitivity because he argues that even eyewitness testimony might sometimes be insensitive.[26] Consider an eyewitness who testifies seeing the defendant in the *Prison Riot* case participating in the killing of the guard. If this testimony is false (for example, because, unknown to the factfinder, the eyewitness is lying and trying to frame the defendant), the factfinder's belief that the defendant is guilty is *in*sensitive: it is *not* true that the factfinder would not have believed that the defendant was guilty, had the defendant not committed the crime. The problem extends beyond false testimonies to cases in which the accused *did* participate in the killing, if, unknown to the factfinder, the eyewitness would have testified that the accused participated even had they not participated. Pundik raised a similar criticism regarding Thomson's account,[27] indicating the similarity between the sensitivity and causal approaches and the insufficiency of both for separating NSE from other types of evidence. In response, it could be argued that sensitivity should be understood not as requiring that the evidence *be* sensitive but only that it *could* be sensitive: while NSE is *always* insensitive, the eyewitness testimony *could be* sensitive under some conditions (for instance, if it is true). Expressed differently, sensitivity operates at the type rather than the token level: eyewitness testimony as a *category* of evidence is sensitive, even if some specific instances of eyewitness testimony are not.

One problem with the sensitivity approach that we find particularly troubling is that the *scope* of the sensitivity requirement is unclear and problematic to delimit. It would be devastating if the requirement of sensitivity extended to all parts of evidentiary inference. However, as Pundik has pointed out elsewhere, the assessment of how strongly a certain piece of evidence supports a hypothesis is always made on the basis of general background knowledge about the possibility that this piece of evidence is found even if the hypothesis is false.[28] For example, factfinders may consider eyewitness identification more credible if the eyewitness observed the perpetrator at close range in excellent lighting conditions. This inference relies on the generalization that, under such conditions, a higher proportion of eyewitness identifications is accurate than under average or poor conditions, and this generalization is *insensitive* to whether the defendant in the case at hand is guilty or innocent. While such generalizations do not pass the sensitivity test, factfinding would become impossible without them.

The same goes for DNA evidence, which is commonly considered the "gold standard" of legal factfinding.[29] How strongly a DNA match supports the hypothesis that the defendant is the source of the DNA found at the crime scene is assessed on the basis of statistical data indicating the probability of a random match (the possibility that the sample from the crime scene happens to match the defendant even though it originates from a different individual). Just like generalizations about errors in eyewitness testimony, the probability of

---

[26] Smith 2018, 1201–22. See also Blome-Tillmann 2015.
[27] Pundik 2008, 470–2.
[28] Pundik 2017a, 210–13.
[29] *United States v. Boyd*, 686 F.Supp.2d 382 (S.D.N.Y. 2010), 384.

a random match is insensitive to whether the DNA found at the crime scene actually comes from the defendant or not. When Enoch and Fisher discuss DNA evidence, they argue that the factual claim that a match was found between the two samples is sensitive to the defendant's guilt.[30] We concur that this is so: had the defendant been innocent, a match would (most likely) not have been found. But the problem for the sensitivity approach is to explain *why* the sensitivity requirement that applies to the match does not also apply to the probability of a random match. This probability is meant to help the factfinder decide between two possible scenarios: in the first, the two samples match because they originated from the defendant (guilt), and in the second, they match randomly despite originating from two different people (innocence). It is unhelpful to stress the sensitivity of the match itself because a match was found in *both scenarios*. The scope of the sensitivity requirement must be limited in some way to avoid the conclusion that all factfinding is unjustified because it relies on insensitive background information. In our view, any attempt to extract such limitations from the sensitivity approach seems ad hoc and difficult to justify.

Smith proposes an epistemic approach based on *normalcy*. According to Smith, NSE fails to provide *normic support* because it would be normal for the defendant to be innocent in spite of the NSE, and their innocence, therefore, requires no further explanation: "it could just so happen" that the defendant is the only prisoner who did not participate in the killing.[31] By contrast, if it turns out that the defendant is innocent despite the eyewitness having testified to seeing them participate in the killing, a further explanation would be required (for instance, that the eyewitness was lying). Notably, unlike sensitivity, the normalcy approach manages to distinguish NSE from the scenario with the lying witness.

However, the normalcy approach also has a problem with scope. Assume that the court convicted the defendant based on the eyewitness identification that was made under excellent conditions but, subsequently, more evidence comes to light and proves that the defendant is innocent. It is unclear why further explanation must be provided. After all, even in the best conditions, eyewitness identification might sometimes be mistaken and, unfortunately, "it could just so happen" that this is one of these cases.[32]

The problem is even more apparent with respect to DNA evidence. Smith acknowledges that DNA evidence is a difficult case for his approach and grapples with it in a dedicated section.[33] He understands the problem to be limited to cases in which such evidence is the only incriminating evidence against the defendant and concludes that his approach would oppose convictions that rest on DNA evidence alone.[34] This conclusion contrasts starkly with legal practice.[35] More importantly, if the background information about the possibility of a random match means that no further explanation is required in cases of mistaken convictions that are based on DNA evidence alone, why cannot the same be said about mistaken

---

[30] Enoch and Fisher 2015, 587–92.
[31] Smith 2018, 1208.
[32] Smith claims in a footnote that background information poses no difficulty for the normalcy approach (ibid., 1213–14, n. 19), but he understands the problem very differently. Smith responds to the claim that some types of background information fail the normalcy test because the probability of error is quantified explicitly and precisely, like in the case of DNA evidence. His response, without any supporting argument, is: "The normic support that the testimony provides for its content is not lost simply because probability has been allowed to enter the picture" (ibid., 1213). By contrast, the challenge we set for the normalcy approach is to explain how eyewitness identification can meet the normalcy test to begin with, *even when the probability of error is not explicitly quantified*.
[33] Ibid., 1211–16.
[34] Ibid., 1214.
[35] e.g., *R v. Adams* [1996] 2 Cr App R 467.

convictions that were based solely on eyewitness testimony? How can the normalcy approach make a distinction between these situations that is anything but arbitrary and ad hoc? Yet, the normalcy requirement must be somehow limited because, as we observed earlier, if its scope included all parts of the inference, it would render factfinding impossible. Therefore, while the normalcy approach overcomes some of the problems that the sensitivity approach faces, it does not seem to do much better than the sensitivity approach when it comes to the problem of scope.

Enoch, Spectre, and Fisher's work has also motivated other philosophers to propose alternative epistemic approaches of their own. Gardiner, for example, highlights the importance of the notion of explanation even further, by arguing that statistical evidence fails to rule out relevant alternatives.[36] Here, instead of presenting and scrutinizing every epistemic approach that has been suggested to date, we offer two arguments for why the epistemic direction is lacking *in general*—that is, irrespective of the exact details of the specific accounts: *context insensitivity* and *inadmissibility*.

Epistemic approaches tend to be insensitive to the context in which the evidence is used as a basis for decision-making. If it were true that NSE does not provide the right kind of justification for beliefs, as the epistemic approaches claim, this should hold across all contexts. However, there are many contexts in which basing beliefs and decisions on NSE is perfectly justified.[37] Assume, for example, that, in a sequel to the *Prison Riot* scenario, one of the prison guards who were on duty at the riot is walking down a dark alley a few years later and notices that one of the one hundred ex-prisoners who had participated in the riot is walking behind him. He knows that ninety-nine of them vowed to kill a guard once they got out of prison. Is the guard not justified in believing that his life is in danger? Although a naked statistic of 99% should be insufficient for a court of law to convict, it is surely sufficient evidence for the guard to believe he is in danger and act on that belief. Furthermore, such a switch from unacceptable to acceptable use of NSE does not only occur when we move from a legal context to a non-legal one. There are some legal issues where it is clear that NSE should be taken into account, for example, the use of average life expectancy in calculations of compensation for loss of earnings in tort cases. The context in which the inference from NSE is drawn is crucial for evaluating that inference because, whatever the reason why convictions should not be based on NSE, that reason has something to do with the fact that NSE is used for a specific purpose: for conviction. The epistemic approaches— which are context insensitive—are therefore incapable of explaining why the use of NSE is problematic in some decisions and unproblematic in others.

Things get even worse for the epistemic approaches when we not only consider the question of *sufficiency* but also that of *admissibility*. So far, our discussion has followed the epistemic approaches' implicit assumption that the main puzzle about NSE is its apparent inability to support a conviction (or the knowledge or justified belief that the accused is guilty). This implicit assumption is understandable, given that philosophers seek to draw parallels between the proof paradoxes in law and other paradoxes in epistemology, such as the lottery paradox (Enoch, Spectre, and Fisher, for example, assert that "There is a need for an epistemological story, one that will treat lottery cases and legal cases ... alike").[38]

---

[36] Gardiner 2019.
[37] Pundik 2017a, 210–13.
[38] Enoch, Spectre, and Fisher 2012, 221.

However, cases like *Crime Rate* highlight not only the importance of context but also that of *admissibility*: the legal problem of NSE involves not only its apparent insufficiency to support a conviction on its own, but also (and perhaps mainly) the exclusion of NSE such as crime rates as evidence for a conviction. Even if the epistemic approaches were capable of somehow explaining the insufficiency of NSE, it would not suffice to address its inadmissibility. Moreover, when the issues of context insensitivity and admissibility are combined, the following conclusion emerges: even if the epistemic approaches were able to justify the exclusion of NSE from criminal trials, it would only be at the price of conceding that such statistics should have no place as evidence in any context, including science, policy-making, and day-to-day life.

In our view, the epistemic approaches fail to solve the problem of NSE because they rest on the incorrect assumption that evidence used in legal factfinding need not only provide sufficient probabilistic support (so the belief it supports is most likely to be true), but it is also subject to further epistemic requirements needed for knowledge or epistemic justification. We hold that the standard of proof entails moral requirements, but does not require any epistemic standard that goes beyond sufficient probability, such as sensitivity or normalcy, even if one of those is required for knowledge. As Enoch, Spectre, and Fisher point out: "To insist that the law should after all care about knowledge is (pretty much) to be willing to pay a price in accuracy."[39] To paraphrase, then, if legal factfinding is going to be constrained in its use of statistical evidence because of some epistemic considerations, more guilty people will evade the law. It is unclear why society should be willing to pay such a price in the name of some abstract notions such as "knowledge" or "epistemic justification."[40]

As we explained in Section 3, the alternative to the epistemic approaches is that of *moral* approaches, which hold that a conviction on NSE in *Prison Riot* and other similar scenarios is unacceptable on moral grounds. In the following two sections, we discuss two possible solutions within the moral approach: incentives and free will.

5. Incentives

The idea that the problem of NSE has to do with incentives has been explored by Posner, Sanchirico, Enoch, Spectre, and Fisher and Dahlman.[41] According to the *incentive approach*, convicting the defendant in the *Prison Riot* case is morally unjustified as the conviction would not contribute in a positive way to the incentive structure for lawful behavior. This idea is based on a Benthamite view on the moral justification of criminal punishment. Jeremy Bentham observes that criminal punishment imposes suffering on the defendant and argues that this can only be morally justified if the incentives for lawful conduct produced by the verdict are expected to prevent suffering exceeding the suffering it inflicts on the defendant.[42] According to Bentham, every single verdict must meet this requirement to be morally justified.[43] When this moral principle is incorporated into the law, the legal standard of proof requires not only that the probability, given the evidence, reaches a certain

---

[39] Enoch, Spectre, and Fisher 2012, 212.
[40] Pundik 2011.
[41] Posner 1999, 1510; Sanchirico 2001, 1262; Enoch, Spectre, and Fisher 2012, 217–18; Dahlman 2020, 173–7.
[42] Bentham 1789, XIII, 2.
[43] Ibid., 3.

threshold but also that it is the *right kind* of evidence—the kind that gives future potential offenders incentives to act lawfully.

In the *Prison Riot* case, a conviction based on NSE alone would not give a prisoner in the defendant's position at a future prison riot any incentive to refrain from participating in an assault on a guard. Since participation in the riot is sufficient for conviction, the prisoner knows that he will be convicted for participating in the killing, whether he decides to participate in the killing or not.[44] Imagine that you are one of one hundred inmates participating in a riot. During the riot, ninety-eight of your fellow inmates start attacking a guard, while one of them refrains from participating in the attack and moves away, to the opposite side of the prison yard. What should you do? Should you join the attackers or join the single prisoner on the other side of the yard? If you are later prosecuted for participating in the killing of the guard, there will be sufficient NSE against you, whether you join the attackers or not. If you join the attackers, the probability that a prisoner who participated in the riot also participated in the attack will be 99%. If you refrain, the probability will be 98%. In a legal system where a probability of 98% based on NSE is sufficient to meet the standard of proof, you will be convicted either way.

This can be contrasted with the alternative scenario, discussed in Section 1, where the evidence against the defendant in the *Prison Riot* case is a fingerprint. A conviction based on a fingerprint does give a prisoner at a future riot an incentive to refrain from attacking a guard because refraining would significantly reduce the probability of conviction. True, it is not 100% certain that there will be trace evidence against him if he attacks the guard (the fingerprint and other traces might accidentally be cleaned off before forensic scientists search the crime scene); and it is not 100% certain that there will be no false trace evidence presented against him if he refrains from attacking the guard (the police might plant his fingerprint at the crime scene). However, it is a good deal more likely that there will be trace evidence against him if he attacks the guard than if he refrains. Note that the incentives for lawful behavior created by convictions on trace evidence are undermined if defendants are also convicted in similar cases where there is only NSE. A conviction on NSE in the *Prison Riot* case would therefore have a negative net effect on the incentive structure for lawful behavior.[45]

There are cases where the incentive structure is more complex and the incentive approach to NSE becomes more complicated. Such situations have been analyzed by Enoch, Spectre, and Fisher[46] and by Dahlman.[47]

An important limitation of the incentive approach is that it only provides an explanation for why NSE is insufficient for conviction. It does not provide an argument for why NSE should be inadmissible. Imagine a variation of the *Prison Riot* case where there is NSE as well as other kinds of evidence (eyewitness and fingerprint). Since a conviction would contribute in a positive way to the incentive structure for lawful behavior, there is no "incentive argument" to make the NSE inadmissible. The reason why the incentive approach cannot justify excluding NSE is rooted in how people respond to an increased risk that depends on factors that they can control as well as factors they cannot. Consider the following example. When a person is told by their doctors that they are likelier to contract skin cancer because

---

[44] Dahlman 2020, 174.
[45] Ibid., 175.
[46] Enoch, Spectre, and Fisher 2012, 218–19.
[47] Dahlman 2020, 174–6.

they have light skin (a factor they cannot control), most would regard their higher risk as an incentive to *reduce* their risk by taking more precautionary measures, such as using sun creams (a factor they can control). Similarly, a verdict in the *Prison Riot* case based on a combination of NSE and trace evidence gives prisoners in future riots an incentive not to participate in the killing of a guard. Since they are participating in the riot, it is not within their control to get rid of the NSE, but, by refraining from participating in the killing of the guard, it *is* within their control not to produce any trace evidence. This illustrates that the incentive approach is limited to extreme cases, like the *Prison Riot*, *Gatecrasher*, and *Blue Bus* cases, where a verdict against the defendant would be based on NSE alone. While, in cases like *Crime Rate*, NSE should clearly not be used at all, the incentive approach cannot justify why this is the case.

6. Free Will

Pundik's free-will approach focuses on certain *uses* of NSE: instances where it is used expressly to attribute culpability to an individual.[48] Pundik argues that NSE supports the prosecution's claim that the defendant committed the alleged crime only if the defendant's conduct was determined by a certain *causal* factor that rendered the conduct unfree. Yet, in the context of attributing culpability, it is necessary to presuppose the exact opposite: that the defendant was free to determine their own conduct. Using these types of generalization to determine culpability is objectionable because it involves *contradicting* presuppositions about the individual's conduct.

The free-will approach begins with the premise that inferences about human conduct, drawn for either prediction or conviction purposes, require reliance on *causal* generalizations—that is, generalizations that reflect a causal connection between the type of fact from which the inference begins and the type of fact the inference seeks to establish. If an inference is based on a non-causal generalization, a mere correlation, it is unlicensed and thus invalid.[49] But, even if inferences about human conduct require reliance on causal generalizations, why cannot free actions be proven with such generalizations? Starting with a simple example, assume that Richard is exposed to radiation of a particular kind that affects his nervous system, resulting in blotches all over his skin and an irresistible urge to attack everyone around him. Assume further that *every* person exposed to this radiation develops these symptoms. When Richard is admitted to hospital, it seems unproblematic to infer from the blotches that, given the opportunity, he will lose control and should therefore be restrained. However, inferring from these marks that a violent action that had taken place before Richard arrived at the hospital was committed by him (rather than by someone else), for the purpose of convicting him of a violent offense, seems intuitively problematic.

According to the free-will approach, this inference should not be used for the purpose of determining culpability because it leads to a contradiction. To infer from Richard's skin marks that he had acted violently, it is necessary to presuppose a *causal* generalization: either one caused the other or they both have a common cause. In this example, the radiation caused both Richard's blotches and his violent conduct. However, Richard's acting violently

---

[48] Pundik 2017a.
[49] This premise is detailed and defended in Pundik 2017a, 198–200.

may be culpable only if he acted *freely*. Establishing Richard's guilt by inferring from his skin marks that it was he who acted violently is, therefore, contradictory: Richard's conduct is treated as free and unfree at the same time. This example also explains why the very same inference seems unproblematic when restraining him in the hospital because, in the medical context, it is not necessary to presuppose that Richard's violent conduct will be free and culpable.

Moving to probabilistic generalizations, consider the following variation on the previous example. Assume that Stephen is exposed to another type of radiation, which affects the nervous system and always causes certain skin blotches but causes an irresistible urge to attack others, when the opportunity arises, in only 80% of cases. According to the subjective interpretation of probability, which is commonly considered the most suitable for legal purposes,[50] probabilistic generalizations reflect the limited state of our knowledge rather than the true nature of the world. While the generalization about the radiation is probabilistic, it imperfectly reflects a reality that may be deterministic. If the world is indeed deterministic, Stephen belongs to one of two possible subgroups. One possibility is that he belongs to the sub-group of people who possess an extra unknown variable, which, together with the radiation, determines that he will lose control and attack someone. The other possibility is that he belongs to the subgroup of people who do not possess the extra variable, in which case the exposure to the radiation will not cause him to do so.

Supporting Stephen's conviction by inferring from the blotches on his skin that he was (80%) likely to have acted violently is problematic. If Stephen does indeed possess the extra variable, then—similarly to deterministic generalizations—this inference leads to a contradiction: his conduct is taken to be both free (in order to be culpable) and unfree (as, together with another unknown variable, his violent actions were determined by the radiation). If Stephen does not possess the extra variable, then inferring from his skin marks that he acted violently is mistaken and misleading because, if he belongs to the subgroup of people who are not caused to act violently by the radiation, then the probability that he acted violently is not affected by his exposure to the radiation. In sum, this inference is either contradictory because it requires inconsistent presuppositions, or misleading because it is mistaken and yet is presented as informative.[51]

Returning to *Crime Rate*, inferring from the crime rate data that the resident was likelier to have committed a crime involving an illegal firearm requires presupposing that there is a causal generalization that makes the resident's conduct predictable to some extent, be it the dangerous character of the neighborhood or its socio-economic conditions, for instance. Such causal factors are outside the control of the individual resident. The inference from crime rates to the resident's committing the alleged crime is, hence, either inconsistent with their being culpable, or mistaken.

Unlike the epistemic and incentives approach, the free-will approach is able to justify the *inadmissibility* of NSE in cases like *Crime Rate* because, irrespective of other evidence available in the case, the use of NSE rests on contradicting presuppositions. Pundik argues that the free-will approach is able to provide a unifying justification for the hostility of criminal factfinding toward various types of predictive evidence, such as NSE, previous convictions,

---

[50]   e.g., Alexander and Ferzan 2009, 31, for criminal law; Perry 1995, 333–5, for tort law.
[51]   As for the proposal that the causal relation itself is probability—that causing is nothing more than raising the probability of the effect—see Pundik 2020, 256–9.

and motive.[52] On the other hand, unlike the epistemic approaches, the free-will approach does not object to NSE per se but only when it is used for decision-making about the defendant's culpability. Furthermore, even when NSE is used to determine the defendant's culpability, the free-will approach does not object to the use of background information to assess pieces of evidence, such as the cases of DNA evidence discussed earlier. Rather than presupposing that the defendant's culpable behavior was caused by their genetic composition, the inference is based on their culpable behavior causing evidence of their genetic composition to be found at the crime scene.[53] Furthermore, the free-will approach explains why NSE should not have been used to prove causation in some known cases of wrongful conviction, such as the British case of Sally Clark and the Dutch case of Lucia de Berk.[54] Lastly, it could support an argument against racial profiling.[55]

Pundik's free-will approach has been criticized by Picinali and Dahlman.[56] Picinali points out that it does not identify the exact theory of free will that it assumes.[57] According to Dahlman, the attribution of culpability does not require such a thick notion of free will as the free-will approach assumes.[58] In response to this challenge, Pundik 2020 outlines a unique type of libertarian theory of free will, which has not received sufficient attention in either law or philosophy (with the notable exception of Bergson),[59] under which a free action is not only undetermined but also *lacks both subjective and objective probabilities*. It is not only the lack of sufficient information that prevents an accurate prediction of how an agent will act freely: free actions cannot be predicted because their probability does not exist. Since these metaphysical commitments are quite radical and counter-intuitive, the free-will approach comes at a heavy price. Its focus on culpability also renders its applicability to non-criminal cases significantly more limited (though still possible).[60] Pundik has sought to explain how free choices under this theory may still be rational and within the agent's control,[61] but scholars who reject this theory of freedom (including Dahlman) still maintain that the free-will approach does not solve the problem of NSE (and the same goes for those who remain skeptical about the significance of the issue of free will to legal factfinding).

Perhaps the free-will approach could be understood in a way that is consistent with, and even motivated by, the incentives approach. Instead of understanding the free-will approach as resting on the metaphysical assumption that "people *have* unpredictable free will," it rests on the view that "criminal law should treat people *as if* they have unpredictable free will." Criminal law sometimes adopts assumptions that are evidently false: ignorance of the law is not a defense because people are assumed to have knowledge of the law, yet it is difficult to believe that every defendant knows about the existence, let alone the exact definition, of all the criminal prohibitions that exist in their jurisdiction. Similarly, irrespective of whether people have unpredictable free will, there could be reasons for why criminal law should

---

[52] Pundik 2020, 249–52.
[53] For a more detailed explanation, see Pundik 2017a, 212–13.
[54] Pundik 2020.
[55] Pundik 2017b.
[56] Picinali 2016; Dahlman 2020.
[57] Picinali 2016.
[58] Dahlman 2020, 172.
[59] Bergson 1910.
[60] Pundik 2020, 254–5.
[61] Ibid., 245–6.

assume that they do (for example, if it encourages lawful conduct). After all, philosophers who are deeply skeptical about free will and consider it a mere illusion sometimes proceed to argue that society could nevertheless benefit from people continuing to believe that they do indeed have it.[62]

More work is clearly needed to identify what benefits, if any, may be gained by treating people as not only having free will but also free will that is unpredictable. In the meantime, we hope this chapter has introduced readers to new approaches to the problem of NSE and its unique characteristics within legal factfinding, and has demonstrated the potential of cross-fertilization between starkly different approaches.

7. Concluding Remarks

The problematic nature of NSE has been discussed since the 1970s and this debate has been revitalized over the last decade or so by a number of new approaches and proposed solutions. In this chapter, we have discussed four approaches from the recent debate: *sensitivity*, *normalcy*, *incentives*, and *free will*. As our review shows, each of these approaches has contributed to a more nuanced understanding of NSE, but serious objections remain against each, and none has yet offered a solution that has received general acceptance.

References

Alexander, L. and Ferzan, K. K. (2009). *Crime and Culpability: A Theory of Criminal Law.* Cambridge: Cambridge University Press.

Allen, R. (1991). "On the Significance of Batting Averages and Strikeout Totals: A Clarification of the 'Naked Statistical Evidence' Debate, the Meaning of 'Evidence,' and the Requirement of Proof beyond Reasonable Doubt," *Tulane Law Review*, 65: 1093–110.

Bentham, J. (1789). An Introduction to the Principles of Morals and Legislation.

Bergson, H. (1910), Time and Free Will: An Essay on the Immediate Data of Consciousness. Frank Lubecki Pogson tr, Kessinger Publishing Company.

Blome-Tillmann, M. (2015). "Sensitivity, Causality, and Statistical Evidence in Courts of Law," *Thought*, 4:102–12.

Bollinger, R. J. (2020). "The Rational Impermissibility of Accepting (some) Racial Generalizations," *Synthese*, 197: 2415–31.

Buchak, L. (2014). "Belief, Credence, and Norms," *Philosophical Studies*, 169: 285–311.

Cohen, L. J. (1977). *The Probable and the Provable.* Oxford: Oxford University Press.

Collins, J., Hall, N., and Paul, L. (eds.) (2004). *Causation and Counterfactuals.* Cambridge, MA: MIT Press.

Dahlman, C. (2020). "Naked Statistical Evidence and Incentives for Lawful Conduct," *International Journal of Evidence and Proof*, 24: 162–79.

Di Bello, M. (2019). "Trial by Statistics: Is a High Probability of Guilt Enough to Convict?" *Mind*, 128: 1045–84.

Enoch, D. and Fisher, T. (2015). "Sense and 'Sensitivity': Epistemic and Instrumental Approaches to Statistical Evidence," *Stanford Law Review*, 67: 557–611.

Enoch, D., Spectre, L., and Fisher, T. (2012). "Statistical Evidence, Sensitivity and the Legal Value of Knowledge," *Philosophy and Public Affairs*, 40: 197–224.

---

[62] See, most notably, Smilansky 2000.

Gardiner, G. (2019). "The Reasonable and the Relevant: Legal Standards of Proof," *Philosophy & Public Affairs*, 47: 288–318.

Kaye, D. (1980). "Naked Statistical Evidence," *Yale Law Journal*, 89: 601–11.

Lewis, D. (1973). "Causation," *Journal of Philosophy*, 70: 556–67.

Moss, S. (2018). *Probabilistic Knowledge*. Oxford: Oxford University Press.

Nesson, C. (1979). "Reasonable Doubt and Permissive Inference: The Value of complexity," *Harvard Law Review*, 92: 1187–99.

Nesson, C. (1985). "The Evidence or the Event? On Judicial Proof and the Acceptability of Verdicts," *Harvard Law Review*, 98: 1357–92.

Nunn, G. A. (2015). "The Incompatibility of Due Process and Naked Statistical Evidence," *Vanderbilt Law Review*, 68: 1407–33.

Pardo, M. (2019). "The Paradoxes of Legal Proof: A Critical Guide," *Boston University Law Review*, 99: 233–90.

Pearl, J. (2000). *Causality*. Cambridge: Cambridge University Press.

Perry, S. (1995). "Risk, Harm, and Responsibility," In D. G Owen (ed.), *Philosophical Foundations of Tort Law*, 321–46. Oxford: Oxford University Press.

Picinali, F. (2016). "Generalisations, Causal Relationships, and Moral Responsibility," *International Journal of Evidence and Proof*, 20: 121–35.

Posner, R. (1999). "An Economic Approach to the Law of Evidence," *Stanford Law Review*, 51: 1477–546.

Pritchard, D. (2017). "Legal Risk, Legal Evidence and the Arithmetic of Criminal Justice," *Jurisprudence*, 9: 108–19.

Pundik, A. (2008). "What is Wrong with Statistical Evidence? The Attempts to Establish an Epistemic Deficiency," *Civil Justice Quarterly*, 27: 461–93.

Pundik, A. (2011). "The Epistemology of Statistical Evidence," *International Journal of Evidence and Proof*, 15: 117–43.

Pundik, A. (2017a). "Freedom and Generalisation," *Oxford Journal of Legal Studies*, 37: 189–216.

Pundik, A. (2017b). "Against Racial Profiling," *University of Toronto Law Journal*, 67: 175–205.

Pundik, A. (2020). "Predictive Evidence and Unpredictable Freedom," *Oxford Journal of Legal Studies*, 30: 238–64.

Pundik, A. (2021). "Rethinking the Use of Statistical Evidence to prove Causation in Criminal Cases: A Tale of (Im)Probability and Free Will," *Law & Philosophy*, 40:97–128.

Redmayne, M. (2008). "Exploring the Proof Paradoxes," *Legal Theory*, 14: 281–309.

Redmayne, M. (2015). *Character in the Criminal Trial*. Oxford: Oxford University Press.

Sanchirico, C. (2001). Character Evidence and the Object of Trial. *Columbia Law Review, 101*(6), 1227–311.

Schauer, F. (2003). *Profiles, Probabilities, and Stereotypes*. Cambridge, MA: Harvard University Press.

Smilansky, S. (2000). *Free Will and Illusion*. Oxford: Oxford University Press.

Smith, M. (2018). "When does Evidence Suffice for Conviction?" *Mind*, 127: 1193–218.

Stein, A. (2005). *Foundations of Evidence Law*. Oxford: Oxford University Press.

Thomson, J. J. (1986). "Liability and Individualized Evidence," *Law and Contemporary Problems*, 49: 199–219.

Tribe, L. (1971). "Trial by Mathematics: Precision and Ritual in the Legal Process," *Harvard Law Review*, 84: 1329–93.

Wasserman, D. (1991). "The Morality of Statistical Proof and the Risk of Mistaken Liability," *Cardozo Law Review*, 13: 935–76.

Wright, R. (1985). "Causation in Tort Law," *California Law Review*, 73: 1735–828.

PART VII
BIASES AND EPISTEMIC INJUSTICE

23

Evidence Law and Empirical Psychology

Justin Sevier

1. Introduction

Empirical psychology is a natural fit for understanding the law of evidence but is also substantially at odds with it. Since psychologist Hugo Münsterberg's provocative critique of the legal system in his 1908 book, *On the Witness Stand*—and the prolific evidence scholar John Henry Wigmore's humorous but scathing rejoinder in an article published in the *Illinois Law Review*—researchers have begun applying the insights from experimental psychology to various aspects of courtroom adjudication, including the assumptions underlying the Federal Rules of Evidence and the effects of the rules on litigants and the public.[1] At the same time, the law has struggled with whether and how to incorporate insights from an academic discipline that embodies goals and methodologies that are, in many ways, dramatically different from its own.

Researchers have noted that evidentiary rule-makers "often, and unavoidably, must act as applied psychologists" when forming legal rules.[2] Indeed, the rules of evidence rest at times almost explicitly on untested folk wisdom about how certain types of evidence—including propensity evidence, expert testimony, and hearsay—affect the perceptions, cognition, and social psychological processes surrounding lay triers of fact.[3] For example, should courts truly be concerned that jurors will overvalue the probative weight of hearsay evidence when people naturally tend to discount unsubstantiated rumors outside the courtroom? Do jurors become so overwhelmed by scientific expertise that they fail to identify critical weaknesses in an expert's testimony? These questions and many others are well suited to evaluation by investigators who are uniquely qualified to examine human cognition, lay attitudes, and corresponding behavior.

At the same time, difficult epistemological questions create significant barriers to importing psychological insights into the law of evidence. The methodological disconnect between psychology and the law provides, perhaps, the biggest challenge. Empirical psychology is the study of averages: in the aggregate, when one aspect of an experimental study is manipulated, researchers examine whether (on average) a difference between the experimental groups, with respect to some outcome, is statistically reliable. For example, psychologists have discovered that, all else equal, cross-racial identifications tend to be less accurate than same-race identifications. But what about *this* particular witness's cross-racial identification in *this* particular case? To the extent that the law of evidence primarily is focused on

---

[1] Münsterberg 1908; Wigmore 1909; for a review, see Bornstein and Neuschatz 2020.
[2] Saks and Spellman 2016, 1.
[3] Sevier 2012.

Justin Sevier, *Evidence Law and Empirical Psychology* In: *Philosophical Foundations of Evidence Law*. Edited by: Christian Dahlman, Alex Stein, and Giovanni Tuzet, Oxford University Press. © Christian Dahlman, Alex Stein, and Giovanni Tuzet 2021. DOI: 10.1093/oso/9780198859307.003.0024

individual cases, witnesses, and parties, these methodological differences pose a substantial obstacle to integrating psychology findings into the law of evidence.[4]

Moreover, there is a philosophical disconnect between evidence law and the field of empirical psychology. To the extent that empirical psychology is a scientific discipline, its goal is to discover truth: to use the scientific method to describe, predict, and explain human behavior. The discovery of truth is, of course, an important goal of the rules of evidence, but it is not the only goal. Trial rules routinely balance the factfinder's quest for the truth with other policy considerations, including the procedural rights of criminal defendants and the protection of important societal relationships. In doing so, evidentiary rules exclude otherwise highly probative information from consideration by the factfinder, potentially at the expense of decision accuracy.[5]

Despite these methodological and philosophical challenges, an increase in receptive, empirically conversant members of the bench and bar, along with innovations in empirical methodology—including more sophisticated research designs, greater realism and ecological validity, a focus on behavioral phenomena from a broader array of psychological disciplines, and a recent influx of researchers who are experienced with the nuances of courtroom adjudication—have allowed psychologists to more fully contribute to discussions of evidentiary policy. Indeed, an array of well-respected psychologists and legal scholars have published books and taught courses at the graduate and undergraduate levels on the relationship of empirical psychology to the legal system and to evidence law more specifically.[6] This chapter therefore seeks not to reinvent the wheel, but instead to highlight some (but not all) of the major contributions that psychologists have made to understanding the most important areas of evidence law, while also highlighting recent cutting-edge research. The chapter also offers suggestions for how future research can continue to establish psychology's relevance to creating sound evidential policy.

2. Character Evidence

The role that character evidence plays—or is forbidden from playing—in legal dispute resolution is complex and contradictory. What is now viewed as the most pernicious form of character evidence—information suggesting that an individual acted in accordance with her "propensity" to commit some bad act—actually predated the modern trial, was routinely legitimized by factfinders, and was viewed as persuasive evidence of a defendant's guilt.[7] But in response to societal changes introduced during the industrial revolution, and changing cultural mores favoring the view that character traits are not immutable, the law of evidence reversed its stance on the utility and admissibility of propensity information, largely banning it from trial.[8]

Despite calls for reform from prominent legal scholars, character evidence initially did not attract much attention from experimental psychologists. Researchers had been, however, exploring several phenomena with direct relevance to how factfinders evaluate

---

[4] Sood 2017.
[5] Merritt and Simmons 2017.
[6] Saks and Spellman 2016.
[7] Vidmar and Hans 2007.
[8] Leonard 1998.

information about character. In the 1940s, social psychologists began publishing studies on the phenomena of person perception and impression formation, both of which examine the factors that people use to evaluate others in their social surroundings.[9] The weight of the research supports an "interactionist model" of social perception, in which our judgments about others are formed in two stages.[10] First, we gather information about others' personality traits from their observed behavior. Second, and with differing degrees of success, we adjust those initial assessments to account for external, situational factors that may have contributed to those observed behaviors. Jurors may be imperfect calibrators, but to the extent that the ban on propensity evidence suggests that jurors, per se, give propensity evidence undue weight, research suggests that this assumption may be misguided.

The first study of propensity evidence was published in 1979 by social psychologist Eugene Borgida, and focused on the effects of character evidence on trial strategy.[11] Borgida's study was sophisticated even by modern standards, insofar as it included a half-hour, videotaped trial and included cleverly edited experimental manipulations. Borgida found that jurors tended to find character evidence presented in the form of reputation testimony less persuasive than character evidence that referenced specific acts, and that the inclusion of too many character witnesses created a boomerang effect that harmed the proponent's case.

Two subsequent studies also examined the manner in which propensity evidence shapes litigation strategy. Lupfer et al. collected data from twenty-eight mock juries regarding their reactions to favorable and unfavorable character evidence. Lupfer found an effect of valence, such that *unfavorable* character evidence had a much stronger effect on jurors than did positive evidence.[12] Along those lines, Hunt and Budesheim conducted a study that found no effect of positive character evidence on mock jurors' judgments, but when a positive character witness was *impeached* on cross-examination, the positive character witness substantially damaged the defendant's case.[13]

Recent research on character evidence has shifted from trial strategy to the assumptions underlying the ban on propensity evidence. To that end, two recent mock juror studies produced conflicting findings with respect to whether jurors place disproportionate weight on a defendant's propensity to commit some act. Cicchini and White randomly presented a sexual assault case to mock jurors where the identity of the alleged perpetrator was at issue; the first group received conclusive evidence in the form of a stipulation that the defendant had been in the room at the time of the alleged crime, whereas the second group heard evidence of the defendant's prior conviction for a similar act.[14] Cicchini and White found a statistically meaningful increase in the conviction rate among participants in the "prior act" experimental condition compared to the "stipulation" condition, suggesting that jurors may afford undue weight to "prior act" propensity evidence.

On the other hand, in a series of studies that surveyed over 1,200 mock jurors, Sevier reported that jurors exhibit substantial competency with propensity evidence.[15] He found

---

[9] Asch 1946.
[10] Bell and Stanfield 1973.
[11] Borgida 1979.
[12] Lupfer et al. 1986.
[13] Hunt and Budesheim 2004.
[14] Cicchini and White 2018.
[15] Sevier 2019.

that, when asked to rank the evidence presented to them in a criminal trial, propensity information ranked well below forensic evidence and police testimony presented by the prosecution, and statistically was perceived as no stronger than the testimony presented by fact witnesses. In a second study in which he varied the frequency, recency, and similarity of a defendant's prior bad act to the current charge in a mock trial, jurors rated a prior bad act that occurred more frequently in the past, more recently in the past, and that was more similar to the act under dispute in the current trial as significantly more persuasive than a bad act that occurred seldomly, longer ago in time, and that was substantially different from the act of which the defendant was accused. This suggests that mock jurors attended to specific features of the evidence and weighed them defensibly. And perhaps most surprisingly, in a third study where participants read about an evidentiary hearing in which a court either included or excluded propensity evidence, participants rated trials in which propensity evidence was excluded as less procedurally fair and less legitimate than trials in which the factfinder was allowed to hear the evidence.

Two final studies have broadened the focus of character evidence research by examining its intersection with race. These studies investigated whether mock jurors evenhandedly weigh propensity evidence or if they weigh the evidence differently depending on whether the defendant is black or white. Tomei and Cramer found that mock jurors differentially attend to positive and negative character evidence consistent with racial stereotypes.[16] Specifically, positive character evidence had a stronger effect on judgments when the defendant was black, and negative character evidence had a greater impact on the strength of the defendant's case when he was white. Psychologist Jennifer Hunt later replicated these findings, concluding that "the same character evidence may be interpreted or used differently, based on how it confirms or challenges [a factfinder's] preexisting expectations."[17]

The handful of studies on propensity evidence produce a complex body of research. There is encouraging empirical evidence that jurors think carefully about propensity information and distinguish "stronger" propensity evidence from "weaker" evidence. Further, the public appears less willing to legitimize trials in which that evidence is kept secret. But other studies suggest that in emotion-invoking cases such as sexual assault, or when a defendant's race is salient at trial, jurors may overvalue propensity evidence or weigh it selectively. More research is necessary to integrate these intriguing findings into a cohesive whole.

3. Hearsay

The rule barring hearsay has been called the "spoiled child" of the law of evidence, insofar as it has received outsized attention from legal scholars and policy makers.[18] But perhaps this is for good reason. Although the rule, which bars secondhand information from trial, is conceptually simple, it contains roughly thirty different exceptions spanning numerous sociolegal contexts. Moreover, the doctrine has a storied history, featuring prominently and villainously in trials from Guildhall to Winchester Castle.[19] Indeed, one of the

---

[16] Tomei and Cramer 2014.
[17] Hunt 2017.
[18] Wigmore 1935, 238.
[19] For a recounting of the trials of Sir Nicholas Throckmorton and Sir Walter Raleigh, see Sevier 2015; 2016.

lasting legacies of hearsay evidence in the United States might be its impact on the Federal Constitution, which bestows upon a criminal defendant the right to confront directly her accusers.

The state of empirical hearsay research mirrors its spoiled-child status among legal scholars. Although this research is relatively young, it embodies numerous studies from a diverse array of methodologies—some exceedingly clever—across various psychological subdisciplines. Initial experiments focused on the valuation question—whether mock jurors discount hearsay compared to firsthand information—while follow-up experiments examined specialized issues, including the assumptions underlying the exceptions to the hearsay rule. The most recent research has challenged the underlying assumptions of the rule itself and explored the rationale from which the rule purports to derive its popular legitimacy.

The first direct examination of the hearsay rule, conducted by Landsman and Rakos in the early 1990s, examined the role of differentially strong hearsay evidence on mock juror verdicts. Although Landsman and Rakos found that the perceived strength of the evidence as a whole affected participants' judgments, and although participants were sensitive to the different strengths of the hearsay evidence, the hearsay evidence did not appreciably affect their verdicts.[20]

In a clever experiment the following year, Meine, Park, and Borgida attempted to replicate these findings while directly comparing the effects of eyewitness testimony against the effects of hearsay testimony on criminal verdicts.[21] The researchers staged a computer theft in a campus classroom that some students observed while others did not. The students who had not observed the theft subsequently learned the details from the eyewitnesses. Other participants then viewed a mock trial in which the direct observers served as eyewitnesses while those who learned about the theft afterward served as hearsay witnesses. The researchers found that the presence of an eyewitness doubled the conviction rate from baseline, while the presence of only a hearsay witness raised the conviction rate just 4%. These findings suggest that jurors might actually undervalue hearsay.

In a similar study, researchers staged a crime and created "good" and "poor" eyewitnesses, who then relayed their observations to a hearsay witness. The hearsay witness then reported the secondhand information either soon afterward (creating a "good" hearsay witness) or after a delay (creating a "poor" hearsay witness). The researchers found that study participants were not sensitive to differences in the quality of the eyewitness testimony, but they *were* sensitive to differences in the quality of the hearsay testimony, preferring the testimony of the "good" hearsay witness over the testimony of the "poor" witness.[22]

Taken together, the initial studies suggest that jurors attend to hearsay evidence but do not afford it undue weight. Indeed, researchers who examined how jurors respond to specific features of hearsay evidence found that mock jurors are attuned to several cognitive factors that can affect the reliability of hearsay statements, such as suggestive questioning of children or the effect of age on the elderly.[23] But jurors are occasionally subject to hearsay blind spots, including the effects of age on the sincerity, narration, perception, and memory of child declarants or the tendency to recall only the "gist" of hearsay statements at the

---

[20] Landsman and Rakos 1991.
[21] Meine, Park, and Borgida 1992.
[22] Bull Kovera, Park, and Penrod 1992.
[23] Pathak and Thompson 1999; Dunlap et al. 2007.

expense of its more detailed information.[24] It is also an open question whether jurors respond well to curative or limiting instructions with respect to hearsay evidence.[25] The most recent studies, however, continue to provide cause for optimism. For example, jurors are skilled at rooting out motivational factors that strengthen or weaken the value of hearsay. One study suggests that jurors subscribe to a "best evidence" model of hearsay, such that they are less likely to credit hearsay evidence when it is clear that more probative, firsthand information is available instead. In that study, jurors discounted hearsay substantially when it appeared that the hearsay was proffered to shield the declarant from damaging cross examination, but not when the declarant was legitimately unable to testify.[26]

Most recently, researchers have examined the validity of the assumptions underlying the hearsay rule. Sevier had participants read a mock trial in which the alleged dangers of hearsay evidence—in which the testimonial capacities of the hearsay witness cannot be tested on cross-examination—were on display.[27] Sevier manipulated not only the testimonial infirmity present in the speaker's information, but also the *identity* of the individual whose testimony was infirm. Sevier found that mock jurors were attuned to the different testimonial infirmities with respect to both the testifying witness *and* the absent hearsay declarant. In a follow-up study in which he systematically increased the levels of hearsay present in the testimony, he found concomitant decreases in the weight that mock jurors afforded the hearsay evidence.

The psychology findings suggest that, with caveats, jurors are better at evaluating hearsay than the evidentiary rules suppose, and they do not give hearsay evidence undue weight. If these findings replicate, then the prevailing rationale for the hearsay rule appears to be unfounded. A solution to this problem might be found in another study that explores the basis for the popular legitimacy of the hearsay rule. The researcher examined lay attitudes toward the doctrine and reported a surprising outcome: a majority of the public does not view the hearsay rule as a rule safeguarding the reliability of trial evidence. Rather, the public perceives the hearsay rule as premised on *procedural justice*—the desire to ensure that defendants have the ability to look their accusers in the eye and to afford them the dignity of questioning their accusers directly in court.[28] To the extent that the public views the hearsay rule as providing procedural safeguards akin to that which is provided by the Sixth Amendment Confrontation Clause, it may be worth examining whether the hearsay rule should follow suit, and rule-makers should consider whether that requires reimagining the current regime and its myriad exceptions.

4. Impeachment

The impeachment of witnesses through cross-examination is arguably the most important procedural feature of the American trial. Wigmore once famously claimed that cross-examination is "beyond any doubt the greatest legal engine ever invented for the discovery of truth," and the Sixth Amendment's Confrontation Clause ensures criminal defendants

---

[24] Warren and Woodall 1999.
[25] Lee, Krauss, and Lieberman 2005, 590–1.
[26] Sevier 2012.
[27] Sevier 2015.
[28] Sevier 2016.

the important procedural right of looking their accusers in the eye and questioning them directly.[29] The law governing impeachment also provides fertile ground for experimental psychologists. Psychological research on the "story model" of jury decision-making suggests that jurors frequently choose between competing trial narratives by examining the fit between each narrative and the credible evidence that the parties present at trial.[30] It is therefore in each party's interest to attack the four testimonial capacities of their adversary's witnesses: their ability to testify in an unambiguous manner, to have perceived the events in question correctly, to have remembered those events correctly, and to testify truthfully.

Whichever of the witness's testimonial capacities an adversary chooses to attack, she does so primarily through contradicting the witness in some manner or by impeaching the witness's character for truthfulness. Psychology studies demonstrate that jurors generally are receptive to successful attacks on the testimonial capacities and discount the witness's testimony accordingly.[31] But at least one type of witness presents a puzzle. Several studies, including a classic study by cognitive psychologist Elizabeth Loftus, have examined "impeachment by contradiction" in the context of eyewitness testimony. Regardless of whether the eyewitness has contradicted herself or whether she was contradicted with other evidence, her testimony remained largely impervious to successful impeachment in the eyes of the jurors, particularly if the eyewitness expressed strong confidence in her identification.[32]

Another area in which jurors appear to struggle involves the impeachment of a testifying witness with a prior conviction. Federal Rule 609 lays out an intricate set of conditions—involving the identity of the witness and the nature of the prior crime—by which prior convictions are admissible to impeach. The rules anticipate the potential unduly prejudicial nature of a criminal defendant's prior conviction and attempt to reduce undue prejudice by allowing the evidence to be introduced in only narrow circumstances. Nonetheless, a body of research suggests that the procedural safeguards inherent in Federal Rule 609 may be insufficient to protect defendants from unfairly prejudicial effects of prior conviction evidence. The initial studies found what attorneys had long suspected: evidence of a defendant's prior crime increased jurors' willingness to convict, although the size of the effect varied.[33] These studies could not demonstrate, however, the pathway through which jurors were more likely to convict the defendant. If jurors convicted because the defendant was viewed as less credible after being impeached, this inference is permissible under the rules. If, however, the increased convictions are a result of beliefs that the defendant is "crime prone," this would be an impermissible inference.

Researchers tested these dueling explanations. Wissler and Saks manipulated the defendant's prior conviction in a murder case: the prior conviction was either for murder, which does not always bear directly on dishonesty, or for perjury, which does.[34] Mock jurors exposed to the prior murder conviction convicted the defendant roughly 70% of the time, but they did so only 50% of the time when the prior conviction was for perjury. Wissler and Saks reported that jurors were not using the prior conviction evidence solely to evaluate the

[29] Wigmore 1974, §1367.
[30] Pennington and Hastie 1992.
[31] Sevier 2015.
[32] Loftus 1975, 189–90; Brewer and Burke 2002.
[33] Doob and Kirshenbaum 1972.
[34] Wissler and Saks 1985.

defendant witness's credibility. Rather, they appeared to use the prior conviction as inadmissible propensity evidence.

These findings have been replicated. Clary and Shaffer conducted a mock trial in which they found that, in an armed robbery case, jurors convicted markedly more often when confronted with a testifying defendant's prior conviction for robbery than for counterfeiting, which bears more directly on dishonesty.[35] Studies by Hans and Doob and by Eisenberg and Hans also suggest that, even if the impermissible use of the prior conviction *itself* is not responsible for jurors' increased willingness to convict a testifying defendant, the prior conviction is associated with increased perceptions of the probative value of *other* evidence against the defendant.[36]

Perhaps the most important contribution of this body of research involves the downstream effects of how jurors evaluate prior conviction evidence. Several studies suggest that criminal defendants—in particular, factually innocent defendants—*believe* that information concerning their prior conviction will so damage their case that they become less willing to testify in their defense and risk cross-examination.[37] Unfortunately, other well-known research suggests that although jurors are forbidden from making inferences about a defendant's silence at trial, jurors subconsciously and sometimes overtly conclude that, by "withholding crime-relevant information," the defendant is deceptive or guilty.[38]

Recently, law professor Jeffrey Bellin conducted the first mock juror experiment pitting the "silence penalty," which a criminal defendant may face if he gives up his right to testify in his defense, against the "prior offender penalty," which he is likely to receive if he testifies and faces impeachment.[39] In a mock robbery case, Bellin manipulated whether the defendant testified, and if he did, whether or not he was impeached with a prior conviction (either for robbery or for criminal fraud). Bellin confirmed that evidence law creates a catch-22 for criminal defendants. In terms of its effect size, the "silence penalty" harms defendants about as much as the "prior offender penalty," and both result in increased convictions. Rule-makers should consider this research in examining the unintended effects of allowing prior conviction evidence to be admitted at trial.

5. Limiting and Curative Instructions

There are two truisms regarding evidentiary rules. First, rules of evidence largely act as rules of exclusion, because most are designed to prevent information from reaching the factfinder. Second, and less obvious, the rules of evidence are largely permissive, insofar as trial judges are afforded vast discretion in terms of the manner in which they implement evidentiary rules at trial. Perhaps signaling their increased importance, however, a few evidentiary rules are mandatory. Federal Rule 103(d), for example, states that "[t]o the extent practicable, the court *must* conduct a jury trial so that inadmissible evidence is not suggested to the jury," and Federal Rule 105 requires that, if the court admits information into evidence for one (legitimate) purpose but not for another (illegitimate) purpose, "the

---

[35] Clary and Shaffer 1985, 245.
[36] Hans and Doob 1976; Eisenberg and Hans 2009.
[37] Blume 2008.
[38] Clary and Shaffer 1980.
[39] Bellin 2018.

court, on timely request, *must* restrict the evidence to its proper scope and instruct the jury accordingly."[40]

These mandatory rules present a puzzle for the presiding judge and a challenge for the jury: they require the factfinder to evaluate the evidence while pretending that she does not know some fact about the underlying dispute, or she must resist the urge to process the evidence in one manner, while explicitly processing it in another manner. The cognitive complexity of both tasks provides fertile ground for experimental psychologists to determine whether jurors are truly capable of correctly undertaking those tasks and whether they are sufficiently motivated to do so.

These questions have generated a wealth of empirical scholarship, including fifty published reports and a meta-analysis. Researchers have explored several psychological theories that might compromise a juror's ability to (1) disregard inadmissible evidence, or (2) evaluate evidence for a permissible purpose (for example, to gauge a witness's credibility) but not for an impermissible purpose (for example, as propensity evidence establishing that the defendant committed the crime at issue). With respect to curative instructions, psychologists have identified cognitive and motivational factors that increase the difficulty of disregarding inadmissible evidence. Many raise the "pink elephant" or "white bear" problem, made famous in Daniel Wegner's ironic processes theory, in which an individual's attempt to suppress certain thoughts makes the thoughts more likely to surface.[41] Other researchers point to the concepts of belief perseverance and the hindsight bias, insofar as these phenomena involve forbidden information exerting subconscious influence over how people process subsequent information.[42] Cognitive psychologists also point to the increased attention that such evidence receives merely due to the judge's instruction, while noting that jurors might encode and perceive the evidence more vividly as well.[43]

Interestingly, motivational factors might influence jurors even if they *could* limit or disregard the inadmissible evidence. Researchers have found support for a "pursuit of justice" theory of decision-making, in which jurors believe that it is unjust to render a verdict that does not account for certain types of inadmissible evidence once they become aware of it.[44] Still, other researchers point to the phenomenon of psychological reactance. Reactive jurors might experience unpleasant motivational arousal to a judicial order restricting their behavior, which causes them explicitly to consider the inadmissible evidence.[45] Relatedly, other studies support a phenomenon that one researcher has dubbed "omission suspicion," in which "secret" evidence has such strong appeal to jurors that they ineluctably consider it in their verdicts.[46] It is, however, worth noting that the extent to which these motivational forces affect verdicts is unclear, because most studies of limiting and curative instructions did not require jurors to deliberate. And when researchers *have* evaluated the behavior of real jurors during deliberation, the evidence is mixed: some jurors explicitly brought up the inadmissible evidence, but other jurors observed that they were told not to take the admissible evidence into account.[47]

---

[40] Federal Rules of Evidence (FRE) 103(d); FRE 105.
[41] Wegner 1994.
[42] Ross, Lepper, and Hubbard 1975; Fischhoff 1975.
[43] Borgida and Howard-Pitney 1983.
[44] Kassin and Sommers 1997.
[45] Brehm and Brehm 1981.
[46] Saks and Spellman 2016; Sevier 2012.
[47] Vidmar and Hans 2007.

With a deep well of psychological phenomena on which to draw, over fifty different studies on the subject, and prevailing legal wisdom that curative and limiting instructions present nothing more than a legal fiction, one would expect greater coherence than currently exists in the literature. Several psychological mechanisms have been proposed, each with some support, but the literature contains studies that are heterogenous and difficult to harmonize, insofar as they vary with respect to the subject matter of the trial, the nature of the objections, and the parties raising the objections. Drawing clear conclusions, therefore, is difficult. At the very least, however, a meta-analysis from psychologist Nancy Steblay and colleagues provides some clarity. They found that inadmissible evidence "has a reliable effect on verdicts consistent with the content of the [evidence]," and that judicial instructions fail to completely mitigate this effect.[48] Promisingly, the researchers also noted that when a judge provides the jury with a meaningful reason for why jurors should disregard evidence or consider it for just one purpose, the effects of the inadmissible evidence on jurors' verdicts appears to diminish, perhaps mitigating the cognitive and motivational forces that draw jurors toward the inadmissible evidence.

6. Scientific Expertise

The volume of scholarship examining the role that scientific and expert information plays in the legal system could fill several legal treatises.[49] But this is unsurprising. The practice of admitting testimony into evidence from partisan scientific experts goes at least as far back as the famous British case of *Folkes v. Chadd* in the 1780s, and is more controversial today as evidence in civil and criminal trials has become more complex.[50] And now that American federal courts have shifted from a model in which expertise that purports to be generally accepted within the relevant scientific community is admissible to the *Daubert* standard—where judges serve as gatekeepers who evaluate the expertise before admitting it into evidence—the competency of jurors and judges to evaluate scientific and expert evidence has become an important research question for empirical psychologists.[51]

The *Daubert* test requires judges to determine if scientific expertise is reliable enough to be considered by the factfinder. As applied to Federal Rule 702, the *Daubert* test requires federal judges—the majority of whom lack specialized training in physical or social science—to examine the evidence according to a litany of non-exhaustive factors: whether the research hypothesis is falsifiable, whether the method has a known error rate, whether the science has been subject to peer review, and whether the purported expertise is generally accepted within the relevant scientific community. Several empirical studies suggest that although federal judges are generally more intelligent than jurors, and they are intrinsically and extrinsically motivated to make correct admissibility decisions, they routinely misunderstand critical scientific concepts. For example, Dobbin and colleagues surveyed judges with respect to their understanding of the scientific concepts embodied in the *Daubert* test. Using predetermined coding criteria, the researchers found several deficiencies. Although a

---

48   Steblay et al. 2006.
49   See, e.g., Faigman et al. 2008.
50   *Folkes v. Chadd* [1782] 3 Doug KB 157, [1782] 99 Eng. Rep. 589.
51   *Daubert v. Merrell Dow Pharmaceuticals, Inc.* [1992] 509 U.S. 579.

high percentage of judges "clearly underst[ood]" the significance of the peer review process (71%) and of general acceptance in the relevant scientific community (82%), judges had difficulty understanding the concept of falsifiability (finding that just 6% of judges demonstrated "clear understanding") and error rates (finding that just 4% demonstrated a "clear understanding").[52] Other research is largely in accord with these findings. For example, Kovera and McAuliff asked scientifically trained and untrained judges to evaluate the admissibility of social science evidence and found that judges were largely insensitive to the differences in the quality of the evidence and were insensitive to its peer-reviewed status. Promisingly, however, scientifically trained judges performed better than untrained judges and were more sensitive to at least some of the deficiencies in the evidence.[53]

Other research suggests that these deficiencies in judges' gatekeeping abilities have substantial downstream effects. Law professor Andrew Jurs, for example, reported that attorneys appear to lack faith that judges will perform their gatekeeping task correctly, and found that only 20% of attorneys agreed that "judges properly screen experts so that only qualified experts are permitted to testify."[54] Perhaps more troubling, Schweitzer and Saks found in a mock trial study that, regardless of the quality of the scientific expertise, the mere fact that a judge had allowed the evidence to reach the jury resulted in jurors evaluating the evidence less critically than they would have if they had been exposed to it outside of the courtroom. Thus, judges who misapply the *Daubert* criteria risk compounding their mistake when the evidence reaches the jury.

Research on the effects of scientific expertise on juror decision-making is complex. Because jurors evaluate facets of both the message (the expertise itself) and the messenger (information about the expert, including her qualifications and bona fides), psychologists have drawn from dual process theories of persuasion in exploring how jurors decide which experts to credit.[55] Dual process theories suggest that to the extent that a message is overly complex, the evaluator may employ superficial, heuristic processing when evaluating the message, compared to when the evaluator has the cognitive capacity and motivation to encode the message (in which the individual will rely on more effortful processing).[56] Jurors tend to evaluate messengers by using a heuristic model. For example, they find experts more persuasive if the expert's gender is congruent with gender stereotypes associated with the expert's scientific field.[57] Moreover, they strongly consider an expert's personal characteristics, such as the extent to which she is paid for her testimony, her communicative ability, and the impressiveness of her credentials, in assessing credibility.[58]

With respect to the expert's substantive message, jurors prefer experts who tailor their expertise closely to the facts of the case, who arrive at firm conclusions about the evidence, and who candidly admit their exposure to biasing information.[59] Although the data does not support the "CSI effect"— that is, jurors are not overly enamored with or skeptical of forensic evidence by virtue of their television habits—jurors are likely to engage in heuristic processing of scientific information that requires high levels of numeracy to interpret,

[52] Dobbin et al. 2002.
[53] Bull Kovera and McAuliff 2002.
[54] Jurs 2016.
[55] Ivković and Hans 2003.
[56] Petty and Cacioppo 1986.
[57] Schuller, Terry, and McKimmie 2001.
[58] Shuman, Champagne, and Whitaker 1996; Rosenthal 1983.
[59] Champagne, Schuman, and Whitaker 1991.

including error risks, likelihood ratios, and DNA evidence.[60] And the presence of additional experts to assist jurors in processing complex evidence appears to help more than it hurts; "battles of the experts" tend to cause jurors to reduce the probative value of the expertise altogether.[61]

Encouragingly, however, researchers have identified a number of reforms that can improve the quality of juridical decision-making with respect to expert evidence. At the judicial level, judges should be more skeptical of scientific "expertise" that has a history of admission in court but a weak record of scientific validity.[62] Moreover, jurors are more likely to take seriously (1) neutral experts, whom judges can appoint pursuant to Federal Rule 706, and (2) experts who have been "blinded" to the identity of the party that hired them.[63] With respect to jurors, under certain circumstances, well-executed cross-examination may focus them on critical shortcomings of scientific expertise.[64] And training on how to be an informed consumer of science may pay dividends regarding how both judges and juries understand and evaluate expertise.[65]

7. Concluding Remarks

The attention of empirical psychologists to the law of evidence has grown substantially since the famous feud between Münsterberg and Wigmore in the early twentieth century. And for good reason, because evidence law is, at its core, deeply rooted in psychology. Indeed, over the ensuing one hundred years, researchers have examined the psychological underpinnings of courtroom adjudication by drawing on an array of phenomena from a variety of psychological perspectives, including the fundamental attribution error, interactionist models of social perception, the elaboration likelihood model of persuasion, metacognition, construal level theory, the ironic processes model, motivated reasoning, procedural justice and legitimacy, and Kalven and Zeisel's seminal work on real American juries. Psychologists have much to say to legal policy-makers about the wisdom of many evidentiary rules.

Whether those rule-makers will (or should) listen is a complex question. As of now, the body of research on propensity evidence, impeachment, and scientific expertise has produced conflicting findings regarding the wisdom of the assumptions underlying each rule. There is growing evidence that jurors are attuned to factors that enhance or diminish the probative value of different types of propensity evidence, but moderator variables such as the defendant's race complicate the empirical narrative. With respect to impeachment evidence, although it appears that jurors are attuned to efforts to attack a witness's testimonial capacities—and discount the probative weight of an impeached witness's testimony defensibly—impeachment by means of a prior conviction tends to lead jurors to engage in inappropriate propensity reasoning. The research on scientific expertise suggests that although judges and jurors sometimes understand the strengths and weaknesses of scientific

---

[60] Koehler 2011.
[61] Boudreau and McCubbins 2009.
[62] Saks and Spellman 2016.
[63] Robertson and Yokum 2012.
[64] Thompson and Scurich 2019.
[65] Schweitzer and Saks 2012.

evidence, they sometimes engage in superficial reasoning that can increase the perceived probative value of junk science that reaches the jury. In light of the nuances of the empirical research, evidence policy-makers fairly may hesitate to incorporate these findings into the evidentiary rules. The burden may therefore fall upon psychologists to continue pursuing these lines of research, using methods that provide convergent evidence, to create a strong body of peer-reviewed scholarship that is accessible to the legal community. Such scholarship may encourage policy-makers that the cost-benefit analysis of altering an evidentiary rule weighs in favor of tweaking the rule accordingly.

The empirical data on hearsay and limiting instructions provides greater clarity to evidence policy-makers and has earned the attention of prominent jurists. The weight of the empirical data suggests that critical assumptions that underly the necessity of the hearsay rule are, at least on average, incorrect. The data support similar conclusions with respect to limiting and curative instructions given to jurors, although the psychological mechanisms that underlie the research findings remain inconclusive. Still, in light of current issues in psychology—including a renewed interest in the replicability of prior studies—evidence rule-makers may be cautious even of the clear conclusions from this body of work.[66] It may behoove psychologists to consider supplementing these findings with field research, including data collected from real trials. Rule-makers may perceive these studies as more directly applicable to courtroom adjudication, which could serve as a tipping point that convinces them to revise evidentiary rules so that their underlying assumptions more closely align with their legal consequences.

References

Asch, S. E. (1946). "Forming Impressions of Personality," *Journal of Abnormal and Social Psychology*, 41: 258–90.

Bell, B. D. and Stanfield, G. G. (1973). "An Interactionist Appraisal of Impression Formation: The 'Central Trait' Hypothesis Revisited," *Kansas Journal of Sociology*, 9: 55–68.

Bellin, J. (2018). "The Silence Penalty," *Iowa Law Review*, 103: 395–434.

Blume, J. H. (2008). "The Dilemma of the Criminal Defendant with a Prior Record—Lessons from the Wrongfully Convicted," *Journal of Empirical Legal Studies*, 5: 477–505.

Borgida, E. (1979). "Character Proof and the Fireside Induction," *Law and Human Behavior*, 3: 189–202.

Borgida, E. and Howard-Pitney, B. (1983). "Personal Involvement and the Robustness of Perceptual Salience Effects," *Journal of Personality and Social Psychology*, 45: 560–70.

Bornstein, B. H. and Neuschatz, J. S. (2020). *Hugo Münsterberg's Psychology and Law: A Historical and Contemporary Assessment*. Oxford: Oxford University Press.

Boudreau, C. and McCubbins, M. D. (2009). "Competition in the Courtroom: When does Expert Testimony improve Jurors' Decisions?" *Journal of Empirical Legal Studies*, 6: 793–817.

Bull Kovera, M. and McAuliff, B. (2002). "The Effects of Peer Review and Evidence Quality on Judge Evaluations of Psychological Science: Are Judges effective Gatekeepers?" *Journal of Applied Psychology*, 85: 574–86.

Bull Kovera, M., Park, R. C., and Penrod, S. D. (1992). "Jurors' Perceptions of Eyewitness and Hearsay Evidence," *Minnesota Law Review*, 76: 703–22.

Brehm, S. S. and Brehm, J. W. (1981). *Psychological Reactance: A Theory of Freedom and Control*. Cambridge: Academic Press.

---

[66] Open Science Collaboration 2015.

Brewer, N. and Burke, A. (2002). "Effects of Testimonial Inconsistencies and Eyewitness Confidence on Mock-Juror Judgments," *Law and Human Behavior*, 26: 353–64.

Champagne, A., Schuman, D., and Whitaker, E. (1991). "An Empirical Examination of the Use of Expert Witnesses in American Courts," *Jurimetrics*, 31: 375–92.

Cicchini, M. D. and White, L. T. (2018). "Convictions Based on Character: An Empirical Test of Other-Acts Evidence," *Florida Law Review*, 70: 347–77.

Clary, E. G. and Shaffer, D. R. (1980). "Effects of Evidence Withholding and a Defendant's prior Record on Juridic Decisions," *Journal of Social Psychology*, 112: 237–45.

Clary, E. G. and Shaffer, D. R. (1985). "Another Look at the Impact of Juror Sentiments toward Defendants on Juridic Decisions," *Journal of Social Psychology*, 125: 637–51.

Dobbin, S. A., Gatowski, S. I., Richardson, J. T., Ginsburg, G. P., et al. (2002). "Applying Daubert: How well do Judges understand Science and Scientific Method?" *Judicature*, 85: 244–7.

Doob, A. N. and Kirshenbaum, H. M. (1972). "Some empirical Evidence on the Effect of s. 12 of the Canada Evidence Act upon an Accused," *Criminal Law Quarterly*, 15: 88–96.

Dunlap E. E., Golding, J. M., Hodell, E. C., and Marsil, D. F. (2007). "Perceptions of Elder Physical Abuse in the Courtroom: The Influence of Hearsay Witness Testimony," *Journal of Elder Abuse & Neglect*, 19: 19–39.

Eisenberg, T. and Hans, V. P. (2009). "Taking a Stand on Taking the Stand: The Effects of a prior Criminal Record on the Decision to Testify and on Trial Outcomes," *Cornell Law Review*, 94: 1353–90.

Faigman, D. L., Cheng, E. K., Mnookin, J., Murphy, E. E. et al. (2008). *Modern Scientific Evidence*. Eagan, MN: Thomson-West.

Fischhoff, B. (1975). "Hindsight is not Equal to Foresight: The Effect of Outcome Knowledge on Judgment under Uncertainty," *Journal of Experimental Psychology: Human Perception & Performance*, 1: 288–99.

Hans, V. P. and Doob, A. N. (1976). "Section 12 of the Canada Evidence Act and the Deliberations of Simulated Juries," *Criminal law Quarterly*, 18: 235–53.

Hunt, J. S. (2017). "The Cost of Character," *Florida Journal of Law and Public Policy*, 28: 241–90.

Hunt, J. S. and Budesheim, T. L. (2004). "How Jurors use and misuse Character Evidence," *Journal of Applied Psychology*, 89: 347–61.

Ivković, S. K. and Hans, V. P. (2003). "Jurors' Evaluations of Expert Testimony: Judging the Messenger and the Message," *Law and Social Inquiry*, 28: 441–82.

Jurs, A. W. (2016). "Expert Prevalence, Persuasion, and Price: What Trial Participants really think about Experts," *Indiana Law Journal*, 91: 353–91.

Kassin, S. M. and Sommers, S. R. (1997). "Inadmissible Testimony, Instructions to Disregard, and the Jury: Substantive versus Procedural Considerations," *Personality and Social. Psychology Bulletin*, 23: 1046–54.

Koehler, J. J. (2011). "If the Shoe Fits they might Acquit: The Value of Forensic Science Testimony," *Journal of Empirical Legal Studies*, 8: 21–48.

Landsman, S. and Rakos, R. F. (1991). "Research Essay: A Preliminary Empirical Enquiry concerning the Prohibition on Hearsay Evidence in American Courts," *Law & Psychology Review*, 15: 65–85.

Lee, D. H., Krauss, D. A., and Lieberman, J. (2005). "The Effects of Judicial Admonitions on Hearsay Evidence," *International Journal of Law and Psychiatry*, 28: 589–603.

Leonard, D. P. (1998). "In Defense of the Character Evidence Prohibition: Foundations of the Rule against Trial by Character," *Indiana Law Journal*, 73: 1161–215.

Loftus, E. F. (1975). "Reconstructing Memory: The Incredible Eyewitness," *Jurimetrics*, 15: 188–93.

Lupfer, M., Cohen, R., Bernard, J. L., and Smalley, D. (1986). "Presenting Favorable and Unfavorable Character Evidence to Juries," *Law and Psychology Review*, 10: 59–71.

Meine, P., Park, R. C., and Borgida, E. (1992). "Juror Decision Making and the Evaluation of Hearsay Evidence," *Minnesota Law Review*, 76: 683–701.

Merritt, D. J. and Simmons, R. (2017). *Learning Evidence: From the Federal Rules to the Courtroom*. St. Paul, MN: West Academic.

Münsterberg, H. (1908). *On the Witness Stand: Essays on Psychology and Crime*. New York: Doubleday.

Open Science Collaboration (2015). "Estimating the Reproducibility of Psychological Science," *Science*, 349: 943.

Pathak, M. K. and Thompson, W. C. (1999). "From Child to Witness to Jury: Effects of Suggestion on the Transmission and Evaluation of Hearsay," *Psychology, Public Policy and Law*, 5: 372–87.

Pennington, N. and Hastie, R. (1992). "Explaining the Evidence: Tests of the Story Model for Juror Decision Making," *Journal of Personality and Social Psychology*, 62: 189–206.

Petty, R. E. and Caccioppo, J. T. (1986). "The Elaboration Likelihood Model of Persuasion," in L. Berkowitz (ed.), *Advances in Experimental Social Psychology*. Cambridge: Academic Press.

Robertson, C. T. and Yokum, D. V. (2012). "The Effect of Blinded Experts on Juror Verdicts," *Journal of Empirical Legal Studies*, 9: 765–94.

Rosenthal, P. (1983). "Nature of Jury Response to the Expert Witness," *Journal of Forensic Science*, 28: 528–31.

Ross, L., Lepper, M. R., and Hubbard, M. (1975). "Perseverance in Self-Perception and Social Perception: Biased Attributional Processes in the Debriefing Paradigm," *Journal of Personality and Social Psychology*, 32: 880–92.

Saks, M. J. and Spellman, B. A. (2016). *The Psychological Foundations of Evidence Law*. New York: NYU Press.

Schuller, R. A., Terry, D., and McKimmie, B. (2001). "The Impact of an Expert's Gender on Jurors' Decisions," *Law and Psychology Review*, 25: 59–79.

Schweitzer, N. J. and Saks, M. J. (2012). "Jurors and Scientific Causation: What Don't They Know, and What can be Done About It?" *Jurimetrics*, 52: 433–55.

Sevier, J. (2012). "Omission Suspicion: Juries, Hearsay, and Attorneys' Strategic Choices," *Florida State University Law Review*, 40: 1–55.

Sevier, J. (2015). "Testing Tribe's Triangle: Juries, Hearsay, and Psychological Distance," *Georgetown Law Journal*, 103: 879–931.

Sevier, J. (2016). "Popularizing Hearsay," *Georgetown Law Journal*, 104: 643–92.

Sevier, J. (2019). "Legitimizing Character Evidence," *Emory Law Journal*, 68: 441–508.

Shuman, D. W., Champagne, A., and Whitaker, E. (1996). "Juror Assessments of the Believability of Expert Witnesses: A Literature Review," *Jurimetrics*, 36: 371–82.

Sood, A. M. (2017). "Applying Empirical Psychology to inform Courtroom Adjudication—Potential Contributions and Challenges," *Harvard Law Review Forum*, 130: 301–15.

Steblay, N., Hosch, H. M., Culhane, S. E., and McWethy, A. (2006). "The Impact on Juror Verdicts of Judicial Instruction To disregard Inadmissible Evidence," *Law and Human Behavior*, 30: 469–92.

Thompson, W. C. and Scurich, N. (2019). "How Cross-Examination on Subjectivity and bias affects Jurors' Evaluations of Forensic Science Evidence," *Journal of Forensic Science*, 64: 1379–88.

Tomei, J. and Cramer, R. J. (2014). "Perceived Credibility of Character Witnesses: Implications for Trial Consultation," *Journal of Forensic Psychology Practice*, 14: 263–75.

Vidmar, N. and Hans, V. P. (2007). *American Juries: The Verdict*. Buffalo, NY: Prometheus.

Warren, A. R. and Woodall, C. E. (1999). "The Reliability of Hearsay Testimony: How Well do Interviewers Recall their Interviews with Children?" *Psychology, Public Policy and Law*, 5: 355–71.

Wegner, D. M. (1994). "Ironic Processes of Mental Control," *Psychological Review*, 101: 34–52.

Wigmore, J. H. (1909). "Professor Münsterberg and the Psychology of Testimony," *University of Illinois Law Review*, 3: 399–445.

Wigmore, J. H. (1935). *A Student's Textbook on the Law of Evidence*. Brooklyn: Foundation Press.

Wigmore, J. H. (1974). *A Treatise on the System of Evidence in Trials at Common Law*. Boston: Little, Brown, and Company.

Wissler, R. L. and Saks, M. J. (1985). "On the Inefficacy of Limiting Instructions: When Jurors use Prior Conviction Evidence to decide on Guilt," *Law and Human Behavior*, 9: 37–48.

Legal Cases and Rules

Daubert v. Merrell Dow Pharmaceuticals, Inc., 509 U.S. 579 (1992)

Folkes v. Chadd [1782] 3 Doug KB 157, [1782] 99 Eng. Rep. 589

Federal Rule of Evidence 103(d)

Federal Rule of Evidence 105

24

Relevance through a Feminist Lens

Julia Simon-Kerr[*]

1. Introduction

A chapter on feminist theory and evidence necessarily begins with the questions: What does it mean to be a feminist and what does it mean to apply "feminist" theory in the context of an evidentiary system designed by men?

As with labels more generally, identifying ideas as "feminist" invites the assumption that the term has a static meaning. If "gender" and, in particular, the treatment of women have been feminism's central preoccupations, we have to take care, as Katharine Bartlett writes, not to "assume a definition of 'woman' or a standard for 'women's experiences' that is fixed, exclusionary, homogenizing, and oppositional."[1] Using the "feminist" label also creates pressure for "feminism to be distinctive," for it to own or claim a unique way of knowing.[2] This pressure to claim, name, divide, and blame is a distraction from the work of "challenging the patterns of thought that historically excluded women."[3]

With these difficulties in mind, it is still the case that both theory and reform require working classifications. Three decades on from the height of feminist legal scholarship, "gender remains a category that can help to analyze and improve our world."[4] To see this, a brief overview is required.[5] American rules of evidence date back to and are informed by the English common law and a legal system that placed white women in a private domestic sphere with few independent rights to speak in courts of law. Black women's voices were even more attenuated in the courts. Only through legislative and court victories driven by the second wave of feminism in the United States in the early 1970s, did women gain significant access to the legal profession and the legal academy.[6] Evidence theory continued to be explicitly biased against women after these reforms. Wigmore's influential treatise, for example, claimed into the 1980s that the evidentiary system should assume women who allege sexual assault are lying.[7]

Perhaps unsurprisingly, feminism's first challenges to discriminatory laws rested on the premise that women and men have essentially the same capabilities, a premise that

[*] I wish to thank the editors of this volume, as well as Kiel Brennan-Marquez, Virginia Kerr, Jamelia Morgan, and participants in the UConn Law Summer WIP Series for helpful comments and suggestions on this and earlier drafts. Morgen Barroso provided excellent research assistance.
[1] Bartlett 1990, 834.
[2] Minow 1989, 131.
[3] Ibid.
[4] Bartlett 1990, 835, n. 1.
[5] The following extremely brief summary of the general evolution of feminist legal scholarship is indebted to Bartlett's 2012 overview. For overviews that focus specifically on evidence, see Kinports 1991; Hunter 1996; Taslitz 1999a; Orenstein 1990. See also Park and Saks 2006.
[6] See, e.g., Wolfson 2005.
[7] Bienen 1983, 236.

Julia Simon-Kerr, *Relevance through a Feminist Lens* In: *Philosophical Foundations of Evidence Law*. Edited by: Christian Dahlman, Alex Stein, and Giovanni Tuzet, Oxford University Press. © Christian Dahlman, Alex Stein, and Giovanni Tuzet 2021. DOI: 10.1093/oso/9780198859307.003.0025

grounded successful challenges to overt discrimination in many areas of substantive law and to a lesser extent procedure.[8] However, this premise of sameness which lies at the heart of liberal or equality feminism did not pose deep challenges to structural social and economic harms women routinely experience in a patriarchal system.[9] It fell to nonsubordination or dominance feminism, most often associated with the work of Catherine MacKinnon, to refocus the feminist lens from inequality to gender subordination.[10] At the same time, difference feminism, spurred by the work of Carol Gilligan, posed a critical corrective to the valorization of modes of reasoning associated with men and the devaluation of qualities associated with women.[11] Although many feminist theorists worried that difference theory's quest to revalue qualities and modes of reasoning identified as "feminine" could be used to revive the kind of gender essentialism that had long been used to justify sex discrimination, difference theory proved an empowering analytic tool and quickly gained adherents.[12] During this period as well, Kimberlé Crenshaw mapped out an intersectional feminism which urged that race, class, and gender are overlapping social categories functioning as interdependent systems of discrimination.[13] Without an intersectional approach, Crenshaw argued, feminist critiques would inevitably track and reproduce existing hierarchies of race and power. These theories were all informed by the work of critical legal theorists who, in turn, drew on postmodernism to question the neutrality and objectivity of legal rules and to argue that systems of power and truth cannot be legitimized by external foundations or authorities, which are simply constituted from their social context.[14]

In a wealth of articles published primarily during the late 1980s and 1990s, feminist evidence scholars drew on this body of theory through gender-based critiques of specific evidentiary rules,[15] explication of the ways in which the evidentiary system constrains narrative,[16] efforts to change the systemic disbelief of women who are victims of sexual assault or domestic violence,[17] and empirical work on the ways in which the system silences women's voices or discounts women's stories.[18] These critiques have led to significant changes in evidentiary rules and substantive law, particularly in the area of rape and sexual assault.

A central claim of feminist accounts of evidence is that, contrary to accepted wisdom, this system of procedural rules is neither neutral nor value-free.[19] This chapter explores this theme through the concept of relevance. In its most basic function, relevance determines whose stories are told and how they are told. As every student of evidence knows,

---

[8] See, e.g., Bader Ginsburg 1978; Williams 1982.

[9] See, e.g., Herma Hill 1985; Littleton 1991.

[10] MacKinnon 1987; 1989.

[11] Gilligan 1982 used social science research to expose an implicit rights-oriented "male norm" by which female modes of reasoning, which she dubbed an "ethic of care" were measured and found wanting. Difference theory has traveled under a number of rubrics, including "cultural," "relational," "connection," and "different voice" theory, with the latter term making explicit Gilligan's influence. See Bartlett 2012, 399, n. 5.

[12] See DuBois et al. 1985 (describing feminist concerns); Bartlett 2012, 399, n. 101 ("different voice scholarship has left virtually no field of law untouched").

[13] See, e.g., Crenshaw 1989.

[14] See Bartlett 2012, 397–8 (discussing the work of Claire Dalton, Fran Olsen, and Mary Joe Frug).

[15] See, e.g., Orenstein 1997.

[16] See, e.g., Kinports 1991; Hunter 1996; Scheppele 1992.

[17] See, e.g., Mack 1993.

[18] See, e.g., Hlavka 2019.

[19] See, e.g., Nicolson 2000, 13, 16; Kinports 1991.

relevant evidence is evidence that tends to make a material fact more or less probable than it would be without the evidence. Materiality is governed by the substantive law, but our beliefs about the tendency of a piece of evidence to make a fact more or less probable will depend on generalizations from experience or expertise.[20]

While evidence theorists have long recognized that relevance is contingent upon generalizing from social understandings or experience, most have viewed as unremarkable the fact that relevance determinations have reflected the experiences of the white men who acted as judges and who comprised the vast majority of jurors.[21] In a 1940 article cited in the commentary to the Federal Rules of Evidence, for example, George James wrote that the relevance inquiry depends on "some general proposition, based most often on the practical experience of the judge and jurors *as men*."[22] His words, which doubtless reflected a truism of his time, substantiate a common critique levied at various evidentiary rules by feminist evidence scholars, which is that they have subtly or overtly privileged the perspective of white men to the exclusion of other voices.[23]

To understand what is at stake when we assess relevance, it is helpful to begin with MacKinnon's assertion that "[e]vidence law lays down what the legal system will take to be real."[24] MacKinnon elaborates that "[a]s law's epistemology, the rules of evidence embody assumptions about reliability and credibility and common knowledge."[25] The requirement of relevance shapes the process of translating "common knowledge" into legal consequences, and in doing so validates and creates knowledge itself. Probing more deeply into relevance allows us to heed Patricia Hill Collins' call, made in the context of Black feminist epistemology, to "challenge all certified knowledge and open up the question of whether what has been taken to be true can stand the test of alternative ways of validating truth."[26] Katharine Bartlett put this more concretely in 1990 when she observed that many reforms that have benefitted women have involved "expanding the lens of legal relevance to encompass the missing perspectives of women and to accommodate perceptions about the nature and role of women."[27]

In sum, because knowledge and experience shape our understanding of relevance, assessing relevance naturally raises fundamental questions that are at the heart of feminist inquiry: Whose knowledge, and whose experience? At the same time, relevance's social contingency holds the potential to validate alternative ways of knowing and to expand the process of arriving at truth. This chapter begins by exploring the contingent nature of the relevance inquiry from a feminist perspective. It then considers the practical importance of relevance in incorporating new baseline positions into legal judgment as a result of legal or non-legal change.[28]

---

[20] Federal Rules of Evidence (FRE) 401.
[21] Thayer 1898 (relevance "tacitly refers to logic and general experience").
[22] James 1940–1, 696, n.15.
[23] See, e.g., Hunter 1996, 131.
[24] MacKinnon 2003, 209.
[25] Ibid.
[26] Collins 2000, 271.
[27] Bartlett 1990, 863.
[28] In using the notion of baseline positions, I am influenced by an article by Carbado and Harris identifying areas of overlap between intersectional and dominance feminist theories. One area of overlap is the attention paid by both theories to the importance of baselines and starting assumptions in the legal system. See Carbado and Harris 2019, 2223.

2. The Contingency of Relevance

Relevance is a foundational concept in the American system of evidence. Indeed, relevance has been conceptualized not as a rule or doctrine, but as a "principle" of evidence, a view that evokes a world of enlightenment rationality in which relevance offers a clear constraint on the front end of admissibility determinations.[29] This view presents logic and rationality as faithful guides to whether evidence makes a fact of consequence more or less probable. The messiness of human subjectivity is left to other rules that touch explicitly on concerns of prejudice, probative value, efficiency, and extra-evidentiary policy concerns. Viewing relevance as a binary inquiry that can be answered by commonsense and logic harmonizes with the conceit that law finds truth through "neutral" rules of procedure. This presumed neutrality also serves to reinforce the impression that judicial outcomes accurately reconstruct external events, an impression that along with other features of the evidentiary system enhances the perceived legitimacy of legal verdicts.

Feminists in many disciplines have argued that such rationalist approaches to knowledge, when they "aim to create scientific descriptions of reality by producing objective generalizations," can serve simply to reinforce the ideologies of those in power.[30] For example, postmodernist feminist theorist Donald Nicolson writes that traditional evidence scholarship and legal positivism more generally, with their focus on the importance of logic, have masked the "inherently political and partial nature of law and facts."[31] Nicolson argues that traditional evidence theory embraces an "Enlightenment myth," which he defines as the idea of an epistemological subject with the "view from nowhere."[32] Hill Collins, in her pathbreaking articulation of Black feminist epistemology, offers a related critique, writing that by privileging "rationality" positivism excludes other ways of knowing, requiring practitioners to "distance themselves from the values, vested interests, and emotions generated by their class, race sex, or unique situation."[33] These perspectives expose a number of interrelated and problematic assumptions in the law's conception of relevance, among them that a presumed scientific rationality offers a value-free method through which the law can uncover objective facts waiting to be discovered.[34] These assumptions also ignore the law's role in producing socially contingent knowledge.[35]

Evidence scholars have long recognized that relevance is not inherent in a piece of evidence. Rather, it depends on the substantive law and "the proposition sought to be proved."[36] In other words, evidence may be "irrelevant" because it is not probative of the fact or proposition in the way its proponent suggests or "because that proposition is not provable in the case."[37] The Federal Rules of Evidence (FRE) express these ideas by explicitly defining relevant evidence as evidence that has a "tendency to make a fact more or less likely

---

[29] Thayer wrote that it is a "principle—not so much a rule of evidence as a presupposition involved in the very conception of a rational system of evidence ... which forbids receiving anything irrelevant, not logically probative." Thayer 1898, 264.

[30] See, generally, Collins 2000.

[31] Nicolson 2000, 16.

[32] Ibid., 23.

[33] Collins 2000, 255.

[34] Nicolson 2000, 16.

[35] Ibid., 23.

[36] See, e.g., James 1940–1, 690 (critiquing earlier scholars for failing to understand that relevance was dependent upon the substantive law).

[37] Ibid., 691.

than it would be without the evidence," when the "fact is of consequence in determining the action."[38]

Feminist theorists have understandably focused primarily on substantive law constraints on relevance, exposing the extent to which an ostensibly neutral inquiry tied to substantive law excludes facts that might contest the gender politics in that law.[39] By design, relevance constraints reinforce the normative judgments contained in the substantive law. To illustrate this, Nicolson, Rosemary Hunter, and others have pointed to the criminal law's treatment of women who killed their batterers in jurisdictions allowing a defense of provocation. Such jurisdictions generally excluded as irrelevant evidence that such women had been subjected to years of physical or mental abuse by the men they were accused of killing.[40] When these women offered a defense of provocation, prosecutors could refute the defense by showing that the battered woman's lethal act was not an immediate response to an act of violence against her. Nicolson argues that this emphasis on immediate and violent reactions to provocation reflects the dominant ideology of the men who constructed the criminal law, to whom such reflexive violence was familiar and understandable. While Nicolson's analysis sounds in a form of essentialism, offering gender as "an opposition of inherently different beings," the example also demonstrates how the substantive law can shape relevance determinations in a way that discounts or discredits women's experiences and stories.[41]

Once the substantive law suggests that certain facts are consequential, the relevance inquiry must still assess whether the proffered evidence tends to make a consequential proposition more or less probable. This inquiry, as is clear from the commentary to the FRE, is expected to hinge on rationality and logic. Factfinders must determine if a piece of evidence is probative using "principles evolved by experience or science, applied logically to the situation at hand."[42] Taking issue with this assumption, feminist scholars have argued that a factfinder's decision that a piece of evidence has any probative value often rests on unexpressed assumptions reflecting that factfinder's own epistemology. Minow makes this point when she questions the claim that judges act neutrally and impartially when they rule on relevance. This assumption, she writes, "presupposes the universality of a particular reference point."[43] Similarly, in *Evidence Engendered*, often cited as the first article to apply feminist theory to evidence, Kinports writes that even though relevance is thought to be "neutral and impartial," it is "in fact in the eye of the beholder."[44]

This stance of neutrality also silently defeats alternative claims of knowledge, illustrating why, as Hill Collins writes, such claims "in and of themselves are rarely threatening to conventional knowledge."[45] Instead, they are "absorbed and marginalized in existing paradigms."[46] The attorneys who propose the relationship between evidence and premises sought to be proved and the judges who evaluate the plausibility of those relational

[38] FRE 401. The federal rules here use the term "likely" as synonymous with "probable."
[39] Nicolson 2000, 19; Hunter 1996, 133.
[40] Ibid.
[41] Flax 1987, 641; Collins 2015, 452, offers an excellent critique of the related prosecutorial use of experts on "battered women's syndrome," and the way in which it essentializes and discredits women while resting on a poor scientific foundation.
[42] Commentary on FRE 401 (citing James 1940–1, 695, n. 15).
[43] Minow 1988.
[44] Kinports 1991.
[45] Collins 2000, 270.
[46] Ibid.

claims maintain the gloss of objectivity even as their epistemologies constrain assessments of relevance.[47] To repurpose a critique Minow levied at essentialist feminism, this process "adopt[s] unstated reference points that hide from view a preferred position and shield[s] it from challenge by other plausible alternatives."[48]

The observation that relevance is socially constructed has been elaborated by evidence theorists far outside any feminist or critical tradition, and it is instructive to consider how those theorists have framed the issue. For example, in writing about inductive reasoning, Cohen implicitly acknowledges the social factors that bear on relevance determinations. Deploying the language of science, he writes that inductive reasoning, which draws upon "background data" comprised of "a vast number of commonplace generalizations about human acts, attitudes, intentions," allows the "*juryman*" to make probabilistic assessments.[49] Cohen finds this unproblematic, explaining that the main generalizations relied upon in this process are "too essential a part of our culture for there to be any serious disagreements about them."[50]

Twining quotes from this portion of Cohen's analysis in his own meditation on the relevance inquiry, which he describes as "one of the more problematic questions in the subject of Evidence."[51] Twining's own description of the way that relevance relies on "the available social stock of knowledge" is apposite here. He turns to biblical times for his example. In Sodom, he proposes, there is an offense of fomenting earthquakes. Also, in Sodom, being gay is "known" to cause earthquakes. Therefore, evidence of a private act of gay sex committed the day before an earthquake in Sodom is relevant evidence in a prosecution of the couple for "fomenting earthquakes." Of course, Twining writes, "[w]e 'know' that there is no connection between the two events." For this reason, "in Sodom the evidence is relevant to the charge, in our culture it is not."[52] Twining suggests that this example demonstrates the relativity of knowledge, another paradoxical problem of proof. Yet for feminist scholars of evidence it has greater significance.

Cohen's reference to "our" culture reinforces the profound sense in which the "background data" of the relevance inquiry is assumed to be universal. Minow charitably describes this type of thinking as the tendency to "treat one's own perspective as truth, rather than as one of many possible points of view."[53] What "we know" in "our culture" about causal or other connections between propositions in myriad arenas depends on how "we" is defined. As Hill Collins writes, "[a] knowledge claim that meets the criteria of adequacy for one group and thus is judged to be acceptable may not be translatable into the terms of a different group."[54] Further, feminist theorists have repeatedly argued against the notion that

---

[47] No matter their backgrounds, attorneys and judges must be trained in law schools, pass bar association licensing exams, and remain in good standing with those associations. These are additional homogenizing forces that push against alternative knowledge claims.

[48] Minow 1988, 48.

[49] Cohen 1977. It is worth noting that Cohen published this description of inductive reasoning in 1977, when women had been serving on juries for over fifty years, and after the Supreme Court held in 1975 that a state law that systematically excluded women from the jury pool violated a defendant's Sixth Amendment rights. *Taylor v. Louisiana*, 419 U.S. 522.

[50] Ibid., 275.

[51] Twining 1990.

[52] Ibid.

[53] Minow 1988, 48.

[54] Collins 2000, 268.

a tradition coded as white and male is universal, demurring from the view that it can speak for those whose experiences have differed along lines of, for example, sex, gender, race, or social privilege. Yet, as the examples suggest, this "convergence between knowledge and power" is often on full display in the legal system's approach to relevance. Finally, because the relevance inquiry lacks "meaningful methodological constraints," a decision-maker's substantive preferences are more likely to "determine a particular outcome."[55] Thus, as Bartlett argues, we should not be surprised when decision-makers' "preferences follow certain patterns reflecting the dominant cultural norms."[56]

Relevance decisions leave us "with a wide range of acceptable substantive results from which to choose."[57] From a feminist perspective, this makes the relevance inquiry available as a mechanism for incorporating changing understandings of the world or ways of knowing.[58] Thus relevance inquiries are one way in which we might answer Bartlett's call for feminist practical reasoning, which she describes as reasoning focused on specific, real-life dilemmas that might be glossed over by unexamined generalizations. This approach resonates with work by evidence theorists seeking to grapple with the problem of generalization and its role in legal proof. Notably, one of the editors of this volume has recently offered a cogent argument that the task is not to eliminate generalizations but rather "to recognize that some generalizations are more problematic than others."[59] Feminist practical reasoning means being engaged in the crucial practice of recognizing and categorizing generalizations, a practice that is not in opposition to "male" rationality. As Bartlett explains, feminists acknowledge greater diversity and are "alert ... to certain forms of injustice that otherwise go unnoticed and unaddressed."[60]

Patricia Hill Collins describes an end goal for Black feminist epistemology as a point where "all people can learn to center in another experience, validate it, and judge it by its own standards without need of comparison or need to adopt that framework as their own."[61] In this world, "one has no need to 'decenter' anyone in order to center someone else; one has only to constantly, appropriately, 'pivot the center.'"[62] I do not argue here that relevance, particularly as it is understood in US law, has the capacity to allow us to fully "pivot the center." As Sotomayor J. has observed, this type of understanding "takes time and effort" which many are not willing to give, assuming they have the capacity or care to do so.[63] In addition, the substantive law often constrains relevance in ways that are impossible to overcome without legal change. Still, relevance inquiries—because they are so contingent, and perhaps even more so if their contingency is better recognized—hold the potential to respond to problems women confront in the legal system by giving voice to different perspectives and sources of knowledge.

---

[55] Bartlett 1990, 845.

[56] Ibid. On this topic, it is worth noting that women are still underrepresented in the federal judiciary. At the time of writing, 73% of Article III judges are white and 66% are men. From 2017–August 2020, 85% of confirmed federal judges have been white and 76% have been men (American Constitution Society).

[57] Bartlett 1990, 845.

[58] Ibid.

[59] Dahlman 2017, 87.

[60] Ibid., 85.

[61] Collins 2000, 270 (quoting Brown 1989, 922).

[62] Ibid.

[63] Sotomayor 2001, 92.

3. Relevance and Practical Justice

In her influential critique of the "reasonable man" tort construct, Bender defined feminism as "an analysis of women's subordination" aimed at both identifying ways to change women's subordinated status and working towards that reform.[64] Precisely because not all women are oppressed in the same way, feminist thinkers have argued forcefully that it is a fallacy to suggest that there is some "essential" women's experience independent of race, sexual orientation, social privilege, and lived experience.[65] Keeping in mind that "women's subordination" is not monolithic, Bender's orientation toward reform still reflects one of feminism's deep virtues: it involves "searching ... for practical justice, not just more theory."[66] Accordingly, this part of the chapter suggests ways in which the relevance inquiry is intertwined with questions of practical justice from a feminist perspective.

3.1 Reshaping Relevance Through Law Reform

Law reform has always been at the core of feminist work to achieve more practical justice. Particularly in the law of rape, feminist reformers have explicitly sought to use the substantive law to reshape the relevance of evidence. The best-known example of this is the widespread enactment of rape shield statutes to constrain defendants' use of victims' sexual histories as evidence in sexual assault prosecutions.[67] Another relevance-related reform to the substantive law is the repeal of marital rape exceptions in all states. Feminist efforts to recenter or redefine the concept of consent are ongoing. They have thus far led towards allowing lack of consent to be proved through words or conduct and away from requiring a showing of physical resistance.[68] Putting aside debates over the efficacy of these reforms, they highlight the continued central role of relevance assessments in rape trials, particularly when courts determine what evidence is admissible on the question of consent.

In recent years, MacKinnon has argued that when used as a dividing line in rape law, consent itself is deeply problematic from a feminist perspective. Consent, she points out, is defined as "voluntarily yielding the will to the proposition of another."[69] From an equality perspective, MacKinnon argues, the consent standard reinforces historically unequal power relations.[70] Accordingly, she argues that rape law should be redefined to eliminate consent because a focus on consent does not account for sex that is the coerced result of "economic, psychological, and social hierarchical threats, so long as severe physical injury ... or death does not ensue."[71]

MacKinnon also stresses the practical consequences of a consent standard for relevance. She writes: "consent is the reason the rape complainant is put on trial. This is what makes the complaining witness's sexual definition—hers as a woman, his as a gay man, for instance, and their sexual histories, despite legal barriers to their introduction—*seem, even*

[64] Bender 1988, 5, 22.
[65] Harris 1990.
[66] Minow 1988, 48.
[67] See, generally, Hunter 1996.
[68] For a critical overview of reforms in the law of rape, see, e.g., Seidman and Vickers 2005; Klein 2008.
[69] MacKinnon 2016, 440.
[70] Ibid., 443.
[71] Ibid.

be, relevant to the accused perpetrator's defense. The distinction between whether someone was raped or just had sex, when seen in consent terms, is ultimately defined by how B felt about it, rather than in terms of what A did to B."[72]

Whether or not one agrees with her analysis, MacKinnon's description highlights both the social construct of relevance—what "seems" relevant—and the way in which the substantive law can itself make certain facts "even be" relevant. MacKinnon acknowledges the power of both features of relevance in her argument for reform. She proposes a definition of rape that includes "use of force, fraud, coercion, abduction, or the abuse of power, trust, or a position of dependency or vulnerability." Crucially, she adds that the definition should make the victim's consent "expressly irrelevant." Why? She recognizes that eliminating consent entirely from the definition of sexual assault is not enough to stop it from *seeming* relevant.[73] Prosecutors and judges, she reasons, will inevitably conclude that consent is relevant to proving one of the listed elements of sexual assault, such as "abuse of power," an outcome MacKinnon suggests might be inevitable where the presence of consent is "socially presupposed from facts on the ground, namely that sex happened."[74] In such circumstances, an express provision instructing factfinders that consent is not relevant is perhaps the only way to eliminate consent entirely from the definition of sexual assault.

MacKinnon similarly took no chances with relevance when she conceptualized the law of sexual harassment.[75] Her definition of sexual harassment does not turn on a person's consent to the sex-related conduct, but instead depends on its welcomeness, so that in a sexual harassment suit, voluntariness is not relevant to the inquiry.[76] This approach also offers instructive guidance for relevance issues in the law of sexual assault. Sexual harassment is defined as discrimination or harassment that is "based on sex." MacKinnon explains that this part of the definition "[i]mplicitly grasps that the central impetus driving the practice is the imposition of a subordinate position within a sexualized social hierarchy of status, regard, reward, dignity, and power."[77] The definition also makes it clear that repeated acts or a pattern of harassment are unquestionably relevant to proof of the offense. This is how a plaintiff shows that the conduct is "based on" sex or gender, rather than motivated by personal animus or some other factor that does not fall within the purview of anti-discrimination law.

Sexual assault law, by contrast, does not recognize similar power dynamics, recognition that would establish the relevance of repeated acts of sexual coercion or violence. For example, in prosecutions under sexual assault statutes that continue to require proof of force, courts are often pressed to admit evidence of the defendant's prior bad acts involving sexual misconduct. At common law, such evidence was viewed as unfair and inadmissible because it tended to put the defendant's character on trial in lieu of a focus on the crime charged. In the 1990s, Congress amended the FRE to make this evidence admissible under a propensity theory, and in the United States over half of the states now allow it.[78] Other states sometimes exclude the evidence as propensity evidence and sometimes admit it if a court determines

---

[72] Ibid., 452 (emphasis added).
[73] Ibid., 474–5.
[74] Ibid., 452.
[75] MacKinnon 1979.
[76] MacKinnon 2016, 451. See also *Meritor Sav Bank v. Vinson* 477 US 57, 68 (1986) (holding that "[t]he fact that sex-related conduct was 'voluntary,' in the sense that the complainant was not forced to participate against her will, is not a defense to a sexual harassment suit brought under Title VI").
[77] MacKinnon 2020, 215.
[78] Holtzman 2020, 1155, n. 1.

that it shows motive, plan or has some other permissible non-propensity relevance to the case.[79] All three approaches are problematic. The federal rules have been rightly criticized for unjustifiably removing procedural protections from criminal defendants, a change that has a disproportionate impact in Black communities with more police contact, while the non-propensity theories offered by courts are often unprincipled at best. Yet, excluding this type of evidence means that it is more difficult to prosecute sexual assault cases, particularly against men who serially sexually assault women.

Although I do not offer a definitive resolution of these difficulties, viewing the problem from a feminist perspective focused on relevance reveals that the substantive law might have more work to do in this area. For example, cases of sexual assault might be distinguished substantively based on whether they involve serial predation. In cases involving repeated acts of sexual assault, as in the law of sexual harassment, these prior bad acts might be framed as relevant not because they speak to the character of the defendant, but rather because they are part of the nature of the offense itself, as one that is "based on" sex.

3.2 Changing Baselines

As described in Section 2, the relevance inquiry depends on both the substantive law and the factfinder's understanding of how a piece of evidence bears on issues that law treats as material. The latter inquiry can serve to exclude or marginalize other voices and to reinforce the beliefs and belief structures of the powerful. At the same time, relevance can also be a site of legal responsiveness to feminist concerns. Evidence that would once have been excluded as irrelevant, as Twining's Sodom example crudely suggests, may become admissible in light of different social beliefs without a corresponding change in either the substantive law or evidentiary rules.

Credibility impeachment provides one example. In prior work on gendered conceptions of credibility in US law, I show that evidence of the alleged "unchastity" of female witnesses was admissible in many states on the theory that it was relevant to their credibility.[80] This form of impeachment happened not just when women were bearing witness to their own sexual assaults, but also when they testified as witnesses in actions involving title to land, assault, arson, or wrongful death.[81] The practice reflected a cultural conviction that a white woman's honor was not contingent upon truthfulness, but rather upon her ability to maintain a reputation for chastity.[82] Hunter and other feminist evidence scholars have critiqued the notion embedded in the relevance inquiry that there are "universally accepted generalizations about human behavior that are available to all triers of fact."[83] The belief that a woman's credibility depended on her chaste appearance was one such accepted generalization.

Indeed, the theory of relevance that led to women being impeached with unchastity evidence depends upon at least two generalizations. First, there is the assumed

---

[79] Ibid.

[80] See Simon-Kerr 2008.

[81] Ibid., 1858; cases cited in n. 5.

[82] Different stereotypes have influenced credibility judgments of Black women, who through courtroom narratives that are both racialized and gendered have been represented as hypersexualized "jezebels," dishonest "welfare queens," and asexual mammy figures. See, e.g., Taslitz 1999b, 32.

[83] Hunter 1996, 131.

interdependence between a woman's honor and her conformity, or apparent conformity, with norms of chaste behavior. And second, is the generalization that a woman who lacked honor also lacked credibility. I have suggested that courts often did not need a third generalization, one that says a woman who lacks honor or credibility is more likely to lie than an honorable woman.[84] Rather, as Rich has observed, women's honesty was not "considered important."[85] Much like incompetency doctrine, which precluded the possibility that enslaved or formerly enslaved people and native Americans could have credibility in courts of law,[86] the legal system was largely uninterested in whether women without honor would in fact lie.[87] Their failure to maintain a chaste reputation meant that they were not worthy of being believed.

It should be no surprise, then, that courts and attorneys invoked "common knowledge" as the basis for their assumptions that a women's chastity determined her credibility, or worthiness of belief.[88] In 1935, Missouri was one of the last jurisdictions to abandon this explicit legal doctrine, and its supreme court did so largely because it concluded that "reason" counselled impeaching witnesses with evidence of truth and veracity.[89] Other courts explained their decisions to stop permitting unchastity impeachment in similar terms.[90] No new substantive or procedural law impelled this doctrinal change. Rather, judicial "reason," which had once suggested that unchastity was acceptable impeachment evidence, now responded to a changed epistemic environment and drew the opposite conclusion.[91]

The story of unchastity impeachment highlights how a feminist perspective on relevance might add insight to the scholarly debate over probabilistic versus explanatory modes of factfinding discussed elsewhere in this volume. One question I have been asked when I present work on the historical entanglement between a woman's chastity and her credibility is whether there might, in fact, have been a correlation. Would an unchaste woman, in other words, be more likely to lie? The answer to this is twofold. First, as described above, this was not, in fact, the empirical question with which factfinders using this elision were primarily concerned. Second, the question starts from the wrong baseline. The belief system that connects two propositions through the relevance inquiry or the broader process of proof itself has the power to create an actual probabilistic connection. The example of a woman's chastity and her credibility illustrates this point. If a particular culture discredits people for behavior separate and apart from lying, while still paying some heed to actual lies, those who will be assumed to be lying regardless of their actual words will have less incentive to be

---

[84] Simon-Kerr 2008, Part I. Thus, I might add "missing generalizations" to Professor Dahlman's taxonomy. See Dahlman 2017, 85.

[85] Rich 1979, 185, 186.

[86] See Simon-Kerr 2017.

[87] Again, it is important to note that this doctrine applied largely to white women whereas Black women were often considered incapable per se of having honor or credibility.

[88] See, e.g., *State v. Sibley* 33 SW 167, 171 (Mo 1895) ("It is a matter of common knowledge that the bad character of a man for chastity does not even in the remotest degree affect his character for truth, when based upon that alone, while it does that of a woman.").

[89] *State v. Williams* 87 SW2d 175, 181 (Mo 1935).

[90] Simon-Kerr 2008, 1884–5.

[91] In sexual assault cases, however, courts continued to admit the same evidence by reframing credibility as consent. Ibid., 1891. For example, one New York court explained why a clergyman accused of raping a woman who worked in his house should have been allowed to question her about her sexual history despite New York precedent holding that a woman's sexual history was not relevant to her credibility. The court held, "it goes to her credibility in the particular matter, to a circumstance relevant to the case in hand, from which the jury are asked to say she did consent." *People v. Abbot*, 19 Wend. 192 (N.Y. Sup. Ct. 1838).

truthful. Whether they lie or not will not change their chances of being believed. Those who have maintained an outward appearance that will not in itself be discrediting might be more concerned about being caught in outright lies. Lying is more costly for this latter group which could make it correspondingly less likely.[92] This suggests one reason why a doctrine holding that women will be disbelieved if they have reputations for unchastity could create the conditions in which they are more likely to lie.[93]

Professors Allen and Pardo describe a related phenomenon when they explain that a "subjective" probabilistic model of proof "provides a means of maintaining consistent belief structures, but has no necessary relationship to advancing accurate outcomes."[94] Allen and Pardo argue that "objective" probabilistic accounts are equally impossible because humans can't have enough knowledge to set the right baselines.[95] A feminist perspective adds to both of these claims. When we use a feminist lens, we see that even potentially measurable probabilistic connections will inevitably be the result of the belief structures that maintain that two propositions are connected. For this reason, probabilistic conceptions of proof, if actualized, might maintain belief structures *and* advance accurate outcomes. Thus, we might find through "objective" measurement that in a system in which women with a reputation for unchastity are disbelieved, those women are more likely to lie. Belief systems can be self-reinforcing, creating the probabilistic connections they espouse. Put another way, the problem is not the risk of error but baseline assumptions that reinforce certain realities at the expense of others. There is no "view from nowhere," and to suggest that probabilistic reasoning will, or could ever, achieve it is one way to ignore the contingency of knowledge. In Allen and Pardo's parlance, the necessity of setting the "reference class" for probabilistic assessment—is it other women in this society or a society that does not hold that credibility and chastity that are intertwined?—unravels the notion of objective probability as a basis for legal judgment.

The two trials of entertainer Bill Cosby, held less than one year apart in front of the same judge, serve as a final illustration of the problem of baselines and the socially contingent nature of relevance.

Andrea Constand, an administrator at Temple University, first accused Cosby of drugging and sexually assaulting her in 2004, but the state declined to prosecute.[96] Thirteen years later, the state decided there was probable cause to proceed with a criminal trial after more than sixty women came forward to make public stories of assault that were markedly similar to Constand's.[97] At Cosby's first trial, the state sought to introduce testimony from other accusers. Because Pennsylvania does not admit evidence of prior acts of sexual misconduct under a propensity theory, the state argued that the evidence was relevant under a modus operandi theory. Under this theory, Cosby's pattern of conduct was unique enough to be identifying—he used his fame to gain the trust of his victims, then drugged and assaulted them.

---

[92] Ironically, this assumes people respond "rationally" to incentives.

[93] Of course, we could also tell a different story, which is that trying to maintain a reputation for chastity above all else creates pressure for all women to lie. Mary Wollstonecraft made this argument in A Vindication of the Rights of Woman. Wollstonecraft 1988, 131–3.

[94] Allen and Pardo 2019, 10.

[95] Ibid., 12, n. 44.

[96] Banner 2019, 39.

[97] Ibid.

As sociologist Banner describes it, Cosby's lawyers "countered that this was not a calling card but a cliché."[98] The defense argued that even if Cosby demonstrated this pattern of behavior repeatedly, its significance was to show that "women and men have been willing to offer up their bodies on a casting couch" and then make accusations for monetary gain.[99] If the number of accusers were more indicative of Cosby's status as a powerful target than of his being a man who serially drugged and assaulted women, the argument that it showed Cosby's modus operandi should fail. The relevance of the other accusers' accounts would simply be to support the vision of Cosby as a powerful man. The trial judge excluded testimony from Cosby's other accusers, and the first trial resulted in a hung jury.

Cosby's second trial took place before the same judge less than a year later, in 2018. By 2018, however, the #MeToo social media movement had brought attention and credence to accounts of powerful men using their positions to coerce or force sex on women or sometimes on men. "The casting couch was starting to look like a strikingly different place," a "hunting ground" rather than a site where women might be imagined as "offering their bodies in a business transaction."[100] Although the defense continued to argue that Constand and the other accusers were "gold diggers" with no real grievances, the trial court allowed five other accusers to testify. Cosby was convicted.

The state in this second trial reframed its relevance theory, arguing that testimony from Cosby's other accusers should be admitted not as proof of modus operandi but on a doctrine of chances theory. This doctrine expresses a probabilistic judgment that it is unlikely that there would be many false complaints alleging very similar conduct against the accused if he is innocent of the charged act. Under this theory, evidence of other uncharged misconduct is admissible as evidence of the probability of the defendant's guilt of the current charge.[101] While the modus operandi theory was that Cosby's behavior with the other accusers was sufficiently distinctive to be probative of his conduct in the Constand case, the doctrine of chances theory held that Cosby's pattern of behavior could not plausibly be understood as a coincidence. It is possible that the judge found the latter probabilistic rationale more persuasive, but it seems more likely that a change in the judge's preliminary assessment of Cosby's accusers made the difference. As a preliminary matter, both theories of relevance required the judge to credit Cosby's other accusers and see his behavior as assaultive rather than ordinary. If the judge had continued to see the claims of the other accusers as a commonplace outgrowth of Cosby's celebrity rather than as representing predatory conduct on his part, a doctrine of chances argument about his behavior towards Constand would have failed. That starting generalization from the accusers' claims, that Cosby was powerful and the target of mercenary women, would not support any theory—including a probabilistic lack of coincidence—suggesting that his prior conduct was relevant to guilt.

The key change between the two trials happened not in the statute books or the evidentiary theory but in the culture. That cultural shift surely reached the consciousness of the judge tasked with understanding the relevance of information offered by the other accusers. In order to accept the doctrine of chances argument, the judge must have been able to understand Cosby's behavior towards women as abusive rather than ordinary and his accusers

---

[98] Ibid.
[99] Ibid., 40.
[100] Ibid., 41.
[101] Evidence scholars have debated whether doctrine of chances evidence is propensity evidence, and if so, what kind. See, e.g., Imwinkelried 2017, 867.

as victimized rather than mercenary. Although we cannot see into the trial judge's mind, his exclusion of the same evidence at the first trial suggests, at a minimum, that he had less clarity about the relevance of the stories being told by so many other accusers. Absent the change in social understanding brought about by the #MeToo movement, a doctrine of chances theory is unlikely to have succeeded.[102]

4. Conclusion

In her recent memoir, author Rebecca Solnit recounts a story about an old boyfriend whose uncle was a nuclear physicist. To amuse the company at a Christmas gathering, the uncle told how a neighbor's wife in his suburban community had run out of her house naked in the middle of the night screaming that her husband was trying to kill her. Solnit asked him how he knew the husband wasn't trying to kill his wife. The uncle explained that they were "respectable middle-class people" so obviously the husband was not actually trying to kill his wife. The real explanation was that the wife herself was "crazy."[103] For Solnit this story exemplifies an epistemic order that "rested on the right and capacity of men to be in charge of meaning and of truth, of which stories mattered and whose got told, as well as of more tangible phenomena"—including law and government—"that maintained the arrangement."[104]

Solnit's anecdote encapsulates many of the themes of this chapter. The human struggle over which "social realities are better" or more real than others plays out at the dinner table, and also in rules of procedure and evidence that set the parameters for whose stories will be heard and believed.[105] At the base of this procedural system is the evidentiary concept of relevance. While too often seen as the product of a combination of rational logic and universal baseline assumptions as constrained by the substantive law, relevance is contingent on social understandings in a way that has served systematically to silence voices and narratives that should be heard. At the same time, the relevance inquiry offers the potential for what Bartlett describes as a "positional" feminist approach to legal epistemology. Such an approach acknowledges empirical truths, values, and knowledge, and also their contingency.[106] Assessing relevance from this positional perspective can be a way to "pivot the center" and to incorporate different sources of knowledge into the evidentiary process.

References

Allen, R. J. and Pardo, M. S. (2019). "Relative Plausibility and its Critics," *The International Journal of Evidence and Proof,* 23(1–2): 5–59.

American Constitution Society, "Diversity of the Federal Bench: Current Statistics on the Gender and Racial Diversity of the Article III Courts." Available at https://www.acslaw.org/judicial-nominations/diversity-of-the-federal-bench/ (Accessed: April 8, 2021).

---

[102] The Pennsylvania Supreme Court will review Cosby's conviction in part to assess whether the testimony of the five other accusers was improperly admitted. *Commonwealth v. Cosby,* 326 A.3d 1045 (2020).

[103] Solnit 2020.

[104] Ibid.

[105] Bartlett 1990, 884.

[106] Ibid., 881–2.

Bader Ginsburg, R. (1978). "Sex, Equality and the Constitution," *Tulane Law Review*, 52(3): 451–75.

Banner, F. (2019). *Crowdsourcing the Law: Trying Sexual Assault on Social Media.* Washington, DC: Rowan and Littlefield, 37–74.

Bartlett, K. T. (1990). "Feminist Legal Methods," *Harvard Law Review*, 103: 829–88.

Bartlett, K. T. (2012). "Feminist Legal Scholarship: A History through the Lens of the California Law Review," *California Law Review*, 100: 381–40.

Bender, L. (1988). "A Lawyer's Primer on Feminist Theory and Tort," *Journal of Law and Education*, 38(1–2): 3–46.

Bienen, L. (1983). "A Question of Credibility: John Henry Wigmore's Use of Scientific Authority in Section 924a of the Treatise of Evidence," *California Western Law Review*, 19: 235–68.

Brown, E. B. (1989). "African-American Women's Quilting: A Framework for Conceptualizing and Teaching African-American Women's History," *Signs*, 14: 921–9.

Carbado, D. W. and Harris, C. I. (2019). "Intersectionality at 30: Mapping the Margins of Anti-Essentialism, Intersectionality, and Dominance Theory," *Harvard Law Review*, 132(8): 2193–39.

Cohen, L. J. (1977). *The Probable and the Provable.* Oxford: Clarendon Press.

Collins, E. R. (2015). "The Evidentiary Rules of Engagement in the War against Domestic Violence," *New York University Law Review*, 90: 397–459.

Collins, P. H. (2000). "Black Feminist Epistemology," in P. Hill Collins, *Black Feminist Thought: Knowledge, Consciousness, and the Politics of Empowerment.* New York: Routledge.

Crenshaw, K. (1989). "Demarginalizing the Intersection of Race and Sex: A Black Feminist Critique of Antidiscrimination Doctrine, Feminist Theory and Antiracist Politics," *The University of Chicago Legal Forum*, 1989(1): 139–67. Available at https://chicagounbound.uchicago.edu/uclf/vol1989/iss1/8 (Accessed: April 9, 2021).

Dahlman, C. (2017). "Unacceptable Generalizations in Arguments on Legal Evidence," *Argumentation*, 31: 83–9.

DuBois, E. C., Dunlap, M. C., Gilligan, C. J., MacKinnon, C. A., Marcus, I. et al. (1985). "Feminist Discourse, Moral Values and the Law: A Conversation," *Buffalo Law Review*, 34: 11–87.

Flax, J. (1987). "Post-Modernism and Gender Relations in Feminist Theory," *Signs*, 12(4): 621–43.

Gilligan, C. (1982). *In a Different Voice: Psychological Theory and Women's Development.* Cambridge, MA: Harvard University Press.

Harris, A. P. (1990). "Race and Essentialism in Feminist Legal Theory," *Stanford Law Review*, 42: 581–93.

Herma Hill, K. (1985). "Models of Equality," *University of Illinois Law Review*, 1985: 39–88.

Hlavka, H. R. and Mulla, S. (2019). "That's how she Talks: Animating Text Messaging Evidence in the Sexual Assault Trial," *Law and Society Review*, 52(2): 401–35.

Holtzman, E. (2020). "Balancing Act: Admissibility of Propensity Evidence under Article I, Section 18(c) of the Missouri Constitution," *Missouri Law Review*, 84(4): 1–22.

Hunter, R. (1996). "Gender in Evidence: Masculine Norms and Feminist Reforms," *Harvard Women's Law Journal*, 19(1): 127–67.

Imwinkelried, E. J. (2017). "Criminal Minds: The Need to Refine the Application of the Doctrine of Objective Chances as a Justification for introducing Uncharged Misconduct Evidence to prove Intent," *Hofstra Law Review*, 45: 851–898.

James, G. F. (1940–1941) "Relevancy, Probability and the Law," *California Law Review*, 29: 689–705.

Kinports, K. (1991). "Evidence Engendered," *University of Illinois Law Review*, 1991: 413–56.

Klein, R. (2008). "An Analysis of Thirty-Five Years of Rape Reform: A Frustrating Search for Fundamental Fairness," *Akron Law Review*, 41(4): 981–1057.

Littleton, C. (1987). "Reconstructing Sexual Equality," *California Law Review*, 75: 1279–337.

Mack, K. (1993). "Continuing Barriers to Women's Credibility: A Feminist Perspective on the Proof Process," *Criminal Law Forum*, 4: 327–53.

MacKinnon, C. A. (1979). *Sexual Harassment of Working Women.* New Haven, CT: Yale University Press.

MacKinnon, C. A. (1988). *Feminism Unmodified: Discourses on Life and Law.* Cambridge, MA: Harvard University Press.

MacKinnon, C. A. (1991). *Toward A Feminist Theory of the State*. Cambridge, MA: Harvard University Press.

MacKinnon, C. A. (2003). "Mainstreaming Feminism in Legal Education," *Journal of Law and Education*, 53(2): 199–212.

MacKinnon, C. A. (2016). "Rape Redefined," *Harvard Law & Policy Review*, 10(2): 431–77.

MacKinnon, C. A. (2020). "Equality," *Daedalus*, 49: 213–21.

Minow, M. (1988). "Feminist Reason: Getting It and Losing It," *Journal of Legal Education*, 38(1–2): 47–60.

Minow, M. (1989). "Beyond Universality," *University of Chicago Legal Forum*, 1989(1): 115–38.

Nicolson, D. (2000). "Gender, Epistemology and Ethics: Feminist Perspectives on Evidence Theory," in M. Childs and L. Ellison (eds.), *Feminist Perspectives on Evidence*, 13–38. London: Cavendish.

Orenstein, A. (1990). "Apology Excepted: Incorporating a Feminist Analysis into Evidence Policy where you would Least expect It," *Southwestern University Law Review*, 28: 221–79.

Orenstein, A. (1997). "'My God!': A Feminist Critique of the Excited Utterance Exception to the Hearsay Rule," *California Law Review*, 85(1): 159–223.

Park, R. C. and Saks, M. J. (2006). "Evidence Scholarship Reconsidered: Results of an Interdisciplinary Turn," *Boston College Law Review*, 47(5): 949–1031.

Rich, A. (1979). "Women and Honor: Some Notes on Lying," in A. Rich, *On Lies, Secrets, and Silence: Selected Prose, 1966–1978*. New York: W. W. Norton & Co.

Scheppele, K. L. (1992). "Just the Facts, Ma'am: Sexualized Violence, Evidentiary Habits, and the Revision of Truth," *New York Law School Law Review*, 37: 123–72.

Seidman, E. and Vickers, S. (2005). "The Second Wave: An Agenda for the Next Thirty Years of Rape Law Reform," *Suffolk University Law Review*, 38: 467–92.

Simon-Kerr, J. (2008). "Unchaste and Incredible: The Use of Gendered Conceptions of Honor in Impeachment," *Yale Law Journal*, 117(8): 1854–98.

Simon-Kerr, J. (2017). "Credibility by Proxy," *The George Washington Law Review*, 85: 152–225.

Solnit, R. (2020). *Recollections of my Nonexistence: A Memoir*. London: Viking Books.

Sotomayor, S. (2002). "A Latina Judge's Voice," *Berkeley La Raza Law Journal*, 13(1): 87–93.

Taslitz, A. (1999a). "What Feminism has to offer Evidence Law," *Southwestern University Law Review*, 28: 171–220.

Taslitz, A. E. (1999b). *Rape and the Culture of the Courtroom*. New York: New York University Press.

Thayer, J. B. (1898). *A Preliminary Treatise on Evidence at the Common Law*. New York: Little Brown.

Twining, W. (1990). *Rethinking Evidence: Exploratory Essays*. Evanston, IL: Northwestern University Press.

Williams, W. (1992). "The Equality Crisis: Some Reflections on Culture, Courts, and Feminism," *Women's Rights Law Reporter*, 14(2–3): 154–74.

Wolfson, A. (2005). "Sex Discrimination in the Legal Profession: Historical and Contemporary Perspectives," *Valparaiso University Law Review*, 39(4): 859–909.

Wollstonecraft, M. (1988). *A Vindication of the Rights of Woman*, 131–33. Second edition. Edited by C. H. Poston. New York: WW Norton. Originally published 1792.

25

Race, Evidence, and Epistemic Injustice

Jasmine B. Gonzales Rose

1. Introduction

In other works, I have explored some of the ways that racism—whether it be racial subordination or racial privilege—takes on evidentiary value in litigation and prosecution.[1] Each time I have concluded that racism should not be used as evidence because it offends well-established principles of evidence law and notions of fairness, justice, and decency. In this essay, I go beyond those evidence law and normative analyses and explore what makes racist evidence wrong as a matter of proof and truth. Racist evidence includes: (1) evidence "that suggests one racial group is inferior to or superior to another racial group in any way,"[2] (2) products of structural racism, (3) racially disparate evidentiary burdens in proving one's racialized reality, and (4) the ways that racism distorts observation, perception and—accordingly—belief, which is then utilized as a basis of proof in legal proceedings. The use of multifaceted racist evidence in legal proceedings in the U.S. results in pervasive, but often overlooked, racialized epistemic injustice.

Historically in the United States, there was a dual-racial system of evidence where white people were deemed to be capable and credible witnesses in all court proceedings, but people of color were not. Race-based witness competency laws allowed white people to testify against anyone but restricted the testimony of witnesses of color.[3] In some jurisdictions, there was a blanket bar prohibiting any testimony by witnesses of color.[4] In other jurisdictions, witnesses of color could testify but not against white people.[5] In its most extreme application, this meant that white people could kill people of color with impunity because Black, Latino, Asian, and Native American eye witnesses were not allowed to provide evidence as to the identity of the murderers.[6] When witnesses of color did testify, their competence and credibility was impugned on the basis of their race.[7] Evidence Law no longer

---

[1] See Gonzales Rose 2017, 2243; 2018, 369; forthcoming (a); forthcoming (b); forthcoming (c).
[2] Kendi, 2019, 20. I base my definition of "racist evidence" off of Ibram X. Kendi's definition of "racist idea."
[3] Gonzales Rose 2017, 2247, citing Capers 2010, 1377. See also Finkelman 1986, 415; Johnson 1996, 261.
[4] Avins 1966, 473–4.
[5] Ibid.
[6] See, e.g., *People v. Hall* 1854, 399, overturning a white defendant's conviction for murder of a Chinese miner because the evidence was based on testimony of witnesses of Chinese descent who were deemed unqualified to testify under the California Crimes and Punishment Act of 1850; *Blyew v. United States* 1871, overturning the convictions of two white men who axe-murdered three generations of a family while they slept in their home because the conviction depended on identifications made by two Black witnesses and a Kentucky statute deemed Black witnesses not competent to testify against white people.
[7] See State v. Mah, 10P. 306, 306-07 (Or. 1886) (finding, "experiences convince everyone that the testimony of Chinese witnesses is very unreliable, and that they are apt to be actuated by motives that are not honest"); State v. Ching Ling, 18 P. 844, 847 (Or. 1888); Gabriel J. Chin, "*A Chinaman's Chance" in Court: Asian Pacific Americans and Racial Rule of Evidence*, 3 U.C. Irvine L. Rev. 965, 989 (2013).

Jasmine B. Gonzales Rose, *Race, Evidence, and Epistemic Injustice* In: *Philosophical Foundations of Evidence Law*. Edited by: Christian Dahlman, Alex Stein, and Giovanni Tuzet, Oxford University Press. © Christian Dahlman, Alex Stein, and Giovanni Tuzet 2021. DOI: 10.1093/oso/9780198859307.003.0026

overtly grants or diminishes testimonial competence on the basis of race. However, this continues to occur in subtle colorblind ways.

Modernly, there are many instances where white people are customarily deemed to be capable and credible witnesses and people of color's testimonial competence and credibility are weakened and doubted. Ironically, this may happen in instances where non-white witnesses likely have superior knowledge about systemic racism, but inferior knowledge by white witnesses is given preferential evidentiary treatment. At times, this might oblige parties of color to augment their evidence with expert witness testimony, which is costly.[8]

Four examples of recurrent evidence scenarios demonstrate the use of racist evidence: 1) impeachment of witnesses by prior convictions, 2) cross-racial identification of suspects, 3) determining whether a victim was threatening such that deadly police force was warranted, and 4) flight from law enforcement. Each is discussed in turn.

2. Impeachment by Prior Conviction

Arguably the most controversial of all evidence rules in the United States is Federal Rule of Evidence (FRE) 609 and its state equivalents which provide, in a broad array of circumstances, that once a witness (including a criminal defendant) takes the stand to testify, their credibility for truthfulness can be impeached with their former convictions.[9] The probative value of a person's former convictions in an unrelated case to demonstrate their general character for truthful testimony is tenuous at best.[10] It also has a chilling effect on testimonial speech, particularly for criminal defendants. Juries tend to rely on former convictions as proof of a defendant's guilt rather than to assess their credibility as a witness, despite jury instructions to the contrary.[11] This forces criminal defendants who have a conviction record to choose not to testify in their own defense..[12] The failure to testify in one's own defense has grave consequences as juries are more likely to render verdicts of guilt when a defendant does not testify.[13] Criminal defendants are caught in a testimonial catch-22.

This raises racial justice concerns because people of color are more likely to have criminal convictions, not because of increased criminality but because of structural racism.[14] In comparison to white people, people of color are more likely to live, work, and otherwise

---

[8] Expert Institute 2018, 17, reporting the 2018 average hourly fee for expert testimony to be $461.53.

[9] FRE 609.

[10] Letwin 1984, 704.

[11] Eisenberg and Hans 2009, 1371, 1373, 1381–3, citing Hannaford-Agor et al. 2002, 29–40, conducting analysis of hung jury data from courts in Los Angeles, Maricopa County, the Bronx, and the District of Columbia and finding a 60% conviction rate in cases where jurors knew of a prior record in contrast to the 20% conviction rate where jurors did not know of the prior record, despite the evidence in all the cases being relatively weak.

[12] Ibid.

[13] Bellin 2018, 409, 414, study revealing the "silence penalty" where 76% of defendants who did not testify were convicted while only 62% of similarly situated testifying defendants were convicted.

[14] Bishop 2020, 1–2, suggesting that racialization, rather than criminality, account for 70% of the racial disparity in sentence length which likely pervades across the entire criminal justice process including adjudication and disposition; see also Tonry 2010, 281 ("Americans, especially white Americans, are predisposed to associate blackness with crime and dangerousness and are prepared to treat black offenders especially harshly as a result"); Gross et al. 2017 ("There is no one explanation for the heavy concentration of black defendants among those convicted of crimes they did not commit. The causes we have identified run from inevitable consequences of patterns in crime and punishment to deliberate acts of racism, with many stops in between. They differ sharply from one type of crime to another.")

exist in areas subject to over-policing.[15] They are more likely to be racially profiled by law enforcement,[16] stopped and frisked,[17] arrested,[18] have charges instituted against them,[19] be indicted by a grand jury, enter a plea for more serious offenses,[20] and be found guilty by a jury.[21] Due to structural racism at every stage of policing and prosecution, people of color are more likely to have convictions for the same conduct and behavior as white people who do not have convictions. Being a Black or Brown person is itself a heightened-risk factor for having a conviction. For example, while people with felony convictions only account for 8% of the population,[22] one-third of Black men have felony convictions[23] even though Black men are not more criminally inclined than men of other races.[24]

A record of criminal convictions has become a racialized trait in the United States.[25] "[T]he development of the population with felony convictions since 1980 has been one of widespread, racialized growth."[26] A collateral evidentiary consequence of this is that one

[15] Desilver et al. 2020; see also Smith 1986, 324, 336, finding police are more likely to use coercion and initiate suspicious persons stops in minority or racially mixed neighborhoods than predominantly white neighborhoods which consist of less than 10% nonwhite residents.

[16] American Civil Liberties Union Foundation of Massachusetts 2014, 6–9, finding that being Black increases the chance of police-civilian encounters, that police target Black people for multiple encounters including frisk and search; see also Desilver et al. 2020, n. 14.

[17] Bureau of Justice and Statistics 2018, 4, 12, Table 12, demonstrating the increased likelihood of Black and Hispanic persons to experience stops and searches or arrests than white persons; see also Jones 2018, explaining that Bureau of Justice Statistics released a report which showed that "Black residents were more likely to be stopped by police than white or Hispanic residents, both in traffic stops and street stops;" Ramirez 2000, iii, 6–7 ("[Dr. John] Lamberth compared the population of people searched and arrested with those violating traffic laws on Maryland highways. He constructed a violator sample using both stationary and rolling surveys of drivers violating the legal speed limit on a selected portion of the interstate. His violator survey indicated that 74.7% of speeders were [w]hite, while 17.5% were Black. In contrast, according to MSP data, Black people constituted 79.2% of the drivers searched. Lamberth concluded that the data revealed dramatic and highly statistically significant disparities between the percentage of Black I–95 motorists legitimately subject to stop by the Maryland State Police and the percentage of Black motorists detained and searched by troopers on this roadway.")

[18] Uniform Crime Reporting Program 2018, Table 43, reporting of all persons arrested in 2018, 69% were white and 27.4% were Black. But see United States Census Bureau 2019, Table 2a, indicating that in 2018 the US population was 60% white and 12.5% Black or African American. See also Srikanth 2020 ("In 800 jurisdictions across the United States, black people were arrested at a rate five times higher than white people over a three-year period ending in 2018, according to an ABC analysis of data voluntarily reported to the FBI. In 250 jurisdictions, black people were 10 times more likely to be arrested than their white counterparts.")

[19] Starr and Rehavi 2013, 28–9, reporting significant racial disparities in the severity of charges, including, for example, that Black men are twice as likely as white men to receive a charge carrying a mandatory minimum; The Sentencing Project 2018.

[20] Berdejó 2018, 1215–16, examining the 74.72% greater likelihood that white defendants get all misdemeanor charges carrying potential imprisonment dropped, dismissed, or amended than Black defendants. See also Demby 2014, study found that "Black defendants were 19% more likely than whites to be offered plea deals that included jail or prison time." Also, "Blacks and Latinos were both significantly more likely to be offered plea deals that included time behind bars for misdemeanor drug offenses. For misdemeanor marijuana cases in particular, blacks were 19% more likely to be offered a plea deal that required time behind bars."

[21] Johnson 1985, 1620–1 ("Nine very recent experiments find that the race of the defendant significantly and directly affects the determination of guilt. White subjects in all of these studies were more likely to find a minority-race defendant guilty than they were to find an identically situated white defendant guilty."); Sommers and Ellsworth 2000, 1367 ("White mock jurors rated the Black defendants more guilty, aggressive, and violent than the [w]hite defendant."); Anwar 2012, 1017, finding 81% of Black defendants are likely to be convicted versus 66% of white defendants.

[22] Shannon et al. 2017.

[23] Ibid.

[24] The disproportionately high criminal convictions and sentencing of Black people is due to structural racism rather than increased criminality. See Rehavi and Starr 2014. See, e.g., Substance Abuse and Mental Health Services Administration 2016, 233, Table 1.28b, showing the minimal 6% greater illicit drug usage of whites compared to Black persons; Carson and Sabol 2012, 27, Appendix, Table 8, evincing the racial disparity in prisoners sentenced for drug related crimes where Black persons account for 46% of the incarcerated population and white persons account for 28%.

[25] Shannon et al. 2017.

[26] Ibid.

out of three Black men could have diminished testimonial capacity in courts at some time. In other words, due to structural racism, one third of Black men might have a limited ability to testify and be believed—due to prior conviction impeachment rules—at a point during their life. Although, Black men (and other people of color) are not directly prohibited from testifying in court, as was the case under eighteenth and nineteenth century race-based witness competency rules, for a large segment of the Black male population the effect is comparable. Acting in concert with the criminal justice system, FRE 609 and its state counterparts disproportionately diminish people of color's capacity to testify and their credibility to be believed when they do testify.

3. Cross-Racial Eyewitness Identification

Another scenario vulnerable to racialized epistemic injustice is eyewitness identification of suspects of color, particularly in cases of cross-racial (mis)identifications. Unlike former conviction impeachment, which serves to systematically diminish people of color's testimonial ability, this evidence law phenomena bestows unjustified epistemic privilege on white witnesses often to the detriment of suspects of color. It also reveals how antiracist perspectives sometimes need to be proven by expert witness testimony while perspectives informed by and based on structural racism do not.

Eyewitness testimony is incredibly influential. Jurors tend to be persuaded by eyewitness testimony over other evidence, even in the face of reasonable doubt.[27] They are more likely to believe white people's eyewitness testimony because white witnesses are considered more credible and convincing than witnesses of color.[28] This is because, as discussed below, white people are given a credibility excess. While eyewitness testimony is often unreliable, cross-racial identifications are particularly unreliable due to cross-race (also called "other-race") bias.[29] Cross-race bias occurs where people are unable to accurately identify people from racial groups that differ from their own.[30] Of all the racial groups, white people are least

[27] McKee 1996, 1, §8; Vidmar and Hans 2007, 194; Loftus 1974, 116–19, studying three scenarios with varying degrees of eyewitness testimony and revealing 18% of mock jurors vote guilty without eyewitness testimony, 72% voted guilty in a scenario with one eyewitness, and 68% voted guilty even when the eyewitness credibility was questionable.

[28] Frumkin and Stone 2020, 123 ("The current study measured accent status, race and age with 254 participants listening to oral witness statements. Results indicate eyewitnesses with higher-status accents were rated more favorably than those with lower-status accents .... White eyewitnesses were more favorably rated than black witnesses ...."). See, e.g., Johnson 1996, 277–8, 285–6, 290, 298, examining three different court cases where Black witness credibility was either blatantly rejected or disproportionately questioned over white witnesses whose credibility was lacking.

[29] Flevaris and Chapman 2015, 866–7, citing Malpass et al. 2009, 3–4, noting in many cases of misidentification the accused and actually guilty criminal did not bare any resemblance; Lindsay and Wells 1980, 306–7, 308–9, 311, extracting data from a study where participants were eyewitnesses to a stolen calculator "robbery" and later had to identify the suspect, which revealed cross-racial misidentification based on the 70% chance that participants erroneously choose an innocent individual from a line-up featuring people of different races from the suspect and where the suspect was not present, versus the 31% chance of choosing an innocent individual in lineups without the suspect but featuring people all of the same race.

[30] Chance et al. 1975, 249, 250–1, expanding on two studies that showed a population group various pictures of Black, white, and Asian faces to determine the rate at which a participant of one race could identify a photo of a different race). See Cutler and Penrod 1995, 104 ("Own-race recognitions are more accurate than other-race identifications. Lindsay and Wells (1983) reviewed 11 separate experiments that all show an interaction between race of witness and race of target (although the patterns of main effects differ). Shapiro and Penrod (1986) included own- versus other-race in their meta-analysis and found that, indeed, own-race recognitions were correctly identified more often ($d = .53$; 63% v. 57%) and falsely identified less often ($d = .44$; 18% v. 22%). Bothwell, Brigham,

likely to accurately identify people who are of a different race than themselves.[31] In short, white witnesses are statistically less able to accurately identify a Black or Brown suspect.[32] However, due to white privilege, white witnesses' identifications of suspects are more likely to be believed by jurors than witnesses of color even though white witnesses are statistically less reliable.[33] To prove the truth of this diminished reliability, the criminal defense would have to obtain an expert witness to testify on cross-race bias,[34] which is often cost prohibitive.[35]

4. Police Violence

A third example is determinations of whether a Black or Brown victim's actions warranted deadly force by law enforcement. On-duty police officers brutalize and kill community members at alarming rates in the United States. In the first nine months of 2020 alone police have killed over 861 people and typically kill about 1,000 people a year.[36] Disproportionately, the victims of police violence are people of color. In 2020, Black people make up 28% of the people killed by police even though they are only 13% of the entire population.[37] Typically, of 42 million Black people and 39 million Latinx people, police kill 32 people per million of the Black population and 24 people per million of the Latinx population.[38] Out of 100,000 men of the same race, roughly forty white men can expect to be killed by police, versus the one hundred Black men that can expect the same fate.[39]

Racialized police killings are frequent, but legal accountability for the killings is uncommon. Prosecutors are reluctant to prosecute law enforcement officers.[40] Grand jurors

---

and Malpass (1989) meta-analyzed 14 separate tests of the own-race recognition bias ($d = .71$ for black subjects and $d = .69$ for white subjects). Thus, the cross-race recognition effect is substantial and comparable in magnitude across races."); Wells and Olson 2001, 230; Wong et al. 2020, 212–13, finding facial recognition was better with own-race faces in a study which showed participants thirty-two various-race faces and later asked participants to identify which faces they had previously seen.

[31] Cutler and Penrod 1995; Wells 2001; Wong 2020, 6, Figure 2, displaying the lower facial recognition by white participants of the remaining three other-race faces than other participants and their corresponding other-race faces; Johnson 1983, 949 ("[T]he own race effect is strongest and most consistent where white subjects attempt to identify black faces.")

[32] See Johnson 1983, 949 ("[T]he risk of misidentification is greatest where the victim is white and the defendant is black."). See also Chance 1975, 251, Table 1, indicating, although cross-racial misidentification occurred in both white and Black participant groups, white participants were more likely to not recognize a face from the Black group.

[33] The increased credibility blindly awarded to whites generally makes it more likely that their inaccurate identifications will be believed. See Johnson 1996, 277–8, 285–6, 290, 298; Wong et al. 2020, 6, Figure 2.

[34] See Connelly 2015, 145, suggesting jurors are more likely to weigh identifications correctly when presented with cross-racial bias information by an expert. See also Rutledge 2001, 220, 227, quoting Devenport 1997, 338, reviewing common critiques of expert testimony on cross-race bias and suggesting it can actually mitigate negative effects from misidentification and improve juror decision-making.

[35] Gonzales Rose 2017, 2288. See also Nellis et al. 2008, 6–7, criticizing the recurring lack of financial resources that indigent defendants, made up predominantly of minorities, possess to hire expert witnesses.

[36] "Mapping police violence;" "990 people have been shot and killed by police in the past year" 2020.

[37] "Mapping police violence."

[38] "990 people have been shot and killed by police in the past year."

[39] Edwards et al. 2019, 16794, analyzing data which suggesting that compared to white men, Black men, Latino men, and Native American men are 2.5, 1.4, and 1.7 times, respectively, more likely to be killed by police.

[40] Gonzales Rose 2018, 377. See also Thompson-DeVaux et al. 2020, citing "Henry Wallace police crime database," analyzing the Stinson data which showed only 110 officers were charged with murder or manslaughter for an on-duty shooting. See also "990 people have been shot and killed by police in the past year."

are disinclined to indict officers.[41] Petit juries are not likely to render guilty verdicts against officers.[42] In the rare instance that there is a conviction, judges rarely sentence law enforcement officers as stringently as if the offender was a civilian.[43]

The civil justice system mirrors this lack of accountability. In civil rights cases seeking redress for police violence, officers often seek to be shielded by qualified immunity which "insulates them from defending the claim for damages."[44] Qualified immunity is supposed to be granted only "where the right asserted by the plaintiff was not 'clearly established' at the time of the challenged conduct."[45] However, too often deadly force against community members of color is considered reasonable.[46] The issue of qualified immunity most frequently arises on summary judgment.

Summary judgment is appropriate when the movant shows that there "is no genuine dispute as to any material fact and the movant is entitled to judgment as a matter of law."[47] In ruling on a motion for summary judgment, a judge must view the facts in the light most favorable to the non-moving party,[48] here the victim's survivors. The advent of police dash and body cameras might be assumed to be a boon for civil rights cases seeking redress for police killings. However, video evidence generated from these cameras may actually serve as a basis for denying these claims before they reach a jury or settlement.[49]

Judges' reliance on video evidence to dispose of a case on summary judgment implicates racialized epistemic injustice because victims of police violence are disproportionately people of color[50] while judges are disproportionately white.[51] In viewing instances of police force against people of color, white people are more likely than people of color to find the use of force was warranted.[52] The case of *Harrison v.*

---

[41] Gonzales Rose 2018, 377–8. See also Burlew 2014, indicating that in the preceding fourteen years, of the twenty-four officers examined for police shootings, zero were indicted. See also Pinkerton 2013, revealing that between 2008 and 2012 grand juries reviewed eighty-one police-involved shootings and indicted only one officer.

[42] Grinberg 2018; Thompson-DeVaux et al. 2020, highlighting that out of 110 officers charged with murder or manslaughter for an on duty shooting only forty-two were convicted.

[43] Chan 2019 ("Of the 104 state and local law enforcement officers who have been arrested for murder or manslaughter for fatal on-duty shootings since 2005, 36 have been convicted of a crime, according to criminologist Philip Stinson, who was a police officer in New Hampshire in the 1980s. By comparison, of the 217 people charged with murder and manslaughter in the nation's 75 largest counties in May 2009 alone, 70% were convicted of murder or other felonies, according to the most recent data from the Bureau of Justice Statistics. Even when officers are convicted, they're often found guilty of lesser offenses and receive more lenient sentences than civilians convicted of the same crimes, according to researchers"); Luongo and Conti-Cook 2017, telling the personal accounts of two criminal defense attorneys who have noticed disparities in officer versus civilian discipline such as paid leave versus a quick arrest.

[44] Levinson and Bodensteiner 2019, 339.

[45] Ibid.

[46] Reinhart 2018, 2087, conducting an analysis of 211 civil cases between 2015–2015 and finding that 78% of all cases where qualified immunity was used resulted in verdicts for the defendants. See also Chung 2020, analyzing data which showed between 2017 and 2019 about 57% of civil cases involving excessive force favored police through qualified immunity.

[47] Federal Rule of Civil Procedure 56(a).

[48] *Reeves v. Sanderson Plumbing Prods.* 2000, 149–50.

[49] See Schwartz 2009, 863, stressing the increased number of summary judgments in favor of officers when videotape evidence is present.

[50] Frye 2019, 1214, examining different datasets and finding Black persons are 21.3% more likely to experience use of force, even when the officer reports them to be compliant, than white people; Obasogie 2020, finding that police are "3.5 times more likely" to kill Black men than white men and "1 in every 1,000 black men will die at the hands of police;" McCarthy 2020.

[51] State trial and appellate judges are 83% and 80% white, respectively. George and Yoon 2020, 1, 7. Additionally, "[o]f the 1,352 [] federal judges, 60 percent are white men, while only 11 percent are Black and 7 percent are Latino." Jawando and Anderson 2016. White men make up only about 37.5% of the U.S. population, which is 76.3% white, 18.5% Latinx, and 13.4% Black ("Quick facts: United States").

[52] See Kahan et al. 2009.

Dallas[53] is a prime example of this. Two white police officers shot and killed a Black man within six seconds of their arrival to help transport him to a hospital because he was twiddling a screwdriver and did not immediately drop "it" when they suddenly drew their guns and yelled at him.[54] The white defendant officers claimed that *after* they pointed their firearms and yelled at the victim, the victim lunged at them with the screwdriver.[55] The victim's Black mother who observed the interaction claims that he did not.[56] In the absence of a video, an issue of material fact would remain, warranting a trial by jury and fostering the circumstances that could lead to a settlement. However, there was a video.[57]

The video is by no means conclusive. It only captures part of the victim's body and actions during the event. It is just as, if not more, likely that the victim tried to escape the police who were screaming with guns drawn at him than he lunged to attack them with a small household tool. However, the white trial judge found the video spoke for itself and granted summary judgment for the white defendant officers. It is likely that a diverse jury, one that was representative of the community, would have come out differently.[58] However, ultimately the white judge's perspective on the video was the only one that would count.

5. Flight from Law Enforcement

This brings us to the final example: Black and Brown flight. Generally, people's perspectives on the police vary based on race.[59] White people tend to have greater trust in and warm feelings for the police in comparison to other racial groups, particularly Black people.[60] Under white racialized reality, police officers are protectors of the public and only guilty people would run from them. Racialized reality evidence is de facto "evidence of the lived experience of a person that is directly shaped by the racially stratified system in which [they] live. Racialized reality is how one experiences our nation's current racial caste system as a benefit or detriment."[61] People of color are more likely to distrust and fear the police.[62] They may flee law enforcement to avoid racial profiling, police brutality, and even death.[63] The lived-reality of generations of Black Americans since the original police force—the slave patrols—serve as racialized reality evidence that law enforcement should be avoided at all costs. Unlike white people who do not have knowledge about the relationship between

---

[53] Harrison *v. City of Dallas* 2014.

[54] Ibid.

[55] *Defendants Andrew Hutchins and John Rogers Joint Motion for Summary Judgment on Qualified Immunity as to the Claims by Plaintiff David Harrison* 2015, No. 3:14-CV-3585-N, 8.

[56] *Plaintiffs Shirley Marshall Harrison and David Sean Harrison's Amended Complaint* 2015, No. 3:14-CV-3585-N, 4.

[57] Gunscom 2015.

[58] See Mezey 2013, 3–4, suggesting that videotape evidence displaces the jury because judges erroneously believe there is only one interpretation of video evidence even when parties dispute it; see also Kahan et al. 2012, 889, concluding a judge's perception of fact can prevent them from understanding what a "reasonable" but culturally different person experiences.

[59] Morin and Stepler 2016, finding that only 14% of Black participants have a lot of confidence in police, whereas 42% of white people and 31% of Hispanic people have a lot of confidence in police.

[60] Fingerhut 2017, showing that 74% of White Americans view law enforcement "warmly," as compared to just 55% of Hispanic Americans and 30% of Black Americans.

[61] Gonzales Rose 2017, 2282.

[62] Morin and Stepler 2016, finding that 35% of Blacks and 58% of Hispanics say the police department in their community does an excellent or good job, compared to 75% of whites.

[63] See *Commonwealth v. Warren* 2016, 342.

people of color and police, many Black people have vast evidence-based knowledge of how police officers treat Black people.[64]

However, the white norm that only the guilty flee is given precedence. In critical evidence terms, it is given implicit judicial notice—it is argued to the jury without any evidentiary support—while the Black experience is subject to the full rigors of evidentiary analysis. White experience with and beliefs about the police and policing is accepted as the established norm and indisputable reality without any need to call a witness or otherwise introduce evidence.[65] On the other hand, if a party wants the jury to consider the dominant perspective of people of color on police and policing, they would have to call a witness. People of color themselves should be able to testify freely about their racialized reality as lay witnesses. However, too often Black and Brown witnesses are subjected to "testimonial quieting."[66] "The problem of testimonial quieting occurs when an audience fails to identify a speaker as a knower."[67] Lay opinion testimony would likely not be deemed sufficient to prove the non-criminal motivations behind Black and Brown flight from law enforcement because it deviates from the white perspective that police are community protectors. Proof of the non-criminal motivations between Black and Brown flight would likely require expert testimony evidence to be persuasive. Expert testimony is often cost prohibitive, especially for a criminal defendant.[68] Moreover, expert witnesses are disproportionately white due to the underrepresentation of people of color in higher education.[69] In such occurrences, Black and Brown evidence is deemed insufficient on its own and must be offered through educationally elite and often white voices, at significant financial expense. This example demonstrates an imbalance in evidentiary burdens placed on people of color versus white people.

6. The Epistemic Injustice of Racist Evidence

At its core, evidence concerns what a factfinder is justified in believing and what is reasonable to believe. Under the concept of evidentialism, beliefs should be established by evidence.[70] However, when racist evidence is employed in a case, knowledge and justified belief become distorted and deteriorate. A prevalent example is how white jurists may unconsciously view Black and Brown people as criminally inclined and dangerous.[71] White

[64] See generally Braman 2005, 29–30, studying the cultural status anxieties based on worldviews of people of color when analyzing risk which are not apparent for whites with the "white male effect."

[65] See Morin and Stepler 2016, finding that whites tend to have much more confidence and trust in the police; Braman 2005, 2–3, emphasizing white male's insensitivity to societal dangers, unlike the experience of people of color, may be reflective of the hierarchical reality that American society faces.

[66] Dotson 2011, 237.

[67] Ibid., 242.

[68] Gonzales Rose 2017, 2288. See Sentencing Project 2008, 6–7, highlighting the great importance of financial resources in navigating the criminal justice system where indigent clients, who are predominantly minorities, often lack the public funding necessary to hire expert witnesses.

[69] Gonzales Rose 2017, 2288, n. 240; Libassi 2018, ("[C]ompared with white students, [B]lack and Hispanic graduates are far more likely to have attended for-profit colleges and less likely to have attended four-year public or nonprofit institutions.")

[70] Way 2016, 805.

[71] According to results from the National Race and Crime Survey, whites are more inclined to believe Black people deserve harsher punishment because whites are influenced by racial stereotypes. The survey asked participants to explain why African Americans tended to receive harsher punishment from the criminal justice system. Conversely, Black participants attributed this to an unfair and bias system. Peffley 2010, 111.

people do not actually have a reasonable epistemic justification that Black and Brown people are criminally inclined or dangerous. This is a conclusion based upon racist rather than justified beliefs. Or more seemingly benign, white people may believe that police are protectors of all populations, including Black and Brown communities.[72] As discussed above, this may be treated in court as unequivocal and commonsensical even though it is not. In the reverse, many Black and Brown people have a reasonable epistemic justification that police are dangerous toward people in their communities.[73] This perception is often based upon justified and reasonable sources of belief. However, this knowledge is given less epistemic respect.

The four examples discussed here illustrate one of the main types of epistemic injustice: testimonial injustice. "Testimonial injustice occurs when prejudice causes a hearer to give a deflated level of credibility to a speaker's word."[74] Testimonial injustice happens when a witness giving testimony is disbelieved due to a conviction that is the result of a racist system of policing and criminal justice; when the prevalent lived-reality of Black and Brown flight from police as a matter of dignity and survival is not known or accepted into evidence; and when a Black or Brown witness's testimony is discounted on the basis of their race. Another type of racialized testimonial injustice arises on the flipside when there is unjust regard bestowed on particular knowers. The converse of witnesses of color's knowing being diminished is white witness's knowing being aggrandized. Here, this was demonstrated by the fact that white people systemically escape prior conviction impeachment at greater rates than people of color, statistically white cross-racial identifications are generally found to be persuasive although highly unreliable, white racialized reality concerning flight from law enforcement is considered commonsense, and where white judges unilaterally determine whether deadly force was warranted against a victim of color, even when reasonable, diverse minds could differ.

Testimonial injustice can manifest into two prejudiced results: "the speaker receiving more credibility than she otherwise would have" (credibility excess) or "in her receiving less credibility than she otherwise would have" (credibility deficit).[75] "Testimonial injustice is . . . in its central case, a matter of credibility deficit, arising from prejudice about someone's social identity."[76] This is also the case where white witnesses are simply considered more credible due to implicit beliefs about white supremacy.[77] In the critical evidence context, this is an example of racial character evidence. "Racial character evidence refers to the way

---

[72] See Morin et al. 2017, 74–5, 88, conducting a survey of 4,538 US adults uncovering that 57% of whites, but only 12% of Black participants, believed the country has taken adequate steps to achieve racial equality between Black people and whites, and 54% of whites versus 79% of Black participants believe deadly Black-police encounters are signs of broader racial issues between Black people and police.

[73] See Bureau of Justice and Statistics 2018, 1, finding Black residents were twice as likely to experience a threat or use of physical force than whites.

[74] Fricker 2007, 1.

[75] Ibid., 18. While Fricker has underestimated the prejudicial impact of credibility excess, other scholars have confirmed it. See Davis 2016; José Medina, *The Relevance of Credibility Excess in a Proportional View of Epistemic Injustice: Differential Epistemic Authority and Social Imaginary*, 25 Soc. Epistemology 15 (2011).

[76] Langton 2010, 459.

[77] See Sue 2006, 16–18, highlighting the history of white supremacy that led to a current system of implicit white privilege which confers unearned benefits on whites while subjecting non-white people to being characterized as inferior. See, e.g., Johnson 1996, 305–6, 330, citing *Withers v. United States* 1979, 125, referencing over ten different cases where white witnesses were argued to be more credible and non-white witnesses were characterized as prone to lying, including one case where an attorney attempted to strengthen their case by emphasizing that "[n]ot one White witness" contradicted their evidence.

a person's race is used as de facto proof of his or her character. More specifically, it describes how race—in tandem with racial stereotypes and biases—is relied upon or emphasized to establish the person's character propensity to be peaceful, violent, truthful, deceptive, or a variety of other traits."[78] A person's race is never a reasonable basis to determine a witnesses' testimonial candor, integrity, or knowing. Yet, the use of racial character evidence goes unrecognized and unmitigated.[79]

Another main type of epistemic injustice is hermeneutical injustice. Hermeneutical injustice occurs when "someone has a significant area of their social experience obscured from understanding owing to prejudicial flaws in shared resources for social interpretation."[80] This occurs in the failure of courts to recognize Black and Brown flight. Here, due to systemic and systematic devaluing of Black and Brown knowing and normalizing of white knowing there is a divide in "collective interpretative resources"[81] which puts people of color at an unfair disadvantage when it comes to white judges and factfinders understanding their lived-reality and experience with police. While testimonial and hermeneutical injustice are separate, they can easily intertwine and make up significant epistemic injustice.

Testimonial and hermeneutical injustice bring different types of harm. The ultimate harm of testimonial injustice is: "[w]hen you are not taken seriously in your capacity as a knower, you are not taken seriously in a fundamental human capacity. You are damaged in your standing as a knower, and as a human being."[82] Additionally, "[n]ot being believed can prevent you from being a participant in the trustful conversation that 'steadies the mind': it can undermine your confidence in your own beliefs, thus your knowledge."[83] In comparison, hermeneutical injustice involves everyone: "all parties are epistemologically damaged," but as Langton notes, not evenly.[84] "The shared ignorance of all manifests the hermeneutical marginalization, not of all, but of only some."[85] Therefore, while everyone is technically damaged, hermeneutical injustice hurts some more than others. In the context of the legal system, particularly in criminal and civil rights cases, the harms of testimonial and hermeneutical injustice are far more than dignitary: life, liberty, and recovery for the loss of life and liberty are literally at stake.

7. Conclusion

The use of racist evidence poses epistemic—as well as ethical and justice—problems. While it is true that the use of racist beliefs as evidence is contrary to evidence law principles and morally repugnant, it is also valuable to examine the epistemic justice implications. This examination reveals how racism causes rightful knowers to be silenced and disbelieved, and those who have less knowledge to be given more credibility and credence in their belief than they are legitimately entitled to. It reveals another way that white privilege operates in the

---

[78] Gonzales Rose 2018, 371.
[79] See Thompson 2015, 322, stressing the trending use of racial character evidence and "stereotypical Blackness" as a replacement for the inadmissible evidence of a Black defendant's character for violence.
[80] Fricker 2007.
[81] Ibid.
[82] Langton 2010, 460.
[83] Ibid.
[84] Ibid., 461.
[85] Ibid.

law to the detriment of people of color. This examination exposes the fact that in some ways, there is still a dual-racial system of evidence in the United States. Evidence law is supposed to ensure fairness and be applied "to the end of ascertaining the truth and securing a just determination,"[86] but too often evidence rules, doctrines, practices, and policy rationales are employed or even more frequently overlooked to quiet, if not silence, the testimony, knowledge, and perspectives of people of color in the courtroom.

References

"990 People have been Shot and Killed by Police in the Past Year," *Washington Post*, December 1, 2020. Available at https://www.washingtonpost.com/graphics/investigations/police-shootings-database/ (Accessed: April 5, 2021).

American Civil Liberties Union Foundation of Massachusetts (2014). *Black, Brown and Targeted: A Report on Boston Police Department Street Encounters from 2007–2010*. Boston, MA: American Civil Liberties Union Foundation of Massachusetts.

Anwar, S., Bayer, P., and Hjalmarsson, R. (2012). "The Impact of Jury Race on Criminal Trials," *Quarterly Journal of Economics*, 127: 1017–55.

Avins, A. (1966). "The Right to be a Witness and the Fourteenth Amendment," *Missouri Law Review*, 31: 471–504.

Bellin, J. (2018). "The Silence Penalty," *Iowa Law Review*, 103: 395–431.

Berdejó, C. (2018). "Criminalizing Race: Racial Disparities in Plea-Bargaining," *Boston College Law Review*, 59: 1187–249.

Bishop, E. T., Hopkins, B., Obiofuma, C., and Owusu, F. et al. (2020). *Racial Disparities in the Massachusetts Criminal System*. Cambridge, MA: Harvard Law School Criminal Justice Policy Program.

Braman, D., Kahan, D. M., Gastil, J., Stovic, P., and Mertz, C. K. (2005). "Gender, Race, and Risk Perception: The Influence of Cultural Status Anxiety," in *GW Law Faculty Publications and Other Works*, 208. Available at "Gender, Race, and Risk Perception: The Influence of Cultural Status An" byDan M. Kahan, Donald Braman et al. (gwu.edu) (Accessed: April 7, 2021).

Bureau of Justice and Statistics (2018). *Contact between Police and the Public, 2015*. Washington, DC: Bureau of Justice & Statistics.

Burlew, J. (2014). "Officers Consistently Cleared by Grand Juries in Police-Involved Shootings," *Tallahassee Democrat*, June 28, 2014. Available at https://www.tallahassee.com/story/news/politics/2014/06/28/officer-involved-shootings-judged-justified/11698753/ (Accessed: April 7, 2021).

Capers, I. B. (2010). "The Unintentional Rapist," *Washington University Law Review*, 87: 1345–95.

Carson, E. A. and Sabol, W. J. (2012). *Prisoners in 2011*. Washington, DC: Bureau of Justice Statistics.

Chan, M. (2019). "A Police Officer Killed their Mother, and her Sons want to know why he hasn't Faced Trial," *Time*, July 18, 2019. Available at https://time.com/5628206/police-shooting-trial-knowlton-garner/(Accessed: April 7, 2021).

Chance, J., Goldstein, A. G., and McBride, L. (1975). "Differential Experience and Recognition Memory for Faces," *Journal of Social Psychology*, 97: 243–53.

Chung, A., Hurley, L., Botts, J., Januta, A., and Gomez, G. (2020). "Shielded," *Reuters*, May 8, 2020. Available at https://www.reuters.com/investigates/special-report/usa-police-immunity-scotus/ (Accessed: April 7, 2021).

Connelly, L. (2015). "Cross-Racial Identifications: Solutions to the "They All Look Alike" Effect," *Michigan Journal on Race and Law*, 21: 125–45.

Cutler, B. L. and Penrod, S. D. (1995). *Mistaken Identification: The Eyewitness, Psychology, and the Law*. Cambridge: Cambridge University Press.

---

[86] FRE 102.

Davis, E. (2016). *Typecasts, Tokens, and Spokespersons: A Case for Credibility Excess as Testimonial Injustice*, 31 Hypatia 485.

Demby, G. (2014). "Study reveals Worse Outcomes for Black and Latino Defendants," *NPR*, July 17, 2014. Available at https://www.npr.org/sections/codeswitch/2014/07/17/332075947/study-reveals-worse-outcomes-for-black-and-latino-defendants (Accessed: April 7, 2021).

Desilver, D., Lipka, M., and Fahmy, D. (2020). "10 Things we know about Race and Policing in the U.S.," *Pew Research Center*, June 3, 2020. Available at https://www.pewresearch.org/fact-tank/2020/06/03/10-things-we-know-about-race-and-policing-in-the-u-s/ (Accessed: April 7, 2021).

Devenport, J. L. (1997). "Eyewitness Identification Evidence: Evaluating Commonsense Evaluations," *Psychology, Public Policy, and Law*, 3: 338–61.

Dotson, K. (2011). "Tracking Epistemic Violence, tracking Practices of Silencing," *Hypatia*, 26: 236–57.

Edwards, F., Lee, H., and Esposito, M. (2019) . "Risk of being Killed by Police Use of Force in the United States by Age, Race–Ethnicity, and Sex," *Proceedings of the National Academy of Sciences*, 116: 16793–8.

Eisenberg T. and Hans, V. P. (2009). "Taking a Stand on Taking the Stand: The Effect of a Prior Criminal Record on the Decision to Testify and on Trial Outcomes," *Cornell Law Review*, 94: 1353–90.

Expert Institute (2018). *Expert Witness Fee Report*. New York: Expert Institute.

Fingerhut, H. (2017). "Deep Racial, Partisan Divisions in Americans' views of Police Officers," *Pew Research Center*, September 15, 2017. Available at https://www.pewresearch.org/fact-tank/2017/09/15/deep-racial-partisan-divisions-in-americans-views-of-police-officers/ (Accessed: April 7, 2021).

Finkelman, F. (1986). "Prelude to the Fourteenth Amendment: Black Legal Rights in the Antebellum North," *Rutgers Law Journal*, 17: 415–82.

Flevaris, T. V. and Chapman, E. F. (2015). "Cross-Racial Misidentification: A Call to Action in Washington State and Beyond," *Seattle University Law Review*, 38: 861–900.

Fricker, M. (2007). *Epistemic Injustice: Power and Ethics of Knowing*. Oxford: Clarendon Press.

Frumkin, L. A. and Stone, A. (2020). "Not all Eyewitnesses are Equal: Accent Status, Race and Age Interact to Influence Evaluations of Testimony," *Journal of Ethnicity in Criminal Justice*, 18: 123–45.

Frye, R. G. (2019). "An Empirical Analysis of Racial Differences in Police Use of Force," *Journal of Political Economy*, 127: 1210–61.

George, T. E. and Yoon, A. H. (2020). *The Gavel Gap: Who sits in Judgement on State Courts?* Washington, DC: American Constitution Society. Available at https://www.prisonlegalnews.org/media/publications/Gavel_Gap_-_Who_Sits_in_Judgment_on_State_Courts_ACSLP_2016.pdf(Accessed: April 7, 2021).

Gonzales Rose, J. (2017). "Toward a Critical Race Theory of Evidence," *Minnesota Law Review*, 101: 2243–311.

Gonzales Rose, J. (2018). "Racial Character Evidence in Police Killing Cases," *Wisconsin Law Review*, 2018: 369–439.

Gonzales Rose, J. (forthcoming (a)). "Civil Rights Summarily Denied: Race, Evidence, and Summary Judgment in Police Brutality Cases," in B. Coleman, S. Malveaux, P. Pedro, and E. Porter (eds.), *A Guide to Civil Procedure: Integrating Critical Legal Perspectives*.

Gonzales Rose, J. (forthcoming (b)). "Race and Evidence," in D. Carbado, K. Bridges, and E. Hough (eds.), *The Oxford Handbook of Race and Law in the United States*. Oxford: Oxford University Press.

Gonzales Rose, J. (forthcoming (c)). "Truth and Evidence," in M. Schwartzberg and P. Kitcher (eds.), *NOMOS LX*. New York: New York University Press.

Grinberg, E. (2018). "Why Police-Involved Shooting Trials rarely end in Convictions for Police Officers," *CNN*, August 29, 2018. Available at https://www.cnn.com/2017/06/23/us/police-deadly-force-trials/index.html (Accessed: April 7, 2021).

Gross, S. R., Possley, M., and Stephens, K. (2017). *Race and Wrongful Convictions in the United States*, National Registry of Exonerations, University of California Irvine, March 7, 2017. Available at https://www.law.umich.edu/special/exoneration/Documents/Race_and_Wrongful_Convictions.pdf (Accessed: April 7, 2021).

Gunscom (2015). "Raw Body Cam: Dallas Police Officers shoot Mentally-Ill Jason Harrison holding Screwdriver," *YouTube*, March 18, 2015. Available at https://youtube.com/watch?v=QMfupZ64T1M (Accessed: April 7, 2021).

Hannaford-Agor, P. L., Hans, V. P., Mott, N. L., and Munsterman, G. T. (2002). *Are Hung Juries a Problem?* National Center for State Courts, National Institute of Justice, September 30, 2002. Available at Are Hung Juries a Problem? Executive Summary (ojp.gov) (Accessed: March 26, 2021).

"Henry Wallace Police Crime Database," *Bowling Green State University*. Available at https://policecrime.bgsu.edu (Accessed: March 26, 2021).

Jawando, M. L. and Anderson, A. (2016). "Racial and Gender Diversity sorely Lacking in America's Courts," *Center for American Progress*, September 15, 2016. Available at https://www.americanprogress.org/issues/courts/news/2016/09/15/144287/racial-and-gender-diversity-sorely-lacking-in-americas-courts/ (Accessed: April 7, 2021).

Johnson, S. L. (1983). "Cross-Racial Identification Errors in Criminal Cases," *Cornell Law Review*, 69: 934–87.

Johnson, S. L. (1985). "Black Innocence and the White Jury," *Michigan Law Review*, 83: 1611–708.

Johnson, S. L. (1996). "The Color of Truth: Race and the Assessment of Credibility," *Michigan Journal on Race & Law*, 1: 261–346.

Jones, A. (2018). "Police Stops are still Marred by Racial Discrimination, New Data Shows," *Prison Policy Initiative*, October 12, 2018. Available at https://www.prisonpolicy.org/blog/2018/10/12/policing/ (Accessed: April 7, 2021).

Kahan, D. M., Hoffman, D., and Braman, D. (2009). "Whose Eyes are you Going to Believe? Scott v. Harris and the Perils of Cognitive Illiberalism," *Harvard Law Review*, 122: 837–906.

Kahan, D., Hoffman, D. A., Braman, D., Evans, D., and Rachlinski, J. J. (2012). "'They saw a Protest': Cognitive Illiberalism and the Speech-Conduct Distinction," *Stanford Law Review*, 64: 851–906.

Kendi, I. X. (2019). *How to be an Antiracist*. London: One World.

Langton, R. (2010). "Epistemic Injustice: Power and the Ethics of Knowing," *Hypatia*, 25: 459–64.

Letwin, L. (1984). "Impeaching Defendants with their Prior Convictions: Reconsidering the Dangerous Propensities of Character Evidence after People v. Castro," *University of California Davis Law Review*, 18: 681–719.

Levinson, R. B. and Bodensteiner, I. E. (2019). *Civil Rights Legislation & Litigation*. Lake Mary, FL: Vandeplas Publishing.

Libassi, C. J. (2018). "The Neglected College Race Gap: Racial Disparities among College Completers," *Center for American Progress*, May 23, 2018. Available at https://www.americanprogress.org/issues/education-postsecondary/reports/2018/05/23/451186/neglected-college-race-gap-racial-disparities-among-college-completers/ (Accessed: April 7, 2021).

Lindsay, R. C. L. and Wells, G. L. (1980). "What Price Justice? Exploring the Relationship of Lineup Fairness to Identification Accuracy," *Law & Human Behavior*, 4: 303–13.

Loftus, E. F. (1974). "Reconstructing Memory: The Incredible Eyewitness," *Psychology Today*, 8: 116–19.

Luongo, T. and Conti-Cook, C. (2017). "Police & Civilians: Two Justice Systems, Criminally Unequal," *Daily News*, October 5, 2017. Available at https://www.nydailynews.com/opinion/police-civilians-justice-systems-criminally-unequal-article-1.3541614 (Accessed: April 7, 2021).

Malpass, R. M., Ross, S. J., Meissner, C. A., and Marcon, J. L. (2009). "The Need for Expert Psychological Testimony on Eyewitness Identification," in B. L. Cutler (ed.), *Expert Testimony on the Psychology of Eyewitness Identification*. Oxford: Oxford University Press, 3–28.

"Mapping Police Violence," https://mappingpoliceviolence.org.

McCarthy, N. (2020). "Police Shootings: Black Americans Disproportionately Affected [Infographic]," *Forbes*, May 28, 2020. Available at https://www.forbes.com/sites/niallmccarthy/2020/05/28/police-shootings-black-americans-disproportionately-affected-infographic/#586041fb59f7 (Accessed: April 7, 2021).

McKee, D. K. (1996). "Challenge to Eyewitness Identification through Expert Testimony," in *American Jurisprudence Proof of Facts*. Toronto: Thomas Reuters.

Mezey, N. (2013). "The Image cannot Speak for Itself: Film, Summary Judgment, and Visual Literacy," *Valparaiso University Law Review*, 48: 1–39.

Morin, R., Parker, K., Stepler, R., and Mercer, A. (2017). *Behind the Badge*. Washington, DC: Pew Research Center.

Morin, R. and Stepler, R. (2016). "The Racial Confidence Gap in Police Performance," *Pew Research Center*, September 29, 2016. Available at https://www.pewsocialtrends.org/2016/09/29/the-racial-confidence-gap-in-police-performance/ (Accessed: April 7, 2021).

Nellis, A., Greene, J., and Mauer, M. (2008). *Reducing Racial Disparity in the Criminal Justice System: A Manual for Practitioners and Policymakers*, The Sentencing Project. Available at Reducing Racial Disparity in the Criminal Justice System: A Manual for Practitioners and Policymakers | The Sentencing Project (Accessed: April 7, 2021).

Obasogie, O. K. (2020). "Police Killing Black People is a Pandemic, Too," *Washington Post*, June 5, 2020. Available at https://www.washingtonpost.com/outlook/police-violence-pandemic/2020/06/05/e1a2a1b0-a669-11ea-b619-3f9133bbb482_story.html (Accessed: April 7, 2021).

Peffley, M. and Hurwitz, J. (2010). *Justice in America*. Cambridge: Cambridge University Press.

Pinkerton, J. (2013). "Hard to Charge: Bulletproof: Part 3," *Houston Chronicle*. Available at https://www.houstonchronicle.com/local/investigations/item/Bulletproof-Part-3-Hard-to-charge-24421.php (Accessed: April 7, 2012).

"Quick Facts: United States," *United States Census Bureau*. Available at https://www.census.gov/quickfacts/fact/table/US/PST045218 (Accessed: April 7, 2021).

Ramirez, R., Farrell, A., and McDevitt, J. (2000). *A Resource Guide on Racial Profiling Data Collection Systems: Promising Practices and Lessons Learned*. Northeastern University School of Law Research Paper. Available at DOI:10.2139/ssrn.2001598 (Accessed: April 7, 2021).

Rehavi, M. and Starr, S. B. (2014). "Racial Disparity in Federal Criminal Sentences," *Journal of Political Economy*, 122: 1320–54.

Reinhart, A. A. (2018). "Qualified Immunity at Trial," *Notre Dame Law Review*, 93: 2065–92.

Rutledge, J. P. (2001). "They all Look Alike: The Inaccuracy of Cross-Racial Identifications," *American Journal of Criminal Law*, 28: 207–28.

Schwartz, M. A., Silbey, J., Ryan, J., and Donoghue, G. (2009). "Analysis of Videotape Evidence in Police Misconduct Cases," *Touro Law Review*, 25: 857–908.

Shannon, S. K. S., Uggen, C., Schnittker, J., Thompson, M. et al. (2017). "The Growth, Scope, and Spatial Distribution of People with Felony Records in the United States, 1948–2010," *Demography*, 54: 1795–818.

Smith, D. A. (1986). "The Neighborhood Context of Police Behavior," *Crime and Justice*, 8: 313–41.

Sommers, S. R. and Ellsworth, P. C. (2000). "Race in the Courtroom: Perceptions of Guilt and Dispositional Attributions," *Personality and Social Psychology Bulletin*, 26: 1367–79.

Srikanth, A. (2020). "Black People 5 Times More Likely to be Arrested than Whites, According to New Analysis," *The Hill*, June 11, 2020. Available at https://thehill.com/changing-america/respect/equality/502277-black-people-5-times-more-likely-to-be-arrested-than-whites (Accessed: April 7, 2021).

Starr, S. B. and Rehavi, M. (2013). "Mandatory Sentencing and Racial Disparity," *Yale Law Journal*, 123: 2–80.

Substance Abuse and Mental Health Services Administration (2016). *2015 National Survey on Drug Use and Health*. Rockville, MD: Substance Abuse and Mental Health Services Administration.

Sue, D. W. (2006). "The Invisible Whiteness of Being: Whiteness, White Supremacy, White Privilege, and Racism," in M. G. Constantine and D. W. Sue (eds.), *Addressing Racism: Facilitating Cultural Competence in Mental Health and Educational Settings*. Hoboken, NJ: John Wiley & Sons.

The Sentencing Project (2018). *Report to the United Nations on Racial Disparities in the U.S. Criminal Justice System*. The Sentencing Project, 15–30. Available at https://www.sentencingproject.org/publications/un-report-on-racial-disparities/ (Accessed: April 7, 2021).

Thompson, M. K. (2015). "Blackness as Character Evidence," *Michigan Journal of Race and Law*, 20: 321–48.

Thompson-DeVaux, A., Rakich, N., and Butchireddygari, L. (2020). "Why It's so Rare for Police Officers to Face Legal Consequences," *FiveThirtyEight*, June 4, 2020. Available at https://

fivethirtyeight.com/features/why-its-still-so-rare-for-police-officers-to-face-legal-consequences-for-misconduct/ (Accessed: April 7, 2012).

Tonry, M. (2010). "The Social, Psychological, and Political Causes of Racial Disparities in the American Criminal Justice System," *Crime and Justice*, 39: 273–312.

United States Census Bureau (2019). "2018 Population Estimates by Age, Sex, Race, and Hispanic Origin," *United States Census Bureau*, June 20, 2019. Available at https://www.census.gov/newsroom/press-kits/2019/detailed-estimates.html (Accessed: April 7, 2021).

Vidmar, N. and Hans, V. P. (2007). *American Juries: The Verdict*. Amherst, NY: Prometheus Books.

Way, J. (2016). "Two Arguments for Evidentialism," The *Philosophical Quarterly*, 66: 805–18. Available at https://academic.oup.com/pq/article/66/265/805/2223554 (Accessed: April 7, 2021).

Wells, G. L. and Olson, E. A. (2001). "The Other-Race Effect in Eyewitness Identification: What do We do About It?" *Psychology, Public Policy and Law*, 7: 230–46.

Wong, H. K., Stephen, I. D., and Keeble, D. R. T. (2020). "The Own-Race Bias for Facial Recognition in a Multiracial Society," *Frontiers in Psychology*, 11: 208–23. Available at Frontiers | The Own-Race Bias for Face Recognition in a Multiracial Society | Psychology (frontiersin.org) (Accessed: April 7, 2021).

26

De-Biasing Legal Factfinders

Frank Zenker

1. Introduction

Vis-à-vis "the largely uncharted frontier of debiasing,"[1] empirical evidence on the efficacy of de-biasing measures is principally valuable for legal factfinders, because factfinding processes are fallible. This entails that some proportion of factfinding decisions are suboptimal given a normative standard. Plausibly explaining (part of) this proportion is the hypothesis that *cognitive* and *social* biases are at play.[2] Cognitive biases entail some broadly erroneous form of reasoning, while social biases entail reasoning based on stereotypes. Both kinds of biases are (rightly) thought to potentially reduce the *accuracy* of the given judgement or evaluation.

De-biasing measures seek to address a bias's negative effects by improving either the legal factfinding process or characteristics of the factfinder. De-biasing measures arguably are already part of the legal system; indeed, the historical development of the legal system may be a progressive institutionalization of such measures. The available evidence for the efficacy and reliability of de-biasing measures, however, is not only scant, but also mixed. What measure might work when, how, and why, is unclear. Worse, the scarcity of theory-driven research already leaves the measure's causal/explanatory antecedent, the bias itself, unclear.

After a brief overview of the research into human biases and de-biasing measures, we point to the problematic evidential basis and identify future research needs.

2. Biases, De-Biasing Measures, and the Legal System

According to an ancient *topos*, human beings are imperfect—*errare humanum est* ("to err is human"). Owing to their first nature or the untrained state, agents regularly accept and act upon *seeming* truths. Subject to passions and appetites, moreover, humans are known to endorse "vain opinions, flattering hopes, false valuations, imaginations as one would, and the like," or so Francis Bacon's essay *Of Truth*[3] echoes a classical idea during the onset of the Renaissance, even mentioning "a natural though corrupt love of the lie itself."[4] Bacon not only sought to make human belief-forming processes more sensitive to the empirical. He also intended to provide a counter-weight to the negative human dispositions that his *idolatry* had identified (idols of the cave, tribe, theater, and marketplace).[5] Like contemporary

---

[1] Lilienfeld et al. 2009, 391.
[2] Langevoort 1998; Enescu and Kuhn 2012; cf. Mitchell 2002.
[3] Bacon 1625.
[4] Ibid.
[5] Lord et al. 1984.

Frank Zenker, *De-Biasing Legal Factfinders* In: *Philosophical Foundations of Evidence Law*. Edited by: Christian Dahlman, Alex Stein, and Giovanni Tuzet, Oxford University Press. © Christian Dahlman, Alex Stein, and Giovanni Tuzet 2021.
DOI: 10.1093/oso/9780198859307.003.0027

Cognitive Biases and Failed Heuristics Addressed by Diagnostic Checklists

Bias or heuristic	Definition*	Role of checklist
Anchoring	The tendency to perceptually lock on to salient features of the patient's presentation too early in the diagnostic process and failing to adjust this impression in light of later information.	Prompt physician to consider diagnoses other than the initially favored one.
Availability	The disposition to judge things as being more likely or frequently occurring, if they readily come to mind.	Prompt physician to consider diagnoses other than those that readily come to mind.
Base-rate neglect	The tendency to ignore the true prevalence of a disease, either inflating or reducing its base rate and distorting Bayesian reasoning.	Remind physician of the relative prevalence of diseases in primary care for the patient's complaint.
Premature closure	The decision-making process ends too soon; the diagnosis is accepted before it has been fully verified. "When the diagnosis is made, the thinking stops."	Prompt physician to reopen the diagnostic process and consider alternative diagnoses before discharging the patient.
Representativeness restraint	The physician looks for prototypical manifestations of disease (pattern recognition) and fails to consider atypical variants.	Prompt physician to consider causes for the symptoms other than the ones that readily fit the pattern.
Search satisticing	The tendency to call off a search once something is found.	Prompt physician to consider additional causes of the complaint after something is found.
Unpacking principle	The failure to elicit all relevant information in establishing a differential diagnosis.	Prompt physician to ask questions that might confirm or rule alternative diagnoses.
Context errors	The critical signal is distorted by the background against which it is perceived.	Encourage physician to rethink assumptions and maintain objectivity.

Figure 26.1

empirical research on human biases,[6] Bacon's early modern taxonomy had thus already recognized the need for prescriptive ameliorative interventions, or *de-biasing measures*.

De-biasing measures arguably are of special relevance if the stakes are as high as in legal factfinding. Following Larrick,[7] de-biasing measures can be analytically classified as in the widest sense *motivational, cognitive*, or *technological*. Motivational and cognitive measures operate at the individual level, even if deployed in a group. Technological measures provide incentives (or nudges) to use more desirable reasoning processes, and can operate both at the group and the institutional level. The same holds for cognitive measures, which equip agents with knowledge, skill, or information to deploy such reasoning processes correctly, for example via environmental props ensuring a procedural standard as institutional due procedure. Since a de-biasing measure targets individual dispositions, abilities, and the structure of collective environments, a successful measure must address aspects of cognition, motivation, and technology *simultaneously*. A measure must raise awareness of the bias (*cognition*) in ways that sustain or increase the impetus to avoid biased reasoning (*motivation*), while providing information and devices that agents can deploy to correct otherwise biased reasoning (*technology*).

A large number of empirical studies report evidence consistent with the operation of cognitive and social biases in various groups and contexts.[8] Although relatively few studies have specifically addressed legal factfinding and decision-making contexts, these studies do report that biases are at play also in legal contexts. Examples include anchoring, hindsight

---

[6] Fischhoff 2010.
[7] Larrick 2008.
[8] Kahneman 2011; cf. Schimmack et al. 2017.

bias, and base-rate neglect.[9] Similar studies typically rely on survey responses (acquired using questionnaires) vis-à-vis a hypothetical case description (vignette). Responses are averaged in order to measure the difference to a relevant normative standard. Moreover, data are evaluated statistically under standards of H_0-hypothesis testing to establish the probability of the observed difference under a random-effect model.

A typical selection of biases[10] includes *anchoring*, where a first proposal sets a reference point for the final judgment or its direction. *Framing effects* and *loss aversion* show that agents may accept different risks depending on whether an otherwise identical state of affairs is presented using a gain-framed or a loss-framed message, such that "losses loom larger."[11] The *omission bias* is at work if, despite identical consequences, risky acts of commission are evaluated differently than risky acts of omission. Virtually all *probabilistic biases* entail that judgments deviate from Bayes' theorem. *Confirmation bias* refers to the relatively increased likelihood of acknowledging, weighing, searching, or somehow favoring confirmatory as opposed to dis-confirmatory evidence for a hypothesis. *Hindsight bias* results in retrospectively overestimating the predictability of facts. The *halo effect* refers to connecting a person's causally independent characteristics. Finally, *overconfidence bias* is at work in overestimating one's own chances of success relative to a base rate.

Like other contexts, legal factfinding is thought to be subject to pure or mixed forms of *psychophysically based* errors (e.g., overweighing most recently received information), *association-based* errors (e.g., using available evidence rather than searching for representative evidence), and *strategy-based* errors (e.g., inferior decision rules such as "a bird in the hand is worth two in the bush").[12] Since the concept of error presupposes a (principally revisable) *normative standard* dictating how agents should act, biases can be thought of as *partial causes* of suboptimal reasoning/decision-making relative to the normative standard, which itself derives from current best expert knowledge. (Examples are the maximization of choice utility via excluding dominated strategies in decision theory, or specific formal constraints such as the complement rule $P(p)=1-P(non\ p)$ in Pascalian probability theory.) By parity of reasoning, a de-biasing measure seeks to align actual reasoning/decision-making processes and outcomes with the normative standard. This entails that a de-biasing measure is needed *only if* natural dispositions fail at this. Conversely, if the alignment remains (too) imperfect despite deploying the de-biasing measure, then the measure itself fails.

Research strongly suggests that humans are particularly challenged in applying a de-biasing measure, the more so in self-application.[13] The primary challenge in overcoming barriers to de-biasing appears to be suspending the bias's latency. Some researchers are therefore more optimistic with respect to institutionalized *rather than* personalized versions of de-biasing measures, also known as de-biasing infrastructures. As barriers to de-biasing, Lilienfeld et al.[14] identify the following: de-biasing may be perceived as irrelevant to personal welfare (*lack of motivation*); present cognitive abilities remain domain-specific and do not transfer to new contexts (*lack of cognition*); "individual and cultural differences in

[9] Guthrie et al. 2001; English and Mussweiler 2001; 2006; Rachlinski et al. 2007; see Zenker and Dahlman 2016.
[10] Schweizer 2005.
[11] Tversky and Kahneman 1974.
[12] Larrick 2008, 319f.
[13] Fischhoff 1982; Pronin and Kugler 2007; Pronin, Lin, and Ross 2002; Willingham 2007; Kahneman 2011; Kenyon 2014.
[14] Lilienfeld et al. 2009.

personality, cognitive styles, and developmental level may predict the efficacy of de-biasing efforts."[15] Given that the consequences of a legal factfinding can be severe, factfinders may even need to distance themselves from the idea of committing errors, because being constantly aware thereof can be a burden (keyword: "paralysis by analysis").

The impotency of instructing agents about biases as a way of removing their effects has been addressed in a variety of ways. These not only include postulating self-defense or immunization mechanisms in response to a perceived *ad personam* criticism, but also veritable null explanations such as the "bias blindspot" (offering the *explanandum* in place of an *explanans*[16]) as well as the non-empirical, because non-testable, Dunning-Kruger effect.[17] It postulates that the principled incompetence of the incompetent to comprehend their own incompetence goes along with a similar incompetence to comprehend the competence of others.

At any rate, it appears to primarily waste time and resources to tell people that they are potentially subject to biases, or to instruct agents to reason harder, better/longer/deeper, to concentrate, or to just put yourself to it. Though brief non-technical tutorials on biases are reportedly effective in reducing the tendency to fall prey to them,[18] teaching *meta-cognitive* rules (engaging cognition about cognition) such as "consider the opposite" appear more promising.[19] Such teaching goes beyond a non-technical level of instruction, which also holds for formal logic instruction as a de-biasing measure.[20] At a less technical level of instruction, however, logic instruction appears ineffective in transferring to all relevant domains.[21]

While the empirical evidence for the effectiveness and reliability of de-biasing measures is both scant and mixed (see Section 4), researchers have nevertheless identified de-biasing measures that also apply to legal factfinders, including "specific testing and training, exposure to stereotype-incongruent models, inducement of more effective deliberative thought processing, and increased post-decision auditing."[22] Such measures may include elements of the jurisprudential procedure that, today, are already too sedimented to understand them as intending to impact natural dispositions.[23] A vivid example, widely endorsed in both Greek and Roman law to counter the arbitrary one-sidedness of legal decision-making,[24] is the *audi alteram partem* principle ("you must listen to the other side"). Its near-equivalent, the *total evidence principle* in inductive reasoning, is what the sciences at large rely upon. Having entire courts, rather than only individual judges, can be similarly interpreted as a traditional and institutionalized de-biasing measure.

The perhaps most basic de-biasing measure rests in a legal factfinder's *accountability* insofar as decisions are subject to review, for example by a higher court.[25] Other measures can be roughly sorted under three categories:

---

[15] Stanovich and West 2000.
[16] Pronin et al. 2002; 2007.
[17] Dunning et al. 2003.
[18] Lilienfeld et al. 2009, 393.
[19] Willingham 2007.
[20] Duthil Novaes 2012, 221–48.
[21] Lilienfeld et al. 2009.
[22] Irwin and Real 2010, 7; see Rachlinski et al. 2007.
[23] Arlen and Tontrup 2014; Farnsworth, 2003; Jolls and Sunstein 2005; 2006; Pi et al. 2013.
[24] Kelly 1964.
[25] Arkes 1998.

- *Consider the opposite* (aka "Devil's Advocate"): reminding agents of the hypothetical possibility of the opposite standpoint sometimes ameliorate instances of hindsight bias, overconfidence, and selective availability owed to anchoring effects.[26] For instance, a positive effect may arise for self-serving bias in litigation negotiations upon considering the weaknesses of one's own case. A specific version thereof is "reframing." Here, presenting the same state of affairs in a gain- versus a loss-framed message can counteract loss-aversion.[27] Similarly, probability information can become more manageable when presented in a frequency rather than a decimal format.[28]

- *Give reasons*: normally falling upon the judge, the requirement to give reasons always depends on the differentially ability to do so.[29] Not only do agents differ in their need for cognition, they are also naturally inclined to give supporting reasons.[30] In fact, it is also natural (though no less problematic) to conclude that a decision was better than it in fact is, because few reasons speak against it.[31] By contrast, generating strong counter-reasons to one's own belief normally requires training.[32] A specific variant is the "Socratic method," where guided questioning can serve to elicit more accurate responses.[33]

- *Reduce discretion*: regarding norms or procedures that leave less room for a factfinder's interpretation/understanding of the legal provisions that guide factfinding (e.g., explicit checklists or the use of formal models), various sources report mixed results from deploying environmental props aimed at reducing reliance on cognition, particularly on memory.[34] This extends to using formal models, for example Bayesian evidence models or causal maps, where lack of detailed knowledge of the formalities regularly risks using the right tool wrongly.[35]

Arguably, the historical development of procedural or substantial law has already put similar de-biasing measures on the ground. The negative effect of self-serving bias, for instance, "… turns out to be an old and familiar problem to the law; indeed, it is possible to view many features of the American [or another] legal system precisely as responses to the threat of such biases and attempts to contain them—but with sensitivity at the same time to the fact that investment in such efforts can reach a point of diminishing returns."[36]

The earliest stages of the legal system are today (rightly) decried for endorsing elements of magic, such as the widely accepted "evidence-standard" *for* witchcraft being equated with the defendant's body floating on water. Particularly in small societies, the legal system's early stages aligned less with fair and well-reasoned decisions, but rather with rapprochement and reconciliation, primarily seeking to allow disagreeing parties to cohabit. Indeed,

---

[26] Lord et al. 1984; Büyükkurt and Büyükkurt 1991; Mumma and Wilson 1995; Mussweiler et al. 2000; Kamin and Rachlinski 1995; Arkes et al. 1988; Babcock et al. 1997.

[27] Hodgkinson et al. 1999.

[28] Lopes 1987; Gigerenzer and Hoffrage 1995; Cosmides and Tooby 1996.

[29] Engel 2004; Zenker et al. 2018.

[30] Larrick 2008, 323; Hodgkinson et al. 1999; Mumma and Wilson 1995; Koriat et al. 1980; Kamin and Rachlinksi 1995.

[31] Koriat et al. 1980.

[32] Lilienfeld et al. 2009.

[33] Büyükkurt and Büyükkurt 1991.

[34] Kamin and Rachlinski 1995.

[35] Pundik 2012.

[36] Farnsworth 2003, 603.

various such magical elements were retained, whereas elements found indispensable today had long remained absent. For instance, "[w]hen the jury system first evolved, the defendant had few of the procedural safeguards which are taken for granted today .... There was no right to counsel of any kind; the defendant did not even have the right to have a copy of the charges against him. Confessions were often obtained by torture, and the defendant could be convicted on the basis of almost any kind of hearsay evidence [or ordeal, even battle]."[37]

Rather than as a *deliberate* successive eradication of a deficient prior system-state, of course, the legal system may instead have developed simply via agents' *spontaneous* coordination.[38] This makes "[l]egal rules ... the 'unintended' by-product of many people's combined actions,"[39] and also implicates terms such as "error," "fallacy," or "interest," which are historically much older than "bias." In fact, psychologists began using "bias" in the relevant sense only in the 1960s, reaching legal and other scholarship via the popularization of the *heuristics and biases program* in the 1980s.[40] The strong claim—that *this* development in rules/procedure (spontaneously or intendedly) had evolved as a de-biasing measure to address *that* bias—would presuppose at least some empirical evidence that a de-biasing measure treats a bias successfully. Thus, all that can properly "piggyback" on experimental research on human biases are contemporary approaches to implementing de-biasing measures such as the *nudging* paradigm.[41]

Addressing any given bias necessarily presupposes a relevant normative standard as it has developed historically. Though researchers keep coining terms for allegedly *new* biases (e.g., "sunk-cost bias," "*status quo* bias," "gender bias"), most terms that associate to "bias" today map onto classical/early modern predecessors, collectively known as *fallacies*.[42] The large number of novel terms also suggests a rather long list of biases, which increasingly includes social biases, stereotypes, and *implicit biases*,[43] that sustain discrimination against individuals or groups (based on age, gender, sexual orientation, origin, religious, political persuasion).

An important distinction is that between addressing a suboptimal form of reasoning and decision-making (assumedly caused by a bias) by means of a specific de-biasing measure, and more fully understanding how to improve reasoning and decision-making processes that involve *no* such biases. While the distinction is analytically clean, it turns "dirty" because presence of bias is hard to separate from conditions that *also* produce suboptimal decisions-making outcomes, or conditions that do so by interacting with a bias. After all, suboptimal outcomes underdetermine their causes (effect of a bias alone, bias plus quasi-facilitating conditions, absence of bias). Therefore, just as value-choices do not require explaining them as *biased* choices,[44] suboptimal decision-making outcomes alone cannot immediately entail the presence of personal or social bias.

---

[37] Neef and Nagel 1974, 146.
[38] Hayek 1982, 48f., 94f.
[39] Heiner 1986, 231.
[40] Tversky and Kahneman 1974; Lopes 1991.
[41] Thaler and Sunstein 2008; Jolls and Sunstein 2005; 2006; Pi et al. 2013.
[42] Hamblin 1970; Hansen and Pinto 1995; Woods 2013.
[43] Project Implicit 2015; Jolls and Sunstein 2006.
[44] Weinstein 2002.

3. De-Biasing

Originating in medical research, exemplary cognitive biases typical of the literature include anchoring, availability, base-rate neglect, premature closure, representativeness restraint, search satisficing, unpacking principle, and context errors.[45] The primary intention here is to motivate a checklist addressing errors, mishaps, and diagnostic failures that presence of bias can effect.

Primarily serving medical practitioners presented with emergency cases, checklists qualify as de-biasing measures in the sense of decision-making props. While their purpose may seem to differ from similar measures in legal factfinding contexts, where time constraints on decision-making are less pressing, factfinders nevertheless have deadlines, too. As a pragmatic tool, moreover, checklists simply meet a need that theorizing has not met yet. Besides rather non-rigorous ideas on dual systems, dual processes, or dual types of human reasoning, little in the way of a theoretically motivated explanation is available why biases exist and persist.[46]

In the early twentieth century, dual system-like ideas appeared in the works of William James or Sigmund Freud, while the distinction between intuition and deliberation dates back at least as far as the classical age.[47] Current dual-systems accounts of reasoning initially sought to separate intuitive from reflective reasoning, but later came to operate with diverse clusters of properties (related to human consciousness, evolutionary considerations, functional characteristics, and individual differences in reasoning).[48] This provided handy terms for interdisciplinary (mis-)use, seemingly at the expense of constructing theories from which differentiable empirical hypotheses can be deduced for predictive or interventionist purposes.

This also implicates scholars who treat the use of a heuristic as an *ecologically rational* affair, given that natural environments are uncertain, rather than risky.[49] In view of agents' limited cognitive resources and time-constraints, or their *bounded rationality*,[50] deploying a heuristics might have resulted from trading off against more effortful, reflective reasoning. Heuristics themselves would thus have evolved as adaptations (or exaptations) to natural environments, that is, in virtue of agents successfully resisting the survival uncertainty that natural contexts present. By definition, if environmental conditions are right, then a heuristic *can* deliver outcomes that are better than those delivered by decision or probability theory. After all, non-vague probabilities (hence well-defined risks) are calculable *only if* the outcome-space is finite; yet genuinely uncertain environments (such as the natural one) fail this condition by featuring "unknown unknowns." *Optimal* reasoning and decision-making would thus be a matter of the best-fit between task, context, and resources, binding the very notions of optimality to features that make a heuristic a *contextually optimal* problem-solution strategy.

---

[45] Croskerry 2009a, b; Ely et al. 2011, Table 1.
[46] Samuels et al. 2002.
[47] Osman 2004.
[48] Evans 2008.
[49] Gigerenzer et al. 1999; Gigerenzer and Todd 1999; Gigerenzer and Brighton, 2009; Gigerenzer and Sturm 2012.
[50] Simon 1982.

Among most researchers working on dual process accounts of reasoning and decision-making,[51] the "consensus is that there are two major sources: innate, hard-wired biases that developed in our evolutionary past, and acquired biases established in the course of development and within our working environments [and that b]oth are associated with abbreviated decision-making in the form of heuristics."[52] Intended again for medical reasoning, Croskerry et al.'s[53] model captures the ongoing dual reasoning processes as agents transition from patient presentation to diagnosis. The model is general enough to transfer to legal factfinding. Information processing here occurs in terms of recognized or unrecognized patterns that trigger either an intuitive or an effortful reasoning response. The dual-process model features a toggle function, representing that decision-makers may "move forth and back between [intuitive] Type 1 and [deliberative] Type 2 processes."[54] As further features of this model, "executive override" denotes the ability to let a type-2 process dominate the type-1 process; "dysrationalia" denotes the inability or unwillingness to reason in effortful ways; and "calibration" refers to the degree to which the intuitive and the deliberative diagnoses align.

De-biasing requires of agents to change the intuitive type-1 reasoning-process whenever this is apt. In order to align the outcome to the normative standard (so as to achieve accuracy-gains in information processing), five conditions are presupposed, here listed in implicational order: (i) awareness of the bias, (ii) motivation to correct it(s effects), (iii) awareness of the bias's direction and magnitude, (iv) ability to apply an appropriate de-biasing technique, and (v) successful de-biasing.[55] Conditions occurring downwards, although fulfilled, may *not* suffice to ameliorate a bias's effects on the decision-making outcome, unless *all* conditions upwards are also fulfilled. For instance, the *ability* to deploy an appropriate de-biasing measure (condition v) is ineffective without *motivation* to do so (condition i). Thus, a de-biasing measure should be more likely to fail if its successful deployment presupposes conditions that are false. Conversely, effective de-biasing measure need to leave *all* relevant conditions fulfilled, while efficient measures avoid wasting resources.

Yet, none of these conditions pertain to agents being *personally* biased, i.e., when what the de-biasing measure addresses originates with a faulty agent—an *imperfect but perfectible* individual—rather than with a misunderstood or unfair task, or a mismatch between agent and task. One may similarly debate the implications of the final step, from successful de-biasing to optimal decision-making. After all, one of the main insights from studying the ecologically rational use of heuristics is that the reasoning-outcome does not presuppose this step.[56] Intuitive and reflective reasoning modes may well differ in their underlying processes, yet nevertheless deliver the same outcome. Conversely, even a fully *de*-biased agent can reach a suboptimal decision, *although* the agent's reasoning *is* licensed by a normative standard, namely when the agent commits run-errors within an otherwise optimal

[51] Osman 2004; Evans 2008.
[52] Croskerry et al. 2013a, ii58.
[53] Croskerry et al. 2013a, Figure 1 (available at https://qualitysafety.bmj.com/content/qhc/22/Suppl_2/ii58/F1.large.jpg (Accessed: April 7, 2021)); see Croskerry et al. 2013b.
[54] Ibid., ii60.
[55] Wilson and Brekke 1994. See Croskerry et al. 2013a, Figure 3 (available at https://qualitysafety.bmj.com/content/qhc/22/Suppl_2/ii58/F3.large.jpg (Accessed: April 7, 2021)).
[56] Betsch and Held 2012.

reasoning process. Run-errors can arise from mundane matters such as fatigue, distraction, or species-typical cognitive limits (e.g., on memory and perception).

Pace this caveat, long-term successful de-biasing at a personal level requires *decoupling* intuitive from quasi-automatic responses. Once an agent can engage in deliberative reasoning, this mode may even become quasi-automatic. As the intuitive mode is lastingly overridden, the seemingly paradoxical claim that expert decision-makers command expert knowledge *in intuitive ways* hence becomes meaningful. A de-biasing measure should thus seek to improve agents' reasoning in ways that make outcome-optimal reasoning modes self-sustaining. In the short run, of course, agents may be *nudged* into better decisions, for instance through formal procedures, conducive decision-making environments, props, or selective hints.[57] Yet nudges do not require that agents are *personally* aware of a bias, nor that they command internal motivation to de-bias. Indeed, nudges are a work-around to the internalist conditions (i) to (iii). If this succeeds, then also because nudges are by definition attuned to agents' *ready* abilities.

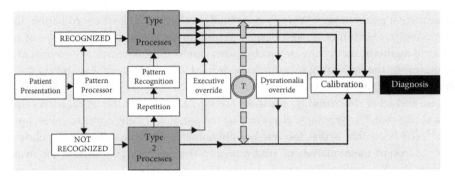

Figure 26.2

4. Solid Evidence, Anyone?

As Hahn and Harris[58] put it, "[a] reader venturing into the psychological literature about human biases soon realizes that the word 'bias' means many things to many people." The term "de-biasing measure" likewise denotes nothing less vague than all "strategies designed to reduce the magnitude of judgment errors."[59] This includes errors owed not to personal bias, but to non-conducive environmental, institutional, or cultural conditions, cognitive limitations ("stupidity"[60]), or simply fatigue.

One can generally speak of *personal* bias only if the decision-task is clear, and if the resources and abilities that a normatively correct decision requires are available.[61] As for an empirical study's "scientific hygiene," moreover, evidence of suboptimal decision-making can be evidence of personal bias only if the bias to be ameliorated *is* a relevant (partial)

---

[57] Thaler and Sunstein, 2008.
[58] Hahn and Harris 2014, 42.
[59] Arkes 1998, 449.
[60] Cipolla 1987.
[61] Cohen 1981.

cause of some instances of poor decision-making. Similarly, empirical evidence in support of a de-biasing measure's efficacy requires the ability to observe that a bias reliably "responds" to this intervention.

Alas, the same decision-making outcome can be caused by more than one bias, that is, be "multiply determined."[62] Moreover, what scant evidence there is includes both cases where one "cannot cure a disease by dancing around the patient," and cases where one cannot "extinguish fire by pouring oil onto it."[63] Rather than ameliorate a bias, a de-biasing measure may well make it worse, for instance, with respect to hindsight bias, confirmation bias, overconfidence, and belief persistence.[64]

Not only does the experimental literature on de-biasing legal factfinders contain many such *mixed* empirical results. Also, the tendency to underreport statistically *non*-significant empirical results entails that the number of studies where de-biasing measures fail is presumably much higher than is reported ("file-drawer" problem). In addition, relevant empirical studies typically suffer from overly small sample sizes given the observed effect sizes, from potentially externally invalid experimental set-ups (e.g., a mock-trial versus its video recording), and from primarily using university students as a presumably non-representative population.[65] Worse yet, partially caused by lack of coordination among (competing) research groups, and despite paying lip-service to the importance of meta-analytical methods, hardly any two such studies can be unproblematically compared as to the bias(es) or the de-biasing measure(s) addressed, the experimental set-up used, or the cohort of participants observed.

These and other shortcomings are widely recognized today as the "replication crisis" in medical research,[66] psychology, elsewhere in the social and behavioral sciences, and beyond.[67] The brute fact is that too few key-phenomena are replicable by independent efforts.[68] A recent meta-analysis of studies in top-tier psychology journals, for instance, estimates that the replicability rate is a mere 35%; more recent estimates reach a similar conclusion.[69] The main reason is that samples are typically too small for the normally small effect sizes to reach acceptable test power, entailing a low chance that an observed effect is independently replicable.

Since current conditions let studies differ far too widely to compare results soundly, and because individual research groups foreseeably lack the resources required to engage with larger samples on their own, the crisis indicates the need to improve research coordination at unprecedented levels. For these reasons, what few empirical results are available today provide only a speculative basis as to how legal factfinders might be reliably de-biased. Future research should invest in conducting, and replicating, well-powered studies that provide robust positive or negative evidence for the presence of biases and the efficacy of de-biasing measures.

---

[62] Larrick 2008.
[63] Wissler and Saks 1985.
[64] Arkes 1998; Fischhoff et al. 1977; Kurtz and Garfield 1978; Kenyon 2014; Wood 1978.
[65] Henrich et al. 2010.
[66] Ioannidis 2005a, b; Baker 2016.
[67] Spellmann 2012; Pashler and Wagenmakers 2012; Sturm and Muehlberger 2012.
[68] Witte and Zenker 2017.
[69] Bakker et al. 2012; Open Science Collaboration 2015.

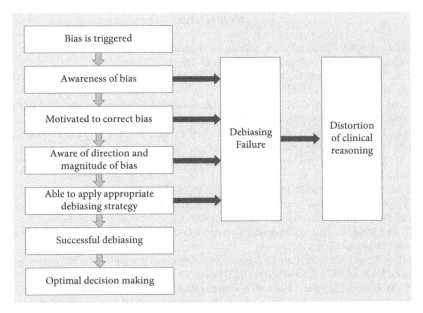

Figure 26.3

5. Conclusion

Regarding the efficacy of de-biasing measures in legal factfinding, empirical research results are both scant and mixed. Rather few instances of empirically tested de-biasing measures are available; the few studies that "test" such measures suffer from overly small sample sizes and await replication. This may seem to deliver less than what one would have hoped for. Analytically, it is nevertheless clear that effective de-biasing measures must simultaneously address aspects of *cognition*, *motivation*, and *technology*, perhaps in ways more similar to personalized medicine than to a typical form of instruction. Being personally de-biasable, whatever this means, also presupposes a conducive institutional environment; some agents may otherwise lack a valid reason to de-bias. Socio-political implications aside, legal fact-finding remains an important high-stake application context for the study of human biases and de-biasing measures.

Acknowledgments

I thank audiences at Lund University, Sweden; the University of Windsor, Canada; Rochester Institute of Technology, USA; The University of Rotterdam, The Netherlands; and Copenhagen University, Denmark, for discussion and comments. I also thank Christian Dahlman and Giovanni Tuzet for constructive comments on an earlier draft. I acknowledge funding from the Ragnar Söderberg Foundation (project: "Judges without bias").

References

Arkes, H. A. (1998). "Principles in Judgment/Decision Making Research Pertinent to Legal Proceedings," *Behavioral Sciences & the Law*, 7 (4): 429–56.

Arkes, H. R., Faust, D., Guilmette, T. J., and Hart, K. (1988). "Eliminating the Hindsight Bias," *Journal of Applied Psychology*, 73 (2): 305–7.

Arlen, J. and Tontrup, S. W. (2014). "Does the Endowment Effect Justify Legal Intervention? The Debiasing Effect of Institutions," *NYU School of Law, Public Law Research Paper*, 473: 1–50.

Babcock, L., Loewenstein, G., and Issacharoff, S. (1997). "Creating Convergence: Debiasing Biased Litigants," *Law & Social Inquiry*, 22(4): 913–25.

Bacon, F. (1625). "Of truth," in C.W. Eliot (ed.), *Essays, Civil and Moral* (1909–1914) (vol. III, Part 1). New York: P. F. Collier & Son.

Baker, M. (2016). "Reproducibility Crisis," *Nature*, 533(26): 353–66.

Bakker, M., Dijk, van A., and Wicherts, J. M. (2012). "The Rules of the Game Called Psychological Science," *Perspectives on Psychological Science*, 7: 543–54.

Betsch, T. and Held, C. (2012). "Rational Decision Making: Balancing RUN and JUMP Modes of Analysis," *Mind and Society*, 11: 69–80.

Büyükkurt, B. K. and Büyükkurt, M. D. (1991). "An Experimental Study on the Effectiveness of Three Debiasing Techniques," *Decision Sciences*, 22(1): 60–73.

Cipolla, C. M. (1987). "The Basic Laws of Human Stupidity," *Whole Earth Review*, (Spring): 2–7.

Cohen, J. L. (1981). "Can Human Irrationality be Experimentally Demonstrated?" *Behavioral and Brain Sciences*, 4: 317–70.

Cosmides, L. and Tooby, J. (1996). "Are Humans Good Intuitive Statisticians after all? Rethinking Some Conclusions from the Literature on Judgment under Uncertainty," *Cognition*, 58(1): 1–73.

Croskerry, P. (2009a). "A Universal Model of Diagnostic Reasoning," *Academic Medicine*, 84: 1022–8.

Croskerry, P. (2009b). "Cognitive and Affective Dispositions to Respond," in P. Croskerry, K. Cosby, S. Schenkel, and R. Wears (eds.), *Patient Safety in Emergency Medicine*, 219–27. Philadelphia, Pa: Lippincott Williams & Wilkins.

Croskerry, P., Singhal, G., and Mamede, S. (2013a). "Cognitive Debiasing 1: Impediments to and Strategies for Change," *BMJ Quality & Safety*, 22 (Suppl. 2): ii58–ii64.

Croskerry, P., Singhal, G., and Mamede, S. (2013b). "Cognitive Debiasing 2: Impediments to and Strategies for Change," *BMJ Quality & Safety*, 22 (Suppl. 2): ii65–ii72.

Dunning, D., Johnson, K., Ehrlinger, J., and Kruger, J. (2003). "Why People Fail to Recognize their own Incompetence," *Current Directions in Psychological Science*, 12(3): 83–7.

Duthil Novaes, C. (2012). *Formal Languages in Logic: A Philosophical and Cognitive Analysis*. Cambridge: Cambridge University Press.

Ely, J., Graber, M., and Croskerry, P. (2011). "Checklists to Reduce Diagnostic Errors," *Academic Medicine*, 86: 307–13.

Enescu, R. and Kuhn, A. (2012). "Serial Effects of Evidence on Legal Decision Making," *European Journal of Psychology Applied to Legal Context*, 4(2): 99–118.

Engel, C. (2004). "The Impact of Representation Norms on the Quality of Judicial Decisions," *MPI Collective Goods Preprint*, No. 2004/13. Available at https://dx.doi.org/10.2139/ssrn.617821 (Accessed: April 7, 2021).

English, B. and Mussweiler, T. (2001). "Sentencing under Uncertainty: Anchoring Effects in the Courtroom," *Journal of Applied Social Psychology*, 31: 1535–51.

English, B., Mussweiler, T., and Strack, F. (2006). "Playing Dice with Criminal Sentences: The Influence of Irrelevant Anchors on Experts' Judicial Decision Making," *Personality and Social Psychology Bulletin*, 32 (2): 188–200.

Evans, J. S. T. B. (2008). "Dual-Processing Accounts of Reasoning, Judgment, and Social Cognition," *Annual Review of Psychology*, 59: 255–78.

Farnsworth, W. (2003). "The Legal Regulation of Self-Serving Bias," *UC Davis Law Review*, 37: 567–603.

Fischhoff, B. (1982). "Debiasing," in D. Kahneman, P. Slovic, and A. Tversky (eds), *Judgment Under Uncertainty: Heuristics and Biases*, 422–44. New York: Cambridge University Press.

Fischhoff, B. (2010). "Judgment and Decision Making," *WIREs Cognitive Science*, 1: 724–35.

Fischhoff, B., Slovic, P., and Lichtenstein, S. (1977). "Knowing with Certainty: The Appropriateness of Extreme Confidence," *Journal of Experimental Psychology: Human Perception and Performance*, 3(4): 552–64.

Gigerenzer, G. and Brighton, H. (2009). "Why Biased Minds make Better Inferences," *Topics in Cognitive Science*, 1: 107–43.

Gigerenzer, G. and Hoffrage, U. (1995). "How to Improve Bayesian Reasoning without Instruction: Frequency Formats," *Psychological Review*, 102: 684–704.

Gigerenzer, G. and Sturm, T. (2012). "How (far) can Rationality be Naturalized?" *Synthese*, 187: 243–68.

Gigerenzer, G, Todd, P. M., and the ABC Research Group (1999). *Simple heuristics that Make us Smart*. New York and Oxford: Oxford University Press.

Guthrie, C., Rachlinski, J. J., and Wistrich, A. J. (2001). "Inside the Judicial Mind," *Cornell Law Review*, 86: 777–830.

Hahn, U. and Harris A. J. L. (2014). "What does it Mean to be Biased: Motivated Reasoning and Rationality," *Psychology of Learning and Motivation*, 61: 41–102.

Hamblin, C. (1970). *Fallacies*. London: Methuen.

Hansen, H. V. and Pinto, R. (eds.) (1995). *Fallacies—Classical and Contemporary Readings*. University Park, PA: Penn State University Press.

Hayek, F. (1982). *Law Legislation and Liberty*. London: Routledge & Kegan Paul.

Heiner, R. A. (1986). "Imperfect Decisions and the Law: On the Evolution of Legal Precedent and Rules," *The Journal of Legal Studies*, 15(2): 227–61.

Henrich, J., Heine, S., and Norenzayan, A. (2010). "The Weirdest People in the World?" *Behavioral and Brain Sciences*, 33(2–3): 61–135.

Hodgkinson, G. P., Bown, N. J., Maule, A. J., Glaister, K. W., and Pearman, A. D. (1999). "Breaking the Frame: An Analysis of Strategic Cognition and Decision Making under Uncertainty," *Strategic Management Journal*, 20(10): 977–85.

Ioannidis, J. P. A. (2005a). "Contradicted and Initially Stronger Effects in Highly Cited Clinical Research," *Journal of the American Medical Association*, 294(2): 218–28.

Ioannidis J. P. A. (2005b). "Why Most Published Research Findings are False," *PLoS Medicine*, 2(8): e124.

Irwin, J. F. and Real, D. L. (2010). "Unconscious Influences on Judicial Decision-Making: The Illusion of Objectivity," *McGeorge Law Review*, 43: 1–20.

Jolls, C. and Sunstein, C. A (2005). "Debiasing through Law," *NBER Working Paper* 11738, 1–49. Available at http://www.nber.org/papers/w11738 (Accessed: April 7, 2021).

Jolls, C. and Sunstein, C. A. (2006). "The Law of Implicit Bias," *California Law Review*, 94(4): 969–96.

Kahneman, D. (2011). *Thinking, Fast and Slow*. New York: Farrar, Strauss and Giroux.

Kamin, K. and Rachlinski, J. (1995). "Ex post ≠ Ex Ante: Determining Liability in Hindsight," *Law and human behavior*, 19(1): 89–104.

Kelly, J. M. (1964). "Audi Alteram Partem," *Natural Law Forum*, 9: 103–10.

Kenyon, T. (2014). "False Polarization: Debiasing as Applied Social Apistemology," *Synthese*, 191(11): 2529–47.

Koriat, A., Lichtenstein, S., and Fischhoff, B. (1980). "Reasons for confidence," *Journal of Experimental Psychology: Human learning and memory*, 6(2), 107–18.

Kurtz, R. M. and Garfield, S. L. (1978). "Illusory Correlation: A Further Exploration of Chapman's Paradigm," *Journal of Consulting and Clinical Psychology*, 46(5): 1009–15.

Langevoort, D. C. (1998). "Behavioral Theories of Judgment and Decision Making in Legal Scholarship: A Literature Review," *Vanderbilt Law Review*, 51: 1499–540.

Larrick, R. P. (2008). "Debiasing," in D. J. Koehler and N. Harvey (eds.), *Blackwell Handbook of Judgment and Decision Making*, 316–37. Malden, MA: Blackwell Publishing.

Lilienfeld, S. O., Ammirati, R., and Landfield, K. (2009). "Giving Debiasing Away: Can Psychological Research on Correcting Cognitive Errors promote Human Welfare?" *Perspectives on Psychological Sciences*, 4(4): 390–8.

Lopes, L. L. (1987). "Procedural Debiasing," *Acta Psychologica*, 64: 167–85.

Lopes, L. L. (1991). "The Rhetoric of Irrationality," *Theory & Psychology*, 1(1): 65–82.

Lord, C. G., Lepper, M. R., and Preston, E. (1984). "Considering the Opposite: A Corrective Strategy for Social Judgment," *Journal of Personality and Social Judgment*, 47(6): 1231–43.

Mitchell, G. (2002). "Why Law and Economics' Perfect Rationality should not be Traded for Behavioral Law and Economics' Equal Incompetence," *Georgetown Law Journal*, 91: 67–167.

Mumma, G. H. and Wilson, S. B. (1995). "Procedural Debiasing of Primacy/Anchoring Effects in Clinical-Like Judgments," *Journal of Clinical Psychology*, 51(6): 841–53.

Mussweiler, T., Strack, F., and Pfeiffer, T. (2000). "Overcoming the Inevitable Anchoring Effect: Considering the Opposite Compensates for Selective Accessibility," *Personality and Social Psychology Bulletin*, 26(9): 1142–50.

Neef, M. and Nagel, S. (1974). "Adversary Nature of the American Legal System from a Historical Perspective," *N.Y.L.F.*, 20: 123–6.

Open Science Collaboration (2015). "Estimating the Reproducibility of Psychological Science," *Science*, 349(6251): aac4716.

Osman, M. (2004). "An Evaluation of Dual-Process Theories of Reasoning," *Psychonomic Bulletin & Review*, 11(6): 988–1010.

Pashler, H. and Wagenmakers, E.-J. (2012). "Editors' Introduction to the Special Section on Replicability in Psychological Science: A Crisis of Confidence?" *Perspectives on Psychological Science*, 7: 528–30.

Pi, D., Parisi, F., and Luppi, B. (2013). "Biasing, Debiasing, and the Law," In E. Zamir and D. Teichman (eds.), Oxford handbooks. The Oxford handbook of behavioral economics and the law, 143–66. Oxford: Oxford University Press.

Project Implicit (2015). Available at https://implicit.harvard.edu/implicit/index.jsp (Accessed: April 7, 2021).

Pronin, E. and Kugler, M. B. (2007). "Valuing Thoughts, Ignoring Behavior: The Introspection Illusion as a Source of the Bias Blind Spot," *Journal of Experimental Social Psychology*, 434: 565–78.

Pronin, E., Lin, D., and Ross, L. (2002). "The Bias Blind Spot: Perceptions of Bias in Self versus Others," *Personality and Social Psychology Bulletin*, 28: 369–81.

Pundik, A. (2012). "Was it Wrong to use Statistics in R v Clark? A Case Study of the Use of Statistical Evidence in Criminal Courts," in F. Zenker (ed.), *Bayesian Argumentation*, 87–109. Dordrecht: Springer.

Rachlinski, J. J., Guthrie, C., and Wistrich, A. J. (2007). "Heuristics and Biases in Bankruptcy Judges," *Journal of Institutional and Theoretical Economics*, 163(1): 167–86.

Samuels, R., Stich, S., and Bishop, M. (2002). "Ending the Rationality Wars: How to Make Disputes about Human Rationality Disappear," in R. Elio (ed.), *Common Sense, Reasoning and Rationality*, 236–68. New York: Oxford University Press,.

Schimmack, U., Moritz, H., and Kesavan, K. (2017). "Reconstruction of a Train Wreck: How Priming Research went Off the Rails." Available at https://replicationindex.com/2017/02/02/reconstruction-of-a-train-wreck-how-priming-research-went-of-the-rails/comment-page-1/#comments (Accessed: April 7, 2021). (Comment by D. Kahman, posted at 8:37 pm, February 14, 2017.)

Schweizer, M. D. (2005). Kognitive Täuschungen vor Gericht: Eine empirische Studie. Ph.D Dissertation, University of Zurich.

Simon, H. A. (1982). *Models of Bounded Rationality*. Cambridge, MA: MIT Press.

Spellman, B. A. (2012). "Introduction to the Special Section on Research Practices," *Perspectives on Psychological Science*, 7: 655–6.

Stanovich, K. E. and West, R. F. (2000). "Individual Differences in Reasoning: Implications for the Rationality Debate?" *Behavioral and Brain Sciences*, 23: 645–726.

Sturm, T. and Mülberger, A. (2012). "Crisis Discussions in Psychology—New Historical and Philosophical Perspectives," *Studies in History and Philosophy of Biological Sciences*, 43: 425–33.

Thaler, R. H. and Sunstein, C. R. (2008). *Nudge: Improving Decisions about Health, Wealth, and Happiness*. New Haven, CT: Yale University Press.

Tversky, A. and Kahneman, D. (1974). "Judgment under Uncertainty: Heuristics and Biases," *Science*, 185: 1124–31.

Weinstein, I. (2002). "Don't Believe Everything you Think: Cognitive bias in Legal Decision Making," *Clinical Law Review*, 9: 783–834.

Willingham, D. (2007). "Critical Thinking: Why is it so Hard to Teach?" *American Educator*, 31(2), 8–19. (Reprinted: (2008) *Arts Education Policy Review*, 109 (4): 21–32.)

Wilson T. D. and Brekke, N. (1994). "Mental Contamination and Mental Correction: Unwanted Influences on Judgments and Evaluations," *Psychological Bulletin*, 116: 117–42.

Wissler, R. L. and Saks, M. J. (1985). "On the Inefficacy of Limiting Instructions: When Jurors use Prior Conviction Evidence to Decide on Guilt," *Law and Human Behavior*, 9(1): 37–48.

Witte, E. H. and Zenker, F. (2017). "From Discovery to Justification. Outline of an Ideal Research Program in Empirical Psychology," *Frontiers in Psychology*, 8: Art. 1847. Available at doi.org/10.3389/fpsyg.2017.01847 (Accessed: May 1, 2021).

Wood, G. (1978). "The Knew-it-all-Along-Effect," *Journal of Experimental Psychology: Human Perception and Performance*, 4: 345–53.

Woods, J. (2013). *Reasoning Errors: Naturalizing the Logic of Inference*. London: College Publications.

Zenker, F. and Dahlman, C. (2016). "Reliable Debiasing Techniques in Legal Contexts? Weak Signals from a Darker Corner of the Social Science Universe," in F. Paglieri, L. Bonelli, and S. Felletti (eds.), *The Psychology of Argument: Cognitive Approaches to Argumentation and Persuasion*, 173–96. London: College Publications.

Zenker, F., Dahlman, C., Bååth, R., and Sarwar, F. (2018). "Reasons *Pro et Contra* as a Debiasing Technique in Legal Contexts," *Psychological Reports*, 121(3): 511–26.

Index

For the benefit of digital users, indexed terms that span two pages (e.g., 52–53) may, on occasion, appear on only one of those pages.

Tables and figures are indicated by *t* and *f* following the page number

1/N-principle (1/n principle) 59, 275–76, 290–91, 292–97

Abduction *see* Reasoning
Accommodation 223–24
Accuracy
  of factfinding *see* Factfinding
  value of 16–17, 20–22, 73
Adjudication 26, 56, 57, 71, 77–78, 102–3, 123, 125–26, 132, 135, 147, 150, 241, 349, 350, 360–61
Admissibility
  admissible evidence *see* Evidence
Adversarial trial/system 15, 16, 17–18, 142–43, 175
Adverse inference 125, 128–29, 174
Aggregation problem 209–10, 325–27
Allen, Ronald J. 110, 111, 138–39, 201–14, 219, 233–34, 291, 301–13, 326–27, 375
Amaya, Amalia 219, 231–47
Analogy *see* Reasoning
Anchoring *see* Biases
Arguments
  argumentation 183, 186–90, 193–95
  argumentation schemes 190, 191, 192, 225
  attacking arguments 187–88, 188*f*
  counterarguments 183, 184, 186–88, 193–94
  dialectical status of 187–89
Ashworth, Andrew 84–85, 86
Assertion 11–12, 18–19, 157, 158–59, 160, 164, 171–73
Austin, John Langshaw 157, 158, 162, 170–71, 172
Authority
  to condemn and punish 84–85, 88, 89, 91–94
  epistemic 54
Autonomy 17–18, 96–97, 99–100, 105
Autopsy 53

Background knowledge *see* Knowledge
Bacon, Francis 395–96
Baehr, Jason 240
Balancing 87–91, 146, 322–23
Barry George case 269
Base rate neglect *see* Probability
Bayesianism
  Bayes' rule 59, 267–68, 280–81, 295, 298
  Bayes' theorem 254–55, 259–60, 261, 280–81, 301–2, 307, 397

Bayesian approach 109, 111, 195, 201–2, 209–11, 225, 267, 270, 274, 280, 287–89, 299
Bayesian framework 267–69, 276–77
Bayesian networks 225, 268–69
Beccaria, Cesare 138
Belief
  confidence in 31–32, 33–34, 110, 115, 124, 130–31, 165, 216, 355, 389
  degree of 41–42, 110, 111, 127–28, 254, 256, 263, 297
  partial 231
  resilience of 130
  set 231, 236–37, 241, 242–43
  tenacity of 130
Bentham, Jeremy 69, 70–73, 76–77, 79, 137, 138, 339–40
Bex, Floris 183–97, 221, 222, 233
Beyond reasonable doubt *see* Burdens
Biases
  anchoring 76, 148–49, 396–97, 399, 401
  availability 76, 148–49, 399, 401
  blindspot 398
  cognitive 148–49, 240–41, 320–21, 395, 401
  coherence 240, 243, 244
  confirmation 17–18, 222–23, 228, 397, 404
  gender 400
  hindsight 357, 396–97, 399, 404
  implicit 400
  omission 397
  overconfidence 148–49, 397, 399, 404
  probabilistic 397
  racial 383–84, 384n.34
  social 395, 396–97, 400
Biedermann, Alex 251–66
Blackstone ratio 140–41
Blue bus case (Blue bus scenario / Blue cab case) 302, 303–5, 317–18, 321, 332, 340–41
BonJour, Lawrence 241, 242–43
Bornstein, Brian H.. 28
Bozza, Silvia 251–66
Bronston case 175–77
Broughton, Gabriel 25–39
Burdens
  beyond reasonable doubt 18, 20, 40–41, 42, 57–58, 102, 103, 108, 109, 113, 115, 116–17, 126–27,

Burdens (*cont.*)
  130–31, 140–41, 180, 202, 207–8, 211, 220–21,
    224, 268, 287–88, 298–99, 383–84
  clear and convincing evidence 42, 102, 103, 108,
    109, 113, 126–27, 202, 207
  of persuasion 108, 123, 124, 127, 128–29, 130, 132,
    133–34, 205, 206–7, 209, 210–11, 321–22
  preponderance of the evidence (balance of
    probabilities) 40–41, 42, 57–58, 63, 101–2, 103,
    108, 109, 112, 113, 115, 116–17, 119, 126–27, 140,
    202, 205, 209, 321, 323, 324–25
  of production 108
  of proof 17, 45–46, 102–4, 108–22, 125, 132, 141,
    189, 202, 205, 206–7, 241, 293, 297, 298–99,
    320, 325–26
  theories of proof burden
  dualist theories 126–27, 130–31
  holistic theories 126–30

Calculator analogy 282
Causation 43, 47, 57–58, 103–4, 117–18, 194–95, 204,
    215–16, 221–22, 225, 227, 233, 271, 273, 282, 303,
    335–36, 341–43
Character evidence 21, 28, 35–36, 104, 141, 146, 372–
    73, 380, 388–89
Cheng, Edward 109, 113–14, 298–99, 326
Cicchini, Michael D. . 351
Civil rights 380, 385, 389
Clermont, Kevin 40–41, 110, 326–27
Cognition 148–49, 244–45, 349, 396, 398, 399, 405
Cohen, L. Jonathan 1, 110, 125–27, 132–33, 318–19,
    323, 326–27, 344, 369–70
Cohen, Neil B. . 110, 130–31
Coherence
  base 232, 236, 237, 238, 239, 244–45
  coherence bias *see* Biases
  coherentism 231, 236–39, 240–45
  narrative 110–11, 113, 205–6, 215, 232–34
  structural 231–32, 241, 243
Collins case 262, 268, 269
Collins, Hill 366, 367, 368–70
Confession 21, 55–56, 85, 134, 135, 179, 399–400
Confidence interval 110, 130, 131, 269, 270
Conjunction 184–86, 224–26, 323–27
Consistency 89, 103–4, 110–11, 113–14, 193, 216,
    226, 227, 231, 232, 243, 301–2
Constraint-satisfaction 234–36
Context
  of discovery 220, 222–23
  insensitivity 338–39
  of justification 220, 222–23, 224
Contrast set 238
Coroner 53
Cost-benefit analysis (CBA) 137–53
  cost minimization model 140–44, 145–49
  costs of evidence 139–40
  search model 139–40, 144
Courtroom interaction 169–70, 173, 174, 175–76
Coverage 110–11, 216, 226, 227, 233–34

Credences *see* Probability
Credibility 16, 22, 43, 48, 54, 100–1, 104–5, 125–26,
    143–44, 174, 233, 321–23, 357, 359, 366, 373–75,
    381, 388–90
Crenshaw, Kimberlé W. . 364–65
Crime
  extended crime scene 276
  rate 333–34, 338–39, 340–41, 342–43
  scene 54, 58–59, 63–64, 160–61, 203, 218, 251–52,
    255, 270, 272, 275–76, 293–94, 307, 308, 332–33,
    336–37, 340
Criminal
  investigation 90, 92–93, 217, 220, 223, 225–26,
    251–52, 275, 279
  justice 30, 31, 84–86, 87, 88–89, 90, 91, 92–93, 150,
    296, 382–83, 388
Critical questions 192, 193, 226
Crombag, Hans 215, 233
Croskerry, Pat 402
Cross-examination 16, 21, 22, 32, 62, 75, 102, 104–5,
    138, 142, 176–77, 180, 351, 354–55, 356, 360
CSI effect 359–60

Dahlman, Christian 53–66, 287–300, 332–45
Daubert
  Daubert case 61
  Daubert factors 61, 359
  Daubert test 358–59
Davidson, Barbara 130–31
Davidson, Donald 242–43
Davis, Christopher 166
Davis, Deborah 309–11
Dawid, Philip 258
Debiasing 76, 240–41, 244, 395–409
Decision
  decision analysis 255–56, 260–61
  decision making 26–27, 41, 42, 45, 46, 48, 50, 56,
    71, 72, 75–79, 88–89, 101, 140, 327–29, 359, 397,
    400, 402
  decision theory 109, 124, 128, 201–2, 251, 261
  rectitude of 19–20
  under uncertainty 123, 254–56
Defeasible 167, 183, 187, 193, 238–39, 242, 243
Defense hypothesis 273, 279
Deflationism *see* Truth
Deixis 170, 179–81
Devil's advocate 399
Diagnostic value 63
Diamond, Shari S. . 29
Direct evidence *see* Evidence
Discretion 21, 56–57, 71, 91, 399
Discrimination 34, 320, 364–65, 372, 400
  discriminating fact 224–26
Discursive dilemma 327–29
Disjunction 323–27
DNA 30, 138, 147–48, 185*f*, 187, 188*f*, 191, 202,
    203, 252–53, 270, 271–73, 271*f*, 274*f*, 277–79,
    279*f*, 279*t*, 280–81, 280*f*, 293, 320, 336–38, 342–
    43, 359–60

Domain of expertise   *see* Expertise
Double counting   276, 289
Dreyfus affair   59–60
Due process   33, 41, 44, 46–49, 50
Duff, Antony   84–85, 86, 91

Economic analysis   109
  of evidence law   137–53
Ekelöf, Per Olof   1
Empirical
  knowledge (science / studies)   25, 26, 63,
    171, 205, 232–33, 302–3, 318–19, 349–63,
    395–409
  support   32
  verification   22
Enoch, David   333, 334–35, 336–37, 338–40
Episode   215–17, 221–22
Epistemic
  authority   *see* Authority
  injustice   380–94
  risk   75–76, 132–33
  warrant   124, 127, 128, 129
Epistemology
  black feminist   367, 370
  feminist   377
  naturalized   25–39
  social   25–26, 244
  virtue epistemology   239–41
Error
  type I   58
  type II   58
  type III   58
European Court of Human Rights (ECtHR)   46, 49–
    50, 83–84
Evidence
  admissible (inadmissible)   13, 21–22, 28, 29, 34,
    35, 45, 61, 62, 73–74, 76, 87–88, 91, 105, 130,
    132, 134–35, 143–44, 146, 157, 158, 160, 169–70,
    171–72, 202, 235–36, 288, 317, 319, 320, 321–22,
    333–34, 350, 355, 356–75, 376
  character   *see* Character evidence
  circumstantial   167
  direct (indirect)   165, 221, 251–52
  evidence discourse   169–70
  forensic   27, 53–54, 55, 56–57, 60, 63–64, 218,
    251–54, 260–61, 262, 269, 273–74, 320,
    340, 359–60
  improperly obtained   83–84, 87, 90–91
  missing   125, 132–33, 216–17
  naked statistical   100–2, 130–31, 132–33, 261–62,
    318–23, 332–45 (*see also* statistical)
  predictive   36, 335, 342–43
  and proof   40, 215, 217–18, 232–33,
    237, 256, 261
  scientific   34, 55–56, 63, 65, 120, 171, 191–92, 202,
    251–66, 321–22, 358–61
  second-personal   96–107
  specific (case-specific)   100–1, 102–3, 125, 132,
    134–35, 305, 319

  statistical   115, 202, 268, 280–81, 318–19 (*see also*
    naked statistical)
  trace   277–78, 292, 335, 340
  trial   288–90, 293–94, 295–97, 298–99, 354
Evidential
  reasoning   44, 45–46, 183–97, 221, 231, 233–34,
    242, 243–45
  value   251–52
  weight   *see* Weight
Exclusion of evidence (Exclusionary
    rules)   21–22, 69–79, 85–86, 87–88, 161–62,
    171–72, 356–57
Excusable preferences   124, 131, 132–33
Experiments   26–28, 30, 32, 34, 117, 148–49, 324,
    349–63, 404
Expertise
  domain of expertise   54, 56–57, 252
  expert testimony   34, 53–54, 55–56, 59–60, 61–63,
    138, 190, 191, 306–7, 319, 349
  expert witness   32–33, 53–66, 148, 219, 254, 269,
    273, 274–75, 277, 358–60, 383, 387
Explanation
  causal   204, 221–22, 225, 227, 395
  of evidence   *see* Inference to the best explanation
  explanationism   113, 201–2, 234
  explanationist approach   231–32, 234
  of fact   125, 135, 224
  of hypothesis   235–36
Eyewitness
  cross-racial   383–84
  eyewitness identification   27, 304–5, 336, 337
  testimony   26–27, 30–34, 54, 100–1, 103–4, 173,
    318, 336–38, 353, 355

Factfinding
  accuracy of   12, 16, 25–26, 115, 138–39, 141–42,
    144, 145, 301
  factfinders/triers of fact   17–19, 21–22,
    42, 53–56, 71–72, 76, 100–1, 110–12, 115–16,
    127, 129–30, 136, 176–77, 205–8, 215, 221, 222,
    226–27, 233–34, 292, 296–97, 302, 336, 357,
    395–409
  factum probandum   57–58
  proven facts   40–52
  verdict   14, 15, 17, 20, 26–29, 30, 33, 34, 40–52, 110,
    117, 127–28, 172–73, 206–7, 261, 322, 325, 328–
    29, 339–40, 353, 357–58
Fair trial   46, 48–49
Fallacy
  defendant's   272
  prosecutor's   269, 270, 272, 273, 282
Falsification   227–28
  Falsificationism   222–23
Federal Rules of Evidence (FRE)   33–34, 35, 157, 158,
    160, 349, 366, 367–68
Feminism   324, 364–79
Fenton, Norman   267–86, 293–94
Ferrer Beltrán, Jordi   40–52
Finetti, Bruno de   258, 259

Fingerprint 203, 218–19, 223, 260–61, 332–33, 335, 340–41
Finkelstein, Michael 306–8
Fisher, Talia 137–53, 333, 334–35, 336–37, 338–40
Flight from law enforcement 386–87
Follette, William 309–12
Forensic
  evidence *see* Evidence
  linguistics 169–70
  science 27, 53–66, 138, 251–54, 340
  statistics 273
Framing 397, 399
Franklin, James 291–92
Free
  evaluation of evidence 40–41, 44
  proof 69–75
  will 334, 341–44
Frequency
  frequency principle 290–92, 294–95, 296–97
  frequentism 103, 257, 305, 306–7
Freud, Sigmund 401
Friedman, Richard 128, 129–30, 206, 289, 296, 310–11, 350

Gardiner, Georgi 338
Gatecrasher case (Gatecrasher scenario) 318, 321, 322–23, 332, 340–41
Gender 359, 364–65, 368, 369–70, 372, 373, 400
Generalizations 100–1, 102–3, 134–35, 183–84, 186–87, 190–93, 217, 219, 301–13, 336–37, 367, 369, 370, 373–74
  causal 104, 341–42
  probabilistic 342
Gilligan, Carol 364–65
Glougie, Jennifer 165, 166
Golding, Martin P. . 13
Goldman, Alvin 303
Gonzales Rose, Jasmine B. . 380–94
Grice, Paul 162–64
  Gricean cooperative principle 162–63, 170, 173–74
  Gricean implicatures *see* Implicatures
  Gricean maxims 163, 174–75, 176
Gunshot residue 252

Haack, Susan 12, 15, 21, 127–28, 129–30
Halo effect 397
Hand, Learned 62
Handwriting 59–60, 252
Hastie, Reid 110–11, 215, 227, 233
Hearsay 15, 21, 69, 75, 104–5, 157–68, 171–72, 352–54, 361
Hempel, Carl 61
Heuristics
  consider the opposite 398, 399
  heuristics and biases program 148–49, 240–41, 400, 401–2
Ho, Hock Lai 11–24, 127–28
Hohfeld, Wesley Newcomb 96, 98

Holism 110, 116, 126–30, 217–18, 221–22, 225, 232–34, 237
Holroyd, Jules 83–95
Holyoak, Keith J. . 236
Hypothesis
  alternative 270
  competing 123, 124, 126, 127, 312
  defense 273, 279
  offense level 270
  prosecution 49–50, 59, 235, 261, 272–73, 275, 278, 287–90, 295–99
  source level 270, 277–78
  ultimate 270, 271, 273–74

Impartiality 368
Impeachment 30–34, 35, 360–61, 373–75, 381–83
Implicatures 163, 173–77, 178, 180, 181, 334, 339–41, 343–44, 396
Improperly obtained evidence *see* Evidence
Inadmissible evidence *see* Evidence
Incentive 17–18, 125, 138, 144–46, 321
Incommensurability 148, 259–60
Indirect evidence *see* Evidence
Inference to the best explanation
  (IBE) 110, 111–12, 194–95, 201–14, 219–22, 223, 224–25, 226, 237–38, 239–40, 242–43, 312, 326–27, 329
Informational failures 143–44
Inquisitorial trial/system 15, 17–18, 127, 142–43
Instructions 31, 32, 35, 108–9, 113, 125, 129–30, 289, 291, 292, 324–25, 353–54, 356–58, 381, *see also* Jury
Integrity 83–95
  as balancing 87–91
Inter-American Court of Human Rights (I/A Court HR) 46, 49–50
Interpretation
  legal 57, 170, 399
  of probability 59, 254, 257, 258–59, 270, 323, 342
  of scenario/evidence 217–18, 233–34, 237–38
Intime conviction 41, 43–44, 47
Investigative phase 220, 223, 225

James, George 366
James, William 401
Judge 11–18, 56–57, 69–70, 71, 75–76, 77, 142–43, 171–72, 295–96, 358–59, 360, 366
Junk science 60, 61, 360–61
Jury
  jurors 32–34, 69–70, 71, 72–73, 74, 75, 76, 77, 142–43, 176, 295–96, 350–52, 353–54, 355–60, 366
  jury instructions 33–34, 356–58
  jury simulations 26–30, 351–52, 353–54, 355–56, 404
Justice
  miscarriage of 13, 19–20, 148, 251, 252
  procedural 147, 297, 354, 360

Kahneman, Daniel 76–77, 148–49, 324
Kalven, Harry 360
Kaplan, John 1, 256
Kaye, David 119, 254, 318, 321
Kelsen, Hans 12–13
Keynes, John Maynard 123, 124
Keynesian weight see Weight
Knowledge
    background/general 54, 190–93, 217–19, 227, 237–
        38, 289–90, 336
    case-specific 216
    empirical 25
    expert 53, 54–55, 58–59, 61–62, 63–64, 397, 403
    probabilistic/statistical 120, 274–75
Kolflaath, Eivind 275, 287–300
Koppen, Peter J. van 215–30, 233

Lagnado, David 267–86, 293–94
Landsman, Stephan 353
Law
    procedural 14–15, 53–54, 72, 140, 142, 364–
        65, 374
    substantive 19, 20, 72, 203–4, 206, 208, 209–10,
        364–66, 367–68, 370–72, 373, 377
Legal proof see Proof
Lehrer, Keith 242–43
Leiter, Brian 25–39
Levin, Bruce 306–8
Lewis, David 335–36
Likelihood ratio 59–60, 63–64, 101–2, 109, 111, 212,
    225, 254, 272–73, 276–80, 298–99, 301–2, 305,
    307–8, 311
Lindley, Dennis 292, 293–95
Linguistic evidentials 157–68
Locked room case 295
Loftus, Elizabeth 355
Loss aversion 397, 399
Lucia de Berk case 269, 342–43

MacCormick, Neil 233
MacKinnon, Catherine 366, 371–72
Mackor, Anne Ruth 215–30
MeToo movement 376–77
Miscarriage of justice see Justice
Missing evidence see Evidence
Mock trial (Mock jury) 26–27, 28–29, 33, 117, 324,
    351–54, 355–56, 359, 404
Motivation
    motivational failures 141–43
    motive 35, 194–95, 218–19, 310, 372–73
Münsterberg, Hugo 349, 360

Naked statistical evidence see Evidence
Nance, Dale 123–36, 209, 210–11, 322, 324–25
Narrative 103, 110–11, 113, 205–6, 215, 232–34, 355,
    360–61, 365
Naturalized epistemology see Epistemology
Negligence 57, 73–74, 124
Neil, Martin 293–94
NESS-test 57, 58

Nesson, Charles 14, 322, 326, 332–33
Norm
    legal 56–57, 172
    non-legal 63, 369–70
    normative reason 47
    normative standard/model 115, 395, 396–98
Normalcy 334–39
Nudging 396, 400, 403

Objectivity 54–55, 61–62, 192, 258, 364–65, 368–69
Opportunity 35, 275, 276
    opportunity prior 275, 276, 293–94

Paradox
    conjunction 210–11, 323–27
    disjunction 317–23
    group decision 327–29
    naked statistical evidence see Evidence
Pardo, Michael S.. 110, 111, 201–14, 219, 233–34,
    291, 301–13, 326–27, 329, 375
Pargetter, Robert 130–31
Park, Roger 310–11, 353
Pearl, Judea 335–36
Pennington, Nancy 110–11, 215, 233
Persuasion 17, 359, 360, 400
    burden of see Burdens
Picinali, Federico 83–95, 343
Poincaré, Henri 59–60
Police violence 384–86
Policy 21, 73, 126–27, 132–35, 138, 147, 317, 320–21,
    350, 360–61, 367
Popper, Karl 61, 222–23
Posner, Richard 139–40, 144, 146–47, 160–61, 296,
    321, 339–40
Possible perpetrators 59, 275–76, 288–89, 290, 291,
    292–95, 296–97
Posterior probability see Probability
Potts, Christopher 166
Practical optimization of weight see Weight
Pragmatics 163–64, 169–82
Prediction 14–15, 223–24, 228, 343
    predictive connection 335
Preference 78–79, 111, 140–42, 148–49, 187–88, 260–
    61, 297, 329, 369–70
    preference structure 124, 131, 132–33, 256
Preponderance of the evidence see Burdens
Presumed prior 295–97, 298, 299
Presumption of innocence 49–50, 57, 59, 287–88,
    289–90, 291, 292, 294, 295–96, 297, 299
    strong interpretation of 290, 294, 295, 297, 299
    weak interpretation of 290
Presupposition 159, 177–79
Primary behavior 105, 144, 145–47
Principle of maximal individualization (PMI) 132–
    33, 134–35
Prior conviction 104, 351, 355–56, 360–61, 381–83
Prior probability see Probability
Priority 235, 237, 241
Prison riot case (Prison yard / Prison riot scenario)
    100, 332–33, 334, 335, 336, 337, 338, 339–41

Privileges 21, 69, 73, 74
Probability
    Baconian 45, 103
    base rate neglect 307–8, 318, 396f
    credences 295–96, 297
    objective 111, 257, 305
    Pascalian 397
    posterior 59, 101–2, 271
    prior 59, 101–2, 259–60, 271, 275–76, 287–
        99, 306
    probabilism 106, 201–2, 208–9, 210–11
    probabilistic inference 195
    probability theory 208–9, 231–32, 251, 254–
        55, 301
    subjective 111, 254, 257–59, 267–68, 375
Probative
    force/strength 34, 119–20, 135, 165, 187–88, 208,
        233–34, 307, 353
    value 27, 32, 36, 69–71, 72–73, 74–75, 88–89, 140,
        146, 157, 202, 208, 212, 251, 254, 260–61, 262,
        273, 275, 278, 301–3, 304–12, 322–23, 356, 359–
        61, 367, 368, 381
Problem of scope 91–94, 337–38
Proof see also Evidence
    juridical 201–2, 204, 206, 208–9, 212, 301–3, 305
    legal 43, 201, 202, 231–32, 234, 242, 243–44,
        245, 370
Propensity 103–4, 275, 349, 350–52, 355–56, 360–61,
        372–73, 375, 388–89
Propositional attitude 43–45
Prosecution hypothesis see Hypothesis
Prosecutor's fallacy see Fallacy
Proven facts see Factfinding
Psychology 27, 34, 35, 55–56, 76–77, 193, 232–33,
        240, 349–63, 404
Pundik, Amit 332–45
Punishment
    authority to condemn and punish
        see Authority
    moral justification of 334, 339–40
P-value 269–70

Questions of law v. questions of fact 56–58
Quick case 55–56

Race 31, 349–50, 352, 360–61, 364–65, 380–94
Rakos, Richard F. . 353
Ramsey, Frank Plumpton 11–12, 232
Random match 53–54, 272, 278, 279, 280–81,
        320, 336–38
Rape 180, 280–81, 365, 371–72
Rationality 79, 137–38, 148–49, 232, 302, 367
    bounded 148–49, 401
Read, Stephen J. . 236, 244–45
Reason
    giving 41, 46–49, 50
    preemptive 54
Reasonable doubt see Burdens
Reasoned verdicts 40–52

Reasoning
    abductive 201, 203–5, 219–20, 221
    by analogy 216, 235
    deductive 184, 203, 216, 220, 221, 223, 231
    economic 137–38, 147
    evidential see Evidential
    explanatory 194–95, 201–2, 219–20, 221, 237–
        38, 243
    indirect 221
    inductive 126, 191–92, 203, 220, 221, 251, 322,
        326–27, 369, 398
    legal/juridical 112–13, 186, 194, 240, 267, 270–75
    types of 216
Rectitude of decision see Decision
Reference class problem 212, 291–92, 301–13,
        320, 375
Relative plausibility 111, 205, 207–8, 209–10, 211–12,
        216, 233–34
Relevance 72–73, 163–64, 174, 189, 218, 259–60,
        291–92, 304–5, 320, 365–77
Reliability 21–22, 30–33, 60–62, 164, 184, 192, 304–5,
        354–55, 358–59, 373, 383–84
Resilience 58–59, 130–31
Right-holders 96, 97
Robustness 58–59, 227–28, 251
Rule of law 12–13, 21, 25–26, 49–50, 141–42, 295–96
Rules of evidence see Evidence

Sally Clark case 269, 342–43
Sanchirico, Chris William 145–46, 339–40
Scenario
    descriptive 215, 218–19, 222–23
    normative 218–19, 222–23
    scenario theory 194–95, 215–30, 233
    sub-scenario 217–19, 218f
Schauer, Frederick 69–82, 297
Scientific evidence see Evidence
Search model see Cost-benefit analysis
Searle, John 158, 162
Second-personal
    evidence see Evidence
    liability 99
    rights 97, 98, 106
Sensitivity 34, 101, 282, 334–39
Separation thesis 91, 92–94
Sevier, Justin 349–63
Sexual assault 351, 352, 364, 365, 371, 372–73
Shoeprint (Shoe mark) 54, 58–59, 63–64, 180, 184–
        86, 185f, 252
Shonubi case 319–20
Simon, Dan 236, 244–45
Simon, Herbert 148–49
Simon-Kerr, Julia 364–79
Smith, Martin 336–338
Snow, Chadwick J. . 236
Solan, Lawrence M. . 157–68
Speas, Margaret 166
Spectre, Levi 333, 334–35, 338–40
Speech acts 11–12, 157, 158–64, 170–73

Spottswood, Mark 108–22, 317–31, 332, 333
Standard of proof *see* Burdens
Statistical evidence *see* Evidence
Stein, Alex 96–107, 132–35, 138–39, 141–42, 143–44,
     176, 296, 297, 325–26
Stenstrom, Douglas M. . 244–45
Stereotype 190, 310, 359, 395, 400
     racial 352, 388–89
Story model 110–11, 112, 114–15, 215, 217, 219, 221–
     23, 226–28, 233, 354–55
Subjective probability *see* Probability
Subjectivism 40–41, 257–58
Subordination 364–65, 371, 380
Sub-scenario *see* Scenario
Sullivan, Sean 109, 322–23
Sunstein, Cass 148
Support 58–60, 103, 127, 278, 322,
     337, 339, 387
Symmetry 235, 259

Taroni, Franco 251–66
Technology 281, 320, 396, 405
Tenacity of belief *see* Belief
Testimony
     expert *see* Expertise
     witness *see* Witness
Thagard, Paul 234–35, 241, 242–43, 275
Thayer, James Bradley 21, 72–73, 74, 75–76
Thomson, Judith Jarvis 1, 335, 336
Tool marks 252
Toulmin, Stephen 189
Trial
     adversarial *see* Adversarial
     inquisitorial *see* Inquisitorial
     trial evidence *see* Evidence
     trial fairness *see* Fair trial
Tribe, Laurence 1, 268, 317–18, 321, 333
Trust 54, 55–56, 61, 71, 187, 192, 224–25, 322–23,
     372, 375, 386–87
Truth *see also* Accuracy
     concept of 11–12
     deflationism 11–12
     goal of 19, 20, 21, 22, 25, 74, 102–3, 138–39, 241,
          242, 350
     legal truth 12–13, 14
     substantive truth 11–12
     truth-related norms 16–19
     veritistic evaluation 25, 27
Tuzet, Giovanni 50, 169–82
Tversky, Amos 76–77, 148–49, 324

Twining, William 1, 183, 190, 369–70, 373
Types of reasoning *see* Reasoning

Uncertainty
     with regard to act 290–91, 295–97
     with regard to identity 290, 291, 292–97
     reticence 63, 64–65
Uniqueness 205, 216, 226–27, 233–34

Validity
     ecological 26–29, 350
     external 27–28, 29
     internal 29
Verdict *see* Factfinding
Viola, Francesco 15
Virtue epistemology *see* Epistemology

Wagenaar, Willem 215, 233
Wahlberg, Lena 53–66
Walton, Douglas 183
Weber, Max 77–78
Weight
     of evidence (evidential) 21–22, 63–64, 69–70, 72–
          73, 110, 111–12, 113, 123–36, 145–46, 283, 318,
          349, 354, 360–61
     Keynesian 123
     practical optimization of weight 124, 126–27,
          130–31, 133–34
Weinstein, Jack B. . 14, 15
White, Lawrence T. . 351
Wigmore, John Henry 72–73, 74, 75–76, 349, 354–55,
     360, 364
Wigmore charts 183, 184–86
Williams, Bernard 43, 159
Witness 16–17, 69, 132–33, 148, 163, 165, 169–70,
     171, 173, 175, 176–77, 178, 302, 349–50, 353–54,
     373–74, 380–81, 387, 388–89
     expert *see* Expertise
     eyewitness *see* Eyewitness
     testimony of 101–2, 105, 110, 125–26, 129–30,
          157–58, 159, 183–86, 187, 190, 191–92, 193, 194,
          221, 222, 224–25, 388
Wrongful
     acquittal 57, 140–41, 144, 150, 296, 298–99
     ascription of civil liability 117
     conviction 30, 57, 140–41, 144, 150, 296, 298–
          99, 332–33

Zeisel, Hans 29, 360
Zenker, Frank 395–409